Online Algorithms

Online algorithms are an optimization paradigm where input is revealed sequentially and an algorithm has to make irrevocable decisions using only causal information. This is a growing area of research with great interest from the theoretical computer science community, having significant practical applications in operations research, big data analysis, design of communication networks, and so on. There are many different mathematical techniques that have been developed to analyse online algorithms, such as potential function arguments, primal–dual methods, and Yao's principle, to name a few. This textbook presents an easy but rigorous introduction to online algorithms for students. It starts with classical online paradigms like ski-rental, paging, list-accessing, and bin packing, where performance of the algorithms is studied under the worst-case input and moves on to newer paradigms like 'beyond worst case', where online algorithms are augmented with predictions using machine learning algorithms. Several other popular online problems, such as metrical task systems, which includes the popular k-server problem as a special case, secretary, knapsack, bipartite matching, load balancing, scheduling to minimize flow-time, facility location, k-means clustering, and travelling salesman, are also covered. A very useful technique for analysing online algorithms called the primal–dual schema is also included together with its application for multiple problems. The book goes on to cover multiple applied problems such as routing in communication networks, server provisioning in cloud systems, communication with energy harvested from renewable sources, and sub-modular partitioning. Finally, a wide range of solved examples and practice exercises are included, allowing hands-on exposure to the concepts. Each exercise has been broken down into simpler parts to provide a clear path towards the solution.

Rahul Vaze is Associate Professor at the School of Technology and Computer Science, Tata Institute of Fundamental Research, Mumbai, India, an institution he has been associated with since 2009. His research interests include online algorithms, wireless communication theory, resource allocation, and network information theory. He has previously published *Random Wireless Networks: An Information Theoretic Perspective* with Cambridge University Press in 2015.

Online Algorithms

Rahul Vaze

CAMBRIDGE
UNIVERSITY PRESS

Shaftesbury Road, Cambridge CB2 8EA, United Kingdom

One Liberty Plaza, 20th Floor, New York, NY 10006, USA

477 Williamstown Road, Port Melbourne, vic 3207, Australia

314–321, 3rd Floor, Plot 3, Splendor Forum, Jasola District Centre, New Delhi - 110025, India

103 Penang Road, #05–06/07, Visioncrest Commercial, Singapore 238467

Cambridge University Press is part of Cambridge University Press & Assessment, a department of the University of Cambridge.

We share the University's mission to contribute to society through the pursuit of education, learning and research at the highest international levels of excellence.

www.cambridge.org
Information on this title: www.cambridge.org/9781009349185

First published 2023

Printed in India by Magic International Pvt. Ltd., Greater Noida

A catalogue record for this publication is available from the British Library

ISBN 978-1-009-34918-5 Paperback

To all the COVID-19 victims and warriors.
This book was mostly written while working from home during full/partial lockdowns.

Contents

Let me begin with a disclaimer! Online algorithms, the subject topic of this book, have nothing to do with the internet or the online connected world. Online algorithms should really be called limited information algorithms or myopic algorithms that have to make decisions with limited information while being compared against the best algorithm in hindsight.

The simplest example of an online algorithm is the game of Tetris, where at each time, the player has to make a decision about where to place the newly arrived tile, given the current state of tile positions and the knowledge of only the newly revealed tile and the next upcoming tile, so as to make as many completed lines with similar colour disappear as possible. Clearly, if all the future arriving tiles were revealed at each time, the optimal placement of the newly arrived tile to maximize the number of completed lines can be computed. However, with the limited information setting of the game, the quest is to get as close to the optimal algorithm in hindsight.

To put online algorithms in perspective, let's ask a question: what does an algorithm usually do? Given a (full) input instance, it provides a routine to optimize an objective function, subject to a set of constraints. When the full input instance is known before the algorithm starts to execute, it is referred to as the *offline* setting.

For many optimization problems of interest, however, the input instance is revealed sequentially, and an algorithm has to execute or make irrevocable decisions sequentially with the partially revealed input amid uncertainty about the future input, e.g., as we discussed for the game of Tetris. This sequential decision setting is generally referred to as the **online** setting, and the corresponding algorithm as an **online algorithm**. Compared to the offline algorithm, an online algorithm's output is a function of its sequentially made decisions and the order in which input is revealed.

To contrast the offline versus the online setting, consider one of simplest problems of memory management in random access memory (RAM) of computing systems. RAM is a fast but limited sized memory, and files before processing have to be loaded in the RAM. At each step of computation, a file is requested. If the requested file is available in the RAM, then execution starts immediately. Otherwise, a fault is counted to model the delay, etc., for loading the requested file into the RAM before execution. Since RAM is of limited size, to load the newly requested file, some existing file has to be ejected. For fast processing, one needs to minimize the total number of faults, which in turn depends on the choice of the file being ejected on each fault by the algorithm. This problem is popularly known as the paging or the caching problem. In the offline setting, a simple algorithm that ejects the file whose next request is farthest in time is optimal. The online setting is more relevant but non-trivial, where an algorithm has to make a decision about which file to eject without knowing the set of files to be requested in future.

Other prominent examples of sequential decision problems include: job scheduling in data/call centres, where jobs arrive sequentially and processing decisions are made causally, the (bin) packing problem, where items of different sizes have to be packed in the smallest number of bins, where each bin has a fixed capacity, e.g., storing differently sized data files on finite sized disks, an ad allocation problem in web-advertising, where on a user's arrival to a webpage an online decision has to be made about which ads to display, and many others.

Because of the sequential input setting, quantifying the performance of an online algorithm is difficult, i.e., directly defining or finding an optimal online algorithm is hard. Hence, a 'strong' performance measure called the *competitive ratio* is used, which is defined as the maximum of the ratio of the objective function of an online algorithm and the optimal offline algorithm (which has access to full input to begin with) over all possible input instances, where inputs can even be chosen adversarially. Thus, the goal is to design online algorithms with small competitive ratios. Even though holding an online algorithm to the standard of the offline optimal algorithm via competitive ratio appears unfair, surprisingly for most of the optimization problems of interest, online algorithms with small competitive ratios have been derived. Thus, even with a limited view of the input, online algorithms can remain 'close' to the offline optimal algorithm, which is remarkable.

Designing optimal or near-optimal online algorithms is not only of theoretical interest but also of profound practical significance. For example, the web advertising business is worth billions of dollars, where on arrival of a user to a webpage, a decision is made about which ads to display depending on the user profile. Each advertiser pays a fixed revenue to the web platform to display an ad and accrues a payoff or utility from the user depending on its profile. The ad display decision has to be made online, as and when a user arrives, without knowing the profiles (consequently the utilities) of users arriving in the future. Other paradigms where sequential decisions are made with progressively accumulating data include cloud computing and big data problems, both of which are multi-billion dollar businesses.

Theoretical results on online algorithms began with the consideration of the classical problems, such as list accessing, bin packing, paging, load balancing, and job scheduling. These are examples of canonical online problems with tremendous impact in the area of operations research, operating systems, and large-scale computing in data centres. As the area evolved, rich combinatorial problems with wide applications were considered, such as the facility location, the travelling salesman, and the knapsack.

Problems motivated by more modern applications such as web advertising (AdWords problem), server allocations in cloud computing (convex optimization with switching costs), and machine learning (k-means clustering) have been considered in depth more recently. Many applied online paradigms have also been studied extensively, e.g., green communication networks, where nodes are powered by harvesting energy from renewable sources, and the transmission decisions have to be made without any knowledge of future harvested energy.

Since online algorithms are compared against optimal offline algorithms, which is a somewhat pessimistic metric, online algorithms endowed with a little more 'power' are also of interest. Typically, this power is either in terms of (i) resource augmentation, where the online algorithm is allowed more resources than the offline algorithm, (ii) lookahead, where the online algorithm is allowed to know the future input of finite length, and (iii) recourse, where the online algorithm is allowed to change a finite number of its prior decisions. For different online problems one or more of these possibilities are relevant.

With the advancement of the machine learning models, for many online problems, future inputs can be reasonably predicted. For example, the arriving user profiles in the web advertising model. Following this, the most recent trend in the area of online algorithms is to design online algorithms that are arbitrarily close to the optimal offline algorithm if the prediction is accurate, while the same online algorithm has a small competitive ratio even if the prediction is inaccurate. Importantly, this needs to be accomplished without knowing the accuracy level of the machine learning model.

BRIEF DESCRIPTION OF THE BOOK

There are many different mathematical techniques that have been developed to analyse online algorithms, such as potential function arguments, primal–dual methods, Yao's principle, and beyond the worst case analysis with machine learning predicted input, to name a few. We present a comprehensive view of most of these techniques and illustrate their use via multiple examples. The book is presented in a cohesive and easy-to-follow manner but without losing the mathematical rigour. The treatment is such that the book is accessible to anyone with mathematical maturity without any necessary advanced prerequisites. Sufficient background and critical details are provided for the advanced mathematical concepts required for solving the considered problems.

In the first part of the book, we cover most of the classical online paradigms, such as the ski-rental, metrical task systems, list accessing, bin packing, metrical task system, k-server, paging, secretary, knapsack, bipartite matching, and load balancing. Next, we discuss a generic technique called the primal–dual schema, and present algorithms built using the primal–dual philosophy for important online problems such as set cover, AdWords, etc. The two related and important problems called the facility location and k-means clustering (a fundamental problem in machine learning) are discussed next. Thereafter, we present three prominent and interrelated scheduling problems in sufficient detail.

In addition to the classical worst-case input setting, we also consider the new paradigm of 'beyond worst case', where online algorithms are augmented with predictions using machine learning algorithms to get competitive ratio results that degrade smoothly with prediction error, without any prior information on the quality of the prediction. We consider this prediction paradigm in depth for multiple problems, such as ski-rental, paging, secretary, and scheduling with deadlines.

The final part of the book covers applied problems such as routing in networks, server provisioning in cloud systems (convex optimization with switching constraints), communication with energy harvested from renewable sources, and submodular partitioning.

As mentioned before, online algorithms with some slightly more power than the optimal offline algorithm, known as resource augmentation, are also of interest. We discuss three different regimes of resource augmentation for the relevant problems at appropriate places in the book mainly via exercises.

TARGET AUDIENCE

Online algorithms is a growing area of research with great interest from the theoretical computer science community, in the field of operations research and combinatorial optimization, for the design of communication networks, and solving resource allocation problems. The book is targeted at interested graduate students and first-time readers looking for an easy and rigorous introduction to the area of online algorithms.

REASONS FOR WRITING THE BOOK

Research on online algorithms primarily began in the 1980s when classical problems like list accessing, bin packing, ski-rental, and paging were considered. The area gained more interest in the 1990s with a lot of work reported on load balancing and scheduling, in addition to the classical problems. In the following two decades, 2000–2020, attention to online algorithms increased rapidly because of the advent of motivating problems from web advertising, machine learning, cloud computing, etc.

The aim of this book is to review this extensive work and present the material in a 'textbook' form that is readily accessible to senior undergraduate and graduate students. There are lecture notes available on the web covering specific topics; however, this book takes a unified view, and presents a cohesive treatment of interrelated concepts, and brings out connections between different problems of interest.

This book is born from the lecture notes that I have been developing while teaching this course for graduate students in 2017, 2019, 2021, and 2022, at the Tata Institute of Fundamental Research, Mumbai. The said lecture notes have been used by the students, and their feedback has been incorporated to improve the readability of the book. Most of the exercises have also been solved by them via homework or exam problems, providing a good gauge of their accessibility. I also maintain video course lectures for the full course at www.youtube.com/playlist?list=PLTtM9ThZ2L-c638AjqTskivmXwVTzTYnl which will keep getting regular updates.

For most of the chapters in the book, the focus is on describing the basic ideas that capture the key concepts that are useful for the considered problem, together with elegant analysis. In the interest of ease of exposition, for certain problems an algorithm with a weaker competitive ratio guarantee is discussed compared to the best-known algorithm. Exercises are presented at the end of each chapter allowing a hands-on exposure to the basic concepts covered in the chapter. Most of the exercises are broken down into several (simpler) parts to provide a clear path towards the solution. Some algorithms are also introduced and analysed via exercises that are not covered in the main body due to space constraints. To really make good use of the book, solving a large fraction of exercises is highly recommended.

The book is much longer than initially planned and even then many important online formulations could not be accommodated. Notable exclusions include discrepancy, graph colouring, disjoint set cover, minimum spanning tree, matching for general graphs, crowdsourcing, network throughput maximization, scheduling to minimize the age of information, and several others. All these problems are important in their own right and should be studied in detail.

HOW TO USE THE BOOK

For instructors

The book is longer than what can be covered in a usual full semester course of roughly 25–26 lectures. For my last two full course offerings, I was able to cover around 12 chapters each time. For a full-semester course, I would recommend covering Chapters 1–6 always, in addition to Chapter 10 on the primal–dual technique. Thereafter, depending on the instructor's taste and students' interests, one can choose either the combinatorial suite, Chapters 7–9, or the scheduling group, Chapters 12–15. Other more applied chapters can be prescribed as student reading.

For students

Essential reading for easy access to all parts of the book should include Chapter 1, Chapter 2 on ski-rental (for Yao's principle), and Chapter 7 (for the secretarial input model). All other chapters are self-contained with these three chapters as pre-requisites.

Classical online problems are reviewed in Chapters 2–6. These chapters should also give the basic flavour of results as well as generic analysis techniques. For students interested in scheduling, they can focus on Chapters 12–15, while for subset selection or combinatorial problems Chapters 7–9 and 20 should be of interest. The most versatile tool used for analysing online algorithms is the primal–dual technique that is reviewed in Chapter 10. Other chapters should be referenced for more applied problems.

FINAL REMARKS

I began the preface with a disclaimer; let me end with another. I am not a theoretical computer scientist working in the broad area of online algorithms. My own contributions to the area of online algorithms are mostly limited to scheduling problems motivated by applications in communication networks, which are only briefly reviewed in the book. However, I am deeply interested in the broad area of online algorithms and remain a sincere student. This book also reflects that passion with special emphasis on it being accessible to beginner students. Experts might find some parts too laborious but it is done keeping student interests in mind. For many problems covered in the book the original proofs are highly clever but very terse. With the aid of additional explanation, relevant examples, and illustrative figures, this book takes special care in presenting the proof ideas for simpler exposition for readers with limited background.

Acknowledgements

I would like to thank everyone who has made this book possible, especially my wife Rashmi, and son Niraad. All of us stuck together during the tough COVID period, during which most of the book was written.

I would like to thank all my colleagues who have made detailed comments on my various drafts that undoubtedly made the book more readable. Their critical comments have also shaped the structure and content of this book. Comments by Arindam Khan made me add a couple of chapters and helped reorganize the book. Discussions with Thomas Kesselheim about the corrected proofs of his papers on the weighted matching and knapsack problem have been very helpful. Comments by Rajshekhar Bhat, Abhishek Sinha, Mohit Sharma, Jaikumar Radhakrishnan, Kumar Appaiah, and Jayakrishnan Nair have helped immensely in polishing the writing. Thanks are also due to all the students who in the recent past have taken my course on online algorithms and helped in proofreading the manuscript. I would especially like to thank Spandan Senapati, Akhil Bhimaraju, Kumar Saurav, Kshitij Gajjar (who was a PhD student at TIFR, now an assistant professor at IIT-Jodhpur), Pranshu Gaba, Hari Krishnan P. A., Praveen C. V., Arghya Chakraborty, Malhar Managoli, Yeshwant Pandit, Agniv Bandyopadhyay, and Soumyajit Pyne.

Critical feedback from reviewers has also been helpful in smoothing the rough edges of the book and to keep a clear and sharp focus.

$\mathcal{A}$	A deterministic online algorithm
$\mathcal{R}$	A randomized online algorithm
OPT	Optimal offline algorithm
σ	input
$\mu_{\mathcal{A}} = \max_{\sigma} \dfrac{C_{\mathcal{A}}(\sigma)}{C_{\text{OPT}}(\sigma)}$	competitive ratio of a deterministic algorithm $\mathcal{A}$
$\mu_{\mathcal{R}} = \max_{\sigma} \dfrac{\mathbb{E}\{C_{\mathcal{R}}(\sigma)\}}{C_{\text{OPT}}(\sigma)}$	competitive ratio of a randomized algorithm $\mathcal{R}$
$\mathbb{P}(A)$	Probability of event A
$\mathbb{E}$	Expectation operator
$\mathbf{A}$	Matrix A
$\mathbf{A}(i,j)$	$(i,j)^{th}$ entry of matrix A
$\mathbf{a}$	vector a
$\mathbf{a}(i)$ or $\mathbf{a}_i$	i^{th} element of vector $\mathbf{a}$
$\mathbf{a}^T, \mathbf{A}^T$	Transpose of vector $\mathbf{a}$ or matrix $\mathbf{A}$
$\mathbb{R}, \mathbb{Z}, \mathbb{N}$	Set of real, integer, and natural numbers, respectively
$\mathbb{R}^+, \mathbb{Z}^+$	Set of non-negative real and integer numbers, respectively
$\mathbb{R}^{++}, \mathbb{Z}^{++}$	Set of positive real and integer numbers, respectively
$\mathbb{R}^d$	Set of real numbers in d dimensions
i.i.d.	independent and identically distributed
$|A|$	Number of elements in set A
For two sets $A, B, A \backslash B$	Set difference, elements of A that are not in B
$|a|$	Absolute value of for a real number a
$\mathbf{1}_E$	Indicator variable which is 1 if event E is true and 0 otherwise
∇f	derivative of f
t^+ and t^-	Just after time t and just before time t, respectively
$[n]$	the set $1, 2, \dots, n$
$\begin{pmatrix} n \\ k \end{pmatrix}$	all possible ways of choosing k elements out of total n elements

$f(n) = \Omega(g(n))$	If $\exists\, k > 0,\ n_0,\ \forall\, n > n_0,\ |g(n)|k \leq |f(n)|$
Big O $f(n) = \mathcal{O}(g(n))$	If $\exists\, k > 0,\ n_0,\ \forall\, n > n_0,\ |f(n)| \leq |g(n)|k$
$f(n) = \Theta(g(n))$	If $\exists\, k_1,\ k_2 > 0,\ n_0,\ \forall\, n > n_0,\ |g(n)|k_1 \leq |f(n)| \leq |g(n)|k_2$
Small O $f(n) = o(g(n))$	If $\lim_{n \to \infty} \frac{f(n)}{g(n)} = 0$

CHAPTER 1

Introduction

1.1 What Is an Online Algorithm

We begin the discussion on what an online algorithm is using a simple example. Consider a vector $\mathbf{X} = (x_1, x_2, \ldots, x_n)$, where $x_i \in \mathbb{R}^+$. Let the objective be to select that element of $\mathbf{X}$ that has the largest value $x_{i^\star}$, where $i^\star = \arg\max_i x_i$. In the usual setting, called **offline**, when the full vector $\mathbf{X}$ is observable/available, the best element $i^\star$ can be found trivially. Here trivially means that it is always possible to find $i^\star$, disregarding the complexity of finding it.

Next, consider an **online** setting, where at step t, an online algorithm observes x_t, the tth-element of $\mathbf{X}$, and needs to make one of the following two decisions: (i) Either select x_t, and declare it to be of the largest value, in which case no future element of $\mathbf{X} \backslash \mathbf{X}^t$ is presented to it, where $\mathbf{X}^t = (x_1, x_2, \ldots, x_t)$, or (ii) does not select x_t, and moves on to observe x_{t+1}, but in this case, it cannot later select any of the elements of $\mathbf{X}^t$ seen already.

Thus, an online algorithm is limited in its view of the input and has to make decisions after observing partial inputs that cannot be changed in the future. Under these online/causal constraints, the online algorithm's objective is still to select the best element $i^\star$. Clearly, this is a challenging task, and depends on the order in which elements of $\mathbf{X}$ are presented, i.e., the online algorithm's decisions might be different with input $\mathbf{X}$ or $\pi(\mathbf{X})$, where π is any permutation, since the online algorithm makes decisions after observing partial inputs. In fact one can argue that no online algorithm can always select the best element $i^\star$ unlike an offline algorithm. Hence, a trivial problem in the offline setting turns out to be quite difficult in the online setting, where it is known as the **secretary** problem. We will discuss the secretary problem in detail in Chapter 7.

To better understand the definition of an online algorithm, consider another example. Let $\mathbf{Y} = \{y_1, y_2, \ldots, y_n\}$ be a set of elements, where y_i represents the 'size' of element i with $0 < y_i < 1, 1 \leq i \leq n$. The objective is to partition the n elements of $\mathbf{Y}$ into as few disjoint subsets as possible, such that the sum of the sizes of all items in each subset is at most 1 (capacity constraint), and the union of all subsets is equal to $\mathbf{Y}$. Disregarding the complexity of finding the solution, if the whole set $\mathbf{Y}$ is available (the offline setting), it is always possible to find such a partition, e.g., using complete enumeration. This problem is popularly called the **bin-packing** problem.

In the online setting, let $\mathbf{Y}^t = \{y_1, y_2, \ldots, y_t\}$ be the prefix of $\mathbf{Y}$ that is revealed until time step t. At each step t, with the knowledge of only $\mathbf{Y}^t$, an online algorithm has to compute its partition under the constraint that in the future, partition can only be augmented. That is, at step t, by observing the newest element t with size y_t, the algorithm can either assign y_t to any of the existing subsets (if the constraint on the sum of the sizes is satisfied) or open a new subset. It cannot 'disturb' the elements already assigned to subsets.

Similar to the secretary problem, the number of subsets used by an online algorithm will depend on the order of arrival of elements of $\mathbf{Y}$, i.e., possibly different with $\mathbf{Y}$ or $\pi(\mathbf{Y})$, while the number of subsets used by the offline algorithm does not depend on π. Compared to the offline setting, complete enumeration is useless for finding an online algorithm given the limited information setting it has to work with in the presence of the augmentation requirement. Thus, even with unlimited complexity, finding an optimal online algorithm is non-trivial.

With these two examples under our belt, we next define an online algorithm abstractly. In general, let σ be the full input, σ^t its t-length prefix, and σ_t the input revealed at time t. A deterministic online algorithm $\mathcal{A}$, at step t, observes σ_t, has the knowledge of σ^{t-1}, and makes an irrevocable decision at time t denoted by D_t using only the information revealed so far, i.e., σ^t. The overall cost of $\mathcal{A}$ with input σ is then represented as

$$f_{\mathcal{A}}(\sigma) = f(D_1(\sigma^1), D_2(\sigma^2), \dots, D_{|\sigma|}(\sigma^{|\sigma|})),$$

where f is the objective function.

To highlight the challenge faced by an online algorithm, consider that the input σ is partitioned into two equal sized parts σ_1 and σ_2, i.e., $\sigma = (\sigma_1, \sigma_2)$. Moreover, let σ_2 take two possible values σ_{21} and σ_{22}. An online algorithm $\mathcal{A}$ until the end of sub-input σ_1 does not know whether σ_2 is equal to σ_{21} or σ_{22}. So the immediate question is: what should $\mathcal{A}$ do until the end of sub-input σ_1?

One possibility is that $\mathcal{A}$ assumes that σ_2 is equal to σ_{21} (σ_{22}) and makes its decisions appropriately until the end of sub-input σ_1. However, if σ_2 is equal to σ_{22} (σ_{21}), then in hindsight $\mathcal{A}$'s cost could turn out be too large compared to if it had guessed the correct input σ_{22} (σ_{21}). A more prudent alternative for $\mathcal{A}$ is to assume that an adversary is going to choose σ_2 among σ_{21} and σ_{22} depending on its decisions until the end of sub-input σ_1 to maximize $\mathcal{A}$'s overall cost. Consequently, $\mathcal{A}$ should make its decisions until the end of sub-input σ_1, such that in hindsight its cost is not too large in either of the two cases. This approach appears more reasonable for the online paradigm when no assumption about the future inputs is made.

Essentially, what this entails is that $\mathcal{A}$ should not overly commit to σ_2 being either σ_{21} or σ_{22}, and keep equal 'distance' from the two hindsight optimal algorithms corresponding to (σ_1, σ_{21}) and (σ_1, σ_{22}). As a result, the cost of $\mathcal{A}$ will be larger than the hindsight optimal algorithm for both cases (σ_1, σ_{21}) and (σ_1, σ_{22}), however, will be guarded against adversarial choice of σ_{21} or σ_{22}. The ensuing penalty compared to the hindsight optimal algorithm controls the performance of $\mathcal{A}$. We next formalize this idea to describe the performance metric for online algorithms.

Consider the offline setting, where the complete input σ is available at time 0 non-causally, and OPT is an optimal algorithm knowing the complete input σ. One could equivalently think of OPT as an hindsight optimal algorithm. For input σ, let the cost of OPT be $f_{\mathrm{OPT}}(\sigma)$, where note that OPT does not make sequential or causal decisions, unlike an online algorithm. Following on from the preceding discussion, since OPT is the hindsight optimal algorithm, we can benchmark the performance of an online algorithm $\mathcal{A}$ against the OPT under the uncertain future input model which could possibly be adversarial.

One such performance metric is the **regret**, that for an online algorithm $\mathcal{A}$ is defined as

$$\mathbf{R}(\mathcal{A}) = \max_{\sigma} |f_{\mathrm{OPT}}(\sigma) - f_{\mathcal{A}}(\sigma)|,$$

the largest difference between the cost of the OPT and that of an online algorithm, over the worst case input. The maximization over the input σ represents the adversary that can choose input at any time depending on prior decisions made by $\mathcal{A}$ to reflect the maximum penalty $\mathcal{A}$ has to pay. With regret as the metric of choice, the quest is to find an online algorithm whose regret is sub-linear in the size $|\sigma|$ of the input σ so that the regret normalized with $|\sigma|$ goes to zero. It turns out that for most of the online problems of interest, sub-linear regret is not possible, and hence a weaker metric called the **competitive ratio**, defined next, is used far more popularly.

For a minimization problem (where the goal is to minimize an objective function), the **competitive ratio** of a deterministic online algorithm $\mathcal{A}$ is defined as

$$\mu_{\mathcal{A}} = \max_{\sigma} \frac{f_{\mathcal{A}}(\sigma)}{f_{\text{OPT}}(\sigma)}, \tag{1.1}$$

i.e., the largest ratio of the cost of an online algorithm and the OPT, maximized over all possible inputs. For a maximization problem, the max is replaced by a min to define

$$\mu_{\mathcal{A}} = \min_{\sigma} \frac{f_{\mathcal{A}}(\sigma)}{f_{\text{OPT}}(\sigma)}. \tag{1.2}$$

Similar to the regret definition, the maximization (minimization) over the input σ to define the competitive ratio represents the adversary that captures the maximum multiplicative penalty $\mathcal{A}$ pays compared to OPT.

The competitive ratio is an unforgiving metric, since an online algorithm that has its cost close to that of the OPT for all almost all inputs, except a few where it is comparatively very large, will be termed bad. To keep the competitive ratio small an online algorithm has to make sure that its cost is close to that of the OPT for all possible inputs. With competitive ratio as the performance metric, the goal is to find online algorithms with constant (and smallest/largest possible depending on whether it is a min/max problem) competitive ratios, i.e., independent of all parameters of the problem specification, and the input. Competitive ratio is a multiplicative metric as compared to the regret that is an additive metric, and thus provides a weaker guarantee even when it is a constant.

One may ask why compare an online algorithm with the OPT (offline setting), isn't that too unfair? The answer to that is multifold. First is the fact that OPT is the absolute benchmark, and if the competitive ratio of an online algorithm is small, this implies that the online algorithm is nearly making optimal decisions even with partial inputs. Second is the difficulty in even defining an optimal online algorithm under the uncertain future input model. Even though the competitive ratio is a pessimistic metric, for many of the problems of interest, the competitive ratio can be shown to be small constants, which is remarkable, and makes the comparison with OPT meaningful. Moreover, considering the competitive ratio metric, robustness to input perturbation is embedded in the online algorithm, since the competitive ratio guarantee is with respect to the worst case input. An added feature of most of the analysis on online algorithms is that their competitive ratios can be bounded without explicitly characterizing the OPT.[1]

---

[1] For most of the problems considered in the chapter, finding OPT that is efficient (polynomial time complexity) is not possible. Thus, the obvious step is to approximate the cost of OPT using efficient algorithms. [1] is an excellent reference for approximation algorithms.

We will discuss the implications of the definition of competitive ratio in a little more detail in Section 1.3. We next outline some of the applications that motivate the study of online algorithms.

1.2 Why Study Online Algorithms

In this section, we discuss some of the motivating online settings that are driven by important practical problems.

Buy/Rent Problems Consider that you need an expensive resource, e.g., a luxury car or a yacht. As is natural, buying it outright costs you much more than renting it. If you knew for how long you were going to need that resource, the problem is easy to solve: pick the choice that costs less. The fact that makes the problem interesting is that you do not know how long you need that resource for, which could be on account of a variety of reasons, such as weather, future appointments, emergencies, etc. Thus, each day you have to decide whether to keep renting or buy, given the unknown remaining use-time. This is a canonical online problem, where the uncertainty is in the number of days for which you need the resource. This problem is popularly known as the **ski-rental** problem, named so for the usual unpredictability of the remaining length of the ski-season.

The ski-rental problem is also closely connected to problems with applications in different areas such as snoopy caching, where there are shared cached systems with a common memory, or the TCP acknowledgment problem, where TCP is the backbone protocol for sending packets reliably over the internet.

Memory Management in Operating Systems Memory systems in most computing platforms typically consist of two parts: one slow but large memory and one fast but small memory, called **cache**. At each step of computation, a file is requested. If a requested file is available in the cache, then execution starts immediately. Otherwise, a fault is counted to model the delay, etc., and the requested file has to be loaded into the cache before execution. Since cache is of limited size, to load the newly requested file, some existing file has to be ejected from the cache. For fast processing, one needs to minimize the number of faults, which in turn depends on the choice of the file being ejected on each fault by the algorithm. This problem is popularly known as the paging or the caching problem, and is another canonical example of an online problem, since the set of future requested files is unknown and depends on the nature of the computation task. The problem got renewed attention because of widespread use of content distribution networks, e.g., YouTube, that want to store small amounts of popular information close to the user end.

Operations Research/Combinatorial Optimization Suppose the task is to plumb a house, which requires pipes of different lengths. Pipes in the market are, however, available only in fixed lengths. Thus, a relatively basic but non-trivial problem is how to cut the fixed length pipes into required lengths so as to waste as little as possible or to minimize the cost of plumbing. A two-dimensional variant of this example occurs in the production setting where glass/metal sheets are produced in fixed rectangular sizes, rather than in customized forms. Using these fixed size sheets, required sizes are cut, and the objective is to use as few sheets as possible, or to minimize the wastage. This decision problem is also encountered in inventory management, where pellets or containers need to be packed with objects of different sizes and weights, subject to a size or weight capacity.

The abstracted version of this problem is called **bin-packing**, whose one-dimensional definition is as follows. A large number of bins are available with a finite weight capacity, and items with different weights have to be packed in as few bins as possible, while respecting the bin weight capacity. The obvious generalization of this is when items arrive sequentially, e.g., demand for a certain shape of glass/metal piece or a new shipment, which gives rise to the online setting, where on an item's arrival, the assignment has to be immediate and irrevocable.

Web Advertising One of the most important problems in the online setting, which is also responsible for the renewed interest in the study of online algorithms, is what is called the **AdWords** problem. In the early 2000s, with the explosion of web traffic, web portals had this massive opportunity for revenue generation by displaying advertisements, or ads, to users arriving on their web pages. Each advertiser had a user-specific utility if its ad was viewed by the particular user, for which it was ready to pay a certain price to the web portal, subject to a total payment budget. The web portal's decision problem was to match or assign an advertiser's ad to a slot on the webpage on the user's arrival, so as to maximize the total revenue it could extract from the advertisers. This business model is worth billions of dollars, and solving this problem is highly important.

The AdWords problem is actually a variation of the maximum weight matching problem defined over graphs. For a graph, let each edge have an associated weight. The problem is to choose a subset of edges so as to maximize the sum of weights of the chosen edges, under the *matching* condition that no two chosen edges should have a common endpoint. The more popularly studied version of the matching problem is when the graph is restricted to being a bipartite graph, where there are only two sets of vertices, left and right, and edges exist only between a left and a right vertex, if at all. The bipartite matching problem models many problems of immense interest such as matching customers and taxis for ride hailing applications such as Uber, Ola, etc. The online aspect is immediately clear for the pertinent examples described above, where once a customer is assigned a taxi it cannot be reassigned, and customers arrive with arbitrary destination requests and paying capacity in future.

Networking A network is typically modelled as a graph, and the edges of the graph are either assigned some capacity that limits the amount of traffic through it, or a cost function that is an increasing function of the amount of traffic passing through it. A canonical problem in networking is *routing* with multiple objectives. For example, one may want to maximize the amount of traffic passing through the network respecting edge capacity constraints or minimize the total delay of the network. For this general setup, the most interesting regime is online, since traffic arrives at arbitrary times for arbitrary source–destination pairs, which is difficult to predict. The routing problem is also connected to the fundamental question of online load balancing. To see this, assume that the objective is to minimize the total delay of the network. Clearly, any such solution will make sure that not much traffic passes through any one particular edge, implying balanced traffic across different edges.

Scheduling At a high level, **scheduling** means allocating limited resources to tasks in a certain order. Scheduling problems arise in many different contexts, e.g., machine scheduling on factory floors, computation jobs, queuing systems, airline schedules, and many others. The simplest abstraction of the scheduling problem is that jobs with different processing requirements (typically called sizes) arrive in a queue where they wait to be dispatched to a server, and depart once their processing is complete. Typical performance metrics studied in scheduling include makespan, total delay or response time, or completion time, which are some specific functions of the difference between the departure and the arrival time of each job. For most of these applications, the natural setting to consider is online, where jobs arrive over time, and decisions about scheduling or job-server assignments have to be made causally without the knowledge of future job arrivals.

Renewable Energy Powered Communication My own interest in studying online algorithms was necessitated by a modern communication problem, where the energy needed for communication is extracted from renewable sources. Traditionally, communication devices have been powered either by conventional energy sources or with batteries. With the increased push for green communication, as well as to increase the usage lifetime for devices installed in the field, harvesting energy from wind, solar, electromagnetic, and kinetic sources, has been envisaged. Even though this basic premise is far reaching, with renewable sources, it is difficult to predict the quantum and arrival times of energy arriving in the future. Initial research on green communication was based on the assumption of certain stochastic models for energy arrivals; however, there was no consensus on what is the 'right' model. To obviate the need for choosing a model, an online communication setting emerges, where an algorithm has to choose its transmission rate or energy usage depending on the energy received so far, without knowing the future energy availability or its distribution. This is a unique online scheduling problem where the resource (energy) needed to process jobs itself arrives over time.

1.3 Metric for Online Algorithms

Recall from (1.1) the definition of the performance metric, called the competitive ratio, for online algorithms. Because of the maximization with respect to the input in (1.1), it is an adversarial metric, where the input can be chosen by an adversary in order to maximize the competitive ratio.

In particular, consider a deterministic online algorithm $\mathcal{A}$. Once the deterministic online algorithm $\mathcal{A}$ is specified, the adversary can choose the input knowing the decisions to be made by $\mathcal{A}$ in order to increase its competitive ratio (1.1) (or decrease (1.2)). For example, for the secretary problem discussed in Section 1.1, if $\mathcal{A}$ is deterministic of the following form: sample the first $n/2$ elements, and record the element with the largest value (called threshold) among the first $n/2$ elements. None of the first $n/2$ elements are selected. Then starting from the $n/2 + 1^{st}$ element, select the earliest element that has a value larger than the threshold. Such an algorithm appears reasonable; however, knowing it, the adversary can ensure that the best element is always part of the first $n/2$ elements. Consequently, the best element will never be selected by $\mathcal{A}$, and $\mu_{\mathcal{A}}$ can be made arbitrarily small (recall that the secretary problem is a maximization problem).

As we will see in many chapters of the book, even under this limitation, there are deterministic online algorithms for many problems with constant competitive ratios.

A natural extension of a deterministic online algorithm is a randomized algorithm, which is essentially equivalent to having a probability distribution over all possible deterministic algorithms. Unlike deterministic online algorithms, for randomized online algorithms, one needs to be careful about the definition of the adversary: whether the adversary is allowed to see the outcome of the random choices made by the randomized online algorithm or not. This question leads to a broad classification of adversaries, the most popular among them being the oblivious adversary.

Definition 1.3.1 *For randomized online algorithms, the* **oblivious adversary** *has to generate the entire input sequence in advance before any requests are served by the online algorithm. Moreover, the adversary's cost is equal to the cost of the optimal offline algorithm* OPT *for that input sequence.*

To belabour the point, this means that the adversary knows the distribution over all possible deterministic algorithms that the randomized algorithm is using but it cannot see the random choices made by the algorithm sequentially.

For a randomized algorithm $\mathcal{R}$ against an oblivious adversary, the competitive ratio (1.1) specializes to

$$\mu_{\mathcal{R}} = \max_{\sigma} \frac{\mathbb{E}\{f_{\mathcal{R}}(\sigma)\}}{f_{\text{OPT}}(\sigma)}, \tag{1.3}$$

where the expectation is over the random choices made by the algorithm.

There are stronger adversaries that are also defined for randomized online algorithms. We review their definitions and the connections between them in Appendix A.1. Throughout the book, whenever we consider a randomized algorithm, by default it is analysed against an oblivious adversary.

1.3.1 Why Adversarial Inputs

One question that is pertinent while considering online algorithms is: why consider adversarial inputs when *nature* is not adversarial? The choice of adversarial input is primarily to avoid making a choice about the true input model (which may be very difficult). To buttress this point, suppose magically the precise input or a class of inputs is known. In this case, one can design an algorithm that is tuned to that input. However, if the input model needs to be redefined for any reason in future or is inexact, a complete redesign of the algorithm might be necessitated. This reworking can be totally avoided if no assumptions are made on the input. Thus a safe choice is to assume that the input is as bad as it can be for an algorithm compared to OPT, and quantify the performance of the algorithm via its competitive ratio. This approach would have been meaningless if algorithms with reasonable competitive ratios did not exist. However, remarkably, as we see in the book, for a large variety of problems, algorithms with competitive ratios that are constant or that grow logarithmically with the parameters of the input have been designed. This book is dedicated to this success story.

1.3.2 Beyond the Worst Case Input

With the advent of very powerful machine learning algorithms, e.g., neural networks, it is not hard to imagine the setting where future input can in fact be predicted with reasonable accuracy. So the obvious challenge in designing online algorithms is whether we can leverage the prediction information and improve the performance of the algorithm when the prediction is highly accurate, while still ensuring the worst case guarantee in case the prediction is noisy. This model also alleviates some criticism about the metric of competitive ratio, since its guarantee is against the worst case input; however, by and large, the observed inputs are not adversarial. This new paradigm (called **beyond the worst case**) has attracted sufficient attention from the online algorithms community in the recent past, and in a remarkably short time, algorithms that achieve these dual objectives have been devised for many problems of interest. In this book, we consider beyond the worst case setting for multiple problems, and highlight the main ideas behind this approach.

1.4 Complexity Implications for Online Algorithms

In the usual offline setting for solving any problem, where the full input is available, any useful algorithm should be efficient, i.e., its complexity should be polynomial in the size of the input. It is instructive to note that we have not enforced any such requirement for online algorithms. The reason for this relaxation is that, unlike the offline setting, in the online setting, the adversary can adapt the input sequentially depending on the decisions made by the online algorithm. Thus, it is not easy to find online algorithms with small competitive ratios even with unlimited complexity. For example, for the secretary problem, there is no brute-force or complete enumeration based algorithm that can be shown to have a small competitive ratio. Thus, throughout this book, we will disregard the complexity of the studied online algorithms, where in most of the cases they will be efficient anyway.

1.5 Overview of the Book

In Chapters 2–15, we consider most of the basic and well-known online problems, while in the subsequent chapters, we consider some applied online problems that have applications in many different areas.

For most of the chapters in the book, the focus is on describing the basic ideas that are useful for the considered problem together with elegant analysis. For certain problems, in the interest of the ease of exposition, an algorithm with a weaker competitive ratio guarantee is discussed compared to the best-known algorithm.

We begin the discussion on online algorithms with perhaps the simplest online problem, called the ski-rental problem. With the ski-rental problem, an algorithm has to decide each day between renting (low cost) and buying (high cost) the ski, given the uncertain length of the total skiing season, with the objective of minimizing the total cost paid till the end of the skiing season. The ski-rental problem captures the uncertainty about the future input that an online algorithm faces in the simplest form, and is a remarkably useful primitive for many applied problems. Using the ski-rental problem as an example, we also discuss the generic technique called the Yao's principle to lower bound the competitive ratio of randomized online algorithms.

The list-accessing and bin-packing, which are two of the earliest studied online problems, are discussed next in Chapters 3 and 4. The paging problem, a canonical online problem and one of the most exhaustively studied in the literature because of its importance in computing systems, is discussed next.

In Chapter 6, we discuss a very general online problem formulation called the metrical task system (MTS) and its special case, the k-server problem. MTS generalizes several other important online problems, such as paging and list-accessing.

Subsequently, the secretary problem and its extensions, the knapsack problem, and the bipartite matching problem are considered. The secretary problem has its origins in the applied probability literature, where exact solutions have been obtained using dynamic programming and the Markov decision theory. The weighted bipartite matching problem is a bit modern and is directly applicable for online web-advertising and auctions.

The classical graph theory problem, the travelling salesman problem, in its online avatar is discussed next, which is useful for unknown graph exploration models. After this, we review the load balancing problem that is of great importance in call centres, supermarket queues, and large-scale cloud servers.

A generic primal–dual technique is discussed in Chapter 10 that is useful for analysing a number of online algorithms for different problems, such as the set cover problem, the bipartite matching problem, and the AdWords problems, to name a few.

In Chapter 11, we discuss the facility location problem, where on arrival of each request, either a new facility is opened (which costs a fixed amount) or the request is assigned to the nearest existing open facility (incurring a distance cost) with an objective of minimizing the total cost after all request arrivals. The k-means clustering problem, which is of immense interest in the machine learning community, is closely related to the facility location problem. We expose this connection and present an online algorithm for the k-means clustering problem and bound its competitive ratio.

Three important variants of the job scheduling problem are presented in Chapters 13–15, where in Chapter 13 we consider that the processor speeds are fixed, while in Chapters 14–15 speed tuneable processors are considered.

In the last part of the book, we consider applied problems, such as multi-commodity routing over an undirected network, server provisioning in large-scale cloud systems, also known as online convex optimization with switching cost, green communication (communication powered with renewable energy sources), and submodular partitioning for welfare maximization.

CHAPTER 2

Ski-Rental

2.1 Introduction

In this chapter, we consider a canonical online problem that captures the basic decision question encountered in online algorithms. Assume that you arrive at a ski resort in the middle of the ski season. To rent a pair of skis, it takes $1 per day, while to buy them outright, it costs P. On each new day, you only get to see whether the season is on-going or not, and have to decide whether to buy the ski or keep renting. The objective is to ski for as long as the season lasts with minimum cost possible without, however, knowing the remaining length of the skiing season. This problem is popularly known as the **ski-rental** problem. The ski-rental problem illustrates the inherent challenge of making decisions under uncertainty, where the uncertainty can even be controlled by an adversary depending on your current or past decisions.

The ski-rental problem models the classic rent/buy dilemma, where the uncertainty about future utility makes the problem challenging. It is highly relevant in various real-world applications, e.g., whether to rent/buy an expensive equipment or a luxury item with unknown number of days of utility, networking/scheduling problems where there are multiple servers with different service guarantees and prices. In scheduling, the following simple problem is equivalent to the ski-rental problem. Consider two servers, where one is shared and follows a FIFO discipline and has a minimal cost while the other is costly but dedicated. The decision to make for each user/packet is whether to stay with the shared server or jump to the dedicated one any time until it is served/processed.

In this chapter, we consider both deterministic and randomized algorithms for the ski-rental problem, and derive optimal algorithms in both settings, which is typically not possible for most of the other online problems considered in the book. We also describe the generic technique to lower bound the competitive ratio of randomized algorithms using Yao's principle. Two extensions of the ski-rental problem – the TCP (transmission control protocol) acknowledgement problem and the Bahncard problem – are also discussed at the end.

2.2 Problem Formulation

To begin the concrete discussion for the ski-rental problem, let the unknown length of the remaining skiing season be L from the day on which you arrive. Renting the ski for any day costs $1, while buying it outright on any day costs P.

Any deterministic algorithm for the ski-rental problem is of the form: rent the ski for $k - 1$ days (consecutively), and buy the ski on the kth day if $L \geq k$. We call such an algorithm $\mathcal{A}_k$. The cost of $\mathcal{A}_k$ is

$$C_{\mathcal{A}_k} = \begin{cases} L & \text{if } L < k, \\ P + k - 1 & \text{otherwise.} \end{cases} \tag{2.1}$$

OPT on the other hand knowing true L always pays the cost of $C_{\text{OPT}} = \min\{L, P\}$, since if $L < P$, then it rents the ski for L days, while, otherwise, it buys the ski on day one itself.

Thus, the competitive ratio of $\mathcal{A}_k$ is

$$\mu_{\mathcal{A}_k} = \max\left\{ \max_{L \geq k} \frac{P + k - 1}{\min\{L, P\}}, \max_{L < k} \frac{L}{\min\{L, P\}} \right\}. \tag{2.2}$$

The goal is to find k with minimum $\mu_{\mathcal{A}_k}$ by choosing an appropriate value of k.

A randomized algorithm $\mathcal{R}$ for the ski-rental problem chooses $\mathcal{A}_k$, $k \in \mathbb{N}$ with probability p_k, and its competitive ratio is

$$\mu_{\mathcal{R}} = \max_L \frac{\mathbb{E}\{C_{\mathcal{A}_k}\}}{\min\{L, P\}}.$$

2.3 Deterministic Algorithms

Theorem 2.3.1 $\mathcal{A}_P$ is the optimal deterministic algorithm for the ski-rental problem that rents for $P - 1$ days and buys the ski on the Pth day if $L \geq P$, and the optimal competitive ratio is $2 - \frac{1}{P}$.

Proof: Among all deterministic algorithms $\mathcal{A}_k$, $k \geq 1$, for the ski-rental problem one intuitively good choice that tries to balance the total renting and buying cost is $k = P$, where P is the price to buy the ski. Depending on L,

$$\frac{C_{\mathcal{A}_P}}{C_{\text{OPT}}} = \begin{cases} 1 & \text{if } L < P, \\ \frac{2P-1}{P} & \text{otherwise,} \end{cases} \tag{2.3}$$

since when $L < P$, $\mathcal{A}_P = \text{OPT}$, while for $L \geq P$, OPT buys the ski on day one itself but $\mathcal{A}_P$ incurs a cost of $P - 1 + P$. Thus, taking the worst case over all L, we get

$$\mu_{\mathcal{A}_P} = 2 - \frac{1}{P}.$$

The remaining question is: can we do better by choosing $k \leq P - 1$ or $k > P$? To answer this question, note that for $\mathcal{A}_k$ the worst-case length of the skiing season (chosen by the adversary) is $L = k$, i.e., ski season ends on the day you buy the ski. This follows since choosing $L > k$, $\mathcal{A}_k$ pays no additional cost from day $k + 1$ onwards, while the cost of OPT remains $\min\{L, P\}$. Similarly, one can argue against $L < k$. Thus to maximize the competitive ratio of $\mathcal{A}_k$, the adversary will always choose $L = k$. Once we have this fact, a simple exercise reveals that for any k (Problem 2.1) algorithm $\mathcal{A}_k$ has

$$\mu_{\mathcal{A}_k} = \begin{cases} \dfrac{P+k-1}{k} & \text{if } k \leq P, \\ \dfrac{P+k-1}{P} & \text{otherwise.} \end{cases} \tag{2.4}$$

From (2.4),

$$\arg\min_k \mu_{\mathcal{A}_k} = P,$$

i.e., the intuitive choice of renting for $P - 1$ days (algorithm $\mathcal{A}_P$) is in fact optimal. Consequently, the best competitive ratio for any deterministic algorithm is $2 - \dfrac{1}{P}$. ∎

An alternate way of thinking about the competitive ratio for the ski-rental problem is to consider that the adversary is solving the problem

$$\max_L \mu_{\mathcal{A}_k},$$

while the algorithm is trying to solve

$$\min_k \max_L \mu_{\mathcal{A}_k}.$$

Thus, the algorithm first fixes a value of k to which the adversary responds by choosing the worst-case L, and then the algorithm chooses k anticipating the response of the adversary to minimize the competitive ratio.

The cost of $\mathcal{A}_k$ is given by (2.1). It is easy to argue that the algorithm will never choose $k > P$, since if $k > P$ the adversary will choose $L = k > P$ and OPT will buy on day one itself, making

$$\mu_{\mathcal{A}_k} = \frac{k+P-1}{P} > \mu_{\mathcal{A}_P} = \frac{2P-1}{P}$$

for any $k > P$. For any choice $k \leq P$ of $\mathcal{A}_k$, the adversary responds to the chosen k by picking $L = k$, which makes the competitive ratio the largest given by

$$\max_L \mu_{\mathcal{A}_k} = \frac{P+k-1}{k}. \tag{2.5}$$

Clearly, for $k \in [1 : P]$ the optimal value of k for the algorithm that minimizes the competitive ratio (2.5) is $k = P$, and the resulting competitive ratio is

$$\min_k \max_L \mu_{\mathcal{A}_k} = \min_k \frac{P+k-1}{k} = \frac{2P-1}{P} = 2 - \frac{1}{P}.$$

This way we can also directly solve the min–max problem. There is an intuitive appeal to Theorem 2.3.1 as a function of P. When $P = 1$, then an algorithm can buy on day one itself and it is equivalent to OPT. As P increases, any algorithm's uncertainty about when to buy increases, and in the limit $P \to \infty$, the competitive ratio converges to 2.

To further identify the limitations of an online algorithm, we illustrate its performance when the length of the skiing season is stochastic and not chosen by an adversary.

Example 2.3.2

Let the length L of the skiing season be geometrically distributed with success probability p (i.e., season ends as soon as the first success event is realized). Then the competitive ratio $\mu_{\mathcal{A}_k}$ of algorithm $\mathcal{A}_k$ that rents for $k - 1$ days and buys on the kth day can be computed as follows.

Conditioned on L, with $L < k$, $\frac{C_{\mathcal{A}_k}}{C_{OPT}} = \frac{L}{\min\{L,P\}}$, while for $L \geq k$, $\frac{C_{\mathcal{A}_k}}{C_{OPT}} = \frac{k-1+P}{\min\{L,P\}}$. Hence the expected competitive ratio[1] is

$$\mathbb{E}\{\mu_{\mathcal{A}_k}\} = \sum_{\ell < k} \mathbb{P}(L = \ell) \frac{\ell}{\min\{\ell, P\}} + \sum_{\ell \geq k} \mathbb{P}(L = \ell) \frac{k - 1 + P}{\min\{\ell, P\}},$$

$$= \sum_{\ell < k} (1 - p)^{\ell - 1} p \frac{\ell}{\min\{\ell, P\}} + \sum_{\ell \geq k} (1 - p)^{\ell - 1} p \frac{k - 1 + P}{\min\{\ell, P\}}.$$

Depending on the value of p, the optimal value of k can be found; however, there is no closed-form expression. The following remarks are in order. It is easy to see that the smaller the value of p (when the season lasts longer) the better it is to choose a small value of k, while if p is close to 1, it is profitable to select a large k and keep renting for a while.

In summary, deterministic algorithms have a limitation in terms of achieving competitive ratios better than 2 for large values of P. Next, we consider randomization to overcome this hurdle and illustrate the power of random choices made by an algorithm in confusing the adversary.

2.4 Randomized Algorithms

In Section 2.3, we saw that the best competitive ratio for any deterministic algorithm for the ski-rental problem is close to 2. In this section, we explore the idea of using randomized algorithms to see whether significant improvement can be made in terms of the competitive ratio if randomization is allowed. Throughout this book, with randomization, we consider an oblivious adversary that does not have access to the outcomes of the random coins of the algorithm, as discussed in Section 1.3.

The power of randomization lies in the fact that the adversary cannot choose the worst-case length of the skiing season depending on the algorithm's random choices that are private

---

[1] Here we are taking the expectation of the competitive ratio rather than the ratio of the expected cost of the algorithm and OPT.

to the algorithm. Thus, the adversary has less freedom to choose the length L, and that helps an algorithm to achieve a competitive ratio better than 2. We illustrate this idea first via a sub-optimal randomized algorithm, which can be generalized to get the optimal randomized algorithm in Problem 2.3.

Let $\mathcal{A}_k$ be a deterministic algorithm that buys the ski on day k (if $L \geq k$) and rents until then. Consider a simple randomized algorithm $\mathcal{R}_2(p)$ that chooses one of the two deterministic algorithms $\mathcal{A}_{P/2}$ and $\mathcal{A}_P$, with probability p and $1 - p$, respectively. Thus, $\mathcal{R}_2(p)$ chooses to buy the ski on day $P/2$ or P and rents until then, with probability p and $1 - p$, respectively.

The adversary does not have access to the random choices that the algorithm is using to randomize and hence it is solving the problem

$$\max_L \frac{\mathbb{E}\{C_{\mathcal{R}_2(p)}\}}{C_{\text{OPT}}},$$

while the algorithm is trying to solve

$$\min_p \max_L \frac{\mathbb{E}\{C_{\mathcal{R}_2(p)}\}}{C_{\text{OPT}}}.$$

Equivalently, the algorithm first fixes a value of p to which the adversary responds, and then the algorithm chooses p anticipating the response of the adversary to minimize the competitive ratio. For $\mathcal{R}_2$, it is easy to compute that

$$\frac{\mathbb{E}\{C_{\mathcal{R}_2(p)}\}}{C_{\text{OPT}}} = \begin{cases} 1 & \text{if } L < \frac{P}{2} \\ \frac{p(P/2-1+P)+(1-p)L}{L} & \text{if } \frac{P}{2} \leq L < P, \\ \frac{p(P/2+P-1)+(1-p)(P-1+P)}{P} & \text{if } L \geq P, \end{cases} \tag{2.6}$$

where importantly note that for $L < \frac{P}{2}$, the competitive ratio is 1. Thus, the adversary is never going to choose $L < \frac{P}{2}$. For $L \geq P$, the competitive ratio is independent of the exact value of L. For $\frac{P}{2} \leq L < P$, for a fixed p, the best (worst for $\mathcal{R}_2(p)$) choice of L for the adversary is $L = \frac{P}{2}$. Using this we get

$$\frac{\mathbb{E}\{C_{\mathcal{R}_2(p)}\}}{C_{\text{OPT}}} = \begin{cases} 1 & \text{if } L < \frac{P}{2} \\ \frac{p(3P/2-1)}{P/2} + (1-p) & \text{if } \frac{P}{2} \leq L < P, \\ \frac{p(3P/2-1)+(1-p)(2P-1)}{P} & \text{if } L \geq P, \end{cases} \tag{2.7}$$

We concentrate on only the two regimes $\frac{P}{2} \leq L < P$ and $L \geq P$ that are of interest to the adversary, since for $L < P/2$, $\frac{\mathbb{E}\{C_{\mathcal{R}_2(p)}\}}{C_{\text{OPT}}} = 1$. From (2.7), as a function of p, $\frac{\mathbb{E}\{C_{\mathcal{R}_2(p)}\}}{C_{\text{OPT}}}$ increases for $\frac{P}{2} \leq L < P$ while decreases for $L \geq P$. Thus, if the algorithm $\mathcal{R}_2(p)$ chooses a value of p, such that $\dfrac{\mathbb{E}\{C_{\mathcal{R}_2(p)}\}}{C_{\text{OPT}}}$ in the two regimes $L = \dfrac{P}{2} \le L$ and $L \ge P$ is equal, then the adversary is indifferent in its choice between $\dfrac{P}{2} \le L < P$ and $L \ge P$. Equating $\dfrac{\mathbb{E}\{C_{\mathcal{R}_2(p)}\}}{C_{\text{OPT}}}$ for $\dfrac{P}{2} \le L < P$ and $L \ge P$, we get the optimal choice of p, $p^\star$, as follows:

$$\frac{p(3P/2 - 1)}{\frac{P}{2}} + (1 - p) = \frac{p(3P/2 - 1) + (1 - p)(2P - 1)}{P},$$

$$\implies p^\star = \frac{2(P - 1)}{5P - 4}.$$

Substituting the value of $p^\star$ for $P = 10$, $\mu_{\mathcal{R}_2} = \max_L \dfrac{\mathbb{E}\{C_{\mathcal{R}_2(p^\star)}\}}{C_{\text{OPT}}} = 1.7$, while the comparable competitive ratio for the optimal deterministic algorithm from Theorem 2.3.1 is $\mu_{\mathcal{A}_P} = 1.9$. Thus, there is a reasonable improvement with a sub-optimal randomized algorithm compared to the optimal deterministic algorithm. Next, we discuss how to get an optimal randomized algorithm whose competitive ratio is $\dfrac{e}{e-1}$.

Consider a randomized algorithm $\mathcal{R}$ that specifies the probability p_i of choosing algorithm $\mathcal{A}_i$. The expected cost of $\mathcal{R}$ is then

$$\mathbb{E}\{C_{\mathcal{R}}\} = \sum_{i=1}^{L} p_i(i - 1 + P) + \sum_{i>L} p_i L, \tag{2.8}$$

while the cost of OPT is $\min\{P, L\}$ depending on the length L. Thus, to find an optimal randomized algorithm, one can solve the following optimization problem:

$$\inf_{\mathbb{E}\{C_{\mathcal{R}}\} \le c \min\{L, P\}} c, \tag{2.9}$$

where the optimal objective value $c^\star$ of (2.9) corresponds to the best competitive ratio, and there is one constraint for each value of L in (2.9).

Theorem 2.4.1 *The optimal competitive ratio of a randomized algorithm for the ski-rental problem is*

$$\frac{e}{e - 1},$$

and the optimal randomized algorithm chooses a distribution over $\mathcal{A}_i$ given by

$$p_i^\star = \frac{\eta}{P}\left(1 - \frac{1}{P}\right)^{P-i}, \quad i = 1, \dots, P, \tag{2.10}$$

where η is the normalization constant found via $\sum_{i=1}^{P} p_i^\star = 1$.

In Problem 2.3, we detail steps on how to prove Theorem 2.4.1. Note that the optimal randomized algorithm has $p_i = 0$ for $i > P$, i.e., there is no need to wait to buy beyond the Pth day. This fact can also be proved directly, summarized in the next lemma, whose proof is left as an exercise in Problem 2.2.

Lemma 2.4.2 *An optimal randomized algorithm has* $p_i = 0$ *for* $i > P$.

An alternate way of showing the optimality of (2.10) is to find a lower bound on the competitive ratio for any randomized algorithm, and then show that that matches with the competitive ratio obtained by using (2.10). Towards that end, in the next section, we first describe a generic technique known as Yao's principle to derive a lower bound on the competitive ratio of a randomized algorithm, and then illustrate its use for the ski-rental problem.

2.5 Lower Bound for a Randomized Algorithm

In this section, we show that no randomized algorithm can achieve a competitive ratio better than $\frac{e}{e-1}$ for the ski-rental problem. Towards that end, we first describe a general recipe called Yao's principle, which is a universal method for deriving lower bounds for randomized online algorithms that will be useful throughout the book.

2.5.1 Yao's Lower Bound Principle

Let $C_{\mathcal{A}}(\sigma)$ be the cost of a deterministic online algorithm $\mathcal{A}$ with input σ. Recall that any randomized algorithm is simply a probability distribution over the set of all deterministic algorithms A. For a particular randomized algorithm let that distribution be D_A. A randomized algorithm is μ-competitive against an oblivious adversary if

$$\mathbb{E}_{A \in A}\{C_A(\sigma)\} \le \mu C_{\text{OPT}}(\sigma), \ \forall \ \sigma, \tag{2.11}$$

where the expectation is with respect to the distribution D_A.

Consider a distribution D_I over the input σ. Note that the competitive ratio of a randomized algorithm (2.11) is with respect to the worst-case input σ. Distribution D_I is only being considered for deriving a lower bound on all possible randomized algorithms.

Taking the expectation on both sides of (2.11) with respect to D_I, we get

$$\mathbb{E}_\sigma\left\{\mathbb{E}_{A \in A}\{C_A(\sigma)\}\right\} \le \mu \mathbb{E}_\sigma\left\{C_{\text{OPT}}(\sigma)\right\}. \tag{2.12}$$

Exchanging the two expectations (using Fubini's Theorem if needed),

$$\mathbb{E}_{A \in A}\left\{\mathbb{E}_\sigma\{C_A(\sigma)\}\right\} \le \mu \mathbb{E}_\sigma\left\{C_{\text{OPT}}(\sigma)\right\}. \tag{2.13}$$

Let $c^\star = \min_{\mathcal{A}} \mathbb{E}_\sigma\{C_{\mathcal{A}}(\sigma)\}$, where the minimum is over all deterministic algorithms $\mathcal{A}$, and $c^\star$ is the minimum expected cost for the best deterministic algorithm over the distribution D_I of input σ.

By definition of $c^\star$, we have $c^\star \le \mathbb{E}_{\mathcal{A} \in A}\left\{\mathbb{E}_\sigma\{C_{\mathcal{A}}(\sigma)\}\right\}$. Thus, from (2.13), we get

$$c^\star \le \mu \mathbb{E}_\sigma\left\{C_{\text{OPT}}(\sigma)\right\},$$

$$\implies \mu \ge \frac{c^\star}{\mathbb{E}_\sigma\left\{C_{\text{OPT}}(\sigma)\right\}}, \tag{2.14}$$

which implies that the competitive ratio of a randomized algorithm against an oblivious adversary is at least as much as the ratio of the expected cost of the best deterministic algorithm and OPT for any fixed distribution D_I over the input sequences σ. Note that the choice of D_I is arbitrary.

Thus, **Yao's recipe** to derive a lower bound on the competitive ratio of a randomized algorithm for a specific online problem is to specify a distribution over the input σ, and try to compute (2.14). This is not always an easy exercise since it involves finding the optimal deterministic algorithm for the chosen input distribution. In the next subsection, we show that for the ski-rental problem, it is possible to compute this lower bound explicitly and which turns out to be tight.

2.5.2 Computing a Lower Bound Using Yao's Principle

Following Yao's principle (2.14), we derive a lower bound on the competitive ratio of any randomized algorithm for the ski-rental problem, where we will choose a distribution over the length L of the ski season such that any deterministic algorithm $\mathcal{A}_k$ that buys the ski on day k performs uniformly poorly for any k. We prove the following result, which shows the optimality of the randomized algorithm defined in (2.10).

Lemma 2.5.1 *The competitive ratio of any randomized algorithm for the ski-rental problem is lower bounded by $e/(e-1)$.*

Before proving this result, to get some intuition we first look at a specific distribution D_I over L, which has a probability mass function $\mathbb{P}(L=1) = \mathbb{P}(L=P) = 1/2$, and using which we can show that the competitive ratio of any randomized algorithm is at least $4/3$.

Example 2.5.2

Under the bi-modal distribution $\mathbb{P}(L=1) = \mathbb{P}(L=P) = 1/2$, the cost of OPT is

$$\mathbb{E}_L\{C_{\text{OPT}}\} = \frac{1}{2} + \frac{P}{2}. \tag{2.15}$$

Similarly, for the deterministic algorithm $\mathcal{A}_k$ that buys on day k, the expected cost is

$$\mathbb{E}_L\{C_{\mathcal{A}_k}\} = \begin{cases} P & \text{if } k = 1, \\ \frac{P+k-1}{2} + \frac{1}{2} & \text{otherwise.} \end{cases} \tag{2.16}$$

From Yao's principle (2.14), the competitive ratio of any randomized algorithm is lower bounded by α, where

$$\alpha = \frac{\min_k \mathbb{E}_L\{C_{\mathcal{A}_k}\}}{\mathbb{E}_L\{C_{\text{OPT}}\}}.$$

From (2.16), $k = 2$ is the optimal choice for $\mathcal{A}_k$ and the lower bound on the competitive ratio is $\alpha = \frac{P+2}{P+1}$. For $P > 1$, the largest value of α is $4/3$, and hence the competitive ratio of any randomized algorithm is at least $4/3$.

The main idea behind the lower bound of $4/3$ is that the adversary should keep sufficient probability mass at both $L = 1$ and $L = P$ so that no randomized algorithm can commit to $\mathcal{A}_1$ beforehand. Next, we formalize this idea and find the optimal distribution D_I over L that maximizes the lower bound on the competitive ratio via Yao's principle.

Proof: [Lemma 2.5.1] Recall that the cost of OPT is $\min\{L, P\}$. Let L be a random variable with distribution D_I. Then the expected cost of OPT with D_I is

$$\mathbb{E}_L\{C_{\mathsf{OPT}}\} = \sum_{\ell=1}^{P-1} \ell \mathbb{P}[L = \ell] + P\mathbb{P}[L \geq P] = \sum_{\ell=1}^{P} \mathbb{P}[L \geq \ell]. \tag{2.17}$$

From Lemma 2.4.2, a randomized algorithm for the ski-rental problem is equivalent to choosing between P different deterministic algorithms $\mathcal{A}_1, \dots, \mathcal{A}_P$ with probability $p_1, \dots, p_P$, such that $\sum_{i=1}^{P} p_i = 1$. Thus, if $L = \ell$, then the cost for $\mathcal{A}_i$ is

$$C_{\mathcal{A}_i} = \begin{cases} \ell & \text{if } \ell \leq i - 1, \\ i - 1 + P & \text{otherwise.} \end{cases} \tag{2.18}$$

Hence, the expected cost of a deterministic algorithm $\mathcal{A}_i$ over D_I is

$$\mathbb{E}_L\{C_{\mathcal{A}_i}\} = \sum_{\ell=1}^{i-1} \ell \mathbb{P}[L = \ell] + (i - 1 + P)\mathbb{P}[L > i - 1],$$

$$= \sum_{\ell=1}^{i-1} \mathbb{P}[L \geq \ell] + P\mathbb{P}[L > i - 1]. \tag{2.19}$$

Following Yao's principle, the next task is to find the optimal $\mathcal{A}_i$ that minimizes the expected cost with respect to input D_I. Instead of doing that directly, we find a distribution D_I for which the expected cost $\mathbb{E}_L\{C_{\mathcal{A}_i}\}$ is same for all i. Since the choice of D_I is arbitrary with Yao's principle, if such a D_I exists, then the expected costs of all $\mathcal{A}_i$'s, including that of the optimal, will be equal. Thus, we need $\mathbb{E}_L\{C_{\mathcal{A}_i}\} = \mathbb{E}_L\{C_{\mathcal{A}_{i+1}}\}$ for all i, which implies from (2.19) that

$$\sum_{\ell=1}^{i-1} \mathbb{P}[L \geq \ell] + P\mathbb{P}[L > i - 1] = \sum_{\ell=1}^{i-1} \mathbb{P}[L \geq \ell] + \mathbb{P}[L \geq i] + P\mathbb{P}[L > i]. \tag{2.20}$$

This is equivalent to

$$P\mathbb{P}[L \geq i] = \mathbb{P}[L \geq i] + P\mathbb{P}[L \geq i + 1],$$

since L only takes integer values, and hence we get

$$\mathbb{P}[L \geq i + 1] = \left(1 - \frac{1}{P}\right)\mathbb{P}[L \geq i].$$

The choice of

$$\mathbb{P}[L \geq i] = \frac{\left(1 - \frac{1}{P}\right)^i}{1 - \frac{1}{P}} \tag{2.21}$$

satisfies (2.20), and results in the same cost for all deterministic algorithms $\mathcal{A}_i$ from (2.19) as

$$\mathbb{E}_L\{C_{\mathcal{A}_i}\} = \frac{1}{1 - \frac{1}{P}} \sum_{\ell=1}^{i-1} \left(1 - \frac{1}{P}\right)^\ell + \frac{P}{1 - \frac{1}{P}} \left(1 - \frac{1}{P}\right)^i = P. \tag{2.22}$$

Moreover, from (2.17), the expected cost of OPT with input distribution (2.21) is given by

$$\mathbb{E}_L\{C_{\text{OPT}}\} = \sum_{\ell=1}^{P} \frac{1}{1 - \frac{1}{P}} \left(1 - \frac{1}{P}\right)^\ell = P\left(1 - \left(1 - \frac{1}{P}\right)^P\right). \tag{2.23}$$

Thus using Yao's principle (2.14), the lower bound on any randomized algorithm for the ski-rental problem obtained by taking the ratio of (2.22) and (2.23) is given by

$$\frac{P}{P\left(1 - \left(1 - \frac{1}{P}\right)^P\right)} = \left(1 - \left(1 - \frac{1}{P}\right)^P\right)^{-1}.$$

Recall that as $P \to \infty$,

$$\left(1 - \left(1 - \frac{1}{P}\right)^P\right)^{-1} = \frac{e}{e - 1},$$

proving Lemma 2.5.1. ∎

Remark 2.5.3 *In light of Lemma 2.5.1, an alternate way to prove Theorem 2.4.1 is to evaluate the competitive ratio for the distribution defined in (2.10), and showing that it meets the lower bound (Lemma 2.5.1).*

Remark 2.5.4 *Theorem 2.4.1 can also be proved via a primal–dual analysis, which will be illustrated via Problem 10.10 in Chapter 10.*

Remark 2.5.5 *The quantity $e/(e - 1)$ has special relevance for online algorithms; it mysteriously appears as the optimal competitive ratio for many online algorithms. We will see many such examples in later chapters of this book.*

In the next section, we discuss some important extensions of the ski-rental problem.

2.6 Extensions of the Ski-Rental Problem

- **TCP acknowledgement problem:** With the TCP protocol that is widely implemented in the internet, all packets correctly received by the destination are acknowledged to the source. Multiple packets can be acknowledged via a single acknowledgement ACK; however, delaying acknowledgements in order to save on the number of ACKs sent (each ACK costs some resource) interferes with the TCP protocol. Thus, there is a trade-off between minimizing delay (the difference between the time at which the packet is acknowledged and its arrival time) and the total acknowledgement cost. One objective function that effectively models this trade-off is defined as follows.

  Let the arrival times of packets at the destination be $a_i, a_{i+1} \geq a_i, i = 1, \ldots, n$. Moreover, let $t_j, t_{j+1} \geq t_j, j = 1, \ldots, k, t_k \geq a_n$ be the time at which the jth ACK is sent back by the destination. Then as a function of a_i and t_j, the delay or latency seen by the subset of packets that are being acknowledged via the jth ACK is given by latency$(j) = \sum_{i:t_{j-1} \leq a_i \leq t_j} (t_j - a_j)$. Assuming that it costs one unit to send an ACK, the problem is to choose a sequence of ACK time indices $t_1 \leq t_2 \leq \ldots \leq t_k$ to minimize

$$k + \sum_{1 \leq j \leq k} \text{latency}(j). \tag{2.24}$$

  Similar to the ski-rental problem, the decision question with the TCP acknowledgement problem at each time instant is whether to send an ACK given the set of unacknowledged packets at that time or wait for one more packet to be received (whose arrival time is unknown).

- **The Bahncard problem**: The problem is described by a triplet (C, α, T), where C is the cost to buy the Bahncard that permits the price of tickets to be discounted by $0 \leq \alpha \leq 1$ fraction for T days from the date of purchase. The problem is to determine when to buy the card without knowing the actual dates of travel.

  Thus, we get a three-way extension of the ski-rental problem. In particular, the discount is available for a fixed number of days T; on each day the cost you pay depends on the ticket you buy (which is then discounted), thus the rent paid on each day is variable; and buying a Bahncard does not guarantee free usage of the facility forever.

2.7 Notes

The ski-rental problem was first introduced in the context of snoopy caching [2] where deterministic algorithms were considered. A randomized algorithm with a competitive ratio of $e/(e-1)$ and the lower bound of $e/(e-1)$ was presented in [3]. Stochastic models for ski-rental problems have been considered in [4, 5]. Generalizations to the basic ski-rental problem with multiple buying options or different renting/buying cost functions can be found in [6–10].

The TCP acknowledgement problem [11] and the Bahncard problem [12] are known generalizations of the ski-rental problem. The lower bound of $e/(e-1)$ on the competitive ratio of any randomized algorithm for the TCP acknowledgement problem was shown in [13] and by John Noga independently, while an algorithm meeting the lower bound was derived in [14]. A primal-dual algorithm achieving the optimal competitive ratio of $e/(e-1)$ for the TCP acknowledgement problem can be found in [15], which is discussed in Problem 10.11, and an extension in the presence of machine learning (ML) augmented prediction in [16]. For the Bahncard problem also, a randomized algorithm achieving the competitive ratio of $e/(e-1)$ can be found in [14].

PROBLEMS

2.1 Show that for deterministic algorithm $\mathcal{A}_k$ that buys the ski on day k

$$\frac{C_{\mathcal{A}_k}}{C_{\text{OPT}}} = \begin{cases} \frac{P+k-1}{k} & \text{if } k \leq P \\ \frac{P+k-1}{P} & \text{otherwise,} \end{cases} \tag{2.25}$$

and the worst-case length of the skiing season (chosen by the adversary) to maximize the competitive ratio of $\mathcal{A}_k$ is $L = k$ if $k \leq P$.

2.2 Prove Lemma 2.4.2.

2.3 Optimal randomized algorithm for the ski-rental problem. For a randomized algorithm $\mathcal{R}$, let p_j be the probability of choosing algorithm $\mathcal{A}_j$ that rents till day $j-1$ and buys on the jth day if $L \geq j$. Minimizing the competitive ratio of a randomized algorithm $\mathcal{R}$ for the ski-rental problem is equivalent to solving the linear program (LP)

$$\inf_{\mathbb{E}\{C_{\mathcal{R}}\} \leq c \min\{L, P\}} c, \tag{2.26}$$

where the expected cost of $\mathcal{R}$ is

$$\mathbb{E}\{C_{\mathcal{R}}\} = \sum_{i=1}^{L} p_i(i-1+P) + \sum_{i>L} p_i L,$$

and $\min\{L, P\}$ is the OPT's cost. For each possible value of L, we get one constraint in (2.26). In the following, whenever we say optimal p's it means optimal for solving (2.26).

1. Argue that the constraint in $\mathbb{E}\{C_{\mathcal{R}}\} \leq c \min\{L, P\}$ corresponding to $L = P$ is redundant and is already captured by constraints for $L > P$. Thus, the constraint corresponding to $L = P$ can be removed.

2. Next argue that without loss of generality we can let optimal $p_{P+1} = 0$ by showing that compared to $p_P > 0$ and $p_{P+1} > 0$, $p'_P = p_P + p_{P+1}$ and $p'_{P+1} = 0$, while keeping all other p_i's the same does not increase the expected cost of $\mathcal{R}$.

3. Iteratively apply the procedure in part 2 to show that for any $i > P$, optimal $p_j = 0, \forall j \in (P, i]$.

4. Let $N \geq 2P$. Then show that for the optimal solution, $\sum_{j \geq N} p_j < 2P/N$, since otherwise the competitive ratio of $\mathcal{R}$ can be made at least 2 by the adversary, which is worse than $2 - 1/P$ (the best deterministic algorithm).

5. For some $0 < \epsilon < 1$, use part 4 with $N(\epsilon) = 2P/\epsilon$ to get that $\sum_{j > N(\epsilon)} p_j < \epsilon$. Moreover, from part 3 with $i = 2P/\epsilon$, we have $p_j = 0$ for $j = (P, i]$. Consider a reassignment of probabilities,

$$p_1' = p_1 + \sum_{j > N(\epsilon)} p_j$$

while keeping $p_i' = p_i, 2 \leq i \leq P$'s same, $p_i' = 0$, $P + 1 \leq i \leq 2P/\epsilon$, and $p_i' = 0$ for $i > 2P/\epsilon$. Show that with the reassigned probabilities, the left-hand side of any constraint in (2.26) increases by at most $(P - 1)\epsilon$. Thus, letting $c' = c + (P - 1)\epsilon$, we get a feasible solution of LP (2.26) with c' and p_i'.

6. Show that part 5 implies that the optimal p_i satisfies $p_i = 0$ for $i \geq P + 1$ (since ϵ can be chosen arbitrarily small with fixed P, and inf in (2.26) with c and p_i is the same as c' and p_i'), and to solve (2.26), we only need to consider the P constraints corresponding to $L = 1, \ldots, P$.

7. Show that with $p_i > 0$ only for $i \leq P$, at optimality, all constraints are tight. Thus, to solve (2.26), we have P variables $p_i, 1 \leq i \leq P$, and P equality constraints. Solving this (using elimination) prove that optimal $p_i = \left(\frac{P-1}{P}\right)^{P-i} \frac{c}{P}$, and using $\sum_{i=1}^{P} p_i = 1$, show that optimal

$$c = \frac{1}{1 - (1 - 1/P)^P} \approx \frac{e}{e - 1}.$$

2.4 [4] Consider a continuous time version of the ski-rental problem, where the length of the skiing season L is exponentially (memoryless) distributed with parameter λ having probability density function $f_L(x) = \lambda e^{-\lambda x}, x \geq 0, \lambda > 0$. In this model, the cost of an online algorithm $\mathcal{A}_k$ that rents the ski for time k is

$$C_{\mathcal{A}_k}(L) = \begin{cases} L & 0 \leq L \leq k, \\ k + P & k < L, \end{cases}$$

while the cost of OPT is $C_{\text{OPT}}(L) = \min\{P, L\}$. Consider the average competitive ratio as

$$\bar{\mu}_{\mathcal{A}_k} = \mathbb{E}_L \left\{ \frac{C_{\mathcal{A}_k}(L)}{C_{\text{OPT}}(L)} \right\}.$$

1. Derive an expression (may not be in closed form) for $\bar{\mu}_{\mathcal{A}_k}$ in two regimes: (i) $0 < k \leq P$ and (ii) $P < k$.

2. Deduce that the optimal algorithm (choice of k) when $\frac{1}{\lambda} \leq P$ is to rent forever, while when $\frac{1}{\lambda} > P$, rent for time k_0 and buy thereafter, where k_0 satisfies $P^2\lambda - \frac{P}{10} < k_0 < P^2\lambda$.

2.5 Consider that each day is of unit length and, similar to Problem 2.4, the length of the ski season L is exponentially (memoryless) distributed with parameter λ. Thus, the number of days in the ski season is

$$D = \min_{d < L < d+1, d \in \mathbb{N}} d.$$

Consider an online algorithm $\mathcal{A}_p$ that chooses to buy on any day with same probability p, and rents otherwise, i.e., it is stationary. Find its competitive ratio $\mu_{\mathcal{A}_p}$ as a function of p and the optimal p that minimizes $\mu_{\mathcal{A}_p}$.

2.6 [14] Continuous time version of the ski-rental problem. Let the length of the skiing season be L that is a non-negative real number, and consider a deterministic algorithm $\mathcal{A}_z$ that buys the ski at time z if $L > z$. Thus, the cost of $\mathcal{A}_z$ is

$$C_{\mathcal{A}_z} = \begin{cases} L & \text{if } L < z, \\ z + P & \text{otherwise,} \end{cases} \tag{2.27}$$

while the cost of OPT is always $C_{\text{OPT}} = \min\{L, P\}$. We can argue that any online algorithm should have $z \leq P$. As a result, we can also assume that $L \leq P$.

Thus, any randomized algorithm is a probability distribution over $\mathcal{A}_z$, where $0 \leq z \leq P$. Let $p(z)$ be the probability with which $\mathcal{A}_z$ is chosen by the randomized algorithm. Then the problem to minimize the competitive ratio can be stated as: minimize c such that

$$\int_0^L p(z)(z + P)dz + L\int_L^P p(z)dz \leq cL. \tag{2.28}$$

for all $L \leq P$.

1. Argue that without loss of generality, we can let (2.28) hold with equality.

2. For any $L < P$, twice differentiating (2.28) with respect to L, show that we get

$$P\frac{dp(L)}{dL} - p(L) = 0,$$

a differential equation whose solution is $p(L) = ae^{L/P}$, where a needs to be determined.

3. Using $\int_0^P p(z)dz = 1$, find a, and using that conclude that the optimal competitive ratio is $\frac{e}{e-1}$ by finding the optimal value of c in (2.28).

2.7 Let there be two stores from which you can rent/buy the ski each day. Let store $i = 1, 2$ have rent r_i and buying price b_i, where both r_i and b_i are not better for any one store simultaneously. The choice of the store has to be made on day one and is then fixed thereafter. Find the optimal deterministic strategy, i.e., which store to pick and for the picked store how long to rent.

2.8 (With predictions of unknown quality [17].) Suppose that there is a black-box that outputs the number of days of the skiing season as $\hat{L}$ while the true length of the skiing season is L days. Thus, the error is $\eta = |\hat{L} - L|$ which importantly is unknown. Show that algorithm PREDICTION has a worst-case competitive ratio of

$$\min\left\{\frac{1+\lambda}{\lambda}, (1+\lambda) + \frac{\eta}{(1-\lambda)C_{OPT}}\right\}, \qquad (2.29)$$

where $0 < \lambda < 1$ is an input to the algorithm. Thus, if error η is small, the competitive ratio can be made close to 1, while if η is large, the competitive ratio is at most $\frac{1+\lambda}{\lambda}$.

Algorithm 1 PREDICTION

1: Input $0 < \lambda < 1$, predicted length $\hat{L}$, and price to buy P.
2: **if** $\hat{L} \geq P$ **then**
3:     Buy on day $\lceil \lambda P \rceil$
4: **else**
5:     Buy on day $\left\lceil \dfrac{P}{\lambda} \right\rceil$
6: **end if**

[Hint: Try to prove each of the two bounds inside the min of (2.29) separately by considering the two distinct cases (i) $\hat{L} \geq P$ and (ii) $\hat{L} < P$, and the respective behaviour of algorithm Prediction and the worst-case choice of L made by the adversary.]

2.9 [14] In this problem, we will propose an algorithm $\mathcal{A}$ for the TCP acknowledgement problem, and show that it is 2-competitive. Let the latest acknowledgement made by the online algorithm $\mathcal{A}$ be at time t_i, where $t_0 = 0$. Then $\mathcal{A}$ selects the next time instant to send back the acknowledgement as t_{i+1}, if there exists a $\tau_{i+1}, t_i \leq \tau_{i+1} \leq t_{i+1}$ such that

$$A(t_i, \tau_{i+1})(t_{i+1} - \tau_{i+1}) = 1, \qquad (2.30)$$

where $A(t_1, t_2)$ is the number of packets that arrive in time interval $(t_1, t_2]$, i.e., the number of indices i such that $t_1 < a_i \leq t_2$. Given that the last acknowledgement was made at time $t_i \leq \tau_{i+1}$, at time $t_{i+1} \geq \tau_{i+1}$ the latency cost for the packets $A(t_i, \tau_{i+1})$ is at least $A(t_i, \tau_{i+1})(t_{i+1} - \tau_{i+1})$. Algorithm $\mathcal{A}$ is trying to make sure that that remains at most 1 by suitably choosing t_{i+1}.

1. Let the acknowledgement times used by $\mathcal{A}$ and OPT be $t_1 \leq t_2 \leq ...$, and $t_1^o \leq t_2^o \leq ...$, respectively. Show that without loss of generality, we can assume that $t_{\ell-1} \leq t_\ell^o \leq t_\ell$ for all ℓ.

[Hint: Suppose it was not true, count the increase and decrease in cost in making it true.]

2. Refer to Figure 2.1 for a geometric interpretation of the latency of any algorithm as a function of the time instants at which acknowledgements are made. For an algorithm $\mathcal{A}$, let region$_{\mathcal{A}}$ be the region spanned by the difference between the two curves $p(t)$ and $\text{Ack}_{\mathcal{A}}(t)$. Note that area of region$_{\mathcal{A}}$ is total-latency$_{\mathcal{A}}$. Moreover, let region$_{\mathcal{A}\backslash\mathcal{B}}$ = region$_{\mathcal{A}}\backslash$region$_{\mathcal{B}}$.

Using part 1, show that the cost of $\mathcal{A}$ satisfies

$$C_{\mathcal{A}} \leq k_{\text{OPT}} + \text{total-latency}_{\text{OPT}} + \text{total-latency}_{\mathcal{A}\backslash\text{OPT}},$$

where k_{OPT} is the number of acknowledgements sent by OPT.

3. Argue that total-latency$_{\mathcal{A}\backslash\text{OPT}} \leq k_{\text{OPT}}$ by exploiting the choice made by the algorithm (2.30) to keep the area of each dotted rectangle as shown in Figure 2.1 to be at most 1.

4. Conclude the proof by showing that $C_{\mathcal{A}} \leq 2C_{\text{OPT}}$.

[Note : Replacing 1 in (2.30) by a variable $z \in [0, 1]$ that is chosen with probability $p(z) = e^z/(e-1)$, this algorithm can be shown to be $e/(e-1)$ competitive [14].]

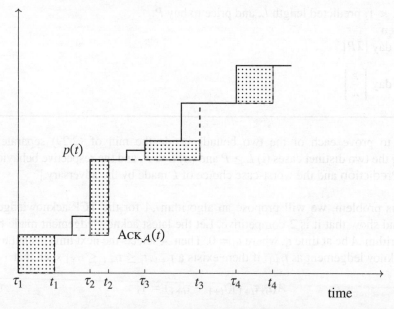

Figure 2.1 An example to show the execution of algorithm (2.30) for the TCP acknowledgement problem. Curve $p(t)$ (solid line) at time t is the number of packets received till time t starting from 0. t_i's are instants where an acknowledgement is sent by the algorithm (2.30), and the dashed curve $\text{Ack}_{\mathcal{A}}(t)$ increases at the acknowledgement time instants t_i's and remains constant between t_i and t_{i+1} with value equal to the number of packets received so far. By definition of the algorithm (2.30), an acknowledgement is triggered as soon as the area of each dotted rectangle is 1. Note that the total latency of the algorithm (2.30) is the sum of the areas of the region spanned by the difference between the two curves $p(t)$ (solid) and $\text{Ack}_{\mathcal{A}}(t)$ (dashed). For any other algorithm, e.g., OPT, it will have a different dashed curve, say $\text{Ack}_{\text{OPT}}(t)$, and its total latency will be the area of the region spanned by the difference between the corresponding two curves $p(t)$ and $\text{Ack}_{\text{OPT}}(t)$.

CHAPTER 3

List Accessing

3.1 Introduction

In this chapter, we will consider one of the earliest studied online problems called list accessing. This problem is motivated by memory systems, where files are stored in a stack or a list, and the cost of accessing any file depends on the location of the file in the list. In particular, with files ordered from left to right, the cost of accessing a file is the number of files preceding it in the list from the left plus one.

Requests for files arrive online, and the memory system is allowed to move or shuffle the files after every file request in the quest for minimizing future costs, without of course knowing the file requests to be made in the future. Thus, the decision variable is how to move files in an online manner after every file request so as to minimize the sum of the costs across all file requests. This problem is non-trivial even in the offline setting, and for very long its complexity was unknown. Only in the early 2000s did it get settled and was shown to be NP-hard.

In the online setting, early progress was made for deterministic algorithms, where a natural algorithm called move-to-front, which moves the requested file to the first place/front of the list, is shown to be optimal and achieves a competitive ratio close to 2. For the randomized setting, an online algorithm with a competitive ratio of 1.6 is known, with the best-known lower bound being 1.5. Thus, there is a gap in characterizing the optimal randomized algorithm.

In this chapter, we will first consider the deterministic setting and show that the move-to-front algorithm is optimal. Next, we present the lower bound of 1.5 on randomized algorithms and a randomized algorithm whose competitive ratio is at most 1.75.

3.2 Problem Definition

Consider that there is a collection of L files that are stored in a horizontal stack of size L called the **list**, where file f_i, $i = 1, \ldots, L$, is in location $\ell_i(t)$ at time t from the left. The input σ is a sequence of file requests, where if at time t, file f_i is requested, then the cost for fulfilling this request is $\ell_i(t)$. Once a file is requested, an algorithm is allowed to move the requested file to any location for free, called the **free exchange**, without, however, knowing the future file requests. An algorithm is also allowed to move a non-requested file by paying a cost of k on moving it k places, called the **paid exchange**. For example, if the current ordered (from left to right) list is $[a, b, c, d]$, the paid exchange cost for moving d to the first location and get a new list as $[d, a, b, c]$ will be three (essentially the number of pairs that need to transposed).

The cost $C_{\mathcal{A}}(\sigma)$ of an online algorithm $\mathcal{A}$ is the sum of the cost for fulfilling all requests in the input and the paid exchanges, and the competitive ratio of $\mathcal{A}$ is

$$\mu_{\mathcal{A}} = \max_{\sigma} \frac{C_{\mathcal{A}}(\sigma)}{C_{\text{OPT}}(\sigma)}. \tag{3.1}$$

Consider the following example to better understand the problem faced by any online algorithm $\mathcal{A}$.

Example 3.2.1

Let $L = 4$ and the four files be a, b, c, d. Let at time 0, the files be indexed in order (from left to right) as $[a, b, c, d]$. Let the first file requested be d. Consider an online algorithm $\mathcal{A}$ that moves file d when requested the first time to the kth position. If $k = 4$, then the next requested file is again d. Otherwise, file c, which is in the fourth position, is requested. Thus, the cost of $\mathcal{A}$ after two file requests is 8. OPT, on the other hand, pays the cost of $4 + 1$ in case 1 with input $\{d, d\}$ by moving file d to the first place, while in the second case with input $\{d, c\}$ keeps d in the fourth place, and pays a cost of $4 + 3$.

In the next example, we discuss an important class of online algorithms, called MOVE(j), that moves the requested file to location j.

Example 3.2.2

Let $L = 4$ and the four files be a, b, c, d. Let at time 0, the files be indexed in order (from left to right) as $[a, b, c, d]$, and the file request sequence be $\{d, d, c, c\}$ (left to right).

Consider an algorithm that moves the requested file to location j (from the left) after it is requested, called MOVE(j), and never attempts any paid exchange. Let $\mathcal{A}$ be MOVE(j). At time 1, the cost of $\mathcal{A}$ is 4, since the requested file d is in the fourth position. Thereafter, $\mathcal{A}$ will move file d to the jth location. Subsequently, at time 2, when file d is requested again, the cost of $\mathcal{A}$ is j, and file d remains in the jth location. At time 3, when file c is requested, if $j \leq 3$, then the cost of $\mathcal{A}$ is 4, otherwise 3, and file c is moved to the jth location. Finally, at time 4, the cost of $\mathcal{A}$ is j when c is again requested. Thus, the total cost of MOVE(j) with this input is $4 + j + 4 - (j - 3)^+ + j$ which is minimized for $j = 1$. The choice of $j = 1$ is optimal for minimizing the competitive ratio of MOVE(j) class of algorithms, and we leave this as an exercise in Problem 3.1.

Let us consider what OPT can do with this input. Either it can make a paid exchange to improve the location of files d and c (the only files to be requested) or pay a similar cost as MOVE(1). It is clear that if no paid exchange is made, then the cost of OPT is equal to MOVE(1). Thus, let OPT make a paid exchange before the first request is made, and move file d to the k_1^{th} location. Note that since d is requested successively twice, OPT will make any number of paid exchanges at most once. Thus, the cost of OPT for paid exchange is $4 - k_1$, on the first request to file d is k_1 and on the second request to d is at least 1 (if OPT moves d to the first location using free exchange).

If file c is at the fourth location at time 3, let OPT *pay* $4 - k_2$ *in paid exchange to move file c to location* k_2. *Otherwise, when it is in the third (original) location, i.e., file d remains in the fourth location on both its requests, the cost in paid exchange for moving file c would be* $3 - k_2$. *Then similar to above, the cost on request to the two successive requests to file c is* k_2 *and at least 1, respectively. Hence the total cost for* OPT *is* $4 - k_1 + k_1 + 1 + 4 - k_2 + k_2 + 1$ *when c is at the fourth location at time 3, and* $8 + 3 - k_2 + k_2 + 1$, *otherwise.*

Thus, it is easy to see that it is better to have file d ahead of file c (c is at the fourth location) at time 3, and the cost of OPT *is at least 10, which is equal to the cost of* MOVE(1). *For this simple input,* OPT = MOVE(1).

The case when MOVE(1) *is not equal to* OPT *will be described in the proof of Theorem 3.3.1, where we will derive a lower bound on the competitive ratio of* MOVE(1).

Example 3.2.3

Another natural algorithm called FREQUENCYCOUNT *is to order the files according to the frequency with which they have been accessed. In particular, initially, the frequency* $F_i = 0$ *for each file* f_i. *On a request to file* f_i, F_i *is incremented by 1, and file* f_i *is moved ahead of* f_j *for which* $F_i > F_j$. *Even though this algorithm has an intuitive appeal, it turns out that its competitive ratio is* $\Omega(L)$. *We leave the proof of this result as an exercise in Problem 3.5.*

In the next section, we consider deterministic algorithms for the list-accessing problem, and derive matching upper and lower bounds on their competitive ratios.

3.3 Lower Bound: Deterministic Algorithms

We begin by lower bounding the competitive ratio of the simple and intuitive algorithm MOVE(1), described in Example 3.2.2.

Theorem 3.3.1 *The competitive ratio of* MOVE(1) *is at least* $\frac{2L}{(L+1)} - \epsilon$ *for any* $\epsilon > 0$.

Proof: Without loss of generality, to begin with, let the indexed file order be $[f_1, f_2, \ldots, f_L]$ for both MOVE(1) and OPT. Consider an L-length input σ^L where the requested file at time t is the file that is in the Lth (last) location after the $t - 1^{st}$ request with the MOVE(1) algorithm, i.e.,

$$\sigma^L = \{f_L, f_{L-1}, \ldots, f_1\}. \tag{3.2}$$

The overall requested file sequence will be

$$\sigma = \sigma^L, \sigma^L, \ldots, \sigma^L, \ldots. \tag{3.3}$$

With this input, the cost of the MOVE(1) algorithm is L for each request, and the overall cost is nL, where $n = |\sigma|$ is the total number of requests. Consider an offline algorithm OFF, which pays a certain number of paid exchanges, and indexes its files as $[f_L, f_{L-1}, \ldots, f_1]$ before any request arrives, and does not shuffle any files in between requests. The total cost in such paid exchanges is at most $\binom{L}{2}$. Then, for each block σ^L of L requests (3.2), the cost of OFF is $\sum_{i=1}^{L} i = L(L+1)/2$. Since there are at most n/L blocks in the input σ, the total cost of OFF without counting the paid exchange is at most $n(L+1)/2$. Thus, the overall cost of OFF is $\leq n(L+1)/2 + \binom{L}{2}$, and the competitive ratio of MOVE(1) algorithm is at least

$$\frac{nL}{n(L+1)/2 + \binom{L}{2}} = \frac{L}{(L+1)/2 + \binom{L}{2}/n} \geq \frac{2L}{(L+1)} - \epsilon,$$

for any $\epsilon > 0$ by choosing n large, since L is fixed. ∎

Theorem 3.3.1 can be extended using an almost identical proof to apply for all deterministic algorithms, as stated next, whose proof is left as an exercise in Problem 3.2.

Theorem 3.3.2 *The competitive ratio of any deterministic algorithm for the list accessing problem is at least* $\frac{2L}{(L+1)} - \epsilon$ *for any* $\epsilon > 0$.

Next, we show that MOVE(1) in fact achieves the lower bound on the competitive ratio of any deterministic algorithm.

3.4 Optimal Deterministic Algorithm

In this section, we prove that the competitive ratio of MOVE(1) is at most $\frac{2L}{(L+1)}$ matching the lower bound (Theorem 3.3.1), and hence showing that MOVE(1) is an optimal online algorithm.

The idea behind MOVE(1) is that it expects the most recently requested file to be requested again more often, which may be reasonable from a practical point of view. The fact that it has an optimal competitive ratio compared to the $\Omega(L)$ competitive ratio of algorithm FREQUENCYCOUNT, however, is somewhat surprising. It turns out that with MOVE(1), the power of the adversary is somewhat limited compared to algorithm FREQUENCYCOUNT, since the adversary can cause maximum 'damage' if recently requested files are requested again soon enough, and not much later, which helps MOVE(1).

Theorem 3.4.1 *The competitive ratio of algorithm* MOVE(1) *is at most* $\frac{2L}{(L+1)}$.

Proof: The relative position for two files f_i and f_j means whether f_i is ahead (to the left) of f_j, or vice versa, in the list. For MOVE(1), the relative position of f_i and f_j changes only when either of f_i or f_j is requested. Consider any input sequence σ, and let $\sigma_{i,j} \subseteq \sigma$ be the punctured input, where all requests to files other than f_i and f_j are removed from σ, while maintaining the order in which f_i and f_j are requested.

Consider the execution of MOVE(1) on input $\sigma_{i,j}$ with a list of only two files f_i and f_j, and let the final relative position of f_i and f_j be r_{ij}. Similarly, execute MOVE(1) on input σ with the full list of files $f_1, \dots, f_L$, and let the final relative position of files f_i and f_j be r. Then it is not hard to see that $r_{ij} = r$. This property is known as the **pairwise independence** property and is very useful for analysing algorithms since an algorithm's performance can be characterized by its performance on a list of length 2. More details about pairwise independence are provided in Section 3.7.

For an illustration of the pairwise independence property for MOVE(1), consider $L = 3$, and to begin with, let the indexed file order be $\mathcal{L} = [f_3, f_1, f_2]$, and let the input σ be $\{f_1, f_3, f_2\}$ (left to right). Let the ordered restriction of the original indexed list $\mathcal{L}$ with just two files f_1, f_2 and f_3, f_1 be $\mathcal{L}_{1,2} = [f_1, f_2]$ and $\mathcal{L}_{1,3} = [f_3, f_1]$. Then with the punctured input $\sigma_{1,2} = \{f_1, f_2\}$ and $\sigma_{1,3} = \{f_1, f_3\}$, following MOVE(1), the final indexed order for $\mathcal{L}_{1,2} = [f_2, f_1]$ and $\mathcal{L}_{1,3} = [f_3, f_1]$. Moreover, for $\mathcal{L}$ with full input $\{f_1, f_3, f_2\}$, the final indexed order is $\mathcal{L} = [f_2, f_3, f_1]$. Thus, the relative order of files is maintained with $\mathcal{L}_{1,2}$ and $\mathcal{L}$ as well as $\mathcal{L}_{1,3}$ and $\mathcal{L}$ with MOVE(1).

For further analysis, we need the following definition.

$$M_{i,j}(t, \sigma) = \begin{cases} 1 + \dfrac{1}{L-1} & \text{if at time } t, f_i \text{ appears before } f_j \text{ in MOVE(1)'s} \\ & \text{list and file } f_j \text{ is requested,} \\ \dfrac{1}{L-1} & \text{if at time } t, f_j \text{ appears before } f_i \text{ in MOVE(1)'s} \quad (3.4) \\ & \text{list and file } f_j \text{ is requested,} \\ 0 & \text{otherwise.} \end{cases}$$

$OPT_{i,j}(t, \sigma)$ is defined similarly with respect to OPT's list at time t.

Definition (3.4) is essentially made so that we can write the total cost of MOVE(1) as

$$C_{\text{MOVE(1)}}(\sigma) = \sum_{t=1}^{|\sigma|} \sum_{1 \leq i,j, \leq L, i \neq j} \left(M_{i,j}(t, \sigma) + M_{j,i}(t, \sigma) \right). \quad (3.5)$$

To see why (3.5) is correct, let at time t, file j be requested which is at the ℓth location. Then for the $\ell - 1$ files that are ahead of j, $M_{i,j}(t, \sigma) = 1 + \dfrac{1}{L-1}$, while for the $L - \ell$ files that are behind j, $M_{i,j}(t, \sigma) = \dfrac{1}{L-1}$, while $M_{j,i}(t, \sigma) = 0$. Summing over all files, we get that $\sum_{1 \leq i,j, \leq L, i \neq j} \left(M_{i,j}(t, \sigma) + M_{j,i}(t, \sigma) \right) = \ell$, and subsequently summing over time, we get (3.5).

From (3.5), exchanging the two summations,

$$C_{\text{MOVE(1)}}(\sigma) = \sum_{1 \leq i,j, \leq L, i \neq j} \sum_{t=1}^{|\sigma|} \left(M_{i,j}(t, \sigma) + M_{j,i}(t, \sigma) \right). \quad (3.6)$$

Let $\sigma_{i,j}$ be the punctured input derived out of σ, where either file f_i or f_j is requested while keeping the same order of requests for f_i and f_j as in σ. Let $t \in \sigma_{i,j}$ mean that either file f_i or f_j is requested at time t.

For $t \in \sigma_{i,j}$, for a two-element list $\mathcal{L}_{i,j}$ that contains only f_i and f_j, let

$$
M_{i,j}^2(t, \sigma_{ij}) = \begin{cases} 1 + \dfrac{1}{L-1} & \text{if at time } t, f_i \text{ appears before } f_j \text{ in MOVE}(1)'s \\ & \text{list and file } f_j \text{ is requested,} \\ \dfrac{1}{L-1} & \text{if at time } t, f_j \text{ appears before } f_i \text{ in MOVE}(1)'s \\ & \text{list and file } f_i \text{ is requested,} \\ 0 & \text{otherwise.} \end{cases}
\tag{3.7}
$$

Now, exploiting the pairwise independence property of MOVE(1), we can rewrite

$$
C_{\text{MOVE}(1)}(\sigma) = \sum_{1 \le i,j, \le L, i \ne j} C_{\text{MOVE}(1)}(\sigma_{i,j}).
\tag{3.8}
$$

where

$$
C_{\text{MOVE}(1)}(\sigma_{i,j}) = \sum_{t \in \sigma_{ij}} M_{i,j}^2(t, \sigma_{ij}) + M_{j,i}^2(t, \sigma_{ij}).
\tag{3.9}
$$

is the cost of MOVE(1) on a list $\mathcal{L}_{i,j}$ of just two elements f_i, f_j on input σ_{ij}, where to begin with, the relative order of f_i and f_j in the list of just two elements is the same as relative order with the full list of L elements. Because of the pairwise independence property, this relative order remains the same throughout for $\mathcal{L}_{i,j}$ with input σ_{ij}, and $\mathcal{L}$ with input σ and we get (3.8).

Using the definition of $\text{OPT}_{i,j}(t, \sigma)$, similar to (3.5), the cost of OPT is

$$
C_{\text{OPT}}(\sigma) = \sum_{t=1}^{|\sigma|} \sum_{1 \le i,j, \le L, i \ne j} \left(\text{OPT}_{i,j}(t, \sigma) + \text{OPT}_{j,i}(t, \sigma) \right) + p_{\text{OPT}},
\tag{3.10}
$$

where $p_{\text{OPT}} \ge 0$ is the total cost of paid exchanges used by OPT. Similar to (3.7), define $\text{OPT}_{i,j}^2(t, \sigma_{ij})$, and

$$
C_{\text{OPT}}(\sigma_{i,j}) = \sum_{t \in \sigma_{ij}} \text{OPT}_{i,j}^2(t, \sigma_{ij}) + \text{OPT}_{j,i}^2(t, \sigma_{ij}),
$$

as the cost of OPT on a list $\mathcal{L}_{i,j}$ of just two elements f_i, f_j on input σ_{ij}, where note that we are not including the paid exchange cost in this two-element list case on account of the following argument. Suppose OPT makes a paid exchange between files f_i and f_j at time t, when f_i precedes file f_j. Then, equivalently, OPT can wait till the next request to f_j after time t, and then move f_j ahead of f_i, paying only the cost equal to the current location of f_j when f_j is requested. Thus, from here on, we let OPT not use any paid exchange when considering the list of size two.

Define $C_{\text{OPT}}^{i,j}(\sigma) = \sum_{\sigma(t) \in \{f_i, f_j\}} \left(\text{OPT}_{i,j}(t, \sigma) + \text{OPT}_{j,i}(t, \sigma) \right)$ as the cost of OPT on the requests to either file f_i or f_j in σ, such that

$$
C_{\text{OPT}}(\sigma) = \sum_{i,j} C_{\text{OPT}}^{i,j}(\sigma).
$$

Then, we have

$$C_{\text{OPT}}^{i,j}(\sigma) \geq C_{\text{OPT}}(\sigma_{i,j}), \tag{3.11}$$

since the decisions made by OPT with list $\mathcal{L}_{i,j}$ for all pairs of files i,j may not be necessarily feasible with the full list. Another way to see this is as follows. Note that the decisions made by OPT over σ whenever it moves file f_i or f_j in σ are feasible even when the input is just $\sigma_{i,j}$. Thus, if $C_{\text{OPT}}^{i,j}(\sigma) < C_{\text{OPT}}(\sigma_{i,j})$, we get a contradiction to the definition of OPT working over just $\sigma_{i,j}$.

Thus, from (3.8) and (3.11), we have

$$\mu_{\text{MOVE}(1)}(\sigma) = \frac{C_{\text{MOVE}(1)}(\sigma)}{C_{\text{OPT}}(\sigma)} \leq \frac{\sum_{1 \leq i,j, \leq L, i \neq j} C_{\text{MOVE}(1)}(\sigma_{i,j})}{\sum_{1 \leq i,j, \leq L, i \neq j} C_{\text{OPT}}(\sigma_{i,j})}. \tag{3.12}$$

From (3.12), we can see that for analysing the competitive ratio of MOVE(1), it is sufficient to consider a list of just two files f_i and f_j, and input $\sigma_{i,j}$ with no paid exchange. In particular, if we can show that for all pairs of files i,j,

$$\frac{C_{\text{MOVE}(1)}(\sigma_{i,j})}{C_{\text{OPT}}(\sigma_{i,j})} \leq c, \tag{3.13}$$

then from (3.12), we can conclude that

$$\mu_{\text{MOVE}(1)}(\sigma) \leq c.$$

Thus, to prove the result, we will show that for a two element list $\mathcal{L}_{i,j}$,

$$\sum_{t \in \sigma_{i,j}} \left(M_{i,j}^2(t, \sigma_{i,j}) + M_{j,i}^2(t, \sigma_{i,j}) \right) \leq \left(\frac{2L}{L+1} \right) \left(\sum_{t \in \sigma_{i,j}} \left(\text{OPT}_{i,j}^2(t, \sigma_{i,j}) + \text{OPT}_{j,i}^2(t, \sigma_{i,j}) \right) \right). \tag{3.14}$$

We define the *cost of pair* (f_i, f_j) with MOVE(1) and OPT at time t as

$$\left(M_{i,j}^2(t, \sigma_{i,j}) + M_{j,i}^2(t, \sigma_{i,j}) \right)$$

and

$$\left(\text{OPT}_{i,j}^2(t, \sigma_{i,j}) + \text{OPT}_{j,i}^2(t, \sigma_{i,j}) \right),$$

respectively. Then we have the following result.

Lemma 3.4.2 *If at time t, the cost of pair (f_i, f_j) with MOVE(1) is $1 + \frac{1}{L-1}$, while the cost of pair (f_i, f_j) with OPT is $\frac{1}{L-1}$, then the next time after t, whenever f_i or f_j is requested, the cost of pair (f_i, f_j) for both MOVE(1) and OPT is the same.*

Proof: Let just before time t, without loss of generality, f_i precede f_j in MOVE(1)'s list. Then, since the cost of MOVE(1) on (f_i, f_j) at time t is $1 + \frac{1}{L-1}$, by the definition of the cost $M_{i,j}^2(t, \sigma)$, f_j is the requested file at time t.

Moreover, since f_j is the requested file at time t, and the cost of OPT on (f_i, f_j) at time t is $\frac{1}{L-1}$, file f_j precedes file f_i in OPT's list just before time t.

At time t, on f_j's request, by definition, MOVE(1) moves f_j ahead of f_i. Thus, f_j precedes f_i in both MOVE(1)'s and OPT's lists. Any subsequent request to file f_j, say at time $t' > t$, will cost both algorithms $\frac{1}{L-1}$, and more importantly, the relative position of f_i and f_j will not be changed. ∎

Lemma 3.4.2 has coupled the cost of two consecutive requests to files f_i or f_j with respect to MOVE(1) and OPT, and if the cost is larger with MOVE(1) than with OPT at any time when either of f_i or f_j is requested, then the cost is the same for both algorithms at the next request time of f_i or f_j. Thus, averaging over time, using Lemma 3.4.2, we can upper bound the ratio of the cost of MOVE(1) and OPT on file pair (f_i, f_j) from (3.14) as

$$\frac{\sum_{t \in \sigma_{i,j}} \left(M_{i,j}^2(t, \sigma_{i,j}) + M_{j,i}^2(t, \sigma_{i,j}) \right)}{\sum_{t \in \sigma_{i,j}} \left(\text{OPT}_{i,j}^2(t, \sigma_{i,j}) + \text{OPT}_{j,i}^2(t, \sigma_{i,j}) \right)} \leq \frac{2 + \frac{2}{L-1}}{1 + \frac{2}{L-1}} = \frac{2L}{L+1}. \tag{3.15}$$

Thus, (3.13) implies that

$$\mu_{\text{MOVE}(1)}(\sigma) \leq \frac{2L}{L+1}.$$

∎

Combining Theorem 3.3.2 and Theorem 3.4.1, we conclude that MOVE(1) is an optimal deterministic algorithm. We next focus on the randomized setting and consider the question whether randomization can improve the competitive ratio fundamentally or not.

3.5 Lower Bound: Randomized Algorithms

In this section, we show that the competitive ratio of any randomized algorithm is at least 1.5. Towards that end, we will follow Yao's principle (Section 2.5.1), where we will specify a distribution over the input σ, and compute the ratio

$$\frac{\min_{\mathcal{A}} \mathbb{E}_\sigma \{C_{\mathcal{A}}(\sigma)\}}{\mathbb{E}_\sigma \{C_{\text{OPT}}(\sigma)\}} \tag{3.16}$$

which is a lower bound on the competitive ratio of all randomized algorithms, and where the min in (3.16) is over all deterministic online algorithms $\mathcal{A}$.

Theorem 3.5.1 *The competitive ratio of any randomized algorithm for the list-accessing problem is at least $1.5 - \epsilon$ for any $\epsilon > 0$.*

Proof: We define the random input using an offline algorithm called OFF (which is not necessarily the OPT) as follows. To begin with, without loss of generality, let the files be indexed in the list for OFF or any algorithm as $[f_1, \ldots, f_L]$ (left to right). The input will be divided in phases, where the length of each phase is random.

Let at the end of phase $i - 1$, OFF's indexed list be $\mathcal{L}_i^o$. Then, in phase i, each file is requested in order as they appear from left to right in $\mathcal{L}_i^o$, k times, where k is a random variable that takes values $\in \{1, 3\}$ with equal probability. For example, with $L = 2$, and the two files being named x, y, with $\mathcal{L}_i^o = [x, y]$, possible inputs in phase i are $(x_1, y_3), (x_1, y_1), (x_3, y_1)$, and (x_3, y_3), where $*_k$ means the symbol $*$ is repeated k times. Phase i ends as soon as all the L distinct files have been requested once or thrice.

OFF, knowing the realization of the random input of the next phase, moves a file on its request to the front only if it is going to be requested more than once. For example, with $L = 2$ and list $\mathcal{L}_i^o = [x, y]$, if (x_1, y_3) is the input in the next phase, OFF keeps x in the front until y's first request arrives, and at that time, OFF's list is updated to $[y, x]$.

Remark 3.5.2 *At the end of phase i, the last file to be requested thrice in phase i is at the front in OFF's list, and the second last file to be requested thrice in phase i is at the second position in OFF's list. In general, the rth last file to be requested thrice in phase i is at the rth location in OFF's list.*

To bound the cost of OFF in phase i, note that OFF pays a cost of j on the first arrival of the jth distinct file request, and since any file requested more than once is moved to the front on the first request, it pays a cost of 1 on subsequent requests (possibly second/third) for the same file. Thus for a request that is at the jth location at the end of phase $i - 1$, its cost in phase i is j if requested once, while the cost is $j + 2$ otherwise when it is requested thrice. Counting across the L distinct files requested in each phase, the cost of OFF in phase i is

$$C_{\mathrm{OFF}}(i) = \sum_{j=1}^{L} \left(\frac{j}{2} + \frac{j+2}{2} \right) < \frac{L(L+1)}{2} + 2L. \tag{3.17}$$

Next, we fix any deterministic algorithm $\mathcal{A}$ and let its indexed list be $\mathcal{L}_i$ at the end of phase $i - 1$. For the moment, we assume that $\mathcal{A}$ performs no paid exchanges, which we will relax later. We next define a potential function using the number of inversions[1] between $\mathcal{L}_i$ and $\mathcal{L}_i^o$. In particular, at the end (or start) of phase $i - 1$ (phase i),

$$\Phi(i) = \sum_{x,y \in \{f_1, \dots, f_L\}} \Phi_i^{xy}, \tag{3.18}$$

where

$$\Phi^{xy}(i) = \begin{cases} 1 & \text{if files } x \text{ and } y \text{ are not in the same relative position in } \mathcal{L}_i \text{ and } \mathcal{L}_i^o, \\ 0 & \text{otherwise.} \end{cases} \tag{3.19}$$

Let $\Delta\Phi(i) = \Phi(i) - \Phi(i - 1)$ be the difference between $\Phi(i)$ in two successive phases. It is easy to see that $\Phi(0) = 0$ and $\Phi(i) \leq \binom{L}{2}$ since in a list of L elements there can at most be $\binom{L}{2}$ inversions. Let $C_{\mathcal{A}}(i)$ be the cost of algorithm $\mathcal{A}$ in phase i. To prove the result, we will show that

$$\mathbb{E}\{\Delta\Phi(i) + C_{\mathcal{A}}(i)\} \geq \frac{3}{4}L(L-1) + 2L = \left(\frac{3}{2} - \frac{5}{L+5} \right) \frac{1}{2}L(L+5), \tag{3.20}$$

---

[1] The number of file pairs that are not in the same relative order with $\mathcal{A}$ and OFF.

which implies that the lower bound on the competitive ratio for any randomized algorithm (3.16) is at least 3/2, as follows. Summing (3.20) over N phases (for any $N > 0$), we get

$$\mathbb{E}\{C_{\mathcal{A}}\} + \mathbb{E}\{\Phi(N)\} - \mathbb{E}\{\Phi(0)\} = \sum_{i=1}^{N} \mathbb{E}\{\Delta\Phi(i) + C_{\mathcal{A}}(i)\},$$

$$\overset{(a)}{\geq} N \cdot \left(\frac{3}{2} - \frac{5}{L+5}\right)\frac{1}{2}L(L+5),$$

$$\overset{(b)}{\geq} \left(\frac{3}{2} - \frac{5}{5+L}\right)\mathbb{E}\{C_{\text{OPT}}\},$$

where (a) follows from (3.20), and (b) from (3.17) since OPT by definition is better than OFF. Since $\Phi(0) = 0$ and $0 \leq \Phi(i) \leq \binom{L}{2}$, we get

$$\frac{\min_{\mathcal{A}} \mathbb{E}_\sigma\{C_{\mathcal{A}}(\sigma)\}}{\mathbb{E}_\sigma\{C_{\text{OPT}}(\sigma)\}} \geq \frac{3}{2} - \epsilon$$

for any $\epsilon > 0$ for large L. Thus, if (3.20) is true, then the proof is complete.

Next, we work towards proving (3.20). We will denote $x < y$ if x precedes (is ahead of) y in the list. For every pair of files (x, y), let $c_{\mathcal{A}}(x, y, i)$ be the number of requests to file y during phase i when $x < y$ in $\mathcal{A}$'s list, while $R_x(i)$ be the number of requests for x in phase i. Then the cost of $\mathcal{A}$ in phase i can be written as

$$C_{\mathcal{A}}(i) = \sum_{(x,y)} \left(c_{\mathcal{A}}(y, x, i) + \frac{1}{L-1}R_x(i)\right) + \sum_{(x,y)} \left(c_{\mathcal{A}}(x, y, i) + \frac{1}{L-1}R_y(i)\right). \quad (3.21)$$

It is easy to see that all possible inputs in a phase i involving x, y are $\{x, y\}$, $\{x, x, x, y\}$, $\{x, y, y, y\}$, and $\{x, x, x, y, y, y\}$ which are equally likely. Thus,

$$\mathbb{E}\left(\frac{1}{L-1}R_x(i) + \frac{1}{L-1}R_y(i)\right) = \frac{4}{L-1}. \quad (3.22)$$

Let at the beginning of phase i, $x < y$ for OFF's list. Then from the definition of input, in phase i, x is requested before y. Recall the definition of $\Phi^{x,y}(i)$ from (3.19), and let

$$\Delta\Phi^{x,y}(i) = \Phi^{x,y}(i+1) - \Phi^{x,y}(i),$$

where note that quantities with index i represent their values at the end of phase $i - 1$ or start of phase i. Since $\Phi^{x,y}(i + 1) \in \{0, 1\}$, we have that $\Delta\Phi^{x,y}(i)$ takes values in $\{-1, 0, 1\}$. Also $\Delta\Phi(i) = \sum_{x,y} \Delta\Phi^{x,y}(i)$.

Let t^- represent the time just before t and after $t - 1$, where actions taken at time $t - 1$ have been incorporated. Moreover, t_i is the start time of phase i.

Case 1: $x < y$ with $\mathcal{A}$ at the start of phase i, i.e., at time t_i^-, i.e., just before phase i begins. Recall that for $x < y$ at time t_i^- with OFF by definition. Thus $\Phi^{x,y}(i) = 0$. Let the arrival time of the first request for x be t_x, while that for y be t_y, where $t_y > t_x$ by the choice of the input. Since x

is requested before y in phase i, on the arrival of any number of requests for x, $x < y$ always for both $\mathcal{A}$ and OFF. Thus, $c_{\mathcal{A}}(y, x, i) = 0$. Therefore, the earliest time of interest is time t_y^-, where $x < y$ for both $\mathcal{A}$ and OFF.

Case 1 (a): For $\mathcal{A}$, let $x < y$ just after time t_y, i.e., right after y is requested for the first time.

Sub-case 1 (a-i): A single y is requested. By definition of this case, $c_{\mathcal{A}}(x, y, i) \geq 1$. Moreover, OFF knowing the input will keep $x < y$, and hence $\Delta\Phi^{x,y}(i) = 0$ in this sub-case.

Sub-case 1 (a-ii): Three y's are requested. In this case, OFF makes $y < x$ after time t_y. Given its decision to keep $x < y$ right after t_y, $\mathcal{A}$ without knowing the future input still has options right after time $t_y + 1$. It either keeps $x < y$ even after time $t_y + 1$, in which case $c_{\mathcal{A}}(x, y, i) = 3$, while $\Delta^{x,y}(i) = 1$ or makes $y < x$ after time $t_y + 1$, in which case $c_{\mathcal{A}}(x, y, i) = 2$, while $\Delta\Phi^{x,y}(i) = 0$. Since a single y or three y's are requested with equal probability,

$$\mathbb{E}\{\Delta\Phi^{x,y}(i) + c_{\mathcal{A}}(x, y, i) + c_{\mathcal{A}}(y, x, i)\} \geq \frac{1}{2}1 + \frac{1}{2}2 = 3/2. \tag{3.23}$$

Case 1 (b): For $\mathcal{A}$, let $y < x$ after time t_y, i.e., right after y is requested for the first time.

Sub-case 1 (b-i): A single y is requested. By definition of this sub-case, $c_{\mathcal{A}}(x, y, i) = 1$. Moreover, OFF knowing the input will keep $x < y$, and hence $\Delta\Phi^{x,y}(i) = 1$ in this sub-case.

Sub-case 1 (b-ii): Three y's are requested. In this case, OFF makes $y < x$ after time t_y. For $\mathcal{A}$, by the definition of this sub-case, $c_{\mathcal{A}}(x, y, i) \geq 1$ and $\Delta\Phi^{x,y}(i) = 0$.

Since a single y or three y's are requested with equal probability,

$$\mathbb{E}\{\Delta\Phi^{x,y}(i) + c_{\mathcal{A}}(x, y, i) + c_{\mathcal{A}}(y, x, i)\} \geq \frac{1}{2}1 + \frac{1}{2}2 = 3/2. \tag{3.24}$$

Case 2: $y < x$ with $\mathcal{A}$ just before the start of phase i, i.e., at time t_i^-. Recall that by definition, $x < y$ at time t_i^- with OFF. Thus $\Phi^{x,y}(i) = 1$.

Case 2 (a): For $\mathcal{A}$, let $y < x$ just before time t_y.

Since $y < x$ at time t_y^-, $c_{\mathcal{A}}(y, x, i) = 1$ if a single x was requested, while $c_{\mathcal{A}}(y, x, i) = 3$ if three x's were requested. Option of $c_{\mathcal{A}}(y, x, i) = 2$ can be ruled out since if $\mathcal{A}$ makes $x < y$ after the second x is requested but makes $y < x$ after the third x is requested, it will lead to $c_{\mathcal{A}}(y, x, i) = 2$, but then it has to pay $c_{\mathcal{A}}(x, y, i) = 1$ on the arrival of the first y at time t_y. Thus, without loss of generality, we can let $\mathcal{A}$ not change the relative position of x and y after the arrival of the second x. Since a single x or three x's are requested with equal probability, we get

$$\mathbb{E}\{c_{\mathcal{A}}(y, x, i)\} = 2.$$

Given that for $\mathcal{A}$, $y < x$ just before time t_y, it pays no more cost when y is requested once or thrice, i.e. $c_{\mathcal{A}}(x, y, i) = 0$. OFF, on the other hand, keeps $x < y$ if a single y is requested after time t_y, while makes $y < x$ after time t_y if three y's are requested. Therefore, when a single y is requested, $\Phi^{x,y}(i + 1) = 1$, which implies $\Delta\Phi^{x,y}(i) = 0$, while when three y's are requested, $\Phi^{x,y}(i + 1) = 0$, which implies $\Delta\Phi^{x,y}(i) = -1$.

Since a single y or three y's are requested with equal probability, therefore,

$$\mathbb{E}\{\Delta\Phi^{x,y}(i) + c_{\mathcal{A}}(x, y, i) + c_{\mathcal{A}}(y, x, i)\} \geq 2 + \frac{1}{2}0 + \frac{1}{2}(-1) = 3/2. \tag{3.25}$$

Case 2 (b): For $\mathcal{A}$, let $x < y$ at time t_y^-. Recall that $\mathcal{A}$ does not use any paid exchange. Thus, since $y < x$ at time t_i^- while $x < y$ at time t_y^-, we have that $c_{\mathcal{A}}(y, x, i) = 1$ independent of the number of x's requested.

Since $x < y$ at time t_y^-, from time t_y onwards this is same as Case 1, where either $x < y$ or $y < x$ just after time t_y. The main difference compared to Case 1 where $\Phi^{x,y}(i) = 0$ is that $\Phi^{x,y}(i) = 1$ in the current case. Thus, in contrast to case 1, where $\Phi^{x,y}(i) = 0$, in this case, it can be that $\Delta\Phi^{x,y}(i)$ might become -1, compared to $\Delta\Phi^{x,y}(i) = 0$ in Case 1. However, since $c_{\mathcal{A}}(y, x, i) = 1$ in this case in comparison to $c_{\mathcal{A}}(y, x, i) = 0$ as in Case 1, the decrease in $\Delta\Phi^{x,y}(i)$ is compensated by the increase in $c_{\mathcal{A}}(y, x, i)$, and using (3.23) and (3.24), we get

$$\mathbb{E}\{\Delta\Phi^{x,y}(i) + c_{\mathcal{A}}(x, y, i) + c_{\mathcal{A}}(y, x, i)\} \geq 3/2. \tag{3.26}$$

Combining (3.23), (3.24), and (3.25), for all cases, we get

$$\mathbb{E}\{\Delta\Phi^{x,y}(i) + c_{\mathcal{A}}(x, y, i) + c_{\mathcal{A}}(y, x, i)\} \geq \frac{3}{2}. \tag{3.27}$$

Since (3.28) is true for any pair x, y, and since there are $\binom{L}{2}$ such pairs, using (3.22) we get

$$\mathbb{E}\{\Delta\Phi(i) + c_{\mathcal{A}}(i)\} = \sum_{x,y} \mathbb{E}\{\Delta\Phi^{x,y}(i) + c_{\mathcal{A}}(x, y, i) + c_{\mathcal{A}}(y, x, i)\} + \sum_{x,y} \frac{4}{L-1},$$

$$\geq \frac{3}{2}\binom{L}{2} + \binom{L}{2}\frac{4}{L-1} = \frac{3}{4}L(L-1) + 2L. \tag{3.28}$$

Thus, we have proved (3.20), as required, as long as $\mathcal{A}$ does not make any paid exchange.

The paid exchange case can be handled easily, by noting an important property of the proof. All we did was to argue based on the relative positions of a pair of files with $\mathcal{A}$. The implication is that the proof applies even if an algorithm maintains a partial order between a pair of files, without maintaining a total order. Thus, if an algorithm makes a paid exchange between two files x and y, and moves y ahead of x, then equivalently (with the same cost) we can consider an algorithm that defers this exchange to the time when y is requested next. Thus, there is no need to consider the case of paid exchange separately, and the proof while assuming no paid exchange is without loss of generality. ∎

With this lower bound of 1.5 on the competitive ratio of any randomized algorithm under our belt, the quest is to find a randomized algorithm with a competitive ratio close to 1.5. In this direction, in the next section, we describe a non-trivial randomized algorithm called BIT and show that it's competitive ratio is at most 1.75.

3.6 Randomized Algorithms

In this section, we consider randomized algorithms for the list-accessing problem. Given that MOVE(1) is an optimal deterministic algorithm, a natural randomized algorithm is to follow MOVE(1) with probability 1/2, while leaving the requested file in its current location with probability 1/2. It turns out that this algorithm does not do any better than MOVE(1) in terms of the competitive ratio (Problem 3.9). Thus, we need a more intelligent randomized algorithm to come close to the lower bound of 1.5 on the competitive ratio of randomized algorithms, which is presented next.

3.6.1 A Randomized Algorithm BIT

In this section, we present a randomized algorithm called BIT that assigns a random bit to all files and moves files depending on their bit status. In particular, for each file f_i, a bit $b(f_i) \in \{0, 1\}$ is initialized, where the bit is chosen uniformly randomly. Whenever f_i is requested, the bit $b(f_i)$ is flipped, and if after flipping $b(f_i) = 1$, then f_i is moved to the first place/front, and if $b(f_i) = 0$ after flipping, file f_i is left in its location as it is.

In Figure 3.1, we illustrate the execution of BIT with $L = 6$, where at a certain time, the bit status of all files is denoted below the file indices. If file f_5 is requested next, whose current bit is 1, then after flipping the bit, its bit status is 0, and hence file f_5 is not moved. On the other hand, if file f_2 is requested next, whose current bit is 0, then after flipping the bit, its bit status is 1, and hence file f_2 is moved to the front.

Remark 3.6.1 *One simple property of* BIT *is that among the two consecutive requests for the same file, the file moves to the front exactly once.*

Another important property of BIT is as follows.

Lemma 3.6.2 *The bit status of each file remains uniformly random throughout the execution of the algorithm.*

The proof follows by noticing that the bit status of file f right after time t is equal to

$$((R_f(t), \mod 2) + b_0(f), \mod 2),$$

where $R_f(t)$ is the number of requests made for file f until time t, while $b_0(f)$ is the initial bit status of file f.

The main result of this section is as follows.

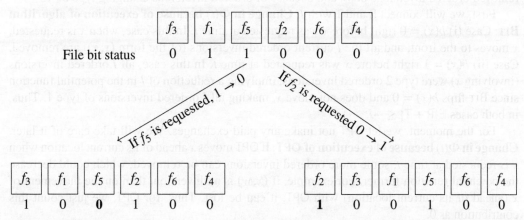

Figure 3.1 Example to show the execution of the BIT algorithm, where the bold bit represents the flipped bit.

Theorem 3.6.3 *The competitive ratio of* BIT *is at most* 7/4.

Proof: We will use a potential function argument to prove the theorem. Define an **ordered inversion** to be an ordered pair of files (y, x) such that y precedes x ($y < x$) in BIT's list and x precedes y ($x < y$) in OPT's list. An ordered inversion is called of **type 1** if $b(x) = 0$, and of **type 2** if $b(x) = 1$, for the file x in the ordered pair (y, x). Following the definition of BIT and Remark 3.6.1, the **type** of an inversion counts the number of requests required for that file to be moved to the front of the list by BIT.

Definition 3.6.4 *At time t, let* $\phi_1(t)$ *and* $\phi_2(t)$ *be the number of type* 1 *and type* 2 *ordered inversions, then the potential function at time t is defined as*

$$\Phi(t) = \phi_1(t) + 2\phi_2(t).$$

Note that $\Phi(0) = 0$, and $\Phi(t) \geq 0$ for all t. Thus, to prove the result, it is sufficient to show that

$$\mathbb{E}\{C_{\text{BIT}}(t)\} + \mathbb{E}\{\Delta\Phi(t)\} \leq \frac{7}{4}C_{\text{OPT}}(t),$$

with $\Delta\Phi(t) = \Phi(t) - \Phi(t-1)$, and $C_{\text{BIT}}(t)$ is the cost of BIT at time t.

Consider time t, when the requested file is x and let I be the number of ordered inversions of the form (y, x) just before the arrival of the request for x. Note that since BIT is randomized, many of the defined quantities are random. For ease of exposition, we avoid writing this fact repeatedly. Let the requested file x be at the kth location from the left in OPT's list at time t, i.e., the cost of OPT is k. Then the cost of BIT at time t is simply

$$C_{\text{BIT}}(t) \leq k + I = C_{\text{OPT}}(t) + I, \tag{3.29}$$

since $I = |\{(y, x) : y < x \text{ in BIT's list but } x < y \text{ in OPT's list}\}|$.

Next, we analyse $\Delta\Phi(t)$. The potential function $\Phi(t)$ can change because of (i) newly created ordered inversions, (ii) removal of old ordered inversions, and (iii) ordered inversions changing type. Let the change in $\Phi(t)$ because of newly created ordered inversions be N, because of newly removed ordered inversions be R, and because of ordered inversions changing type be T.

First, we will connect R and T with I. **Change in $\Phi(t)$ because of execution of algorithm BIT**: Case (i) $b(x) = 0$ right before x was requested at time t. In this case, when x is requested, x moves to the front, and all the I current ordered inversions (of the form (y, x)) are removed. Case (ii) $b(x) = 1$ right before x was requested at time t. In this case, all I ordered inversions (involving x) were type 2 ordered inversions, implying a reduction of I in the potential function since BIT flips $b(x) = 0$ and does not move x, making all I ordered inversions of type 1. Thus, in both cases $\mathbb{E}\{R + T\} \leq -I$.

For the moment, we let OPT not make any paid exchanges. We will take care of it later. **Change in $\Phi(t)$ because of execution of OPT**: If OPT moves x ahead of its current location when x is requested at time t, some more ordered inversions can be removed, which could decrease the potential function further. For example, if (x, w) is an inversion, then on the movement of x (ahead of its current location) with OPT, it can be lost. Thus, for OPT, we just count this contribution as 0.

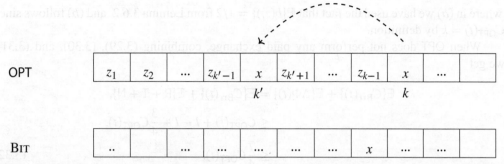

Figure 3.2 Illustration to count the number of new ordered inversions created because of movement by OPT and the BIT algorithm. In the top list, OPT moves the requested file x from position k to k'. Depending on the bit $b(x)$, if $b(x) = 0$, then BIT moves x to the front, in which case new inversions of type $1 + b(z_i)$ for $i = 1, 2, \ldots, k' - 1$ are created, while if $b(x) = 1$, in which case BIT leaves x as it is, and because of movement of x with OPT, new ordered inversions are created with $z_{k'+1}, \ldots, z_{k-1}$.

Overall, counting for both BIT's and OPT's contribution, we get

$$\mathbb{E}\{R + T\} \le -I. \tag{3.30}$$

Next, we bound $\mathbb{E}\{N\}$ (the new ordered inversions that can be created). Towards that end, consider Figure 3.2. Recall that new ordered inversions can be created only when OPT moves x ahead. Let x be in location k with OPT just before x is requested at time t, and let OPT move it to location $k' \le k$, as shown in Figure 3.2. Let $z_1, \ldots, z_{k-1}$ be the files ahead of x in OPT's list before the movement of x.

If $b(x) = 0$ when x is requested, then BIT moves x to the front, and in this case, for any $z_i, i = 1, 2, \ldots, k' - 1$, (x, z_i) is an ordered inversion since $x < z_i$ with BIT while $z_i < x$ with OPT. Thus, OPT and BIT together, create a new ordered inversion of type $1 + b(z_i)$ for $i = 1, 2, \ldots, k' - 1$.

Otherwise, if $b(x) = 1$, x's location remains unchanged with BIT and $b(x)$ is made 0. Thus, the new ordered inversions of type 1 (since the bit index for file x changes to 0) are created between files $(z_j, x), j = k', \ldots, k - 1$.

Since $b(x)$ is equally likely to be 0 or 1 from Lemma 3.6.2, we have

$$\mathbb{E}\{N\} \le \mathbb{E}\left\{ \sum_{i=1}^{k'-1} \frac{1}{2}(1 + b(z_i)) + \sum_{i=k'}^{k-1} \frac{1}{2} 1 \right\},$$

$$= \sum_{i=1}^{k'-1} \frac{1}{2}(1 + \mathbb{E}\{b(z_i)\}) + \sum_{i=k'}^{k-1} \frac{1}{2} 1,$$

$$\overset{(a)}{\le} \frac{3}{4}(k - 1),$$

$$\overset{(b)}{\le} \frac{3}{4} C_{\text{OPT}}(t), \tag{3.31}$$

where in (a) we have used the fact that $\mathbb{E}\{b(z_i)\} = 1/2$ from Lemma 3.6.2, and (b) follows since $C_{\text{OPT}}(t) = k$ by definition.

When OPT does not perform any paid exchange, combining (3.29), (3.30), and (3.31), we get

$$\mathbb{E}\{C_{\text{BIT}}(t)\} + \mathbb{E}\{\Delta\Phi(t)\} = \mathbb{E}\{C_{\text{BIT}}(t)\} + \mathbb{E}\{R + T + N\},$$

$$\leq C_{\text{OPT}}(t) + I - I + \frac{3}{4}C_{\text{OPT}}(t),$$

$$\leq \frac{7}{4}C_{\text{OPT}}(t). \tag{3.32}$$

So far we have not accounted for the fact that OPT can also perform paid exchanges. If OPT performs a paid exchange,[2] then it pays a cost of 1; while doing so it can at most create one new inversion between its own and BIT's list. Since the file with respect to which a new inversion can be created is equally likely to have its bit 0 or 1, it is equally likely that the newly created inversion is of type 1 or 2. Since type 2 inversion is weighted by a factor of 2 in the potential function, it follows that the expected increase in $\Phi(t)$ on one paid exchange is at most

$$\frac{1}{2}1 + \frac{1}{2}2 = 3/2. \tag{3.33}$$

Recall that file x is requested at time t, which is at location k in OPT's list. Let OPT perform r paid exchanges just after x is requested at time t to move any files. Then the cost of OPT at time t is $k + r$. Thus, with r paid exchanges, analogous relations to (3.29) and (3.31) are

$$\mathbb{E}\{C_{\text{BIT}}(t)\} = k + I = C_{\text{OPT}}(t) - r + I, \tag{3.34}$$

and

$$\mathbb{E}\{N\} \leq \frac{3}{4}(k-1) \leq \frac{3}{4}(C_{\text{OPT}}(t) - r). \tag{3.35}$$

Combining (3.33), (3.34), and (3.35), we get

$$\mathbb{E}\{C_{\text{BIT}}(t)\} + \mathbb{E}\{\Delta\Phi(t)\} \leq C_{\text{OPT}}(t) - r + I - I + \frac{3}{2}r + \frac{3}{4}C_{\text{OPT}}(t) - \frac{3}{4}r \leq \frac{7}{4}C_{\text{OPT}}(t). \tag{3.36}$$

Since (3.32) is the same as (3.36), with or without paid exchanges made by OPT,

$$\mathbb{E}\{C_{\text{BIT}}(t)\} + \mathbb{E}\{\Delta\Phi(t)\} \leq \frac{7}{4}C_{\text{OPT}}(t). \tag{3.37}$$

Summing (3.37) over all time slots,

$$\mathbb{E}\{C_{\text{BIT}}\} \leq \sum_{t=1}^{T} \left(C_{\text{BIT}}(t) + \mathbb{E}\{\Delta\Phi(t)\} \right) \leq \frac{7}{4}C_{\text{OPT}}(t) + \Phi(T) - \Phi(0). \tag{3.38}$$

---

[2] One paid exchange corresponds to one transposition.

Recalling the fact that $\Phi(0) = 0$ and $\Phi(t) \le 3\binom{L}{2}$ for any t, since the maximum number of ordered inversions in a list of size L is at most $\binom{L}{2}$. Thus, for large T such that $C_{\text{OPT}}(T)$ much much larger than L, we get

$$\mu_{\text{BIT}} = \frac{\mathbb{E}\{C_{\text{BIT}}\}}{C_{\text{OPT}}} \le \frac{7}{4}.$$

$\blacksquare$

3.7 Pairwise Independence Property

In this section, we will formalize the pairwise independence property that we exploited while analysing the competitive ratio of the MOVE(1) algorithm. Towards that end, we first modify the cost structure, called the **partial cost model**, for any file request as follows. For algorithm $\mathcal{A}$, if the requested file is at the ℓth location, then the cost of that request with $\mathcal{A}$ is $\ell - 1$. Thus, compared to the cost earlier defined, this new cost captures just the number of files that need to be searched before the requested file is found.

The original cost model and the partial cost model share an interesting property: if an online algorithm $\mathcal{A}$ has a competitive ratio $\mu_{\mathcal{A}}$ with the partial cost model, then $\mathcal{A}$ also has a competitive ratio $\mu_{\mathcal{A}}$ with the original cost model. This fact is proven in Problem 3.7. Thus, for analysing any algorithm, without loss of generality, the partial cost model can be considered. Compared to the original cost model, the partial cost model simplifies some of the computations and helps in characterizing certain properties that we describe as follows.

For any online algorithm $\mathcal{A}$, let

$$C_{\mathcal{A}}(x,j) = \begin{cases} 1 & \text{if } x \text{ precedes the file requested at time } j, \ \sigma_j \\ 0 & \text{otherwise.} \end{cases} \tag{3.39}$$

Using (3.39), the cost of $\mathcal{A}$ can be written as

$$C_{\mathcal{A}}(\sigma) \doteq \sum_{j=1}^{|\sigma|} \sum_{x \in L} C_{\mathcal{A}}(x,j) = \sum_{x \in L} \sum_{j=1}^{|\sigma|} C_{\mathcal{A}}(x,j). \tag{3.40}$$

Since the requested file at time j, σ_j, is some element $y \in L$, (3.40) can also be written as

$$C_{\mathcal{A}}(\sigma) = \sum_{x \in L} \sum_{y \in L} \sum_{j:\sigma_j = y}^{|\sigma|} C_{\mathcal{A}}(x,j). \tag{3.41}$$

Now notice that for any j, and any pair x, y, one of the two costs $C_{\mathcal{A}}(x,j)$ and $C_{\mathcal{A}}(y,j)$ is zero. Thus, the cost (3.41) can be rewritten as

$$C_{\mathcal{A}}(\sigma) = \sum_{x,y \in L:\sigma_j = \{x,y\}} C_{\mathcal{A}}(x,j) + C_{\mathcal{A}}(y,j), \tag{3.42}$$

$\sigma_j = \{x, y\}$ means that at time t, either file x or y is requested.

The way to interpret cost (3.42) is that for a fixed pair x, y,

$$C_{\mathcal{A}}^{x,y}(\sigma) = \sum_{j:\sigma_j=\{x,y\}} C_{\mathcal{A}}(x,j) + C_{\mathcal{A}}(y,j),$$

is the cost that $\mathcal{A}$ incurs whenever x or y is requested in the input σ.

Compared to σ, consider the punctured input σ_{xy} that is obtained from σ by removing all requests to files other than x and y, while keeping the same order of requests to x, y in σ. Let the cost of $\mathcal{A}$ with input σ_{xy} on a list of size two that contains only x and y be $C_{\mathcal{A}}^2(\sigma_{x,y})$.

An algorithm is defined to satisfy the **pairwise independence** property if for each pair x, y

$$C_{\mathcal{A}}^{x,y}(\sigma) = C_{\mathcal{A}}^2(\sigma_{x,y}). \tag{3.43}$$

Not surprisingly, there is a simple characterization of all algorithms that satisfy the pairwise independence property.

Lemma 3.7.1 *An algorithm satisfies the pairwise independence property if and only if for every request sequence σ, and the punctured input $\sigma_{x,y}$ for any pair of files x, y, the relative order of x, y for $\mathcal{A}$ is the same with σ and $\sigma_{x,y}$.*

The proof of 3.7.1 is left as an exercise. The forward direction is simple, while the only if condition can be proven via contradiction.

The bigger advantage of an algorithm having the pairwise independence property is that to characterize its competitive ratio it is sufficient to consider a list of size 2, i.e., $L = 2$, because of the following result.

Lemma 3.7.2 *Let $\mathcal{A}$ be a deterministic or randomized online algorithm that does not use any paid exchange and satisfies the pairwise independence property. Then for any $\mu \geq 1$, $\mathcal{A}$ has a competitive ratio of μ for any L as long as it has competitive ratio of μ for $L = 2$.*

The proof of Lemma 3.7.2 is discussed in Problem 3.8. We already saw that algorithm MOVE(1) satisfies the pairwise independence property. The same can be said about the randomized algorithm BIT as well.

Lemma 3.7.3 BIT *satisfies the pairwise independence property.*

Remark 3.7.4 *Even though* BIT *satisfies the pairwise independence property, in the proof of Theorem 3.6.3, we did not make use of it.*

3.8 Notes

The list-accessing problem may be by far the earliest studied online problem. The competitive ratio for this problem was first studied in [18], where it was shown that MOVE(1)'s competitive ratio is at most 2 using the potential function method as discussed in Problem 3.6. The competitive ratio of Move(1) was improved to $\frac{2L}{L+1}$ in [19], using the analysis presented in the chapter. The lower bound of $\frac{2L}{L+1}$ on the competitive ratio of any deterministic algorithm was derived in [20]. Another deterministic algorithm called TIMESTAMP was proposed in [21], and shown to be 2-competitive. The randomized algorithm BIT presented in the chapter was proposed and analysed in [22] where it was shown to have a competitive ratio of 1.75. A combination of TIMESTAMP and BIT, where each of them is used on any instance with a specific probability, was shown to be 1.6 competitive in [23], which is currently the best-known competitive ratio.

The lower bound presented for randomized algorithms in the chapter was derived in [24] that showed that no randomized algorithm can have a competitive ratio better than 1.5, using Yao's principle. The best-known lower bound in the partial cost model is known to be 1.50084 [25].

A new class of algorithms, other than Move(j) and TIMESTAMP, have been proposed in [26], whose competitive ratio is at most 3. A primal–dual approach to prove competitive ratio results for many of the algorithms for the list-accessing problem can be found in [27]. Extensions to the list-accessing problem, where input is randomized, has been studied in [28] and references therein, while performance in the presence of lookahead can be found in [29].

The list-accessing problem is also of interest in the offline setting, where it is not obvious whether an efficient optimal algorithm exists. Early results in this direction can be found in [30]; however, in a surprising result in a Ph.D. thesis [31], it was shown that the offline problem is in fact NP-hard. For a survey on the list-accessing problem, one can refer to [32].

PROBLEMS

3.1 Prove that $j = 1$ is optimal for minimizing the competitive ratio for the MOVE(j) class of algorithms. To show this, derive a lower bound on the competitive ratio of MOVE(j) for $j > 1$ similar to Theorem 3.3.1.

[Hint: The cost of MOVE(j) on each request can be made as large as L; however, for an offline algorithm it is sufficient to restrict attention to a list of size $L - j + 1$.]

3.2 Prove Theorem 3.3.2 by considering an input where the requested file at time t is the file that is in the Lth location after the $t - 1^{st}$ request for any deterministic algorithm $\mathcal{A}$. Argue that for this input, there exists an offline algorithm (not necessarily OPT) for which the average cost per request is $(L + 1)/2$.

[Hint: Consider a random permutation of the L files as the choice for OPT's list to begin with, which is never updated or shuffled. Compute the expected cost to OPT in this case, and then argue that the same cost can be achieved by a specific permutation that can be used by OPT.]

3.3 [30] Show that OPT requires paid exchanges. Consider the following input. Let $L = 3$ and the initial list configuration be $[1, 2, 3]$ and the request sequence $\{3, 2, 2, 3\}$ (left to right). Show that without any paid exchange, any offline algorithm must incur a cost of 9, while with two paid exchanges the cost can be reduced to 8.

3.4 [30] Let O be an offline algorithm performing free and paid exchanges. Then there exists an algorithm O' performing only paid exchanges with the same cost as O. [Hint: Show that if O uses a free exchange for item i, then O' can use paid exchanges just before i arrives.]

3.5 Show that the competitive ratio of algorithm FREQUENCYCOUNT described in Example 3.2.3 is $\Omega(L)$.

[Hint: The following input might be helpful. For file $f_i, i = 1, \ldots, L$, let it be requested exactly i times, in order. Thereafter, repeatedly for k times, let the following block of requests arrive for $i = 1$ to L, request file f_i, L times consecutively. Choose k large to conclude the result.]

3.6 In this problem, we will show that the competitive ratio of MOVE(1) is at most 2 using a potential function argument as follows.

Let $\sigma = (\sigma_1, \sigma_2, \ldots, \sigma_n)$ be the request sequence, where σ_j is the file requested at time j. Let $\pi = (\pi_1, \pi_2, \ldots, \pi_n)$, where π_i is the ordered list of the L files (permutation) with MOVE(1) after fulfilling request σ_i. Let π^{OPT} be similarly defined for the OPT. Note that $\pi_0 = \pi_0^{\text{OPT}}$.

Define an inversion to be a file pair (f_j, f_k) with respect to π_t and π_t^{OPT} at time t, if either (i) $\pi_t(f_j) < \pi_t(f_k)$ while $\pi_t^{\text{OPT}}(f_j) > \pi_t^{\text{OPT}}(f_k)$ or (ii) $\pi_t(f_j) > \pi_t(f_k)$ while $\pi_t^{\text{OPT}}(f_j) < \pi_t^{\text{OPT}}(f_k)$. Essentially an inversion is where the order in which two files appear is reversed with π_t and π_t^{OPT}.

Using the definition of inversion, we define the potential function as

$$\Phi(t) = \text{\# of inversions with respect to } \pi_t \text{ and } \pi_t^{\text{OPT}}.$$

Note that since $\pi_0 = \pi_0^{\text{OPT}}$ (initial conditions), $\Phi(0) = 0$, and $0 \leq \Phi(t) \leq \binom{L}{2}$ for all t.

With $\mathcal{A}$ as MOVE(1), the cost $C_{\mathcal{A}}(t)$ paid by $\mathcal{A}$ at time t on arrival of request σ_t is $\pi_{t-1}(\sigma_t)$, the position of the file requested at time t in list π_{t-1} from the left. Similarly, define OPT's cost $C_{\text{OPT}}(t)$.

To prove the result, we need to show that

$$(C_{\mathcal{A}}(t) + \Phi(t) - \Phi(t-1)) \leq 2C_{\text{OPT}}(t) - 1, \tag{3.44}$$

since the actual cost $\sum_{t=1}^{n} C_{\mathcal{A}}(t) \leq \sum_{t=1}^{n}(C_{\mathcal{A}}(t) + \Phi(t) - \Phi(t-1)) = \Phi(n) - \Phi(0) + \sum_{t=1}^{n}(C_{\mathcal{A}}(t))$ and $\Phi(0) = 0$ and $0 \leq \Phi(n) \leq \binom{L}{2}$. For large n, the competitive ratio approaches 2.

To prove (3.44), bound the change in the potential function $\Phi(t) - \Phi(t-1)$ as follows.

Let f_j be the file requested at time t, i.e., $\sigma_t = f_j$. With respect to π_{t-1} and π_{t-1}^{OPT}, let k be the number of files that appear before f_j in both MOVE(1)'s list and OPT's list, and let ℓ be the number of files that appear before f_j in MOVE(1)'s list but come after f_j in OPT's list.

1. Show that $C_{\mathcal{A}}(t) = \ell + k + 1$, while $C_{\text{OPT}}(t) \geq k + 1 + p_{\text{OPT}}(t)$, where $p_{\text{OPT}}(t)$ is the number of paid exchanges OPT makes just after time t.

2. Once f_j is requested, MOVE(1) moves it to the first place/front while OPT moves it somewhere. Argue that because of these movements, exactly ℓ inversions are destroyed, while at most $k + p_{OPT}(t)$ new inversions are created.

3. Combining parts 1 and 2, conclude that $C_{\mathcal{A}}(t) + \Phi(t) - \Phi(t-1) \leq 2C_{OPT}(t) - 1$, proving (3.44).

3.7 Show that if an online algorithm $\mathcal{A}$ has a competitive ratio $\mu_{\mathcal{A}}$ in the partial cost model, i.e., the cost at time t is $\ell_i(t) - 1$ if the requested file $f_i, i = 1, \dots, L$ is in location $\ell_i(t)$ at time t from the left, then $\mathcal{A}$ also has competitive ratio $\mu_{\mathcal{A}}$ in the original cost model, where the cost at time t is $\ell_i(t)$.

[Hint: For any $\mathcal{A}$ including OPT, the cost of $\mathcal{A}$ in the original cost model is equal to the cost of an algorithm $\mathcal{A}$ in the partial cost model plus the number of total requests.]

3.8 [33] Let $\mathcal{A}$ be a deterministic or randomized online algorithm that does not use any paid exchange and satisfies the pairwise independence property. Then under the **partial cost model**, let $\mathcal{A}$ have a competitive ratio of μ for $L = 2$, i.e., $C_{\mathcal{A}}^2(\sigma_{x,y}) \leq \mu C_{OPT}^2(\sigma_{x,y})$, where the superscript 2 in the cost means that the algorithms are working over a list of size $L = 2$ list, and $\sigma_{x,y}$ is the punctured input derived from the full input σ with only those instants where either x or y is requested.

Then show that $\mathcal{A}$ has a competitive ratio of μ over the full list for any L in the partial cost model by proving the following claims.

i. Fix any two files, x, y. Construct an offline algorithm OFF for the punctured input $\sigma_{x,y}$ using the actions of OPT on σ as follows.

   (a) If OPT working over σ switches the relative order of x and y for free on any request to either x, y, then OFF does the same on the punctured input $\sigma_{x,y}$.

   (b) If OPT working over σ uses a paid exchange to switch x and y between two requests for items x, y, then OFF does the same at the corresponding times on the punctured input $\sigma_{x,y}$.

   Using (a) and (b) justify (ii) in (3.45), while (i) is by definition

$$C_{OPT}^2(\sigma_{x,y}) \overset{(i)}{\leq} C_{OFF}^2(\sigma_{x,y}) \overset{(ii)}{\leq} C_{OPT}^{x,y}(\sigma) + C_{OPT}^{y,x}(\sigma) + \text{paid}(x, y), \qquad (3.45)$$

   where $\text{paid}(x, y)$ is the number of paid exchanges used by OPT to switch the relative order of x and y with input σ, $C_{OPT}^{x,y}(\sigma)$ is defined as the number of times y is requested and x precedes y in OPT's list, with input σ.

ii. Using (3.45), in conjunction with the property that $\mathcal{A}$ does not use any paid exchange and satisfies the pairwise independence property, conclude the result. Combining this result together with what we showed in Problem 3.7 implies the result for the full cost model.

3.9 Show that the following randomized algorithm, called RANDOM, which, on request for file f_i, moves f_i to the first place/front with probability 1/2, and keeps the location of f_i unchanged with probability 1/2, is 2-competitive.

[Hint: Consider a list of only three files, and an input that consists of alternating blocks of long repeated requests for a single file.]

3.10 [30] [With lookahead] Let $L = 2$, and an online algorithm have a lookahead of 1, i.e., at time t it knows the file requested at time t and $t + 1$. Consider the following algorithm, and show that it is optimal among all lookahead−1 algorithms.

Algorithm: After each request, move the requested file to the front, if the next request is also for that file. Otherwise do nothing.

[Hint: Use induction on the length of the input sequence.]

CHAPTER 4

Bin-Packing

4.1 Introduction

In this chapter, we consider a very basic packing problem, called bin-packing, where the objective is to pack items with different weights or sizes in boxes or bins of fixed capacity using as few bins as possible. In particular, assuming that the capacity of each bin is 1 and the weight of each item is at most 1, the problem is to divide the set of items into as few partitions (corresponding to individual bins) as possible, such that the sum of the weight of items in each partition is at most 1. The offline problem when the full set of items is available ahead of time is known to be NP-hard.

Applications of the bin-packing problem in both offline and online settings include inventory management where pellets or containers need to be packed with objects of different sizes and weights, subject to a size or weight capacity, job scheduling where each server can process jobs subject to a maximum capacity, and storing large data sets on disks of finite size, and many others.

Bin-packing is one of the most well-studied problems in the area of online algorithms for which multiple classes of algorithms have been studied. In this chapter, we review two such classes: ANYFIT algorithms that try to fit an item in a bin using some local rule and (ii) the HARMONIC algorithm that creates special classes of bins ahead of time and assigns an item to a bin of a particular class. The philosophy behind these two classes of algorithms is entirely different; however, they result in very similar competitive ratios when the number of items is large.

We show that with a large number of items, the competitive ratio of ANYFIT class of algorithms is 1.7, while the competitive ratio of the HARMONIC algorithm is 1.691, where both the ratios are tight. We also show that for arbitrarily many number of items, the lower bound on the competitive ratio of any deterministic online algorithm is 5/3.

4.2 Problem Formulation

Consider that there is an infinite supply of bins each with a capacity 1. Items with weight w_i arrive sequentially that have to be placed in one of the bins (subject to the sum-weight of the items placed in any bin being less than its capacity) irrevocably with an objective of minimizing the number of bins used. Here, irrevocably means that once an item is placed in a bin it cannot be placed in any other bin in the future. Let the number of bins used by an online algorithm $\mathcal{A}$ be $\mathbf{b}_{\mathcal{A}}$, and by OPT be $\mathbf{b}_{\mathsf{OPT}}$. Then the competitive ratio of $\mathcal{A}$ is

$$\mu_{\mathcal{A}} = \max_{\sigma} \frac{\mathbf{b}_{\mathcal{A}}(\sigma)}{\mathbf{b}_{\mathsf{OPT}}(\sigma)}. \tag{4.1}$$

Throughout this chapter, without loss of generality, we will assume that the capacity of each bin is 1, and the weight of each arriving item is ≤ 1.

To illustrate the non-triviality of the problem, consider the following example.

Example 4.2.1

Let three items each of weight 1/4 arrive together. An online algorithm $\mathcal{A}$ can pack all of them either in a single bin or in two or more bins. If $\mathcal{A}$ uses two or more bins, the input stops and the competitive ratio of $\mathcal{A}$ is at least 2 since OPT *can pack all these items in a single bin. Thus, let $\mathcal{A}$ pack all three items in a single bin. Then, next, three items each with a weight of 3/4 arrive. Clearly,* OPT *would have used a total of three bins by packing one item each with weight 1/4 and 3/4 together in a single bin. $\mathcal{A}$, however, has to use a total of four bins, since it has already assigned the first three items in a single bin, and none of the three items with a weight of 3/4 can fit together or in the first bin. Thus, the competitive ratio of $\mathcal{A}$ is at least 4/3.*

For the bin-packing problem, the asymptotic regime is also very well studied, where the asymptotic competitive ratio is defined as

$$\mu_{\mathcal{A}}^{\infty} = \lim_{b \to \infty} \sup \left\{ \max_{\sigma : \mathbf{b}_{\mathsf{OPT}}(\sigma) = b} \left\{ \frac{\mathbf{b}_{\mathcal{A}}(\sigma)}{b} \right\} \right\}, \tag{4.2}$$

where the class of inputs of interest is those with which the number of bins used by OPT is large. To differentiate the asymptotic competitive ratio (4.2) and (4.1), (4.1) is referred to as the absolute competitive ratio.

4.3 Algorithms

In this section, we concentrate on the asymptotic competitive ratio and present two classes of algorithms for the bin-packing problem and derive upper bounds on their asymptotic competitive ratios.

4.3.1 ANYFIT Class of Algorithms

A bin is defined to be **open** if some item has been assigned to it. The **occupied weight** of a bin is defined as the sum of the weights of all the items assigned to it. Consequently, the **remaining capacity** of a bin is the difference between its capacity and the occupied weight. An item is defined to **fit** in a bin if its weight is less than or equal to the remaining capacity of the bin.

In ANYFIT class of algorithms, a newly arrived item is assigned to an open bin as long as it fits in any one of them (the precise choice gives rise to a particular algorithm); otherwise, a new bin is opened and the item is assigned to the newly opened bin.

Lemma 4.3.1 *The asymptotic competitive ratio of any algorithm that belongs to the* ANYFIT *class of algorithms is at most* 2.

Proof: Let $\mathcal{A}$ be an algorithm belonging to the ANYFIT class of algorithms. After assigning the ith item to some bin, let $\mathbf{b}_i$ be the total number of bins that have been opened by $\mathcal{A}$ so far. Note that with $\mathcal{A}$ at any time, at most one bin is less than half full. To see this, let A and B be two bins that are less than half full, and A was opened before B. Then algorithm $\mathcal{A}$ would have had space to assign all items of B to A. Since $\mathcal{A}$ opens a new bin only if there is no bin where a newly arriving item can fit, we get a contradiction. Thus, the sum-weight of items after assigning the ith item is at least $(\mathbf{b}_i - 1)/2$. Since the same set of items has to be assigned by OPT as well, by the pigeon-hole principle at least $(\mathbf{b}_i - 1)/2$ bins are needed by OPT since the capacity of each bin is at most 1. Since this is true for all i, the result follows.   ∎

There are multiple algorithms that belong to the ANYFIT class of algorithms; the popular ones among them are: FIRSTFIT, which assigns an item on its arrival to the oldest (earliest opened) bin into which it fits, and BESTFIT, which assigns an item on its arrival to the bin with the most occupied weight among the bins where it can fit. Asymptotically (in the number of items) the competitive ratio of both FIRSTFIT and BESTFIT is 1.7. Next, we present the analysis of the competitive ratio for the BESTFIT algorithm.

4.3.2 BESTFIT Algorithm

BESTFIT can equivalently be thought of as follows. Consider that the algorithm keeps a sorted list of already open bins in decreasing order of their occupied weight, and assigns a new item to the first (ordered) bin where it fits. If the item cannot fit into any of the open bins, then a new bin is opened, and the item is assigned to the newly opened bin.

We next derive a more refined analysis of BESTFIT compared to the simple upper bound derived in Lemma 4.3.1.

Theorem 4.3.2 *The asymptotic competitive ratio of* BESTFIT *is at most* 1.7.

Before presenting the proof, we need the following definitions.

Definition 4.3.3 *At any time instant, the* **level of a bin** *is the total weight of the items currently present in the bin. The* **level of item** i *is the level of the bin where it is placed just before the arrival of item i. For example, if the item i is placed in bin j, and the level of bin j just before the arrival of item i is ℓ_j^{-i}. Then level of item i is ℓ_j^{-i}.*

Definition 4.3.4 *An item i is called light if its weight* $w_i \le 1/6$, *medium if* $w_i \in (1/6, 1/2]$, *and heavy if* $w_i > 1/2$.

Definition 4.3.5 *The occupied weight of a bin b, and the weight of a subset S is defined as* $w(b) = \sum_{i:\, assigned\ to\ bin\ b} w_i$, *and* $w(S) = \sum_{i \in S} w_i$, *respectively.*

Using these definitions, we next describe some elementary properties of BESTFIT that will be useful for the proof of Theorem 4.3.2.

Proposition 4.3.6   *At any time during the execution of* BESTFIT, *the following holds:*

1. *The sum of levels of any two open bins is greater than 1. In particular, there is at most one open bin with the level at most 1/2.*

2. *An item i assigned to a bin with the level at most 1/2 on its arrival (i.e., a new bin or the single bin with the level at most 1/2 following (1)) does not fit into any bin open at the time of its arrival, except for the bin where item i is assigned.*

3. *If there are two bins B and B′ both with level at most 2/3, where B is opened before B′, then either B′ contains a single item or the first item that was assigned to B′ is heavy.*

Proof:

1. Suppose to the contrary, consider any two open bins b_1 and b_2, where b_1 was opened before b_2, and let the sum of their levels be at most 1. Clearly, this contradicts the algorithm's description, since all items in b_2 can be assigned to b_1 as $w(b_1) + w(b_2) \leq 1$.

2. If item i is assigned to a new bin, clearly by definition, it does not fit in any currently open bin. Otherwise, let $\ell \leq 1/2$ be the level of the bin just before item i arrives where item i is assigned. From (1), there is at most one bin with level at most 1/2. Thus, at the time of assigning of item i, all other bins are at levels strictly greater than ℓ. Thus, if item i could fit in any of these bins, the algorithm would have assigned item i there. Therefore item i does not fit into any of these bins.

3. Let $B′$ have two items and its first item (the item that was assigned to $B′$ first) be not heavy. Clearly, the first item of $B′$ does not fit into B, since otherwise $B′$ would not have been opened. Moreover, since the first item is not heavy, the level of $B′$ just before the arrival of the second item is at most 1/2. Then by Property 2, the second item of $B′$ also cannot fit into B. Since the level of B is at most 2/3 and each of the first two items of $B′$ does not fit into B, this means they have weights larger than 1/3 individually. Thus the level of $B′$ is larger than 2/3, providing a contradiction.   ∎

Using Proposition 4.3.6, we next prove Theorem 4.3.2.

Proof: [Theorem 4.3.2] We define a value function v_i for each item i that is related to the weight of the item as follows. For item i, let its *value* be defined as $v_i = \bar{v}_i + \bar{\bar{v}}_i$

where
$$\bar{v}_i = \begin{cases} 0, & \text{if } w_i \leq 1/6, \\ \frac{3}{5}\left(w_i - \frac{1}{6}\right), & \text{if } w_i \in (1/6, 1/3), \\ 0.1, & \text{if } w_i \in [1/3, 1/2], \\ 0.4, & \text{if } w_i > 1/2, \end{cases}$$

and
$$\bar{\bar{v}}_i = \frac{6}{5}w_i. \tag{4.3}$$

Lemma 4.3.7   *For any subset of items S with cumulative weight less than 1, i.e., $w(S) = \sum_{i \in S} w_i \leq 1$, we have $v(S) = \sum_{i \in S} v_i \leq 1.7$.*

Note that Lemma 4.3.7 is independent of any algorithm.

Since $\bar{\bar{v}}_i \leq 1.2 w_i$ for each item i, we have

$$\bar{\bar{v}}(S) \leq 1.2 \sum_{i \in S} w_i \leq 1.2.$$

Thus to prove Lemma 4.3.7, it is sufficient to show that $\bar{v}(S) \leq 0.5$, which we do as follows.

Proof: In case set S has no heavy items, then all items $i \in S$ with $\bar{v}_i > 0$ have weights either $w_i \in (1/6, 1/3)$ or $w_i \in [1/3, 1/2]$. By hypothesis, the total weight of items in S is at most 1, $\sum_{i \in S} w_i \leq 1$, which implies that S contains at most 5 items that have $\bar{v}_i > 0$, since if there were 6 or more items, then $\sum_{i \in S} w_i > 1$ as the weight of each item is at least $1/(6 - \epsilon)$ when $\bar{v}_i > 0$. Since for each item with $w_i \in (1/6, 1/3)$ or $w_i \in [1/3, 1/2]$, $\bar{v}_i \leq 0.1$, and there are at most 5 of them, the claim follows.

Otherwise, let there be a heavy time in S. Then since $\sum_{i \in S} w_i \leq 1$, either there is at most one other item in S with weight $\in [1/3, 1/2]$ with no item with weight belonging to $(1/6, 1/3]$, or at most two other items i, j in S with weights belonging to $(1/6, 1/3]$ that have $\bar{v}_i > 0$. In the first case, it is clear from the definition of $\bar{v}$ that $\bar{v}(S) \leq 0.5$, since $\bar{v} = 0.4$ for the heavy item and $\bar{v}_i \leq 0.1$ for the other item i with weight $w_i \in [1/3, 1/2]$. In the second case, when there are at most two other items i, j in S with weights in $[1/6, 1/3]$, because of the presence of the heavy item and the constraint that $\sum_{i \in S} w_i \leq 1$, we get $w_i + w_j \leq 1/2$. Therefore, from the definition of $\bar{v}$, we get that the sum of the values $\bar{v}_i + \bar{v}_j \leq 0.1$. Since $\bar{v} = 0.4$ for the heavy item, the total value is $\bar{v}(S) \leq 0.5$. ∎

Let $\mathcal{I}$ be the total set of items, and let OPT place subset $O_i \subseteq \mathcal{I}$ in bin b_i ($\cup_{i \in \{1, \ldots, \mathbf{b}_{\text{OPT}}\}} O_i = \mathcal{I}, O_i \cap O_j = \varnothing$), with total number of bins being $\mathbf{b}_{\text{OPT}}$. Since the capacity of each bin is 1, the set O_i satisfies $\sum_{j \in O_i} w_j \leq 1$ for each bin i. Thus, applying Lemma 4.3.7 for the value function, we get $v(O_i) \leq 1.7$ for each O_i. Hence

$$v(\mathcal{I}) = \sum_{i=1}^{\mathbf{b}_{\text{OPT}}} v(O_i) \leq \sum_{i=1}^{\mathbf{b}_{\text{OPT}}} 1.7 = 1.7 \mathbf{b}_{\text{OPT}} \tag{4.4}$$

Therefore the value of the whole instance is less than 1.7 times the number of bins used by OPT. To prove the result of the theorem, we will lower bound $v(\mathcal{I})$ as a function of the number of bins used by BestFit.

Lemma 4.3.8 *Let the set of items S assigned to bin b have weight*

$$w(S) = \sum_{j \in S} w_j \geq 2/3,$$

and two items k, ℓ be such that $w_k > 1 - w(S)$ and $w_\ell > 1 - w(S)$, i.e., both k and ℓ cannot be placed in bin b. Then,

$$\bar{\bar{v}}(S) + \bar{v}_k + \bar{v}_\ell \geq 1.$$

Note that Lemma 4.3.8 holds independently of the choice of the algorithm.

Proof: If $\sum_{j \in S} w_j \geq 5/6$, then from the definition of $\bar{\bar{v}}$, $\bar{\bar{v}}(S) \geq 1$ irrespective of items k, ℓ.

Thus, let $\sum_{j \in S} w_j = 5/6 - x$ for some $0 < x \leq \frac{1}{6}$ since $\sum_{j \in S} w_j \geq 2/3$. Moreover, since for items k and ℓ, $w_k > 1 - w(S)$ and $w_\ell > 1 - w(S)$, we get $w_k > 1/6 + x$ and $w_\ell > 1/6 + x$. Therefore, $\bar{v}_k, \bar{v}_\ell > \frac{3}{5}x$, and hence we get

$$\bar{\bar{v}}(S) + \bar{v}_k + \bar{v}_\ell > \frac{6}{5}\left(\frac{5}{6} - x\right) + \frac{3}{5}x + \frac{3}{5}x = 1. \qquad \blacksquare$$

Next we will estimate the value v of each bin when using BESTFIT. If any bin b_i with BESTFIT contains a heavy item j, we denote it as a heavy bin h_i, where $\bar{v}_j \geq 0.4$ and $\bar{\bar{v}}_j = \frac{5}{6}w_i > \frac{5}{6} \times \frac{1}{2} = 0.6$. Thus, the value of a heavy bin

$$v(h_i) = \sum_{j \in h_i} v_j > 1. \tag{4.5}$$

From Proposition 4.3.6, we know that with BESTFIT there is at most one bin with occupied weight/level at most $1/2$ (call it bin E_1) and there is at most one bin b with two or more items such that $w(b) \leq 2/3$ and that contains no heavy item, (call it bin E_2). Excluding bins E_1, E_2, and any heavy bin (bin that contains a heavy item), consider bins $b_1, b_2, \ldots, b_M$ opened by BESTFIT with $w(b_i) > 2/3$ and containing no heavy items, where the bins are indexed in the order in which they were opened by BESTFIT.

Note that all bins among $b_1, \ldots, b_M$ have levels more than $2/3$ and contain no heavy items. Thus, there are at least two items in each bin among $b_1, \ldots, b_M$. Consider the first two items k, ℓ, respectively, with individual weights at most $1/2$ that are assigned to bin b_{i+1}.[1] Since bin b_{i+1} is opened after bin b_i, the first item k could not have fit in bin b_i, and the level of bin b_i just before the arrival of item k, $\ell_{b_i}^{-k} > 1 - w_k$, where $w_k \leq \frac{1}{2}$. Thus, given that item ℓ is the second item assigned to bin b_{i+1} when its level was at most $w_k \leq \frac{1}{2}$, from Proposition 4.3.6 (2) we can conclude that item ℓ also could not have fit in bin b_i. Moreover, $w(b_i) > 2/3$ by definition of b_i.[2] Since items k and ℓ did not fit in bin i on their respective arrivals, they do not fit in bin i after all arrivals also. Thus, using Lemma 4.3.8, we have

$$\bar{\bar{v}}(b_i) + \bar{v}(b_{i+1}) \geq \bar{\bar{v}}(b_i) + \bar{v}_k + \bar{v}_\ell \geq 1. \tag{4.6}$$

Equation (4.6) allows amortisation of the value across the two successively opened bins (among $b_1, \ldots, b_M$) by BESTFIT, which will be used as follows to bound the overall value of items.

Next, counting across all bins, we relate the valuation of the full instance $\mathcal{I}$ of items in terms of the assignments made by BESTFIT, as follows.

$$v(\mathcal{I}) = \sum_{i=1}^{M} v(b_i) + \sum_{i \in \text{heavy bin}} v(h_i) + v(E_1) + v(E_2),$$

$$\stackrel{(a)}{=} \sum_{i=1}^{M} \left(\bar{\bar{v}}(b_i) + \bar{v}(b_i)\right) + \sum_{i \in \text{heavy bin}} v(h_i) + v(E_1) + v(E_2),$$

---

[1] Since none of the bins $b_1, \ldots, b_M$ are heavy.

[2] After all item arrivals, and not necessarily at the time when item k or ℓ arrived.

$$= \bar{v}(b_1) + \sum_{i=1}^{M-1} \left(\bar{v}(b_i) + \bar{v}(b_{i+1}) \right) + \bar{v}(b_M) + \sum_{i \in \text{heavy bin}} v(h_i) + v(E_1) + v(E_2),$$

$$= \sum_{i=1}^{M-1} \left(\bar{v}(b_i) + \bar{v}(b_{i+1}) \right) + \sum_{i \in \text{heavy bin}} v(h_i) + v(E_1) + v(E_2) + \bar{v}(b_1) + \bar{v}(b_M),$$

$$\overset{(b)}{>} \sum_{i=1}^{M-1} 1 + \sum_{i \in \text{heavy bin}} 1 + v(E_1) + v(E_2) + \bar{v}(b_1) + \bar{v}(b_M),$$

$$\overset{(c)}{=} M - 1 + \# \text{ of heavy bins} + 3 - 3 + v(E_1) + v(E_2) + \bar{v}(b_1) + \bar{v}(b_M),$$

$$\overset{(d)}{=} \mathbf{b}_{BF} - 3 + v(E_1) + v(E_2) + \bar{v}(b_1) + \bar{v}(b_M),$$

$$\overset{(e)}{\geq} \mathbf{b}_{BF} - 3, \tag{4.7}$$

where in (a) we write $v(b_i)$ in the expanded form $\left(\bar{v}(b_i) + \bar{v}(b_i) \right)$ since we want to combine values $\bar{v}(b_i)$ and $\bar{v}(b_{i+1})$ using (4.6), and (b) follows using (4.6) and (4.5), respectively, on the first two summations, in (c) we have added and subtracted 3 since there are two bins E_1, E_2 whose values have not been lower bounded, and among bins $b_1, \dots, b_M$ we have lower bounded the contribution from only $M - 1$ bins, in (d) we recall the definition $\mathbf{b}_{BF}$ as the total number of bins used by BestFit, which by definition includes bins $1, \dots, M$, the set of heavy bins, and bins E_1 and E_2, and finally (e) follows since $v(.) \geq 0$.

Combining (4.7) with the lower bound on $\mathbf{b}_{OPT}$ (4.4), we get

$$1.7\mathbf{b}_{OPT} > \mathbf{b}_{BF} - 3,$$

which implies that the asymptotic competitive ratio of BestFit is at most 1.7, completing the proof of Theorem 4.3.2. ∎

The main idea of this proof is the use of the value function (4.3) that is split in two parts, where the two parts are essentially defined to connect the weights in two consecutive bins opened by BestFit via (4.6).

4.3.3 Harmonic Algorithm

In this section, we present a conceptually different algorithm compared to the AnyFit class, called the Harmonic, that reserves bins for items that belong to a certain interval of weights, and keeps only one open bin for each interval. In particular, the algorithm chooses a parameter C (the number of distinct classes it creates) and each class $c \in C$ corresponds to interval $I_c = \left(\frac{1}{c+1}, \frac{1}{c} \right]$ for $1 \leq c \leq C - 1$ and $I_C = \left(0, \frac{1}{C} \right]$. An item i of weight $w_i \in I_c$ is called a c-item, and an interval I_c is called a c-interval. Each c-interval corresponds to a c-bin, which is used to allocate only c-items.

Algorithm: On arrival of a new c-item, $1 \leq c \leq C$, the algorithm tries to fit it in the currently open c-bin. A c-bin is defined to be *closed* as soon as the newly arrived c-item cannot fit anymore in that bin. A c-bin that is not closed is defined to be *open*. When a c-item encounters a closed bin, a new c-bin is opened and the item is assigned to it. Once a bin is closed, no new items are assigned to it ever in future. Thus, the algorithm keeps at most one open c-bin for each c. The algorithm gets its name from the harmonic partitioning it makes of the unit interval.

Example 4.3.9

Let $C = 3$. Then HARMONIC *creates three classes of bins, a 3-bin, a 2-bin, and a 1-bin, corresponding to intervals $I_3 = (0, 1/3], I_2 = (1/3, 1/2]$, and $I_1 = (1/2, 1]$, and keeps at most one bin open for these three classes. Let items with weights $\{1/2, 1/2, 1/4, 1/4, 1/4, 1/3, 1/4\}$ arrive in order (left to right). Then the algorithm first opens a 2-bin and assigns item 1 to it, next assigns item 2 to the same bin and closes that bin since its capacity is completely exhausted. Thus, after the arrival of the first two items, there is one closed 2-bin, and no other open bin. On the arrival of the third item with weight 1/4, a 3-bin is opened and item 3 is assigned to it. Items 4 and 5 with weight 1/4 each are also assigned to the open 3-bin. Next, on the arrival of item 6 with weight 1/3, since it cannot fit in the open 3-bin, the currently open 3-bin is closed, and a new 3-bin is opened and item 6 is assigned to it. Finally, on the arrival of item 7 with weight 1/4, it is assigned to the currently open 3-bin, even though it can fit in the closed 3-bin.*

One can see with a small number of total items HARMONIC *is inefficient, since even though the seventh item fits in the closed 3-bin, it assigns it to the currently open 3-bin, thus potentially leaving unused capacity in closed bins. We will show that asymptotically in the number of items, the competitive ratio of* HARMONIC *is strictly better than* BESTFIT.

Some properties of algorithm HARMONIC are useful to note. (i) Each closed c-bin for $1 \leq c < C$ contains exactly c c-items, (ii) with $|\mathcal{I}| = n$, the complexity of the algorithm is $\mathcal{O}(n \log C)$ since on each new item arrival only a classification problem as to which interval I_c it belongs to needs to be solved that can be done in $\mathcal{O}(\log C)$ and there is at most one c-bin for each c, and (iii) which we leave as an exercise (Problem 4.7) is that, except for the number of C-bins, the number of c-bins $c < C$ used by the algorithm is independent of the order of arrival of items.

Theorem 4.3.10 *The asymptotic competitive ratio of* HARMONIC *is at most* 1.691.

Thus, compared to BESTFIT, HARMONIC performs only slightly better but the improvement is fundamental. We next prove Theorem 4.3.10.

Proof: Among the total n arriving items, let n_c be the number of c-items, and w_C denote the sum of the weights of all the C-items, $w_C = \sum_{w_i \in I_C} w_i$. Let b_c be the number of c-bins used by HARMONIC.

For $c = 1$, since no two items with weight more than $1/2$ can fit in any single bin, we have $b_1 = n_1$. Moreover, for $2 \leq c < C, b_c = \left\lceil \frac{n_c}{c} \right\rceil$, and $b_C < \left\lceil \frac{w_C}{(C-1)/C} \right\rceil$ since each C-item has weight at most $1/C$, making the occupied fraction of each C-bin at least $(C-1)/C$.

Therefore, the total number of bins used by HARMONIC is

$$\mathbf{b}_H = n_1 + \left\lceil \frac{n_2}{2} \right\rceil + \cdots + \left\lceil \frac{n_{C-1}}{C-1} \right\rceil + b_C,$$

$$< \sum_{c=1}^{C-1} \frac{n_c}{c} + \frac{Cw_C}{C-1} + (C-1), \tag{4.8}$$

by upper bounding $\lceil x \rceil$ by $x + 1$, and since there are $C - 1$ terms with a $\lceil . \rceil$.

Next, we compare the performance of OPT on the same input. Towards that end, we define a function g as follows.

$$g(x) = \begin{cases} \dfrac{1}{c} & \text{if } x \in I_c \text{ for } 1 \le c < C, \\[2mm] \dfrac{Cx}{C-1} & \text{if } x \in I_C. \end{cases} \tag{4.9}$$

Let $S = \{(y_1, y_2, \ldots, y_p) | y_i > 0, y_i \ge y_j, j \ge i, \sum_{i=1}^p y_i \le 1\}$ be the set that contains all possible partitions with sum at most 1 having p elements (ordered in non-increasing weights y_i). For a fixed element (p-tuple) $s = (y_1, y_2, \ldots, y_p) \in S$ with $\sum_{i=1}^p y_i \le 1$, let

$$z_s = \sum_{i=1}^p g(y_i), \tag{4.10}$$

and let

$$z^* = \sup_{s \in S, \, p \in \mathbb{N}} z_s. \tag{4.11}$$

Using the definition of g (4.9), we can rewrite the upper bound (4.8) on the number of bins used by HARMONIC as (where there are total $|\mathcal{I}| = n$ items and item $j \in \mathcal{I}$ has weight w_j)

$$\mathbf{b}_H \le \sum_{j=1}^n g(w_j) + C - 1. \tag{4.12}$$

Let $g_S = \sum_{i \in S} g(w_i)$. Since OPT also has to assign all items to some bins, using conservation of the total g-weight $\sum_{j=1}^n g(w_j)$, we have

$$\sum_{j=1}^n g(w_j) \overset{(a)}{=} \sum_{i=1}^{\mathbf{b}_{OPT}} g_{S_i^{OPT}} \overset{(b)}{\le} z^* \mathbf{b}_{OPT}, \tag{4.13}$$

where (a) is obtained by writing the g-weight bin-wise by letting $\mathbf{b}_{OPT}$ to be the number of bins opened by OPT and S_i^{OPT} to be the set of items assigned by OPT to bin i, and the inequality (b) follows from definition (4.11). Next, we work towards upper bounding z^*.

Define a sequence ℓ_i, where

$$\ell_1 = 1, \text{ and } \ell_{i+1} = \ell_i \cdot (\ell_i + 1) \text{ for } i \in \mathbb{N}, i \ge 2. \tag{4.14}$$

Thus, $\ell_1 = 1, \ell_2 = 2, \ell_3 = 6, \ell_4 = 42$, and so on.

Let $U_C = \sum_{j=1}^{i} \frac{1}{\ell_j} + \frac{C}{\ell_{i+1} \cdot (C-1)}$, where $i > 1$, C is such that $\ell_i < C \leq \ell_{i+1}$ and ℓ_i is defined in (4.14).

A non-obvious fact is that U_C is a non-increasing sequence. To see this, let $C = 3$, in which case $i = 2$, satisfies $\ell_i < C \leq \ell_{i+1}$. Thus, $U_3 = \sum_{j=1}^{2} \frac{1}{\ell_j} + \frac{3}{\ell_{i+1}(2)} = 1.75$, while for $C = 4$,

i remains 2 that satisfies $\ell_i < C \leq \ell_{i+1}$. Therefore, $U_4 = \sum_{j=1}^{2} \frac{1}{\ell_j} + \frac{4}{\ell_{i+1} \cdot (3)} = 1.72$. Moreover,

$$\lim_{C \to \infty} U_C = \sum_{j=1}^{\infty} \frac{1}{\ell_j} = 1 + \frac{1}{2} + \frac{1}{6} + \frac{1}{42} + \cdots = 1.691.$$

For any choice of C made by HARMONIC in Lemma 4.3.12 we show that $z^* \leq U_C$. Since U_C is a non-increasing sequence of C, and $\lim_{C \to \infty} U_C = 1.691$, if C is chosen large enough we can get the competitive ratio of HARMONIC using (4.12) and (4.13),

$$\lim_{n \to \infty} \frac{b_H}{b_{OPT}} \leq z^* \approx 1.691, \qquad (4.15)$$

as required. ∎

Note that $U_C \leq 1.692$ for $C \geq 12$. Thus, in practice, choosing $C = 12$ is sufficient for executing HARMONIC.

In the rest of the section, we prove Lemma 4.3.12, for which we need the following preliminary result whose proof is immediate.

Proposition 4.3.11 *If $x < 1/c$ and $1 \leq c < C$, we have*

$$\frac{g(x)}{x} \leq \frac{c+1}{c}.$$

Lemma 4.3.12 *For $i > 1$, with $\ell_i < C \leq \ell_{i+1}$, where ℓ_i is defined in (4.14), we have*

$$z^* = U_C,$$

where recall that $U_C = \sum_{j=1}^{i} \frac{1}{\ell_j} + \frac{C}{\ell_{i+1}(C-1)}$.

Proof: From the definition of U_C, each C corresponds to a particular choice of i. To avoid confusion we call that $i = i_C$ for the particular choice.

To prove the lemma, we will prove that $z_s \leq U_C$ for any $s = (y_1, \ldots, y_p) \in S$ where $S = \{(y_1, y_2, \ldots, y_p) | y_j > 0, y_j \geq y_k, k \geq j, \sum_{j=1}^{p} y_j \leq 1\}$.

Towards this end, we will classify any s in three possible cases as follows.

Case I: $y_1 \notin I_1$, i.e., $y_1 \leq 1/2$. Recall that in s, $y_j's$ are ordered in non-increasing order. Thus, this implies that $y_j \leq 1/2 \ \forall j \geq 1, s = (y_1, \ldots, y_p)$. Therefore, from Proposition 4.3.11, we have $g(y_i) \leq 3y_i/2$. Using the definition of z_s (4.10), thus we get that $z_s \leq 3/2 \sum_{i=1}^{p} y_i \leq 3/2$, for all $s \in S$. Therefore, $z^* \leq U_C$ for $C > \ell_2$, i.e. $i_C = 2$.

Case II: Let $y_1 \in I_{\ell_1}, y_2 \in I_{\ell_2}, \ldots, y_{j-1} \in I_{\ell_{j-1}}, y_j \notin I_{\ell_j}$ for some $j \leq i_C$. It could be that $j = 1$ itself. The definition of intervals I_{ℓ_j} implies that

$$\frac{1}{\ell_k + 1} < y_k \leq \frac{1}{\ell_k} \quad \text{for } k \leq j - 1. \tag{4.16}$$

From (4.16), the sum of the weights of the first $j - 1$ items

$$\sum_{k=1}^{j-1} y_k > \sum_{k=1}^{j-1} \frac{1}{\ell_k + 1}.$$

Given that $\sum_{j=1}^{p} y_k \leq 1$, therefore the left-over sum of weights of items of s,

$$\sum_{k=j}^{p} y_k \leq 1 - \sum_{k=1}^{j-1} y_k \leq 1/\ell_j. \tag{4.17}$$

Recall that $y_{j-1} \in I_{\ell_{j-1}}$, i.e., $\frac{1}{\ell_{j-1}+1} < y_{j-1}$. Moreover, since $y_j \leq y_{j-1}$ and $y_j \notin I_{\ell_j}$, either $\frac{1}{\ell_{j-1}+1} \leq y_j \leq y_{j-1}$ or $y_j \leq \frac{1}{\ell_j+1}$. From (4.17), we know that $y_j \geq \frac{1}{\ell_{j-1}+1}$ is not possible. Thus, $y_j < \frac{1}{\ell_j+1}$. Hence, we have

$$y_k < \frac{1}{\ell_j + 1} \text{ for } j \leq k \leq p. \tag{4.18}$$

Thus, we can upper bound z_s as follows.

$$z_s = \sum_{k=1}^{p} g(y_k)$$

$$\overset{(a)}{\leq} \sum_{k=1}^{j-1} \frac{1}{\ell_k} + \sum_{k=j}^{p} g(y_k),$$

$$\overset{(b)}{\leq} \sum_{k=1}^{j-1} \frac{1}{\ell_k} + \sum_{k=j}^{p} \frac{y_k(\ell_j + 2)}{\ell_j + 1},$$

$$= \sum_{k=1}^{j-1} \frac{1}{\ell_k} + \frac{(\ell_j + 2)}{\ell_j + 1} \sum_{k=j}^{p} y_k,$$

$$\overset{(c)}{\leq} \sum_{k=1}^{j-1} \frac{1}{\ell_k} + \frac{1 + 1/(\ell_j + 1)}{\ell_j},$$

$$\overset{(d)}{=} \sum_{k=1}^{j+1} \frac{1}{\ell_k},$$

$$\overset{(e)}{\leq} \sum_{k=1}^{i_C+1} \frac{1}{\ell_k},$$

$$< U_C,$$

where (a) follows since $y_k \in I_{\ell_k}$ for $k \leq j-1$ as in (4.16) for which $g(y_k) \leq \frac{1}{\ell_k}$, (b) follows by applying (4.18) since $y_k < \frac{1}{\ell_j+1}$ for $k \geq j$ and Proposition 4.3.11, (c) follows from (4.17), (d) follows by using the definition of $\ell_{i+1} = \ell_i(\ell_i + 1)$, and finally (e) follows since $i_C \geq j$ to begin with.

Finally we consider Case III: If $y_1 \in I_{\ell_1}, y_2 \in I_{\ell_2}, \ldots, y_{i_C} \in I_{\ell_{i_C}}$. Similar to case II, we have $\sum_{k=1}^{i_C} g(y_k) \leq \sum_{k=1}^{i_C} \frac{1}{\ell_k}$. Moreover, similar to (4.17), we have $\sum_{k=i_C+1}^{p} y_k \leq \frac{1}{\ell_{i_C+1}}$. Since y'_j are ordered in non-increasing order in s, we also have $y_k \leq y_{i_C}$ for $k > i_C$. Moreover, by definition, $\ell_{i_C} < C$. Recalling that $I_C = \left(0, \frac{1}{C}\right]$, we get $y_k \in I_C$ for $k > i_C$ since $y_{i_C} \in I_{\ell_{i_C}}$. Thus, we get

$$z_s = \sum_{k=1}^{i_C} g(y_k) + \sum_{k=i_C+1}^{p} g(y_k),$$

$$\overset{(a)}{\leq} \sum_{k=1}^{i_C} \frac{1}{\ell_k} + \frac{C}{C-1} \sum_{k=i_C+1}^{p} y_k,$$

$$\overset{(b)}{\leq} \sum_{k=1}^{i_C} \frac{1}{\ell_k} + \frac{C}{C-1} \frac{1}{\ell_{i_C+1}},$$

$$\leq U_C,$$

where (a) follows since $\sum_{k=1}^{i_C} g(y_k) \leq \sum_{k=1}^{i_C} \frac{1}{\ell_k}$ and definition of function $g(x) = \frac{C-1}{C}x$ for $x \in I_C$, and (b) follows since $\sum_{k=i_C+1}^{p} y_k \leq \frac{1}{\ell_{i_C+1}}$ as argued earlier.

Thus, we have shown that $z_s \leq U_C$ for any $s = (y_1, \ldots, y_p) \in S$. Note for a particular choice of $y_k = \frac{1}{\ell_k} + \epsilon$ for $1 \leq k \leq i$ and $\sum_{k=i+1}^{p} y_k = \frac{1}{\ell_{i+1}} - \epsilon$, we have $\lim_{\epsilon \to 0} z_s = U_C$. This implies that $z^* = U_C$ as required. ∎

Remark 4.3.13 *In the asymptotic regime, the best known algorithm for the bin-packing problem is based on a modification of* HARMONIC *[34] and has a competitive ratio of* 1.58889.

4.4 Lower Bounds

To complement the results derived in the previous sections, we next present lower bounds for HARMONIC, BESTFIT, and for all deterministic algorithms.

Lemma 4.4.1   *The asymptotic competitive ratio bound for* HARMONIC *derived in Theorem 4.3.10 is tight.*

Proof: We show that the upper bound U_C on the competitive ratio of HARMONIC derived in Theorem 4.3.10 is tight, when $C = \ell_{i+1}$ for some i, where ℓ_i has been defined in (4.14). The basic idea to do this is to construct an input that has just one item per each class that the HARMONIC algorithm creates, but where the sum of the weights of most of the items is at most 1, i.e., they can all fit in a single bin. Thus, OPT can assign most of the items to the single bin, while HARMONIC will assign only one item to one bin, thereby needing a lot more bins than OPT. The precise input sequence is as follows.

Let $C = \ell_{i+1}$ for some i. Recall the definition (4.14) and consider items with $i + 2$ distinct weights, $w_j = \frac{1}{\ell_j + 1} + \frac{1}{a}$ for $1 \le j \le i$, $w_{i+1} = \frac{1}{\ell_{i+1}} - \frac{i}{a}$ and $w_{i+2} = \frac{1}{b}$ where $a \ge i\ell_{i+1}$ to make sure that $w_{i+1} \ge 0$, while $b \ge \ell_{i+1}$ so that w_{i+2} is a $C = \ell_{i+1}$-item with this input, where the exact values of a, b will be chosen later. By definitions of c-items, items j for $1 \le j \le i$ are ℓ_j items while item $i + 1$ is a C-item. Importantly, the sum of the weights of the first $i + 1$ items $\sum_{j=1}^{i+1} w_j \le 1$, i.e., they all can fit in a single bin. Let $w^{i+1} = (w_1, \dots, w_i, w_{i+1})$, and the input (arriving from left to right) is

$$\sigma = \underbrace{\underbrace{w^{i+1}, \dots, w^{i+1}}_{C-1 \text{ times}} w_{i+2}, \dots, \dots, \underbrace{w^{i+1}, \dots, w^{i+1}}_{C-1 \text{ times}} w_{i+2}}_{\frac{M}{C-1} \text{ times}}$$

for any $M \in \mathbb{N}$. On input σ, HARMONIC assigns each of the items with weight w_j, $1 \le j \le i$, to a distinct bin, and each such bin can contain at most ℓ_j items of weight w_j before it is closed. Thus to assign all items of weight w_j, $1 \le j \le i$, the number of bins used by HARMONIC is $\sum_{j=1}^{i} \frac{M}{\ell_j}$.

Only items with weight w_{i+1} and w_{i+2} remain. Since items with weight w_{i+1} and w_{i+2} are C-items with input σ, HARMONIC assigns $C - 1$ items of weight w_{i+1} and one item of weight w_{i+2} to a single C-bin, which thereafter cannot accommodate any other items with weight w_{i+1} or w_{i+2}. Thus, the total number of bins used by HARMONIC is

$$\sum_{j=1}^{i} \frac{M}{\ell_j} + \frac{M}{C-1}.$$

Given that $\sum_{j=1}^{i+1} w_j \le 1$, consider an offline algorithm that packs one item each of weight $w_1, w_2, \dots, w_{i+1}$ into a single bin, and packs the b items of weight $w_{i+2} = 1/b$ into a single bin. Thus, the total number of bins used by this offline algorithm with input σ is $M + \frac{M}{(C-1)b}$. Since OPT is better than any offline algorithm, $\mathbf{b}_{\text{OPT}} \le M + \frac{M}{(C-1)b}$. Thus, the competitive ratio of HARMONIC is at least

$$\frac{\sum_{j=1}^{i} \frac{M}{\ell_j} + \frac{M}{C-1}}{M + \frac{M}{(C-1)b}} = \frac{\sum_{j=1}^{i} \frac{M}{\ell_j} + \frac{MC}{\ell_{i+1}(C-1)}}{M + \frac{M}{(C-1)b}}$$

since $C = \ell_{i+1}$. Choosing b very large, $M + \dfrac{M}{(C-1)b} \to M$. Thus,

$$\frac{\sum_{j=1}^{i} \dfrac{M}{\ell_j} + \dfrac{MC}{\ell_{i+1}(C-1)}}{M + \dfrac{M}{(C-1)b}} \to \sum_{j=1}^{i} \frac{1}{\ell_j} + \frac{C}{\ell_{i+1}(C-1)} = U_C.$$

Equivalently, for any $\epsilon > 0$, $\mu_{\text{HARMONIC}} \geq U_C - \epsilon$. Since this is true for any C, letting $C \to \infty$, we get that $\mu_{\text{HARMONIC}} \geq 1.691 - \epsilon$ for any $\epsilon > 0$. ∎

Lemma 4.4.2 *The asymptotic/absolute competitive ratio of the* BESTFIT/FIRSTFIT *algorithm is at least* 1.7.

Proof Sketch: We present the idea for BESTFIT. The argument for FIRSTFIT follows similarly. Consider an input where for some $k \in \mathbb{N}$, initially $10k$ items each with weight $\approx 1/6$ arrive. BESTFIT will pack all these items in at least $2k$ bins. Then another set of $10k$ items each with weight $\approx 1/3$ arrive that are assigned in pairs by BESTFIT into $5k$ bins. And finally, $10k$ more items arrive each with weight $1/2 + \epsilon$ for some small $\epsilon > 0$ that are assigned in individual $10k$ bins by BESTFIT, since none of them can be assigned to any of the currently open bins that are occupied with at least half of their capacities and no two of them can fit together. Thus the total number of bins used by BESTFIT is $17k$. One can show that choosing the exact weights, three items (one each from the three sets of $10k$ items with different weights) can fit in a single bin, and, thus, OPT needs only $10k$ bins to pack these $30k$ items, proving the result. The exact computation we leave as an exercise in Problem 4.8. Similar ideas can be used to prove a lower bound of 1.7 on the absolute competitive ratio of BESTFIT. ∎

Lemma 4.4.3 *The absolute competitive ratio* (4.1) *of any online algorithm for the bin-packing problem is at least* 5/3.

Proof: Consider an input where initially 6 items each with weight $1/7$ arrive. If any online algorithm $\mathcal{A}$ packs these 6 items into more than one bin, then the input stops and the competitive ratio is at least 2.

Thus without loss of generality, assume that all the 6 items are assigned to one bin by $\mathcal{A}$. Then 6 more items arrive each with weight $1/3 + \epsilon/2$ for $\epsilon \in (0, 1/42)$. Then $\mathcal{A}$ has to use at least 3 more bins. If $\mathcal{A}$ uses 4 more bins, then the input stops and the competitive ratio is at least $5/3$. Thus, the only possibility left to explore is if $\mathcal{A}$ uses 3 more bins. In this case, let 6 more items arrive each with weight $1/2 + \epsilon/2$, that are assigned to individual 6 new bins by $\mathcal{A}$, since none of them can be assigned to any of the existing bins that are occupied with at least half of their capacities and no two items with weight $1/2 + \epsilon/2$ can fit together. Thus the total number of bins used by $\mathcal{A}$ is 10. It is easy to see that OPT needs only 6 bins (with appropriate choice of ϵ) to pack these 18 items proving the result. ∎

Thus, if a lower bound of 5/3 is achievable, then clearly BESTFIT is not optimal since its competitive ratio is lower bounded by 1.7 (Lemma 4.4.2). Only recently it has been shown that a clever fix to BESTFIT actually can achieve the lower bound of 5/3 [35], where the algorithm tries to avoid having bins with only two items that are not heavy.

4.5 What about Randomized Algorithms?

So far in this chapter, we have only considered deterministic algorithms. It turns out that there is a generic technique to convert a lower bound on the deterministic algorithms for the bin-packing problem that applies to a randomized algorithm as well [36]. We illustrate one such example in Problem 4.6 to prove a lower bound of 4/3 on any randomized algorithm. Thus, for the bin-packing problem, randomized algorithms are not typically considered.

4.6 Notes

The FIRSTFIT algorithm has been considered widely in literature starting with [37–39], where the asymptotic competitive ratio of 1.7 was proved in [40]. Similarly, the asymptotic competitive ratio of BESTFIT has been well studied [37–39, 41] with the most tight analysis presented in [42]. In particular, the result presented in this chapter that $\mathbf{b}_{BF} \leq 1.7\mathbf{b}_{OPT} + 3$ was proved in [37], which was improved to $\mathbf{b}_{BF} \leq 1.7\mathbf{b}_{OPT} + 2$ in [38], and $\mathbf{b}_{BF} \leq \lceil 1.7\mathbf{b}_{OPT} \rceil$ in [41], and $\mathbf{b}_{BF} \leq \lfloor 1.7\mathbf{b}_{OPT} \rfloor$ in [42]. The analysis for the asymptotic competitive ratio upper bound on BESTFIT presented in this chapter can be found in [42].

The HARMONIC algorithm was proposed and analysed in [43], whose extension called the HARMONIC++ was studied in [34] with an asymptotic competitive ratio bound of 1.58889. The best known lower bound on the asymptotic competitive ratio is 1.54037 [44] improving upon the bound of 1.54014 [45]. A simple proof of the lower bound of 1.536 can be found in [46]. Converting the lower bounds on the deterministic algorithms to randomized algorithms was described in [36], proving that randomization does not help for the bin-packing problem.

For the non-asymptotic regime, called the absolute competitive ratio defined over arbitrary number of items, [35] presented a variation of the FIRSTFIT algorithm which achieves the lower bound of 5/3 on the competitive ratio of any online algorithm, making it optimal.

Comprehensive but bit dated surveys on the offline and the online bin-packing problems can be found in [47] and [48], respectively. A more recent survey that also includes the multi-dimensional bin-packing problem can be found in [49]. Bin-packing when lookahead in terms of cost is allowed has been considered in [50], while the model where some information about the input is available, called advice, has been studied in [51].

Throughout the chapter, we considered the worst-case input; however, there is a large body of literature on the bin-packing problem when the item weights are stochastic. With stochastic input, typically the problem of minimizing the regret of expected wastage is considered, where wastage is the sum of the unused capacity of all the open bins. Initial work in this direction includes [52–54], while more recently, algorithms with sum-of-squares [55] and primal–dual techniques [56] have been used to show that the regret can be made to grow sublinearly in the number of items. Most recently, [57] showed that constant regret is also possible. The bin-packing problem has also been considered in the secretarial model, where the order of arrival of items is uniformly random, for which BESTFIT is shown to have an asymptotic competitive ratio of at most 1.5 [58].

PROBLEMS

4.1 For the offline case, show that for any algorithm $\mathcal{A}$ that sorts the items in decreasing size and then applies an ANYFIT assignment rule has an asymptotic approximation ratio of at least 5/4.

4.2 **Item–bin assignment restriction** If any item can be assigned to only some specific bins, show that no deterministic algorithm can have a competitive ratio smaller than 2.

4.3 Let an item be defined to be *light* if its weight $w_i \leq 1/3$. Show that for BESTFIT, if the input does not contain any light item, then the asymptotic competitive ratio of BESTFIT is at most 3/2. Repeat the exercise when the input contains no heavy item.

4.4 **Repacking** On the arrival of a new item, let an online algorithm be allowed to change the bin assignment of at most one of the items that have arrived in the past. For this case, show a lower bound of 3/2 on the absolute competitive ratio of any online algorithm. [Hint: Consider the input with eight items of weight 1/12 and two items of weight 2/3.]
[Remark: When repacking of any constant number of items at any step is allowed, a lower bound on the asymptotic competitive ratio of 4/3 [59] and 1.3871 [60, 61] is known.]

4.5 **Lookahead** Show that the competitive ratio of any online algorithm cannot be improved even if the weights of the next arriving set of items with bounded size is known to it. [Hint: Pad a sequence with many items of very small size.]

4.6 [36] **Randomization** Show that the competitive ratio of any randomized algorithm for the bin-packing problem is at least 4/3. To show this, consider set S_1 of k items each with weight 0.49 and S_2 of k items with weight 0.51 each. Consider two instances of input $\sigma_1 = S_1$ and $\sigma_2 = \{S_1, S_2\}$, where in σ_2 set of items in S_1 arrive before S_2. Now notice that any randomized algorithm will put the same distribution on the bins it uses for the first k items irrespective of whether the input instance is σ_1 or σ_2.

4.7 Show that for HARMONIC, except for the number of C-bins, the number of c-bins for any $c < C$ used by the algorithm is independent of the order of arrival of items.

4.8 [42] Complete the proof of Lemma 4.4.2, where the exact input is as follows. Let $\delta_j = \dfrac{\delta}{4^j}$ and $\epsilon < \delta_{10k+4}$, where $\delta < 1/50$. Consider items a_j^+ with weight $1/6 + \delta_j$ and $b_j^- = 1/3 - \delta_j - \epsilon$ for $j = 1, \ldots, 5k$, and items $a_j^- = 1/6 - \delta_j$ and $b_j^+ = 1/3 + \delta_j - \epsilon$ for $j = 0, \ldots, 5k - 1$. The order in which the items arrive is : phase (i) first $10k$ items arrive, all of a_j^+ and a_j^- are released in order so that the assignments made by FIRSTFIT and BESTFIT are identical. Show that at the end of phase (i), except the last bin that has been opened by FIRSTFIT or BESTFIT, no item among b_j^+ or b_j^- can fit in any of the other open bins. In phase (ii) $10k$ more items arrive, all of b_j^+ and b_j^- are released in order so that the assignment made by FIRSTFIT and BESTFIT are identical. Show that at the end of phase (ii) no open bin has remaining capacity of at least $1/2 + \epsilon$. In final phase (iii) another $10k$ items arrive with weight $1/2 + \epsilon$. Show that the number of bins used by BESTFIT or FIRSTFIT is $17k$ while $\mathbf{b}_{OPT} = 10k$.

4.9 Bin-Packing Problem with Cardinality Constraint: Consider that there is an infinite supply of bins each with capacity 1. As usual, n items with weight $w_i \in [0, 1]$ arrive sequentially that have to be placed in one of the bins (subject to sum-weight of any bin being less than its capacity). **An additional cardinality constraint is now enforced, that each bin can at most contain two items.**

The objective remains the same: minimize the number of bins used once all the n items have arrived.

Consider a modified BESTFIT that assigns a newly arrived item to the most full bin if it fits **and** if it contains at most 1 other item, otherwise opens a new bin and assigns it there.

1. Show that the competitive ratio of the modified BESTFIT algorithm is at most $3/2$, by showing the following:

   Define a bin to be **heavy** if it contains two items, and **light** otherwise. Let x be the number of heavy bins and y be the number of light bins with modified BESTFIT after all n items have arrived. You can assume that y is even.

   (a) Show that if either $x = 0$ or $y = 0$, then the competitive ratio of the modified BESTFIT is 1.
   (b) Show that the number of bins used by OPT is at least

   $$\begin{cases} x + y/2, & \text{if } x > y/2 \\ y & \text{if } x = y/2 \\ y & \text{if } x < y/2. \end{cases}$$

   [Hint: Note that items in any two y light bins cannot be put in a single bin even by OPT. You can assume that y is even.]
   (c) Conclude that the competitive ratio is at most $3/2$ for modified BESTFIT.

2. Show that the competitive ratio of any deterministic online algorithm is at least $3/2$, under the considered cardinality constraint that each bin can contain at most two items.

CHAPTER 5

Paging

5.1 Introduction

In this chapter, we consider a classical online problem, called *paging*, where a file request sequence is served from two memories – one fast, called the *cache*, with finite size, and the other slow, which contains all the files. On a file request, if that file is not found in the cache, then it is loaded from the large memory into the cache by ejecting one of the existing files of the cache. Each such ejection is called a *fault* and the goal is to minimize the total number of faults without knowing the future file request sequence.

The paging problem is directly relevant for the critical question of what to store in the random access memory (RAM) of a computer system so as to minimize the number of memory overwrites. It has also received renewed attention recently with the advent of large content distribution networks (CDNs), e.g., Youtube, where multiple limited-sized caches serve fast-evolving contents that are located closer to the end-users.

For the paging problem, we first consider the deterministic setting, for which we first find a lower bound on the competitive ratio of any online algorithm and then describe an algorithm whose competitive ratio matches the lower bound. Similar strategy is adopted for randomized algorithms, where we first derive a lower bound, and then discuss an almost optimal randomized algorithm. Machine learning augmented algorithms are also considered, where prediction about the future request arrivals is available, albeit with uncertain accuracy. The goal in this paradigm is to design online algorithms that are close to optimal when the accuracy of prediction is very good, and have a reasonable competitive ratio otherwise. We also discuss the randomized input setting, where we show that all natural deterministic algorithms perform poorly, and non-trivial algorithms are required to achieve close to optimal competitive ratios.

To address the modern application of paging in CDNs, we finally consider the multiple cache paging problem, where the input at each time is a vector of file requests that are served by multiple caches parallelly. Under this setting, in addition to deciding which file to eject, if needed, one extra question is which file to serve from which cache, a matching problem. Thus, in a multiple cache problem, the file matching and ejection decisions need to be taken jointly to minimize the total number of faults. We show a surprising result for the multiple cache paging problem, that no deterministic algorithm has a bounded competitive ratio, which is fundamentally different from the classical results on paging with a single cache.

5.2 Problem Formulation

Let the file universe (the set of all files) be $\mathcal{U}$, where each file $f_i \in \mathcal{U}$ is stored in some large but slow memory space. Let the cache (fast memory) be of size k, i.e., at any time instant it can contain at most k files of $\mathcal{U}$. The input sequence $\sigma = \{f_i\}_{i=1}^n$ consists of file requests $f_i \in \mathcal{U}$ that need to be served via the cache. If a file on arrival is found in the cache, no further action is required. Otherwise, when the requested file is not found in the cache, it is loaded from the large memory space into the cache by ejecting one of the current files of the cache. Each such ejection is called a *fault*, and the goal is to minimize the total number of faults F without knowing the sequence σ in advance. The competitive ratio for any online algorithm $\mathcal{A}$ for the paging problem is then

$$\mu_{\mathcal{A}} = \max_{\sigma} \frac{F_{\mathcal{A}}(\sigma)}{F_{OPT}(\sigma)}.$$

Consider the following example to better understand the fault counting mechanism. Throughout this chapter, we interchangeably use time i or the ith request to denote/represent step i of the input.

Example 5.2.1

Let $k = 4$, and cache contents at time t be $C(t)$ a four-tuple. Let $C(0) = \{f_1, f_{10}, f_4, f_{23}\}$ and the input sequence be $\sigma = \{f_4, f_9, f_{23}, f_{10}, f_9, f_1, f_4\}$ (left to right). First, consider an online algorithm $\mathcal{A}$. On the arrival of request f_4 at time 1, no updates are made by $\mathcal{A}$ to the cache since $f_4 \in C(0)$, and $C(1) = C(0)$. Further, on the arrival of request f_9 at time 2, since f_9 is not found in $C(1)$, one file, say f_{23}, is ejected (without knowing that the next file request is f_{23}), and f_9 is brought into the cache. Consequently $C(2) = \{f_1, f_{10}, f_4, f_9\}$.

Now at time 3, $C(2)$ does not contain file f_{23} which was ejected at time 2, and one more fault is incurred by deleting some file, say f_{10}, by $\mathcal{A}$, and $C(3) = \{f_1, f_{23}, f_4, f_9\}$. At time 4, on the arrival of request f_{10}, some file, say f_1, is ejected, and $C(3) = \{f_{10}, f_{23}, f_4, f_9\}$. At time 5, no file is ejected since $f_9 \in C(3)$ and $C(4) = C(3)$. At time 6, on the arrival of request f_1, some file is ejected, say f_9, and finally at time 7, on the arrival of request f_4 some file is ejected, say f_{23}. Hence to serve σ, in total 5 faults are incurred by $\mathcal{A}$.

Knowing the request sequence $\sigma = \{f_4, f_9, f_{23}, f_{10}, f_9, f_1, f_4\}$ ahead of time, an offline algorithm at time 2 would not eject file f_{23} and instead choose one among f_1, f_4, f_{10} to eject. The choice among files f_1, f_4, f_{10} to eject affects the number of faults incurred by the offline algorithm in total. Moreover, note that all of f_1, f_4, f_{10} are requested in future. One choice is to eject the file among f_1, f_4, f_{10} that appears the farthest in the input sequence, which in this case is f_4. Following this ejection rule, file f_4 is ejected at time 2, then all the requests arriving from time 3 until time 6 are found in the cache, and the next ejection is needed only at time 7 on the arrival of request for file f_4. Thus, following the ejection rule that ejects the file that appears the farthest in the input sequence, an offline algorithm needs to incur only two faults in total. Consequently, the competitive ratio of $\mathcal{A}$ is $\mu_{\mathcal{A}} = \dfrac{5}{2}$.

The above example points to the fact that if the request sequence σ is known ahead of time, a natural choice for OPT could be to eject the file (if needed) whose request comes the farthest in time. In fact, this algorithm called LFD, which stands for the longest forward distance, is actually an optimal offline algorithm, which we discuss next.

5.3 Optimal Offline Algorithm

Algorithm LFD (longest forward distance): Eject a file (if needed) from the cache whose next request appears the farthest in the input request sequence.

Theorem 5.3.1 *Algorithm* LFD *is an optimal offline algorithm for the paging problem.*

LFD appears intuitively optimal, and the intuition stems from the fact that if an algorithm $\mathcal{A}$ deviates from the LFD policy on the ith file request by ejecting a file $f_{\mathcal{A}}$ instead of LFD's choice of file f_{LFD}, where f_{LFD} is requested after $f_{\mathcal{A}}$, then it incurs a larger number of faults between the time of the ith file request and the time at which file f_{LFD} is requested. We formalize this in Problem 5.1.

5.4 Lower Bound on the Competitive Ratio for Deterministic Algorithms

In this section, we show that the competitive ratio of any deterministic online algorithm for the paging problem is lower bounded by the size of the cache k. Towards that end, we consider an input sequence where the universe size is $|\mathcal{U}| = k + 1$. This restriction helps in finding a good upper bound on the number of faults incurred by the optimal offline algorithm LFD as a function of the length of the input sequence as follows.

Lemma 5.4.1 *With* $|\mathcal{U}| = k + 1$, *the maximum number of faults incurred by* LFD *on an input sequence* σ *of length n is at most* $\left\lceil \dfrac{n}{k} \right\rceil$.

Proof: Let LFD incur a fault at time i by ejecting a file f_i. Then since $|\mathcal{U}| = k + 1$, the contents of cache at time i,[1] $C(i) = \mathcal{U} \backslash \{f_i\}$. Moreover, since LFD has ejected f_i from the set $C(i - 1)$, f_i must be the last file among the files present in $C(i - 1)$ to be requested in future after time i, i.e., all files in $C(i - 1) \backslash \{f_i\}$ must be requested before f_i. Since $|C(i - 1) \backslash \{f_i\}| = k - 1$, at least $k - 1$ distinct files must be requested before the next request of f_i. Hence starting from time $i + 1$ till time $i + k - 1$ (may be for more time), there are no more faults incurred by LFD. Thus, LFD incurs at most one fault per k length input subsequence. Since the total length of input is n, the result follows. ∎

Using Lemma 5.4.1, we establish the following negative result on the competitive ratio of any deterministic online algorithm.

---

[1] After serving the request made at time i.

Theorem 5.4.2 *Let $\mathcal{A}$ be any deterministic online algorithm to solve the paging problem. Then*

$$\mu_{\mathcal{A}} \geq k.$$

Proof: We consider $|\mathcal{U}| = k + 1$. Let the contents of the cache be $C(0)$ to begin with for any algorithm, and, without loss of generality, let $f_0 \notin C(0)$. Then let the first element of the input sequence be $\sigma_1 = f_0$. For an online algorithm $\mathcal{A}$, let f_i be the only file that is missing from its cache at the end of time $i - 1$, i.e., after serving $i - 1$ file requests. Then, at time i, $\sigma_i = f_i$. Thus, $\mathcal{A}$ faults on each file request, and the total number of faults is equal to the length n of the input sequence σ.

From Lemma 5.4.1, we know that for the LFD algorithm, the total number of faults is at most $\left\lceil \dfrac{n}{k} \right\rceil$ when $|\mathcal{U}| = k + 1$. Thus, the competitive ratio of $\mathcal{A}$ for this input is at least k. ∎

An important point to note in this lower bound proof is that the worst-case input sequence can be constructed from a file universe that contains only $k + 1$ files. Thus, the only missing file from the cache is sufficient to 'fool' any deterministic online algorithm. To show that this lower bound is tight, in the next section we discuss some natural online algorithms, and show that some of them achieve this lower bound on the competitive ratio.

5.5 Deterministic Algorithms

One natural choice of a deterministic algorithm for the paging problem is to eject the file that has been requested the least number of times so far, called the LFU, which stands for least frequently used. However, under an adversarial input, LFU performs poorly, and cannot be α-competitive for any $\alpha > 1$, as shown next.

Given the initial contents of cache $C(0) = \{f_1, \dots, f_k\}$ to begin with, consider the adversarial input (from left to right)

$$\sigma = \underbrace{f_1, \dots, f_1}_{\ell \text{ times}} \underbrace{f_2, \dots, f_2}_{\ell \text{ times}} \cdots \cdots \underbrace{f_{k-1}, \dots, f_{k-1}}_{\ell \text{ times}} \underbrace{f_k, f_{k+1}, \dots, f_k, f_{k+1}}_{\ell \text{ times}}.$$

Then at the first and all subsequent arrivals of file requests for file f_{k+1}, file f_k is the LFU file, and will be ejected repeatedly by the LFU algorithm. Consequently, the total number of faults of LFU is $2\ell - 1$. OPT, however, can just eject f_1 on the first request for f_{k+1}, and incurs only 1 fault, making the competitive ratio of LFU $2\ell - 1$ for any ℓ. Essentially, with the adversarial input, the LFU file (that is ejected) is being requested next often enough.

A similar idea precludes the possibility that the last-in-first-out (LIFO) algorithm for ejection can be α-competitive for any α, and we leave that as an exercise (Problem 5.2). This brings us to the alternate choice of the first-in-first-out (FIFO) and the least recently used (LRU) algorithms for file ejections. We illustrate the difference between the LRU and the FIFO sequences of file ejection in Example 5.5.1.

Example 5.5.1

Let the cache size be $k = 4$, and the input sequence be $\{f_5, f_2, f_6, f_3\}$ (left to right) with the initial contents of cache being $C(0) = \{f_1, f_2, f_3, f_4\}$. Since we are beginning from time 0, for the execution of the FIFO algorithm, as a convention we assume that f_i came into the cache before f_{i+1} for $1 \le i \le 3$. As shown in Table 5.1, to easily represent the evolving contents of the cache, we follow the notation throughout the chapter that if a file f_k is ejected to serve file f_j at time t, then in row t we write f_j directly below the location where file f_k was placed earlier. So the final contents with FIFO are f_5, f_6, f_3, f_4, while with LRU are f_5, f_2, f_6, f_3, and they incur 2 and 3 faults, respectively, for this input.

Table 5.1

input	FIFO				LRU			
	f_1	f_2	f_3	f_4	f_1	f_2	f_3	f_4
f_5	f_5				f_5			
f_2								
f_6		f_6					f_6	
f_3								f_3

It turns out that both LRU and FIFO are optimal deterministic algorithms for the paging problem, i.e., both have competitive ratios equal to k. We present the analysis of the LRU algorithm, and leave the (similar) computation of the competitive ratio of FIFO as an excercise (Problem 5.3).

Before proving this result, we describe a counter-intuitive property of some paging algorithms, known as the **Belady's anomaly**. It turns out that for some algorithms, increasing the cache size can actually lead to an increased number of faults. One such example is the FIFO algorithm, for which with the following input $\{f_4, f_3, f_2, f_1, f_4, f_3, f_5, f_4, f_3, f_2, f_1, f_5\}$ (from left to right), the number of faults is 10 when $k = 4$, while it is 9 with $k = 3$, as shown in Tables 5.2 and 5.3, where we are following the same notation to write the evolving contents of the cache as shown in Table 5.1, except that now the table is illustrated horizontally for saving space and initially the cache is empty. Intuition for FIFO having Belady's anomaly is that the recently requested pages can remain at the bottom of the FIFO queue longer.

It is worth noting that LRU or the optimal offline algorithm LFD does not suffer from Belady's anomaly. The proofs of these facts are left as an exercise in Problem 5.4 and Problem 5.5, respectively.

Table 5.2 FIFO with $k = 3$

f_4			f_1			f_5					
	f_3			f_4					f_2		
		f_2			f_3					f_1	

Table 5.3 FIFO with $k = 4$

f_4						f_5				f_1	
	f_3						f_4				f_5
		f_2						f_3			
			f_1						f_2		

Next, we show that LRU is an optimal deterministic online algorithm for the paging problem.

Lemma 5.5.2 *The competitive ratio of* LRU *is at most k.*

Proof: To show this result, we will consider any input subsequence where LRU makes k faults, and for which we will show that at least $k + 1$ distinct files have been requested within that subsequence. Since the total cache size is k, this will imply that OPT has to incur at least one fault in that subsequence.

Let the input $\sigma = \{\sigma_i\}_{i=1}^n$ (where i denotes the time of arrival of the ith request) be partitioned into phases, where in each phase LRU makes k faults. Let σ_i be the first time (file request) at which LRU makes a fault, then phase 1 starts at σ_{i+1} and ends at σ_j, where

$$j = \min\{t : \text{LRU makes } k \text{ faults from } \sigma_{i+1} \text{ till } \sigma_t\}.$$

Phase ℓ starts with the next request after the end of phase $\ell - 1$ and is defined similarly.

There are two ways in which LRU makes k faults in a phase: (i) either it faults at the same file request at least twice or (ii) makes k faults on k distinct file requests. Note that case (i) cannot happen if $k = 2$. In case (i) for $k > 2$ if LRU faults on a file request p twice, i.e., file p is requested twice in a phase and it is not found in the cache at both times, then in between the two requests for file p, at least k other distinct files must have been requested for LRU to remove p before the second request to p. Thus, the total number of distinct file requests in that phase is at least $k + 1$, for which OPT has to incur at least one fault.

For case (ii), consider phase i, when LRU makes k faults on k distinct files, and let the last file on which LRU faulted in phase $i - 1$ be p. Since the phase ends on the last fault made by LRU, p is the last file requested in phase $i - 1$. Therefore, OPT contains file p in its cache at the start of phase i (defined with respect to LRU alone). Then in phase i, either (a) LRU faults on p or (b) LRU makes no fault on p, or p is not requested. With subcase (a) necessarily, before the fault on file p in phase i, k other distinct files must have been requested for LRU to remove p. That is, $k + 1$ distinct files have been requested in phase i (including p), and hence OPT has to incur at least one fault in phase i. With subcase (b) since LRU is making k faults on files other than p, at least k other distinct files have been requested, and to serve all of them OPT has to remove p, which it contains in its cache at the start of phase i.

Therefore, for each phase, where k faults are incurred by LRU, at least one fault is incurred by OPT, and consequently,

$$\mu_{\text{LRU}} \leq k.$$

∎

Combining Lemma 5.5.2 and Theorem 5.4.2, we get that LRU is an optimal deterministic online algorithm for the paging problem. Even though LRU is an optimal deterministic algorithm, its competitive ratio increases linearly in the size of the cache, which is quite poor from a system design point of view. For the paging problem, the lower bound (Theorem 5.4.2) suggests that the adversary is too 'powerful', and to compensate for that, we next consider randomized algorithms. With randomization, we show that significant improvement can be made to the competitive ratio. In particular, it can be made to scale logarithmically in the size of the cache. Similar to this section, we first derive a lower bound on the competitive ratio of all randomized algorithms, and then consider a randomized algorithm called MARKING, which is order-wise optimal.

5.6 Randomized Algorithms

5.6.1 Lower Bound on the Competitive Ratio

To derive a lower bound on the competitive ratio of any randomized algorithm, we once again use Yao's lower bound recipe described in Section 2.5.1. To recall, the competitive ratio μ of any randomized algorithm is lower bounded by

$$\mu \geq \frac{\min_{\mathcal{A}} \mathbb{E}_D\{F_{\mathcal{A}}(\sigma)\}}{\mathbb{E}_D\{F_{OPT}(\sigma)\}}, \tag{5.1}$$

where the expectation is over any distribution D for input σ, and the minimization is over all possible deterministic online algorithms $\mathcal{A}$.

For further exposition, we need a result on the coupon collector problem that we describe via an example as follows.

Example 5.6.1

[*Coupon Collector Problem*] *Consider a six-faced dice where the probability of seeing any face on any roll is* 1/6, *and successive rolls of the dice are independent. Then consider* T_c *(random variable) to be the earliest roll of dice such that all the six distinct faces have been seen at least once.*

The first roll always shows the first new face, and subsequently, the time at which the $i^{th}, i \geq 2$, *new face is seen is a geometric random variable with probability* $(6 - i + 1)/6$, *with expected time* $\frac{6}{(6-i)}$. *Thus*

$$\mathbb{E}\{T_c\} = 1 + \sum_{i=2}^{6} \frac{1}{(6 - i + 1)/6}. \tag{5.2}$$

The generalized version of this problem, where a dice has k faces (called coupons) and the probability of seeing any face on each roll is $1/k$, where each roll is independent, is called the coupon collector problem. The collection time T_c is defined as the first time at which all the k distinct coupons have been seen at least once. Similar to (5.2), we get that

$$\mathbb{E}\{T_c\} = 1 + \sum_{i=2}^{k} \frac{1}{(k-i+1)/k} = k\left(\sum_{i=1}^{k} \frac{1}{i}\right) = kH_k, \tag{5.3}$$

where H_k is the k-th harmonic number.

Using Yao's recipe for lower bound, we next show the following result.

Lemma 5.6.2 *The competitive ratio of any randomized algorithm for the paging problem is lower bounded by H_k.*

Comparing with the lower bound in the deterministic case (Theorem 5.4.2), we see that there is a large improvement going from k to $H_k \sim \ln k$ with randomization in terms of the competitive ratio.

Proof: Let the universe size be $|\mathcal{U}| = k + 1$, and the distribution D over the input be such that input at time i, σ_i is uniformly distributed over the $k + 1$ elements of $\mathcal{U}$ and independent across i. For an input $\sigma = \{\sigma_i\}_{i=1}^{j}$ of size $|\sigma| = j$, with uniform distribution D, it is easy to see that

$$\min_{\mathcal{A}} \mathbb{E}_D\{\mathsf{F}_{\mathcal{A}}(\sigma)\} = \sum_{i=1}^{j} \frac{1}{k+1} = \frac{j}{k+1}, \tag{5.4}$$

since the probability of having a fault with any online algorithm on file request σ_i is $\frac{1}{k+1}$ for any $i \in 1, \dots, j$. Thus, to find the lower bound (5.1), we need to compute an upper bound on $\mathbb{E}_D\{\mathsf{F}_{\mathsf{OPT}}(\sigma)\}$, which we do as follows.

We partition the input σ into phases $\mathcal{P}_i$, $i \geq 0$, where phase $\mathcal{P}_i$ consists of requests made at time $[\tau_i, \tau_i + 1, \dots, \tau_{i+1} - 1]$ where $\tau_0 = 1$, and

$$\tau_{i+1} = \min\{r : \{\sigma_{\tau_i}, \sigma_{\tau_i+1}, \dots, \sigma_r\} = \{1, 2, \dots, k+1\}\}.$$

Thus, in each phase $\mathcal{P}_i$, exactly k distinct file requests are made. Phase $\mathcal{P}_1$ begins with the first request and ends at time $\tau_1 - 1$ if the $k + 1^{st}$ distinct file request is made at time τ_1. Phase i begins as soon as phase $i - 1$ is completed. Length of phase i is denoted by $|\mathcal{P}_i| = \tau_i - \tau_{i-1}$.

Recall that OPT is LFD, and hence if one fault is incurred in any phase, no more faults can be incurred in that phase because of the LFD ejection rule. Thus, the total number of faults incurred by OPT until time j is bounded by at most the number of completed phases by time j. Let $\sigma^j = (\sigma_1, \dots, \sigma_j)$. Hence, we have

$$\mathsf{F}_{\mathsf{OPT}}(\sigma^j) \leq 1 + \mathbb{E}\{\max\{\ell : \tau_\ell \leq j\}\}. \tag{5.5}$$

Note that since the distribution D is uniform and i.i.d., the length of each phase $|\mathcal{P}_i| = \tau_i - \tau_{i-1}$ is also i.i.d. Hence, applying Theorem 5.6.4, with renewal intervals $X_i = \tau_i - \tau_{i-1}$, we get

$$\lim_{j \to \infty} \frac{1 + \mathbb{E}\{\max\{\ell \,:\, \tau_\ell \leq j\}\}}{j} = \frac{1}{\mathbb{E}\{|\mathcal{P}_1|\}}. \tag{5.6}$$

since $\mathcal{P}_i$'s are i.i.d. The relation (5.6) essentially says that over a long input length, the number of completed phases normalized with the length of the input converges to the reciprocal of the expected length of a phase. Therefore, using (5.5)

$$\lim_{j \to \infty} \frac{\mathsf{F}_{\mathsf{OPT}}(\sigma^j)}{j} \leq \frac{1}{\mathbb{E}\{|\mathcal{P}_1|\}}. \tag{5.7}$$

It is worth noting that by the definition of a phase, $|\mathcal{P}_1| + 1$ is identically distributed as the finish time T_c in the coupon collector problem with $k + 1$ coupons (Example 5.6.1). Hence, from (5.3), we have $\mathbb{E}\{|\mathcal{P}_1| + 1\} = (k+1)H_k + 1$.

Therefore, from (5.1), using (5.4) and (5.7), the lower bound on the competitive ratio of any randomized algorithm is

$$\mu \geq \frac{(k+1)H_k}{k+1} = H_k. \tag{5.8}$$

∎

Definition 5.6.3 *Consider a renewal process with i.i.d.* **renewal times** X_i $i \geq 1$. *For $k \geq 1$, let*

$$Z_k = \sum_{i=1}^{k} X_i$$

be the kth renewal instant, where $Z_0 = 0$. Moreover, for $t \geq 0$, let

$$M(t) = \sup\{k \geq 0 \,:\, Z_k \leq t\}$$

be the number of renewals in time $[0, t]$.

Theorem 5.6.4 *(The Elementary Renewal Theorem [62]) Given a sequence of mutually i.i.d. random variables X_i, $i \geq 1$, with $0 < \mathbb{E}\{X_1\} \leq \infty$, then*

$$\lim_{t \to \infty} \frac{M(t)}{t} = \frac{1}{\mathbb{E}\{X_1\}} \quad \text{with probability } 1.$$

In the next section, we confirm the optimism suggested by the improved lower bound (Lemma 5.6.2), and show that a randomized algorithm can achieve a competitive ratio of $2H_k$. Even though the competitive ratio is off by a factor of 2 compared to the lower bound, it is still far better than the competitive ratio of k in the deterministic case. The optimal randomized algorithm that achieves the lower bound of H_k is a little more complicated and can be found in [63].

5.6.2 Almost Optimal Randomized Algorithm

In this section, we consider a randomized algorithm called MARKING, and show that its competitive ratio is at most $2H_k$.

The algorithm is as follows. At the start, **mark** all files present in the cache. On the arrival of a new file request p

1. If p is not in cache
   (a) If all files in the cache are marked, unmark all files
   (b) Eject a file uniformly at random from all the unmarked files and bring p into the cache
   (c) Mark p
2. Otherwise: Mark p in cache

Remark 5.6.5 *It turns out that the purely random algorithm RANDOM that ejects any one file in the cache with equal probability of $1/k$ every time a newly requested file is not found in the cache has a lower bound of k on its competitive ratio as discussed in Problem 5.7. Thus, some intelligence is needed even for a randomized algorithm to come closer to the competitive ratio lower bound (Lemma 5.6.2) for randomized algorithms, e.g., as in algorithm MARKING.*

For a better understanding of the working of algorithm MARKING, consider the following example.

Example 5.6.6

Let the cache size be $k = 4$, and to begin with let the cache contents with any algorithm be $\{f_1, f_2, f_3, f_4\}$. As shown in Table 5.4, for each file, the index inside the bracket () is 0 if that file is unmarked and 1 otherwise. Let all the existing files $\{f_1, f_2, f_3, f_4\}$ be marked at the beginning. Let the next input request be f_9, which is not present in the cache. All files are then unmarked, and one of them (f_3 in the Table 5.4) is ejected uniformly randomly, and f_9 is brought into the cache and is marked. Next, let file f_1 be requested, which is present in the cache, and hence the algorithm marks f_1 and continues. Next, when file f_5 is requested, only files f_2 and files f_4 are unmarked, and one of them is ejected uniformly randomly, say file f_4. Then file f_4 is ejected and file f_5 is brought into the cache and is marked, as shown in Table 5.4.

Table 5.4 Example for MARKING's execution

input	MARKING			
	$f_1(1)$	$f_2(1)$	$f_3(1)$	$f_4(1)$
f_9	$f_1(0)$	$f_2(0)$	$f_3(0)$	$f_4(0)$
				$f_9(1)$
f_1	$f_1(1)$			
f_5				$f_5(1)$

Next, we define a *phase* using which we will analyse the competitive ratio of algorithm MARKING.

Definition 5.6.7 *Let the input σ be partitioned in phases $\mathcal{P}_i$ as follows. Phase $\mathcal{P}_1$ begins at time τ_0, where MARKING makes its first fault, and ends at time τ_1 if the $k + 1^{st}$ distinct file request starting from τ_0 is made at time $\tau_1 + 1$. Thus, in a phase, exactly k distinct file requests are made. Phase i begins as soon as the phase $i - 1$ is completed at time τ_i and is defined similarly to phase P_1. Length of phase i is denoted by $|\mathcal{P}_i|$.*

An important property of this definition of a phase is that it does not depend on the randomization used in MARKING; it only depends on the input sequence.

Using this definition of phases, some remarks on MARKING are in order. First point to note is that at the end of a phase, the k contents of the cache are exactly the k distinct files that have been requested in that phase. Thus, when a new phase begins at the arrival of the $k + 1^{st}$ distinct file, all the existing files in the cache are unmarked, and any one file is ejected randomly on the first fault in a new phase. As more files become marked, there is less room available with MARKING to randomize the choice of unmarked files to eject, which can be exploited by the adversary in designing the input. Roughly, the rate at which the randomization power of MARKING is decreasing is $1/u$, where u is the number of unmarked files $u = k, k - 1, \dots, 1$, which will also reflect in the competitive ratio of this algorithm.

Subsequently, on the ℓth distinct file request in a phase that is not found in the cache, the previous $\ell - 1$ distinct files requested in the same phase are already marked, and are not considered for ejection by the algorithm, and one among the remaining $k - \ell$ files are ejected uniformly at random. This behaviour is reminiscent of LRU, where instead of ejecting the LRU file, the unmarked set is defined that consists of all files that have not been requested in that phase, and one file in the unmarked set is ejected uniformly at random.

Also note that once a fault occurs on a file request p in a given phase, no more fault is incurred if p is requested again in the same phase.

Lemma 5.6.8 *The competitive ratio of MARKING is upper bounded by $2H_k$.*

Proof: For analysis, we will use Definition 5.6.7 of phases.

Let $C(i)$ be the contents of the cache with MARKING at the beginning of phase i. Then within phase i, (i) when a file $p \notin C(i)$ is requested (called a new request) one fault is incurred and (ii) when a file $q \in C(i)$ (called an old request) is requested, a fault is incurred only if q that has been ejected by MARKING before the arrival of q in the same phase.

Let the number of new requests in phase i be $n(i)$. Since a total of k distinct files are requested in a phase, the number of old files requested in phase i is $k - n(i)$. We next compute the probability of incurring a fault on an old request given that a certain number of new and old requests have already been made.

Lemma 5.6.9 *Given that there have been n new and o old requests in a phase so far,*

$$\mathbb{P}(a\ subsequent\ old\ file\ requested\ is\ not\ found\ in\ cache) = \frac{n}{k - o}.$$

Proof: One way to prove this result is via a direct computation and induction as follows. Let p be a file that is part of the cache at the start of the phase. Let $n - 1$ and $o = 1$; then the event that the old request for file p is not found in the cache is either because (i) to serve the first new request, MARKING ejected file p, or (ii) to serve the first new request, MARKING ejected a file q, and the single old request is for q and to serve that, MARKING ejected p. Thus,

$$\mathbb{P}(\text{file } p \text{ is not found in cache after } n = 1 \text{ and } o = 1) = \frac{1}{k} + \frac{1}{k(k-1)} = \frac{1}{k-1}.$$

Then using induction, we can show the general result.

A more subtle argument for proving Lemma 5.6.9 is as follows. After n new and o old requests, on the arrival of an old request for file p (not requested before in this phase) at time j, let the set of old requests of size o be O. Then at time j, the n new requests occupy the n uniformly distributed slots among the $k - o$ slots in the cache. This follows from the fact that all the old requests of set O are present in the cache at the start of the phase as well as at time j, as each old request in O arriving in this phase is marked on its arrival and never deleted subsequently. See for example Figure 5.1, where the initial file contents are on the left with $k = 4$, and after one new (dark grey) and one old (medium grey) file request, the dark grey file occupies one of the three slots uniformly randomly. Thus, the event that p is not in the cache happens if one among the $k - o$ slots occupied by it at the start of the phase is now occupied by one of the n new requests, whose probability is

$$\frac{n}{k-o}.$$

∎

Given that there are $n(i)$ new requests in phase i, the number of old requests is $k - n(i)$. The old and the new requests can arrive in any order; however, in light of Lemma 5.6.9, to upper bound the number of faults incurred by MARKING in phase i, we let all the $n(i)$ new requests arrive first and then the $k - n(i)$ old requests arrive. Thus, the expected number of faults incurred on all old requests in phase i is at most

$$F_o(i) \leq \frac{n(i)}{k} + \frac{n(i)}{k-1} + \cdots + \frac{n(i)}{k - (k - n(i) - 1)}.$$

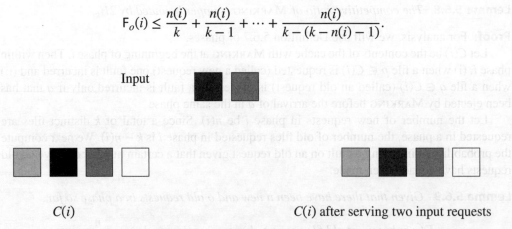

Input

$C(i)$ $C(i)$ after serving two input requests

Figure 5.1 Example to show the counting argument to see that new requests occupy $k - o$ slots uniformly randomly, where the dark grey request is uniformly distributed in 3 slots other than the slot occupied by the medium grey request that is old.

Since each new request implies a fault, the total number of faults incurred by MARKING in phase i is

$$F_{\text{MARKING}}(i) = n(i) + F_o(i) \leq n(i)H_k.$$

Summing across (total) ℓ phases, the total faults incurred by MARKING are at most

$$F_{\text{MARKING}} \leq \left(\sum_{i=1}^{\ell} n(i)\right) H_k. \tag{5.9}$$

To complete the proof, we next lower bound the number of faults incurred by OPT across all phases. To accomplish that, we introduce a potential function argument that is quite versatile and will be used for analysing the competitive ratio of many online algorithms in this book.

The phase definition remains as it is (Definition 5.6.7), and for phase i, let the potential V_i be the number of files that are present in OPT's cache but not in the cache of MARKING at the start of phase i. Recall that MARKING receives $n(i)$ new requests in phase i, i.e., all the $n(i)$ requests are not present in the cache of MARKING at the start of phase i. Thus, it follows that at least $n(i) - V_i$ of the new requests are also not present in the cache of OPT at the start of phase i. Thus, OPT also incurs at least $n(i) - V_i$ faults in phase i.

Moreover, at the end of phase i, all the files in the cache of MARKING are the k distinct files requested in phase i. By definition of V_{i+1}, OPT does not contain V_{i+1} of these k files requested in that phase, which means that OPT must have ejected these V_{i+1} files in phase i, and hence the number of faults incurred by OPT in phase i is at least V_{i+1}.

Combining the two bounds,[2] we get

$$F_{\text{OPT}}(i) \geq \frac{n(i) - V_i}{2} + \frac{V_{i+1}}{2}.$$

Summing across (total) ℓ phases, we get

$$\sum_{i}^{\ell} F_{\text{OPT}}(i) \geq \sum_{i}^{\ell} \frac{n(i) - V_i}{2} + \frac{V_{i+1}}{2},$$

$$= \frac{1}{2}\left(\sum_{i=1}^{\ell} n(i) - V_1 + V_{\ell+1}\right),$$

$$\geq \frac{1}{2}\left(\sum_{i=1}^{\ell} n(i)\right), \tag{5.10}$$

where the last inequality follows since $V_1 = 0$ and $V_{\ell+1} \geq 0$.

Combining (5.9) and (5.10), we get that the competitive ratio of MARKING is at most $2H_k$ as desired. ∎

---

[2] If $f(x) \geq a$, and $f(x) \geq b$, then $f(x) \geq \lambda a + (1 - \lambda)b$, for $\lambda \in [0, 1]$.

5.7 Beyond the Worst-Case Input: Incorporating Predictions

In this section, we will study a simple modification of MARKING when prediction about the next arrival time of each request is available, albeit with uncertain accuracy. Let the input be $\sigma = (z_1, z_2, \ldots, z_n)$, where $z_i \in \mathcal{U}$ is the file requested at time i. We are departing from our earlier notation of $\sigma = \{f_i\}_{i=1}^n$ for simplicity of further exposition. Given σ, the true next arrival time of file requested at time i, z_i, is denoted as

$$y_i = \min_{\tau > i}\{\tau \,:\, z_\tau = z_i\}.$$

If the file z_i is never requested again, then we set $y_i = |\sigma| + 1$.

This is an overloaded definition; thus it is useful to see an example.

Example 5.7.1

Let $(f_1, f_2, f_1, f_3, f_9, f_4, f_5, f_1, f_8)$ be the requested input. Then at time 1, f_1 is requested, so $z_1 = f_1$. Moreover, $y_1 = 3$ since the next time file f_1 is requested is 3. At time 2, f_2 is requested and it is never requested again. Thus, $y_2 = 10$, since $|\sigma| = 9$. At time 3, f_1 is requested again, which is next requested at time 8; thus $y_3 = 8$. Similarly, at time 5, $z_5 = f_9$, and $y_5 = 10$, since f_9 is not requested again.

Let the predicted value of y_i by a machine learning algorithm be $\hat{y}_i$, with error

$$\eta = \sum_{i=1}^n |\hat{y}_i - y_i|. \tag{5.11}$$

Note that if prediction is perfect, i.e., $\eta = 0$ is known, we can implement the LFD algorithm, which is OPT. However, in the practical setting η is unknown, and hence a non-trivial algorithm is needed to make use of the prediction. Next, we consider a modification of MARKING that makes use of the prediction.

The definition of a phase remains the same as defined in Definition 5.6.7 (now with respect to the new algorithm to be described as follows), and a file is *old* in phase i if it has been requested in phase $i - 1$, and *new* otherwise. Algorithm PREDICTIVE-MARKING is defined as follows: At the start, **mark** all files present in the cache. On the arrival of a file request p in any phase

1. If p is not in cache, and if all files in the cache are marked, unmark all files
   (a) If p is new
      i. Eject the file with the largest predicted next arrival time from all the unmarked files, and bring p into the cache and mark it.
   (b) Otherwise
      i. Eject any file uniformly randomly among all the unmarked files, and bring p into the cache
2. Otherwise: Mark p in cache

In short, the algorithm evicts the unmarked file with the highest predicted arrival time if the incoming request is new, and otherwise evicts a random unmarked file. Thus, prediction is trusted or used only on a new file arrival.

For analysing algorithm PREDICTIVE-MARKING, we define the concept of a *chain* as follows.

Definition 5.7.2 *With* PREDICTIVE-MARKING, *in any phase, a new request's arrival evicts some old file, whose next appearance evicts another old file, and so forth, until an old file is evicted which never reappears in the phase. This (interdependent) sequence of files ejected by* PREDICTIVE-MARKING *starting from a new request is defined to be an **eviction chain**.*

Each request in the eviction chain after the first new request must be old, since to be evicted it must have been present in the cache to begin with. Eviction chains are disjoint, each new request starts a new chain, and the total number of faults incurred by an algorithm is the sum of the lengths of all the eviction chains.

For proceeding further, we need the following definition, and a corresponding basic combinatorial result stated in Lemma 5.7.5.

Definition 5.7.3 *Let $A = (a_1, a_2, \ldots, a_n)$ be an integer sequence, i.e., a_i's are integers. Then $inv(A)$ is the number of pairs $i < j$ such that $a_i \geq a_j$. For example, for $A = (1, 3, 2, 1, 1)$, $inv(A) = 8$ for inverted pairs*

$$(1, 1), (1, 1), (3, 2), (3, 1), (3, 1), (2, 1), (2, 1), (1, 1).$$

Moreover if $M = (m_1, m_2, \ldots, m_n)$ is a strictly increasing integer sequence, i.e., $m_i < m_{i+1}$, then define $Cost(A) = \sum_{i=1}^{n} |a_i - m_i|$, and $\Delta(A) = 2Cost(A) - inv(A)$.

Proposition 5.7.4 *For an integer sequence $A = (\underbrace{a, a, \ldots, a}_{\ell})$ with identical entries of length ℓ,*

$$inv(A) = \binom{\ell}{2}, \text{ and } Cost(A) \geq \frac{\binom{\ell}{2}}{2}.$$

The proof of first claim is immediate, while the second claim follows by noting that since M is a strictly increasing integer sequence, $|a - m_i|$ for $i = 1, \ldots, \ell$ takes ℓ distinct positive integer values.

Lemma 5.7.5 *For Definition 5.7.3,*

$$inv(A) \leq 2Cost(A).$$

Proof: Let all elements of A be bounded between m_1 and m_n, the smallest and the largest element in M. This does not change the result, since elements lying outside of this range $[m_1, m_n]$ can be thresholded without decreasing $inv(A)$ or increasing $cost(A)$. Thus, the set of sequences A under consideration are finite. Let A be the set of sequences that minimize $\Delta(A)$. Let $A^\star \in A$ be such that it has the largest sum of its elements.

The claim is that with sequence $A^\star = (a_1^\star, \ldots, a_n^\star)$, there is no pair $i < j$ such that $a_i^\star > a_j^\star$. To prove this, we use contradiction, and let for $A^\star$, $\exists i$ such that $a_i^\star > a_{i+1}^\star$. For such an $A^\star$, define two sequences A^L and A^R, where the ith element $A^L(i) = a_{i+1}^\star$ and the $i + 1^{st}$ element $A^R(i+1) = a_i^\star$, while A^L and A^R agree with $A^\star$ on all other locations. Then, by definition,

$$inv(A^\star) - inv(A^L) = inv(A^R) - inv(A^\star). \tag{5.12}$$

Moreover,

$$\text{cost}(A^\star) - \text{cost}(A^L) = |a_i^\star - m_i| - |a_{i+1}^\star - m_i|,$$

$$\overset{(a)}{\geq} |a_i^\star - m_{i+1}| - |a_{i+1}^\star - m_{i+1}|,$$

$$= \text{cost}(A^R) - \text{cost}(A^\star), \tag{5.13}$$

where (a) follows since $m_i < m_{i+1}$. Consider

$$\Delta(A^R) - \Delta(A^\star) = 2\text{Cost}(A^R) - \text{inv}(A^R) - 2\text{Cost}(A^\star) + \text{inv}(A^\star),$$

$$\overset{(a)}{\leq} 2\text{Cost}(A^\star) + \text{inv}(A^L) - 2\text{Cost}(A^L) - \text{inv}(A^\star),$$

$$= \Delta(A^\star) - \Delta(A^L),$$

$$\overset{(b)}{\leq} 0,$$

where (a) follows from (5.12) and (5.13), and (b) follows from the optimality of $A^\star$ in minimizing Δ. Thus, we get that A^R also minimizes Δ, but A^R has a larger sum of elements than $A^\star$; and hence we get a contradiction.

Therefore, with $A^\star = (a_1^\star, \dots, a_n^\star)$, there is no pair $i < j$ such that $a_i^\star > a_j^\star$. The only possibility is that

$$A^\star = (\underbrace{a_1^\star, \dots, a_1^\star}_{\ell_1}, \underbrace{a_2^\star, \dots, a_2^\star}_{\ell_2}, \dots, \underbrace{a_k^\star, \dots, a_k^\star}_{\ell_k}) \tag{5.14}$$

for some k, where $a_i^\star < a_j^\star$ for $i < j$. From Proposition 5.7.4, we get that for $A^\star$ of the type (5.14), $\Delta(A^\star) \geq 0$. ∎

After this brief detour, we are ready to state the main result of this section as follows.

Theorem 5.7.6 *For any input σ, with* PREDICTIVE-MARKING

$$\frac{\mathbb{E}\{F_{\text{PREDICTIVE-MARKING}}(\sigma)\}}{F_{\text{OPT}}(\sigma)} = \mathcal{O}\left(1 + \min\left\{\log\left(\frac{\eta}{F_{\text{OPT}}(\sigma)}\right), \log(k)\right\}\right),$$

where $F_{\text{OPT}}(\sigma)$ is the number of faults incurred by the OPT with input σ.

Thus in terms of dependence on k, the bound is optimal in light of Lemma 5.6.2. In presence of prediction, to get a competitive ratio better than $\mathcal{O}(\log k)$, the error needs to satisfy $\eta/F_{\text{OPT}} = o(\log k)$.

Proof: Consider a particular phase r (Definition 5.6.7) where as we know exactly k distinct file requests are made. Let $i_1, \dots, i_k$ be the earliest arrival times of these k distinct requests in this phase. Among these k requests, consider a new request that arrives at time i_t. To fulfil this new request, from the definition of PREDICTIVE-MARKING, among the old files, the file with the highest predicted next arrival time is evicted. The evicted file is an old file that can either (i) be requested again at time $i_{t+1}, \dots, i_k$ in this phase, or (ii) never requested in this phase. If case (ii) occurs, there are no further faults to be counted because of the arrival of this new request at time i_t. Thus, we concentrate on case (i) hereafter. In particular, let the evicted file at time t be $z_{i_{e(t)}}, e(t) \leq k$, which will be requested next at time $i_{e(t)}$.

Definition 5.7.7 *For $1 \leq a \leq b \leq k$, let $N_a(b)$ be the number of old files that are unmarked and in the cache at time i_a,[3] and have (true) arrival times[4] after time i_b.*

The quantity of interest will be $N_t(e(t))$, which is equal to the number of old files that are unmarked and in cache at time i_t and have true arrival times after time $i_{e(t)}$.

Lemma 5.7.8 *If the new file request arriving at time i_t evicts an old file arriving at time $i_{e(t)}$, then the expected length of the eviction chain that begins at time i_t is at most*

$$\mathcal{O}\left(\mathbb{E}\{(1 + \log(N_t(e(t))))\}\right).$$

Proof: Let D_t be the distribution over the execution of PREDICTIVE-MARKING up to time i_t. Thus, given D_t, $N_t(e(t))$ is deterministic.

As defined earlier, the file evicted on the arrival of the new request at time i_t is $z_{i_{e(t)}}$, which is requested next at time $i_{e(t)}$. The length of the chain started by the new file arriving at time i_t will be maximum if each evicted old file evicts another old file until it is no longer possible. By definition of $N_t(e(t))$, there are at most $N_t(e(t))$ old unmarked files at time $i_{e(t)}$ (just before time $i_{e(t)}$). In general, let the number of old unmarked files at time $i_{e(t)}$ be $m \leq N_t(e(t))$. Let these m unmarked files be indexed in increasing order of their future (true) arrival times.

At time $i_{e(t)}$, $z_{i_{e(t)}}$ arrives, which is an old request, and hence any one of the m unmarked old files is ejected uniformly randomly to fulfil request for $z_{i_{e(t)}}$. Let the jth file (in order) be evicted at time $i_{e(t)}$. Then the next fault occurs on this chain at the time at which the jth file ejected at time $i_{e(t)}$ is requested next. When the jth file is requested next, there are at most $m - j$ unmarked old files, since the first $j - 1$ files must have been requested before the jth file ejected at time $i_{e(t)}$, as the unmarked files are ordered in increasing order of their next arrival time at time $i_{e(t)} - 1$.

Thus, conditioned on D_t, the expected length of the eviction chain that begins on the arrival of the new request at time i_t is bounded above by $R_{N_t(e(t))}$ defined by the recurrence relation[5]

$$R_m = 1 + \frac{1}{m} \sum_{j=1}^{m} R_{m-j}, \qquad (5.15)$$

since the jth file is chosen from among the m files uniformly with probability $\frac{1}{m}$, and on the next step of the chain (next subsequent eviction) the number of unmarked old files is $m - j$, and the process continues.

Solving for recursion (5.15), we get $R_m = \mathcal{O}(\log m)$. Since $m \leq N_t(e(t))$, and unconditioning with respect to D_t, we get that the expected length of the eviction chain that begins at time i_t is at most

$$\mathcal{O}\left(\mathbb{E}\{(1 + \log(N_t(e(t))))\}\right),$$

where the $+1$ is counted for the first fault incurred when the new request arrived. ∎

---

[3] That is just before the arrival of request at time i_a.

[4] Whenever we write arrival time, we mean the earliest next arrival time.

[5] The following sequence dominates the actual sequence from above.

The remaining part of the proof is to connect $N_t(e(t))$ with the prediction error η via using the notion of inversions and Lemma 5.7.5.

For phase r, among the k distinct file request times $i_1, \ldots, i_k$, let i_s be the arrival time of an old file[6] z_{i_s}. For each old file z_{i_s}, let j_s be the time of its most recent appearance in the previous phase $r - 1$. Let $J = \{j_s | z_{i_s}$ is old in phase $r\}$.

Note that the predicted next arrival time for any file is revealed only at the time of that file's request. Since j_s is the time of the most recent appearance of any old file of phase r in phase $r - 1$, the predicted time for file z_{i_s} before it arrives for the first time in phase r is same as $\hat{y}_{j_s}$.

Since file $z_{i_{e(t)}}$ is evicted by the algorithm on the arrival of a new request z_{i_t} at time i_t, then at time i_t, all the unmarked old files in the cache with true arrivals in time-set $\{i_{e(t)+1}, \ldots, i_k\}$ must have an earlier predicted next arrival time than $z_{i_{e(t)}}$. Thus, comparing the two sequences $\{i_u\} : u = e(t) + 1, \ldots, i_k$ and $\{\hat{y}_{j_u}\} : u = e(t) + 1, \ldots, i_k$, the number of indices $u > e(t)$ for which file z_{i_u} is old, and $\hat{y}_{j_{e(t)}} > \hat{y}_{j_u}$ is at least $N_t(e(t))$. Thus, for each new request, we get that the sequence of predicted next arrival times $\{\hat{y}_j\}_{j \in J}$ has at least $N_t(e(t))$ inversions compared to the true sequence of increasing old request arrival times.

Defining $N(r) = \sum_{i_t: \text{ new request arrives at time } i_t \text{ in phase } r} N_t(e(t))$ for phase r, we get that there are at least $N(r)$ inversions compared to the true sequence of increasing old request arrival times. Thus, using Lemma 5.7.5, we get

$$\sum_{j \in J} |\hat{y}_j - i_s| \geq N(r)/2, \tag{5.16}$$

where $\hat{y}_j$'s are indexed as j while i_s as s, following the definition of

$$J = \{j_s | z_{i_s} \text{ is old in phase } r\}.$$

Recall the definition of total error in prediction η (5.11), and let $N = \sum_r N(r)$ be the total number of new requests. Relation (5.16) is quite useful for connecting the error η and N, which we do as follows.

Let η_{r-1} be the total error made in prediction in phase $r - 1$, i.e., $\eta = \sum_r \eta_r$. Note that J is a subset of time instants that are part of phase $r - 1$; thus we have

$$\eta_{r-1} \geq \sum_{j \in J} |\hat{y}_j - i_s|,$$

as i_s's are the true arrival times of the first request to file j in phase r since the last arrival of file j in phase $r - 1$ at which time its predicted next arrival was $\hat{y}_j$. Hence from (5.16) we get $\eta_{r-1} \geq N(r)/2$, which implies $2\eta \geq \sum_r N(r)$. Moreover, by linearity of expectation,

$$2\eta \geq \sum_r \mathbb{E}\left\{ \sum_{i_t: \text{ new request arrives at time } i_t \text{ in phase } r} N_t(e(t)) \right\}. \tag{5.17}$$

---

[6] By definition, this means that file was requested in the previous phase.

From Lemma 5.7.8, recall that

$$\mathbb{E}\{\text{Faults in phase } r\} \leq \sum_{i_t:\text{ new request arrives at time } i_t \text{ in phase } r} \mathcal{O}\left(\mathbb{E}\{(1 + \log(N_t(e(t))))\}\right),$$

$$\overset{(a)}{\leq} \sum_{i_t:\text{ new request arrives at time } i_t \text{ in phase } r} \mathcal{O}\left((1 + \log(\mathbb{E}\{N_t(e(t))\}))\right), \quad (5.18)$$

where (a) follows from Jensen's inequality. Next, we sum across all phases and bound (5.18) in two ways. First, by using (5.17) and Jensen's inequality, and then by upper bounding $N(r) \leq k$. Using (5.17), and Jensen's inequality one more time on (5.18),[7] and recalling that $N = \sum_r N(r)$ is the total number of new requests, we get

$$\mathbb{E}\{\text{Faults in all phases}\} \leq N + \mathcal{O}\left(N\log\left(\frac{2\eta}{N}\right)\right), \quad (5.19)$$

while noting that $N(r) \leq k$, since at most k distinct requests arrive in any phase, we also get

$$\mathbb{E}\{\text{Faults in all phases}\} \leq N + N\log(k). \quad (5.20)$$

Combining (5.19) and (5.20), and using (5.10) from which we have $\mathsf{F}_{\mathrm{OPT}} \geq N/2$ which is still valid since the definition of the phase is same with MARKING for PREDICTIVE-MARKING, we get that for any input σ,

$$\frac{\mathbb{E}\{\mathsf{F}_{\text{PREDICTIVE-MARKING}}(\sigma)\}}{\mathsf{F}_{\mathrm{OPT}}(\sigma)} \leq \mathcal{O}\left(1 + \min\left\{\log\left(\frac{\eta}{\mathsf{F}_{\mathrm{OPT}}(\sigma)}\right), \log(k)\right\}\right).$$

$\blacksquare$

5.8 Paging with Lookahead

One important extension of the paging problem is to allow an algorithm to have a *lookahead*, i.e., at each time, information about some fixed number of future requests is made available to an online algorithm which it can use for making the ejection decision.

There are two types of lookaheads that have been discussed in literature – weak and strong – for which the competitive performance of online algorithms differs significantly. We discuss the effects of lookahead via Problem 5.11.

5.9 Random Input

In this section, we consider the randomized input setting, and assume that file requests are being made from a distribution that is derived from a Markov chain. The Markov chain assumption is reasonable since typically in a practical setting, some correlation is observed in subsequent file requests.

---

[7] Multiplying and dividing by n.

We begin by showing that the optimal deterministic algorithms in the adversarial setting, namely LRU and FIFO, are no longer optimal in this random input setting; actually far from optimal. This motivates the study of 'new' algorithms that explicitly use the randomness of the input, and we describe one such algorithm whose performance is only a constant factor away from the optimal.

Under the Markov chain input model, one can show using the Markov decision process results that there exists a deterministic optimal algorithm. Let that algorithm be OPT, and the resulting minimum expected number of faults for OPT be $\mathbb{E}\{F_{OPT}\}$.

5.9.1 Sub-Optimality of LRU

To show the sub-optimality of the LRU algorithm, consider the Markov chain input called the lollipop graph, as shown in Figure 5.2. For positive integers (a, b), the lollipop graph $L(a, b)$ is formed by attaching one end of a path through a nodes to a complete graph K_b on b nodes. Let the Markov chain be a simple random walk on a lollipop graph $L(k/2, k/2 + 1)$, as shown in Figure 5.2, where k is the size of the cache and there are in total $k + 1$ files. By simple random walk, we mean that the probability of transitioning out from any state to any of the connected states in the Markov chain is $1/d$, where d is the degree of that state.

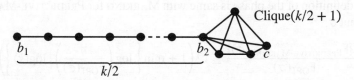

Figure 5.2 Lollipop graph with total $k + 1$ nodes

Lemma 5.9.1 *The expected number of faults incurred by the* LRU *algorithm for input coming from the lollipop graph as shown in Figure 5.2 is at least* $(\log k)\mathbb{E}\{F_{OPT}\}$.

The proof of this lemma is easy and developed in Problem 5.10. The main reason for this behaviour is the local correlation between subsequent file requests resulting from the underlying Markov chain that defines the structure of files over which consecutive faults are made by LRU. Recall that in the proof of Lemma 5.6.2, we have shown that for another randomized input, the competitive ratio of LRU (in fact any deterministic algorithm) is $\mathcal{O}(\log k)$.

5.9.2 Sub-Optimality of the Maximum Hitting Time (MHT) Algorithm

The MHT algorithm, on the arrival of file p, ejects a file q (if required) such that the expected (hitting) time to reach file q starting from p on the Markov chain is maximized. One might expect better (close to optimal) performance from the MHT algorithm compared to LRU; however, even MHT is not close to optimal, and the expected number of faults it incurs is at least k times the optimal expected number of faults. To show this, we consider a particular Markov chain, called a forked lollipop graph, as shown in Figure 5.3 with a total of $k + 1$ nodes (possible file requests). Since the size of the cache is k, at any time, there is only one file missing from the cache. Note that the expected hitting time from t_1 to t_2 or vice versa is $\dfrac{4k^2}{9}$, while the expected

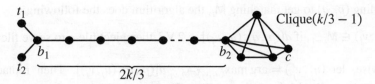

Figure 5.3 Forked lollipop graph with total $k + 1$ nodes

hitting time from t_1 or t_2 to any node in the clique is $2k^2/9 + \mathcal{O}(k)$ for the Markov chain shown in Figure 5.3.

Eventually the file on any one tip (t_1 or t_2) of the fork will be ejected. When the ejected file among t_1 or t_2 is requested next, the other among t_1 or t_2 is ejected, since that has the largest hitting time. Thus, the MHT algorithm will alternatively eject t_1 and t_2, and its expected number of faults is $\Omega\left(\frac{1}{k^2}\right)$.

OPT on the other hand will alternatively eject one of the files c in the clique and the one at the tip of the fork – let that be t_1. Note that the hitting time from t_1 to node c in the clique is $\mathcal{O}(k^2)$, but the hitting time from c to t_i is $\mathcal{O}(k^3)$. Moreover, the (stationary) probability of file t_1 being requested is $\mathcal{O}\left(\frac{1}{k}\right)$. Hence the expected number of faults incurred by OPT is only $\mathcal{O}\left(\frac{1}{k^3}\right)$.

5.9.3 Almost Optimal Algorithm

We now describe an almost optimal online algorithm (called COMMUTE) when the input distribution is derived from a Markov chain. Let in a phase ℓ (defined subsequently) p_i be the ith new file requested that is not present in the cache at that time. Then the *window* W_i at time i is defined as $W_i = C(\ell - 1) \cup \{p_1, \dots, p_{i-1}, p_i\}$, where $C(\ell - 1)$ are the contents of the cache at the end of phase $\ell - 1$.

Let the algorithm maintain a matching $M_{i-1} = \{(u_1, v_1), \dots, (u_{i-1}, v_{i-1})\}$ between files u_j, v_j for each $1 \le j \le i - 1$, and where $u_j \ne u_k$ and $v_j \ne v_k$ for $j \ne k$.

Let $\mathcal{T}_{a,b}$ be the expected (hitting) time to reach state b from a in the Markov chain. Let

$$q = \arg \max_{j \in W_i,\, j \notin M_{i-1}} \mathcal{T}_{p_i, j}$$

be the element in W_i but not in M_{i-1}, i.e., j does not belong to any pair of nodes that is part of M_{i-1} such that the hitting time from p_i to q is the maximum over the Markov chain. Then we match p_i to q, i.e., add the pair (p_i, q) to the matching, i.e., $M_i = M_{i-1} \cup (p_i, q)$. The algorithm will only keep exactly one of u_j or v_j in its cache for $1 \le j \le i$.

We need the following definition for the subsequent description of this algorithm. Let

$$d[(a, b), (u, v)] = \frac{\min\{\mathcal{T}_{a,u}, \mathcal{T}_{b,u}, \mathcal{T}_{a,v}, \mathcal{T}_{b,v}\}}{\mathcal{T}_{a,b}}.$$

The 'distance' $d[(a, b), (u, v)]$ corresponds to the distance in terms of time needed to reach a from b in comparison to reaching u or v. Large $d[(a, b), (u, v)]$ corresponds to the case where a and b are much farther from both u and v than they are from each other.

On adding (p_i, q) to get matching M_i, the algorithm does the following:

- For $(u_j, v_j) \in M_{i-1}$, if $d[(p_i, q), (u_j, v_j)] \leq 2 \, \forall \, j$, then eject file q to serve file p_i.

- Otherwise, let $(u_j^*, v_j^*) = \arg\max_{(u_j, v_j) \in M_{i-1}} d[(p_i, q), (u_j, v_j)]$. Then replace (p_i, q) with (u_j, p_i) and (u_j, v_j) with (q, v_j) in M_i. Eject file u_j or v_j whichever is in cache to serve file p_i.

The phase ends as soon as the $k + 1^{st}$ distinct file is requested, at which time the window size is shrunk to size k that contains the k most recently requested files, and the contents of the cache at the end of phase are equal to the contents of the window.

We have already seen that the MHT algorithm that ejects the file with the largest hitting time is far from optimal. Thus, the COMMUTE algorithm uses the hitting time in a clever way, so as to avoid the limitation of a simple maximum hitting time algorithm.

Lemma 5.9.2 *The expected number of faults incurred by the* COMMUTE *algorithm with Markov input is at most* $c\mathbb{E}\{F_{OPT}\}$ *for some constant c.*

The proof is long and technical, and can be found in [64].

5.10 Multiple Cache Paging

Consider a bank of m caches, each of which can store k out of the $|\mathcal{U}|$ files in the universe. In each time step, m parallel requests arrive that have to be fulfilled by or matched with the m caches, such that each cache is allocated exactly one request. Once the requests are matched to the caches, if the requested content is not stored in the corresponding cache, the cache ejects one of the currently stored contents with the requested content to serve the request, and a single fault is counted. See Figure 5.4 for an illustration of the setup. We call this problem multiple cache paging (MCP) and the goal is to design an online algorithm that minimizes the number of faults made to serve the requests, where both the matching and the ejection problems have to be jointly solved. For $m = 1$, this is the classical paging problem, which we have discussed in detail in this chapter.

The m-length request vector at time t is denoted by $\sigma(t) = (r_1, \ldots, r_m)$. The k contents of cache j at time t are denoted as $c_j(t)$, and $C(t) = (c_j(t), j = 1, \ldots m)$.

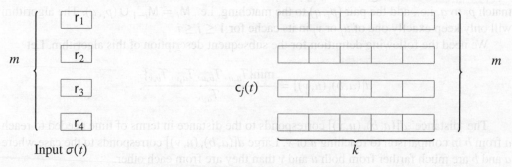

Figure 5.4 Schematic for the multiple cache problem with m caches

5.10.1 Lower Bound

In this section, we present a surprising result that the competitive ratio of any deterministic online algorithm for solving MCP with more than one cache is unbounded, in contrast to the single cache case.

Theorem 5.10.1 *The competitive ratio of any deterministic online algorithm for solving MCP with $m > 1$ is unbounded.*

Proof: We will prove it for the specific case of $m = 2$ and $k = 4$, which suffices for proving the theorem. We will produce a sequence of input requests for which no matter what a deterministic online algorithm does, the number of faults is unbounded, while OPT makes only two faults. First we state two rules that any online algorithm must follow, since otherwise there is an easy construction of 'bad' sequences for which the competitive ratio is unbounded. The proof is left as an exercise in Problem 5.13.

1. Let the weight of an edge between the ith file of the input vector $\sigma(t)$ and cache j be defined as 1 if cache j contains requested file i, and zero otherwise. Let $M(t)$ be a set of maximum weight matchings of the input vector $\sigma(t)$ and the contents of cache $C(t)$ at time t. Then any deterministic online algorithm at time t must serve the input vector $\sigma(t)$ via any one of the maximum weight matchings.

2. Once an online algorithm decides on a matching (which content will be served by which cache), then it should always eject the oldest arrived content from each cache, if required. It will be clear from the following input construction that if the online algorithm ejects the most recently requested content to serve the current request, then the adversary can repeatedly ask for two tuples of contents a, b, for which any online algorithm will repeatedly fault on each request. A similar argument can be extended for any other policy that does not eject the oldest arrived content.

We prove the result for the case of two caches $m = 2$ each with size $k = 4$. Assume that the contents of the two caches at a certain time are $c_1 = \{x_1, f_2, f_3, f_4\}$ and $c_2 = \{x_2, b_2, b_3, b_4\}$. Without loss of generality, since files are only placeholders, we will follow a convention that f_k, b_k came earlier than f_{k-1}, b_{k-1} in caches 1 and 2, respectively, for $k = 2, 3, 4$. Moreover, we assume that $x_i, i = 1, 2$, are the oldest contents in cache i, respectively, at this time.

Let at next time slot the request vector be $\{f_1, b_1\}$. Not knowing the future input sequence, let any online algorithm $\mathcal{A}$ make the following allocation, serve f_1 from cache 1 and b_1 from cache 2 by evicting x_1 and x_2, respectively. Then $c_1(\mathcal{A}) = \{f_1, f_2, f_3, f_4\}$, and $c_2(\mathcal{A}) = \{b_1, b_2, b_3, b_4\}$. Moreover, let the OPT, knowing the future input, serve f_1 from c_2 and b_1 from c_1 by evicting x_2 and x_1, respectively. Thus, the updated contents of the two caches with OPT are $c_1(OPT) = \{b_1, f_2, f_3, f_4\}$ and $c_2(OPT) = \{f_1, b_2, b_3, b_4\}$. Note that for competitive ratio definition, the adversary is allowed to give inputs depending on the current state of the deterministic algorithm $\mathcal{A}$. If suppose $\mathcal{A}$ makes the opposite allocation, then we can replace the role of f_1 and b_1 in future input sequence, and get the same result as f_1 and b_1 are only placeholders, as will be evident as follows.

Table 5.5 'Bad' input for any online algorithm $\mathcal{A}$ for MCP

input	c_1				c_2			
	f_1	f_2	f_3	f_4	b_1	b_2	b_3	b_4
(f_1, f_2)								f_2
(b_1, b_2)				b_2				
(f_1, f_3)							f_3	
(f_3, b_3)						b_3		
(f_1, f_4)					f_4			
(f_3, b_4)								b_4
(f_1, f_2)								f_2
(b_1, b_2)						b_1		
(f_1, f_3)							f_3	
(f_3, b_3)							b_3	
(f_1, f_4)				f_4				
(f_3, b_4)						b_4		
(f_1, f_2)					f_2			
(b_1, b_2)								b_1
(f_1, f_3)				f_3				
(f_3, b_3)						b_3		
(f_1, f_4)					f_4			
(f_3, b_4)								b_4

Now we construct a sequence of inputs so that OPT does not have to incur any fault, while any online algorithm $\mathcal{A}$ makes at least one fault at each subsequent request. Let

$$\sigma = \{(f_1, f_2), (b_1, b_2), (f_1, f_3), (b_2, b_3), (f_1, f_4), (b_4, b_2)\}.$$

From hereon, we will use $\sigma = \{\sigma, \sigma, \dots\}$ that uses σ repeated infinitely many times, as the request vector sequence.

For $u, v \in \{1, 2\}$, without loss of generality, we follow that if the input is $(*_i, *_j)$, $i < j$, $* \in \{a, b\}$ and $*_i, *_j \in \mathsf{c}_u(\mathcal{A})$ and $*_i, *_j \notin \mathsf{c}_v(\mathcal{A})$, we follow that $*_i$ is served from cache u, and $*_j$ is served from cache v after evicting some content from $\mathsf{c}_v(\mathcal{A})$, since the content names are only placeholders.

For input σ as described above, Table 5.5 illustrates the evolving contents of the two caches with any online algorithm following rules 1 and 2 and our convention that if a file f_k is ejected to serve file f_j at time t, then in row t, we write f_j directly below the location where file f_k was placed earlier. For example, at time 2, b_2 replaces f_4 in cache 1.

The main idea to notice from Table 5.5 is that after one full cycle of σ in $\boldsymbol{\sigma}$, contents of cache 1, c_1, are never changed and it always contains $\{f_1, f_2, f_3, b_2\}$. The request sequence at each subsequent time is such that only one content can be served from c_1 without any fault, while the other content is missing from c_2 and at least one fault has to be made. Since c_1 is never updated, there is no way for any online algorithm to make cache contents c_1, c_2 equal to OPT's $c_1(OPT)$ and $c_2(OPT)$ up to a permutation. Thus, the number of faults made by $\mathcal{A}$ in each cycle is at least 6, and the total number of faults made with input $\boldsymbol{\sigma}$ is at least $6|\sigma|$.

Moreover, it is easy to check that the full request sequence $\boldsymbol{\sigma}$ can be served by OPT that has contents $c_1(OPT) = \{b_1, f_2, f_3, f_4\}$ and $c_2(OPT) = \{f_1, b_2, b_3, b_4\}$ without incurring any fault, and the total number of faults made by OPT is 2.

Thus, the competitive ratio of any online algorithm is at least $3|\sigma|$. Since $|\sigma|$ can be chosen to be arbitrarily large, the result follows. ∎

Theorem 5.10.1 shows that even if there are only two caches, no deterministic online algorithm can have a bounded competitive ratio for MCP, which is a surprising result given that the competitive ratio of a simple LRU algorithm is bounded for the single cache case. The added decision of matching needed with MCP makes it fundamentally different than the single cache problem, and if any online algorithm makes one mistake in matching the requests, then that algorithm can be forced to make repeated mistakes.

This result also shows that MCP with $m > 1$ and k-sized caches is not related to MCP with single cache and memory size of mk, since otherwise the LRU algorithm would achieve a competitive ratio of at most mk.

One challenging question that remains open is: what is the best competitive ratio a randomized algorithm can achieve for MCP? For the case when the input is random, for example, the m parallel requests are i.i.d., a parallel LRU policy is asymptotically optimal, where the matching is fixed ahead of time between requests and cache, and each cache implements an independent LRU policy for some input distributions [65], e.g., Zipf or Power-law.

5.11 Notes

The paging problem was first considered in the classical work of Belady [66], which showed that LFD is an optimal offline algorithm. For online algorithms, the lower bound on the competitive ratio of k for all deterministic algorithms and the fact that LRU and FIFO achieve it was derived in [67]. The randomized algorithm MARKING with competitive ratio of $2H_k$ was analysed in [68], while a 'pure' random algorithm that ejects any file uniformly randomly was considered in [69] to show that its competitive ratio is k against any adaptive online adversary. A lower bound of H_k was also shown in [68] for all randomized algorithms. Optimal randomized algorithms that achieve the lower bound of H_k have been derived in [63] and [70], where the algorithm in [70] is easier to state and analyse. The weighted paging problem has also been considered in literature, where each file f has an associated cost c_f, and every time file f is requested and not found in the cache, a cost of c_f is incurred, and the objective is to find an ejection algorithm to minimize the sum of the cost. An optimal k-competitive deterministic algorithm has been proposed in [71] for the weighted paging problem, while an $\mathcal{O}(\log k)$ randomized algorithm was derived in [72].

A less adversarial and a more practical setting for the paging problem, where the power of the adversary is restricted by allowing only certain input distributions, has been studied in [73].

With stochastic or randomized input, [64] showed that the well-known algorithms such as LRU or maximum hitting time algorithms are far from optimal, and proposed the COMMUTE algorithm whose competitive ratio is at most a constant. The paging problem with multiple caches was considered in [65], where the un-competitiveness of any deterministic algorithm was shown together with some asymptotically optimal algorithms for random inputs.

The machine learning augmented setup was first considered in [74], with improved results obtained in [75] as presented in Section 5.7. In addition to upper bounds, [75] also proved a lower bound for all randomized algorithms in the presence of predicted input.

PROBLEMS

5.1 Prove that LFD (longest distance forward) is an optimal offline algorithm for the paging problem that ejects the file that is going to be requested last among the existing files in the cache.

[Hint: Consider the first time instance i at which OPT and LFD diverge (make different decisions about which page to eject), where LFD discards page q instead of page p discarded by OPT. Let t be the earliest time thereafter where OPT discards q. Alter the algorithm OPT to OPT' between time i and t, such that the cost of OPT' is less than or equal to OPT and the cost of OPT' is less than or equal to LFD.]

5.2 Show that the LIFO algorithm is not α-competitive for any $\alpha > 1$ for solving the paging problem.

5.3 Show that the competitive ratio of the FIFO algorithm is at most k for solving the paging problem.

5.4 For an input σ, let the number of faults made by LRU with cache size k be $F_{LRU}(k, \sigma)$. Then show that $F_{LRU}(k, \sigma) \geq F_{LRU}(k + 1, \sigma)$. Thus, LRU does not have Belady's anomaly.

[Hint: Use the critical property of LRU to show that the cache contents $C_k(t)$ at time t with capacity k satisfies the relation $C_k(t) \subset C_{k+1}(t)$.]

5.5 Show that the optimal offline algorithm for the paging problem, LFD, does not have Belady's anomaly.

5.6 Consider the following *cat* and *mouse* game on a **complete graph** over n vertices. At time 0, the cat and mouse are at two distinct vertices. At any time, the cat does not know the vertex at which mouse is located while the mouse knows the vertex where cat is located. Moreover the mouse also gets to observe if the cat is moving towards its current location. What this means is that if the cat chooses an edge between its current vertex and the vertex at which currently the mouse is, the mouse gets to see that and can jump to any other vertex before the cat reaches its chosen vertex.

In particular, let at each discrete time $t, 1 \leq t \leq T$, cat chooses a vertex, say c_t and the mouse sees the cat's choice, and chooses a vertex $m_t \neq c_t$, to avoid the cat. Both move to their destination simultaneously. If $m_t \neq m_{t-1}$, the mouse incurs a cost of 1. The objective of the mouse is to stay alive (never end up at the same vertex as the cat), while incurring minimum total movement cost. Consider the moves made by the mouse be an algorithm while treat the cat moves as an adversary.

1. Propose a deterministic online algorithm with competitive ratio of at most n.

2. Show that no deterministic algorithm can have competitive ratio less than n.

3. Propose a randomized online algorithm with competitive ratio of at most $O(\log n)$.

   [Hint: The idea behind the MARKING algorithm for the paging problem might be helpful.]

5.7 **Resource Augmentation.** In this problem, we will consider that an online algorithm for solving the paging problem has a cache size of $k + r$ while OPT is restricted to using a cache of size k. Show that the competitive ratio of LRU in this setting is at most

$$\frac{k+r}{r+1}.$$

[Hint: Rework the argument used for proving Lemma 5.5.2.]

5.8 **[76]** Consider a randomized online paging algorithm RANDOM for solving the paging problem that on each fault evicts a (uniformly) random file from the cache. Prove that its competitive ratio is at least k, where k is the cache size. The following basic result might be useful. Let W be the (random) waiting time for the first success in a sequence of Bernoulli trials with success probability p. Define

$$W_k = \begin{cases} W & \text{if } W \leq k, \\ k & \text{otherwise.} \end{cases} \tag{5.21}$$

Then $\mathbb{E}\{W_k\} = \frac{1-(1-p)^k}{p}$.

[Hint: Input sequence of the type $a_1 a_2 \ldots a_k (b_1 a_2 \ldots a_k)^2 (b_2 a_2 \ldots a_k)^3 \ldots$ may be useful, where a_i, b_i are distinct files and $(s)^i$ denotes i repetitions of sequence s. Consider the jth segment $(b_j a_2 \ldots a_k)^j$ and lower bound the expected number of faults incurred by RANDOM in the jth segment by $\frac{(1-(1-p)^j)}{p}$ where $p = \frac{1}{k}$.]

5.9 Consider the paging problem where the original cache capacity is k units. The novelty now is that one can buy more capacity, with each extra unit of cache capacity costing c dollars. Note that this capacity can be bought at any time during the total time horizon of the input, and at the same price. For an input σ with size $|\sigma| = T$, the overall cost of an algorithm $\mathcal{A}$ is the total cost paid (to buy all the extra capacity) plus the number of faults (ejections) made by $\mathcal{A}$ to serve all the different files requested in the input. Thus, the competitive ratio of any online algorithm $\mathcal{A}$ is

$$\mu_{\mathcal{A}} = \max_{\sigma} \frac{c \, r_{\mathcal{A}} + \#\text{Faults}_{\mathcal{A}}}{c \, r_{\text{OPT}} + \#\text{Faults}_{\text{OPT}}},$$

where $r_{\mathcal{A}}, r_{\text{OPT}}$ is the total extra capacity bought by $\mathcal{A}$ and the OPT, respectively. Let $c < k$.

1. Show that the lower bound on the competitive ratio of any deterministic online algorithm is at least c.

2. Show that the competitive ratio of any online algorithm that buys an additional unit capacity every time it is about to make a fault is at most c for $c \geq 1$, and 1 otherwise.

5.10 LRU is not universally good. Show that the LRU algorithm is $\log k$ competitive in expectation for the simple random walk on the lollipop graph $L(k/2, k/2 + 1)$ as shown in Figure 5.2, where k is the size of the cache and there are total $k + 1$ files. By simple random walk, we mean that the probability of transitioning out from any state to any of the connected states in the Markov chain is $1/d$, where d is the degree of the state.

[Hint: Consider the leftmost node on the path of a nodes and call it ℓ. Break the request sequence into phases, where each phase begins when the kth distinct request is made. Show that a constant fraction of the phases start on ℓ. Once a phase starts on ℓ, show that on average LRU makes $\log k$ faults in that phase (phase ends when each page in the clique has been requested once). An algorithm that just toggles between evicting one page inside the clique and ℓ incurs just one fault on average.]

5.11 Lookahead. Let an online algorithm for the paging problem have a *weak* lookahead of ℓ if it knows the next ℓ requests at each time t. A lookahead is called *strong* if the algorithm at time t knows the next ℓ **distinct** requests to be made after time t, other than the request made at time t. For example, if the request sequence is $\sigma = \{\sigma_1, \sigma_2, \dots, \}$, then with weak lookahead the information at time t is $\{\sigma_1, \sigma_2, \dots, \sigma_{t+\ell}\}$, while with strong lookahead it is $\{\sigma_1, \sigma_2, \dots, \sigma_m\}$, where $|\{\sigma_t, \sigma_{t+1}, \sigma_{t+2}, \dots, \sigma_m\}| = \ell + 1$.

1. Show that with weak lookahead, no deterministic online algorithm can have a competitive ratio better than k in the worst case.

2. Show that with strong lookahead no deterministic online algorithm can have competitive ratio better than $k - \ell$ in the worst case with $\ell \leq k - 2$ and $k \geq 3$.

3. Show that a natural extension of LRU can achieve the competitive ratio of $k - \ell$.

5.12 Multiple Cache Paging. Consider that there are two memories each of size k and the request is a two tuple (a, b). Any of the two entries of the request vector can be served by any of the two caches, and each cache can only serve one request. To be specific, if (a, a) is the request and a single copy of a is in one of the two caches, then an extra copy of a has to be loaded in the other cache to serve the request. Assuming that each entry of the request vector is likely to be requested with probability p_i and is i.i.d. across time and space (tuple), find the optimal storage strategy for each cache for $k = 3$. [Note that storing the most likely contents in each cache is not optimal.]

5.13 Show that if any algorithm does not follow the two rules stated in the proof of Theorem 5.10.1, then its competitive ratio is unbounded.

CHAPTER 6

Metrical Task System

6.1 Introduction

In this chapter, we consider a very general and abstract online problem that generalizes various problems already studied in this book, e.g., paging and list accessing. For any generic problem, the cost paid by any online algorithm on the arrival of a new request is a function of its current state and the action taken to fulfil the new request. Typically, the chosen action also alters the state of the algorithm, which then determines the subsequent costs. To model this interplay between cost and state transitions, an abstract paradigm called the metrical task system (MTS) is defined, where there is a set of all possible states (one of them is occupied by any online algorithm at any time).

Requests arrive over time, and the cost of an online algorithm to serve or fulfil each request depends on the state from which it chooses to fulfil the request. This cost is called the state dependent cost. If the online algorithm serves the newly arrived request from its current state, then the only cost it pays is the state dependent cost. Otherwise, it first transitions to a new state and then serves the request. In the event of a transition, the algorithm pays the state dependent cost of the new state in addition to the switching cost to move from the present state to the new state. The switching cost is restricted to satisfying the usual metric properties, e.g., the triangle inequality. The overall cost of an online algorithm is the sum of the state dependent cost and the switching cost, summed over all requests. This is a very generic formulation and can model any finite state dependent dynamical system.

We begin this chapter by deriving a lower bound on the competitive ratio of any deterministic algorithm for the MTS. Because of the generality of the MTS, the power of deterministic online algorithms is limited, and the competitive ratio of any deterministic online algorithm is at least $2|\mathcal{S}| - 1$, where $|\mathcal{S}|$ is the total number of states. Thus, more the number of states, more is the power that adversary has over an online algorithm. We next present a simple algorithm called *work-function*, based on the broad principle of dynamic programming, that achieves this lower bound exactly.

As remarked earlier, the special cases of the MTS include paging and list accessing. Another important special case of the MTS is the k-server problem, where there are k servers located in a metric space and a request corresponds to a location in the metric space that is defined to be fulfilled by moving at least one of the k servers to that location. The cost of an online algorithm is the sum of the distance covered by the k servers. Direct application of the guarantee available for the MTS results in very poor competitive ratio guarantee for the k-server problem. Thus, finer analysis of the work-function algorithm is done to show that it can achieve a competitive ratio of $2k - 1$. This analysis is fairly involved and in the chapter, we restrict our attention to the one-dimensional k-server problem, where the locations of the servers lie on a line. For this simpler setting, we present an optimal online algorithm that achieves a competitive ratio of k. The fact that k is a lower bound on the competitive ratio for the k-server problem follows from the respective lower bound for the paging problem.

6.2 Metrical Task System

Definition 6.2.1 *A metric space $\mathcal{M}$ is a set endowed with a 'distance' or metric d such that*

$$d : \mathcal{M} \times \mathcal{M} \to \mathbb{R},$$

and

1. $d(u, v) \geq 0 \ \forall \ u, v \in \mathcal{M}$,
2. $d(u, v) = 0$ *if and only if* $u = v$,
3. $d(u, v) = d(v, u) \ \forall \ u, v \in \mathcal{M}$,
4. $d(u, v) + d(v, w) \geq d(u, w) \ \forall \ u, v, w \in \mathcal{M}$.

In short, we call $(\mathcal{M}, d)$ as the metric space.

We define the MTS as follows. Let the set of all possible states be $\mathcal{S}$. Let a distance metric be defined over $\mathcal{S}$, i.e., $d(x, y), x, y \in \mathcal{S}$, such that $(\mathcal{S}, d)$ is a metric space. Let the time horizon be T, and for any $1 \leq t \leq T$, let an online algorithm $\mathcal{A}$ be in state $s_{\mathcal{A}}(t) \in \mathcal{S}$ at time t.[1] The initial state is $s(0)$, which is common for all algorithms.

For each $1 \leq t \leq T$, let r_t be a cost-function defined over $\mathcal{S}$:

$$r_t : \mathcal{S} \to \mathbb{R}^+. \tag{6.1}$$

Essentially, for each state $s \in \mathcal{S}$, r_t represents the cost to serve the request made at time t from state s.

At time $t + 1$, input that is expressed via function r_{t+1} arrives and defines the **state cost** equal to $r_{t+1}(s_{\mathcal{A}}(t + 1))$ that $\mathcal{A}$ has to pay depending on the state $s_{\mathcal{A}}(t + 1)$ it chooses for time $t + 1$. Moreover, there is a **switching** cost $\mathcal{A}$ has to pay if it changes its state from $s_{\mathcal{A}}(t)$ to $s_{\mathcal{A}}(t + 1)$ at time $t + 1$ that is given by $d(s_{\mathcal{A}}(t), s_{\mathcal{A}}(t + 1))$.

Note that since $(\mathcal{S}, d)$ is assumed to be a metric space, d satisfies the **symmetry** property, i.e., $d(x, y) = d(y, x)$. There are cases when the symmetry property does not hold, and that can also be handled, similar to our treatment of the symmetric case with an additional penalty in the competitive ratio [77].

The cost for $\mathcal{A}$ at time $t + 1$ is

$$C_{\mathcal{A}}(t + 1) = r_{t+1}(s_{\mathcal{A}}(t + 1)) + d(s_{\mathcal{A}}(t), s_{\mathcal{A}}(t + 1)),$$

---

[1] We are following the convention that the state at time t means the state from which the request that arrives in time t is fulfilled.

the sum of the state and the switching cost, and the overall cost of $\mathcal{A}$ is

$$C_{\mathcal{A}} = \sum_{t=1}^{T} C_{\mathcal{A}}(t).$$

Consequently, the competitive ratio of $\mathcal{A}$ is

$$\mu_{\mathcal{A}} = \max_{\sigma} \frac{C_{\mathcal{A}}(\sigma)}{C_{\mathrm{OPT}}(\sigma)},$$

where $\sigma = \{r_1, r_2, \ldots, r_T\}$ in the input.

The MTS is an abstractly defined object. Concretely, MTS models input as job requests that require a certain cost when processed in a particular state or configuration by a machine, and there is a cost to changing the configuration of the machine.

Proposition 6.2.2 *The paging problem discussed in Chapter 5 is a special case of the MTS.*

Proof: Let the universe of all files be $\mathcal{U}$, and let the cache size for the paging problem be k. Then the set of all states $\mathcal{S}$ is the set containing all possible subsets of $\mathcal{U}$ with cardinality k. Moreover, the switching cost $d(C, C')$ between two states $C, C' \in \mathcal{S}$ is the minimum number of elements that need to be replaced to get C' from C. Moreover, if file f_i is requested at time t,

$$r_t(C) = \begin{cases} \infty & \text{if } f_i \notin C, \\ 0 & \text{otherwise.} \end{cases} \tag{6.2}$$

Thus, any algorithm would be forced to keep the requested f_i in its cache at the end of time t. Hence, for the paging problem, the only cost is the switching cost (that is equal to 1 every time a newly requested file is not found in the cache) which is equal to the fault definition (Chapter 5) at each time t, and the objective is to minimize the total number of faults or the total switching cost. ∎

Similarly, we can show that the list accessing problem discussed in Chapter 3 is a special case of the MTS, which we leave as an exercise.

Proposition 6.2.3 *The list accessing problem discussed in the Chapter 3 is a special case of the MTS.*

6.3 Lower Bound on the Competitive Ratio of Deterministic Online Algorithms

In this section, we show that the competitive ratio of any deterministic online algorithm for the MTS is at least $2|\mathcal{S}| - 1$. This is essentially a negative result, and shows that the power of deterministic online algorithms in this very general formulation of the MTS is rather limited. In contrast, we know that for the special cases of the MTS, namely the paging problem and the list accessing problem, deterministic online algorithms with much smaller competitive ratios are known.

In the following, we first illustrate this result for the simple case when $|\mathcal{S}| = 2$ and show that the competitive ratio of any deterministic algorithm is at least 3. The basic idea remains the same, and can be generalized readily for general $\mathcal{S}$.

Consider that $|\mathcal{S}| = 2$, i.e., there are only two states, s_1 and s_2, and, without loss of generality, let the starting state for any algorithm be s_1. Let $\mathcal{A}$ be any deterministic online algorithm and its state at time t be $s_{\mathcal{A}}(t)$. Depending on $s_{\mathcal{A}}(t)$, the request at time $t + 1$ is such that

$$r_{t+1}(s) = \begin{cases} \epsilon & \text{if } s = s_{\mathcal{A}}(t), \\ 0 & \text{otherwise,} \end{cases} \tag{6.3}$$

i.e., if $\mathcal{A}$ does not change its state, it pays a cost of ϵ, otherwise the cost is zero. In this case, $\mathcal{A}$ always pays a cost of at least $\min\{\epsilon, d(s_1, s_2)\}$ at each time,[2] no matter what it does. So one option for $\mathcal{A}$ is to never change its state and pay a cost ϵT, where T is the total time horizon. However, in this case, OPT can move to s_2 at time 1 by paying a cost $d(s_1, s_2)$ and pay no further cost. Thus, the overall cost of OPT is just $d(s_1, s_2)$, making the competitive ratio $\mathcal{O}(T)$. Thus, $\mathcal{A}$ should never make this choice.

Given $d(s_1, s_2) = d(s_2, s_1)$, with input (6.3), the only other option for $\mathcal{A}$ is to repeatedly move between the two states at certain time instants so as to increase the cost of OPT. Let $\mathcal{A}$ move between the two states k times in time horizon T. Then the cost of $\mathcal{A}$ is $C_{\mathcal{A}} = (T - k)\epsilon + kd(s_1, s_2)$. Now, the question is what is OPT's cost in this case.

Towards that end, consider three algorithms B_1, B_2 and B_3. For these three algorithms, the following invariant is maintained at each time t:

1. exactly two of them are in the state opposite of the state that $\mathcal{A}$ is in,
2. exactly one of them has the same state as the state that $\mathcal{A}$ is in, and
3. at most one of them switches state at any time t.

It is easy to see that such B_1, B_2, and B_3 exist. For example, let at time t, $\mathcal{A}$ be in state s_1, B_1, B_2 be in state s_2, while B_3 be in state s_1. If $\mathcal{A}$ switches state, so does B_1, say, in which case B_1, B_3 are in opposite states compared to $\mathcal{A}$, while $\mathcal{A}$ and B_2 are in the same state. In case $\mathcal{A}$ does not switch states, B_1, B_2, B_3 also do not switch states.

To count the sum of the costs of B_1, B_2, and B_3, note that the total number of times any of B_1, B_2, or B_3 switches states is k. Moreover, one among B_1, B_2, and B_3 shares the same state as $\mathcal{A}$, thus counting the state cost $(T - k)\epsilon$ for that, while for the other two algorithms the state cost is $2k\epsilon$. Letting F be some fixed cost to get to the initial configuration required to implement B_1, B_2, B_3, the sum of the costs of B_1, B_2, and B_3 is

$$\sum_{i=1}^{3} C_{B_i} \leq (T - k)\epsilon + 2k\epsilon + kd(s_1, s_2) + F.$$

Since OPT by definition is better than any of the B_1, B_2, or B_3, $C_{\text{OPT}} \leq C_{B_i}$ for $i = 1, 2, 3$, and hence $C_{\text{OPT}} \leq \frac{\sum_{i=1}^{3} C_{B_i}}{3}$.

---

[2] Recall that $d(s_1, s_2) = d(s_2, s_1)$.

Recall that $C_\mathcal{A} \geq kd(s_1, s_2)$, i.e., $k \leq \frac{C_\mathcal{A}}{d(s_1, s_2)}$. Hence we get

$$3C_{\text{OPT}} - F \leq \left(\frac{2\epsilon}{d(s_1, s_2)} + 1 \right) C_\mathcal{A}.$$

$$\mu_\mathcal{A} = \frac{C_\mathcal{A}}{C_{\text{OPT}}} \geq \frac{3}{\left(\frac{2\epsilon}{d(s_1, s_2)} + 1 \right)} - \frac{F}{C_{\text{OPT}} \left(\frac{2\epsilon}{d(s_1, s_2)+1} \right)}.$$

First letting $\epsilon \to 0$, and then $T \to \infty$, which implies $C_{\text{OPT}} \to \infty$, we get that

$$\mu_\mathcal{A} \to 3.$$

This result essentially exhibits the power of averaging over multiple algorithms to bound the cost of OPT and lower bound the competitive ratio of any online algorithm. Let $\mathcal{A}$ be the online algorithm under consideration. Then the idea is to construct a set of algorithms where, on a specific input, a few of the algorithms have a cost similar to $\mathcal{A}$, while most of the others have a smaller cost than $\mathcal{A}$. Since OPT is at least as good as any individual algorithm, the cost of OPT is at most the average cost of the set of the algorithms, which is typically much smaller than that of $\mathcal{A}$.

For the general set of states $\mathcal{S}$, we have the following result.

Theorem 6.3.1 *The competitive ratio of any deterministic online algorithm for the MTS is at least $2|\mathcal{S}| - 1$.*

The proof follows similarly to the $|\mathcal{S}| = 2$ case, where the input is as defined in (6.3). There are of course more choices of states for any deterministic online algorithm $\mathcal{A}$; however, that only helps OPT. Compared to B_1, B_2, and B_3 defined for the $|\mathcal{S}| = 2$ case, in the general case, define $2|\mathcal{S}| - 1$ algorithms $B_1, B_2, \ldots, B_{2|\mathcal{S}|-1}$ such that the following (as in $|\mathcal{S}| = 2$ case) invariant holds at each time t:

1. exactly two algorithms among $B_1, B_2, \ldots, B_{2|\mathcal{S}|-1}$ are in each state $s \in \mathcal{S}$ other than the state that $\mathcal{A}$ is in,

2. exactly one algorithm among $B_1, B_2, \ldots, B_{2|\mathcal{S}|-1}$ has the same state as the state that $\mathcal{A}$ is in, and

3. at most one algorithm among $B_1, B_2, \ldots, B_{2|\mathcal{S}|-1}$ switches state at any time t.

Rest of the proof remains the same, and is left as an exercise in Problem 6.1.

Remark 6.3.2 *The continuous state space version of the MTS is when the set of states $\mathcal{S}$ is a continuous set, e.g., a closed subset of $\mathbb{R}^n$, while the cost to serve a request in state $s \in \mathcal{S}$ is $r(s)$, as usual. Applying Theorem 6.3.1 directly results in unbounded competitive ratio for any deterministic online algorithm, since $|\mathcal{S}|$ is unbounded. The MTS can be made meaningful in this case by considering a relation between $r(s_1)$ and $r(s_2)$ for any $s_1, s_2 \in \mathcal{S}$, e.g., r being L-Lipschitz $|r(s_1) - r(s_2)| \leq L|s_1 - s_2|$ or β-smooth, i.e., $|\nabla r(s_1) - \nabla r(s_2)| \leq \beta |s_1 - s_2|$. We will see one such example in Chapter 17, where we will consider r that is strongly convex, and for which a deterministic online algorithm for the MTS with constant competitive ratio can be derived over a continuous state space.*

6.3.1 Optimal Deterministic Algorithm

In this section, we present an algorithm called *work-function* (WFA), that has an optimal competitive ratio of at most $2|\mathcal{S}| - 1$. At any time t, for each state $s \in \mathcal{S}$, WFA computes the *locally optimal* cost for serving all the requests seen so far and reaching the state s, using only the request sequence seen so far. Then given its current state, WFA moves to a new state that minimizes the sum of the *locally optimal* cost of that state and the switching cost from the current state to that state.

To be precise, let $\sigma^i = (r_1, r_2, \ldots r_i)$ be the i-length prefix of the input that has been revealed so far. For each state $s \in \mathcal{S}$, define $w_i(s)$ to be the cost of OPT that serves σ^i and then transitions to state s. This cost can be written out as the following recursion:

$$w_0(s) = d(s(0), s), \tag{6.4}$$

$$w_i(s) = \min_{x \in S}\{w_{i-1}(x) + r_i(x) + d(x, s)\}, \tag{6.5}$$

where for the second equality $w_{i-1}(x)$ is OPT's cost till the previous step if its final state is x, $r_i(x)$ is cost of serving request r_i in state x, and $d(x, s)$ is the switching cost from state x to the final state s.

By definition, for OPT,

$$C_{\text{OPT}}(\sigma) = \min_{s \in S} w_T(s), \tag{6.6}$$

where T is the length of the input.

OPT, knowing the full input in advance, can compute the set of states $s_{\text{OPT}}(t)$ for all $1 \le t \le T$ using the backward recursion to solve $\min_{s \in S} w_T(s)$. For an online algorithm that is not possible, since at time i, its knowledge is only σ^i. Thus, WFA tries to mimic OPT using only σ^i while incorporating the switching cost, defined as follows.

WFA: Let WFA be in state s_{i-1} after serving σ^{i-1}. Then on the arrival of request r_i, WFA moves to state s_i such that

$$s_i = \arg\min_{x \in S}\{w_i(x) + d(s_{i-1}, x)\}. \tag{6.7}$$

The motivation for (6.7) is that knowing only σ^i, OPT will be in state $s_i^\star$ at time i, where $s_i^\star = \arg\min_{s \in S} w_i(s)$. However, given its sub-optimal decisions so far, WFA is currently in state s_{i-1} from which moving to $s_i^\star$ might be costly. Thus, (6.7) chooses a linear combination of the two costs and moves to a state with the smallest sum of the costs.

We illustrate the working of WFA and OPT using the following simple example.

Example 6.3.3

Let there be only two states s_1 and s_2, and, without loss of generality, let the state at time 0 be $s(0) = s_1$ for any algorithm. Let the input at time 1 be $r_1(s_1) = 1, r_1(s_2) = a$, and at time 2 be $r_2(s_1) = b, r_2(s_2) = c$, and let the distance cost be $d(s_1, s_2) = d(s_2, s_1) = x$. Computing the recursion (6.5), we get $w_1(s_1) = \min\{1, 2x + a\}, w_1(s_2) = \min\{1 + x, x + a\}$. Let $x + a < 1 < 2x + a$. Then, we get $w_1(s_1) = 1, w_1(s_2) = x + a$. Continuing on, we get $w_2(s_1) = \min\{1 + b, x + a + c + x\}, w_2(s_2) = \min\{1 + b + x, x + a + c\}$. Choosing $b > a + c$, we get that OPT *will choose to be in state s_2 after serving the second request and $C_{OPT} = x + a + c$. Thus, the optimal solution is to switch to state s_2 at time 1 and then stay there at time 2.*

For WFA, $1 = w_1(s_1) + d(s_1, s_1) < w_1(s_2) + d(s_1, s_2) = 2x + a$, and thus it will choose to remain in state s_1 at time 1. Given its state s_1 at the end of time slot 1, the two possible costs for WFA in second time slot are $w_2(s_1) + d(s_1, s_1) = \min\{1 + b, x + a + c + x\}$ and $w_2(s_2) + d(s_1, s_2) = \min\{1 + b + x, x + a + c\} + x$. Now depending on the exact values of x, b, a, c even when $b > a + c$ and $x + a < 1 < 2x + a$, WFA will either choose state 1 or 2 at the end of time slot 2. This example also illustrates why WFA is not OPT.

In place of WFA, a more natural algorithm is greedy, which given that it is in state s_{i-1} at time t_{i-1}, chooses a state s_i that minimizes $r_i(s_i) + d(s_{i-1}, s_i)$. One can show that this algorithm has an arbitrarily large competitive ratio. For example, for the special case of the MTS, the k-server problem, this result is discussed in Problem 6.4.

It is worth noting that there might be multiple solutions to (6.7). The one that WFA picks satisfies

$$w_i(s_i) = w_{i-1}(s_i) + r_i(s_i). \tag{6.8}$$

What (6.8) implies is that the choice of the state s_i made by WFA is such that the cost of OPT after serving σ^i and moving to state s_i is equal to the cost of OPT after serving σ^{i-1} and moving to state s_i plus the cost of serving the ith request in state s_i. We next show that there exists s_i satisfying both (6.7) and (6.8).

Lemma 6.3.4 *There exists s_i that satisfies both (6.7) and (6.8).*

Proof: Let $u \in \mathcal{S}$ that satisfies (6.7), i.e.,

$$w_i(u) + d(s_{i-1}, u) \le w_i(x) + d(s_{i-1}, x), \forall x \in \mathcal{S}, \tag{6.9}$$

for a given s_{i-1}. Let $v \in \mathcal{S}$ be the optimizer of (6.5) for the state u, i.e.,

$$w_i(u) = w_{i-1}(v) + r_i(v) + d(v, u). \tag{6.10}$$

We want to show that $s_i = v$ is a possible option for WFA, i.e., v satisfies both (6.7) and (6.8).
Towards that end, consider

$$w_i(v) + d(s_{i-1}, v) \overset{(a)}{\le} w_{i-1}(v) + r_i(v) + d(s_{i-1}, v), \tag{6.11}$$

$$\overset{(b)}{=} w_i(u) - d(v, u) + d(s_{i-1}, v),$$

$$\overset{(c)}{\le} w_i(u) + d(s_{i-1}, u), \tag{6.12}$$

where (a) follows since by definition, $w_i(v) \le w_{i-1}(v) + r_i(v)$, while (b) follows from (6.10), and finally (c) follows from the triangle inequality $d(s_{i-1}, v) \le d(s_{i-1}, u) + d(v, u)$.
Since (6.9) is true for any $x \in \mathcal{S}$, choosing $x = v$, we get

$$w_i(u) + d(s_{i-1}, u) \le w_i(v) + d(s_{i-1}, v). \tag{6.13}$$

Combining (6.13) with (6.12), we get

$$w_i(v) + d(s_{i-1}, v) = w_i(u) + d(s_{i-1}, u),$$

and as a result (6.11) is also an equality which gives us

$$w_i(v) = w_{i-1}(v) + r_i(v).$$

Thus, v satisfies both (6.7) and (6.8). ∎

In light of Lemma 6.3.4, we can equivalently say that WFA chooses a state s_i satisfying both (6.7) and (6.8). This property is also useful in the following proof where we bound the competitive ratio of WFA.

Theorem 6.3.5 *The competitive ratio of* WFA *is at most* $2|\mathcal{S}| - 1$.

Proof: Let the choice of state made by WFA be s_t in time t. Define a potential function

$$\Phi(t) = w_t(s_t) + \sum_{s \neq s_t} 2w_t(s). \tag{6.14}$$

We will show that the cost of WFA at time t, $C_{\text{WFA}}(t)$, satisfies

$$C_{\text{WFA}}(t) \leq \Phi(t) - \Phi(t - 1). \tag{6.15}$$

Towards that end, recall that

$$C_{\text{WFA}}(t) = r_t(s_t) + d(s_{t-1}, s_t). \tag{6.16}$$

We will bound both of these terms separately as a function of $\Phi(t)$. From the definition of the state s_t chosen by WFA, i.e., (6.7), we have

$$w_t(s_t) + d(s_{t-1}, s_t) = \arg\min_{x \in S}\{w_t(x) + d(s_{t-1}, x)\},$$
$$\leq w_t(s_{t-1}) + d(s_{t-1}, s_{t-1}),$$
$$= w_t(s_{t-1}),$$

where the last equality follows since $d(s_{t-1}, s_{t-1}) = 0$. Thus, we get

$$d(s_{t-1}, s_t) \leq w_t(s_{t-1}) - w_t(s_t). \tag{6.17}$$

Moreover, from (6.8) we also have

$$r_t(s_t) = w_t(s_t) - w_{t-1}(s_t). \tag{6.18}$$

Combining (6.16), (6.17), and (6.18), we get

$$C_{\text{WFA}}(t) \leq w_t(s_{t-1}) - w_{t-1}(s_t). \tag{6.19}$$

Next, we bound the difference $\Phi(t) - \Phi(t-1)$ as follows.

$$\Phi(t) - \Phi(t-1) = w_t(s_t) + \sum_{s \neq s_t} 2w_t(s) - \left(w_{t-1}(s_{t-1}) + \sum_{s \neq s_{t-1}} 2w_{t-1}(s) \right),$$

$$= \sum_{s \neq s_t, s_{t-1}} 2(w_t(s) - w_{t-1}(s)) + 2w_t(s_{t-1}) + w_t(s_t) - 2w_{t-1}(s_t) - w_{t-1}(s_{t-1}),$$

$$\overset{(a)}{\geq} 2w_t(s_{t-1}) - w_{t-1}(s_{t-1}) + w_t(s_t) - 2w_{t-1}(s_t),$$

$$\overset{(b)}{\geq} w_t(s_{t-1}) - w_{t-1}(s_t),$$

$$\overset{(c)}{\geq} C_{\text{WFA}}(t),$$

where (a) and (b) follow since $w_t(s) \geq w_{t-1}(s)$ by definition, while (c) follows from (6.19). Thus, we have shown (6.15).

Next, using (6.15), we complete the proof of the theorem. By definition,

$$C_{\text{WFA}} = \sum_{t=1}^{T} C_{\text{WFA}}(t),$$

$$\overset{(a)}{\leq} \Phi(T) - \Phi(0),$$

$$\overset{(b)}{\leq} (2|\mathcal{S}| - 1) \max_{s \in \mathcal{S}} w_T(s) - \Phi(0),$$

$$\overset{(c)}{=} (2|\mathcal{S}| - 1) \max_{s \in \mathcal{S}} \min_{x \in \mathcal{S}} \{w_{T-1}(x) + r_T(x) + d(x, s)\} - \Phi(0),$$

$$\overset{(d)}{\leq} (2|\mathcal{S}| - 1) \min_{x \in \mathcal{S}} \{w_{T-1}(x) + r_T(x)\} + (2|\mathcal{S}| - 1) \max_{x, y \in \mathcal{S}} d(x, y) - \Phi(0),$$

$$\overset{(e)}{\leq} (2|\mathcal{S}| - 1) \min_{x, s \in \mathcal{S}} \{w_{T-1}(x) + r_T(x) + d(x, s)\} + (2|\mathcal{S}| - 1) \max_{x, y \in \mathcal{S}} d(x, y) - \Phi(0),$$

$$\overset{(f)}{\leq} (2|\mathcal{S}| - 1) \min_{s \in \mathcal{S}} w_T(s) + \eta,$$

$$\overset{(g)}{\leq} (2|\mathcal{S}| - 1) C_{\text{OPT}} + \eta,$$

where (a) follows from (6.15), (b) is a trivial upper bound that follows from the definition of $\Phi(T)$ (6.14) by upper bounding each term $w_T(s)$ of $\Phi(T)$ by $\max_{s \in \mathcal{S}} w_T(s)$, (c) follows by writing out the definition of $w_T(s)$ from (6.5), to obtain (d) we separate the terms involving $w_{T-1}(x) + r_T(x)$ and $d(x, s)$ inside the maximum, while (e) follows since $d(x, s) \geq 0$, to get (f) we reuse the definition of $w_T(s)$ from (6.5) and $\eta = (2|\mathcal{S}| - 1) \max_{x, y \in \mathcal{S}} d(x, y) - \Phi(0)$ is a constant, and finally, (g) follows from the definition of C_{OPT} (6.6). ∎

So far we have shown that the competitive ratio of any deterministic algorithm is at least $2|\mathcal{S}| - 1$, and that can be achieved by WFA. An immediate question is: what about randomized algorithms? We discuss this in Section 6.3.3 after introducing a continuous time model for the MTS in the next section.

6.3.2 Continuous Time Model

So far we have considered a discrete model for the MTS, where any online algorithm can transition between states at consecutive integer time instants at which a request arrives. It is useful sometimes to make the MTS applicable in continuous time, where an algorithm is allowed to switch states in between two requests as well. We describe this model as follows. Let the discrete time instants at which the requests arrive be $t_1, t_2, \ldots$, where $t_j - t_{j-1} = 1 \; \forall \, j$.

Let the instants at which a continuous-time online algorithm $\mathcal{A}_c$ for the MTS switches states be $\tau_1, \tau_2, \ldots$ where compared to the discrete-time model, τ_i's can be arbitrary positive real numbers. For $\mathcal{A}_c$, let the state it occupies between time $[\tau_i, \tau_{i+1}]$ be s_i. For a unit length interval $[t_j, t_j + 1]$ that corresponds to the arrival times of two consecutive requests, the cost for $\mathcal{A}_c$ is then defined as

$$C_{\mathcal{A}_c}(j) = \sum_i \rho_i r_j(s_i) + \sum_i d(s_i, s_{i+1}),$$

where the sum is over index i that corresponds to the epochs where $\mathcal{A}_c$ switched states within $[t_j, t_j + 1]$, and ρ_i is the fraction of time in time interval $[t_j, t_j + 1]$ for which $\mathcal{A}_c$ occupied state s_i. The overall cost of $\mathcal{A}_c$ is

$$C_{\mathcal{A}_c} = \sum_{j=1}^{T} C_{\mathcal{A}_c}(j).$$

Importantly, there is a way to connect the cost of $\mathcal{A}_c$ with a discrete-time algorithm $\mathcal{A}_d$ for the MTS. In particular, we will show that $C_{\mathcal{A}_d} \le C_{\mathcal{A}_c}$ as follows. Let the set of states visited by $\mathcal{A}_c$ in interval $[t_j, t_j + 1]$ be $\mathcal{S}_j$, where r_j is requested at time t_j. The corresponding discrete algorithm $\mathcal{A}_d$ changes state at time t_j to $s_j^\star$, where $s_j^\star = \arg\min_{s \in \mathcal{S}_j} r_j(s)$. Thus, the state cost of $\mathcal{A}_d$ is at most the state cost of $\mathcal{A}_c$. Moreover, the movement cost of $\mathcal{A}_c$ is $\sum_i d(s_i, s_{i+1})$ while that of $\mathcal{A}_d$ is just $d(s_{j-1}, s_j^\star)$. Using the definition of $s_j^\star$ and the triangle inequality, it is easy to argue that $d(s_{j-1}, s_j^\star) \le \sum_i d(s_i, s_{i+1})$. We leave the formal argument as an exercise. Hence $C_{\mathcal{A}_d} \le C_{\mathcal{A}_c}$ and, therefore, considering a continuous time model does not entail any extra cost penalty; however, it can be useful for analysis, as we show in Problem 6.2.

6.3.3 Randomized Algorithms

The major question that we want to address in this section is: what is the competitive ratio of randomized online algorithms for the MTS? In this section, we will restrict our attention to the uniform MTS, where $d(x, y) = c$ for all $x, y \in \mathcal{S}$ and $c > 0$ is a constant, while $d(x, x) = 0$. For the uniform MTS, we next propose a randomized online algorithm and show that its competitive ratio is $\mathcal{O}(\log |\mathcal{S}|)$, which is a fundamental improvement from the $\Omega(|\mathcal{S}|)$ lower bound we derived for any deterministic online algorithm.

For proceeding further, without loss of generality, we let uniform MTS constant $c = 1$. Consider the following continuous-time algorithm. Let phase i begin at time τ_{i-1}, with $\tau_0 = 0$. Consider a time $t > \tau_{i-1}$ in phase i and recall that $j \in \mathbb{N} \cap [\tau_{i-1}, t]$ are all the time instants where a new request r_j arrives in interval $[\tau_{i-1}, t]$. Within a phase i, a state $s \in \mathcal{S}$ is defined to be *saturated* at time $t > \tau_{i-1}$ if the state cost to stay continuously in state s during the interval $[\tau_{i-1}, t]$ is at least 1, i.e.,

$$\sum_{j \in \mathbb{N} \cap [\tau_{i-1}, t]} \ell_j r_j(s) \geq 1,$$

where ℓ_j is the time interval within $[\tau_{i-1}, t]$ for which r_j is the request (that arrives at time t_j and stays until $t_j + 1$). A state that is not saturated at time t is called *unsaturated*. Notice that several states can become saturated at the same time.

Algorithm RAND-MTS: At the start of a new phase, all states are made unsaturated, and the algorithm chooses a state uniformly randomly among all the states. During a phase, the algorithm remains in the same state until it becomes saturated, at which point it switches to any of the unsaturated states at that time uniformly randomly. The phase ends when all the states become saturated.

A careful look suggests a distinct similarity between RAND-MTS and MARKING described in Chapter 5 for the paging problem.

Theorem 6.3.6 *The competitive ratio of* RAND-MTS *is at most* $2H_{|\mathcal{S}|}$, *where* H_n *is the harmonic number with index n.*

Proof is left as an exercise in Problem 6.2. To complement this upper bound, we have the following lower bound.

Theorem 6.3.7 *The competitive ratio of any randomized algorithm is at least* $H_{|\mathcal{S}|}$.

Proof of Theorem 6.3.7 is very similar to the lower bound proof for any randomized algorithm for the paging problem (Lemma 5.6.2) and is left as an exercise.

After discussing the abstract MTS problem in sufficient detail, we next turn our attention to a famous special case of the MTS, namely the k-server problem.

6.4 k-Server Problem

In this section, we consider a very popular special case of the MTS, called the k-server problem. The metric version of the k-server problem is as follows.

Definition 6.4.1 *Consider a metric space $\mathcal{M}$ with distance metric d. There are k servers, and let the location vector of the k servers at time t be X_t, where each element of $X_t \in \mathcal{M}$. The input $\sigma = (r_1, \ldots, r_n)$ is a stream of points in $\mathcal{M}$, where a newly arrived point r_t at time t is defined to be* **served**, *if r_t is an element of X_t. The cost for serving request r_t is equal to $d(X_{t-1}, X_t)$, and the objective is to minimize the sum of the costs for serving all the requested points $\sum_t d(X_{t-1}, X_t)$.*

Remark 6.4.2 *The paging problem considered in Chapter 5 is a special case of the k-server problem, where $d(u, v) = 1$ for all $u \neq v$.*

In light of Remark 6.4.2, we get from Lemma 5.4.2 that no deterministic algorithm can have a competitive ratio of less than k. The k-server problem is inherently a hard problem, and optimal results (competitive ratio of k) are available only for specific values of k. For example, the case of $k = 1$ (which is trivial), $k = 2$, and $k = |\mathcal{M}| - 1$.

One natural choice for solving the k-server problem is to move the server that is located closest to the newly requested point. One can show that this 'greedy' algorithm is uncompetitive (Problem 6.4). A randomized version of the greedy algorithm called HARMONIC, however, has a bounded competitive ratio. With HARMONIC, instead of moving the closest server, move any server with probability that is proportional to the distance from the newly requested point. For example, let x be the requested point, and the existing locations of servers be $x_1, ..., x_k$. Then move server i to location x with probability $p_i = \dfrac{c}{d(x_i, x)}$, for some constant c to satisfy $\sum_{i=1}^k p_i = 1$.

Lemma 6.4.3 *Algorithm* HARMONIC *is* $\left(\dfrac{5}{4}k2^k - 2k\right)$-*competitive.*

The analysis for proving this result is fairly involved and we refer the reader to [78] for more details. We solve the special case of $k = 2$ in Problem 6.8.

A more powerful algorithm is WFA that has been defined for the MTS in Section 6.3.1, for which the following stronger guarantee is available.

Lemma 6.4.4 [79] WFA *is* $2k - 1$-*competitive for the k-server problem.*

The analysis for proving this result is long and complex and we refer the reader to [79] for more details.

In the rest of the chapter, we consider the k-server problem in one-dimension and show that the *double coverage* DC algorithm, which moves two servers on each new request, has the optimal competitive ratio of k.

Algorithm DC: Let the ordered locations (left to right) of the k servers for DC just before the request r_t is made be $x_1(t) \leq ... \leq x_k(t)$. Then if request r_t is such that $r_t < x_1(t)$ or $r_t > x_k(t)$, then $x_1(t^+) = r_t$ or $x_k(t^+) = r_t$, respectively, while keeping the locations of all the other $k - 1$ servers the same. Otherwise, let $x_i(t) \leq r_t \leq x_{i+1}(t)$ for some i. Let $L = \min\{|x_i(t) - r_t|, |x_{i+1}(t) - r_t|\}$. Then move both $x_i(t)$ and $x_{i+1}(t)$ a distance of L towards r_t. Clearly, at least one among $x_i(t^+)$ and $x_{i+1}(t^+)$ is equal to r_t, i.e., one of the servers is at r_t making DC feasible. A pictorial description of DC is provided in Figure 6.1. It is not entirely obvious why it is better to move two servers compared to a single server with the greedy algorithm that has an unbounded competitive ratio.

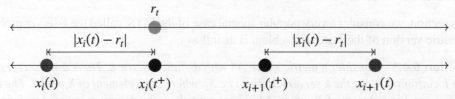

Figure 6.1 Illustration of algorithm DC that moves two servers on each request, where the light grey dot represents the location of the new request r_t, dark grey dots are the locations of the two nearest servers to r_t just before the request r_t's arrival, and the black dots represent their new locations.

Theorem 6.4.5 *The competitive ratio of DC is at most k.*

Proof: Let $x_1^o(t) \leq \ldots \leq x_k^o(t)$ be the ordered locations (left to right) of the k servers for OPT just before request r_t. Define the potential function

$$\Phi(t) = k \underbrace{\sum_{i=1}^{k} |x_i(t) - x_i^o(t)|}_{\Phi_1(t)} + \underbrace{\sum_{i<j} (x_j(t) - x_i(t))}_{\Phi_2(t)}, \tag{6.20}$$

where Φ_1 counts the distance between the locations of DC and OPT, while Φ_2 captures how the locations are spread with DC, respectively. To prove the result we will use the following Lemma, where $\Delta\Phi(t) = \Phi(t) - \Phi(t-1)$.

Lemma 6.4.6 *The contribution to $\Delta\Phi(t)$ because of OPT's actions is*

$$\Delta\Phi(t) \leq k\Delta C_{OPT}(t),$$

where $\Delta C_{OPT}(t)$ is the change in the cost of OPT at time t, while the contribution to $\Delta\Phi(t)$ because of DC's actions is

$$\Delta\Phi(t) \leq -\Delta C_{DC}(t),$$

$\Delta C_{DC}(t)$ is the change in the cost of DC at time t.

From Lemma 6.4.6,

$$\sum_{t=1}^{T} \Delta\Phi(t) \leq \sum_{t=1}^{T} k\Delta C_{OPT}(t) - \sum_{t=1}^{T} \Delta C_{DC}(t) = kC_{OPT} - C_{DC}. \tag{6.21}$$

Moreover,

$$\sum_{t=1}^{T} \Delta\Phi(t) = \Phi(T) - \Phi(0).$$

Note that $\Delta\Phi(t) \geq 0$ for any t by definition. Thus, we get from (6.21) that

$$C_{DC} \leq kC_{OPT} + \Phi(0).$$

Note that $\Phi(0)$ only depends on the initial location of the k servers, making it a fixed constant. Thus, one can argue that for a long enough input, both C_{OPT} and C_{DC} are large enough, and we can ignore $\Phi(0)$. Another workaround is to assume that the initial location for all servers is the same for any algorithm and in which case $\Phi(0) = 0$. In either case, we get the required result. ∎

Next, we present the remaining proof of Lemma 6.4.6.

Proof: [Proof of Lemma 6.4.6] First, we count the contribution of OPT's action to $\Delta\Phi(t)$. It can be argued that for the k-server problem, OPT only moves one server on the arrival of each new request (see Problem 6.3). Using this fact, let on request at r_t, OPT move the server located at $x_j^o(t)$ to r_t. Thus, $\Delta C_{\text{OPT}}(t) = |x_j^o(t) - r_t|$. The action of OPT only changes $\Phi_1(t)$, and even for $\Phi_1(t)$ only one term in the summation changes, in particular the jth term. Because of $x_j^o(t)$ moving to r_t, the change in $\Phi_1(t)$ is at most k times $|x_j^o(t) - r_t|$. Thus, we get

$$\Delta\Phi(t) \leq k\Delta C_{\text{OPT}}(t).$$

Next, we count the contribution of DC's action to $\Delta\Phi(t)$.

- Case 1 $r_t < x_1(t)$ or $r_t > x_k(t)$. Without loss of generality, let $r_t < x_1(t)$. Thus, DC only moves $x_1(t)$ to r_t and $x_1(t^+) = r_t$, which implies

$$\Delta C_{\text{DC}}(t) = |x_1(t) - r_t|.$$

To bound $\Delta\Phi(t)$ we proceed as follows. Given that OPT has moved its jth server to r_t, and $j \geq 1$, and $r_t < x_1(t)$, we know that $|x_1^o - x_1|$ decreases by distance $|x_1(t) - r_t|$. Thus, $\Delta\Phi_1(t) = -k|x_1(t) - r_t|$. While for $\Phi_2(t)$, distance between $x_1(t)$ and $x_j(t)$ for each $j = 2, \ldots, k - 1$ increases by $|x_1(t) - r_t|$. Thus, overall

$$\Delta\Phi(t) \leq -k|x_1(t) - r_t| + (k - 1)|x_1(t) - r_t| = -|x_1(t) - r_t| = -\Delta C_{\text{DC}}(t).$$

- Case 2 $x_i(t) \leq r_t \leq x_{i+1}(t)$. Without loss of generality, let $x_i(t)$ be closer to r_t than $x_{i+1}(t)$. Since DC moves both x_i and x_{i+1} by distance $|x_i(t) - r_t|$,

$$\Delta C_{\text{DC}}(t) = 2|x_i(t) - r_t|. \tag{6.22}$$

Similar to Case 1, if $j \leq i$, then $x_i^o(t^+) \geq r_t$, and thus the change in $|x_i^o - x_i|$, $\Delta|x_i^o - x_i| = -|x_i(t) - r_t|$. However, for location x_{i+1}^o, it can be either $x_{i+1}^o(t^+) \geq x_{i+1}(t^+)$ or $x_{i+1}^o(t^+) < x_{i+1}(t^+)$. Thus, $\Delta|x_{i+1}^o(t) - x_{i+1}(t)| \leq |x_i(t) - r_t|$. Otherwise, when $j > i$, $x_{i+1}^o(t^+) \leq r_t$, and we get $\Delta|x_i^o - x_i| \leq |x_i(t) - r_t|$ and $\Delta|x_{i+1}^o(t) - x_{i+1}(t)| = -|x_i(t) - r_t|$. Thus, essentially, irrespective of whether $j \leq i$ or $j > i$,

$$\Delta\Phi_1(t) = 0. \tag{6.23}$$

Next, we consider $\Delta\Phi_2(t)$. By definition of i, there are $i - 1$ servers to the left of $x_i(t)$ and $k - i$ on the right side of $x_i(t)$. Similarly, there are i servers to the left of $x_{i+1}(t)$ and $k - i - 1$ on the right side of $x_{i+1}(t)$. The movement of $x_i(t)$ to r_t (i.e. $x_i(t^+) = r_t$) increases the distance of the $i - 1$ servers to the left while decreases the distance of the $k - i$ servers to the right by the same amount of $|x_i(t) - r_t|$. An exact opposite relationship holds for the movement of $x_{i+1}(t)$. Thus, we get

$$\Delta\Phi_2(t) = ((i - 1) - (k - i))|x_i(t) - r_t| + (-i + (k - i - 1))|x_i(t) - r_t|,$$
$$= -2|x_i(t) - r_t|. \tag{6.24}$$

Combining (6.22), (6.23), and (6.24), we get

$$\Delta\Phi(t) = -\Delta C_{DC}(t), \tag{6.25}$$

as required.   ∎

Remark 6.4.7 *For the greedy algorithm that moves only one server that is nearest to the request, (6.24) will not be true.*

After this brief discussion on the k-server problem, we present a generic technique to combine multiple online algorithms to create a single algorithm that has better competitive ratio performance than all the original online algorithms. In principle, this strategy is feasible for any online problem; however, to make it work, the precise nature of the problem has to be exploited. Next, we show that it is possible for the uniform k-server problem.

6.4.1 Combining Multiple Online Algorithms

Using the k-server problem in the uniform metric space (where distance between any two states is 1, i.e., $d(x, y) = 1$ for all $x, y \in \mathcal{S}$) as an example, in this subsection, we describe a strategy for combining multiple online algorithms to produce a 'better' online algorithm. This technique can be called bootstrapping or boosting.

Let $\mathcal{B}_1, \ldots, \mathcal{B}_m$ be m distinct deterministic online algorithms for the k-server problem. As usual, an online algorithm $\mathcal{A}$ is μ_i competitive against $\mathcal{B}_i$ if

$$C_{\mathcal{A}}(\sigma) \leq \mu_i C_{\mathcal{B}_i}(\sigma)$$

for all inputs σ.

Definition 6.4.8 *For a given $\mathcal{B}_1, \ldots, \mathcal{B}_\ell$, a sequence $\boldsymbol{\mu} = (\mu_1, \ldots, \mu_\ell)$ is defined to be realizable if there exists a deterministic online algorithm $\mathcal{A}$ such that*

$$C_{\mathcal{A}}(\sigma) \leq \mu_i C_{\mathcal{B}_i}(\sigma), \ \forall \ \sigma \ and \ i = 1, \ldots, \ell.$$

We next show that if and only if

$$\sum_{i=1}^{\ell} \frac{1}{\mu_i} \leq 1, \tag{6.26}$$

a realizable sequence $\boldsymbol{\mu}$ exists.

Theorem 6.4.9 *A realizable sequence $\boldsymbol{\mu}$ exists if and only if (6.26) is satisfied.*

Before providing the proof, we discuss an important ramification of Theorem 6.4.9 as follows.

Let the set of all possible inputs be σ, and consider its two disjoint subsets σ_1 and σ_2 such that $\sigma \subseteq \sigma_1 \cup \sigma_2$. Let there be two deterministic online algorithms $\mathcal{B}_1$ and $\mathcal{B}_2$ such that

$$C_{\mathcal{B}_i}(\sigma) \leq \mu_i' C_{OPT}(\sigma), \ \forall \ \sigma \in \sigma_i \ and \ i = 1, 2.$$

Thus, $\mathcal{B}_i$ is being compared against OPT only for input belonging to σ_i, implying that $\mu_i' \leq \mu_i''$, where

$$C_{\mathcal{B}_i}(\sigma) \leq \mu_i'' C_{\text{OPT}}(\sigma), \ \forall \, \sigma \in \sigma, \ i = 1, 2.$$

Then Theorem 6.4.9 implies that there exists a deterministic online algorithm $\mathcal{A}$ with a competitive ratio of at most $2 \max\{\mu_1', \mu_2'\}$ against OPT over all inputs belonging to σ by choosing $\mu_1 = \mu_2 = 2$. At this stage, an obvious temptation is to partition σ into, say, ℓ partitions (with ℓ large) for which we can find a 'good' (with competitive ratio close to 1) online algorithm for each partition, and then combine these ℓ good online algorithms to produce a single online algorithm. Taking this to the extreme, choosing $\ell = |\sigma|$ with partition i, σ_i, of size $|\sigma_i| = 1$, we know that we can find $\mathcal{B}_i = \text{OPT}$ for each σ_i, i.e., $\mu_i' = 1$. However, making ℓ large results in an effective competitive ratio of ℓ from (6.26) choosing $\mu_i = \ell, \ \forall \, i$. Thus, the power of Theorem 6.4.9 has to be extracted non-trivially by choosing the number of partitions ℓ judiciously, and constructing an online algorithm with a small competitive ratio for each partition.

Proof: [Proof of Theorem 6.4.9] We only prove the sufficiency part of the theorem. For necessity, see [80]. Recall that we are considering the uniform k-server problem, where $d(x, y) = 1$ for all $x, y \in \mathcal{S}$ and $\mathcal{S}$ is the set of all states.

The algorithm $\mathcal{A}$ that we will construct will be required to be *lazy*, i.e., it moves a server only on a request to a state that is not already covered by a server.

Consider a fixed input σ. For any state $v \in \mathcal{S}$ and for an online algorithm $\mathcal{G}$, a time interval $[t_1, t_2)$ is defined to be a v-interval if on input σ, $\mathcal{G}$ moves a server to v at time t_1, leaves the server at v until just before time t_2, and then moves the server from v on request made at time t_2.

We need one more definition to relate the cost of $\mathcal{A}$ with the cost of $\mathcal{B}_i$'s. An online algorithm $\mathcal{G}_1$ is defined to *punish* another online algorithm $\mathcal{G}_2$ at time t_2 if there exists a $v \in \mathcal{S}$ and time $t_1 < t_2$, such that $[t_1, t_2)$ is a v-interval for $\mathcal{G}_1$, while for some t_1', t_2' such that $t_1' \leq t_1 < t_2' \leq t_2$, $[t_1', t_2')$ is a v-interval for $\mathcal{G}_2$.

Cost-punishing instance relation: An important implication of this definition is that the cost of $\mathcal{G}$ on input σ is at least as much as the number of time slots where $\mathcal{A}$ punishes $\mathcal{G}$ with input σ, since $\mathcal{A}$ is lazy, and the cost of moving between any two states is 1.

Consider time t where the tth request is made and the input revealed so far is $\sigma^t = \{\sigma_1, \dots, \sigma_t\}$. Let the set of k states that the servers of $\mathcal{A}$ cover just before the arrival of the tth request be $S_{\mathcal{A}}(t^-)$ and let $\sigma_t \notin S_{\mathcal{A}}(t^-)$. Thus, the cost of $\mathcal{A}$ at time t will be 1. Similarly, let $S_{\mathcal{B}_i}(t + 1^-)$ be the set of k states that the servers of $\mathcal{B}_i$ cover just before the arrival of the $t + 1^{st}$ request. Note that since the request σ_t has to be fulfilled by $\mathcal{B}_i$, $\sigma_t \in S_{\mathcal{B}_i}(t + 1^-)$. Since $|S_{\mathcal{A}}(t^-)| = |S_{\mathcal{B}_i}(t + 1^-)| = k$ and $\sigma_t \in S_{\mathcal{B}_i}(t + 1^-)$ while $\sigma_t \notin S_{\mathcal{A}}(t^-)$, we get that there exists a state $u \in \mathcal{S}$ that has a server with $\mathcal{A}$ at time t^- but not with $S_{\mathcal{B}_i}$ at time $t + 1^-$. Thus, $\mathcal{A}$ punishes $\mathcal{B}_i$ at time t by moving a server from u to σ_t.

Let $\text{PUN}(i, \sigma^s)$ be the number of time instances where $\mathcal{A}$ punishes $\mathcal{B}_i$ with σ^s. Let $C_{\mathcal{A}}(\sigma^s)$ be the cost of $\mathcal{A}$ with σ^s. Now let for some time instant t, $\sigma_t \notin S_{\mathcal{A}}(t^-)$, and $\mathcal{A}$ needs to move one server located at one of the states of $\mathcal{S}$ to the newly requested state σ_t. We will let $\mathcal{A}$ choose that state to move its server from, such that it punishes $\mathcal{B}_{i^\star}$ at time t, where $i^\star = \arg\min \mu_i(\text{PUN}(i, \sigma^{t-1}) + 1)$, and recall that μ_i is the desired competitive ratio of $\mathcal{A}$ against $\mathcal{B}_i$. From the above discussion we know that $\mathcal{A}$ can punish $\mathcal{B}_i$ when $\sigma_t \notin S_{\mathcal{A}}(t^-)$.

This is the point at which we use the fact that $\sum_{i=1}^{\ell} \frac{1}{\mu_i} \leq 1$. From the above construction, by the time $\mathcal{A}$ incurs a total cost of r, $\mathcal{A}$ punishes $\mathcal{B}_i$ for at least $\left\lceil \frac{r}{\mu_i} \right\rceil$ time slots as long as $\sum_{i=1}^{\ell} \frac{1}{\mu_i} \leq 1$. Thus, from the cost-punishing instance relation, we get

$$C_{\mathcal{A}}(\sigma) \leq \mu_i C_{\mathcal{B}_i}(\sigma), \ \forall \ \sigma \text{ and } i = 1, \ldots, \ell,$$

as long as $\sum_{i=1}^{\ell} \frac{1}{\mu_i} \leq 1$. ∎

6.5 Notes

The MTS problem was introduced in [77], where both the lower bound (of $2|\mathcal{S}| - 1$) presented in the chapter and the optimality of WFA were shown. For the uniform MTS, where all the distances or movement costs between states are equal, a randomized algorithm was also presented in [77] that was shown to be order-wise optimal (with expected competitive ratio $\Theta(\log |\mathcal{S}|)$). For general metric spaces, a lower bound of $\Omega\left(\frac{\log |\mathcal{S}|}{\log \log |\mathcal{S}|}\right)$ on the competitive ratio is known [81, 82], while an online algorithm with a competitive ratio $\mathcal{O}(\log |\mathcal{S}|)$ is known for a weighted star metric [72]. In a recent work [83], an $\mathcal{O}(D \log |\mathcal{S}|)$-competitive randomized algorithm for the MTS has been derived for any $|\mathcal{S}|$-point tree metric with a combinatorial depth of D. The MTS with untrusted predictions has been recently considered in [84].

An unfair version of the MTS was considered in [85], where an online algorithm is charged more state cost than an offline algorithm.

For the k-server problem, [86] showed that for no metric space can there be a deterministic online algorithm with a competitive ratio less than k with at least $k + 1$ points. Moreover, [86] also proposed the k-server conjecture that states that for any metric space, there exists an online algorithm with a competitive ratio at most k. The conjecture remains unproven till date; however, significant work has been reported in deriving algorithms with competitive ratios close to k. To begin with, [87] showed that there is an $\mathcal{O}((k!)^3)$-competitive online algorithm for all metric spaces. An 11-competitive algorithm for the $k = 3$-server problem was derived in [88]. Special cases of line, trees, and circles were studied in [89–91], respectively. WFA was shown to have a competitive ratio of 2 for the $k = 2$-server problem [92]. Moreover, for a metric space with $k + 1$ points, WFA is known to have a competitive ratio of k [93, 94]. The most general result for WFA was derived in [79] that showed its $2k - 1$-competitiveness. A simpler proof of $2k - 1$-competitiveness of WFA was derived in [95].

A class of algorithms that balance the cost incurred by each of the servers has been extensively studied in the literature starting with [86], where BALANCE was shown to be k-competitive for a metric space with $k + 1$ points. BALANCE, however, has an unbounded competitive ratio for larger metric spaces. A modification of BALANCE was proposed in [96] called BALANCE2 that is shown to have a competitive ratio of 10 when $k = 2$ for arbitrary metric spaces, and a lower bound of 6 [89] is known for BALANCE2. A generalized lower bound of $\frac{5+\sqrt{7}}{2}$ was derived in [97] for any algorithm belonging to the balance class with $k = 2$.

Prior to the best-known result for WFA [79], a randomized algorithm called HARMONIC [78] was known with a competitive ratio $\mathcal{O}(k2^k)$ whose de-randomized counterpart has a competitive ratio of $\mathcal{O}(k^2 4^k)$ [98]. For uniform metric spaces (where all distances are equal), the competitive ratio of any randomized algorithm is known to be $\Omega(\log k)$ [80], while the best-known randomized algorithm has a competitive ratio of at most $\mathcal{O}(\log^2 k \log^3 |\mathcal{S}| \log \log |\mathcal{S}|)$ [99], where $|\mathcal{S}|$ is the number of points in the metric space. It is believed that the optimal competitive ratio for the k-server problem in the randomized setting is $\Theta(\log k)$; however, a substantial gap remains in order to show this. An efficient algorithm to solve the k-server problem in the offline setting was derived in [100] that is based on finding the minimum cost flow in an appropriately defined acyclic flow network.

The basic idea of combining bootstrapping or combining multiple online algorithms was first proposed in [80] for the paging problem, and later extended to a general k-server problem in [101], and for the MTS in [102].

The book by Borodin and El-Yaniv [103] covers both the MTS and the k-server problem in more detail than this chapter. A review article [94] nicely summarizes the history of the k-server problem.

PROBLEMS

6.1 Prove Theorem 6.3.1.

6.2 Prove Theorem 6.3.6. Towards that end, show the following:

1. Show that for each phase, the cost of OPT is at least 1.

2. For any phase, define $\mathcal{T}(\ell)$ to be the expected number of state transitions that RAND-MTS makes until the end of that phase, given that there are ℓ unsaturated states remaining. We are interested in finding $\mathcal{T}(|\mathcal{S}|)$, since at the beginning of any phase all $|\mathcal{S}|$ states are unsaturated. First note that $\mathcal{T}(1) = 1$. Next, show that for $\ell > 1$,

$$\mathcal{T}(\ell) = \frac{1}{\ell} + \mathcal{T}(\ell - 1).$$

Conclude that the expected cost incurred in each phase by RAND-MTS is at most $2H_{|\mathcal{S}|}$.

3. Combine parts 1 and 2 to complete the proof of Theorem 6.3.6.

6.3 Show that for the k-server problem, OPT only moves one server on any request arrival.

6.4 Show that a greedy algorithm that moves the server that is located closest to the newly requested point has an unbounded competitive ratio for the k-server problem.

[Hint: Considering $k = 2$ and requests belonging to a line interval with distance metric being the Euclidean distance are sufficient.]

6.5 [86] In this problem, we consider a natural algorithm for the k-server problem called BALANCE. At any time t, let the cumulative distance moved by the ith-server $i = 1, 2, \ldots, k$ so far be $d^i(t)$. Then on the new request arrival at location r_t, if there is any one server at r_t, then no action is needed. Otherwise, for the ith server, let the distance needed to reach r_t from its current location be $d_i(t)$. BALANCE moves server $i^\star$ to r_t, where

$$i^\star = \arg \min_{i, i=1,\ldots,k} d^i(t) + d_i(t).$$

Thus, BALANCE moves that server which will have the least cumulative cost after movement.

1. Show that the competitive ratio of BALANCE is unbounded for $k = 2$ when there are 4 points in the metric space.

   [Hint: Consider a rectangle with vertex pairs (a, b) and (c, d) with appropriate width and height, and construct an input that makes the two servers toggle between location pairs (a, b) and (c, d) repeatedly.]

2. Remove any one vertex from the rectangular metic space example in part 1 to get a metric space with only 3 points. Show that with $k = 2$, BALANCE is at most 3-competitive.[3]

6.6 In this problem, we will consider a modification of BALANCE called BALANCE2. Compared to BALANCE, the only difference with BALANCE2 is that server $i^\star$ is moved to r_t (on its arrival), where

$$i^\star = \arg \min_{i, i=1,\ldots,k} d^i(t) + 2d_i(t),$$

where the notation has been defined in Problem 6.5. Surprisingly, BALANCE2 is 10-competitive for $k = 2$-server problem for any sized metric space in contrast to BALANCE which is un-competitive as we saw in Problem 6.5. We will not prove this result here. Instead, we will show a lower bound on its competitive ratio as follows.

Show that the competitive ratio of BALANCE2 is at least 6 using the metric space shown in Figure 6.2.

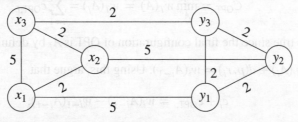

Figure 6.2 Metric space for Problem 6.6, where the number on any edge corresponds to the distance between the two end points.

---

[3] In fact a stronger result is known that BALANCE is k-competitive with $k + 1$ sized metric space.

[One possible idea: At the beginning, the servers for BALANCE2 as well as OPT are at the same points. Referring to Figure 6.2, construct an input such that at some time t, server 1 and server 2 for BALANCE2 are at x_1 and x_3, respectively, while for OPT they are at x_1 and y_2, respectively, and, importantly, $d^2(t) - d^1(t) = 1$ at this time. After time t, consider the input $r_{t+1} = y_2$, for which, importantly, $d^1(t) + 2d_1(t) = d^2(t) + 2d_2(t)$. Because of the tie, BALANCE2 will arbitrarily choose one of the two servers to move which can be exploited by the adversary.]

6.7 [93] Show that WFA has a competitive ratio of k for the k-server problem when the metric space contains $k + 1$ points.

For any algorithm, its *configuration* is the set of k points occupied by the k servers among the $k + 1$ points of the metric space. For the WFA, let the configuration just after the arrival of request r_{i-1} be A_{i-1}, i.e., $r_{i-1} \in A_{i-1}$. Let $w_i(A)$ be the optimal cost of fulfilling the first i requests and then reaching configuration A. For the k-server problem, WFA on arrival of request r_i chooses a configuration $A = A_i$ such that

$$A_i = \arg \min_A w_i(A) + d(A_{i-1}, A).$$

1. Show that to bound the competitive ratio of WFA, without loss of generality, we can assume that the configuration in which WFA ends (after all T requests have arrived) is the same as the final configuration of OPT. Let the final configuration be A_f.

   [Hint: If not, augment the input.]

2. For WFA, let on arrival of request r_i, some server moved from point $p \in A_{i-1}$ to $r_i \in A_i$ where $A_i = A_{i-1} \setminus \{p\} \cup \{r_i\}$, where A_i is such that

$$A_i = \arg \min_A w_i(A) + d(A_{i-1}, A).$$

   Define the cost of servicing r_i as $c_i = d(p, r_i)$, i.e., $C_{\text{WFA}} = \sum_i c_i$. Let $c_{\text{OPT},i} = w_i(A_i) - w_{i-1}(A_{i-1})$.

   Argue that

$$C_{\text{OPT}} = \min_A w_T(A) \stackrel{(a)}{=} w_T(A_f) = \sum_{i=1}^{T} c_{\text{OPT},i},$$

   where (a) is true since the final configuration of OPT is A_f by definition.

3. Show that $w_i(A_i) + d(p, r_i) = w_i(A_{i-1})$. Using this, argue that

$$c_i + c_{\text{OPT},i} = w_i(A_{i-1}) - w_{i-1}(A_{i-1}),$$

   which implies that

$$c_i + c_{\text{OPT},i} \leq \max_A \left(w_i(A) - w_{i-1}(A) \right).$$

Let

$$\text{EXT}_i = \max_A \left(w_i(A) - w_{i-1}(A) \right), \text{ and } \text{EXT} = \sum_{i=1}^{T} \text{EXT}_i.$$

4. Argue that if $\text{EXT} \le (\mu + 1)C_{\text{OPT}} + \text{constant}$, then the competitive ratio of WFA is μ.

5. Next, show that EXT is at most $(\mu + 1)C_{\text{OPT}} + \text{constant}$ for $\mu = k$. Towards that end, define the potential function $\Phi_{i-1} = \sum_A w_{i-1}(A)$.

   (a) Show that $\Delta \Phi = \Phi_i - \Phi_{i-1} \ge w_i(X^\star) - w_{i-1}(X^\star)$, where

   $$X^\star = \arg \max_X w_i(X) - w_{i-1}(X).$$

   (b) Using part 3 conclude that $\Phi_T - \Phi_0 \ge \text{EXT}$.
   (c) Argue that $\Phi_T \le (k+1) \max_A w_T(A)$. Moreover, letting $A^\star = \arg \max_A w_T(A)$, argue that

   $$\Phi_T \le (k+1)w_T(A_f) + (k+1)d(A^\star, A_f),$$

   where A_f is the common ending configuration for WFA and the OPT as argued in part 1.
   (d) Conclude that

   $$\text{EXT} \le (k+1)w_T(A_f) + \text{constant},$$

   where the constant can depend on the metric space and $k+1$.

6.8 [104] In this algorithm we will consider a simple randomized algorithm for the k-server problem called HARMONIC for $k = 2$ servers. Let x be the requested point, and the existing locations of the two servers with HARMONIC be x_1, x_2. Then move server i to location x with probability $p_i = \dfrac{c}{d(x_i, x)}$, for some constant c to satisfy $\sum_{i=1}^{2} p_i = 1$.

We will show that the competitive ratio of HARMONIC with $k = 2$ is at most 18.

To prove this, let at time t the location of the 2 servers with HARMONIC be $x_1(t)$ and $x_2(t)$, while that of OPT be $a_1(t)$ and $a_2(t)$, respectively. Since both HARMONIC and OPT have to fulfil each request, HARMONIC and OPT have at least one server at the same location, i.e., $x_i(t) = a_j(t)$ at least for one i, j pair for each t.

Consider the potential function at time t as

$$\Phi(t) = \frac{M_1(t)M_2(t)}{M_1(t) + M_2(t)}, \tag{6.27}$$

where $M_1(t) = d(a_1(t), x_1(t)) + d(a_2(t), x_2(t))$ and $M_2(t) = d(a_1(t), x_2(t)) + d(a_2(t), x_1(t))$.

Let $\Delta \Phi(i) = \Phi(i) - \Phi(i-1)$, then show that on each new request r_i at time i,

$$C_{\text{HARMONIC}}(i) - 6C_{\text{OPT}}(i) + 4\Delta \Phi(i) \le 0, \tag{6.28}$$

where $C_{\mathcal{A}}(i)$ is the cost of algorithm $\mathcal{A}$ at time i.

Note that OPT moves a server to a location only when a request is made for that location. To show (6.28), consider two cases when OPT moves a_1 or a_2 on a new request, and use the property that once a request is made, HARMONIC and OPT share at least one common location for the two servers. The following inequality for positive real numbers $x, y \in \mathbb{R}^{++}$

$$\frac{xy}{x+y} \leq \frac{x(y+z)}{x+y+z}$$

may be useful.

6.9 (Lookahead) For the k-server problem, for any online algorithm $\mathcal{A}$ with a lookahead size of ℓ (location of next ℓ requests are known ahead of time) that has a competitive ratio of $\mu_{\mathcal{A}}$, show that there exists an online algorithm with no lookahead that can achieve a competitive ratio of $\mu_{\mathcal{A}}$. Thus, lookahead is not useful for the k-server problem.

CHAPTER 7

Secretary Problem

7.1 Introduction

In this chapter, we encounter another canonical online problem (called the *secretary* problem), where items (secretaries) arrive sequentially, and the objective is to select the best item (hire the best secretary); however, the selecting (hiring) decision has to be made right after the item is presented (secretary is interviewed). Moreover, once an item is selected (secretary is hired), the process stops, and no more items are presented (secretaries are interviewed), while if an item is not selected (secretary is not hired), then that item (secretary) cannot be selected later in hindsight.

Secretary problem captures the basic limitation of online algorithms: its limited view of the input and the requirement to make decisions after observing partial inputs that cannot be changed in the future. The secretary problem is trivial in the offline setting but turns out to be quite difficult in the online setting. In this chapter, we will first show that in the adversarial input setting, the competitive ratio of any online algorithm is unbounded. Thus, a randomized input setting called *the secretarial input* is considered, where the value or rank of items can be chosen adversarially; however, the order of arrival of items is uniformly random. Under the secretarial input, we present the optimal online algorithm that belongs to the class of algorithms that observes a constant fraction of the total number of items and builds a threshold using that; thereafter it selects the earliest arriving item whose value is more than the threshold. The optimal competitive ratio turns out to be $1/e$ for a large number of items. We also consider the natural generalization of the secretary problem, called the k-secretary, where multiple items are allowed to be selected.

The basic decision question encountered in the secretary or the k-secretary problem is faced in many real-life situations such as selling a house, accepting a marriage proposal, business opportunity needing massive investment, university admissions with acceptance deadlines, and many others.

7.2 Problem Formulation

Let the set of items be $\mathcal{I}$ with item $i \in \mathcal{I}$ having value $v(i)$. Without loss of generality, we will assume that all items have distinct values, i.e., $v(i) \neq v(j)$ for $i \neq j$. We are interested in selecting the item $i^\star$ with the largest value in $\mathcal{I}$, i.e.,

$$i^\star = \arg \max_{i \in \mathcal{I}} v(i).$$

If $\mathcal{I}$ is revealed completely (offline setting), it is a trivial problem. In the online setting, the items from $\mathcal{I}$ are revealed sequentially, and item i has to be selected on its arrival (in which case no further item is presented) or rejected (in which case item i cannot be selected thereafter) irrevocably. If the item is rejected, the next item is revealed. Under this setting, we still want to select the best item $i^\star$, and the competitive ratio of any online algorithm $\mathcal{A}$ that selects an item i is

$$\mu_\mathcal{A} = \min_\sigma \frac{v(i)}{v(i^\star)},$$

where σ is the order of arrival of items from $\mathcal{I}$.

Remark 7.2.1 *For the rest of the chapter, we will assume that an online algorithm $\mathcal{A}$ knows the length of the input $n = |\mathcal{I}| = |\sigma|$, except Section 7.7.*

Let $\mathcal{A}$ be any deterministic online algorithm. Then it is easy to see that if the order of arrival of the items of $\mathcal{I}$ is controlled by an adversary, then the competitive ratio of $\mathcal{A}$ is arbitrarily bad. To be precise, let the value of first $\ell \leq n-1$ items in the order specified by σ be $1, \beta, \beta^2, \ldots, \beta^\ell$ for $\beta > 1$. If $\mathcal{A}$ accepts the jth item $j \leq \ell$, the next item presented by σ has value β^{j+1}. Otherwise, if $\mathcal{A}$ rejects all the first $n-1$ items, then the final item presented by σ has value 1. Thus, in the two cases, the value of item selected by $\mathcal{A}$ is either β^{j-1} for some $j \leq \ell$, or 1, while the valuation of OPT is β^j or β^{n-1}, respectively. Thus, the competitive ratio of $\mathcal{A}$ is

$$\min_{j \leq n-1} \max \left\{ \frac{\beta^{j-1}}{\beta^j}, \frac{1}{\beta^{n-1}} \right\} \leq \frac{1}{\beta}. \tag{7.1}$$

Choosing $\beta > 1$, the adversary can make the competitive ratio of $\mathcal{A}$ as small as it likes.

Typically, under online settings when all deterministic algorithms are uncompetitive, their randomized counterparts can recover lost ground, and have bounded expected competitive ratios. The secretary problem is one such exception, where even the randomized algorithms are uncompetitive. To be precise, if the number of items in set $\mathcal{I}$ are n, and the order of arrival of items is controlled by the adversary, then the probability that any randomized algorithm selects the best item $i^\star$ is at most $1/n$. We leave it as an exercise to prove this claim via Problem 7.1.

To circumvent these worst-case results, one meaningful direction is to randomize the input. A simple form of such randomization is to assume that the values of the items are still chosen by the adversary, while the order in which they arrive or are presented is uniformly random.

Definition 7.2.2 *The input model where the order in which items arrive is chosen uniformly randomly while the value of the items is allowed to be arbitrary is known as the **secretarial** input model. In particular, let π be a uniformly random permutation over $[1 : n]$, the n items, then the kth item that arrives has value $v(\pi^{-1}(k))$.*

Under the secretarial input, the competitive ratio (7.1) for algorithm $\mathcal{A}$ is then defined as

$$\mu_\mathcal{A} = \min_\sigma \frac{\mathbb{P}_\pi(\mathcal{A} \text{ selecting item } i^\star)}{\mathbb{P}_\pi(\text{OPT selecting item } i^\star)} = \min_\sigma \mathbb{P}_\pi(\mathcal{A} \text{ selecting item } i^\star), \tag{7.2}$$

where π is the uniformly random permutation over the n items of $\mathcal{I}$ and the input is $\sigma = \pi(\mathcal{I})$, and $\mathcal{I} = \{v(1), \ldots, v(n)\}$ where values $v(i)$ are arbitrary. The second equality in (7.2) follows since OPT knows the entire input sequence and always selects the best item; hence $\mathbb{P}_\pi(\text{OPT selecting item } i^\star) = 1$.

Definition 7.2.3 *The problem to maximize* $\min_\sigma \mathbb{P}_\pi(\mathcal{A} \text{ selecting item } i^\star)$ *is called the* **secretary** *problem.*

Under the secretarial input, a simple strategy can be shown to have a constant competitive ratio as follows.

Example 7.2.4

Let a deterministic online algorithm $\mathcal{A}$ observe and not select the first $n/2$ items of $\mathcal{I}$, and record the value of the best item (denoted by $i^\star_{n/2}$) among the first $n/2$ items. Then on the arrival of the ℓth item $\ell > n/2$, $\mathcal{A}$ selects it only if $v(\ell) > v(i^\star_{n/2})$.

Rather than finding an exact expression for $\mathbb{P}_\pi(\mathcal{A} \text{ selecting item } i^\star)$ with this algorithm, a simple but instructive lower bound on probability of selecting the best item can be found as follows.

Let events $\mathcal{E}_1 = \{$second best item of $\mathcal{I}$ is among the first $n/2$ items$\}$ and $\mathcal{E}_2 = \{$the best item of $\mathcal{I}$ is among the last $n/2$ items$\}$. By definition of $\mathcal{A}$, whenever $\mathcal{E}_1$ and $\mathcal{E}_2$ happen together, $\mathcal{A}$ definitely selects the best item. Since the permutation over the n items that describes the order of arrival of items is uniformly random, $\mathbb{P}(\mathcal{E}_1 \cap \mathcal{E}_2) = \mathbb{P}(\mathcal{E}_1)\mathbb{P}(\mathcal{E}_2) = \frac{1}{2} \times \frac{1}{2} = \frac{1}{4}$. Thus, the competitive ratio of $\mathcal{A}$ is at least

$$\mu_{\mathcal{A}} \geq \frac{1}{4}. \tag{7.3}$$

Note that there are many other events under which the algorithm $\mathcal{A}$ selects the best item $i^\star$, and the lower bound (7.3) is strict and can be improved upon. But the motivation remains the same as identifying events of type $\mathcal{E}_1$ and $\mathcal{E}_2$.

Example 7.2.4 is a special case of the class of algorithms called *sample and price*, where an algorithm divides the input into two parts: sampling and decision. No item is accepted in the sampling phase, and an offline algorithm is run at the end of the sampling phase to generate a price or threshold, which is then later used to make decisions in the decision phase. In the previous example, the sampling phase is of length $n/2$, and the price or threshold is the value of the best item seen in the sampling phase.

7.3 Sample and Price Algorithm

There is nothing special about using $n/2$ as the length of the sampling phase in Example 7.2.4. In general, an algorithm of *sample and price* class for the secretary problem observes the first t items and records the value (called the price) of the best item among the first t items. Thereafter, it selects the earliest item arriving after item t if its value is larger than the price. Compared to the lower bound of Example 7.2.4, deriving an exact expression for the probability of selecting the best item, and optimizing over the choice of t, we next show that the probability of selecting the best item with the sample and price class of algorithms is at least as large as $1/e$ as follows.

Theorem 7.3.1 *As $n \to \infty$, the optimal competitive ratio of the sample and price class of algorithms is $\dfrac{1}{e}$ and that is achieved by using $t = n/e$.*

Proof: Let $i^\star$ be the index of the best item of $\mathcal{I}$ that arrives at location $\pi(i^\star)$. Let $\mathcal{E}_\ell^1$ be the event that the ℓth item is selected by the sample and price algorithm $\mathcal{A}$, and $\mathcal{E}_\ell^2$ be the event that ℓ^{th} item is the best item, i.e., $\ell = \pi(i^\star)$.

Then

$$\mathbb{P}_\pi(\mathcal{A} \text{ selecting item } i^\star) = \sum_{\ell=t+1}^{n} \mathbb{P}(\mathcal{E}_\ell^1 \cap \mathcal{E}_\ell^2),$$

$$= \sum_{\ell=t+1}^{n} \mathbb{P}(\mathcal{E}_\ell^1 | \mathcal{E}_\ell^2) \mathbb{P}(\mathcal{E}_\ell^2),$$

$$\overset{(a)}{=} \sum_{\ell=t+1}^{n} \mathbb{P}(\mathcal{E}_\ell^1 | \mathcal{E}_\ell^2) \frac{1}{n},$$

$$\overset{(b)}{=} \sum_{\ell=t+1}^{n} \frac{t}{\ell-1} \frac{1}{n}, \tag{7.4}$$

where (a) follows since the permutation π is uniformly random and the best item can arrive at any location with equal probability of $1/n$. To get (b), given $\mathcal{E}_\ell^2$, i.e., the best item arrives at location ℓ, the event that allows the algorithm to select the ℓth (best) item is when the best item among the items that have arrived till then, i.e., until location $\ell - 1$, appears in the sampling phase from location 1 to t. The probability of this event is $\dfrac{t}{\ell-1}$, since the order of arrival of items is uniformly random.

For large n, the sum in (7.4) can be closely approximated by

$$\frac{t}{n} \int_t^n \frac{1}{x} dx = \frac{t}{n} \ln\left(\frac{n}{t}\right), \tag{7.5}$$

which is maximized for $t = \dfrac{n}{e}$, and the optimal

$$\mathbb{P}_\pi(\mathcal{A} \text{ selecting item } i^\star) = \frac{1}{e}.$$

∎

One immediate question is whether this algorithm is optimal or not, and can we get competitive ratios better than $1/e$ for the secretary problem under the secretarial input? The answer unfortunately is negative, and indeed this algorithm is optimal as shown next via dynamic programming arguments.

7.4 Optimal Algorithm

We use a dynamic programming framework to determine the optimal algorithm for the secretary problem. Note that by the optimal algorithm, we mean the algorithm that has optimal probability of selecting the best item with causal information under the secretarial input without knowing the future item values unlike OPT. We index all the n items with ranks according to their values, where items with lower rank (higher value) are better than those with higher rank, and item with rank 1 (largest value) is the best item that we wish to select with as large a probability as possible.

Definition 7.4.1 *Let m be the number of items seen so far. Then the **relative rank** r of the mth item is $r = j$ if the mth item is the jth best item among the first m items. For example, if the values (ranks) of the first $m = 5$ items in order of arrival are $10(4), 12(3), 1(5), 100(1), 14(2)$, then the relative rank of the 5th item is 2.*

Definition 7.4.2 *The success event for an algorithm is the event when it selects the best item. Consequently, the success probability or the probability of success is the probability of choosing the best item.*

Define the **state** of the system to be (m, r), where m is the number of items seen so far, and r is the relative rank of the mth item. The following remarks are in order:

1. The optimal algorithm will not select item m if its relative rank > 1. This follows since m is not the best item seen so far, and the objective is only to select the best item.

2. If the relative rank of item m is 1, then the probability that indeed the mth item is the best among all the n items is the probability that the best item (with absolute rank 1) is presented among the first m items and is equal to $\frac{m}{n}$.

Let $V(m, r)$ be the maximum probability of success (over all possible algorithms) when the state of the system is (m, r), where the decision any algorithm makes is whether to select the mth item or move on to the next item. If $r > 1$, any algorithm definitely moves on to the next item. Else, if $r = 1$, then an algorithm either selects the mth item and stops, or rejects the mth item and moves on to the next item. With $r = 1$, selecting the mth item, the success probability is $\frac{m}{n}$ (from point 2 above), while moving on to the next item, the state of the system updates to $(m + 1, r')$, and the success probability is

$$\frac{1}{m + 1} \sum_{r'=1}^{m+1} V(m + 1, r')$$

since the relative rank r' of the $m + 1^{th}$ item is equally likely to be one among $\{1, 2, \ldots, m + 1\}$. Thus, we get the dynamic program where if $r = 1$,

$$V(m, r) = \max \left\{ \frac{m}{n}, \frac{1}{m + 1} \sum_{r'=1}^{m+1} V(m + 1, r') \right\}. \tag{7.6}$$

While if $r > 1$, the algorithm moves on to the next item, and

$$V(m, r) = \frac{1}{m+1} \sum_{r'=1}^{m+1} V(m+1, r'), \tag{7.7}$$

and for the last item $m = n$,

$$V(n, r) = \begin{cases} 1 & \text{if } r = 1, \\ 0 & \text{otherwise.} \end{cases} \tag{7.8}$$

Example 7.4.3

Let $n = 4$. Then after all item arrivals $V(4, 1) = 1$ and $V(4, r') = 0$ for $r' > 1$. Continuing backwards,

$$V(3, 1) = \max\left\{ \frac{3}{4}, \frac{1}{4} \right\} = \frac{3}{4}, V(3, 2) = \frac{1}{4}, \text{and } V(3, 3) = \frac{1}{4}.$$

Moreover,

$$V(2, 1) = \max\left\{ \frac{1}{2}, \frac{1}{3}\left(\frac{3}{4} + \frac{1}{4} + \frac{1}{4} \right) \right\} = \max\left\{ \frac{1}{2}, \frac{5}{12} \right\} = \frac{1}{2}, V(2, 2) = \frac{5}{12},$$

while

$$V(1, 1) = \max\left\{ \frac{1}{4}, \frac{1}{2}\left(\frac{1}{2} + \frac{5}{12} \right) \right\} = \max\left\{ \frac{1}{4}, \frac{11}{24} \right\} = \frac{11}{24}.$$

Thus, we see that on the arrival of the first item, selecting it has the probability of success $\frac{1}{4}$, while moving on to the next item, the probability of success increases to $\frac{11}{24}$. On the arrival of the second, the third, or the fourth item, if the relative rank is 1, then selecting it has higher probability of success (probability of success 1/2, 3/4, and 1, respectively) than moving on to the next item. So the optimal algorithm with $n = 4$ items is to select the earliest item among items 2, 3, and 4 that has relative rank 1.

Solving the dynamic program for the general case, (7.6), (7.7), and (7.8), we get

$$V(m, 1) = \max\left\{ \frac{m}{n}, \frac{m}{n}\left(\frac{1}{m} + \frac{1}{m+1} + ... , + \frac{1}{n-1} \right) \right\}. \tag{7.9}$$

Defining $a_m = \frac{1}{m} + \frac{1}{m+1} + ... , + \frac{1}{n-1}$, we get

$$V(m, 1) = \max\left\{ \frac{m}{n}, a_m \frac{m}{n} \right\}. \tag{7.10}$$

Thus, if $a_m < 1$, it is better to select item m in state $(m, 1)$, while if $a_m > 1$, an optimal algorithm will not select the item in state $(m, 1)$ and move on to the next item.

Note that a_m is a decreasing sequence. Thus, let $m^\star$ be such that

$$a_{m^\star} < 1 \le a_{m^\star - 1}.$$

Then the optimal algorithm rejects the first $m^\star - 1$ items, and accepts the first item thereafter that has relative rank 1 (best among the items seen so far). Thus, the optimal algorithm belongs to the sample and price class of algorithms.

To compute the success probability of the optimal algorithm, let $\mathcal{E}(i, m^\star)$ be the event that the second best item among the first i items lies among the first $m^\star - 1$ items. Then the probability of success with the optimal algorithm is

$$\mathbb{P}_{\text{suc}} = \sum_{i=m^\star}^{n} \mathbb{P}\left(\text{item } i \text{ is selected} \cap i \text{ is the best item}\right),$$

$$= \sum_{i=m^\star}^{n} \mathbb{P}\left(\text{item } i \text{ is selected} | i \text{ is the best item}\right) \mathbb{P}\left(i \text{ is the best item}\right),$$

$$= \sum_{i=m^\star}^{n} \mathbb{P}\left(\mathcal{E}(i, m^\star)\right) \mathbb{P}\left(i \text{ is the best item}\right),$$

$$\stackrel{(a)}{=} \frac{1}{n} \sum_{i=m^\star}^{n} \frac{m^\star - 1}{i},$$

$$= \frac{m^\star - 1}{n} a_{m^\star - 1},$$

where (a) follows since $\mathbb{P}\left(i \text{ is the best item}\right) = \frac{1}{n}$, $\forall\, i$ because of the uniformly random permutation π. As the number of items $n \to \infty$, one can show that $\mathbb{P}_{\text{suc}} \to \frac{1}{e}$.

Thus, the optimal algorithm under the secretarial input is deterministic, and randomization is not required. Moreover, recall that this also proves that the sample and price class of algorithms (discussed in Section 7.3) contain the optimal algorithm, which observes or samples a fixed number of items and selects the first item that is better than the best item found in the sampling phase. Since the optimal success probability is $1/e$ with the optimal algorithm, we can also deduce that the choice of $t = n/e$ (length of the sampling phase) made in Theorem 7.3.1 is also optimal.

7.5 Selecting Multiple Secretaries

A natural generalization of the secretary problem is to select multiple items instead of selecting just one item, called the k-secretary problem. The k-secretary problem is an online version of the classical subset selection problem, where the goal is to select the 'best' k-sized subset of a given set. We consider the *additive valuation* case, where the value of the subset is the sum of the values of the items belonging to the subset, for which the offline problem is trivial, while its online counterpart is still challenging.

Since the secretary problem is a special case of the k-secretary problem, the competitive ratio of any algorithm for the k-secretary problem can be arbitrarily bad with the worst-case input. Thus, here again, we consider the secretarial input.

Let the set of items be $\mathcal{I}$, where each item $i \in \mathcal{I}$ arrives sequentially and has to be accepted or rejected on its arrival irrevocably. We consider additive value functions $v(S) = \sum_{s \in S} v(s)$ for any subset $S \subseteq \mathcal{I}$. Let k be the number of items to be selected from the arriving set of items $\mathcal{I}$, and the optimal subset be $\mathcal{I}_k^\star \subseteq \mathcal{I}$ that contains the k items with the largest values in $\mathcal{I}$. Let an online algorithm $\mathcal{A}$ select the subset $S_\mathcal{A} \subseteq \mathcal{I}$ of at most k elements; then its competitive ratio under the secretarial input model is

$$\mu_\mathcal{A} = \min_{S \subseteq \mathcal{I}, |S| \leq k} \frac{\mathbb{E}_\pi \{v(S_\mathcal{A})\}}{v(\mathcal{I}_k^\star)}. \tag{7.11}$$

Remark 7.5.1 *This definition of competitive ratio (7.11) tries to maximize the expectation of the value of the selected items rather than maximizing the probability of selecting the full-subset $\mathcal{I}_k^\star$. Hence (7.11) is a weaker problem formulation compared to the $k = 1$-secretary problem (7.2).*

From the previous section on the secretary problem, which is $k = 1$-secretary problem, we get the following upper bound on the competitive ratio for any randomized online algorithm for the k-secretary problem, whose proof is left as an exercise in Problem 7.2.

Theorem 7.5.2 *For any randomized online algorithm $\mathcal{A}$, the competitive ratio $\mu_\mathcal{A}$ (7.11) is at most $1/e$.*

Next, we work towards finding an algorithm that can achieve this upper bound.

Algorithm 2 VIRTUAL Algorithm

1: %**Sampling Phase**
2: The first t elements $\mathcal{I}_t(\pi) \subset \mathcal{I}$ under permutation π
3: No item is selected from $\mathcal{I}_t(\pi)$
4: $R = \{k$ largest elements of $\mathcal{I}_t(\pi)\} = \{i_1, \ldots, i_k\}$ ordered in decreasing order of item values, item $i_k \in R$ has the least value.
5: %**Decision Phase**
6: Initialize $S = \varnothing$%The set to be selected
7: For every new item $i \geq t + 1$
8:   **if** $v(i) > v(i_k)$ **then**
9:     **if** i_k was sampled in the Sampling phase **then**
10:       $S = S \cup \{i\}$ %select item i
11:     **end if**
12:     Update $R = R\backslash\{i_k\} \cup \{i\}$
13:     Order the elements of R in decreasing order of their values, item $i_k \in R$ has the least value
14:   **else**
15:     Do nothing
16:   **end if**

Consider algorithm VIRTUAL to maximize (7.11) that achieves the upper bound (Theorem 7.5.2) for a large number of items n. VIRTUAL is similar to the sample and price algorithm where it divides the input into two phases: sampling and decision. No item arriving in the sampling phase is selected. At the end of the sampling phase, a reference set R is selected that consists of the k best items observed in the sampling phase. The set R is updated on the arrival of each new item in the decision phase, such that it always consists of the k best items observed so far including the sampling phase.

In the decision phase, a newly arrived item is *selected* (made part of the selected item set S) if

(i)   its value is larger than the lowest valued item currently present in the reference set R, and

(ii) 'more importantly' the currently lowest valued item in set R arrives in the sampling phase.

The second condition is key for avoiding complicated correlations that would result with a more greedy algorithm that selects any item with value larger than the value of any item of R. With this restriction, the probability of selecting an item belonging to set $\mathcal{I}_k^{\star}$ can be computed easily, as shown in Lemma 7.5.4. We first describe the selection criterion of VIRTUAL with an example as follows.

Example 7.5.3

Let $k = 2$ and assume that at the end of the sampling phase, the two best items that are contained in the reference set be $R = \{i_1, i_2\}$, with $v(i_1) = 6, v(i_2) = 5$. In the decision phase, let the value of the first item i_{t+1} be $v(i_{t+1}) = 5.5$. Then item i_{t+1} is selected since its value is larger than the value of the worst item i_2 in the reference set R at time $t + 1$ and i_2 was sampled in the sampling phase. Crucially, the set R is next updated to $R = R\backslash\{i_2\} \cup \{i_{t+1}\} = \{i_1, i_{t+1}\}$, and the item with the least value in R has arrived in the decision phase and not in the sampling phase. Thus, after time $t + 1$, until an item with value greater than 6 arrives, the item with the least value in R will always be an item sampled in the decision phase. Consequently, no new item can be selected by VIRTUAL even though its value might be larger than the lowest value of the item currently in reference set R until an item with value greater than 6 arrives.

Lemma 7.5.4 *The competitive ratio of VIRTUAL approaches $1/e$ as $n \to \infty$.*

Proof: With VIRTUAL, item $i \in \mathcal{I}_k^{\star}$ (the optimal subset of k items) that appears in the decision phase at time $s > t$ is selected if and only if at time s, the item i_k with the smallest value in the reference set R is sampled at or before time t, and $v(i) > v(i_k)$. Note that R always contains the k best items seen so far. Since $i \in \mathcal{I}_k^{\star}$, by definition $v(i) > v(i_k)$. We only need to check whether i_k is sampled in the sampling phase or the decision phase.

Since the permutations are uniformly random, the probability that on the arrival of the sth-item, the item with the smallest value in the reference set R is sampled in the sampling phase, i.e., at or before time t (length of sampling phase), is $\dfrac{t}{s-1}$. Moreover, the probability of any item $i \in \mathcal{I}_k^{\star}$ arriving at the sth location is $\dfrac{1}{n}$ independent of s.

Hence, the probability of selecting an item $i \in \mathcal{I}_k^\star$ when it arrives at position $s \in [t+1, n]$ is

$$P(i \in \mathcal{I}_k^\star \text{ is selected}) = \sum_{s=t+1}^{n} \frac{1}{n} \frac{t}{s-1} = \frac{t}{n} \sum_{s=t+1}^{n} \frac{1}{s-1}$$

$$> \frac{t}{n} \int_t^n \frac{dx}{x} = \frac{t}{n} \ln\left(\frac{n}{t}\right). \tag{7.12}$$

Choosing $t = \frac{n}{e}$ maximizes the lower bound, and we get

$$P(i \in \mathcal{I}_k^\star \text{ is selected}) = 1/e.$$

Hence, by linearity of expectation, we get that the expected value of the set of selected items S by VIRTUAL is at least

$$\mathbb{E}\{v(S)\} \geq \sum_{i \in \mathcal{I}_k^\star} \frac{1}{e} v(i) = \frac{1}{e} v(\mathcal{I}_k^\star), \tag{7.13}$$

and the competitive ratio (7.11) of VIRTUAL is at least $1/e$. ∎

Remark 7.5.5 VIRTUAL *ensures that the probability of selecting any of the best k items is exactly the same as the optimal probability of selecting the best item in the* 1*-secretary problem. Thus, for the considered expected 'weaker' notion (Remark 7.5.1) of the competitive ratio (7.11) for the k-secretary problem,* VIRTUAL *is optimal using Theorem 7.5.2.*

7.6 Recall

For the $k = 1$-secretary problem with recall, at the arrival of the tth item, any item among the $m \geq 1$ previously arrived items is allowed to be selected. Thus, the algorithm keeps a recall window W_t of length m at the tth item's arrival

$$W_t = \{i_{t-m+1}, \dots, i_t\}$$

containing the m most recently arrived items. The algorithm terminates as soon as any item is selected.

Under the secretarial input, with recall, the optimal algorithm[1] [105], following the dynamic programming idea presented in Section 7.4, takes the following form. Let $r^\star$ be some constant that depends on n and m.

Algorithm: Do not select any item before the arrival of item $r^\star$. From the arrival of $r^\star$-th item onwards, select the item with the best relative rank on the arrival of item t; if moving on to considering the next item, the presently relatively best item falls out of the recall window. If the final item arrives, choose the relatively best item in the recall window.

---

[1] Causal optimal algorithm under the secretarial input.

7.7 Unknown Number of Items

So far we have only considered the case where the number of items n to be presented is known ahead of time. This is definitely a limitation, and for many applications, either n is entirely unknown or arbitrary or follows a distribution. It turns out that handling the unknown n case is fundamentally more challenging, and only structural results are known. For example, when n is distributed as uniform, Poisson, or Geometric, the optimal algorithm[2] is known to have the following structure [106]. There exists an item $n^\star$ such that the algorithm does not select any item $i < n^\star$, and selects the first best item seen after item $n^\star$.

7.8 Notes

The exact beginnings of the study of the secretary problem are not well founded, and are attributed to a variety of papers [107, 108]. There is also a paper [109] titled "Who solved the secretary problem" in this regard. The first analytical paper that rigorously solved the basic version is [110]. The stochastic version of the problem was posed in [111], where values of items were independent and identically distributed. Solutions for the uniform and some other distributions were derived in [112, 113]. Most of the early papers used the idea of dynamic programming to analyse the secretary problem, while a new Markov chain based technique was employed by [114], which then became very popular.

There are many variants of the secretary problem, including recall [105], where items previously rejected can be selected, minimizing the expected rank of the selected item [110] rather than maximizing the probability of selecting the best item, unknown number of items [106], selecting more than one item and declaring that the best item has been selected as long as it belongs to the set of selected items [108, 105]. There are many other interesting variants that have been beautifully summarized in [115].

Most of this work is classical. In more recent works, the k-secretary problem was considered in [116, 117], where the objective is to maximize the expected sum of the values of the k selected items. With multiple items being selected, there is also work on submodular valuations on subsets of items [118], which is then extended to matroids [119, 120]. Enforcing the constraint on the number of selected items in expectation has been considered in [121]. When selecting multiple items, rather than enforcing a strict constraint on selecting exactly k items, a more general approach is to include a cost of selecting items that is increasing in the number of selected items, and subtracting it from the value of the selected items [122, 123].

There is also more recent work on stochastic arrival models, called the prophet secretary problem [124–126], where at each time an item with value drawn according to distribution D_i arrives, and the algorithm is aware of all D_i's.

More advanced versions of the secretary problem include the non-uniform arrival model [127] and robust algorithms with respect to outlier arrivals placed by the adversary [128]. Very recently, improved algorithms in the presence of prediction via machine learning have been

---

[2] See note 1.

considered in [129], in what is called the beyond the worst-case paradigm. We consider one such algorithm in Problem 7.9. A detailed book chapter reviewing online problems under the secretarial model can be found in [130].

PROBLEMS

7.1 Show that the maximum probability of selecting the best item from a set $\mathcal{I}$ of $|\mathcal{I}| = n$ items in a secretary problem with adversarial input for any randomized algorithm is at most $\frac{1}{n}$. Thus, any online algorithm for the secretary problem with the worst-case input is un-competitive.

To prove this, consider a cyclic latin square with n letters

$$
\mathcal{L} = \begin{pmatrix} 1 & 2 & 3 & \dots & n \\ n & 1 & 2 & \dots & n-1 \\ n-1 & n & 1 & \dots & n-2 \\ \vdots & \vdots & \vdots & \ddots & \vdots \\ 2 & 3 & & \dots & 1 \end{pmatrix}, \tag{7.14}
$$

where k in any row represents the location of the kth best item. Let any one row j of $\mathcal{L}$ be the input σ chosen by the adversary. Then let any online algorithm select the ith item (i^{th} element of the jth row) as the best item. Then the success matrix is

$$
S = \begin{pmatrix} 1 & 0 & 0 & \dots & 0 \\ 0 & 1 & 0 & \dots & 0 \\ \vdots & \vdots & \vdots & \ddots & \vdots \\ 0 & 0 & & \dots & 1 \end{pmatrix}, \tag{7.15}
$$

where a 1 represents the optimal selection of the best item (with input row j of $\mathcal{L}$ and selection i by the algorithm), and a 0 denotes when the selected item is not the optimal. Let the adversary choose each row of the latin square with equal probability $q_j = \frac{1}{n}$. Then show that for any strategy (choosing the ith item with probability p_i) of the online algorithm, the maximum probability of choosing the best item is $\frac{1}{n}$.

Alternatively, consider the following input. For $1 \le t \le n$, let

$$
x_t = (1, 2, \dots, t, \underbrace{0, \dots, 0}_{n-t}),
$$

and the input $\sigma = x_t$ for $1 \le t \le n$ with probability $1/n$. Using Yao's principle, show that the maximum probability of choosing the best item for any randomized algorithm is at most $\frac{1}{n}$ with the adversarial input.

7.2 In this problem, we will prove Theorem 7.5.2 via showing the following:

1. Consider $k = 1$ and show that the optimal probability of selecting the best item approaches $1/e$ as $n \to \infty$ that only depends on the relative ranks of the items and not their actual values.

2. For $k = 1$, construct input sequences (values of the n items) such that the expected value of the selected item by any algorithm is arbitrarily close to the probability of selecting the best item times the value of the best item.

3. Combining parts 1 and 2, conclude the proof of Theorem 7.5.2.

7.3 For the secretary problem with the secretarial input, consider a relaxed problem where the **expected number** of items that can be selected is 1, with the expectation being over the secretarial input. For any algorithm $\mathcal{A}$, let $S_{\mathcal{A}}$ be the set of selected items. Then the constraint implies $\mathbb{E}\{|S_{\mathcal{A}}|\} = 1$.

1. Show that with the t-Threshold algorithm, the set of selected items S satisfies the constraint $\mathbb{E}\{|S|\} = 1$ by choosing $t = n/e$.

2. Let $i^{\star}$ be the best item in the input. Show that with the t-Threshold algorithm, $\mathbb{P}(i^{\star} \in S) = 1 - \frac{1}{e}$ by choosing $t = n/e$.

   Thus, there is a significant improvement in the competitive ratio from $1/e$ to $1 - 1/e$ by relaxing the hard constraint on the number of selectable items to an expected constraint with the secretary problem.

3. Moreover, show that $\mathbb{P}(i^{\star} \in S) \leq 1 - \frac{1}{e}$ with $\mathbb{E}\{|S|\} = 1$ for any deterministic algorithm.

   To show this, consider any deterministic online algorithm $\mathcal{A}$ for which p_r is the probability that it selects r items at the end of the input sequence σ. Let q_r be the probability that $r \geq 1$ items selected by $\mathcal{A}$ contain the best item $i^{\star}$.

Algorithm 3 t-Threshold Algorithm

1: %**Sampling Phase**
2: Do not select the first t items $\mathcal{I}_t(\pi) \subset \mathcal{I}$ under permutation π
3: $b = $ best item of $\mathcal{I}_t(\pi)$
4: %**Decision Phase**
5: Initialize $S = \varnothing$ %The set to be selected
6: For every new item $i > t$ in the decision phase
7: **if** $v(i) > v(b)$ **then**
8:     Select item i, $S = S \cup \{i\}$
9:     $b = \{i\}$
10: **else**
11:     Do not select item i
12: **end if**

Thus, $\max_{\mathcal{A}} \mathbb{P}(i^\star$ is selected by $\mathcal{A})$ under the expected capacity constraint of 1 is

$$\max \quad \sum_{r=1}^{n} p_r q_r,$$
$$\sum_{r=1}^{n} r p_r \leq 1, \tag{7.16}$$
$$p_r \in [0,1], \ \forall \ 1 \leq r \leq n.$$

Show that $1 - \dfrac{1}{e}$ is an upper bound on the optimal value of (7.16) .

7.4 [126] Consider the $k = 1$-secretary problem, and a stochastic input where values $v(i)$ of item $i \in [1:n]$ are independent and identically distributed according to any continuous distribution $\mathcal{D}$.

Let a deterministic algorithm $\mathcal{A}$ select the first item i for which $v(i) > \tau$, where τ is such that

$$\mathbb{P}_{\mathcal{D}}(\max\{v(i)\}_{i=1}^{n} \leq \tau) = \mathcal{P},$$

and $\mathcal{P} = \left(1 - \dfrac{1.501}{n}\right)^{n} \approx \exp(-1.501)$. Let $p = \mathbb{P}(v(i) > \tau) = 1 - \mathcal{P}^{1/n}$.

1. Let $\mathcal{K}$ be the number of items $j \in [1:n]$ such that $v(j) > \tau$. Show that the item selected by the algorithm is uniformly distributed over the $\mathcal{K}$ items.

2. Using part 1, show that the probability of selecting the best item is

$$\geq \sum_{k=1}^{n} \left(\frac{1}{k} \mathbb{P}(\mathcal{K} = k)\right).$$

3. Show that

$$\mathbb{P}(\mathcal{K} = k) = \binom{n}{k} p^k (1-p)^{n-k},$$

where $p = \mathbb{P}_{\mathcal{D}}(v(i) > \tau)$.

4. Using Le-Cam's Theorem which states that for Bernoulli random variables, $Y_i \in \{0, 1\}$ with $\mathbb{P}(Y_i = 1) = q_i$ and $\lambda = \sum_{i=1}^{n} q_i$,

$$\sum_{k=0}^{\infty} \left| \mathbb{P}\left(\sum_{k=1}^{n} Y_i = k\right) - \frac{\lambda^k \exp(-\lambda)}{k!} \right| < 2 \sum_{i=1}^{n} q_i^2,$$

argue that

$$\sum_{k=1}^{\infty} \left| \frac{1}{k} \mathbb{P}(\mathcal{K} = k) - \frac{1}{k} \frac{\lambda^k \exp(-\lambda)}{k!} \right| < 2np^2 < \frac{6}{n},$$

where $\lambda = np = 1.501$ and $p = \dfrac{1.501}{n}$, since $\mathcal{P} = (1-p)^n = \left(1 - \dfrac{1.501}{n}\right)^n$.

5. Using the approximation $\sum_{k=1}^{n} \frac{1}{k} \frac{\lambda^k \exp -\lambda}{k!} \geq .5173$ for large enough n and $\lambda = 1.501$, and combining parts 2, 3, and 4, conclude that the probability of selecting the best item

$$\sum_{k=1}^{n} \frac{1}{k} \mathbb{P}(\mathcal{K} = k) \geq 0.517$$

for large enough n.

7.5 Consider the $k = 1$-secretary problem, and a stochastic input where values $v(i)$ of item $i \in [1 : n]$ are drawn i.i.d. uniformly randomly from $[0, 1]$. Let the value of the item selected by the online algorithm $\mathcal{A}$ be $v_{\mathcal{A}}$, while the optimal item be $i^\star$; then the competitive ratio of $\mathcal{A}$ is defined as

$$\mu_{\mathcal{A}} = \frac{\mathbb{E}\{v_{\mathcal{A}}\}}{v(i^\star)}. \tag{7.17}$$

Consider an online algorithm $\mathcal{A}$ that waits till time t (does not select any item among the first t items) and selects the first item thereafter if it is the best item seen so far. Moreover, $\mathcal{A}$ always selects the last item if no other item has been selected previously. In the following, we will show that the optimal choice of t to maximize $\mathbb{E}\{v_{\mathcal{A}}\}$ is $t^\star \approx \sqrt{n}$.

$\left[\vphantom{\sum}\right.$ Recall that for $V_t = \max\{v(i), i = 1, \ldots, t\}$ with $v(i)$ being i.i.d. uniformly distributed over $[0, 1]$, $\mathbb{E}\{V_t\} = \frac{t}{t+1}$ $\left.\vphantom{\sum}\right]$.

Express

$$\mathbb{E}\{v_{\mathcal{A}}\} = \sum_{\ell=t+1}^{n-1} \mathbb{P}(\text{item } \ell \text{ is selected})\mathbb{E}\{v(\ell)|\text{item } \ell \text{ is selected}\}$$

$$+ \mathbb{P}(\text{item } n \text{ is selected})\mathbb{E}\{v(n)|\text{item } n \text{ is selected}\}.$$

1. Show that $\mathbb{E}\{v(n)|\text{item } n \text{ is selected}\} = \frac{1}{2}$, while

$$\mathbb{E}\{v(\ell)|\text{item } \ell \text{ is selected}\} = \frac{\ell}{\ell+1} \text{ for } t+1 \leq \ell < n.$$

2. Show that for $\ell \leq n - 1$,

$$\mathbb{P}(\text{item } \ell \text{ is selected}) = \left(\prod_{k=t+1}^{\ell-1} \frac{k-1}{k}\right)\frac{1}{\ell} = \frac{t}{\ell-1}\frac{1}{\ell}.$$

3. Finally, show that $\mathbb{P}(\text{item } n \text{ is selected}) = \left(\prod_{k=t+1}^{n-1} \frac{k-1}{k}\right)$, using which prove that

$$\mathbb{E}\{v_{\mathcal{A}}\} = \frac{2(t+1)n - (t+1)^2 + (t+1) - n}{2(t+1)n}.$$

4. Show that $t + 1 = \sqrt{n}$ optimizes $\mathbb{E}\{v_{\mathcal{A}}\}$.

7.6 [131] In this problem, we will consider the $k = 1$-secretary problem with the worst-case input by letting the value of any item to lie in $[v_{min}, v_{max}]$. Recall that the competitive ratio of any online algorithm for the secretary problem is arbitrarily bad with the worst-case input. However, in this case with $v(i) \in [v_{min}, v_{max}]$, we can recover some lost ground.

Let n items arrive sequentially, where item i has value $v(i) \in [v_{min}, v_{max}]$. Let the values v_{min} and v_{max} be known to any online algorithm. The problem is to select only one item, irrevocably, with the largest value. As soon as one item is selected, the input is terminated. We will consider the **worst-case arrival model**, where the adversary can also choose the order of arrival of items.

Let the value of the item chosen by an online algorithm $\mathcal{A}$ be $v_{\mathcal{A}}$ while the value of the best item be $v_{OPT} \in [v_{min}, v_{max}]$; then the competitive ratio of $\mathcal{A}$ is $\mu_{\mathcal{A}} = \frac{v_{\mathcal{A}}}{v_{OPT}}$. Define $r = \frac{v_{max}}{v_{min}}$ to be the efficiency ratio of the problem.

1. Show that the following deterministic algorithm that chooses the first item with value at least as much as $\sqrt{v_{min}v_{max}}$ is an optimal deterministic online algorithm. Conclude that the optimal competitive ratio is $\sqrt{r}$.

2. Randomized setting is more interesting. Let $r = 2^k$ for some $k \in \mathbb{N}$. Consider a deterministic algorithm $\mathcal{A}_\ell$ that chooses the first item with value at least as much as $v_{min}2^\ell$. The randomized algorithm $\mathcal{R}$ chooses one out of $\mathcal{A}_\ell$ for $\ell = 0, \dots, k-1$ with uniform probability $1/k$ before the input arrives, and plays the chosen deterministic algorithm throughout. Show that the competitive ratio of $\mathcal{R}$ is at most

$$c(r)\log(r),$$

where the constant $c(r) \to 1$ as $r \to \infty$.

To show this result, let the largest value of the item presented by the adversary be v_{OPT} where $v_{min}2^j \le v_{OPT} < v_{min}2^{j+1}$ for some $j \le k$. Show that as a function of j, the expected value of the item chosen by $\mathcal{R}$ is

$$\frac{v_{min}}{k}\left(k - j + \sum_{1 \le i \le j} 2^i\right). \tag{7.18}$$

Using this, show that the competitive ratio for $\mathcal{R}$ is

$$k\frac{2^{j+1}}{2^{j+1} + k - j - 2} \tag{7.19}$$

by arguing about the choice of value v_{OPT} made by the adversary. Conclude the result by maximizing over the choice of j.

7.7 For the $k = 1$-secretary problem with a total of n items, instead of a fully adversarial input model, consider the case when the adversary can only choose the position of the best item, while the rest of the $n - 1$ positions are chosen uniformly randomly. A randomized sample and price algorithm uses $\mathcal{A}_k$ wth probability p_k, for $k = 1, \ldots, n - 1$, where $\mathcal{A}_k$ is the algorithm that rejects the first k items and selects the earliest item with the largest value seen so far.

Show that in this case the probability of selecting the best item using a randomized sample and price algorithm is at most

$$\frac{1}{1 + \sum_{j=1}^{n-1} \frac{1}{j}}.$$

Thus, even with limited control, the adversary can make the probability of selecting the best secretary as small as $\frac{1}{\ln n}$ compared to $\frac{1}{e}$, when the input is uniformly random.

Essentially, let q_r be the probability that the adversary puts the best item in the rth location, and p_k be the probability that the algorithm uses sample and price algorithm $\mathcal{A}_k$. Show that

$$\min_{q_r} \max_{p_k} \mathbb{P}(\text{selecting the best item}) = \frac{1}{1 + \sum_{j=1}^{n-1} \frac{1}{j}}.$$

7.8 [110] Typically in the secretary problem, we are only interested in finding the probability of selecting the best item. An alternative objective is to minimize the expected rank of the selected item. Let the rank utility function be $n - i$ if the ith best item is accepted. Hence, maximizing this utility function corresponds to minimizing the expected rank of the accepted item.

Consider the $k = 1$-secretary problem with secretarial input having a total of n items. After m item arrivals, let the state of an algorithm be (m, r), where r is the relative rank of the mth item among the first m items. Let $V(m, r)$ be the optimal expected rank utility function when in state (m, r).

If an algorithm selects item m in state (m, r), then the expected utility

$$U(m, r) = \sum_{i=r}^{n+r-m} (n - i) p_{i,n}(m, r),$$

where

$$p_{i,n}(m, r) = \frac{\binom{i-1}{r-1}\binom{n-i}{m-r}}{\binom{n}{m}}$$

is the probability that the true rank of the mth item is i over all the n items. If the algorithm rejects item m and moves on to the next item, then the state moves to $(m + 1, r')$.

Then using the dynamic programming formulation, we have

$$V(m, r) = \max \left\{ U(m, r), \frac{1}{m+1} \sum_{r'=1}^{m+1} V(m + 1, r') \right\},$$

where after all arrivals $V(n, r) = n - r$.

1. Show by direct computation that $U(m, r) = n - \frac{n+1}{m+1}r$.

2. Using part 1 argue that causal optimal algorithm under the secretarial input to maximize the expected rank utility is of the form: for each m, stop and accept item m if its relative rank is $r \leq r^*(m)$, and continue otherwise.

7.9 [129] (With Machine Learning (ML) Prediction) In this problem we will consider the secretary problem with the secretarial input model, where an estimate of the value of the best item is available beforehand.

Consider the $k = 1$-secretary problem, and let the value of the item chosen by an online algorithm $\mathcal{A}$ be $v_{\mathcal{A}}$, while the value of the optimal item is $v(i^\star)$; then the competitive ratio of $\mathcal{A}$ for maximizing the expected value of the selected item is defined as

$$\mu_{\mathcal{A}} = \frac{\mathbb{E}\{v_{\mathcal{A}}\}}{v(i^\star)}. \tag{7.20}$$

Let an estimate $\hat{v}$ for $v(i^\star)$ be available from prediction beforehand, through with error $\eta = |v(i^\star) - \hat{v}|$ that is unknown.

Consider the following algorithm (ML AUGMENTED) for selecting the secretary where $\epsilon \leq \hat{v}$ is a tradeoff or trust parameter that the algorithm uses to lean towards the prediction compared to the uncertainty about the future input. Smaller the value of ϵ, more is the trust of ML AUGMENTED in the prediction, and as ϵ increases, ML AUGMENTED is catered more towards the uncertain future input.

Algorithm 4 ML AUGMENTED

1: Input: Predicted value $\hat{v}$, confidence parameter $0 \leq \epsilon \leq \hat{v}$, and $c \geq 1$ that determines t_1, t_2
2: %**Sampling Phase**
3: Do not select the first t_1 items $\mathcal{I}_{t_1}(\pi) \subset \mathcal{I}$ under permutation π
4: $b = $ best item of $\mathcal{I}_{t_1}(\pi)$
5: Threshold $T_1 = \max\{v(b), \hat{v} - \epsilon\}$
6: %**Decision Phase I**
7: For every new item i, for $t_1 + 1 \leq i \leq t_2$
8: **if** $v(i) > T_1$ **then**
9:     Select item i, and STOP
10: **end if**
11: Let $\mathcal{I}_{t_2}(\pi)$ be the set of first t_2 items of $\mathcal{I}$ under permutation π
12: Threshold $T_2 = \max\{v(i), i \in \mathcal{I}_{t_2}(\pi)\}$ the value of the best item seen so far
13: %**Decision Phase II**
14: For every new item i, for $t_2 + 1 \leq i \leq n$
15: **if** $v(i) > T_2$ **then**
16:     Select item i, and STOP
17: **end if**

For any $c \geq 1$, let $x_2 > x_1$ be the two solutions of the equation $-x \ln x = \dfrac{1}{ce}$, where recall that this equation appears naturally in maximizing the probability of selecting the best item for $k = 1$-secretary, e.g., see (7.4). Let $f(c) = x_2 - x_1$, $t_1 = \lfloor nx_1 \rfloor$, and $t_2 = \lfloor nx_2 \rfloor$.

1. First we show that independent of parameter ϵ and η, in the worst case the competitive ratio of ML AUGMENTED is bounded.

   (a) Case I: Let $\hat{v} - \epsilon > v(i^\star)$. Show that in this case, no item is selected in Decision Phase I, and ML AUGMENTED is equivalent to sampling the first t_2 items, and then among the last $n - t_2$ items, selecting the first item that is better than all items seen so far. Conclude that the competitive ratio of ML AUGMENTED in this case is $\dfrac{1}{ce}$.

   (b) Case II: Let $\hat{v} - \epsilon \leq v(i^\star)$. In this case, ML AUGMENTED is equivalent to sampling the first t_1 items, and then selecting the first item that is better than all items seen so far. Conclude that the competitive ratio of ML AUGMENTED in this case again is $\dfrac{1}{ce}$.

2. Now we consider the case when the prediction error is small, i.e., $0 \leq \eta < \epsilon$. This implies that $\hat{v} - \epsilon < v(i^\star)$. Note that the best item $i^\star$ appears in Decision Phase I with probability $f(c)$.

   (a) Case I: Let $\hat{v} > v(i^\star)$. Argue that ML AUGMENTED will select an item with value at least $v(i^\star) - \epsilon$ with probability $f(c)$.

   (b) Case II: Let $\hat{v} \leq v(i^\star)$. In the worst case, $\hat{v} = v(i^\star) - \eta$ and argue that ML AUGMENTED will select an item with value at least $v(i^\star) - \epsilon - \eta$ with probability $f(c)$.

   Conclude that the competitive ratio when $0 \leq \epsilon < \eta$ and $v(i^\star) - \epsilon - \eta > 0$ is $f(c)\left(1 - \dfrac{\epsilon + \eta}{v(i^\star)}\right)$.

Combining parts 1 and 2, conclude that the competitive ratio of ML AUGMENTED is

$$\mu \leq \begin{cases} \max\left\{ \dfrac{1}{ce}, f(c)\left(1 - \dfrac{\epsilon + \eta}{v(i^\star)}\right)\right\} & \text{if } 0 \leq \epsilon < \eta, \\ \dfrac{1}{ce} & \text{otherwise.} \end{cases} \qquad (7.21)$$

Recall that without predictions, the competitive ratio is $1/e$. Thus, improved competitive ratio can be obtained if η is small while paying a small penalty of $1/c$ with $c \geq 1$ otherwise. Choice of c and ϵ is inter-dependent and should be chosen judiciously.

CHAPTER 8

Knapsack

8.1 Introduction

In this chapter, we discuss the online version of one of the most versatile combinatorial problems, called the *knapsack*. In the classical offline version of the knapsack problem, we are provided with a set of items $\mathcal{I}$ and a knapsack of size or capacity C. Each item $i \in \mathcal{I}$ has value $v(i)$ and size $w(i)$, and the problem is to select a subset of $\mathcal{I}$ that maximizes the sum of the value of the selected items, subject to the sum of the sizes of the selected items being less than the capacity C of the knapsack.

Because of the two unrelated attributes for each item, value and size, the knapsack problem is sufficient to model various real-world problems where the objective is to maximize a utility function subject to an independent capacity constraint. Important examples of the knapsack problem are scheduling with resource capacity constraints, budgeted auctions, combinatorial resource allocation, etc.

In the online version, the knapsack capacity constraint is available ahead of time, but each item is presented sequentially when its value and size are revealed. An item on its arrival has to be permanently accepted or rejected, irrevocably. It is worth mentioning that the secretary problem considered in Chapter 7 is a special case of the online knapsack problem, where the size of each item is 1 and the knapsack capacity is also 1. Thus, unfortunately, the result that no algorithm is competitive for the secretary problem under the adversarial input carries over for the knapsack problem. Therefore, in this chapter, we primarily consider the secretarial input and present an online algorithm whose competitive ratio is a constant.

We show that a randomized algorithm based on the sample and price philosophy is $1/10e$-competitive in expectation for the knapsack problem with the secretarial input model. We also consider the worst-case input, though with resource augmentation, where an online algorithm is allowed more capacity than the optimal offline algorithm, and an online algorithm is also allowed to reject previously accepted items.

8.2 Problem Formulation

8.2.1 Linear Programming Formulation of the Offline Knapsack Problem

Let the complete item set be $\mathcal{I}$, and for item $i \in \mathcal{I}$, its value and size be $v(i)$ and $w(i)$, respectively. If all items $i \in \mathcal{I}$ are available beforehand (offline setting), then the knapsack problem with capacity C is to select items $i \in \mathcal{I}$ that maximize the sum of their values, subject to the sum of the sizes of the selected items being at most C.

Formally, the following integer program solves the offline knapsack problem:

$$\max \quad \sum_{i \in \mathcal{I}} v(i) x_{\mathcal{I}}(i, C),$$

$$\sum_{i \in \mathcal{I}} w(i) x_{\mathcal{I}}(i, C) \le C, \tag{8.1}$$

$$x_{\mathcal{I}}(i, C) \in \{0, 1\}, \ \forall \, i \in \mathcal{I},$$

where $x_{\mathcal{I}}(i, C) = 1$ if item i is selected, and 0 otherwise. We index the solution $x_{\mathcal{I}}(i, C)$ with $\mathcal{I}$ and C to make explicit the set of items being considered and the capacity of the knapsack.

Before dealing with the online version of the knapsack problem, it is instructive to discuss the following linear programming (LP) relaxation of the offline version of the knapsack problem (8.1):

$$\max \quad \sum_{i \in \mathcal{I}} v(i) x_{\mathcal{I}}(i, C),$$

$$\sum_{i \in \mathcal{I}} w(i) x_{\mathcal{I}}(i, C) \le C, \tag{8.2}$$

$$x_{\mathcal{I}}(i, C) \in [0, 1], \ \forall \, i \in \mathcal{I},$$

where we have relaxed the condition that $x_{\mathcal{I}}(i, C) \in \{0, 1\}$ in (8.1) to $x_{\mathcal{I}}(i, C) \in [0, 1]$.

Definition 8.2.1 *Let $x_U^\star(i, C)$ be the optimal solution for (8.2) while only considering set of items $U \subseteq \mathcal{I}$ and capacity C, i.e., $x_U^\star(i, C)$ solves*

$$\max \quad \sum_{i \in U} v(i) x_U(i, C).$$

$$\sum_{i \in U} w(i) x_U(i, C) \le C, \tag{8.3}$$

$$x_U(i, C) \in [0, 1], \ \forall \, i \in U,$$

Moreover, let the value of items of set $S \subseteq U$ using the optimal solution $x_U^\star(i, C)$ be

$$v_U^C(S) = \sum_{s \in S} v(s) x_U^\star(i, C),$$

and the ensuing total size of selected items of set S be

$$w_U^C(S) = \sum_{s \in S} w(s) x_U^\star(i, C).$$

We define the *cost–benefit ratio* of item i as $\mathsf{b}_i = \frac{w(i)}{v(i)}$. For technical reasons, we assume throughout that b_i is distinct for distinct items. Using the definition of cost–benefit ratio, we state two important properties of the LP formulation (8.2), which will be used later, as follows.

Proposition 8.2.2 *For the LP relaxation (8.2), with knapsack size C, there exists a threshold $\mathsf{b}_{\mathcal{I}}^\star(C)$ such that all items i with cost–benefit ratio $\mathsf{b}_i < \mathsf{b}_{\mathcal{I}}^\star(C)$ are selected completely, i.e., $x_{\mathcal{I}}^\star(i, C) = 1$ for $\mathsf{b}_i < \mathsf{b}_{\mathcal{I}}^\star(C)$ in (8.2), while items j with $\mathsf{b}_j > \mathsf{b}_{\mathcal{I}}^\star(C)$ are not selected at all, i.e., $x_{\mathcal{I}}^\star(j, C) = 0$ for $\mathsf{b}_j > \mathsf{b}_{\mathcal{I}}^\star(C)$ in (8.2). The only non-triviality is for items with $\mathsf{b}_i = \mathsf{b}_{\mathcal{I}}^\star(C)$, where the relaxed solution may be non-integral.*

The proof of Proposition 8.2.2 is discussed in Problem 8.1. As a corollary of Proposition 8.2.2 we get the following result.

Proposition 8.2.3 *Consider the offline LP relaxation* (8.2) *with capacities x and y, respectively. If* $x \geq y$, *then*

$$\mathsf{b}_{\mathcal{I}}^{\star}(x) \geq \mathsf{b}_{\mathcal{I}}^{\star}(y),$$

where $\mathsf{b}_{\mathcal{I}}^{\star}(c)$ *is defined in Proposition 8.2.2.*

Proposition 8.2.3 implies that the cost–benefit ratio threshold increases with increase in the capacity, and items with poorer cost–benefit ratio are accepted with a larger capacity constraint, which is intuitive.

In light of Proposition 8.2.2, an easy temptation for approximating the optimal solution of the integral offline knapsack problem (8.1) is to order the items in increasing cost–benefit ratio, and pick as many items in order until the capacity is exhausted–essentially a greedy algorithm. The following example shows that such a strategy fails entirely.

Example 8.2.4

Consider the case when there are only two items, $v(1) = 1, w(1) = 1,$ $\mathsf{b}_1 = 1,$ *and* $v(2) =$ $C - 1, w(2) = C,$ $\mathsf{b}_2 = \frac{C}{C-1},$ *and the knapsack capacity is C. The optimal solution* OPT *is to just choose item 2, while a greedy (with respect to the cost–benefit ratio) algorithm will choose item 1 first since it has a smaller value of* b, *and cannot choose item 2 since the capacity constraint is violated. Thus, the total value of* OPT *is* $C - 1$, *while the total value of the greedy algorithm is 1, making the approximation ratio of the greedy algorithm* $\frac{1}{C-1}$.

Using Definition 8.2.1, next, we state a scaling property that relates the value of the LP relaxation (8.2) when the knapsack capacity is scaled.

Lemma 8.2.5 *For* $U \subseteq \mathcal{I}$, *let* $S_C(U) = \{i \in U : x_U^{\star}(i, C) > 0\}$, *where* $x_U^{\star}(i, C)$ *is as stated in Definition 8.2.1, i.e.,* $S_C(U)$ *is the set of items of U that have been (partially) selected in* (8.2) *with item set U and capacity C. By definition,* $v_U^C(U) = v_U^C(S_C(U)) = \sum_{i \in S_C(U)} x_U^{\star}(i, C) v(i)$. *Then*

$$v_U^{2C}(U) \leq 2 v_U^C(U),$$

i.e., doubling the knapsack capacity, the objective function (8.2) *increases at most two times. In general, we have*

$$v_U^y(U) \leq \frac{y}{x} v_U^x(U), \tag{8.4}$$

for any $x, y > 0$ *with* $y/x > 1$.

Note that property (8.4) is not necessarily true when considering the integral problem (8.1). Proof of Lemma 8.2.5 follows from Proposition 8.2.2, and we leave it as an exercise.

After discussing some basic properties of the offline LP relaxation of the knapsack problem in this section, we turn to the main object of interest, the online setting, next.

8.2.2 Online Setting

In the online setting, the knapsack capacity constraint C is known ahead of time. Items arrive one by one, and the value and the size of the item are revealed only at the time of the item's arrival. Moreover, an item has to be permanently accepted or rejected on its arrival, subject to the constraint that the sum of the sizes of all the accepted items is at most C. With σ (some permutation π of the set of items $\mathcal{I}$) as the input, let the set of items selected by an online algorithm $\mathcal{A}$ be $S_{\mathcal{A}}(\sigma)$. Then the profit of $\mathcal{A}$ is $v_{\mathcal{A}}(\sigma) = \sum_{i \in S_{\mathcal{A}}(\sigma)} v(i)$, and the competitive ratio of $\mathcal{A}$ is

$$\mu_{\mathcal{A}} = \min_{\sigma} \frac{v_{\mathcal{A}}(\sigma)}{v_{\text{OPT}}(\sigma)}. \tag{8.5}$$

It is easy to see that the secretary problem is a special case of the knapsack problem when sizes of all items $w(i) = C$, $\forall\, i \in \mathcal{I}$, and the knapsack capacity is C. Thus, from (7.1), we know that no online algorithm has a bounded competitive ratio with the worst-case input. Thus, in this chapter, we consider the secretarial input, i.e., $\sigma = \pi(\mathcal{I})$, where the permutation π is uniformly random over the set of $\mathcal{I}$ items. Hence, the competitive ratio (in expectation) is

$$\mu_{\mathcal{A}} = \min_{\sigma} \frac{\mathbb{E}_{\pi}\{v_{\mathcal{A}}(\sigma)\}}{v_{\text{OPT}}(\sigma)}. \tag{8.6}$$

Moreover, we let the number of items be $|\mathcal{I}| = n$, which is known ahead of time. In the secretarial input setting, it is tempting to extend the sample and price algorithm discussed for the secretary problem in Section 7.3 to the knapsack problem, where it would take the following shape. Use the first t items to build a 'threshold' on the cost–benefit ratio, and then in the decision phase, select any item with a cost–benefit ratio lower than the threshold cost–benefit ratio, subject to the capacity constraint. Example 8.2.4 precludes this possibility immediately and we leave the proof of this claim as an exercise in Problem 8.2.

Next, we consider a more complicated version of the sample and price algorithm that is shown to be $1/10e$-competitive for the online knapsack problem. For the rest of the chapter, without loss of generality, we let the capacity of the knapsack be $C = 1$, and scale the sizes of each item by $1/C$, resulting in $w(i) \leq 1$ for all $i \in \mathcal{I}$.

8.3 Simple Algorithm via k-Secretary Problem

Before describing the actual algorithm, we discuss a simple case to build some intuition. Suppose the item sizes take only few distinct values, e.g., $w(i) \in \left\{ \frac{1}{2}, \frac{1}{4} \right\}$ $\forall\, i \in \mathcal{I}$. Then we show that VIRTUAL (Algorithm 2) for the k-secretary problem can be used to get a reasonable competitive ratio guarantee for the knapsack problem as follows.

Example 8.3.1

Let the size of all items be $\frac{1}{2}$. Then we know that solving the knapsack problem with capacity 1 is to select the 2 best items with the largest value, which is identical to the $k = 2$-secretary problem. Thus, under the secretarial input, Lemma 7.5.4 implies that VIRTUAL (Section 7.5) with $k = 2$ is a $1/e$-competitive algorithm (in expectation) for the knapsack problem.

Example 8.3.2

Generalizing Example 8.3.1, let the size of any item be either $\frac{1}{2}$ or $\frac{1}{4}$. Here again, we know that the optimal solution to the knapsack problem with capacity 1 contains at most 4 items, but we cannot directly apply the k-secretary solution. A simple randomization, however, can be made to work as follows.

Let $I_x \subseteq \mathcal{I}$ be the set of items with size $x \in \left\{ \frac{1}{2}, \frac{1}{4} \right\}$, and $I_x^{\text{OPT}} \subseteq I_x$ be the subset of items of I_x that are part of the optimal offline solution. Moreover, let $O_x^\star \subseteq I_x$ for $x \in \left\{ \frac{1}{2}, \frac{1}{4} \right\}$ be the set that consists of $1/(2x)$ items with the largest values of I_x. With $v(S) = \sum_{i \in S} v(i)$, clearly,

$$v(I_{1/2}^{\text{OPT}}) \leq 2v(O_{1/2}^\star), \tag{8.7}$$

since $|I_{1/2}^{\text{OPT}}| \leq 2$, i.e., OPT can select at most 2 items of size $1/2$. Similarly,

$$v(I_{1/4}^{\text{OPT}}) \leq 2v(O_{1/4}^\star), \tag{8.8}$$

since $|I_{1/4}^{\text{OPT}}| \leq 4$, i.e., OPT can select at most 4 items of size $1/4$.

Consider an **online algorithm** $\mathcal{A}$ that tosses a fair coin once. If the coin toss shows heads (call it event $\mathcal{E}_{1/2}$), $\mathcal{A}$ considers items from $I_{1/2}$ alone and disregards any item of $I_{1/4}$. Otherwise, when the coin toss shows tails (call it event $\mathcal{E}_{1/4}$), $\mathcal{A}$ considers items from $I_{1/4}$ alone. With event $\mathcal{E}_{1/2}$, $\mathcal{A}$ executes VIRTUAL with $k = 1$, while in the other case when event $\mathcal{E}_{1/4}$ happens, $\mathcal{A}$ executes VIRTUAL with $k = 2$. Let the set of items selected by algorithm $\mathcal{A}$ be $I_\mathcal{A}$ in either of the two cases.

Recall that from Lemma 7.5.4, VIRTUAL algorithm is an $1/e$-competitive algorithm for any k. Thus, we get that when $\mathcal{E}_{1/2}$ happens, $\mathbb{E}\{v(I_\mathcal{A})\} \geq v(O_{1/2}^\star)/e$, while, in the other case, when $\mathcal{E}_{1/4}$ happens, $\mathbb{E}\{v(I_\mathcal{A})\} \geq v(O_{1/4}^\star)/e$.

Then, we get the following:

$$v(\text{OPT}) = v(I_{1/2}^{\text{OPT}}) + v(I_{1/4}^{\text{OPT}}),$$

$$\overset{(a)}{\leq} 2e\mathbb{E}\{v(I_\mathcal{A})|\mathcal{E}_{1/2}\} + 2e\mathbb{E}\{v(I_\mathcal{A})|\mathcal{E}_{1/4}\},$$

$$\overset{(b)}{=} 4e\mathbb{P}(\mathcal{E}_{1/2})\mathbb{E}\{v(I_\mathcal{A})|\mathcal{E}_{1/2}\} + \mathbb{P}(\mathcal{E}_{1/4})\mathbb{E}\{v(I_\mathcal{A})|\mathcal{E}_{1/4}\},$$

$$= 4e\,\mathbb{E}\{v(I_\mathcal{A})\},$$

where (a) follows from (8.7) and (8.8), while (b) follows since $\mathbb{P}(\mathcal{E}_{1/2}) = \mathbb{P}(\mathcal{E}_{1/4}) = 1/2$. Thus, we get that algorithm $\mathcal{A}$ is $1/4e$-competitive.

The idea described in Example 8.3.1 will now be extended to the case when item sizes are arbitrary as follows.

8.4 1/10e-Competitive Online Algorithm

Recall that the knapsack capacity $C = 1$.

Algorithm MULTIPARTSEC: Choose a uniformly randomly from $\{0, 1, ..., 4\}$. For $a = \{0, 1, 2, 3\}$, fix $k = 3^a$ and use VIRTUAL (Section 7.5) to select the k-best items among the set of items with size at most $1/k$.

The case of $a = 4$ is handled separately following the sample and price philosophy as follows. Recall that the total number of items presented is $|\mathcal{I}| = n$, which is known to the algorithm. Sample $t \in \{1, 2, ..., n\}$ from a Binomial distribution with n trials and success probability $1/2$, denoted as Binomial $(n, 1/2)$. The input is partitioned into two parts: first part X contains the first t items, i.e., $X = \{1, ... t\}$ (sampling phase), and the second part Y contains the rest of the items $Y = \{t + 1, ... n\}$ (decision phase).

After the arrival of the final item of X at time step t, the algorithm computes the optimal cost–benefit ratio threshold $b_X^\star(1/2)$ (Proposition 8.2.2) from the LP formulation (8.2), with capacity $1/2$ using items belonging to set X. No item from set X is selected. Any item i that appears subsequently in set Y is selected (or added to selected set S) if

1. $w(i) \leq 1/3^4$, and
2. $b_i \leq b_X^\star(1/2)$, and
3. the updated occupied capacity $w(S \cup \{i\}) \leq 1$ (that there is enough room in the knapsack to include item i).

Let $S^{\text{OPT}} \subseteq \mathcal{I}$ be the optimal subset of items for the offline knapsack problem with capacity $C = 1$. Arrange the items belonging to S^{OPT} in decreasing order of their sizes $w(i)$, and let the ordered set be $S^{\text{OPT}} = \{i_1, i_2, ..., i_m\}$. Partition S_{OPT} into five sets, $S_0^{\text{OPT}}, S_1^{\text{OPT}}, ..., S_4^{\text{OPT}}$, where set

$$S_j^{\text{OPT}} = \{i_\ell | 3^j \leq \ell \leq 3^{j+1} - 1\}, j = 0, ..., 3, \tag{8.9}$$

and set $S_4^{\text{OPT}} = \{i_{81}, ..., i_m\}$. For example, $S_0^{\text{OPT}} = \{i_1, i_2\}$, $S_1^{\text{OPT}} = \{i_3, ..., i_8\}$, and so on.

For any $a \in \{0, 1, ..., 4\}$, let G_a be the set of selected items output by the algorithm MULTIPARTSEC. Similar to Example 8.3.2, we show the following result.

Lemma 8.4.1 *For $a = \{0, 1, ..., 3\}$,*

$$\mathbb{E}\{v(G_a)\} \geq \frac{v(S_a^{\text{OPT}})}{2e}, \tag{8.10}$$

where S_a is as defined in (8.9).

A non-trivial result is stated next, which claims that a guarantee similar to (8.10) holds for $a = 4$ as well, whose proof appears after Theorem 8.4.3.

Lemma 8.4.2 *For $a = 4$, $v(G_a) \geq \frac{v(S_a^{OPT})}{2e}$.*

Combining Lemma 8.4.1 and 8.4.2, we get that algorithm MULTIPARTSEC is $1/10e$ competitive as follows.

Theorem 8.4.3 *Algorithm MULTIPARTSEC is $1/10e$-competitive (in expectation).*

Proof: By definition,

$$v(\text{OPT}) = \sum_{i=0}^{4} v(S_i^{OPT}),$$

$$\overset{(a)}{\leq} 2e \sum_{i=0}^{4} \mathbb{E}\{v(G)|a = i\},$$

$$= 10e \sum_{i=0}^{4} \frac{1}{5} \mathbb{E}\{v(G)|a = i\},$$

$$= 10e \sum_{i=0}^{4} \mathbb{P}(a = i)\mathbb{E}\{v(G)|a = i\},$$

$$= 10e \, \mathbb{E}\{v(G)\},$$

where (a) follows from Lemma 8.4.1 and 8.4.2. ∎

Note that there are two sources of randomness here, the secretarial input and the random choices of Algorithm MULTIPARTSEC.

To prove Lemma 8.4.1, we prove the following claims. From the definitions of set partitions S_a^{OPT} for the set of items chosen by OPT, S_{OPT}, an immediate bound on the size of sets S_a^{OPT} is as follows.

Lemma 8.4.4 $|S_a^{OPT}| \leq 2.3^a, a = 0, \dots, 3$.

Important to note that for S_4^{OPT}, there is no such upper bound.

Lemma 8.4.5 *The size of each item in set $S_a^{OPT}, a = 0, \dots, 3$ is at most $1/3^a$.*

Proof: For subset $S_a^{OPT}, a = 0, \dots, 3$, there are $3^a - 1$ bigger items in subsets $\cup_r S_r^{OPT}, r = 0, \dots, a - 1$ 'ahead' of it (indexed in the decreasing order of their sizes), and the total size of the selected items in S_{OPT} is at most 1. Thus, the size of any item in S_a^{OPT} is at most $1/3^a$. ∎

Proof: [Lemma 8.4.1]
Let

$$Q_a = \{i \in \mathcal{I} | w(i) \leq 1/3^a\}$$

be the subset of items with size less than $1/3^a$. Then from Lemma 8.4.5, $S_a^{OPT} \subseteq Q_a$.

Among all possible subsets of Q_a of size 3^a, let R_a be the subset with the largest sum of the value of items in it, i.e.,

$$R_a = \arg \max_{T \subseteq Q_a : |T| = 3^a} v(T).$$

Note that for any $a = 0, \dots, 3$, $|S_a^{\text{OPT}}| \leq 2.3^a$ from Lemma 8.4.4, and $S_a^{\text{OPT}} \subseteq Q_a$. Thus, we have

$$v(S_a) \leq 2v(R_a), \tag{8.11}$$

for $a = 0, \dots, 3$.

An important byproduct of this deduction is that for $a = 0, \dots, 3$, using VIRTUAL with $k = 3^a$, we have $\mathbb{E}\{v(G_a)\} \geq \frac{v(R_a)}{e}$, where G_a is the output of VIRTUAL for $k = 3^a$, $a = 0, \dots, 3$.

Using (8.11), $\mathbb{E}\{v(G_a)\} \geq \frac{v(R_a)}{e}$ implies $\mathbb{E}\{v(G_a)\} \geq \frac{v(S_a^{\text{OPT}})}{2e}$, as required. ∎

Next, we prove the non-trivial Lemma 8.4.2, to complete the proof of Theorem 8.4.3.

Proof: Consider the fifth partition of the OPT solution S_{OPT},

$$S_4^{\text{OPT}} = \{i_{81}, \dots, i_m\}.$$

Note that $w_{81} \leq 1/81$, since there are 80 bigger items in the S_{OPT} that are part of $S_0^{\text{OPT}}, \dots S_3^{\text{OPT}}$, and the total size of the selected items by OPT is at most 1.

The subset of items that is considered for selection with algorithm MULTIPARTSEC when $a = 4$ is $Q_4 = \{i \subseteq \mathcal{I} : w(i) \leq 1/81\}$, and $S_4^{\text{OPT}} \subseteq Q_4$. Let the sum of values accrued by OPT from set S_4^{OPT} be

$$s_4 = v(S_4^{\text{OPT}}) = \sum_{i \in S_4^{\text{OPT}}} v(i).$$

From Definition 8.2.1, we have

$$s_4 \leq v_{Q_4}^1(Q_4), \tag{8.12}$$

since $S_4^{\text{OPT}} \subseteq Q_4$, where $v_{Q_4}^1(Q_4)$ is the value of the optimal (fractional) LP solution (8.2) with set of items Q_4 and knapsack capacity 1.

Moreover, from Lemma 8.2.5,

$$v_{Q_4}^1(Q_4) \leq \frac{4}{3} v_{Q_4}^{3/4}(Q_4). \tag{8.13}$$

Recall that with the secretarial input, the input sequence is $\sigma = \pi(\mathcal{I})$, where the permutation π is chosen uniformly randomly. We concentrate on an item $j \in Q_4$ that appears at location $\pi(j)$ with the online input, for which

$$x_{\pi(Q_4)}^\star(\pi(j), 3/4) > 0,$$

i.e., item j is selected by the offline LP solution (8.2) with items from set Q_4 and capacity $3/4$. Whenever we say LP solution, we mean offline, so we drop the prefix offline from here on. Note that even though the LP solution $x_{\pi(Q_4)}^\star(\pi(j), 3/4)$ does not depend on π, we have included the permutation in the definition of $x_{\pi(Q_4)}^\star(\pi(j), 3/4)$ to make it explicit for ease of exposition when we connect it with the online case, where item j appears at location $\pi(j)$.

The main ingredient to prove Lemma 8.4.2 is presented next.

Lemma 8.4.6 *If* $x^\star_{\pi(Q_4)}(\pi(j), 3/4) > 0$ *for* $j \in Q_4$ *for the LP solution* (8.2) *with capacity* 3/4 *and set of items* Q_4, *then the online algorithm* MULTIPARTSEC *selects item* $\pi(j)$ *with probability larger than* 0.3 *when the knapsack size is* 1.

Using Lemma 8.4.6 and linearity of expectation,

$$\mathbb{E}\{v(G)|a = 4\} \geq \sum_{x^\star_{\pi(Q_4)}(\pi(j),3/4)>0, \, j \in Q_4} \frac{3}{10} v_j = \frac{3}{10} v^{3/4}_{\pi(Q_4)}(Q_4). \tag{8.14}$$

From (8.12) and (8.13), we also have $s_4 = v(S^{\mathrm{OPT}}_4) = \sum_{i \in S^{\mathrm{OPT}}_4} v(i) \leq \frac{4}{3} v^{3/4}_{\pi(Q_4)}(Q_4)$. Combining this with (8.14), we get

$$s_4 \leq \frac{40}{9} \mathbb{E}\{v(G)|a = 4\} \leq 2e \mathbb{E}\{v(G)|a = 4\},$$

which proves Lemma 8.4.2 modulo Lemma 8.4.6 that we prove next. ∎

In the rest of this section, we prove Lemma 8.4.6. Towards that end, consider an item $\pi(j) \in Q_4$ for which $x^\star_{\pi(Q_4)}(\pi(j), 3/4) > 0$. If $\pi(j)$ is encountered by MULTIPARTSEC in the decision phase, i.e., $\pi(j) \in Y$, then we show the following two events happen together with probability at least 0.3, (i) $b_{\pi(j)} \leq b^\star_X(1/2)$, and (ii) the total size of the accepted items just before the arrival of $\pi(j)$ is at most $1 - 1/81$. Since the size of item $\pi(j)$ is at most $1/81$ by definition, both the above conditions imply that item $\pi(j)$ is accepted by MULTIPARTSEC if encountered in the decision phase with probability at least 0.3.

The proof sketch is as follows: to control the event that the total size of the accepted items just before the arrival of item $\pi(j)$ is at most $1 - 1/81$, an LP with capacity 3/2 is considered, while for the other event that $b_{\pi(j)} \leq b^\star(1/2)$, an LP with capacity 3/4 is considered.

Note that the LP with capacity 3/2 selects all items i with $b_i < b^\star_{\pi(Q_4)}\left(\frac{3}{2}\right)$. Intuitively, the connection with the LP having capacity 3/2 is made since the LP with capacity 3/2 is expected to select more items than algorithm MULTIPARTSEC with capacity 1. Therefore, if we can show that $b^\star_X(1/2) \leq b^\star_{\pi(Q_4)}\left(\frac{3}{2}\right)$, then this helps in proving that if LP with capacity 3/2 has room to select an item $\pi(j)$, then algorithm MULTIPARTSEC can also select item $\pi(j)$.

For the other event $b_{\pi(j)} \leq b^\star_X(1/2)$, note that the LP with capacity 3/4 is more limited than the algorithm MULTIPARTSEC that has capacity 1. Thus, if an item $\pi(j)$ is selected by the LP with capacity 3/4, its cost–benefit ratio must be smaller than the threshold $b^\star_{\pi(Q)}\left(\frac{3}{4}\right)$. Hence, showing that $b^\star_{\pi(Q)}\left(\frac{3}{4}\right) \leq b^\star_X\left(\frac{1}{2}\right)$ is sufficient to claim that the cost–benefit ratio of $\pi(j)$ is smaller than $b^\star_X\left(\frac{1}{2}\right)$ as required.

Now we proceed with the proof of Lemma 8.4.6.

Let $x^\star_{\pi(Q_4)}(i, c)$ be the optimal LP solution (8.2) for items $i \in Q_4$ with capacity c, where $x^\star_{\pi(Q_4)}(i, c)$ does not depend on π. For an item $i \in \mathcal{I}$, define $\chi_i = 1$ if item $i \in X$ (belongs to the sampling phase where no items are selected), and $\chi_i = 0$ otherwise, i.e., $i \in Y$. Let[1]

$$Z_1 = w^{3/4}_{\pi(Q_4)}(X \backslash \pi(j)) = \sum_{i \in \pi(Q_4) \backslash \{\pi(j)\}} w(i) x^\star_{\pi(Q_4)}(i, 3/4) \chi_i$$

and

$$Z_2 = w^{3/2}_{\pi(Q_4)}(Y \backslash \pi(j)) = \sum_{i \in \pi(Q_4) \backslash \{\pi(j)\}} w(i) x^\star_{\pi(Q_4)}(i, 3/2)(1 - \chi_i).$$

Note that Z_1 and Z_2 are the **random** sums of the sizes of the items belonging to set $X \cap Q_4$ and $Y \cap Q_4$ without item $\pi(j)$, when (8.2) is solved using set Q_4 of items (or $\pi(Q_4)$ since $x^\star_{\pi(Q_4)}(i, *)$ does not depend on π), with capacities 3/4 and 3/2, respectively.

Because of the uniformly random permutation π, and t being Binomial, $\chi_i's$ are independent random variables with $\mathbb{P}(\chi_i = 1) = \mathbb{P}(\chi_i = 0) = \frac{1}{2}$. Hence

$$\mathbb{E}\{Z_1\} = \frac{1}{2} \sum_{i \in \pi(Q_4) \backslash \{\pi(j)\}} w(i) x^\star_{\pi(Q_4)}(i, 3/4)$$

and

$$\mathbb{E}\{Z_2\} = \frac{1}{2} \sum_{i \in \pi(Q_4) \backslash \{\pi(j)\}} w(i) x^\star_{\pi(Q_4)}(i, 3/2).$$

From the definition of Q_4, for any item $i \in Q_4$, $w_i \leq 1/81$. Hence, both Z_1 and Z_2 are sums of i.i.d. random variables with support belonging to $[0, 1/81]$. We need the following Chernoff bound in the sequel.

Lemma 8.4.7 *Let $z_1, \ldots, z_n$ be independent random variables that take values in $[0, z_{max}]$. Let $Z = \sum_{i=1}^{n} z_i$; then for all $\delta > 0$,*

$$\mathbb{P}(Z \geq (1 + \delta)\mathbb{E}\{Z\}) < \exp\left(-\frac{\mathbb{E}\{Z\}}{z_{max}}\left[(1 + \delta)\ln(1 + \delta) - \delta\right]\right).$$

Note that

$$\mathbb{E}\{Z_1\} = \frac{1}{2} \sum_{i \in \pi(Q_4) \backslash \{\pi(j)\}} w(i) x^\star_{\pi(Q_4)}(i, 3/4) \in [1/2(3/4 - 1/81), 3/8].$$

and

$$\mathbb{E}\{Z_2\} = \frac{1}{2} \sum_{i \in \pi(Q_4) \backslash \{\pi(j)\}} w(i) x^\star_{\pi(Q_4)}(i, 3/2) \in [1/2(3/2 - 1/81), 3/4].$$

---

[1] Whenever we write set X or Y within the considered set of items as Q_4, we mean $X \cap Q_4$ and $Y \cap Q_4$.

Applying the Chernoff bound to both Z_1 and Z_2 with $z_{max} = \frac{1}{81}$, and using $\delta = \frac{1}{3} - \frac{8}{243}$, we get

$$\mathbb{P}\left(Z_1 \geq \frac{1}{2} - \frac{1}{81}\right) < 0.3, \tag{8.15}$$

and

$$\mathbb{P}\left(Z_2 \geq 1 - \frac{2}{81}\right) < 0.1. \tag{8.16}$$

Let $\mathcal{E}$ be the event that $Z_1 < \frac{1}{2} - \frac{1}{81}$ and $Z_2 < 1 - \frac{2}{81}$. Using a simple union bound from (8.15) and (8.16), we get

$$\mathbb{P}(\mathcal{E}|a = 4) > 0.6. \tag{8.17}$$

Using the preceding discussion, we next connect the size of the LP solution with different capacities.

Lemma 8.4.8 *Conditioned on event $\mathcal{E}$,*

$$w_{\pi(Q_4)}^{3/2}(X) > \frac{1}{2} > w_{\pi(Q_4)}^{3/4}(X).$$

Proof: From the definition of Z_1 and Z_2, $w_{\pi(Q_4)}^{3/4}(X) \leq Z_1 + w_{\pi(j)}$ and $w_{\pi(Q_4)}^{3/2}(Y) \leq Z_2 + w_{\pi(j)}$. Moreover, the size of item $\pi(j) \in Q_4$ is at most $\frac{1}{81}$. Thus, conditioned on event $\mathcal{E}$, i.e., $Z_1 < \frac{1}{2} - \frac{1}{81}$,

$$w_{\pi(Q_4)}^{3/4}(X) \leq Z_1 + w_{\pi(j)} < \frac{1}{2},$$

proving one part of the lemma. Under event $\mathcal{E}$, we also have $Z_2 < 1 - \frac{2}{81}$, hence

$$w_{\pi(Q_4)}^{3/2}(Y) \leq Z_2 + w_{\pi(j)} < 1 - \frac{1}{81}. \tag{8.18}$$

Moreover, the total size of the LP (8.2) with capacity $\frac{3}{2}$ with the set of items Q_4 satisfies $w_{\pi(Q_4)}^{3/2}(X \cup Y) = \frac{3}{2}$. Thus, we get

$$w_{\pi(Q_4)}^{3/2}(X) \geq \frac{3}{2} - w_{\pi(Q_4)}^{3/2}(Y).$$

Using (8.18), it follows that

$$w_{\pi(Q_4)}^{3/2}(X) > \frac{1}{2},$$

which implies the other remaining part of the Lemma. ∎

With the set of items U and knapsack capacity c, recall that $\mathsf{b}_U^\star(c)$ is the threshold on the cost–benefit ratio for solving the LP (8.2) as defined in Proposition 8.2.2. Next, we connect the thresholds $\mathsf{b}_U^\star(c)$ with different capacities and item sets.

Lemma 8.4.9 *Conditioned on event $\mathcal{E}$, the cost–benefit ratio satisfies*

$$b^\star_{\pi(Q_4)}\left(\frac{3}{4}\right) \le b^\star_X\left(\frac{1}{2}\right) \le b^\star_{\pi(Q_4)}\left(\frac{3}{2}\right).$$

Proof: We first prove $b^\star_X\left(\frac{1}{2}\right) \le b^\star_{\pi(Q_4)}\left(\frac{3}{2}\right)$; the other claim follows similarly.

Conditioned on event $\mathcal{E}$, from Lemma 8.4.8; we have

$$w^{3/2}_{\pi(Q_4)}(X) > \frac{1}{2}, \tag{8.19}$$

which implies that the items from set $X \cap Q_4$ occupy more than half the size in the LP solution with capacity $\frac{3}{2}$ with set of items Q_4. See Figure 8.1.

[Contradiction] Let the assertion be false, i.e., let $b^\star_X\left(\frac{1}{2}\right) > b^\star_{\pi(Q_4)}\left(\frac{3}{2}\right)$. Under this hypothesis, we show that the items of set $X \cap Q_4$ would occupy less than $\frac{1}{2}$ of the size with the knapsack problem with the set of items Q_4 and capacity $\frac{3}{2}$, contradicting (8.19) as follows.

From Proposition 8.2.2,

$$w^{\frac{3}{2}}_{\pi(Q_4)}(X) = \sum_{i \in Q_4 \cap X, b_i \le b^\star_{Q_4}\left(\frac{3}{2}\right)} x^\star_{\pi(Q_4)}\left(i, \frac{3}{2}\right) w(i), \tag{8.20}$$

while the total size of the LP solution (8.2) with capacity $\frac{1}{2}$ is

$$\sum_{i \in X, b_i \le b^\star_X\left(\frac{1}{2}\right)} x^\star_X\left(i, \frac{1}{2}\right) w(i) = \frac{1}{2}. \tag{8.21}$$

Thus, if the claim is false, i.e., $b^\star_{\pi(Q_4)}\left(\frac{3}{2}\right) < b^\star_X\left(\frac{1}{2}\right)$, then from Proposition 8.2.2, we have $x^\star_{\pi(Q_4)}\left(i, \frac{3}{2}\right) \le x^\star_X\left(i, \frac{1}{2}\right)$ for $i \in X \cap Q_4$. Thus, from (8.20), we get

$$w^{3/2}_{\pi(Q_4)}(X) = \sum_{i \in X \cap Q_4, b_i \le b^\star_{\pi(Q_4)}\left(\frac{3}{2}\right)} x^\star_{\pi(Q_4)}\left(i, \frac{3}{2}\right) w(i),$$

$$\le \sum_{i \in X \cap Q_4, b_i \le b^\star_X\left(\frac{1}{2}\right)} x^\star_X\left(i, \frac{1}{2}\right) w(i),$$

$$\le \frac{1}{2}, \tag{8.22}$$

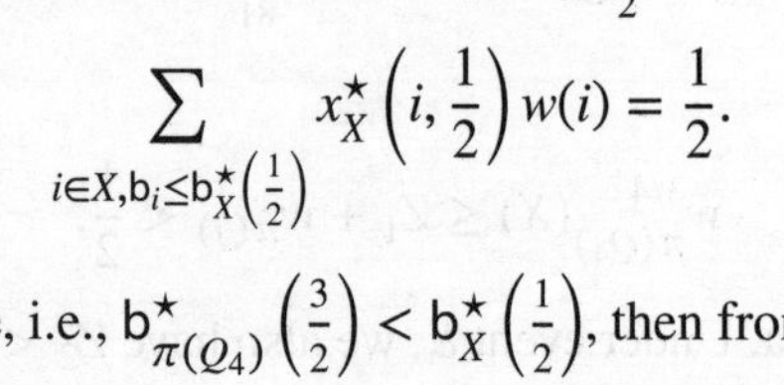

Figure 8.1 Items from set $X \cap Q_4$ occupy more than 1/2 of the capacity in the knapsack of capacity 3/2 under event $\mathcal{E}$

where the final inequality follows from (8.21). Relation (8.22) implies that items of set $X \cap Q_4$ occupy at most half size in $\pi(Q_4)$ with knapsack problem with capacity $\frac{3}{2}$, contradicting (8.19). Thus, we conclude that $b_X^\star \left(\frac{1}{2} \right) \le b_{\pi(Q_4)}^\star \left(\frac{3}{2} \right)$.

To prove the other claim $b_{\pi(Q_4)} \left(\frac{3}{4} \right) \le b_X \left(\frac{1}{2} \right)$, note that under event $\mathcal{E}$, Lemma 8.4.8 implies that items from set $X \cap Q_4$ occupy less than size $1/2$ in the LP solution for the knapsack with capacity $\frac{3}{4}$. Thus, continuing as above via contradiction, the result follows immediately. ∎

Let $\mathcal{I}^{\text{el}} \subseteq (Y \cap Q_4) \backslash \{\pi(j)\}$ be the set of (eligible) items appearing in the decision phase of algorithm MULTIPARTSEC whose cost–benefit ratio is less than or equal to $b_X^\star \left(\frac{1}{2} \right)$, other than item $\pi(j)$. The algorithm MULTIPARTSEC will select all items of $\mathcal{I}^{\text{el}}$ until it runs out of capacity. We next bound the sum of the sizes of items of $\mathcal{I}^{\text{el}}$ and show that it is at most $1 - \frac{1}{81}$, conditioned on event $\mathcal{E}$. This will imply that at the time of arrival of $\pi(j)$, there is enough room for $\pi(j)$, which has size at most $1/81$, to be accepted.

Recall that $b_X^\star \left(\frac{1}{2} \right) \le b_{\pi(Q_4)}^\star \left(\frac{3}{2} \right)$ from Lemma 8.4.9. Thus, by definition of $\mathcal{I}^{\text{el}}$, all items of set $\mathcal{I}^{\text{el}}$ are **selected, where all but one is selected completely, and at most one partially,** in the LP with capacity $3/2$ and set of items Q_4. To be precise, from Proposition 8.2.2 for the LP, for all items $i \in \mathcal{I}^{\text{el}}$ with cost–benefit ratio $b_i < b_{\pi(Q_4)}^\star \left(\frac{3}{2} \right)$, the optimal solution $x_{\pi(Q_4)}^\star \left(i, \frac{3}{2} \right) = 1$, and possibly only for one item $k \in \mathcal{I}^{\text{el}}$, $0 < x_{\pi(Q_4)}^\star \left(k, \frac{3}{2} \right) < 1$ (where we are using the fact all items have distinct b_i). Since the size of item k is at most $1/81$, the total size of items of $\mathcal{I}^{\text{el}}$ is bounded as follows:

$$w(\mathcal{I}^{\text{el}}) \le w_{\pi(Q_4)}^{3/2}(Y \backslash \{\pi(j), k\}) + w(k),$$

$$\le w_{\pi(Q_4)}^{3/2}(Y \backslash \{\pi(j)\}) + \frac{1}{81},$$

$$\overset{(a)}{=} Z_2 + \frac{1}{81},$$

$$\overset{(b)}{<} 1 - \frac{1}{81},$$

where (a) follows from the definition of Z_2, and (b) follows from the definition of event $\mathcal{E}$. Thus, the total size of items of set $\mathcal{I}^{\text{el}}$ is at most $1 - \frac{1}{81}$. Hence, when item $\pi(j)$ with size at most $1/81$ arrives with algorithm MULTIPARTSEC, there is enough room in the knapsack to accept it.

Finally, we show that conditioned on event $\mathcal{E}$, for item $\pi(j)$, its cost–benefit ratio $b_{\pi(j)} \le b_X^\star \left(\frac{1}{2} \right)$. Since item $\pi(j)$ is selected by the LP with capacity $3/4$, i.e., $x_{\pi(Q)}^\star \left(j, \frac{3}{4} \right) > 0$, we know $b_{\pi(j)} \le b_{\pi(Q_4)}^\star \left(\frac{3}{4} \right)$. Combining this with Lemma 8.4.9, we get $b_{\pi(j)} \le b_X^\star \left(\frac{1}{2} \right)$ as required.

Thus, as long as $\pi(j) \in Y$ and event $\mathcal{E}$ holds, item $\pi(j)$ will be selected by algorithm MULTIPARTSEC. Since event $\pi(j) \in Y$ is independent of $\mathcal{E}$, its probability given $\mathcal{E}$ is simply the probability $\pi(j) \in Y$, which is $\frac{1}{2}$. Recall that we have already lower bounded the probability of event $\mathcal{E}$ by 0.6 in (8.17), and hence we get that the probability that item $\pi(j)$ is selected by algorithm MULTIPARTSEC is

$$\mathbb{P}(\pi(j) \in G | a = 4) > 0.3,$$

as required to prove Lemma 8.4.6.

Remark 8.4.10 *The basic idea of algorithm* MULTIPARTSEC *is to separate items into different classes depending on their sizes, and apply different algorithms for each class to accept items into the knapsack. This is a general principle and has been applied subsequently in* [132, 133] *to get a competitive ratio bound of 1/8.06 and 1/6.65, respectively. We will discuss the algorithm of* [132] *in Problem 8.7, where items are separated in only two classes, heavy $w > 1/2$ and light $w \le 1/2$.*

8.5 Resource Augmentation

We already know that the knapsack problem under the adversarial input has an unbounded competitive ratio. In this section, we consider giving the online algorithm more resources than the OPT, where the online algorithm has capacity $C > 1$, while the OPT has capacity 1. In addition, we allow the algorithm to reject or delete items that have been accepted before. Note that allowing deletion of already accepted items without capacity augmentation keeps the competitive ratio of any online algorithm unboundedly large (Problem 8.4).

Under the adversarial input, with capacity augmentation and when item removal is allowed, we next show that a simple greedy algorithm has competitive ratio (8.6) $\ge C - 1$, for $1 < C \le 2$. Thus, for the greedy algorithm to get the same value as OPT, it needs double the capacity $C = 2$ to that of OPT.

The greedy algorithm is as follows: On the arrival of item i_t, let the currently accepted set of items be $i_1, i_2, \ldots, i_{k_t}$. Then sort the $k_t + 1$ ($i_t, i_1, i_2, \ldots, i_{k_t}$) items in the non-decreasing order of their cost–benefit ratio. Accept the first k items such that $\sum_{i=1}^{k} w(i) \le C$, and $\sum_{i=1}^{k+1} w(i) > C$. Essentially, the algorithm always maintains the largest subset of items with the smallest cost–benefit ratio that satisfy the capacity constraint C. With the ability to delete any number of previously selected items, this greedy algorithm is equivalent to the offline setting, and chooses as many 'good' items in terms of the cost–benefit ratio as possible. Let S_g be the set of items chosen by the greedy algorithm.

Lemma 8.5.1 *For the greedy algorithm with capacity C, where $1 < C \le 2$,*

$$\min_{\sigma} \frac{v(S_g)}{v(S_{OPT})} \ge C - 1,$$

when OPT *is allowed capacity 1.*

Proof: Let S_{OPT} and S_g be the set of items selected by OPT with capacity 1, and the greedy algorithm with capacity C, after all item arrivals, respectively.

By definition, the set S_g is the set of k items ordered in non-decreasing order of their cost–benefit ratio, where the first k of them satisfy $\sum_{i=1}^{k} w(i) \le C$, and $\sum_{i=1}^{k+1} w(i) > C$.

Moreover, since $w(i) \leq 1$ for each item i, we have

$$\sum_{i=1}^{k} w(i) > C - 1, \tag{8.23}$$

since otherwise the greedy algorithm would have accepted $k + 1$ items. Let $\sum_{i=1}^{k} w(i) = C'$, i.e., $C' > C - 1$.

We consider two cases (i) $C' \geq 1$ and (ii) $C' < 1$. In case (i), given that the first k items selected by the greedy algorithm have the lowest cost–benefit ratio and OPT has capacity 1, Propositions 8.2.2 and 8.2.3 imply $v(S_{\text{OPT}}) \leq v_{\mathcal{I}}^{1}(\mathcal{I}) \leq \sum_{i=1}^{k} v(i) = v(S_g)$. Thus, the only case of interest is case (ii). For this case, consider the LP relaxation (8.2) with the complete set of items $\mathcal{I}$ and capacity C'. Since $\sum_{i=1}^{k} w(i) = C'$ and the first k items selected by the greedy algorithm have the lowest cost–benefit ratio, we get from Proposition 8.2.2 that $v_{\mathcal{I}}^{C'}(\mathcal{I}) = \sum_{i=1}^{k} v(i) = v(S_g)$. Next, invoking the scaling property, Lemma 8.2.5, we have $v_{\mathcal{I}}^{1}(\mathcal{I}) \leq \frac{1}{C'} v_{\mathcal{I}}^{C'}(\mathcal{I})$ since $C' < 1$. Given that $v(S_{\text{OPT}}) \leq v_{\mathcal{I}}^{1}(\mathcal{I})$, we get $v(S_{\text{OPT}}) \leq \frac{v(S_g)}{C'} \leq \frac{v(S_g)}{C-1}$, where the last inequality follows since $C' \geq C - 1$. ∎

We next show that the result of Lemma 8.5.1 is tight.

Example 8.5.2

Consider the case when there are only two items, $v(1) = C - 1 + \epsilon$, $w(1) = C - 1 + \epsilon/2$, and $v(2) = 1$, $w(2) = 1$ for $1 < C \leq 2$ with $\epsilon > 0$. OPT is allowed capacity 1, while an online algorithm is allowed capacity of C. For this instance, the greedy algorithm only chooses item 1 and has value $C - 1 + \epsilon$ while OPT chooses item 2 and gets value 1. Thus, the competitive ratio of the greedy algorithm is at most $C - 1 + \epsilon$ for any $\epsilon > 0$ from which we can conclude that the result of Lemma 8.5.1 is tight for the greedy algorithm.

It turns out that this greedy algorithm is actually optimal under this setting, and one can show an upper bound of $C - 1 + \epsilon$ for any online algorithm for any $\epsilon > 0$. We develop this upper bound in Problem 8.5.

8.6 Notes

Under the secretary model, [117] proposed and analysed the algorithm presented in Section 8.4, and showed that its competitive ratio is at least $1/10e$. Improved algorithms with competitive ratios of $1/8.06$ and $1/6.65$ have since been developed in [132, 133], respectively. A common idea in algorithms [117, 132, 133] is to split the input according to item sizes and then employ algorithms tailored for these restricted instances separately [117, 132] or jointly [133]. We will discuss the improved competitive ratio obtained by [132] in Problem 8.7. Assuming that the maximum value of any single item is 'small' compared to the total value of the optimal solution, [134] proposed an algorithm with a competitive ratio of at least $1/2e$. Enforcing the capacity constraint in expectation, a $1/4e$-competitive algorithm can be found in [121].

Constraining the cost–benefit ratio to lie within a range $[1/U, 1/L]$, [137] proposed an algorithm with competitive ratio of at most $\ln\left(\dfrac{U}{L}\right) + 1$. Extension to this result with multi-dimensional constraints can be found in [138] as well as [139]. The knapsack problem under the stochastic input model, where the item sizes and their values are drawn from a fixed distribution, has been considered in [135, 136], and additive loss bound (regret) of $\Theta(\log n)$ has been established where n is the number of presented items.

Resource augmentation and item recall has also been considered for the online knapsack problem, where with recall, previously accepted items can be removed. Knapsack problem with recall has been studied in [140, 141], while recall together with resource augmentation has been considered in [142], which we discussed in Section 8.5.

The multiple knapsack problem has also been considered; for example, see [143–145]. The stochastic setting where the values and sizes of items are drawn from a distribution that may or may not be known has also been considered with the best-known result being [138].

PROBLEMS

8.1 Show that for the LP relaxation (8.2) of the offline knapsack problem with set of items $\mathcal{I}$ and capacity C, there exists a threshold $b^\star_{\mathcal{I}}(C)$ such that all items i with $b_i < b^\star_{\mathcal{I}}(C)$ are selected completely $x^\star_{\mathcal{I}}(i, C) = 1$, while items j with $b_j > b^\star_{\mathcal{I}}(C)$ are not selected at all, $x^\star_{\mathcal{I}}(j, C) = 0$.

[Hint: Arrange the items in increasing order of b_i. Let there be an index j such that $x^\star_{\mathcal{I}}(j, C) < 1$ but $x^\star_{\mathcal{I}}(j + 1, C) > 0$. Then claim that $x^\star_{\mathcal{I}}(j, C) = x^\star_{\mathcal{I}}(j, C) + x^\star_{\mathcal{I}}(j + 1, C)\dfrac{w(i+1)}{w(i)}$ and $x^\star_{\mathcal{I}}(j + 1, C) = 0$ increases the value of the objective function.]

8.2 Extend the idea presented in Example 8.2.4 to show that any online algorithm of the sample and price type with the secretarial input that builds a threshold on the cost–benefit ratio using the first t items, and then selects items with cost–benefit ratio less than the threshold subject to the capacity constraint subsequently, has an unbounded competitive ratio.

8.3 Prove Lemma 8.2.5. Using Problem 8.1 might be helpful.

8.4 [140] Show that any online algorithm for the knapsack problem has an unbounded competitive ratio even if it is allowed to remove a previously accepted item. Let the knapsack capacity be $C = 1$. Consider a sequence of items (with (w, v), w is the size and v is the value) $\{(1, 1), (\epsilon^2, \epsilon), (\epsilon^2, \epsilon) \ldots, \}$ for some small $0 < \epsilon \ll 1$. Show that for this sequence of items, the competitive ratio of any online algorithm is at most ϵ even if a previously accepted is allowed to be removed.

8.5 [140] With capacity augmentation of $1 < C \leq 2$ for an online algorithm compared to OPT that is allowed capacity of 1, show that for any online algorithm to solve the knapsack problem that can remove an already accepted item, the competitive ratio is upper bounded by $(C-1) + \epsilon$ for any $\epsilon > 0$.

Consider a sequence of items (with (w, v), w is the size and v is the value) $\{(1,1), \mathbf{s}_1, \mathbf{s}_2, \dots\}$, where subsequence

$$\mathbf{s}_i = \{\underbrace{((1 + (i-1)\delta)\epsilon, \epsilon), \dots, ((1 + (i-1)\delta)\epsilon, \epsilon)}_{\frac{1}{\epsilon}}\}.$$

Show that for this sequence,

1. If any online algorithm removes item 1 with $(v, w) = (1, 1)$ before the end of subsequence $\mathbf{s}_1$, then the competitive ratio is at most $C - 1 + \epsilon$.

2. If any online algorithm removes item 1 with $(v, w) = (1, 1)$ before the end of subsequence $\mathbf{s}_i$, $i \geq 2$, then the competitive ratio is at most

$$\frac{C - 1 + \epsilon}{\left\lceil \frac{1}{\epsilon} \right\rceil \epsilon} \frac{1 + (i-1)\delta}{1 + (i-2)\delta}.$$

3. If the online algorithm never removes item 1, then at the end of sub-sequence $\mathbf{s}_i$, $i \geq 2$, the competitive ratio is at most

$$\frac{C - 1 + \epsilon}{\left\lceil \frac{1}{\epsilon} \right\rceil \epsilon} \frac{\left(1 + (i-1)\delta + \frac{1}{C}\right)}{1 + (i-1)\delta}.$$

8.6 (Expected Capacity Constraint) In this problem, we consider the knapsack problem where the capacity constraint is enforced in expectation. We consider the secretarial input, with an additional assumption defined as follows.

Assumption 8.6.1 *Given two items i, j arriving at locations $\pi(i)$ and $\pi(j)$, if $b_i > b_j$, then $\mathbb{P}(w(i) > w(j)) = \frac{1}{2}$.*

1. Show that algorithm AUG $-$ ON satisfies the capacity constraint of C, i.e., the sum of the size of the items accepted in the decision phase is less than C.

2. First show that without considering the condition $w(i) \leq w(i_k)$ for selection, competitive ratio of the AUG $-$ ON algorithm with respect to OPT that has capacity 1 is at least $1/e$ with $C = 2$. Next, including the condition $w(i) \leq w(i_k)$ for selection, and using Assumption 8.6.1, show that the competitive ratio of the AUG $-$ ON algorithm with respect to OPT that has capacity 1 is at least $1/2e$ with $C = 2$.

Algorithm 5 AUG – ON

1: Input: capacity C
2: %**Sampling Phase**
3: Do not select the first $t = n/e$ items $\mathcal{I}_t(\pi) \subset \mathcal{I}$ under permutation π
4: $R = \{i_1, \dots, i_k\} \subseteq \mathcal{I}_t(\pi)$ ordered in non-decreasing order of cost-benefit ratio values, such that $\sum_{i=1}^{k} w(i) \leq C$ and $\sum_{i=1}^{k+1} w(i) > C$.
5: (worst) Item $i_k \in R$ has the largest cost-benefit ratio value b_{i_k}.
6: %**Decision/Online Phase**
7: Initialize $S = \varnothing$ %The set to be selected
8: For every new item $i \geq t + 1$ in the decision phase
9: **if** $\mathsf{b}_i < \mathsf{b}_{i_k}$ **then**
10:     **if** i_k was sampled in offline phase AND $w(i) \leq w(i_k)$ **then**
11:         $S = S \cup \{i\}$ % select item i
12:     **end if**
13:     Update $R = R \backslash \{i_k\} \cup \{i\}$
14:     Order the items of R in non-decreasing order of their cost–benefit ratio, item $i_k \in R$ has the largest cost–benefit ratio value b_{i_k}
15: **else**
16:     Do not select item i
17: **end if**

---

3. Finally, using part 2, show that the competitive ratio of algorithm ON is $1/4e$ and it satisfies the expected capacity constraint of 1.

Algorithm 6 ON Algorithm

1: Flip a fair coin
2: **if** Heads **then**
3:     Run Algorithm AUG – ON with $C = 2$
4:     Accept all items accepted by AUG – ON
5: **else**Tails
6:     Do not select any item, Break;
7: **end if**

8.7 [132] Consider the following algorithm called REPEATED ASSIGNMENT to solve the knapsack problem with the secretarial input. Let $v_{\mathcal{A}}$ be the sum of the value of the items selected by REPEATED ASSIGNMENT. An item is called **heavy** if its size $> 1/2$ and **light** otherwise. For OPT, let $v_{\text{OPT}}^{\text{heavy}}$ and $v_{\text{OPT}}^{\text{light}}$ be the sums of the value of the items selected by it, while considering only heavy and light items, respectively, with capacity 1 in each case.

1. Show that $\mathbb{E}\{v_{\mathcal{A}} | \text{Heads}\} \geq \dfrac{v_{\text{OPT}}^{\text{heavy}}}{e}$.

Algorithm 7 REPEATED ASSIGNMENT

1: Input: n (the total number of items), capacity $C = 1$
2: Items arrive with uniformly random permutation π
3: Flip a coin with $\mathbb{P}(\text{Heads}) = q, \mathbb{P}(\text{Tails}) = 1 - q$
4: **if** Heads **then**
5:     Consider only heavy items with size $> 1/2$
6:     Execute VIRTUAL Algorithm (Section 7.5) for $k = 1$-Secretary Problem
7: **else** Tails
8:     If item $1 \leq j \leq n$ is heavy, then replace it with a light item of $w(j) = 0, v(j) = 0$
9:     Consider only (light) items with size $\leq 1/2$
10:     Do not select any of the first np light items, for some $0 < p < 1$
11:     Initialize $S = \varnothing$ %The set of items to be selected
12:     On arrival of the kth light item for $k > np$
13:     Visible (light) Set of Items $I_k = \{$all the light items seen so far$\}$
14:     Find $x_{I_k}^{\star}(t, 1)$ for $t = 1, \dots, k$ by solving the LP (8.2) with set I_k and capacity 1
15:     **if** there is room to accept item k, i.e., $w(S) + w(k) \leq 1$ **then**
16:         $S = S \cup \{k\}$ with probability $x_{I_k}^{\star}(k, 1)$
17:     **end if**
18: **end if**

---

2. With the coin showing tails, on the kth light item arrival for $k > np$, notice that the set of visible items I_k is a random subset of all light items I^{light}, with cardinality k. At step k, let $x_{I_k}^{\star}(t, 1)$ for $t = 1, \dots, k$ be the optimal solution obtained by solving the LP (8.2) with item set I_k and capacity 1. Argue that the expected sum valuation

$$\mathbb{E}\left\{\sum_{t=1}^{k} v(t) x_{I_k}^{\star}(t, 1)\right\} = \frac{k}{n} v_{\text{OPT}}^{\text{light}}.$$

Using this, argue that the expected value obtained by REPEATED ASSIGNMENT (i.e., by selecting item k with probability $x_{I_k}^{\star}(k, 1)$) at step k is

$$\mathbb{E}\{v_{\mathcal{A}}(k)\} = \frac{1}{k}\mathbb{E}\left\{\sum_{t=1}^{k} v(t) x_{I_k}^{\star}(t, 1)\right\} = \frac{1}{n} v_{\text{OPT}}^{\text{light}}.$$

3. With the coin showing tails, i.e., while considering only light items, show that the expected capacity used up by a light item selected at step k is $\frac{1}{k}$.

4. With the coin showing tails, using part 3 and Markov's inequality, show that the probability that the total used up capacity just before the arrival of item $k > np$ is at most $1/2$ is

$$\geq 1 - 2 \sum_{k'=pn+1}^{k-1} \frac{1}{k'}$$

5. Using parts 2 and 4 and the fact that all the considered items when the coin toss is tails has size $\leq 1/2$, show that

$$\mathbb{E}\{v_A | \text{Tails}\} \geq \sum_{k'=pn+1}^{n} \frac{v_{\text{OPT}}^{\text{light}}}{n} \left(1 - 2 \sum_{k'=pn+1}^{k-1} \frac{1}{k'}\right)$$

$$\geq v_{\text{OPT}}^{\text{light}} \left(3(1-p) - 2\ln\left(\frac{1}{p}\right)\right).$$

[Using the bound $\sum_{k'=pn+1}^{n} \frac{1}{k'} < \int_{pn}^{n} \frac{1}{t} dt = \ln(1/p)$ will be useful.]

6. Choosing $p = 2/3$, using part 5, show that $\mathbb{E}\{v_A | \text{Tails}\} \geq \frac{3}{16} v_{\text{OPT}}^{\text{light}}$.

7. Choosing $q = \frac{1}{1+16/3e}$, using parts 1 and 6, conclude that REPEATED ASSIGNMENT is $1/8.1$-competitive in expectation.

8.8 [137] In this problem we consider the knapsack problem with worst-case input, though under the condition that the cost–benefit ratio $b_i = \frac{w(i)}{v(i)}$ for each item i, satisfies $\frac{1}{U} \leq b_i = \frac{w(i)}{v(i)} \leq \frac{1}{L}$. For this setting, consider algorithm BOUNDEDVALUE.

Algorithm 8 BOUNDEDVALUE

1: Total Capacity C
2: Let $f(x) = \left(\frac{Ue}{L}\right)^x \frac{L}{e}$
3: On arrival of item i, let α_i be the fraction of the capacity already filled, then select item i if and only if

$$\frac{1}{b_i} = \frac{v(i)}{w(i)} \geq f(\alpha_i).$$

Let S^A and S^{OPT} be the set of items selected by BOUNDEDVALUE and OPT, respectively. Let $W = \sum_{i \in S^A \cap S^{\text{OPT}}} w(i)$, while $V = \sum_{i \in S^A \cap S^{\text{OPT}}} v(i)$. Moreover, for the algorithm BOUNDEDVALUE, let $0 \leq \alpha^c \leq 1$ be the fraction of the capacity used when it terminates.

1. Show that BOUNDEDVALUE satisfies the capacity constraint.

2. Appealing to a property of the function f and BOUNDEDVALUE's definition, show that

$$v_{OPT} = \sum_{i \in S^{OPT}} v(i) \leq V + f(\alpha^c)(C - W).$$

3. By definition, $v_A = \sum_{i \in S^A} v(i) = V + v(S^A \setminus S^{OPT})$. Using this, we get

$$\mu_A \geq \frac{V + v(S^A \setminus S^{OPT})}{V + f(\alpha^c)(C - W)}.$$

4. Show that

$$V \geq \sum_{j \in S^A \cap S^{OPT}} f(\alpha_j) w_j$$

and

$$v(S^A \setminus S^{OPT}) \geq \sum_{j \in S^A \setminus S^{OPT}} f(\alpha_j) w_j,$$

where α_j is the fraction of the occupied capacity encountered on the arrival of item j.

5. Using part 4 show that

$$\mu_A \geq \frac{\sum_{j \in S^A} f(\alpha_j) \Delta \alpha_j}{f(\alpha^c)},$$

where $\Delta \alpha_j = \alpha_{j+1} - \alpha_j = w_j / C$.

6. Assuming that $\frac{\max_{j \in \mathcal{I}} w(j)}{C}$ is small, approximate the summation

$$\sum_{j \in S^A} f(\alpha_j) \Delta \alpha_j$$

by assuming it to be close to $\int_0^{\alpha^c} f(x) dx$ and show that

$$\int_0^{\alpha^c} f(x) dx = \frac{f(\alpha^c)}{(\ln(U/L) + 1)}.$$

The following observation about the function f might be useful. For any $x \in [0, c]$ where $c = \frac{1}{1+\ln(U/L)}, f(x) \leq L.$

Conclude that the competitive ratio of BOUNDEDVALUE is at least $1/(\ln(U/L) + 1)$.

It is worth noting that if the assumption that $\frac{\max_{j \in \mathcal{I}} w(j)}{C}$ is small was not needed for this problem, we could have used this algorithm and solved Problem 7.6 using a deterministic algorithm with the same guarantee.

CHAPTER 9

Bipartite Matching

9.1 Introduction

In this chapter, we consider a rich combinatorial problem of *matching* over bipartite graphs, with two sets of vertices, left and right, and an edge can exist only between a left and a right vertex. A matching is a subset of edges such that no two edges in the matching have any common left or right vertex. In the online setting, one side of the vertices, say, right, are available ahead of time, and the left vertices are revealed sequentially. Once a left vertex arrives, its associated edges and the edge weights are also revealed. For a given bipartite graph, the objective is to maximize the number of edges that are part of the matching in the unweighted (weights are 1/0) case, or to maximize the sum-weight of all the edges that are part of matching in the weighted case.

The matching problem is a fundamental combinatorial object that models large classes of association problems, such as web advertising, scheduling jobs to servers, where each server can handle at most one job, crowdsourcing, where each agent can only accomplish at most one job, etc.

In this chapter, we will consider both the unweighted and the weighted case. For the unweighted case, any deterministic algorithm is shown to have a competitive ratio of at most $1/2$, which is easily achieved by a greedy algorithm. The main challenge in the unweighted case is to find an optimal randomized algorithm under the worst-case or adversarial input. We first present an upper bound of $1 - 1/e$ on the competitive ratio of any randomized algorithm, and then analyse an algorithm whose competitive ratio approaches $1 - 1/e$ with an increasing number of left or right vertices.

The weighted case is a generalization of the secretary problem, and hence adversarial inputs result in the competitive ratio being unboundedly large for any online algorithm. Thus, for the weighted case, typically the secretarial input is considered. Under the secretarial input, we first discuss an algorithm with a competitive ratio of $1/8$ that is based on the sample and price philosophy, and then describe an algorithm called ROM whose competitive ratio is $1/e - 1/n$, where n is the number of left vertices. Since the competitive ratio of any online algorithm for the secretary problem (Chapter 7) is at most $1/e$, ROM is an almost optimal algorithm.

9.2 Problem Formulation

Consider a bipartite graph $G = (L \cup R, E)$, where L and R are the sets of left and right vertices, respectively, with edge set E. By bipartite we mean that an edge can exist only between a left vertex $\ell \in L$ and a right vertex $r \in R$. i.e. $E = \{(\ell, r), \ell \in L, r \in R\}$. Throughout the chapter, we let $|L| = n$ and $|R| = m$ with $n \leq m$, unless stated otherwise. The set of right vertices R is known ahead of time, while the left vertices of L arrive sequentially. In particular, on the arrival of the left vertex $\ell \in L$, all the edges e from ℓ to the set R and their weights $v(e)$ are revealed. Any online algorithm $\mathcal{A}$ has to match the left vertex ℓ on its arrival to any previously unmatched right vertex of R, if at all, irrevocably.

Definition 9.2.1 *A matching* M *over* $G = (L \cup R, E)$ *is a subset of edges of E such that no two edges in the matching have any common left or right vertex.*

Let the matching output by an online algorithm $\mathcal{A}$ be $\mathsf{M}_{\mathcal{A}}$, and its weight be $v(\mathsf{M}_{\mathcal{A}}) = \sum_{e \in \mathsf{M}_{\mathcal{A}}} v(e)$. Let OPT's matching be $\mathsf{M}_{\mathsf{OPT}}$. Then the competitive ratio of $\mathcal{A}$ is

$$\mu_{\mathcal{A}} = \min_{\sigma} \frac{v(\mathsf{M}_{\mathcal{A}}(\sigma))}{v(\mathsf{M}_{\mathsf{OPT}}(\sigma))},$$

where the input σ is the order in which the left vertices of L arrive, and the corresponding weights of edges incident on the arriving left vertices.

We consider two cases: unweighted, where $v(e) = 1$ if edge e is present and $v(e) = 0$ otherwise, and weighted, where $v(e) \geq 0$ are arbitrary. In the unweighted case, the weight of the matching is also equal to the number of edges that are part of it, and for this reason weight is referred to as the size of the matching. The secretary problem (Chapter 7) is a special case of the weighted case, with $|R| = 1$, and hence we will consider the secretarial input for the weighted case. For the unweighted case, however, we will consider the arbitrary or the worst-case input.

Definition 9.2.2 *A matching* M *is called maximal if addition of any edge e to* M *violates the matching condition. Moreover, for the unweighted case, a matching* M *is called maximum if it contains the largest number of matchable edges.*

The following result is immediate and will be useful for further exposition.

Proposition 9.2.3 *In the unweighted case, the size of any maximal matching is at least half of the size of the maximum matching.*

Remark 9.2.4 *In the offline case, it is easy to approximate* $v(\mathsf{M}_{\mathsf{OPT}}(\sigma))$ *or to find the optimal matching* $\mathsf{M}_{\mathsf{OPT}}(\sigma)$. *For example, the greedy algorithm that selects edges in decreasing order of weights (as long as they satisfy the matching condition) is 2-approximate, while an augmentation-based algorithm (Hungarian algorithm [146, 147]) that runs in polynomial time is optimal.*

9.3 Unweighted Case

A left (right) vertex $\ell \in L$ ($r \in R$) is called *matched*, once an edge incident on $\ell(r)$ is matched (accepted) by an online algorithm $\mathcal{A}$. The problem is to match the newly arrived left vertex ℓ to any of the currently unmatched right vertices to which it has an edge (accept the corresponding edge), if at all, so as to maximize the size (number of matched left or right vertices) of the matching at the end of all left vertex arrivals.

Example 9.3.1

We illustrate the challenge faced by an online algorithm $\mathcal{A}$ when the input is revealed sequentially. Consider Figure 9.1, where there are 4 right vertices. Let the first left vertex that arrives has an edge to all the 4 right vertices, and an online algorithm $\mathcal{A}$ accepts or matches edge $e = (\ell_1, r_1)$. Then let the second left vertex that arrives has an edge only to r_1, and since r_1 is already matched, ℓ_2 remains unmatched. OPT, on the other hand, knowing the input, matches ℓ_1 to any of the right vertices $r_2, \ldots, r_4$, and matches ℓ_2 to r_1. Thus, the size of OPT's matching is 2, while that of $\mathcal{A}$ is 1.

Definition 9.3.2 *We define the edge set of a bipartite graph as a matrix $\mathbf{E}$, where $e_{ij} = 1$ if the left vertex ℓ_i (in order of arrival with σ) has an edge to the right vertex r_j, and 0 otherwise. For example, for Figure 9.1,*

$$\mathbf{E} = \begin{bmatrix} 1 & 1 & 1 & 1 \\ 1 & 0 & 0 & 0 \end{bmatrix}.$$

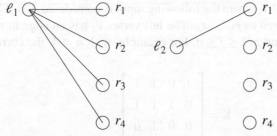

Figure 9.1 Example of an input for a bipartite graph, where the left vertex ℓ_1 has edges to all $r_i, i = 1, \ldots, 4$, while ℓ_2 has only one edge to r_1

Lemma 9.3.3 *A natural greedy online algorithm that matches a newly arrived left vertex ℓ to any currently unmatched right vertex is 1/2-competitive.*

Proof: The greedy algorithm always ends up with a maximal matching, and whose size is at least one-half of the size of the maximum matching (Proposition 9.2.3).

Alternatively, let edge $e = (\ell, r)$ be part of the matching output by the greedy algorithm. Since M_{OPT} can have at most one edge incident on either ℓ or r, each edge accepted by the online greedy algorithm can block at most two other edges that can potentially be part of M_{OPT}. Counting across all edges, we get the result. ∎

Surprisingly, this simple online algorithm is also the best one can hope for in the deterministic setting.

Lemma 9.3.4 *Any deterministic online matching algorithm is at most 1/2-competitive.*

Proof: Consider the input where each of the first (in order of arrival) $|L|/2$ left vertices has an edge to all the right vertices. Let the matching found by any deterministic online algorithm be $M_{1/2}$ after the arrival of the first $|L|/2$ left vertices, where the set of right vertices that are part of $M_{1/2}$ is $R_{1/2}$. Clearly, $v(M_{1/2}) = |L|/2$. Knowing $M_{1/2}$, the adversary chooses the rest of the input, where each subsequently arriving left vertex has only one edge to a right vertex that is already part of $R_{1/2}$. Thus, no new edge can be added to $M_{1/2}$ and the matching size is at most $|L|/2$. OPT, however, knowing the input in advance, matches the first $|L|/2$ left vertices to $R \backslash R_{1/2}$, and assigns the subsequently arriving left vertices to their respective right vertices to which they have an edge. Hence, the matching size obtained by OPT is $|L|$. ∎

Thus, the really interesting paradigm for the matching problem in the unweighted case is the randomized setting. A natural randomized algorithm, called RANDOM, that matches a newly arrived left vertex to any unmatched right vertex to which it has an edge uniformly randomly is $1/2$-competitive, as shown next in Lemma 9.3.5. Therefore, to achieve a competitive ratio better than $1/2$, a randomized algorithm needs to be slightly more clever.

Lemma 9.3.5 RANDOM *algorithm, which matches a left vertex ℓ to any unmatched right vertex to which it has an edge, chosen uniformly randomly, is at most $1/2$-competitive in expectation in the unweighted case.*

For proof, see Problem 9.1, where the following input is considered. Let $|L| = |R| = n$, and the n right vertices are ordered as $r_1, \dots, r_n$. The left vertex ℓ_i has an edge to right vertex r_j if $j = i$ or when $1 \leq i < n/2$ and $n/2 \leq j \leq n$. For example, with $n = 4$, the corresponding edge set matrix is

$$
\mathbf{E} = \begin{bmatrix} 1 & 0 & 1 & 1 \\ 0 & 1 & 1 & 1 \\ 0 & 0 & 1 & 0 \\ 0 & 0 & 0 & 1 \end{bmatrix}.
$$

Essentially, with this input, a left vertex ℓ_i that arrives in the first half (arrival order) has an edge to its corresponding indexed right vertex r_i, and edges to all right vertices in the bottom half. Thus, with sufficient probability, a left vertex ℓ_i that arrives in the first half gets matched to some right vertex in the bottom half. Since any left vertex ℓ_i that arrives in the second half has only one edge to r_i, on its arrival very few left vertices can find an unmatched right vertex to which it has an edge.

In particular, with this input, the expected number of left vertices ℓ_i for $i = 1, \dots, n/2$ (among the first $n/2$ left vertices) not matched to the right vertex r_i by the RANDOM algorithm is $\geq \frac{n}{2} - \log (n/2 + 1)$. As a result, at most $\mathcal{O}(\log(n))$ of the second half of the left vertices will have their corresponding right vertex still available to match with. Thus, the expected size of the matching produced by the RANDOM algorithm is at most $\frac{n}{2} + \mathcal{O}(\log n)$, while OPT's matching is of size n.

Next, we derive a universal upper bound on the competitive ratio for any randomized algorithm.

9.3.1 Upper Bound on All Randomized Algorithms

Lemma 9.3.6 *The expected size of matching obtained by any randomized online algorithm in the unweighted case is at most*

$$n(1 - 1/e) + o(n).$$

The key idea of the proof is to consider the upper triangular edge matrix $\mathbf{T}$ as the edge set matrix $\mathbf{E}$ (input), and derive a lower bound on the competitive ratio of the RANDOM algorithm. Next, using the Yao's recipe (Section 2.5.1) for deriving lower bounds on randomized algorithms, a coupling argument can be used to connect the competitive ratio of any randomized algorithm on row permutations of $\mathbf{T}$ with the competitive ratio of the RANDOM algorithm on $\mathbf{T}$ itself.

We next prove one part of the proof of Lemma 9.3.6, which bounds the size of the matching obtained by the RANDOM algorithm on $\mathbf{E} = \mathbf{T}$, while leaving the coupling argument to complete the proof of Lemma 9.3.6 in Problem 9.2.

Lemma 9.3.7 *With edge matrix $\mathbf{E} = \mathbf{T}$ as input, the expected size of matching obtained by the* RANDOM *algorithm is at most*

$$n(1 - 1/e) + o(n).$$

Proof: Let $|L| = |R| = n$, i.e., the number of left and right vertices are equal. Let the set of left vertices ℓ_i, $i = 1, 2, \ldots, n$, be indexed in order of their arrival times, i.e., ℓ_1 arrives before ℓ_2, and so on.

Let the edge matrix $\mathbf{E}$ be

$$\mathbf{T} = \begin{bmatrix} 1 & 1 & \ldots & \ldots & \ldots & 1 \\ 0 & 1 & 1 & \ldots & \ldots & 1 \\ 0 & 0 & 1 & 1 & \ldots & 1 \\ 0 & \ldots & 0 & 1 & \ldots & 1 \\ 0 & \ldots & 0 & \ddots & 1 & 1 \\ 0 & \ldots & 0 & \ldots & 0 & 1 \end{bmatrix},$$

i.e., for the left vertex ℓ_i, there is an edge to all right vertices r_j, $i \leq j \leq n$. A right vertex r is defined to be *eligible* on arrival of left vertex ℓ_i if there is an edge from ℓ_i to r (the i, r^{th} entry in $\mathbf{T}$ is 1) and r is still unmatched.

We also define the (dynamic) eligible edge matrix $\mathbf{T}^i$ whose i, j^{th} entry is 1 only if the right vertex r_j is eligible on arrival of left vertex ℓ_i. For example, with $|L| = |R| = n = 4$, if left vertex ℓ_1 is matched to the right vertex r_2 by the RANDOM algorithm, then $\mathbf{T}^2$ on arrival of the second left vertex is

$$\mathbf{T}^2 = \begin{bmatrix} - & * & - & - \\ 0 & 0 & 1 & 1 \end{bmatrix},$$

where $*$ stands for the previously matched edge.

With input $\mathbf{T}$, at the time of arrival of ith left vertex ℓ_i, the ith row of $\mathbf{T}$ is revealed. Note that algorithm RANDOM chooses any one of the eligible right vertices to match the newly arrived left vertex, uniformly at random. Hence, if at the arrival of ℓ_i, there are k eligible right vertices among the potential $n - i + 1$ right vertices to which ℓ_i has an edge, then the k-sized eligible right vertices subset is equally likely to be any one of the $\binom{n-i+1}{k}$ possible subsets. Essentially, if the eligible edge matrix $\mathbf{T}^i$ contains k $1's$ in the ith row out of a possible $n - i + 1$ 1's that can be present in the ith row of $\mathbf{T}$, then these k 1's are uniformly distributed.

Let on the arrival of tth left vertex ℓ_t, $x(t) = n - t$ be the number of rows (number of left vertices yet to arrive) of $\mathbf{T}$ that are yet to be revealed, and $y(t)$ be the (random) number of right vertices that are still eligible. The eligible right vertices for the tth left vertex are those that have entry 1 in row t of $\mathbf{T}^t$.

The idea is to find a relation between $y(t)$ and $x(t)$, and find the value of $x(t)$ when $y(t) = 1$, i.e., there is at most one eligible right vertex remaining. Once $y(t) = 1$, then no further left vertex $\ell_k, k > t + 1$ can be matched, and hence the value of $n - x(t)$ when $y(t) = 1$ gives an upper bound on the size of the matching possible with the RANDOM algorithm.

Clearly, at each subsequent left vertex arrival, $x(t)$ decreases by 1 and hence $\Delta x = x(t + 1) - x(t) = -1$. The change in $y(t)$ is more complicated. If suppose on the arrival of the left vertex ℓ_t, the right vertex r_t is eligible but is not matched by the RANDOM algorithm, then $y(t)$ decreases by 2, since ℓ_t gets matched to right vertex $r_j, j > t$, and thus right vertex r_t always remains unmatched since no left vertex arriving after ℓ_t has an edge to r_t. Thus, two vertices r_t and $r_j, j > t$, become ineligible at the same time. Alternatively, either the right vertex t is not eligible or the right vertex t is eligible and is matched. In both these cases $y(t)$ decreases by 1, since only one right vertex is made ineligible in either case.

The probability that right vertex r_t is eligible at time t is $\frac{y(t)}{x(t)}$, because of equally likely subsets of right vertices being eligible at time t. Moreover, the probability that right vertex r_t is not chosen by the RANDOM algorithm to match ℓ_t is $\frac{y(t)-1}{y(t)}$ (not choosing one among the $y(t)$ candidates). Thus,

$$\mathbb{E}\{\Delta y\} = y(t+1) - y(t) = -1\left(1 - \frac{y(t)}{x(t)}\frac{y(t)-1}{y(t)}\right) - 2\left(\frac{y(t)}{x(t)}\right)\left(\frac{y(t)-1}{y(t)}\right).$$

Hence,

$$\mathbb{E}\{\Delta y\} = -1 - \frac{y(t)-1}{x(t)}$$

and

$$\frac{\mathbb{E}\{\Delta y\}}{\Delta x} = 1 + \frac{y(t)-1}{x(t)},$$

since $\Delta x = -1$. Using Kurtz's Theorem [148], it can be shown that the solution of this difference equation is well approximated (with probability 1 as $n \to \infty$) by the solution of the following differential equation as $n \to \infty$,

$$\frac{dy}{dx} = 1 + \frac{y-1}{x}.$$

With initial conditions being $x = y = n$, the solution of the differential equation is

$$y = 1 + x\left(\frac{n-1}{n} + \ln\frac{x}{n}\right).$$

Thus, when only one right vertex remains eligible, $y = 1$, the number of rows (left vertices) x yet to be revealed are $\frac{n}{e} + o(n)$ since for $x = \frac{n}{e} + o(n)$, $\ln\frac{x}{n} \sim -\frac{n-1}{n}$, and none of those left vertices can be matched thereafter. Therefore the expected number of left vertices that are unmatched by RANDOM with input $\mathbf{T}$ is $\frac{n}{e} + o(n)$.

Thus, the expected size of the matching obtained by RANDOM on $\mathbf{T}$ is at most $n - \frac{n}{e} + o(n)$. ∎

The remaining part that completes the proof of Lemma 9.3.6 is to use Yao's principle (Section 2.5.1) and couple the competitive ratio of any randomized algorithm with the competitive ratio of the RANDOM algorithm on $\mathbf{T}$ itself. These steps are detailed in Problem 9.2.

Next, to achieve the lower bound (Lemma 9.3.6) up to the lower order terms, we describe a variation of the RANDOM algorithm that uses a particular permutation on the set of right vertices for matching each incoming left vertex.

9.3.2 RANKING Algorithm

Choose a random permutation π on the set of right vertices R that defines a rank $\pi(r)$ for each right vertex r. On the arrival of the left vertex $\ell \in L$, let the set of unmatched right vertices that have an edge to ℓ be $U(\ell)$. If $U(\ell) \neq \varnothing$, then match ℓ to $r \in U(\ell)$ such that $r = \arg\min_{r \in U(\ell)} \pi(r)$. Thus, a newly arrived left vertex is matched to an unmatched vertex with the lowest rank under π.

Recall that $G = (L \cup R, E)$ is the bipartite graph under consideration. To index the execution of RANKING for graph G with permutation π, we refer to it as RANKING with (G, π) and the resulting matching as $M_\pi(G)$, whenever it is necessary to identify π and G.

Example 9.3.8

Let there be 5 right vertices $r_1, \ldots, r_5$, and the permutation π be $\{2, 4, 1, 5, 3\}$, with rank $\pi(2) = 1$, $\pi(4) = 2$, $\pi(1) = 3$, $\pi(5) = 4$, $\pi(3) = 5$. Thus, the right vertices are arranged in increasing order of rank as shown in Figure 9.2. Then on the arrival of a left vertex ℓ that has an edge to r_1 and r_4, and both r_1 and r_4 are unmatched, ℓ is matched to r_4 because it has a lower rank.

Theorem 9.3.9 RANKING *is* $1 - \left(1 - \frac{1}{n+1}\right)^n$*-competitive in expectation that approaches* $1 - 1/e$ *as* $n \to \infty$, *where n is the number of left vertices.*

We prove Theorem 9.3.9 by noting the following properties of RANKING. For the full bipartite graph $G = (L \cup R, E)$, consider a subgraph $G\backslash\{x\} = (L \cup R\backslash\{x\}, E\backslash e_x)$ or $G\backslash\{x\} = (L\backslash\{x\} \cup R, E\backslash e_x)$ obtained by removing either one left or one right vertex x, and all the edges e_x

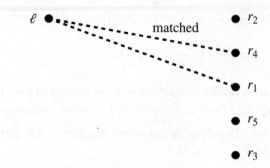

Figure 9.2 Illustration of RANKING

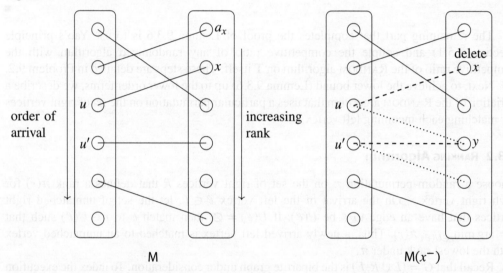

Figure 9.3 Alternating path starting at x where dashed line is the deleted edge from M while dotted is the newly matched edge in $M(x^-)$.

incident on x. Let the order of arrival of left vertices be σ. Then, if a left vertex x is removed, we consider $\sigma(x)$, while if a right vertex x is removed, $\pi(x)$ is considered, where with $\sigma(x)$, the relative order of arrival of left vertices other than x is kept as it is, while with $\pi(x)$, the ranks of all right vertices other than x are unchanged.

Let matching M and $M(x^-)$ be the matching output by RANKING with (G, σ) and $(G \backslash \{x\}, \sigma(x))$, or (G, π) and $(G \backslash \{x\}, \pi(x))$, respectively.

Proposition 9.3.10 *If the matching M and $M(x^-)$ are different, then they differ in an alternating path starting at x.*

The proof is easiest to see via Figure 9.3, where, without loss of generality, we only consider the case when x is a right vertex, and consider matching M and $M(x^-)$ obtained by RANKING with (G, π) and $(G \backslash \{x\}, \pi(x))$. First consider the set of right vertices S_x that have lower rank than x with π (lying above x) in Figure 9.3. By the definition of RANKING, which matches a newly arrived left vertex to the lowest ranked unmatched right vertex, the left vertices matched to any right vertex that is part of the subset S_x with $M(x^-)$ and M are identical.

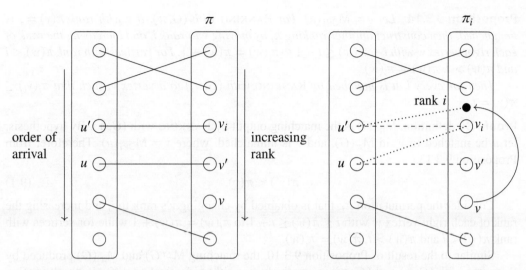

Figure 9.4 Dotted lines indicate the new matched edges after moving right vertex v to rank i, while the dashed lines are the matched edges before moving right vertex v.

Let u be the left vertex that was matched to right vertex x in M. Then in $M(x^-)$, u is matched to a right vertex y with rank higher than x.[1] This starts a 'chain' or an alternating path from x, since any left vertex arriving thereafter that was earlier matched to y in M has to be matched to a right vertex with higher ranked right vertex, and so on. The alternating path is denoted by a path of alternating dashed and dotted lines in Figure 9.4. Also recall that if x was unmatched in M, then $M(x^-) = M$.

Remark 9.3.11 *Proposition 9.3.10 helps us to restrict our attention to bipartite graphs that have perfect matching, i.e., all left or right vertices are matched by* OPT. *From Proposition 9.3.10, we know that with* RANKING, *the size of the matching with G is at least as much as with $G \backslash \{x\}$. Therefore, if G does not have a perfect matching, and say vertex x was not part of the maximum matching (matching that has the largest number of edges), then we can remove x and only increase (make the job of online algorithm harder) the competitive ratio, since the size of* OPT*'s matching remains the same, while that of* RANKING *can only decrease, if at all. Repeatedly removing vertices that are not part of the maximum matching implies that the competitive ratio of* RANKING *is characterized by graphs that have a perfect matching. Thus, without loss of generality, we consider graphs G that have a perfect matching, and $|L| = |R| = n$.*

Definition 9.3.12 *Recall that* M_{OPT} *is the offline optimal matching. We define $v = M_{OPT}(u)$ to mean that left vertex u is matched to right vertex v in* M_{OPT}.

Proposition 9.3.13 *For $v = M_{OPT}(u)$, if v is unmatched by* RANKING *with (G, π), then u is matched by* RANKING *to a right vertex v' such that $\pi(v') < \pi(v)$.*

Proof: Since v is unmatched by RANKING with (G, π), and since RANKING matches u with the lowest ranked unmatched right vertex (let that be v'), then $\pi(v') \leq \pi(v)$. Note that such a v' exists to which u has an edge, since $v = M_{OPT}(u)$ and v is unmatched by RANKING. ∎

---

[1] If there is no y ranked higher than x for which u has an edge to y, then $M(x^-) = M \backslash \{(u, x)\}$.

Proposition 9.3.14 *Let $v = M_{OPT}(u)$. For RANKING with (G, π), if v with rank $\pi(v) = t$ is unmatched, then construct another ranking π_i by moving v to rank i, and increasing the rank of each right vertex w with $i \le \pi(w) \le t - 1$ to $\pi_i(w) = \pi(w) + 1$. For vertices with rank $\pi(w) < i$ and $\pi(w) > t$, $\pi(w) = \pi_i(w)$.*

Then for every i, u is matched by RANKING with (G, π_i) to a vertex v_i such that $\pi_i(v_i) \le \pi(v) = t$.

Proof: By definition, $M_\pi(G)$ is the matching output by RANKING with (G, π). By hypothesis, let u be matched to v' in $M_\pi(G)$, and v is unmatched, where $v = M_{OPT}(u)$. Therefore, from Proposition 9.3.13,

$$\pi(v') < \pi(v). \tag{9.1}$$

Consider the permutation π_i; that is obtained by changing v's rank to i, and increasing the rank of each right vertex w with $i \le \pi(w) \le t - 1$ to $\pi_i(w) = \pi(w) + 1$ while for vertices with rank $\pi(w) < i$ and $\pi(w) > t$, $\pi(w) = \pi_i(w)$.

Similar to the result of Proposition 9.3.10, the matching $M_\pi(G)$ and $M_{\pi_i}(G)$ produced by RANKING with (G, π) and (G, π_i), respectively, are either identical or differ in an alternating path starting at v, and the path is **monotone**. By monotone, we mean that the right vertices encountered in order on the alternating path have increasing ranks in π_i. Therefore, with $M_{\pi_i}(G)$, u is matched to a vertex v_i where

$$\pi_i(v_i) \le \pi_i(v'), \tag{9.2}$$

where u is matched to v' in $M_\pi(G)$.

As an example see Figure 9.4, where we isolate two left vertices u' and u, where u' arrives before u, and for RANKING with (G, π), u' is matched to a right vertex v_i with rank equal to i and u is matched to v', where $i = \pi(v_i) < \pi(v') < \pi(v)$. Left vertices that are matched to right vertices with rank lower than i will not see any change in their matched edges between π and π_i. Therefore, for RANKING with (G, π_i), on the arrival of u', it is matched to v (assuming it has an edge), and consequently v_i is unmatched when u arrives. Thus, for RANKING with (G, π_i), u is matched to v_i (assuming an edge exists between u and v_i), and we get

$$\pi_i(v_i) \le \pi_i(v'), \tag{}$$

where u is matched to v' in $M_\pi(G)$.

Moreover, for all right vertices other than v, the relative rank movement with π and π_i is at most 1; thus,

$$|\pi_i(v') - \pi(v')| \le 1, \ \forall \ v' \ne v. \tag{9.3}$$

From (9.1), we have $\pi(v') < \pi(v)$. Combining this with (9.2) and (9.3), we get

$$\pi_i(v_i) < 1 + \pi(v),$$

which implies that

$$\pi_i(v_i) \le \pi(v),$$

since ranks π, π_i are integers. ∎

Next, we prove the most important lemma that allows us to prove Theorem 9.3.9.

Lemma 9.3.15 *Let q_t be the probability that the right vertex with rank t is matched by* RANKING. *Then*

$$1 - q_t \leq \sum_{1 \leq s \leq t} \frac{q_s}{n},$$

where n is the number of left or right vertices.

This result tells us that with RANKING the probability of right vertices with different ranks being matched are related and is the main reason that RANKING performs better than the RANDOM algorithm.

Proof: Let ρ be a uniformly random permutation over the set of right vertices R. For RANKING with (G, ρ), let $L_t(\rho)$ be the set of left vertices matched to right vertices with rank at most t.

Select a right vertex v randomly among the total $|R|$ right vertices, and move it in the ranking order to rank t (by increasing the ranks of all right vertices with rank between t and $\rho(v)$ by one), and call the new permutation ρ_t. Let $v = \mathsf{M_{OPT}}(u)$.[2] To apply Proposition 9.3.14, we will let $\rho_t = \pi$ as our starting permutation, and $\rho = \pi_i$ for an appropriate i. Thus, applying Proposition 9.3.14 with $\rho_t = \pi$ and $\rho = \pi_i$, we get that if v (that has rank t in ρ_t) is not matched by RANKING with (G, ρ_t) (which happens with probability $1 - q_t$), we have u matched by RANKING (G, ρ) to some $\tilde{v}$, where $\rho(\tilde{v}) \leq t$. This implies that $u \in L_t(\rho)$.

With $v = \mathsf{M_{OPT}}(u)$, define events

$$E_1 = \{\text{right vertex } v \text{ that has rank } t \text{ is not matched by RANKING with } (G, \rho_t)\}$$

and

$$E_2 = \{u \in L_t(\rho)\}.$$

Thus, with $v = \mathsf{M_{OPT}}(u)$, we have

$$E_1 \implies E_2. \tag{9.4}$$

More importantly, the choice of u is independent of ρ and consequently of $L_t(\rho)$. Let $\mathbf{1}_E$ be an indicator function such that $\mathbf{1}_E = 1$ when event E is true, and 0 otherwise. Thus, for a given ρ,

$$\mathbb{P}_\rho(u \in L_t(\rho)) = \frac{|L_t(\rho)|}{n} = \frac{1}{n} \sum_{1 \leq s \leq t} \mathbf{1}_{\{\text{left vertex matched to right vertex with rank } s \text{ under } \rho\}},$$

and unconditioning over ρ, we get

$$\mathbb{P}(u \in L_t) = \frac{1}{n} \sum_{1 \leq s \leq t} q_s.$$

From (9.4), we get

$$1 - q_t = \mathbb{P}(\text{right vertex } v \text{ that has rank } t \text{ is not matched by RANKING}),$$
$$\leq \mathbb{P}(u \in L_t),$$
$$= \frac{1}{n} \sum_{1 \leq s \leq t} q_s.$$

∎

---

[2] Such a u exists, since G has a perfect matching.

Now we complete the proof of Theorem 9.3.9.

Proof: Recall from Remark 9.3.11 that G has a perfect matching, i.e., all the left or right vertices are matched by OPT, and hence OPT's matching M_{OPT} is of size $|L| = n$. Moreover, the expected size of the matching output by RANKING is $\sum_{1 \leq s \leq n} q_t$.

Thus, the expected competitive ratio of algorithm RANKING is

$$\inf_n \frac{\sum_{1 \leq s \leq n} q_s}{n}.$$

Let $Q_t = \sum_{1 \leq s \leq t} q_t$. Then from Lemma 9.3.15, we have

$$Q_t \left(1 + \frac{1}{n}\right) \geq 1 + Q_{t-1} \text{ for } 1 \leq t \leq n. \tag{9.5}$$

Note that (9.5) is not tight for $t = 1$, since with $Q_0 = 0$, from (9.5) we get $Q_1 = \frac{n}{n+1}$, while in reality $Q_1 = q_1 = 1$. Since we are interested in finding a lower bound, this is sufficient. The quantity of interest is Q_n and the infimum of Q_n occurs when all the inequalities in (9.5) are tight. With equality in (9.5), starting from $Q_1 \geq \frac{n}{n+1}$, we get

$$Q_t = \sum_{s=1}^{t} \left(1 - \frac{1}{n+1}\right)^s.$$

Hence, the expected competitive ratio of RANKING is at least

$$\inf_n \frac{\sum_{s=1}^{n} \left(1 - \frac{1}{n+1}\right)^s}{n} = 1 - \left(1 - \frac{1}{n+1}\right)^n.$$

∎

We next consider the more general weighted matching problem, when each edge also has a weight associated with it, and the objective is to maximize the sum of the weights of all the matched edges.

9.4 Weighted Case

We continue to consider a bipartite graph $G = (L \cup R, E)$, but now each edge has an associated non-negative weight. On the arrival of a new left vertex ℓ, the weights $v(e) \geq 0$ of all edges $e = (\ell, r), r \in R$, incident on ℓ are revealed, and the problem is to match ℓ to any of the currently unmatched right vertex, if at all, so as to maximize the sum of the weights of all the matched edges at the end of all the left vertex arrivals. This problem is referred to as the maximum weight bipartite matching problem (MWBPM).

Remark 9.4.1 *Suppose that there is only one right vertex $|R| = 1$; then the MWBPM is equivalent to the secretary problem. Hence, in this section, we consider the secretarial input for left vertex arrivals to obtain non-trivial competitive ratios for MWBPM.*

Remark 9.4.2 *Since the secretary problem is a special case of the MWBPM, in light of Theorem 7.5.2, the best competitive ratio we can hope for with the secretarial input is $\frac{1}{e}$.*

In this section, we will consider two algorithms for solving the MWBPM. In the first, the philosophy is similar to the sample and price class of algorithms proposed for the secretary problem in Chapter 7, of building a threshold after sampling a subset of arrivals, and then using that threshold to select or reject edges. In the second algorithm, on each new left vertex arrival, an optimal matching is found given the input revealed so far, and the newly arrived left vertex is matched if the right vertex to which it is matched in the current optimal matching found on its arrival is currently unmatched.

9.4.1 Sample and Threshold Class of Algorithm

Before discussing an online algorithm we begin with two offline algorithms, SIMULATE and SAMPLEANDPERMUTE, that are 'almost' online, and will be made completely online for our purposes thereafter.

SIMULATE is a randomized offline matching algorithm that first orders the edges in decreasing order of their weights and then maintains two sets M_{1s} and M_{2s} of subsets of edges, where M_{1s} is a matching while M_{2s} is only a pseudo-matching, that possibly contains more than one edge that is incident on the same right vertex.

For each edge $e = (\ell, r)$ in (decreasing) order, a coin with probability of heads p is flipped independently. If the coin shows heads, then $e = (\ell, r)$ is added to M_{1s} if $M_{1s} \cup \{e\}$ is matching, and discarded otherwise. If the coin shows tails, then e is added to M_{2s}. Once an edge $e = (\ell, r)$ has been considered (either added to M_{1s} or M_{2s} or discarded), then no other edge incident on the left vertex ℓ is considered again for being added to M_{1s} or M_{2s}. At the end, M_{2s} is made a matching, called M_{3s}, by deleting all edges of M_{2s} that have more than one common right vertex.

Definition 9.4.3 *An edge e is defined to be considered in algorithm SIMULATE if the coin is flipped for it to assign it to either M_{1s} or M_{2s}.*

An immediate property of SIMULATE that follows trivially is recorded next.

Proposition 9.4.4 *Once any edge incident on $\ell \in L$ is considered, no other edge incident on ℓ can be considered later. Moreover, once an edge incident on $r \in R$ has been added to M_{1s}, no subsequent edge incident on r will be considered.*

Next, we lower bound the expected weight of the matching M_{1s} output by SIMULATE.

Lemma 9.4.5 $\mathbb{E}\{v(M_{1s})\} \geq p \frac{v(\text{OPT})}{2}$.

Proof: Let $L_p \subseteq L$ be the subset of left vertices for which the coin toss results in heads in SIMULATE. Then it is easy to check that the matching M_{1s} is equivalent to a greedy matching on graph $L_p \cup R$. Thus, if OPT_p is the optimal matching on $L_p \cup R$, we have from Remark 9.2.4,

---

Algorithm 9 SIMULATE

1: **Input:** Graph $G = (L \cup R, E)$
2: **Output:** Matching M_{1s}, M_{2s}
3: Sort edges of G in decreasing order of their weights
4: $M_{1s} = \emptyset, M_{2s} = \emptyset$
5: Mark each left vertex $\ell \in G$ as unassigned
6: For each edge $e = (\ell, r)$ in sorted order
7: **if** ℓ is unassigned **AND** $M_{1s} \cup \{e\}$ is a matching **then**
8:     Mark ℓ as assigned
9:     Flip a coin with probability p of Heads
10:    If Heads, $M_{1s} \leftarrow M_{1s} \cup \{e\}$
11:    else $M_{2s} \leftarrow M_{2s} \cup \{e\}$
12: **end if**
13: $M_{3s} \leftarrow M_{2s}$
14: **for** each $r \in R$ **do**
15:    **if** degree of r in $M_{3s} > 1$ **then**
16:        Delete all edges incident on r in M_{3s}
17:    **end if**
18: **end for**

$v(M_{1s}) \geq \frac{v(OPT_p)}{2}$. Moreover, we also have $\mathbb{E}\{v(OPT_p)\} = p\mathbb{E}\{v(OPT)\}$. Thus, we get $\mathbb{E}\{v(M_{1s})\} \geq p\frac{v(OPT)}{2}$. ∎

We can also compare the weight of the matchings M_{1s} and M_{2s} as follows.

Lemma 9.4.6 $(1-p)\mathbb{E}\{v(M_{1s})\} = p\mathbb{E}\{v(M_{2s})\}$.

Proof: Any edge which is **not considered** by SIMULATE provides no contribution to either M_{1s} or M_{2s}. Thus, it is sufficient to restrict attention to only the considered edges. Each considered edge is assigned to M_{1s} with probability p and to M_{2s} with probability $1 - p$, for any history of coin tosses of previously considered edges. Thus, the expected contribution of each considered edge e is $pv(e)$ to M_{1s} and $(1 - p)v(e)$ to M_{2s}. Using linearity of expectation, hence it follows that

$$(1 - p)\mathbb{E}\{v(M_{1s})\} = p\mathbb{E}\{v(M_{2s})\}.$$

∎

Next, we relate the weight of the actual matching M_{3s} to that of OPT in Lemma 9.4.7 via M_{1s} and M_{2s} using Lemmas 9.4.5 and 9.4.6. The result of Lemma 9.4.7 is obtained via a crude analysis, and will be improved via a finer analysis in Lemma 9.4.9 to get the best competitive ratio of 8.

Lemma 9.4.7 $\mathbb{E}\{v(M_{3s})\} \geq \frac{p^2(1-p)}{2}v(OPT)$.

Proof: For each right vertex $r \in R$, let its revenue $\text{rev}_2(r)$ be the sum of the weights of the edges incident on r in M_{2s}. Let $\mathbb{E}\{\text{rev}_2(r)|e\}$ denote the expected revenue of r in M_{2s} given that e is the first edge incident to r that is selected by SIMULATE for M_{2s}. The first claim is that

$$\mathbb{E}\{\text{rev}_2(r)|e\} \leq \frac{v(e)}{p}.$$

To prove this, consider the event when e is added to M_{2s}. Once e is added to M_{2s}, exactly $i - 1$ more edges incident to r are selected by M_{2s} if the $i - 1$ future edges incident on r have coin toss tails (making it part of M_{2s}) and the ith edge incident on r is part of M_{1s} (because of its coin toss being heads). More importantly, once any edge incident on r becomes part of M_{1s}, no other edge incident on r is considered thereafter. Hence the probability of r having i edges ($i - 1$ other than e) incident to it is $(1 - p)^{i-1}p$. Since edges are added in decreasing order of their weights, the total revenue $\text{rev}_2(r)$ is at most $iv(e)$ given that r has i edges incident to it and e was the first edge. Therefore

$$\mathbb{E}\{\text{rev}_2(r)|e\} \leq v(e) \sum_{i=1}^{\infty} i(1 - p)^{i-1}p = \frac{v(e)}{p}. \tag{9.6}$$

Similarly, let the revenue $\text{rev}_3(r)$ of any right vertex $r \in R$ be the weight of the edge incident on r in M_{3s}. Let $\mathbb{E}\{\text{rev}_3(r)|e\}$ denote the expected revenue of r in M_{3s} given that e is the first edge incident to r that is selected by SIMULATE for M_{2s}. Under this conditioning, edge e is part of M_{3s} only if the next edge after e that is incident on r considered by SIMULATE is part of M_{1s}, in which case no further edge incident on r is considered. This event happens with probability p, and hence

$$\mathbb{E}\{\text{rev}_3(r)|e\} \geq pv(e),$$
$$\geq p.p\mathbb{E}\{\text{rev}_2(r)|e\},$$

where the second inequality follows from (9.6). Hence, we have

$$\mathbb{E}\{v(M_{3s})\} = \sum_{r \in R} \mathbb{E}\{\text{rev}_3(r)\} \geq \sum_{r \in R} p^2\mathbb{E}\{\text{rev}_2(r)\} = p^2\mathbb{E}\{M_{2s}\},$$

which together with Lemma 9.4.5 and Lemma 9.4.6 implies

$$\mathbb{E}\{v(M_{3s})\} \geq \frac{p^2(1 - p)}{2}v(\text{OPT}),$$

as required. ∎

With algorithm SIMULATE we removed all edges of M_{2s} that were incident on a right vertex with degree > 1. Clearly, we can obtain a larger weighted matching, if instead of removing all edges, we keep only one edge that arrives the earliest, and then reject all others. The algorithm SAMPLEANDPERMUTE is a simple modification of the SIMULATE algorithm motivated by this idea, where for right vertices with degree at most 1 in M_{3s}, $M_{3p} = M_{3s}$, while for right vertices r with degree > 1 in M_{3s}, M_{3p} contains the only edge incident on r in M_{2s} that arrived the earliest. Moreover, we have the following relations for the matchings produced by SIMULATE and SAMPLEANDPERMUTE.

Proposition 9.4.8 *The matching produced by* SIMULATE *and* SAMPLEANDPERMUTE *satisfy* $M_{1s} = M_{1p}$ *and* $M_{2s} = M_{2p}$ *for identical coin tosses.*

Proof: For SIMULATE, once a coin is tossed for an edge making the left vertex assigned, no other coin is tossed for any edge that shares a common left vertex with it. So it is essentially identical to tossing a coin once for each left vertex instead of each individual edge as done in the algorithm SAMPLEANDPERMUTE. Moreover, in SIMULATE, since the edges are processed in decreasing order of their weights, the matching M_{1s} is essentially a GREEDY matching on the set of edges for which coin tosses were heads, similar to the matching M_{1p} produced by SAMPLEANDPERMUTE.

Algorithm 10 SAMPLEANDPERMUTE

1: **Input:** Graph $G = (L \cup R, E)$
2: **Output:** Matching M_{2p}, M_{3p}
3: %Offline Phase
4: $L' = \varnothing$
5: **for** each $\ell \in L$ **do**
6:     With probability p, $L' \leftarrow L' \cup \{\ell\}$
7: **end for**
8: $(M_{1p}) \leftarrow$ GREEDY$(G(L' \cup R, E(L')))$
9: **for** each $r \in R$ **do**
10:     Set price$(r) = v(e)$ if $e = (\ell, r) \in M_{1p}$
11:     Set price$(r) = 0$ if $e = (*, r) \notin M_{1p}$
12: **end for**
13: %Decision Phase
14: $M_{2p} = \varnothing, M_{3p} = \varnothing$
15: **for** each $\ell \in L \backslash L'$ in random order **do**
16:     Let $e = (\ell, r)$ be the edge with largest weight such that $v(e) \geq$ price(r)
17:     Add e to M_{2p}.
18:     If $M_{3p} \cup e$ is a matching $M_{3p} \leftarrow M_{3p} \cup \{e\}$
19: **end for**

With SAMPLEANDPERMUTE for each right vertex r that has some edge incident on it which is part of M_{1p}, a threshold price(r) is set. In the decision phase (where all left vertices whose coin tosses were tails, and their associated edges are considered in a random order), an edge $e = (\ell, r)$ is added to M_{2p} if $v(e) \geq$ price(r).

Consider an edge $e = (\ell, r)$ that is part of M_{2s} with SIMULATE. Since e is part of M_{2s}, the coin toss for ℓ was tails, so ℓ belongs to the decision phase of SAMPLEANDPERMUTE. Since $e = (\ell, r)$ is part of M_{2s}, from Proposition 9.4.4, we know that no edge considered before $e = (\ell, r)$ that is incident on r is part of M_{1s}, since otherwise $e = (\ell, r)$ would not have been considered. Therefore, any edge that is part of M_{1s} and is incident on r must have been considered after $e = (\ell, r)$. Moreover, since edges are considered in decreasing order of weights, this implies that any edge that is part of M_{1s} and is incident on r must have a weight less than that of $e = (\ell, r)$. Since price(r) is found using edges that are only part of $M_{1p} = M_{1s}$, $v(e) \geq$ price(r). Thus, an edge that belongs to M_{2s} also belongs to M_{2p}.

The reverse direction argument follows similarly, and we can conclude that whenever coin tosses are identical for SAMPLEANDPERMUTE and SIMULATE, the matching $M_{1s} = M_{1p}$ and pseudo-matching $M_{2s} = M_{2p}$ produced by SIMULATE and SAMPLEANDPERMUTE are also identical. ∎

For matching M_{3p} with SAMPLEANDPERMUTE, however, the following improved guarantee can be obtained compared to matching M_{3s} of SIMULATE.

Lemma 9.4.9 $\mathbb{E}\{v(M_{3p})\} \geq \frac{p(1-p)}{2}\mathbb{E}\{v(OPT)\}$. *Hence,* SAMPLEANDPERMUTE *is 8-approximate by choosing* $p = \frac{1}{2}$ *that maximizes the approximation ratio* $\frac{p(1-p)}{2}$.

Compared to Lemma 9.4.7, by retaining the first edge for right vertices with degree > 1 in M_{2s} we are able to get a p-fraction improvement in the approximation ratio.

Proof: From Lemma 9.4.8, $M_{2s} = M_{2p}$. Thus, we essentially use the properties of algorithm SIMULATE to bound the performance of M_{2p}. Let $\mathbb{E}\{\text{rev}_3(r)\}$ and $\mathbb{E}\{\text{rev}_2(r)\}$ be the (expected revenue) expectation of weight of the (at most one) edge incident on vertex $r \in R$ in M_{3p}, and the sum of the expectation of weights of edges incident on $r \in R$ in M_{2p}, respectively. Also, let $\mathbb{E}\{\text{rev}_3(r)|i\}$ and $\mathbb{E}\{\text{rev}_2(r)|i\}$ be the expected revenues in M_{3p} and M_{2p} conditioned on the right vertex r being incident to i edges in M_{2p} respectively.

Let r be incident to i edges in M_{2p} with $p_i = \mathbb{P}(r$ is incident to i edges in $M_{2p})$. Then, since M_{3p} accepts the first edge among the i edges, and the order of arrival is uniformly random, we have

$$\mathbb{E}\{\text{rev}_3(r)|i\} = \frac{\mathbb{E}\{\text{rev}_2(r)|i\}}{i}. \tag{9.7}$$

Moreover, also note that

$$\mathbb{E}\{\text{rev}_2(r)\} = \sum_i p_i \mathbb{E}\{\text{rev}_2(r)|i\}. \tag{9.8}$$

$$\mathbb{E}\{\text{rev}_3(r)\} = \sum_i p_i \mathbb{E}\{\text{rev}_3(r)|i\}. \tag{9.9}$$

We are interested in the condition that maximizes the ratio of $\mathbb{E}\{\text{rev}_2(r)\}$ and $\mathbb{E}\{\text{rev}_3(r)\}$. From earlier analysis in Lemma 9.4.7, we know that this ratio is at least $\frac{1}{p^2}$. We want to show that the ratio is actually lower bounded by $\frac{1}{p}$. Towards that end, we will prove the following. Let $S_i = \mathbb{E}\{\text{rev}_2(r)|i\}$. To prove Lemma 9.4.10, instead of considering the algorithm SAMPLEANDPERMUTE we appeal to the algorithm SIMULATE, since both have identical valuation for matchings they produce in expectation.

Lemma 9.4.10

$$S_i \leq \frac{i}{i-1}S_{i-1}.$$

Proof:

$$S_i = \mathbb{E}\{\text{rev}_2(r) \text{ from the first } i-1 \text{ edges}\} + \mathbb{E}\{\text{rev}_2(r) \text{ from the } i^{th} \text{ edge}\}.$$

Since the edges are presented in decreasing order of their weights in algorithm SIMULATE, the weight of the ith edge is smaller than each of the individual weights of the first $i - 1$ edges, and we have

$$\mathbb{E}\{\text{rev}_2(r) \text{ from the } i^{th} \text{ edge}\} \leq \frac{\mathbb{E}\{\text{rev}_2(r) \text{ from the first } i - 1 \text{ edges}\}}{i - 1}.$$

Moreover, $S_{i-1} = \mathbb{E}\{\text{rev}_2(r) \text{ from the first } i - 1 \text{ edges}\}$. Therefore,

$$S_i \leq S_{i-1} + \frac{S_{i-1}}{i - 1}.$$

$\blacksquare$

Lemma 9.4.11

$$p_i \leq (1 - p)p_{i-1}.$$

Proof: Again considering any fixed realization of the order of arrival of left vertices, let $i - 1$ edges be added to M_{2p} that are incident on r. Then for r to have a final degree i in M_{2p}, the next considered edge that is incident on r has to have its coin toss as tails and the one thereafter to have its coin toss heads and become part of M_{1p}, since otherwise the degree of r is either $i - 1$ or $i + 1$. Thus, given that the current degree is $i - 1$, the final degree of r is i with probability $p(1 - p)$, and $i - 1$ with probability p. Since this holds for each realization, we have $p_i \leq (1 - p)p_{i-1}$. $\blacksquare$

The ratio of $\mathbb{E}\{\text{rev}_2(r)\}$ and $\mathbb{E}\{\text{rev}_3(r)\}$ quantifies how much of rev_2 can be extracted via rev_3. The claim is that the ratio of $\mathbb{E}\{\text{rev}_2(r)\}$ and $\mathbb{E}\{\text{rev}_3(r)\}$ is minimized when both conditions in Lemmas 9.4.10 and 9.4.11 are tight, i.e., $S_i = \frac{i}{i-1}S_{i-1}$ and $p_i = (1 - p)p_{i-1}$. We leave this claim as an exercise in Problem 9.6. With $S_i = \frac{i}{i-1}S_{i-1}$ and $p_i = (1 - p)p_{i-1}$, from (9.8) and (9.9), we get

$$\mathbb{E}\{\text{rev}_2(r)\} = \sum_i i p_1(1 - p)^{i-1}\mathbb{E}\{\text{rev}_2(r)|1\} = \frac{\mathbb{E}\{\text{rev}_2(r)|1\}p_1}{p^2}.$$

$$\mathbb{E}\{\text{rev}_3(r)\} = \sum_i p_1(1 - p)^{i-1}\mathbb{E}\{\text{rev}_2(r)|1\} = \frac{\mathbb{E}\{\text{rev}_2(r)|1\}p_1}{p} = p\mathbb{E}\{\text{rev}_2(r)\}.$$

Hence, we have

$$\mathbb{E}\{v(M_{3p})\} = \sum_{r \in R} \mathbb{E}\{\text{rev}_3(r)\} = \sum_{r \in R} p\mathbb{E}\{\text{rev}_2(r)\} = p\mathbb{E}\{M_{2p}\},$$

which, together with Lemmas 9.4.5 and 9.4.6, implies

$$\mathbb{E}\{v(M_{3p})\} \geq \frac{p(1 - p)}{2}v(\text{OPT}),$$

as required to prove Lemma 9.4.9. $\blacksquare$

Next, we make SAMPLEANDPERMUTE truly online in algorithm SAMPLEANDPRICE.

The connection between SAMPLEANDPERMUTE and SAMPLEANDPRICE is that the output matching M_{3p} of SAMPLEANDPERMUTE and M_{ON} produced by SAMPLEANDPRICE are almost identical, except for the difference in defining the set L' (set of left vertices used to generate the matching M_1). With SAMPLEANDPERMUTE, coins are tossed for all left vertices ahead of time that decide which left vertices are part of the offline phase (so it is offline), while in SAMPLEANDPRICE, a random number of left vertices are made part of the offline phase. But with both these definitions, a left vertex is selected to be part of L' with probability $1/2$ independently. Consequently, the utilities of matchings M_{3p} and M_{ON} are identical in expectation. So whatever guarantee we have on SAMPLEANDPERMUTE for the weight of matching M_{3p} carries over for the SAMPLEANDPRICE algorithm with matching M_{ON}, and we have this final result.

Theorem 9.4.12 SAMPLEANDPRICE *algorithm is 8-competitive in expectation.*

Proof: Choosing $p = \frac{1}{2}$, we get the result from Lemma 9.4.12. ∎

Algorithm 11 SAMPLEANDPRICE

1: **Input:** L, the set of left vertices that arrive sequentially with uniformly random permutation π, R, set of right vertices
2: %Offline Phase
3: $p = \frac{1}{2}$, $k \leftarrow Binomial(|L|, p)$
4: Let L' be the first k vertices of L
5: $M_1 \leftarrow$ GREEDY$(G(L' \cup R))$
6: **for** each right vertex $r : e = (\ell, r) \in M_1$ **do**
7:     Set price$(r) := v(e)$
8: **end for**
9: **for** each right vertex $r : (*, r) \notin M_1$ **do**
10:     Set price$(r) := 0$
11: **end for**
12: %Decision Phase
13: $M_{ON} = \varnothing$
14: **for** every new left vertex $\ell \in L \backslash L'$ **do,**
15:     Let $e^\star = (\ell, r)$ be the edge with the largest weight such that $v(e^\star) \geq$ price(r)
16:     **if** $M_{ON} \cup \{e^\star\}$ is a matching **then**
17:         $M_{ON} = M_{ON} \cup \{e^\star\}$
18:     **else**
19:         Let ℓ be permanently unmatched
20:     **end if**
21: **end for**

9.4.2 Repeated Optimal Matching (ROM) Algorithm

In the previous subsection, we showed that under the secretarial input, the competitive ratio of the SAMPLEANDPRICE algorithm is at least $1/8$, while from Remark 9.4.2 we know that the upper bound on the competitive ratio of any algorithm is $1/e$. In this subsection, we present an algorithm, named repeated optimal matching (ROM), whose competitive ratio is at least $1/e - 1/n$, where n is the number of left vertices.

The basic idea of ROM (Algorithm 12) is that the first τ left vertices are not matched, and on each subsequent left vertex ℓ'_t's arrival at time $t > \tau$, an optimal matching M^t is found between the set of left vertices that have arrived till time t, and the set of right vertices R. If ℓ_t is matched to a right vertex r in M^t, and if r is currently unmatched, then ℓ_t is matched to r.

ROM's philosophy is in contrast to the SAMPLEANDPRICE algorithm, where a single optimal matching is computed after the arrival of a subset of left vertices, and thereafter a newly arrived left vertex is matched to the 'best' right vertex, as long as the weight of the edge between the newly arrived left vertex and the 'best' right vertex is larger than the weight associated with the 'best' right vertex in the optimal matching.

Even though the complexity of ROM is much larger than the SAMPLEANDPRICE algorithm, its competitive ratio guarantee is significantly better and the analysis is remarkably simple, as discussed next.

Theorem 9.4.13 *The competitive ratio of* ROM *is at least* $\dfrac{1}{e} - \dfrac{1}{n}$ *where* $n = |L|$ *by choosing* $\tau = \left\lceil \dfrac{n}{e} \right\rceil$.

Proof: Let $e^t = (\ell_t, r_t)$ be the edge that is matched to ℓ_t at time $t \geq \tau + 1$ in the locally optimal matching M^t at time t. Note that e^t becomes part of the matching M output by ROM only if the right vertex r_t is unmatched when ℓ_t arrives.

We prove the result in two parts. First we lower bound (Lemma 9.4.14) the expected weight of the edge e^t, which is an easy step, using the secretarial input assumption. Thereafter, we lower bound (Lemma 9.4.15) the probability that the right vertex r_t is unmatched when ℓ_t arrives.

Lemma 9.4.14

$$\mathbb{E}\{v(e^t)\} \geq \frac{1}{n} v(\mathsf{M}_{\mathsf{OPT}}),$$

where $\mathsf{M}_{\mathsf{OPT}}$ *is the optimal matching over the full graph* $G = (L \cup R, E)$.

Let $\mathcal{E}_{t'} = (\ell_{t'+1} = u_{t'+1}, \ell_{t'+2} = u_{t'+2}, \ldots, \ell_n = u_n)$ for some fixed set of left vertices $(u_{t'+1}, \ldots, u_n)$.

Lemma 9.4.15 *At time* $t \geq \tau + 1$ *on left vertex* ℓ'_t's *arrival, the probability that* $M \cup \{e^t\}$ *is a matching,*

$$\mathbb{P}(M \cup \{e^t\} \text{ is a matching} | \mathcal{E}_{t-1}) \geq \frac{\tau}{t-1}.$$

Given Lemmas 9.4.14 and 9.4.15, we complete the proof of Theorem 9.4.13 as follows. Let $\mathbf{1}_t$ be the indicator variable; $\mathbf{1}_t = 1$ if $M \cup \{e^t\}$ is a matching at time t, and 0 otherwise. Consider

$$\mathbb{E}\{\mathbf{1}_t v(e^t) | \mathcal{E}_{t-1}\} \overset{(a)}{=} v(e^t)\mathbb{E}\{\mathbf{1}_t | \mathcal{E}_{t-1}\},$$
$$= v(e^t)\mathbb{P}(M \cup \{e^t\} \text{ is a matching} | \mathcal{E}_{t-1}),$$
$$\overset{(b)}{\geq} v(e^t)\frac{\tau}{t-1},$$

Algorithm 12 ROM

1: **Input:** Right vertices R, left vertices L, Graph $G = (L \cup R, E)$ where left vertices (and their edge weights) are revealed sequentially in uniformly random order
2: **Output:** Matching M
3: $M = \varnothing$
4: $L^\tau \subset L$ be the first τ left vertices of L
5: Do not match any left vertex of L^τ
6: **for** each newly arrived left vertex $\ell_t \in L \backslash L^{t-1}, t \geq \tau + 1$ **do**
7:      $L^t = L^{t-1} \cup \ell_t$
8:      $E^t = E(L^t, R)$ %edge set to consider
9:      $M^t =$ optimal matching $G(L^t \cup R, E^t)$
10:      $e^t = (\ell_t, r_t)$ be the edge matched to ℓ_t in M^t
11:      **if** $M \cup \{e^t\}$ is a matching **then**
12:          $M = M \cup \{e^t\}$
13:      **end if**
14: **end for**

---

where (a) follows since conditioning over $\mathcal{E}_{t-1}$ fixes the left vertex arriving at time t, and hence $v(e^t)$ is deterministic, while (b) follows from Lemma 9.4.15.

Unconditioning over $\mathcal{E}_{t-1}$ and using Lemma 9.4.14, we get

$$\mathbb{E}\left\{\mathbf{1}_t v(e^t)\right\} \geq \mathbb{E}\{v(e^t)\}\frac{\tau}{t-1},$$

$$\geq \frac{1}{n} v(M_{OPT})\frac{\tau}{t-1}. \tag{9.10}$$

The total expected weight of the matching M found by ROM is

$$\mathbb{E}\{v(M)\} = \sum_{t=\tau+1}^{n} \mathbb{E}\left\{\mathbf{1}_t v(e^t)\right\},$$

$$\geq \sum_{t=\tau+1}^{n} \frac{1}{n} v(M_{OPT})\frac{\tau}{t-1},$$

$$= \frac{\tau}{n} v(M_{OPT}) \sum_{t=\tau}^{n-1} \frac{1}{t},$$

$$\overset{(a)}{\geq} \left(\frac{1}{e} - \frac{1}{n}\right) v(M_{OPT}),$$

where (a) follows by choosing $\tau = \left\lceil \frac{n}{e} \right\rceil$ and using the fact that for this choice $\tau/n \geq \left(\frac{1}{e} - \frac{1}{n}\right)$ and $\sum_{t=\tau}^{n-1} \frac{1}{t} \geq \ln\left(\frac{n}{\tau}\right) \geq 1$. ∎

Next, we prove Lemmas 9.4.14 and 9.4.15.

Proof: [Lemma 9.4.14] First we show that $\mathbb{E}\{v(\mathsf{M}^t)\} \geq \frac{t}{n}v(\mathsf{M}_{\mathsf{OPT}})$. Recall that $\mathsf{M}_{\mathsf{OPT}}$ is the optimal matching on the whole graph $G = (L \cup R, E)$, and $\mathsf{M}_{\mathsf{OPT}}$ does not depend on the order in which left vertices of L arrive, since it is an optimal offline matching. We will index the set of left vertices in order of their arrival, i.e., ℓ_1 arrives before ℓ_2, and so on. Let $\mathsf{M}^t_{\mathsf{OPT}}$ be the restriction of $\mathsf{M}_{\mathsf{OPT}}$ to set $L^t \subseteq L$, where $L^t = \{\ell_1, \dots, \ell_t\}$ is the set consisting of the first t left vertices, i.e., $\mathsf{M}^t_{\mathsf{OPT}} = \mathsf{M}_{\mathsf{OPT}} \cap E^t$, where E^t is the set of edges between L^t and R. Since each left vertex of L belongs to L^t uniformly randomly, we have

$$\mathbb{E}\{v(\mathsf{M}^t_{\mathsf{OPT}})\} = \frac{t}{n}v(\mathsf{M}_{\mathsf{OPT}}).$$

Since the matching M^t found by ROM at time t has $\mathsf{M}^t_{\mathsf{OPT}}$ as a feasible solution, we get

$$v(\mathsf{M}^t) \geq v(\mathsf{M}^t_{\mathsf{OPT}}),$$

and consequently

$$\mathbb{E}\{v(\mathsf{M}^t)\} \geq \frac{t}{n}v(\mathsf{M}_{\mathsf{OPT}}). \tag{9.11}$$

Note that $v(\mathsf{M}^t) = \sum_{i=1}^{t} v(e^i)$, where e^i is the edge matched to the left vertex ℓ_i in the locally optimal matching M^t that is computed between $L^t \cup R$ on arrival of vertex ℓ_t. Moreover,

$$v(\mathsf{M}^t) \overset{(a)}{=} \mathbb{E}\{v(\mathsf{M}^t)|L^t\}$$

$$= \mathbb{E}\left\{\sum_{i=1}^{t} v(e^i)|L^t\right\}$$

$$\overset{(b)}{=} \sum_{i=1}^{t} \mathbb{E}\{v(e^i)|L^t\},$$

$$\overset{(c)}{=} t\mathbb{E}\{v(e^t)|L^t\},$$

where (a) follows since given L^t, M^t is deterministic, (b) follows from linearity of expectation, and (c) follows from the fact that $\mathbb{E}\{v(e^i)|L^t\} = \mathbb{E}\{v(e^j)|L^t\}$ for $i \neq j$, $1 \leq i, j \leq t$ since any left vertex belonging to set L^t occupies any of the $|L^t|$ locations uniformly randomly.

Thus, we get

$$\mathbb{E}\{v(e^t)|L^t\} = \frac{1}{t}v(\mathsf{M}^t),$$

and unconditioning over L^t,

$$\mathbb{E}\{v(e^t)\} = \frac{1}{t}\mathbb{E}\{v(\mathsf{M}^t)\}. \tag{9.12}$$

Combining (9.11) and (9.12), we get $\mathbb{E}\{v(e^t)\} \geq \frac{1}{n}v(\mathsf{M}_{\mathsf{OPT}})$, as required. ∎

Proof: [Lemma 9.4.15] We prove Proposition 9.4.16, from which choosing $r = r_t$ and $t' = t - 1$ implies Lemma 9.4.15. ∎

Proposition 9.4.16 *On the arrival of left vertex $\ell_{t'}$ at time $t' \geq \tau + 1$, for any right vertex $r \in R$, and all choices of $(\ell_{t'+1} = u_{t'+1}, \dots, \ell_n = u_n)$, we have*

$$\mathbb{P}(\cap_{k=\tau+1}^{t'} r \notin e^k | \ell_{t'+1} = u_{t'+1}, \dots, \ell_n = u_n) \geq \frac{\tau}{t'}.$$

The event $\cap_{k=\tau+1}^{t'} r \notin e^k$ means that starting from time $\tau + 1$ till time t', the right vertex r remains unmatched, and Proposition 9.4.16 lower bounds this event's probability.

Proof: We prove Proposition 9.4.16 using induction on t' starting from $t' = \tau + 1$. The base case is true, i.e., for $t' = \tau + 1$, as follows. We need to prove that $\mathbb{P}(r \notin e^{\tau+1} | \mathcal{E}_{\tau+1}) \geq \frac{\tau}{\tau+1}$, where $e^{\tau+1} = (\ell_{\tau+1}, r_{\tau+1})$, and $\mathcal{E}_{t'} = (\ell_{t'+1} = u_{t'+1}, \ell_{t'+2} = u_{t'+2}, \dots, \ell_n = u_n)$ for some fixed $(u_{t'+1}, \dots, u_n)$. Given $\mathcal{E}_{\tau+1}$, the locally optimal matching $\mathsf{M}^{\tau+1}$ at time $\tau + 1$ is deterministic, and moreover $L^{\tau+1}$ (first $\tau + 1$ arriving left vertices) is fixed up to the random order. Let S be the set of vertices $S \subseteq L^{\tau+1}$ that are not matched to r in matching $\mathsf{M}^{\tau+1}$. Since $\mathsf{M}^{\tau+1}$ is a matching, $|S| \geq L^{\tau+1} - 1$.

Then

$$\mathbb{P}(r \notin e^{\tau+1} | \mathcal{E}_{\tau+1}) = \mathbb{P}(\ell_{\tau+1} \in S | \mathcal{E}_{\tau+1}) \overset{(a)}{=} \frac{|S|}{|L^{\tau+1}|} \geq \frac{|L^{\tau+1}| - 1}{|L^{\tau+1}|} = \frac{\tau}{\tau+1},$$

where (a) follows since $\ell_{\tau+1}$ is chosen uniformly randomly from the set $L^{\tau+1}$.

Next, we assume that the claim is true for time $t' - 1$ and then show that this implies the claim for t'. Recall the definition of $\mathcal{E}_{t'} = ((\ell_{t'+1} = u_{t'+1}), \mathcal{E}_{t'+1})$ for some fixed $(u_{t'+1}, \dots, u_n)$. Thus, conditioning on $\mathcal{E}_{t'}$, matching $\mathsf{M}^{t'}$ is actually deterministic, since it only depends on the set of participating left vertices (that have arrived so far till time t') and not on their relative ordering. Let $\mathcal{I}_{t'}$ be the set of left vertices that have arrived till time t', i.e., $L \backslash \{u_{t'+1}, \dots, u_n\}$, but are not matched to the right vertex r in $\mathsf{M}^{t'}$. Since $\mathsf{M}^{t'}$ is a matching, note that

$$|\mathcal{I}_{t'}| \geq t' - 1. \tag{9.13}$$

Using the law of total probability, we write

$$\mathbb{P}(\cap_{k=\tau+1}^{t'} r \notin e^k | \mathcal{E}_{t'}) = \sum_{u \in \mathcal{I}_{t'}} \mathbb{P}(\ell_{t'} = u | \mathcal{E}_{t'}) \mathbb{P}(\cap_{k=\tau+1}^{t'-1} r \notin e^k | \ell_{t'} = u, \mathcal{E}_{t'}),$$

$$\overset{(a)}{=} \sum_{u \in \mathcal{I}_{t'}} \frac{1}{t'} \mathbb{P}(\cap_{k=\tau+1}^{t'-1} r \notin e^k | \ell_{t'} = u, \mathcal{E}_{t'}),$$

$$\overset{(b)}{\geq} \sum_{u \in \mathcal{I}_{t'}} \frac{1}{t'} \frac{\tau}{t'-1},$$

$$\overset{(c)}{\geq} \frac{t'-1}{t'} \frac{\tau}{t'-1} = \frac{\tau}{t'},$$

where to get (a) we have used the fact that $\mathbb{P}(\ell_{t'} = u | \mathcal{E}_{t'}) = \frac{1}{t'}$ since conditioning over $\mathcal{E}_{t'}$ restricts the set of left vertices arriving until time t' but the relative order remains uniformly random, and (b) follows from the induction hypothesis. Finally, (c) follows from (9.13). ∎

9.5 Notes

The unweighted online bipartite matching problem with adversarial input was first studied in [149], which is now regarded as seminal work, where it was shown that RANKING has the optimal competitive ratio of $1 - 1/e$. There was, however, a subtle mistake in the analysis of [149], noticed by Krohn and Varadarajan. The result, however, is true and the first rigorous proof was presented in [150]. Independently of [150], the proof presented in this chapter for RANKING was derived in [151]. Using a primal–dual analysis, an alternate proof of the $1 - 1/e$-competitiveness of RANKING was presented in [152] that we will discuss in Chapter 10. When the input is not adversarial, but secretarial or randomized, [153, 154] showed that algorithms achieving competitive ratio better than $1 - 1/e$ is possible.

The unweighted online bipartite matching problem under the secretarial input was considered in [150], where a greedy algorithm (MATCH-ANY) that matches the arriving left vertex to any of the unmatched right vertices to which it has an edge is shown to have a competitive ratio of $1 - 1/e$. The result follows from the analysis of RANKING in the adversarial model, presented in this chapter, since MATCH-ANY with secretarial input simulates RANKING with adversarial input, with the roles of the two algorithms switched. Monograph [155] reviews the unweighted bipartite matching problem and its variants.

The competitive ratio of the weighted online bipartite matching problem with adversarial input is unbounded, similar to the secretary problem. Therefore, secretarial input was considered in [156], and showed that an algorithm following the sample and price philosophy has a competitive ratio of 1/8. An algorithm with an almost optimal competitive ratio of $1/e - 1/n$, where n is the total number of left vertices, was derived in [157]. An expected competitive ratio of $1 - 1/e$ for the weighted case with adversarial input was derived in [158], when all edges incident to the same vertex on the right-hand side have identical weights. The case of batch arrivals where more than one left vertex arrives together has also been considered in [156].

Very recently, improved algorithms in the presence of prediction via machine learning has been considered in [129], in what is called the beyond the worst-case paradigm. In particular, prediction about the value of the edge incident on each right vertex in the optimal matching is extracted from a machine learning oracle, and an algorithm whose performance degrades smoothly with prediction error has been derived. The case of online matching over general graphs has also been considered, where either a vertex or an edge arrives sequentially [159, 160].

There is also recent fundamental work on the free-disposal model for MWBMP, where a right vertex r can be matched any number of times; however, the weight of only the heaviest edge incident on r is counted towards the total weight of the matching. With the free-disposal model, one does not need to assume that the left vertex arrival model is secretarial, and an online algorithm with competitive ratio of 0.5086 has been derived in [161] for the worst-case input.

PROBLEMS

9.1 To prove Lemma 9.3.5 consider the following input, with $|L| = |R| = n$, where left vertex i has an edge to right vertex j if $j = i$ or when $1 \leq i \leq n/2$ and $n/2 + 1 \leq j \leq n$.

1. For this input, show that the probability that left vertex i is matched to right vertex i for $1 \leq i \leq n/2$ is at most $\frac{1}{n/2 - i + 2}$.

2. Using part 1, show that the expected number of left vertices i for $i = 1, \dots, n/2$ (among the first $n/2$ left vertices) not matched to right vertex i by the RANDOM algorithm is $\geq \frac{n}{2} - \log(n/2 + 1)$.

3. Show that the expected size of the matching produced by the RANDOM algorithm is $\frac{n}{2} + \mathcal{O}(\log n)$, while the size of OPT's matching is n.

4. Conclude the proof of Lemma 9.3.5.

9.2 We will prove Lemma 9.3.6 in this problem. Let $|L| = |R| = n$, and the edge matrix be the complete upper triangular matrix $\mathbf{T}$. For π as a permutation over $[1 : n]$, let $\mathbf{T}^\pi$ be obtained from $\mathbf{T}$ by permuting the columns of $\mathbf{T}$ using π. Then consider two input instances $\mathcal{I}_1$ and $\mathcal{I}_2$, where the input is $\mathbf{T}$ and $\mathbf{T}^\pi$, respectively, and the order of arrival is row number $1, 2, \dots, n$ in both instances.

When π is uniformly random over the $n!$ permutations, then we call $\mathcal{I}_2$ as input with distribution D.

Let $\mathcal{G}$ be a 'greedy' deterministic algorithm that always matches the incoming left vertex to some right vertex if there is at least one eligible right vertex.

Then show the following, which, together with Lemma 9.3.7, is sufficient to prove Lemma 9.3.6.

1. Show that for $\mathcal{G}$ with input distributed according to D, on arrival of the kth left vertex, the number of eligible (unmatched and that have an edge) right vertices is identically distributed as the number of eligible right vertices for RANDOM algorithm on arrival of the kth left vertex with input $\mathbf{T}$.

   [Hint: Use induction.]

   Thus, the expected size of the matching obtained by $\mathcal{G}$ with input distributed according to D is the same as the expected size of matching obtained by the RANDOM algorithm on $\mathbf{T}$.

2. Argue that, without loss of generality, we can consider the greedy algorithm as the optimal deterministic algorithm.

   [Hint: Simulate any deterministic algorithm $\mathcal{A}$ by $\mathcal{G}$.]

3. Let M_* be the matching obtained by algorithm $*$. Using Yao's principle, show that for a randomized algorithm $\mathcal{R}$,

$$\min_{\pi} \mathbb{E}\{M_{\mathcal{R}}(\mathbf{T}, \pi)\} \leq \max_{\mathcal{A}} \mathbb{E}_D\{M_{\mathcal{A}}(\mathbf{T}, \pi)\} = \mathbb{E}_D\{M_{\mathcal{G}}(\mathbf{T}, \pi)\},$$

i.e., the expected size of the matching obtained by any randomized online algorithm with input $\mathbf{T}^{\pi}$ for any permutation π is upper bounded by the expected size of matching obtained by the greedy algorithm with input $\mathbf{T}^{\pi}$ distributed according to D as the (random) input.

4. Combining parts 1 and 3, conclude that the expected size of the matching obtained by any randomized online algorithm with input $\mathbf{T}^{\pi}$ for any permutation π is upper bounded by the expected size of matching obtained by RANDOM algorithm on $\mathbf{T}$.

9.3 Consider RANKING, where π is the rank function (chosen uniformly randomly) over the right vertices, while σ is the arbitrary order in which left vertices arrive. Let the matching output by RANKING in this case be M_1. Next, we interchange the roles of left and right vertices, i.e., right vertices arrive sequentially according to order π, and all left vertices are available ahead of time, and left vertices are rank ordered using σ. Under this setting, on the arrival of a right vertex it is matched to the unmatched left vertex with the lowest rank with σ. Let the matching output be M_2. Show that the two matchings M_1 and M_2 are identical for any π and σ.

[Hint: Use induction on the number of left and right vertices.]

9.4 For the unweighted online bipartite matching problem, assign an arbitrary rank (among 1 to $|R|$) to all the right vertices. Let the left vertices arrive uniformly randomly (secretarial input), and on the arrival of a left vertex it is matched to an unmatched right vertex with the lowest rank. Show that the competitive ratio (in expectation) of this algorithm is $1 - 1/e$ under the secretarial input by exploiting the result that the competitive ratio of RANKING with the adversarial input is $1 - 1/e$.

[Hint: Using Problem 9.3 will be useful.]

9.5 Consider a bipartite graph $G = (L \cup R, E)$ and a special subgraph $F \subseteq G$, where $F = (L \backslash \{L'\} \cup R, E \backslash \{E'\})$ that is obtained by removing a subset L' of left vertices of G (and deleting all edges E' incident on the left vertices of L'). Let the offline greedy matching on graphs G and F be called GREEDY(G) and GREEDY(F), respectively. Prove that the weight of GREEDY(F) is at most the weight of GREEDY(G), by showing that for each right vertex, the weight of the matched edge in GREEDY(G) is at least as much as in GREEDY(F).

[Note: This is not true for arbitrary subgraphs, where only some edges are removed.]

9.6 Show that for the SAMPLEANDPERMUTE algorithm, the worst-case ratio of $\mathbb{E}\{\text{rev}_3(r)\}$ and $\mathbb{E}\{\text{rev}_2(r)\}$ occurs when the $p_i = (1 - p)p_{i-1}$ and $S_i = \frac{i}{i-1}S_{i-1}$.

9.7 (Reassignments) Consider an unweighted bipartite graph in the online setting, where on each new left vertex arrival (all right vertices are available beforehand) all edges incident on it are revealed. At each new left vertex arrival, a maximum matching has to be found over the subgraph revealed so far, where reassignment of previously matched edges is allowed. The objective is to minimize the number of reassignments while maintaining maximum matching at each step of the sequentially revealed left vertices.

[162] Show that when the order of arrival of left vertices is secretarial, the greedy algorithm, which on each new left vertex arrival re-computes the matching using the AUGPATH Algorithm (details follow next) over the subgraph revealed so far, requires a total of $\mathcal{O}(n \log n)$ reassignments in expectation, where n is the number of total left vertices (equal to the number of right vertices).

To show this result it is sufficient to show that, given that k left vertices are yet to arrive, the expected number of right vertices that the considered algorithm needs to reassign in order to match the next arriving left vertex is at most $\frac{n}{k}$.

[**Augmentation Algorithm Details**] For a bipartite graph $(V \cup W, E)$, let M be a matching, and suppose that

$$v_1, w_1, v_2, w_2, \ldots, v_k, w_k$$

is a sequence of vertices such that no edge in M is incident on v_1 or w_k, and moreover for all $1 \leq i \leq k$, edge $(v_i, w_i) \in$ M, while for all $1 \leq i \leq k - 1$, the edge $(w_i, v_{i+1}) \notin$ M. Then the sequence of vertices $v_1, w_1, \ldots$, together with the edges joining them in order is an **alternating** path.

An **augmentation** path is an alternating path that starts and begins at a vertex that is not part of a matching.

For an unweighted bipartite graph, an algorithm (AUGPATH) that finds augmentation paths is an optimal algorithm to find the maximum (optimum) matching.

Algorithm 13 AUGPATH Algorithm

1: **Input:** Bipartite graph G
2: Initialize M $= \varnothing$
3: Repeat
4: $P = AugmentingPath(G, M)$
5: M $=$ M $\oplus P$
6: Until $P = \varnothing$

---

where $\oplus$ denotes the symmetric difference set operation (everything that belongs to both sets individually, but does not belong to their intersection).

9.8 Consider the following search problem – a robot stands on the x-axis at the origin, and is searching for a bomb, which it knows exists somewhere on the x-axis at some integer distance $d \geq 1$ either to the left or to the right of the origin. The robot can only travel on the x-axis. Neither the distance to the bomb nor the side on which it exists is known to the robot.

1. Let D_A be the total distance travelled by the robot, and the competitive ratio for A is

$$\mu_A = \max_{d,\text{direction}} \frac{D_A}{D_{\text{OPT}}}.$$

   Derive an algorithm A with a competitive ratio of at most 9.

   [Hint: Exponentially increasing the probing distance might be helpful.]

2. Prove that the competitive ratio of any deterministic algorithm for this problem is at least 3.[3]

9.9 Consider the real line, where there are two sets (of same size n) of points, red and blue, are located arbitrarily. The objective is to match a red point with a blue point, such that the sum of the distance between the matched pair of points is minimized. Offline problem is trivial. We consider the online case, where n blue points are available at given locations. The red points arrive sequentially, and have to be matched to a previously unmatched blue point, irrevocably on their arrival, with the same objective as above. Show that a greedy algorithm that matches the newly arrived red point to the nearest unmatched blue point has a competitive ratio of $\Omega(n)$. One can view this as a *lazy* version of the k-server problem (Section 6.4), where each server can move at most once.

9.10 Show that Problem 9.8 is a special case of Problem 9.9.

---

[3] The best-known lower bound is $9 - \epsilon$ for any $\epsilon > 0$. [163]

CHAPTER 10

Primal–Dual Technique

10.1 Introduction

In this chapter, we describe a generic primal–dual technique to bound the competitive ratio for a variety of online problems, whose relaxations can be posed as linear programs (LPs). The basic idea of this approach is to interpret the relaxation of the problem that we are interested in solving as the primal program (let it be a minimization problem). Then considering the primal and its dual together, an algorithm is proposed that updates both the primal and the dual solutions on each new request of the input sequence, such that the increment in the primal cost is upper bounded by c (for some $c > 1$) times the increment in the dual cost. Combining this with the *weak duality* of LPs, that means that the primal cost is lower bounded by the optimal value of the dual, it follows that the competitive ratio of the proposed algorithm is at most c.

We first describe this recipe in detail, and then discuss three versatile problems that are well suited for this primal–dual schema's application.

The first problem we consider is the set cover problem, where we are given a universe of elements and a collection of subsets of the universe, with each subset having an associated cost. The elements of the universe arrive online, and on each new element's arrival, if that element is not part of the current cover (collection of subsets), then at least one subset that contains that element has to be included in the cover. The objective is to choose that set of subsets that minimizes the sum of the cost of the cover at the end of all element arrivals in the input.

The set cover problem is a special case of what is known as *covering* problems, where the objective is to minimize the cost of selected resources under some generic coverage constraints. The dual of the covering problem is a packing problem, such as the knapsack problem (Chapter 8), where the objective is to maximize the profit of included items subject to some capacity constraints on the total size of the included items.

The next problem we consider is a packing problem, called the AdWords, that is highly relevant for online web portals like Google, Facebook, etc., where items (ad slots) arrive online and their valuation from multiple interested buyers (advertisers) are revealed. The problem is to assign items to buyers so as to maximize the total accrued valuation subject to a constraint on each buyer's budget.

The final problem we consider is the unweighted bipartite matching problem (studied in Chapter 9), and present the primal–dual analysis of RANKING (Section 9.3.2), which is much simpler than the combinatorial analysis presented in Section 9.3.2.

10.2 Primal–Dual Programs

Consider a *primal program* as the minimization problem

$$
\min \quad \mathbf{c}^T \mathbf{x},
$$
$$
\mathbf{A}\mathbf{x} \geq \mathbf{b}, \tag{10.1}
$$
$$
x_i \geq 0, \ \forall \, i,
$$

where $\mathbf{x} = [x_1, \ldots, x_n]^T$, $\mathbf{c} = [c_1, \ldots, c_n]^T$, $\mathbf{A} = [a_{j,i}], j = 1, \ldots, m, i = 1, \ldots, n$, and $\mathbf{b} = [b_1, \ldots, b_m]^T$. The *dual* program of (10.1) is given by

$$
\max \quad \mathbf{b}^T \mathbf{y},
$$
$$
\mathbf{A}^T \mathbf{y} \leq \mathbf{c}, \tag{10.2}
$$
$$
\mathbf{y} \geq 0,
$$

where $\mathbf{y} = [y_1, \ldots, y_m]^T$. The dual of the primal program is not an artificial object but has close connections with the optimal value of the primal program. To see this, consider one particular way of solving an optimization problem of the form

$$
\min_{x \in X} \quad f(x). \tag{10.3}
$$

Let z be a universal lower bound on $f(x)$, i.e., $f(x) \geq z, \ \forall \, x$; then an $x^\star$ such that $f(x^\star) = z$ is the optimal solution to (10.3). The dual is precisely a quest for finding such a universal lower bound z, where the optimal objective function of the dual lower bounds the objective function of the primal program for any feasible primal solution.

We now discuss this in detail as follows by starting to write the primal program (10.1) in slightly expanded form as

$$
\min \quad \sum_{i=1}^{n} c_i x_i,
$$
$$
\sum_{i=1}^{n} a_{j,i} x_i \geq b_j, \forall \, j \tag{10.4}
$$
$$
x_i \geq 0, \ \forall \, i.
$$

The idea for finding a lower bound on the optimal value of (10.4) is to leverage the constraints that lower bound how small the values of x_i can be. Suppose $\sum_{j=1}^{m} a_{j,i} \leq c_i$ for each i. Then, clearly, the objective function in (10.4) has the following lower bound:

$$
\sum_{i=1}^{n} c_i x_i \geq \sum_{i=1}^{n} \sum_{j=1}^{m} a_{j,i} x_i \geq \sum_{j=1}^{m} b_j. \tag{10.5}
$$

Thus, the primal objective function $\sum_{i=1}^{n} c_i x_i$ is lower bounded by $\sum_{j=1}^{m} b_j$ as long as $\sum_{j=1}^{m} a_{j,i} \leq c_i$ for each i.

In general, $\sum_{j=1}^{m} a_{j,i} \leq c_i$ may not be true for each i, but a simple generalization of this idea where we take weighted linear combinations of constraints can be made to work as follows.

Let us associate a non-negative variable $y_j \geq 0$ corresponding to the constraint $\sum_{i=1}^{n} a_{j,i} x_i \geq b_j$ of (10.4) for each j. Let $y_j \geq 0$ be such that $\sum_{j=1}^{m} a_{j,i} y_j \leq c_i$ for each i. Unlike (10.5), where we fixed $y_j = 1$, with $y_j \geq 0$, we can always find y_j's that satisfy $\sum_{j=1}^{m} a_{j,i} y_j \leq c_i$. Thus, with $\sum_{j=1}^{m} a_{j,i} y_j \leq c_i$,

$$\sum_{i=1}^{n} c_i x_i \geq \sum_{i=1}^{n} \sum_{j=1}^{m} a_{j,i} y_j x_i = \sum_{j=1}^{m} \left(\sum_{i=1}^{n} a_{j,i} x_i \right) y_j.$$

The primal constraints $\left(\sum_{i=1}^{n} a_{j,i} x_i \geq b_j \right)$ then imply that

$$\sum_{i=1}^{n} c_i x_i \geq \sum_{j=1}^{m} b_j y_j. \qquad (10.6)$$

Thus, we get a lower bound for the objective function of the primal program in terms of $y_j's$ as long as they are dual feasible, i.e., satisfy $\sum_{j=1}^{m} a_{j,i} y_j \leq c_i$ and $y_j \geq 0$. In particular, for any feasible primal and dual solutions $\mathbf{x}, \mathbf{y}$, we have

$$\mathbf{c}^T \mathbf{x} \geq \mathbf{b}^T \mathbf{y}. \qquad (10.7)$$

To find the largest such lower bound on the primal objective function, naturally we can solve the following problem:

$$\max \qquad \mathbf{b}^T \mathbf{y} = \sum_{j=1}^{m} b_j y_j,$$

$$\sum_{j=1}^{m} a_{j,i} y_j \leq c_i, \forall\, i \qquad (10.8)$$

$$y_j \geq 0, \forall\, i,$$

which is exactly the *dual* (10.2) of the primal program.

Relation (10.7) is referred to as the *weak duality* that states that for any feasible primal and dual solutions, the objective function of the primal program is at least as much as the objective function of the dual program. In fact, something stronger is known for this linear programming formulation, called the *strong duality*, that states that if $\mathbf{x}^\star$ and $\mathbf{y}^\star$ are optimal solutions to the primal and dual programs, respectively, then the optimal primal cost and the optimal dual cost are equal, i.e.,

$$\mathbf{c}^T \mathbf{x}^\star = \mathbf{b}^T \mathbf{y}^\star.$$

For the purposes of this chapter, it will suffice to consider just the weak duality property.

10.2.1 Recipe for Bounding the Competitive Ratio of Online Algorithms

The recipe for using the primal–dual schema for bounding the competitive ratio of an online algorithms is as follows. Let the online problem to solve be a minimization problem.[1] Let the relaxation of the online problem be an LP similar to (10.1), whose dual is (10.2). Throughout this chapter, we will call the objective value of the primal and dual programs for any solution $\mathbf{x}$ and $\mathbf{y}$, respectively (the solutions may be infeasible), primal cost $P(\mathbf{x})$ and dual cost $D(\mathbf{y})$.

Consider an online algorithm that incrementally builds the primal and the dual solutions, starting from $\mathbf{x} = 0, \mathbf{y} = 0$. Thus, to begin with, the online algorithm's primal solution is infeasible, while the initial dual solution is feasible but has zero dual cost. On each new request arrival with the input, the algorithm updates both the primal and the dual solutions while ensuring two properties: (i) the primal solution is feasible and (ii) increment or change in the dual cost ΔD is lower bounded by a fraction of the increment in the primal cost ΔP, e.g., $\Delta D \geq \frac{1}{\beta}\Delta P$ for some $\beta > 1$. Let the final primal and dual solutions be $\mathbf{x}_f$ and $\mathbf{y}_f$, respectively. Then property (ii) implies that

$$D(\mathbf{y}_f) \geq \frac{1}{\beta}P(\mathbf{x}_f). \tag{10.9}$$

The final dual solution $\mathbf{y}_f$ of the online algorithm may not be necessarily feasible. To make it feasible, the final dual solution $\mathbf{y}_f$ is scaled by a scalar s, i.e., $\mathbf{y}_f/s$ is a dual feasible solution. For some peculiar problems, this scaling may not be sufficient to make it dual feasible; however, for most problems of interest, it does work.

From the weak duality (10.7), we know that for any feasible primal and dual solutions $\mathbf{x}$ and $\mathbf{y}$, $P(\mathbf{x}) \geq D(\mathbf{y})$. Let $\mathbf{x}^\star$ be the optimal solution of the primal program. Thus, since $\mathbf{x}^\star$ and $\mathbf{y}_f/s$ are primal and dual feasible, using (10.9),

$$P(\mathbf{x}^\star) \geq D(\mathbf{y}_f/s) = \frac{D(\mathbf{y}_f)}{s} \geq \frac{1}{s\beta}P(\mathbf{x}_f). \tag{10.10}$$

Thus,

$$\frac{P(\mathbf{x}_f)}{P(\mathbf{x}^\star)} \leq \beta s.$$

Let $\mathbf{x}_{\mathrm{OPT}}$ be the primal feasible solution of OPT knowing the full input sequence in advance. Note that $P(\mathbf{x}_{\mathrm{OPT}}) \geq P(\mathbf{x}^\star)$ (since $\mathbf{x}^\star$ is allowed to be fractional, while $\mathbf{x}_{\mathrm{OPT}}$ may be required to be integral); we conclude that the primal solution $\mathbf{x}_f$ output by the online algorithm satisfies

$$\frac{P(\mathbf{x}_f)}{P(\mathbf{x}_{\mathrm{OPT}})} \leq \beta s. \tag{10.11}$$

Therefore, if the two properties are satisfied by an online algorithm, then its competitive ratio is at most βs.

Using this recipe, we next discuss three different problems and present their competitive ratio analysis using the primal–dual schema.

---

[1] Similar ideas work for a maximization problem as presented in Section 10.4.

10.3 Set Cover Problem

Let the universe consist of n different elements $\mathcal{U} = \{1, 2, \dots, n\}$. Let $\mathcal{S} = \{S : S \subseteq \mathcal{U}\}$ be a collection of subsets of $\mathcal{U}$. Let $\mathcal{S}_j \subseteq \mathcal{S}$ be the set of subsets of $\mathcal{S}$ that contains the element j. Each subset of $S \in \mathcal{S}$ has an associated cost c_S.

With the input, a subset of elements of $\mathcal{U}$ are requested sequentially, where, without loss of generality, we assume that only distinct elements are requested. In particular, element $e(i) \in \mathcal{U}$ is requested at time step i. Let $\mathcal{C}^i$ be the cover (collection of elements of $\mathcal{S}$) just before the ith step when element $e(i) \in \mathcal{U}$ is requested. If $e(i) \in S$ for some $S \in \mathcal{C}^i$, no further action is needed. Otherwise, a subset S belonging to $\mathcal{S}_{e(i)}$ has to be included in the cover, and the cover is updated to $\mathcal{C}^{i+1} = \mathcal{C}^i \cup S$ for some $S \in \mathcal{S}_{e(i)}$. The cost C of the cover $\mathcal{C}$ is the sum of the costs of all the subsets contained in $\mathcal{C}$, and the objective is to maintain a cover with the minimum cost.

We assume that the universe size n is known to the algorithm; however, the input need not request all the n elements. We also assume that $c_S \geq 1 \; \forall \; S \in \mathcal{S}$, and let $d = \max_{j=1,\dots,n} |\mathcal{S}_j|$ be the maximum number of subsets in $\mathcal{S}$ that contain any one element of the universe.

Let the input until time step i be σ^i, which is a permutation over some i elements of $\mathcal{U}$. Let the cost of the cover of an online algorithm $\mathcal{A}$ at step i of input σ be $C_{\mathcal{A}}(\sigma^i)$. Then the competitive ratio of $\mathcal{A}$ is

$$\mu_{\mathcal{A}} = \max_{\sigma^i, i=1,\dots,n} \frac{C_{\mathcal{A}}(\sigma^i)}{C_{\text{OPT}}(\sigma^i)},$$

where note that the competitive ratio explicitly depends on the step index i of the input, since the adversary need not request all elements of the universe $\mathcal{U}$. To highlight this fact, consider the following example.

Example 10.3.1

Let the universe size be n, and consider $\mathcal{S} = \{S_1, S_2, \dots S_n\}$, where S_i contains the first i elements $S_i = \{1, \dots, i\}$ with cardinality $|S_i| = i$, and the cost of set S_i is i.

Let the rows of the matrix (10.12) be indexed as the sets S_i, while the columns by the elements $1, \dots, n$, where $*$ in the (i,j) set–element matrix represents that set S_i contains element j.

Consider the following input sequence $\{1, 2, 3, \dots, j\}, j \leq n$, i.e., elements are requested in sequence up to element j. Consider any deterministic online algorithm $\mathcal{A}$. If $\mathcal{A}$ picks subset $S_k, k \geq j$, to be included in the cover when the first element $\{1\}$ is requested, then the adversary will terminate the sequence right there, and the competitive ratio for $\mathcal{A}$ will be $k \geq j$, since OPT will just choose subset S_1 and pay a cost of 1. Alternatively, if $\mathcal{A}$ selects subset S_i to be part of the cover when the ith element is requested, then $\mathcal{A}$ pays a total cost of $1 + 2 + \dots + j = j(j+1)/2$ once all the j elements have been requested. OPT, on the other hand, will just choose one subset S_j and pay a cost of j. The resulting competitive ratio for $\mathcal{A}$ will be $\frac{j+1}{2}$. Thus, an online algorithm with competitive ratio $o(j)$ is non-trivial.

	Set	Element {1}	Element {2}	...	...	Element {n}
	S_1	*	–	–	–	–
	S_2	*	*	–	–	–
	$\vdots$	$\vdots$		$\ddots$	$\ddots$ $\ddots$	$\vdots$
	S_{n-1}	*	*	*	*	–
	S_n	*	*	*	*	*

(10.12)

10.3.1 Fractional Set Cover Problem

The online set cover problem as described above is an integral problem, where the decision is to either include a subset fully or not at all, so as to maintain a cover at all times. A simpler problem, which we will use to build the integral solution, is the fractional set cover problem, where on each element's arrival a subset can be included fractionally by paying its fractional cost, and maintaining a fractional cover for all the elements seen so far.

The fractional set cover problem can be written as a (primal) LP:

$$\min \quad \sum_S c_S x_S,$$
$$\sum_{S \in \mathcal{S}_j} x_S \geq 1, \ \forall j \in \mathcal{U} \tag{10.13}$$
$$x_S \geq 0, \ \forall S,$$

where x_S is the fractional contribution from set $S \in \mathcal{S}$, and constraint $\sum_{S \in \mathcal{S}_j} x_S \geq 1$ guarantees that each element $j \in \mathcal{U}$ is covered, fractionally. Restricting $x_S \in \{0, 1\}$ in (10.13) is the actual integral set cover problem we want to solve.

Let $\mathbf{x}^\star$ be the optimal solution of (10.13), which by definition is allowed to be fractional. Since OPT for the set cover problem has to produce an integral solution, $P(\mathbf{x}_{\mathsf{OPT}}) \geq P(\mathbf{x}^\star)$.

Remark 10.3.2 *As we have remarked before, the input need not request all the elements of the universe. However, for ease of exposition, we have considered all elements of $\mathcal{U}$ are requested in (10.13). In case only a subset of $\mathcal{U}$ is requested, replacing $\mathcal{U}$ in (10.13) with only the subset of requested elements, the following analysis will go through as is.*

The dual of (10.13) is given by

$$\max \quad \sum_{j \in \mathcal{U}} y_j,$$
$$\sum_{j | S \in \mathcal{S}_j} y_j \leq c_S, \ \forall S \in \mathcal{S}, \tag{10.14}$$
$$y_j \geq 0, \ \forall j.$$

To solve the fractional online set cover problem consider the MULTIPLICATIVE-WEIGHTS algorithm (MWA), Algorithm 14, where on request for a new element j, if the new element j is not already covered $\left(\sum_{S \in \mathcal{S}_j} x_S < 1 \right)$, the weight x_S (primal solution) of all subsets S that contain element j is multiplicatively increased incrementally, until the element is fractionally covered, where the multiplier depends on the cost of the subsets. The dual variable y_j corresponding to element j is also incremented by 1 for each iteration of the While loop when x_S is incremented. The choice of the multiplier controls the competitive ratio of MWA.

Algorithm 14 MULTIPLICATIVE-WEIGHTS Algorithm MWA

1: Input: The size of universe n, $\mathcal{S}$
2: Initialize $x_S = 0$, $\forall\, S$, $y_j = 0$ $\forall\, j \in \mathcal{U}$,
3: On request for element $j \in \mathcal{U}$
4: **while** $\sum_{S \in \mathcal{S}_j} x_S < 1$ **do**

5: $\qquad \forall\, S \in \mathcal{S}_j, x_S \leftarrow x_S \left(1 + \dfrac{1}{c_S}\right) + \dfrac{1}{c_S |\mathcal{S}_j|}$;

6: $\qquad y_j \leftarrow y_j + 1$;
7: **end while**

Theorem 10.3.3 *The competitive ratio of* MWA *is* $\mathcal{O}(\log d)$ *for the fractional set cover problem, where* $d = \max_j |\mathcal{S}_j|$ *is the maximum number of subsets that contain any element of the universe.*

Note that for the set cover problem, d is clearly a quantity of interest, since if $d = 1$, any algorithm will be equal to OPT. The fact is that as d increases, the number of options an online algorithm has about which subset to include increases, and this can be exploited by the adversary.

To prove Theorem 10.3.3, we state the following lemma whose proof appears after the proof of Theorem 10.3.3.

Lemma 10.3.4 *On a new element's request, after each iteration of the While loop in* MWA, *the increment* ΔP *in primal cost* (10.13) *is at most two times the increment* ΔD *in the dual cost* (10.14). *Moreover, if* $\mathbf{y}_f = [y_1, \dots, y_n]$ *is the final dual solution of the algorithm after all elements have arrived, then* $\mathbf{y}_f / \mathcal{O}(\log d)$ *is dual feasible.*

Proof: [Theorem 10.3.3] From Lemma 10.3.4, the final primal and dual solutions $\mathbf{x}_f$ and $\mathbf{y}_f$ satisfy $P(\mathbf{x}_f) \le 2D(\mathbf{y}_f)$, and the dual solution $\mathbf{y}_f / \mathcal{O}(\log d)$ is feasible. Thus, following our recipe from (10.11),

$$P(\mathbf{x}_f) \le \mathcal{O}(\log d) P(\mathbf{x}^\star) \le \mathcal{O}(\log d) P(\mathbf{x}_{\mathrm{OPT}}),$$

where the last inequality follows since $P(\mathbf{x}_{\mathrm{OPT}}) \ge P(\mathbf{x}^\star)$, as pointed out before. ∎

Next, we present the proof of Lemma 10.3.4, for which we need this intermediate result.

Proposition 10.3.5 *With* MWA, $x_S \le 3$ *for all* S. *Moreover, for any iteration* i *of the While loop* (*executed on request for any new element*),

$$x_S(i) \ge \frac{1}{d}\left(\left(1 + \frac{1}{c_S}\right)^{t_S(i)} - 1\right), \tag{10.15}$$

for $t_S(i) = \sum_{j|S \in \mathcal{S}_j} y_j(i)$, where $x_S(i)$ and $y_j(i)$ is the value of x_S and y_j at the end of iteration i, respectively.

Proof: From the definition of MWA, once $x_S \geq 1$ for any subset S, then x_S is never updated. Thus, consider an iteration i where $x_S < 1$ at which time it is updated. The increment in x_S in any iteration of the While loop can be bounded as

$$\Delta x_S \leq \frac{x_S}{c_S} + \frac{1}{|\mathcal{S}_j|c_S} \leq 2,$$

since $c_S \geq 1$, $\forall S$ and $|\mathcal{S}_j| \geq 1$ for all the requested elements. Therefore,

$$x_S \leq 1 + \Delta x_S \leq 3.$$

We next show that (10.15) is true via induction on the number of requested elements. To begin the induction, note that initially $x_S = 0$ for all S. Let the new element requested be k, and the While loop is on iteration i. Then, from the definition of MWA,

$$x_S(i) = x_S(i-1)\left(1 + \frac{1}{c_S}\right) + \frac{1}{c_S|\mathcal{S}_k|},$$

$$\overset{(a)}{\geq} x_S(i-1)\left(1 + \frac{1}{c_S}\right) + \frac{1}{c_S d},$$

$$\overset{(b)}{\geq} \frac{1}{d}\left(\left(1 + \frac{1}{c_S}\right)^{t_S(i-1)} - 1\right)\left(1 + \frac{1}{c_S}\right)^{\Delta y_k} + \frac{1}{c_S d},$$

$$= \frac{1}{d}\left(\left(1 + \frac{1}{c_S}\right)^{t_S(i-1)+\Delta y_k} - 1\right) - \frac{1}{c_S^{\Delta y_k} d} + \frac{1}{c_S d},$$

$$= \frac{1}{d}\left(\left(1 + \frac{1}{c_S}\right)^{t_S(i-1)+\Delta y_k} - 1\right),$$

$$\overset{(c)}{=} \frac{1}{d}\left(\left(1 + \frac{1}{c_S}\right)^{t_S(i)} - 1\right),$$

where (a) follows since $d \geq |\mathcal{S}_k|$ for all k, and in (b) we apply the induction hypothesis to x_S at iteration $i-1$, where $t_S(i-1) = \sum_{j|S \in \mathcal{S}_j} y_j(i-1)$, and $\Delta y_k = 1$ since y_k increases by 1 in iteration i, and finally (c) follows from the definition of $t_S(i)$. ∎

Finally we are ready to prove Lemma 10.3.4.

Proof: [Lemma 10.3.4] Initially, $\mathbf{x} = \mathbf{y} = \mathbf{0}$, and $P(\mathbf{x}) = D(\mathbf{y}) = 0$. Consider the request for element j, where in each iteration of the While loop (hereafter only referred to as the iteration) until $\sum_{S\in\mathcal{S}_j} x_S \geq 1$, let Δx_S be the increment in the value of x_S for $S \in \mathcal{S}_j$. Consequently, the increment in the primal cost (10.13) in any iteration on the request for element j is

$$\sum_S c_S \Delta x_S = \sum_{S\in\mathcal{S}_j} c_S \left(\frac{x_S}{c_S} + \frac{1}{c_S|\mathcal{S}_j|} \right),$$

$$= \sum_{S\in\mathcal{S}_j} x_S + \sum_{S\in\mathcal{S}_j} \frac{1}{|\mathcal{S}_j|},$$

$$\leq 1 + 1, \tag{10.16}$$

where the last inequality follows as $\sum_{S\in\mathcal{S}_j} x_S < 1$, since otherwise the While loop would have terminated in the previous iteration. Moreover, on any iteration, the increment in y_j is $\Delta y_j = 1$. Therefore, from (10.16), we get $\Delta P \leq 2\Delta D$. Consequently, $P(\mathbf{x}_f) \leq 2D(\mathbf{y}_f)$.

Next, we complete the proof by arguing that $\mathbf{y}_f / \mathcal{O}(\log d)$ is dual feasible. Combining (10.15) with the fact that $x_S \leq 3$ (Proposition 10.3.5), we have

$$\frac{1}{d} \left(\left(1 + \frac{1}{c_S} \right)^{t_S(i)} - 1 \right) \leq 3,$$

from which using the fact that $c_S \geq 1$ it follows that

$$t_S(i) = \sum_{j|S\in\mathcal{S}_j} y_j(i) \leq c_S \log(3d+1),$$

which implies that $\mathbf{y}_f / \mathcal{O}(\log d)$ is dual feasible (10.14). ∎

10.3.2 Integral Set Cover Problem

Now we consider the integral version of the set cover problem, where any subset of $\mathcal{U}$ has to be either completely included or not at all so as to maintain a cover at all times. Thus, for OPT the problem to solve is (10.13) but with integral constraints $x_S \in \{0, 1\}$ instead of $x_S \in [0, 1]$ as in (10.13). Therefore, we have $P(\mathbf{x}_{\text{OPT}}) \geq P(\mathbf{x}^\star)$, where $\mathbf{x}^\star$ is the optimal fractional solution to (10.13).

The online algorithm we consider called the Integral-MWA (IMWA) (Algorithm 15) implements randomized rounding of the output of MWA to select its subsets. The basic idea with IMWA is to include a subset S selected by MWA (fractionally with weight x_S) in the cover if x_S is greater than the minimum of $2\log n$ uniformly distributed random variables between $[0, 1]$.

Remark 10.3.6 *Note that we are assuming that the algorithm is aware of the size of the universe n. If that is not exactly available and only an upper bound $n_b \geq n$ is known, then n can be replaced by n_b in IMWA without any change in the analysis.*

Algorithm 15 INTEGRAL-MULTIPLICATIVE-WEIGHTS Algorithm (IMWA)

1: Input: The size of universe n, $\mathcal{S}$
2: For each $S \in \mathcal{S}$, generate $2 \log n$ independent and uniformly distributed random variables $Z_{S,i}$ with support $[0, 1]$ for $i = 1, \ldots, 2 \log n$
3: $w_S = \min_{i \in [1:2 \log n]} Z_{S,i}$
4: Initialize $x_S = 0$, $\forall S$, $y_j = 0$ $\forall j \in \mathcal{U}$
5: On request for element j
6: **while** $\sum_{S \in \mathcal{S}_j} x_S < 1$ **do**
7: $\quad \forall S \in \mathcal{S}_j, x_S \leftarrow x_S \left(1 + \frac{1}{c_S}\right) + \frac{1}{c_S |S_j|}$
8: $\quad y_j \leftarrow y_j + 1$
9: **end while**
10: **if** $x_S \geq w_S$ **then**
11: $\quad$ add subset S to cover $\mathcal{C}$, $\mathcal{C} = \mathcal{C} \cup S$
12: **end if**

Theorem 10.3.7 IMWA *is* $\mathcal{O}(\log n \log d)$-*competitive in expectation for the integral set cover problem, and all n requested elements are covered with high probability, where* $d = \max_j |\mathcal{S}_j|$ *is the maximum number of subsets that contain any element of the universe, and n is the size of the universe.*

Let $\mathbf{x}$ and $\hat{\mathbf{x}}$ be the fractional solution output by MWA for the primal program (10.13), and the integral solution output by IMWA, respectively. Let w_S be as defined in IMWA. Then the rounding mechanism used in IMWA to make the fractional solution x_S integral is: $\hat{x}_S = 1$ if $w_S \leq x_S$, and $\hat{x}_S = 0$ otherwise. To prove Theorem 10.3.7, we state Lemma 10.3.8, whose proof appears after the proof of Theorem 10.3.7.

Lemma 10.3.8

$$\mathbb{E}\left\{\sum_S \hat{x}_S c_S\right\} \leq (2 \log n) \sum_S c_S x_S = (2 \log n) P(\mathbf{x}), \tag{10.17}$$

where x_S is the fractional solution output by MWA, and each requested element is covered with high probability with IMWA.

Proof: [Theorem 10.3.7] From Theorem 10.3.3, we know that the fractional solution x_S output by MWA satisfies

$$\sum_S c_S x_S \leq \mathcal{O}(\log d) \sum_S c_S x_S^{\star}, \tag{10.18}$$

where $x_S^{\star}$ is the optimal fractional solution, and both x_S and $x_S^{\star}$ are feasible, i.e., $\sum_{S \in \mathcal{S}_j} x_S^{\star} \geq 1$ and $\sum_{S \in \mathcal{S}_j} x_S \geq 1$ for all the requested elements. Thus, from Lemma 10.3.8, using (10.18), we get

$$\mathbb{E}\left\{\sum_S \hat{x}_S c_S\right\} \leq (2 \log n) P(\mathbf{x}) = 2 \log n \sum_S c_S x_S \leq \mathcal{O}(\log n \log d) \sum_S c_S x_S^{\star}. \tag{10.19}$$

As remarked before, for the integral problem, $P(\mathbf{x}_{OPT}) \geq P(\mathbf{x}^\star)$. Hence, we get that IMWA is $\mathcal{O}(\log d \log n)$-competitive in expectation. The fact that all elements are covered with high probability directly follows from Lemma 10.3.8. ∎

Next, we present the remaining proof of Lemma 10.3.8.

Proof: [Lemma 10.3.8] Let $\mathbf{x}$ be any fractional feasible primal solution to (10.13). First, we show that the primal cost $P(\hat{\mathbf{x}})$ (10.13) with the integral solution $\hat{\mathbf{x}} = \{\hat{x}_S\}$ is at most $2 \log n \, P(\mathbf{x})$ in expectation. Note than any subset S is chosen by IMWA if $w_S = \min_{i \in [1:2\log n]} Z_{S,i} \leq x_S$. Thus, the probability of choosing S in the set cover, i.e., of having $x_S = 1$, is $\mathbb{P}(\cup_i Z_i \leq x_S)$. Since $Z_i \sim \text{Uniform}[0, 1]$, $\mathbb{P}(Z_i \leq x_S) = x_S$. Thus, by the union bound,

$$\mathbb{P}(\cup_i Z_i \leq x_S) \leq \sum_i \mathbb{P}(Z_i \leq x_S) \leq (2 \log n) \, x_S.$$

Therefore, the *expected* cost of the integral (rounded) solution is

$$\mathbb{E}\left\{\sum_S \hat{x}_S c_S\right\} = \sum_S \mathbb{P}(\cup_i Z_i \leq x_S) c_S \leq (2 \log n) \sum_S c_S x_S = (2 \log n) \, P(\mathbf{x}).$$

Next, we work towards showing that the rounded solution is feasible, i.e.,

$$\sum_{S \in \mathcal{S}_j} \hat{x}_S \geq 1$$

for all the requested elements j with high probability. We begin by bounding the probability that a single requested element j of the universe is not covered by the rounded solution $\hat{\mathbf{x}}$, and then use the union bound over all the n requested elements. Recall that element j is covered with IMWA as long as

$$x_S \geq \min_{i=1,\ldots,2\log n} Z_{S,i}$$

for some $S \in \mathcal{S}_j$. Thus, for an element j to remain uncovered, for a fixed i, the uniform random variables $Z_{S,i}$ for all $S \in \mathcal{S}_j$ have to be greater than x_S, and which happens with probability

$$\mathbb{P}(\text{element } j \text{ remains uncovered for fixed } i) = \prod_{S \in \mathcal{S}_j} \mathbb{P}(Z_{S,i} > x_S) = \prod_{S \in \mathcal{S}_j} (1 - x_S).$$

Noting that $1 - x \leq \exp(-x)$, we get

$$\mathbb{P}(\text{element } j \text{ remains uncovered for fixed } i) = \exp\left(-\sum_{S \in \mathcal{S}_j} x_S\right).$$

But since the fractional solution of MWA is feasible, i.e., $\sum_{S \in \mathcal{S}_j} x_S \geq 1$, we get

$$\mathbb{P}(\text{element } j \text{ remains uncovered for fixed } i) = \exp(-1).$$

Since $i = 1, 2, \ldots, 2 \log n$ independent random variables are used for each subset S, we get

$$\mathbb{P}(\text{element } j \text{ remains uncovered}) \leq \exp\left(-2 \log n\right) \leq \frac{1}{n^2}.$$

Taking the union bound over all the requested elements that are at most n,

$$\mathbb{P}(\text{any of the requested elements remain uncovered}) \leq \frac{n}{n^2}.$$

and hence the integral (rounded) solution covers all requested elements, i.e., it is feasible, with probability at least $1 - \frac{1}{n}$. Thus, if n (or an upper bound n_b) is large, the competitive ratio of IMWA increases as $\log n$, while the probability of missing any element in the cover decreases as $1/n$. ∎

10.4 AdWords Problem

Consider n buyers, where buyer i has a total budget of B_i that is known ahead of time, offline. m products arrive sequentially in an online manner, where on product j's arrival its bid or valuation v_{ij} by buyer i is revealed. The online algorithm can allocate each product to at most one buyer, and the total revenue made from each buyer is equal to the minimum of its budget and the sum of the valuation of the products allocated to it. The objective is to maximize the total revenue, summed across all the buyers.

This problem is called AdWords because of its close connection to the revenue maximization problem in web advertising, where products correspond to ads and the bid or valuation is the payoff or utility that the advertiser accrues by displaying an ad to the user that depends on the user profile. The budget constraint is enforced by the advertisers that indicates the maximum amount of money they are willing to spend on their campaigns.

Let A_i be the set of products allocated to buyer i. Then the revenue from buyer i is $r_i = \min\left\{\sum_{j \in A_i} v_{ij}, B_i\right\}$ and the problem to solve is

$$R = \max_{\substack{A_i, A_i \cap A_k = \varnothing \\ i \neq k, i, k = 1, \ldots, n,}} \sum_{i=1}^{n} r_i. \tag{10.20}$$

To solve this problem in the online setting, we first look at its fractional LP formulation, where x_{ij} denotes the fraction of product j that is allocated to buyer i, as follows.

$$\max \quad \sum_{i=1}^{n} \sum_{j=1}^{m} v_{ij} x_{ij},$$

$$\text{For each buyer } i \quad \sum_{j=1}^{m} v_{ij} x_{ij} \leq B_i, \forall\, i,$$

$$\text{For each product } j \quad \sum_{i=1}^{n} x_{ij} \leq 1, \forall\, j, \tag{10.21}$$

$$x_{ij} \geq 0, \forall\, i, j,$$

where $\sum_{j=1}^{m} v_{ij}x_{ij} \le B_i$ represents the budget constraint for each buyer i, while $\sum_{i=1}^{n} x_{ij} \le 1$ ensures that the sum of the fractions of any product assigned to different buyers is at most 1. Restricting $x_{ij} \in \{0, 1\}$ is our actual integral problem (10.20), and considering (10.21) as a **dual** program, we get the optimal dual cost

$$D(\mathbf{x}^{\star}) \ge R_{\text{OPT}}, \tag{10.22}$$

where $\mathbf{x}^{\star}$ is the optimal solution of (10.21), and R_{OPT} is the optimal revenue (10.20).

Considering (10.21) as a dual program, its corresponding **primal** program is

$$\min \quad \sum_{i=1}^{n} B_i y_i + \sum_{j=1}^{m} z_j,$$

$$\text{For each } (i, j) \quad v_{ij}y_i + z_j \ge v_{ij}, \tag{10.23}$$

$$\text{For each } i, j \quad y_i \ge 0, z_j \ge 0,$$

where for each buyer i, there is a variable y_i, and for each product j, a variable z_j, that are connected via the constraint $v_{ij}y_i + z_j \ge v_{ij}$.

Algorithm 16 AW-ASSIGN Algorithm

1: Let $\gamma > 1\%$ to be chosen
2: Initially $x_{ij} = 0, \forall i, j\ y_i = 0, \forall i$ (buyers); rembudget$_i = B_i$
3: On request for a new product j, assign it to the buyer $i^{\star}$ such that

$$i^{\star} = \arg\max_i v_{ij}(1 - y_i).$$

4: **if** $y_{i^{\star}} \ge 1$ **then** do nothing;
5: **else**

    1. Charge the selected buyer $i^{\star}$, $\min\{v_{i^{\star}j}, \text{rembudget}_{i^{\star}}\}$, Set $x_{i^{\star}j} = 1$

    2. $z_j \leftarrow v_{i^{\star}j}(1 - y_i^{\star})$ (for product j)

    3. $y_{i^{\star}} \leftarrow y_{i^{\star}}\left(1 + \dfrac{v_{i^{\star}j}}{B_{i^{\star}}}\right) + \dfrac{v_{i^{\star}j}}{(\gamma-1)B_{i^{\star}}}$ (for the assigned buyer $i^{\star}$ only)

    4. rembudget$_{i^{\star}} = $ rembudget$_{i^{\star}} - \min\{v_{i^{\star}j}, \text{rembudget}_{i^{\star}}\}$

6: **end if**

Consider algorithm AW-ASSIGN (Algorithm 16) for solving (10.21), where $y_i \in [0, 1]$ corresponds to the efficiency ratio of buyer i, the ratio of the valuation extracted from buyer i and its total budget B_i. The effective valuation of a newly arrived product j for buyer i is defined as $v_{ij}(1 - y_i)$, which represents how much of the budget capacity of buyer i can be exploited and counted towards the objective function in (10.21). The algorithm greedily assigns the product to the buyer with the largest effective valuation. After each product assignment to buyer i, the variable y_i is updated to reflect the amount of budget used up because of the greedy assignment. The variable z_j is updated to ensure feasibility of the primal constraint $v_{ij}y_i + z_j \ge v_{ij}$. With the greedy assignment, if product j is assigned to buyer i, then the dual variable $x_{ij} \leftarrow 1$. Thus, the dual solution x_{ij} output by the algorithm is always integral, but not necessarily dual feasible.

Remark 10.4.1 *With* AW-ASSIGN, *the revenue obtained by assigning any product j to buyer i, except the last product assigned to any buyer i, is v_{ij}. For any buyer i, the revenue obtained from the last product (say product j_i) assigned to it is the minimum of v_{i,j_i} and the remaining budget of buyer i at the time of request for product j_i. As a result, the solution output by* AW-ASSIGN *is feasible in terms of counting the revenue (10.20). The same cannot be said for the dual LP (10.21), since* AW-ASSIGN *assigns $x_{i\star j} = 1$ on product j's arrival even if $v_{i\star j}$ is larger than the remaining budget of buyer i. Thus, we need to rescale the dual solution $(\mathbf{x})$ to make it dual feasible as will be done in Lemma 10.4.5.*

Let $\rho_{\max} = \max_{i,j} \left\{ \frac{v_{ij}}{B_i} \right\}$ be the maximum of the ratio of the valuation of any product for any buyer and the buyer budget. $\rho_{\max}$ is a fundamental quantity of interest for this problem since it quantifies how closely one can exploit the available buyer budget. For example, consider two products and two buyers, with $B_1 = B_2 = B$. On the first product's arrival, let $v_{11} = B/2$ and $v_{21} = B/2$. Without loss of generality, let an online algorithm assign product 1 to buyer 1. Then let the next product's valuation be $v_{12} = 3B/2$ and $v_{22} = 0$. Assigning product 2 to buyer 1, the total revenue obtained is B, while with OPT it would be $2B$ by assigning product 1 to buyer 2, and product 2 to buyer 1. Essentially, $\rho_{\max}$ being large provides a distinct advantage to OPT compared to an online algorithm. Smaller the value of $\rho_{\max}$, better is the ability of an online algorithm to exploit the maximum profit by avoiding wastage of the usable budget of any buyer.

Next, we derive the competitive ratio of AW-ASSIGN in terms of $\rho_{\max}$ as follows.

Theorem 10.4.2 AW-ASSIGN *is* $\left(1 - \frac{1}{\gamma}\right)(1 - \rho_{max})$-*competitive, choosing* $\gamma = (1 + \rho_{max})^{\frac{1}{\rho_{max}}}$. *Moreover, the competitive ratio tends to $1 - 1/e$ as $\rho_{max} \to 0$.*

Remark 10.4.3 AW-ASSIGN *requires the knowledge of ρ_{max}.*

We prove the theorem via the following three Lemmas that together imply the result.

Lemma 10.4.4 *The final primal solutions y_i, z_j of* AW-ASSIGN *are primal feasible (10.23).*

Proof: For buyer i and product j, if at some iteration of the algorithm $y_i \geq 1$, then the primal constraint $v_{ij}y_i + z_j \geq v_{ij}$ is trivially satisfied. Otherwise, if on request for product j, let $y_i < 1$ for some buyer i. The algorithm assigns the product j to buyer $i^\star$ with the largest $v_{i\star j}(1 - y_{i\star})$ and sets $z_j = v_{i\star j}(1 - y_{i\star})$. Thus, $z_j = v_{i\star j}(1 - y_{i\star}) \geq v_{ij}(1 - y_i)$ for all $i \neq i^\star$. Therefore, for any buyer i, $v_{ij}y_i + z_j \geq v_{ij}$, implying primal feasibility.

Note that this is the only place in the entire proof of Theorem 10.4.2 where the property of AW-ASSIGN that product j is assigned to buyer $i^\star$ such that $i^\star = \arg\max_i v_{ij}(1 - y_i)$ will be used. ∎

Lemma 10.4.5 *Let P be the primal cost (10.23) and D be the dual cost (10.21), and Δ be their increments with* AW-ASSIGN. *Then*

$$\Delta P \leq \left(1 + \frac{1}{\gamma - 1}\right) \Delta D.$$

Proof: If product j is assigned to buyer i, then $x_{ij} = 1$, and the increment in the dual cost ΔD is v_{ij}, even if the remaining budget of buyer i on request for product j is less than v_{ij}. Moreover, the change in the primal cost is

$$\Delta P = B_i \Delta y_i + z_j,$$

$$= B_i \left(\frac{v_{ij} y_i}{B_i} + \frac{v_{ij}}{(\gamma - 1)B_i} \right) + v_{ij}(1 - y_i),$$

$$= v_{ij} \left(1 + \frac{1}{(\gamma - 1)} \right).$$

■

Thus, from our recipe (Section 10.2.1) the ratio β between the primal cost and the dual cost is at most $\left(1 + \frac{1}{\gamma - 1} \right)$.

Lemma 10.4.6 *The solution x_{ij} may not be dual feasible (10.21), but $x_{ij}\psi_{ij}$ is dual feasible, where $\psi_{ij} = \dfrac{B_i}{B_i + \max_j v_{ij}}$.*

Proof: For buyer i, if on some product arrival $y_i \geq 1$, then henceforth the dual variable x_{ij} is never updated, since the effective valuation of buyer i for any subsequent product k is $v_{ik}(1 - y_i) = 0$. Next, we show that for the first time when the assignment made by AW-ASSIGN violates the dual constraint $\sum_{j=1}^{m} v_{ij} x_{ij} \leq B_i$, then $y_i \geq 1$, and hence thereafter the dual solution x_{ij} is never updated. Since in any one iteration, the change in dual cost is at most $\max_{ij} v_{ij}$, the final solution output by AW-ASSIGN always satisfies $\sum_{j=1}^{m} v_{ij} x_{ij} \leq B_i + \max_{ij} v_{ij}$. Thus, the rescaled solution $x_{ij} \dfrac{B_i}{B_i + \max_{ij} v_{ij}}$ is dual feasible.

To prove the claim, we will show that after the request for any subset S of products

$$y_i \geq \frac{1}{\gamma - 1} \left(\gamma^{\frac{\sum_{j \in S} v_{ij} x_{ij}}{B_i}} - 1 \right),$$

for $\gamma = (1 + \rho_{\max})^{\frac{1}{\rho_{\max}}}$, from which it is immediate that whenever $\sum_{j=1}^{m} v_{ij} x_{ij} > B_i$, for any m, $y_i \geq 1$, since $\gamma > 1$. Using induction on the order of product arrivals, consider the iteration where the subset S of products has already arrived and the newly arrived product is k, and that is assigned to buyer i, where y_i is updated as

$$y_i = y_i \left(1 + \frac{v_{ik}}{B_i} \right) + \frac{v_{ik}}{(\gamma - 1)B_i},$$

$$\overset{(a)}{\geq} \frac{1}{\gamma - 1} \left(\gamma^{\frac{\sum_{j \in S} v_{ij} x_{ij}}{B_i}} - 1 \right) \left(1 + \frac{v_{ik}}{B_i} \right) + \frac{v_{ik}}{(\gamma - 1)B_i},$$

$$= \frac{1}{\gamma - 1} \left(\gamma^{\frac{\sum_{j \in S} v_{ij} x_{ij}}{B_i}} \left(1 + \frac{v_{ik}}{B_i}\right) - 1 \right),$$

$$\overset{(b)}{\geq} \frac{1}{\gamma - 1} \left(\gamma^{\frac{\sum_{j \in S} v_{ij} x_{ij}}{B_i}} \gamma^{\left(\frac{v_{ik}}{B_i}\right)} - 1 \right),$$

$$\overset{(c)}{=} \frac{1}{\gamma - 1} \left(\gamma^{\frac{\sum_{j \in S} v_{ij} x_{ij}}{B_i}} \gamma^{\left(\frac{v_{ik}}{B_i}\right)^{x_{ik}}} - 1 \right),$$

$$= \frac{1}{\gamma - 1} \left(\gamma^{\frac{\sum_{j \in S \cup \{k\}} v_{ij} x_{ij}}{B_i}} - 1 \right),$$

where (a) follows from the induction hypothesis, (b) from the choice of $\gamma = (1 + \rho_{\max})^{\frac{1}{\rho_{\max}}}$ which ensures that $\left(1 + \frac{v_{ik}}{B_i}\right) > \gamma^{\left(\frac{v_{ik}}{B_i}\right)}$ since $\frac{\ln(1+x)}{x} \geq \frac{\ln(1+y)}{y}$ for $0 \leq x \leq y \leq 1$ and using the fact that $\rho_{\max} \geq \frac{\max_j v_{ij}}{B_i}$, and (c) follows since when product k is assigned to buyer i, $x_{ik} = 1$ from the algorithm. For buyers $j \neq i$, there is no change in y_j when product k is assigned to buyer i. ∎

Next, we complete the proof of Theorem 10.4.2.

Proof: [Theorem 10.4.2] Recall from Remark 10.4.1 that the revenue (10.20) obtained from buyer i on assignment of product j, except the last product assigned to any buyer i, is v_{ij}. Thus, the revenue extracted from buyer i using AW-ASSIGN is

$$\sum_{j \in A_i \setminus \{j_i\}} v_{ij} x_{ij} + \min\{v_{ij_i}, \mathsf{rembudget}_{i,j_i}\}, \tag{10.24}$$

where j_i is the last product assigned by AW-ASSIGN to buyer i, and $\mathsf{rembudget}_{i,j_i}$ is the remaining budget of buyer i when product j_i arrives.

To count the revenue extracted from buyer i using AW-ASSIGN, counting over all products m, note that either $\sum_{j=1}^{m} v_{ij} x_{ij} < B_i$ or $\sum_{j=1}^{m} v_{ij} x_{ij} \geq B_i$. In the first case, the revenue (10.24) is then just $\sum_{j=1}^{m} v_{ij} x_{ij}$, while in the second case, the revenue (10.24) is B_i.

Moreover, from Lemma 10.4.6, we know that as soon as $\sum_{j=1}^{m} v_{ij} x_{ij} \geq B_i$, then $y_i \geq 1$ and no more products are assigned to buyer i, and $\sum_{j=1}^{m} v_{ij} x_{ij} \leq B_i + \max_{ij} v_{ij}$ for all i. Thus, $B_i \geq \frac{\sum_{j=1}^{m} v_{ij} x_{ij}}{B_i + \max_{ij} v_{ij}} B_i$.

Hence, the revenue extracted from buyer i using AW-ASSIGN (10.24) in either of the two cases is at least

$$\sum_{j \in A_i \setminus \{j_i\}} v_{ij} x_{ij} + \min\{v_{ij_i}, \mathsf{rembudget}_{i,j_i}\} = \min\left\{\sum_{j=1}^{m} v_{ij} x_{ij}, B_i\right\},$$

$$\geq \sum_{j=1}^{m} v_{ij} x_{ij} \left(\frac{B_i}{B_i + \max_j v_{ij}}\right),$$

$$\geq \sum_{j=1}^{m} v_{ij} x_{ij} (1 - \rho_{\max}), \tag{10.25}$$

and the total revenue $R_{\text{AW-ASSIGN}}$ extracted from all buyers i using AW-ASSIGN is at least

$$R_{\text{AW-ASSIGN}} \geq \sum_{i=1}^{n} \sum_{j=1}^{m} v_{ij} x_{ij} (1 - \rho_{\max}). \tag{10.26}$$

From Lemma 10.4.5, with final solution $\mathbf{x}_f, \mathbf{y}_f, \mathbf{z}_f$ output by AW-ASSIGN, the final dual cost

$$D(\mathbf{x}_f) = \sum_{i=1}^{n} \sum_{j=1}^{m} v_{ij} x_{ij} \geq P(\mathbf{y}_f, \mathbf{z}_f)(1 - 1/\gamma), \tag{10.27}$$

and the final primal solution $\mathbf{y}_f, \mathbf{z}_f$ is feasible from Lemma 10.4.4.

Since $\left(\dfrac{B_i}{B_i + \max_j v_{ij}} \right) \geq 1 - \rho_{\max}$, scaling each element of the final solution $\mathbf{x}_f$ with $1 - \rho_{\max}$ instead of $(i,j)^{th}$ element of $\mathbf{x}_f$ with ψ_{ij} for appropriate indices, the scaled solution $\mathbf{x}_f (1 - \rho_{\max})$ is still dual feasible, similar to Lemma 10.4.6. Combining this with weak duality, we get

$$P(\mathbf{y}_f, \mathbf{z}_f) \geq D(\mathbf{x}^\star) \geq D(\mathbf{x}_f (1 - \rho_{\max})) \geq P(\mathbf{y}_f, \mathbf{z}_f)(1 - \rho_{\max})(1 - 1/\gamma), \tag{10.28}$$

where $\mathbf{x}^\star$ is the optimal solution of (10.21).

From (10.26), we know that the revenue extracted by AW-ASSIGN is at least $D(\mathbf{x}_f (1 - \rho_{\max}))$. Thus, combining (10.28) and (10.22) (i.e., $D(\mathbf{x}^\star) \geq R_{\text{OPT}}$ where R_{OPT} is the optimal revenue (10.20)), we get that

$$R_{\text{AW-ASSIGN}} \geq (1 - \rho_{\max})(1 - 1/\gamma) R_{\text{OPT}}$$

as required. $\blacksquare$

10.5 Unweighted Bipartite Matching Revisited

In this section, we revisit the unweighted bipartite matching problem, first discussed in Section 9.3. Recall that $G = (L \cup R, E)$ is the bipartite graph between the set L of left vertices and set R of right vertices. The set of right vertices R is available ahead of time, while the left vertices $\ell \in L$ arrive sequentially. On its arrival, the left vertex $\ell \in L$ reveals all the edges between itself and the right vertices. The problem is to match each newly arrived left vertex (where the arrival order is arbitrary) to an unmatched right vertex, if at all, irrevocably, with the objective of finding the matching with the largest size (the number of edges) at the end of all left vertex arrivals.

For this problem, we considered the RANKING algorithm in Section 9.3.2 where a random permutation π is chosen on the set of right vertices R that defines a rank $\pi(r)$ for each right vertex r, and each arriving left vertex is matched with the currently unmatched right vertex (to which it has an edge) with the least rank.

In this section, we analyse the RANKING algorithm using the primal–dual schema. The following discussion also serves as a good example on how to analyse randomized algorithms using the primal–dual setup. Towards that end, the RANKING algorithm is reinterpreted as follows. Right vertex r is assigned a random number n_r that is uniformly distributed in $[0, 1]$ independent of all other right vertices. Each arriving left vertex is matched with the currently unmatched right vertex (to which it has an edge) with the least number.

Let $G = (L \cup R, E)$ be the graph under consideration. The bipartite matching problem over G can be written as

$$\max \quad \sum_{(i,j)\in E} x_{ij},$$

For each left vertex $i \in L$ $\quad \sum_j x_{ij} \leq 1,$

For each right vertex $j \in R$ $\quad \sum_i x_{ij} \leq 1,$ $\qquad\qquad$ (10.29)

For each edge $(i,j) \in E$ $\quad x_{ij} \in \{0, 1\},$

where $x_{ij} = 1$ means that the edge between left vertex i and right vertex j is part of the matching. The LP relaxation (dual program) of (10.29) is

$$\max \quad \sum_{(i,j)\in E} x_{ij},$$

For each left vertex $i \in L$ $\quad \sum_j x_{ij} \leq 1,$

For each right vertex $j \in R$ $\quad \sum_i x_{ij} \leq 1,$ $\qquad\qquad$ (10.30)

For each edge $(i,j) \in E$ $\quad x_{ij} \geq 0,$

where x_{ij} is now the fractional weight of the matched edge between left vertex i and right vertex j.

The primal program corresponding to the dual (10.30) is given by

$$\min \quad \sum_{i\in L} y_i + \sum_{j\in R} z_j,$$

For each edge $(i,j) \in E$ $\quad y_i + z_j \geq 1,$ $\qquad\qquad$ (10.31)

$z_j, y_i \geq 0, \ \forall \ i,j,$

where L and R are the set of left and right vertices.

We define a **monotone and non–decreasing** function g such that $g : [0, 1] \to [0, 1]$, whose specific form that allows the competitive ratio bound will be discussed later. Let c be the competitive ratio we are aiming for.[2] We define the dual variables z_j and y_i using g and c as follows. Initially, $z_j = y_i = 0, \ \forall \ i,j$. Whenever, left vertex i is matched to right vertex j by RANKING, i.e., $x_{i,j} = 1$, set

$$z_j = g(n_j)/c, \quad y_i = (1 - g(n_j))/c, \qquad\qquad (10.32)$$

where n_j is the random number chosen by the right vertex j. For unmatched vertex pairs (i,j), $z_j = y_i = 0$.

The main result of this section is as follows.

---

[2] $c < 1$ since we are solving a maximization problem.

Theorem 10.5.1 *The competitive ratio of* RANKING *with the primal–dual interpretation is* $1 - 1/e$ *for the particular choice of* $g(x) = \exp(x - 1)$.

Thus, we recover the result of Section 9.3.2, where the analysis is combinatorial.

Proof: When left vertex i is matched to right vertex j, from (10.32) we know that the increment ΔP in the primal cost (10.31) is

$$z_j + y_i = g(n_j)/c + (1 - g(n_j))/c = 1/c.$$

Similarly, when left vertex i is matched to right vertex j, $x_{ij} = 1$, i.e., the dual cost (10.30) is incremented by 1 and $\Delta D = 1$. Thus, $c\Delta P = \Delta D$, which implies that

$$D(\mathbf{x}_f) = cP(\mathbf{y}_f, \mathbf{z}_f), \tag{10.33}$$

where $\mathbf{x}_f, \mathbf{y}_f, \mathbf{z}_f$ are final solutions output by RANKING. Also, note that the dual solution x_{ij}'s are feasible. Thus, to make use of the weak duality and our recipe (Section 10.2.1) all we need to show is that the final primal solution $\mathbf{y}_f, \mathbf{z}_f$ output by RANKING is primal feasible.

By definition, for any edge $(i, j) \in E$ that is part of the matching, $z_j = g(n_j)/c$, $y_i = (1 - g(n_j))/c$, and hence $y_i + z_j \geq 1/c \geq 1$ since $c \leq 1$. Thus, primal feasibility is guaranteed for any $(i, j) \in E$ that is part of the matching. So, the only remaining case is for $(i, j) \in E$ that may not be part of the matching. For any $(i, j) \in E$ that may not be part of the matching, we show that $\mathbb{E}\{y_i + z_j\} \geq 1$ in Lemma 10.5.2 as long as $c = 1 - 1/e$ and $g(x) = \exp(x - 1)$. In effect, we prove primal feasibility in expectation for the choice of $c = 1 - 1/e$ and $g(x) = \exp(x - 1)$.

Note that RANKING is randomized, and we are seeking a competitive ratio bound only in expectation. From Problem 10.7 we will prove that if (10.33) holds and the final primal solution $\mathbf{y}_f, \mathbf{z}_f$ output by RANKING is primal feasible in expectation, following our recipe the competitive ratio is c in expectation. ∎

Lemma 10.5.2 *If* g, c *satisfy the following relation,*

$$\int_0^\theta g(x)dx + 1 - g(\theta) \geq c, \quad \forall \, \theta \in [0, 1], \tag{10.34}$$

together with $g(1) = 1$, *then*

$$\mathbb{E}\{y_i + z_j\} \geq 1,$$

for any $(i, j) \in E$. *Note that* $g(x) = \exp(x - 1)$ *and* $c = 1 - 1/e$ *satisfy* (10.34).

Essentially, Lemma 10.5.2 is exploiting the property that for any edge $(i, j) \in E$, there is sufficient probability of selecting some edge incident on $i \in L$ or $j \in R$ with RANKING.

Towards proving Lemma 10.5.2, we begin with the following two intermediate propositions. Consider any fixed realization of random numbers

$$\bar{n} = [n_1, \ldots, n_{|R|}]$$

for all right vertices. Consider the graph $G = (L \cup R, E)$ and an edge $(i, j) \in E$. Remove the right vertex j to get a subgraph

$$G_{-j} = (L \cup R\backslash\{j\}, E\backslash\mathbf{e}_j),$$

where $\mathbf{e}_j$ is the set of all edges incident on j, while keeping the random numbers of all $j' \neq j$, same as in $\bar{n}$. In graph G_{-j}, i.e., without the right vertex j, let the left vertex i be matched to right vertex j' by RANKING. Then define the critical number $n^c = n_{j'}$, and $n^c = 1$ if i is not matched. Moreover, let the critical $y_i^c = (1 - g(n^c))/c$ (the value of y_i with G_{-j}) in the execution of RANKING on G_{-j}, and $g(1) = 1$.

Fixing a right vertex j and its realization n_j helps us in deriving the following properties.

Proposition 10.5.3 [*Monotonicity Property*] *Given $\bar{n}\setminus\{n_j\}$, the right vertex j is always matched by* RANKING *while considering the full graph G to some left vertex as long as $n_j \leq n^c$.*

We leave the proof as an exercise (Problem 10.8) where the basic idea is to consider that if without the right vertex j, left vertex i is matched to j', then on left vertex i's arrival in the input, j' has the smallest number $n_{j'}$ among the available right vertices. Thus, with full graph G, if $n_j \leq n^c = n_{j'}$, then j will get matched to some vertex i' that is either i or arrives before i. A pictorial description of this idea is presented in Figure 10.1.

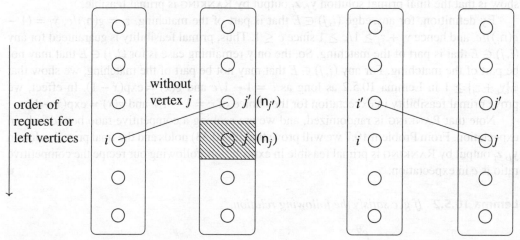

Figure 10.1 Structural property of RANKING, such that if i is matched to j' in absence of j, then j is definitely matched to some left vertex i or some i' that arrives before i as long as $n_j \leq n_{j'}$.

Proposition 10.5.4 [*Domination Property*] *Given $\bar{n}\setminus\{n_j\}$, for all choices of n_j, when* RANKING *is executed on full graph G, $y_i \geq y_i^c$.*

Proof: The first claim we need is that if the algorithm is executed in parallel on G and G_{-j}, then on the arrival of each new left vertex, the unmatched right vertices of R in G is a superset of the unmatched right vertices of R in G_{-j} (Problem 10.9). Thus, when the left vertex i arrives, its unmatched neighbors (right vertices to which i has an edge) in R when the algorithm is executed on G is a superset of its unmatched neighbors when the algorithm is executed on G_{-j}.

Therefore, similar to G_{-j}, for G also, the left vertex i has an unmatched neighbor in R with (random) number n^c. To match the left vertex i with full graph G, RANKING chooses the neighbor (say k with number n_k) in R with the smallest number, and hence $n_k \leq n^c$. Moreover, since $y_i = (1 - g(n_k))/c$ and $y_i^c = (1 - g(n^c))/c$, and g is monotonic by choice, we have $y_i \geq y_i^c$. ∎

Using the preceding two propositions, we next prove the main technical lemma (Lemma 10.5.2).

Proof: [Lemma 10.5.2] We show that the final solution $\mathbf{y}_f, \mathbf{z}_f$ output by RANKING is primal feasible in expectation using (10.34). By definition for any edge $(i, j) \in E$ that is part of the matching, $z_j = g(n_j)/c$, $y_i = (1 - g(n_j))/c$, and hence $y_i + z_j \geq 1/c \geq 1$ since $c \leq 1$. Next, we show that for $(i, j) \in E$ that may not be part of the matching, $\mathbb{E}\{y_i + z_j\} \geq 1$.

From the Monotonicity property (Proposition 10.5.3) we have that the right vertex j is matched whenever $n_j \leq n^c$. Hence, from (10.32), conditioned on n^c,

$$\mathbb{E}\{z_j\} \geq \int_0^{n^c} \frac{g(x)}{c} dx.$$

Moreover, from the Dominance property (Proposition 10.5.4), $y_i \geq y_i^c = (1 - g(n^c))/c$ for all choices of n_j. Therefore, conditioned on n^c,

$$\mathbb{E}\{z_j\} + \mathbb{E}\{y_i\} \geq \int_0^{n^c} \frac{g(x)}{c} dx + \frac{(1 - g(n^c))}{c}.$$

Note that n^c can take any value between $[0, 1]$. Therefore, if

$$\int_0^{\theta} g(x) dx + 1 - g(\theta) \geq c, \quad \forall \, \theta \in [0, 1],$$

(the hypothesis of the Lemma) then unconditionally,

$$\mathbb{E}\{z_j\} + \mathbb{E}\{y_i\} \geq 1,$$

making the solution output by RANKING, primal feasible in expectation. ∎

10.6 Notes

Analysing online algorithms using the primal–dual technique is very popular in literature, e.g., the set cover problem [164, 165], the packing and covering problems [166], AdWords problem [15, 167], convex optimization [168, 169], speed scaling [170] (provides the best-known competitive ratio for the speed scaling problem with multiple servers that we discuss in Chapter 14), bipartite matching [152], matching with stochastic input [171], paging [72] (the problem discussed in Chapter 5, facility location [172] (that we discuss in Chapter 11), learning [173], and non-clairvoyant scheduling under precedence constraints [174]. This is clearly an incomplete list, and the application of primal–dual technique is far more widespread. The monograph [165] reviews many of the problems where primal–dual techniques are useful.

For the set cover problem discussed in this chapter, the analysis presented can be found in [165], which shows a competitive ratio of $\mathcal{O}(\log m \log n)$ that can be specialized to

$\mathcal{O}(\log d \log n)$, where m is the number of subsets of $\mathcal{U}$. A deterministic algorithm that achieves a competitive ratio of $\mathcal{O}(\log m \log n)$ (and $\mathcal{O}(\log d \log n)$) can be found in [175] where the analysis does not use the primal–dual technique. A lower bound of $\Omega\left(\dfrac{\log m \log n}{\log \log m + \log \log n}\right)$ on the competitive ratio for all deterministic algorithms is also derived in [175]. A variant of the set cover problem called the disjoint set cover problem has been analysed in [176, 177], where subsets arrive online and have to be partitioned so as to maximize the number of set covers that have no common subsets.

The analysis presented in the chapter for the AdWords problem can be found in [15]. A similar analysis is also available in [167]. An algorithm with a better guarantee for the AdWords problem in the secretarial input model can be found in [178], and for the adversarial stochastic input in [138]. Compared to AW-Assign, [138] shows that a greedy algorithm achieves a competitive ratio of $1 - 1/e$ for the adversarial stochastic input even when the $\rho_{max} = \max_{i,j}\left\{\dfrac{v_{ij}}{B_i}\right\}$, the worst valuation-to-budget ratio is not small. The AdWords problem with a strict capacity constraint where products can be assigned to a buyer only if its remaining budget is at least as much the product's valuation has been analysed in [179]. The primal–dual based analysis of Ranking for the unweighted bipartite matching problem was derived in [152], which is presented in Section 10.5.

All the problems we encountered in this chapter had linear objective functions. The primal–dual schema can also be applied to online problems with convex objective functions [180, 181, 170]. For a brief review, see [182].

PROBLEMS

10.1 For the set cover problem, let the fractional solution of MWA be $x_S, S \in \mathcal{S}$. We make the solution integral as follows: $\hat{x}_S = 1$ if $x_S \geq 1/d$, and $\hat{x}_S = 0$ otherwise, where $d = \max_j |\mathcal{S}_j|$. Show that the integral solution is primal feasible (10.13), and $P(\hat{x}) \leq d \cdot P(x)$.

10.2 Consider the offline version of the set cover problem, where the cost of each subset is 1. Show that a greedy algorithm that repeatedly picks the subset that covers the most new elements, i.e., elements that are not already covered, has an approximation ratio of $\log(n)$, where n is the size of the universe.

10.3 Recall the simple class of inputs requested in Example 10.3.1,

$$\sigma^j = \{1, 2, \dots, j\}$$

for $j = 1, \dots, n$, where with σ^j, the j elements are requested in sequence. The collection of subsets is $\mathcal{S} = \{S_1, \dots, S_n\}$, where $S_i = \{1, 2, \dots, i\}$ with cost $c_{S_i} = i$ for $i = 1, 2, \dots, n$. Consider an online algorithm $\mathcal{A}$ that includes the set S_{2k-1} in the cover on the request for singleton element $\{k\}, 1 \leq k \leq n$, if the element k is not already part of the cover. In particular, on request for element $\{1\}$, set S_1 is chosen, on request for element $\{2\}$ set S_3 is chosen, while on request for element $\{3\}$ no new set is chosen since it is already contained in S_3 which is part of the cover already, and so on.

Show that the competitive ratio of this online algorithm $\mathcal{A}$ is upper bounded by a constant for the considered class of input, i.e.,

$$\mu_{\mathcal{A}} = \max_{\sigma^j, \, j=1,2,\ldots,n} \frac{C_{\mathcal{A}}(\sigma^j)}{C_{\text{OPT}}(\sigma^j)} \leq c,$$

for some constant c.

10.4 [183] In this problem, we will show that the competitive ratio of any randomized algorithm for the set cover problem is at least $1 + \log_2 n$, where n is the number of elements in the universe.

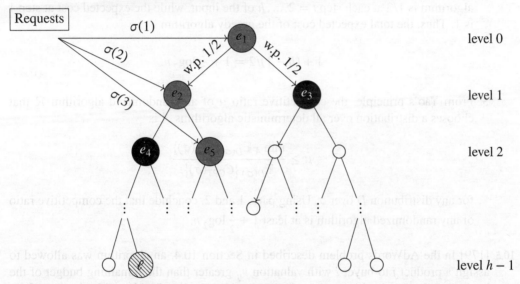

Figure 10.2 Binary tree from which the input sequence is constructed for Problem 10.4. Grey nodes are the requested elements, while the black nodes are the other choices of elements that are not selected as being part of the input. For each leaf node ℓ (element e_ℓ of the universe) there is a corresponding subset $S_\ell \in \mathcal{S}$ that contains all the elements encountered on the path from the root to ℓ.

Let the universe size be $n-1$, and let these $n-1$ elements be represented as the $n-1$ nodes of a binary tree as shown in Figure 10.2 with $h = \log_2 n$ levels where there are $n/2$ leaf nodes. To each leaf node ℓ attach a subset S_ℓ of the universe that contains all the elements on the path from the root to ℓ (all its ancestors). Thus, there are a total of $n/2$ subsets of the universe available, i.e., $\mathcal{S} = \{S_1, \ldots, S_{n/2}\}$, and let the cost of each subset be $c_S = 1$.

For a leaf node $\ell = 1, \ldots, n/2$, let the path from the root to ℓ be denoted as p_ℓ. The input sequence σ will be a path p_ℓ from the root to one of the leaves $\ell = 1, \ldots, n/2$, i.e., the $\log_2 n$ elements (till level $h-1$) on the path p_ℓ will be requested with any input.

The input is chosen as follows: choose any path p_ℓ for $\ell = 1, \ldots, n/2$ uniformly randomly, i.e., the h elements on the path p_ℓ are requested sequentially, where p_ℓ is chosen uniformly randomly. Equivalently, start at the root node, and choose the next element in the input among the two children of root with equal probability. Continue this at each node of the tree corresponding to the previously selected element in the input. The grey coloured nodes in Figure 10.2 represent one realization of the input.

1. For any realization of the input sequence σ, show that the cost of OPT is 1.

2. Without loss of generality, consider a greedy algorithm that chooses to include just one subset to cover the newly requested element with the input if it is not already covered as the best deterministic algorithm. Show that the expected cost paid by the greedy algorithm is $1/2$ at each step $t = 2, \ldots, h$ of the input, while the expected cost at step 1 is 1. Thus, the total expected cost of the greedy algorithm is

$$1 + (h-1)/2 = 1 + \frac{1}{2}\log_2 n.$$

3. From Yao's principle, the competitive ratio μ of any randomized algorithm $\mathcal{R}$ that chooses a distribution over all deterministic algorithms $\mathcal{A}$ is

$$\mu \geq \frac{\min_{\mathcal{A}} \mathbb{E}_{D(\sigma)}\{C_{\mathcal{A}}(\sigma)\}}{\mathbb{E}_{D(\sigma)}\{C_{\text{OPT}}(\sigma)\}}$$

for any distribution D over σ. Using parts 1 and 2, conclude that the competitive ratio of any randomized algorithm is at least $1 + \frac{1}{2}\log_2 n$.

10.5 [179] In the AdWords problem described in Section 10.4, an algorithm was allowed to assign a product j to buyer i with valuation v_{ij} greater than the remaining budget of the buyer i, while charging him or her only the remaining budget. In this problem, we preclude this possibility, and a product j can be assigned to buyer i only if the valuation v_{ij} is at most the remaining budget of buyer i. Show that under this strict budget constraint, no deterministic online algorithm has a bounded competitive ratio.

10.6 [179] In this problem, we consider the AdWords problems with strict budget constraint as defined in Problem 10.5, but where product lives are temporary. Each product j has a valuation v_{ij} and lifespan t_j. Each product has to be assigned to one of the buyers, if at all, on its arrival irrevocably.

Thus, if a product j is assigned to a buyer i on its arrival, then for the next t_j time units, the used-up budget of buyer i because of product j is v_{ij}. The strict budget constraint is enforced at all times, i.e., at each time throughout the total time horizon the total used-up budget of buyer i should be at most B_i.

Let there be only one buyer with budget B, and the objective is to maximize the total accrued revenue summed over time. Show that even if $v_j \leq B/2$ for all products j, the competitive ratio of any deterministic algorithm is unbounded.

[Hint: Considering the following input might be helpful. Let the total time horizon be T. For each product, let (v, ℓ) be the two-tuple representing its valuation and lifespan, respectively. Consider two input sequences

$$\sigma_1 = \{(\epsilon, T), \underbrace{(0, 1), \dots, (0, 1)}_{T-1}\}$$

and

$$\sigma_2 = \{(\epsilon, T), \underbrace{\left(\frac{B}{2}, T-1\right), \left(\frac{B}{2}/0, 1\right), \dots, \left(\frac{B}{2}/0, 1\right)}_{T-1}\},$$

with $\epsilon << \frac{B}{2}$, and where $\frac{B}{2}/0$ means either the valuation of that product is $\frac{B}{2}$ or 0 depending on earlier assignments.]

10.7 [152] Recall the maximization problem (10.30) (considered as the dual) with the corresponding primal as (10.31). Let the output of a randomized algorithm $\mathcal{R}$ be such that (i) it is dual feasible, (ii) it is primal feasible **in expectation**. Then, if for all realizations of randomization, the final dual and primal solutions are $\mathbf{y}_f$, $\mathbf{z}_f$ and $\mathbf{x}_f$ with dual cost $D(\mathbf{x}_f)$ and primal cost $P(\mathbf{y}_f, \mathbf{z}_f)$, respectively, satisfy the relation $D(\mathbf{x}_f) \geq cP(\mathbf{y}_f, \mathbf{z}_f)$ for $c < 1$. Then show that $\mathbb{E}\{D(\mathbf{x}_f)\} \geq c\, \text{Profit}_{\text{OPT}}$, where $\text{Profit}_{\text{OPT}}$ is the optimal objective function value of (10.30). Thus, conclude that $\mathcal{R}$ is c-competitive in expectation.

[Hint: Consider the solution that is the expected value of the random solutions output by $\mathcal{R}$.]

10.8 Prove Proposition 10.5.3.

10.9 Prove the claim used in Proposition 10.5.4 that if the algorithm is executed in parallel on G and G_{-j}, then on the request for each new left vertex, the unmatched right vertices of R in G is superset of the unmatched right vertices of R in G_{-j}.

10.10 [15, 165] In this problem, we will consider a primal–dual algorithm to solve the **fractional** ski-rental problem that we considered in Chapter 2. Let the price to buy the ski be \$P and rent for each day be 1\$. The unknown factor is the number of skiing days left before the snow melts. Then the problem we want to solve is to minimize the cost subject to skiing for as many days as possible. The LP (primal) for this is

$$\min \quad \mathsf{P}x + \sum_{i=1}^{k} z_i,$$

$$\text{for each day } i \quad x + z_i \geq 1, \tag{10.35}$$

$$x \geq 0, z_i \geq 0 \text{ for each day } i,$$

whose *dual* is given by

$$\max \quad \sum_{i=1}^{k} y_i,$$

$$\sum_{i=1}^{k} y_i \leq \mathsf{P}, \tag{10.36}$$

$$0 \leq y_i \leq 1 \; \forall \, i.$$

Variable z_i indicates whether to rent on the i-th day, and x indicates whether we buy a ski. For any day i, we have to either rent or buy a ski, which is reflected in constraints of (10.35).

For a given γ (to be chosen later and which will determine the competitive ratio), consider the algorithm SKI-RENT to solve the problem.

1. Show that the increment in primal cost $\Delta P = 1 + 1/(\gamma - 1)$ and dual cost $\Delta D = 1$, respectively, in each iteration.

2. Show that the solution output by SKI-RENT is primal feasible.

3. Show that the solution output by SKI-RENT is also dual feasible. Essentially, you have to show that $\sum_{i=1}^{k} y_i \leq P$. Towards that end, try to argue that $x \geq 1$ after at most P days of skiing by choosing a value of γ. Essentially, bound how much x increases in each iteration. Since y_i increases by 1 in each iteration, and once $x = 1$, no more updates to y_i are made, this will imply dual feasibility.

4. Argue that the competitive ratio of SKI-RENT is at most $1 + 1/(\gamma - 1)$.

Algorithm 17 SKI-RENT

1: Initially $x = 0, y_i = 0, z_i = 0, \forall i$;
2: On the i-th day ;
3: **if** $x = 1$ **then**, do nothing
4: **else**
5:     $z_i = 1 - x$
6:     $x = (1 + 1/P)x + 1/((\gamma - 1)P)$
7:     $y_i = 1$;
8: **end if**

10.11 [15] In this problem, we will consider a primal–dual algorithm for the TCP acknowledgement problem defined in Section 2.6. We consider a discretized version of the TCP acknowledgement problem defined as follows. Time is discretized, where each considered time slot t's width is some multiple of $\frac{1}{d}$, and d can be arbitrarily small.

Let packet j arrive at time slot a_j. Let $x_t = 1$ if the algorithm sends an acknowledgement at time slot t and 0 otherwise. Similarly, let $z(j, t) = 1$ if the packet j that arrived at time a_j is not acknowledged by time slot $t > a_j$ and 0 otherwise. Thus, the latency seen by packet j is $\sum_{t:t \geq a_j} \frac{1}{d} z(j, t)$ where $1/d$ is the width of each time slot.

With $x_t \in \{0, 1\}$, the overall cost for the TCP acknowledgement problem is just

$$\sum_t x_t + \sum_j \sum_{t:t \geq a_j} \frac{1}{d} z(j, t),$$

where $\sum_t x_t$ is the total number of acknowledgements made. A pictorial description of the problem can be found in Figure 10.3. The optimization problem is then represented as the following primal problem:

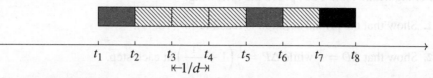

$$t_1 \quad t_2 \quad t_3 \quad t_4 \quad t_5 \quad t_6 \quad t_7 \quad t_8$$
$$\mapsto 1/d \mapsto$$

Figure 10.3 Pictorial description of the TCP acknowledgement problem, where grey slots are the slots in which packets arrive, black slot is where an acknowledgement is sent while the shaded slots are empty where nothing happens, and slot width is $1/d$. For this example, one packet arrives in slot t_1 and t_5, single acknowledgement is made in slot t_7 and hence the acknowledgement cost is 1, while the latency for packet 1 is $(t_7 - t_1)$ and the latency for packet 2 is $(t_7 - t_5)$.

$$\min \qquad \sum_t x_t + \sum_j \sum_{t:t \geq a_j} \frac{1}{d} z(j,t),$$

$$\text{for each } j, t : t \geq a_j \quad \sum_{k=a_j}^{t} x_k + z(j,t) \geq 1, \qquad (10.37)$$

$$x_t \geq 0, z(j,t) \geq 0.$$

If $x_t, z(j,t) \in \{0,1\}$, i.e., the solution to (10.37) was constrained to be integral, the constraint $\sum_{k=a_j}^{t} x_k + z(j,t) \geq 1$ ensures that in any time slot either an acknowledgement has been sent already for a packet that arrives by time slot t, or the latency of each unacknowledged packet increases by 1. By allowing $x_t \geq 0, z(j,t) \geq 0$, (10.37) is a relaxation.

The *dual* of (10.37) is given by

$$\max \qquad \sum_j \sum_{t:t \geq a_j} y(j,t),$$

$$\text{for each } t \in T, \qquad \sum_{j:t \geq a_j} \sum_{t' \geq t} y(j,t') \leq 1, \qquad (10.38)$$

$$\text{for each } j, t : t \geq a_j \quad y(j,t) \leq \frac{1}{d}.$$

Consider the following algorithm AcK-TCP.

Algorithm 18 Algorithm AcK-TCP

1: Fix $c > 0$.

2: Initially $x_t, y(j,t), z(j,t) = 0, \; \forall j, t$

3: At each time slot t (of width $1/d$), consider each of the packets j for which $\sum_{k=a_j}^{t} x_k < 1$

4: For each such packet j do

    1. $z(j,t) = 1 - \sum_{k=a_j}^{t} x_k.$

    2. $x_t = x_t + \frac{1}{d} \sum_{k=a_j}^{t} x_k + \frac{1}{(c-1)d}$

    3. $y(j,t) = \frac{1}{d}$

The condition for each packet j for which $\sum_{k=a_j}^t x_k < 1$ in Ack-TCP means that no packet (including j) has been acknowledged since the arrival of packet j at time a_j.

For algorithm Ack-TCP, prove the following:

1. Show that the primal solution is feasible for (10.37).

2. Show that $\Delta D = \frac{1}{d}$ while $\Delta P = \frac{1}{d}\left(1 + \frac{1}{c-1}\right)$ at each step.

3. Consider any time t for which we want to show that the dual constraint $\sum_{j:t\geq a_j} \sum_{t'\geq t} y(j,t') \leq 1$ is satisfied. Note that whenever any $y(j,t)$ is updated, it is set as $1/d$. Thus, if Ack-TCP ensures that at most d such updates are made for variables $y(j,t')$ involved in the dual constraint $\sum_{j:t\geq a_j} \sum_{t'\geq t} y(j,t') \leq 1$ for each time t, we are done.

   Towards this end, using induction show that $\sum_{k\geq t} x_k \geq \frac{(1+1/d)^q - 1}{c-1}$, where q is the number of updates made to $y(j,t')$ that are involved in the dual constraint $\sum_{j:t\geq a_j} \sum_{t'\geq t} y(j,t') \leq 1$ for each time t.

4. Choose $c = (1 + 1/d)^d$, and using part 3 conclude that Ack-TCP produces a solution that is dual feasible.

5. Argue that the competitive ratio of Ack-TCP is $e/(e-1)$ by choosing $d \to \infty$.

6. Ack-TCP produces a fractional solution x_t for $t = 1, 2, \ldots$. To make it integral, do the following. Choose some real number p uniformly at random in the interval $[0,1]$. For each x_t output by Algorithm-TCP, consider an interval I_t of length x_t, and place the intervals next to each other on the real line starting from 0. Acknowledge packets at time t if the interval I_t corresponding to x_t contains $p + k$ for any $k \in \mathbb{N}$.

   Show that the expected cost of this integral solution is the same as the fractional cost of Ack-TCP. The main point of this correlated rounding strategy is to ensure that at any time slot t, the probability that at least one acknowledgement has been sent between slots $t - \ell$ and t is at least $\sum_{i=t-\ell}^t x_i$. If independent rounding is employed, this would not be true.

11

Facility Location and *k*-Means Clustering

11.1 Introduction

In this section, we consider two related combinatorial online problems that have wide applications in the area of operations research and machine learning, called the facility location problem, and the *k*-clustering problem. With the facility location problem, requests arrive sequentially whose locations belong to a metric space. On the arrival of a new request, the decision to be made is whether to assign this request to any one of the currently open facilities or open a new facility. The cost of assigning a request to an open facility is equal to the distance between the location of the request and the location of the open facility, while opening a new facility incurs a fixed cost. The cost of an online algorithm is the sum of the costs of all requests plus the total facility opening cost, and the objective is to find online algorithms to minimize the competitive ratio.

The facility location problem is a rich object and captures important problems such as: where to install charging stations for electric vehicles with routing and infrastructure costs. In this chapter, we first derive lower bounds on the competitive ratios of both deterministic and randomized algorithms, and show that the best competitive ratio possible for any online algorithm is at least $\Omega\left(\frac{\log n}{\log\log n}\right)$, where n is the number of requests. On the positive side, we present a randomized algorithm whose competitive ratio is at most $\mathcal{O}(\log n)$. We also consider a secretarial input setting where the order of arrival of requests is uniformly random, for which the same randomized algorithm is at most 8-competitive. A deterministic algorithm with a competitive ratio of at most $\mathcal{O}(\log n)$ is also established for a more general setting, where the facility-opening cost depends on the location.

Next, we consider a related problem called the *k*-clustering problem, where requests arrive online and the objective is to partition the set of requests into at most *k*-clusters that minimizes the total cost defined as follows. The cost of each cluster is the distance of all requests that belong to the cluster from its centroid (called the centre), and the total cost is the sum of the cost of all the clusters. The *k*-clustering problem essentially models the classification problem, a fundamental object in machine learning.

For the *k*-clustering problem, it turns out that in the online setting, either an algorithm needs to open more than *k*-clusters or incur an unbounded cost with respect to the optimal offline algorithm. Thus, the quest is to design an online algorithm with a small competitive ratio that creates as few clusters as possible while the optimal offline algorithm creates exactly *k*-clusters.

Facility location and *k*-clustering are closely related problems: i) opening new facilities is similar to creating more cluster centres, both leading to less distance cost, and ii) paying the facility opening cost is similar to creating a new cluster, which limits the ability of an algorithm to create more clusters later since at most k clusters can be created. Similar to the facility location problem, we present a randomized algorithm whose competitive ratio is logarithmic in the total number of requests.

11.2 Facility Location Problem

11.2.1 Problem Formulation

Consider a metric space $\mathcal{M}$ endowed with a distance measure d, (Definition (6.2.1)). Essentially, all we will need is that for the triangle inequality to hold, e.g., $\mathcal{M} = \mathbb{R}^2$, and d as the Euclidean distance.

A set of n requests arrive online, where the ith request arrives at location $x_i \in \mathcal{M}$. Let the set of open facilities just before the arrival of the ith request be F_{i-1}, where the elements of F_{i-1} represent the location of the open facilities. On the arrival of the ith request, any online algorithm can choose to open a new facility by paying a cost of f at location $y_i \in \mathcal{M}$ (that can depend on the whole sequence $x_1, \ldots, x_i$ revealed so far), in which case $F_i = F_{i-1} \cup \{y_i\}$. If no new facility is opened, then $F_i = F_{i-1}$. In either case, the ith request is assigned to the nearest open facility belonging to F_i. The distance of x_i to the nearest open facility belonging to F_i is defined as the **distance cost** of the ith request. The assignment is irrevocable in the sense that if the ith request is assigned on its arrival to some open facility, it cannot be reassigned in future, even if a new facility opens closer to it than the open facility to which it is assigned on its arrival.

We are assuming that the cost of opening a facility is independent of its location, called the **uniform facility cost** case. We will discuss the non-uniform facility cost case in Section 11.2.5.

Definition 11.2.1 *For any set of points $S \subseteq \mathcal{M}$, and $x \in \mathcal{M}$, let*

$$d(x, S) = \min_{s \in S} d(x, s),$$

i.e., $d(x, S)$ is the nearest distance of x from any point of S.

The cost of any online algorithm $\mathcal{A}$ for the facility location problem after the arrival of the ith request is given by

$$C_i^{\mathcal{A}} = \underbrace{f|F_i|}_{\text{facility cost}} + \underbrace{\sum_{k=1}^{i} d(x_k, F_k)}_{\text{distance cost}}, \tag{11.1}$$

where note that for the kth request arrival at x_k, $d(x_k, F_k)$ is computed over the set of facilities F_k available just after the kth arrival, and is equal to the distance cost. The cost (11.1) automatically captures the irrevocable assignment constraint of an online algorithm, that once a request is assigned to an open facility it cannot be reassigned later even if a facility opens closer to it in future. With complete input, $\sigma = (x_1, \ldots, x_n)$ having n requests, the total cost of an online algorithm $\mathcal{A}$ is then just $C_n^{\mathcal{A}}(\sigma)$. Note that n need not be known in advance.

Any offline algorithm, however, is aware of the full input sequence σ and can open facilities depending on σ. The competitive ratio for an online algorithm $\mathcal{A}$ is then

$$\mu_{\mathcal{A}} = \max_{\sigma} \frac{C_n^{\mathcal{A}}(\sigma)}{C_n^{\text{OPT}}(\sigma)}. \tag{11.2}$$

Example 11.2.2

To exhibit the limitations of an online algorithm, consider the following input sequence. Let the metric space be the interval $\mathcal{M} = (0, 1/2]$, i.e., all requests are going to lie in $(0, 1/2]$, and the ith request's location is $x_i = \dfrac{1}{2^i}$, $i = 1, \ldots, n$.

An algorithm that knows the full input sequence in advance can open just one facility at location $1/2^n$ and pay a total cost of $f + \sum_{i=1}^{n} \dfrac{1}{2^i} \leq f + 1$. Thus, the cost of OPT is at most $f + 1$.

An online algorithm $\mathcal{A}$, on the other hand, has a challenging decision to make on the arrival of the tth request, $1 \leq t \leq n$, without knowing the future locations or the total number of requests n: should it open a new facility or not? For example, let $\mathcal{A}$ open a facility at every k^{th} request, i.e., at locations $1/2, 1/2^k, 1/2^{2k}$, and so on, for some $k \in \mathbb{N}$. Then choosing k small, $\mathcal{A}$ has a very large facility-opening cost, while if it chooses a large value of k, then the input might terminate just before a new facility is opened by $\mathcal{A}$, making the distance cost of $\mathcal{A}$ large. Thus, an online algorithm has to choose k so as to balance the facility-opening and the distance cost.

11.2.2 Lower Bound

We begin this section by presenting an easy lower bound on the competitive ratio of any deterministic online algorithm for solving the facility location problem.

Lemma 11.2.3 *The competitive ratio of any deterministic online algorithm for solving the facility location problem cannot be a constant.*

Proof: Let the competitive ratio of a deterministic online algorithm $\mathcal{A}$ be a constant $\mu_{\mathcal{A}}$. We will use the input sequence presented in Example 11.2.2 to contradict the fact that $\mu_{\mathcal{A}}$ is a constant. Recall from Example 11.2.2 that $\mathcal{M} = (0, 1/2]$, and the ith request location is chosen to be $x_i = \dfrac{1}{2^i}$, $i = 1, \ldots, n,$. From Example 11.2.2, we know that $C_n^{\text{OPT}}(\sigma) \leq f + 1$.

Therefore, for $\mathcal{A}$ to be $\mu_{\mathcal{A}}$-competitive, $\mathcal{A}$ can open at most $\mu_{\mathcal{A}} + 1$ (letting $f \geq 1$) facilities, since the cost of opening any new facility is f. Since $\mu_{\mathcal{A}}$ is a constant, there is a last facility opened by $\mathcal{A}$. Let the location of the last facility opened by $\mathcal{A}$ belong to $\left[\dfrac{1}{2^\ell}, 1\right]$ for some $\ell \in \mathbb{N}$.

Then the distance cost of each of the k requests $k = \ell + 1, \ldots, n$, with $\mathcal{A}$ is at least $\dfrac{1}{2^{\ell+1}}$. Thus, the cost of $\mathcal{A}$ is at least $f + (n - \ell)\dfrac{1}{2^{\ell+1}}$.

Since $\mu_{\mathcal{A}}$ is a constant, and there are at most $\mu_{\mathcal{A}} + 1$ open facilities, ℓ is bounded, and hence choosing n arbitrarily large, we get that the cost of $\mathcal{A}$ is arbitrarily large compared to OPT. Thus, reaching a contradiction to the fact that $\mu_{\mathcal{A}}$ is a constant. ∎

Lemma 11.2.3 highlights the basic limitation of any deterministic algorithm for solving the facility location problem. We next present a more refined analysis to claim a lower bound of $\Omega\left(\dfrac{\log n}{\log\log n}\right)$ for any deterministic algorithm for solving the facility location problem.

Theorem 11.2.4 *The competitive ratio of any deterministic online algorithm for solving the facility location problem is $\Omega\left(\dfrac{\log n}{\log\log n}\right)$, where n is the number of requests.*

Proof: We will consider a **binary tree** over which the request sequence will be constructed. The metric space over this binary tree is the hierarchically well-separated tree described at the end of the proof using the following description. Let the root of the tree be v_o, and let the height of the tree be h. There are 2^j nodes at level j in this tree, for $j = 0, \ldots, h, h \in \mathbb{N}$. Let T_v denote the subtree with node v as its root. Hence, the full tree is denoted as T_{v_o}.

The distance between a node at level j and any of its children at level $j + 1$ is defined to be D/m^j, where D, m, and h will be suitably chosen later. See Figure 11.1 for reference.

Proposition 11.2.5 *Let v be a node at level j. Then for any node $u \in T_v$ (subtree rooted at v), the distance $d(u, v)$ between u and v satisfies*

$$d(u, v) \leq \frac{D}{m^j}\frac{m}{m-1}.$$

Moreover, for $u \notin T_v$,

$$d(u, v) \geq \frac{D}{m^{j-1}}.$$

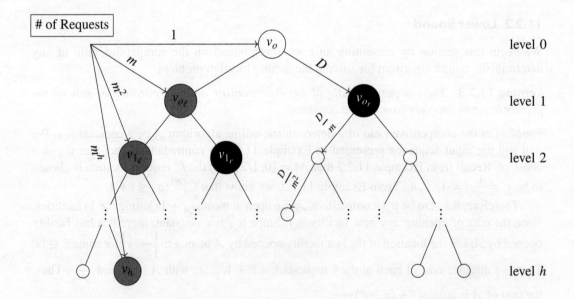

Figure 11.1 A node v is coloured black at level j if algorithm $\mathcal{A}$ opens a facility on a request arrival in phase $j - 1$ somewhere in subtree T_v rooted at v, while a grey node is the location of the request made in phase j.

Proof: Let $u \in T_v$ be a node at level k for $j \le k \le h$. Then by the definition of distance between a node v at level j and its children, also seen from Figure 11.1,

$$d(u, v) = \sum_{\ell=j}^{k-1} \frac{D}{m^\ell} = \frac{D}{m^j} \sum_{\ell=0}^{k-j-1} \frac{1}{m^\ell} \le \frac{D}{m^j} \frac{m}{m-1}.$$

This proves the first claim. For the second claim, recall that v is at level j. Thus, the distance between v and its parent that is at level $j - 1$ is D/m^{j-1}. To reach any $u \notin T_v$ from v, first the parent of v has to be reached from v, and hence the claim follows. ∎

Consider any deterministic online algorithm $\mathcal{A}$. The request sequence consists of $h + 1$ phases, where h is the height of the binary tree under consideration. To begin with, in phase 0, a single request is made for the root of the tree v_o, i.e., $\sigma_0 = v_o$. Among the two children of root v_o, v_{o_ℓ} and v_{o_r}, (denoting left and right children), let $\mathcal{A}$ open a facility in subtree $T_{v_{o_r}}$ ($T_{v_{o_\ell}}$) to fulfil the request made in phase 0. Then in phase 1, m requests are made for $v_{o_\ell}(v_{o_r})$, i.e, $\sigma_j = v_{o_\ell}(v_{o_r})$ for $j = 1, \dots, m$. Therefore, the m requests of phase 1 are at locations that do not belong to the subtree in which $\mathcal{A}$ has opened a facility in phase 0.

In case $\mathcal{A}$ opens a facility at v_o in phase 0, then m requests are made for either $\sigma_j = v_{o,\ell}$ or $\sigma_j = v_{o,r}$, choice being immaterial, for $j = 1, \dots, m$. Note that the requests made in phase 1 depend on the decisions made by $\mathcal{A}$ in phase 0 which is allowed, since we are considering a deterministic algorithm.

The location (node) of the m identical requests made in phase 1 is recorded as v_1. In subsequent phases $j \ge 2$, m^j identical requests will be made for some particular location, let it be v_j. See Figure 11.1 for reference, where $\mathcal{A}$ opens a facility in the black nodes' subtree in the previous phase, while the grey nodes are the actual locations of requests made in the current phase.

Let at the end of phase $j - 1$, among the two children v_{j-1_ℓ}, v_{j-1_r} of v_{j-1} (request location of phase $j - 1$), let the subtree $T_{v_{j-1_\ell}}$ ($T_{v_{j-1_r}}$) contain no open facility with $\mathcal{A}$.[1] Then in phase $j \le h + 1$, m^j requests are made for location v_{j-1_ℓ} (v_{j-1_r}). It could be that both $T_{v_{j-1_\ell}}$ and $T_{v_{j-1_r}}$ contain no open facility with $\mathcal{A}$, in which case, in phase j, m^j requests are made for either v_{j-1_ℓ} or v_{j-1_r}. For this sequence that depends on the decisions of $\mathcal{A}$, we first upper bound the cost of OPT and then lower bound the cost of $\mathcal{A}$.

OPT : Let OPT open only one facility located at v_h, the location of the m^h requests in phase $h + 1$, which is one of the leaf nodes at level h. Using Proposition 11.2.5, we know that the distance from the location v_j of requests made in phase j to v_h is at most $D\frac{m}{m-1}$, since v_h belongs to the subtree T_{v_j} of v_j for each phase $0 \le j \le h$. Thus, the distance cost (11.1) in each of the first h phases is at most $D\frac{m}{m-1}$ for OPT, while for the last phase, the distance cost is zero, since the request is made for v_h, where OPT opens the facility. Since OPT opens only one facility, the total cost of OPT is at most

$$f + hD\frac{m}{m-1}. \tag{11.3}$$

---

[1] This is true, since, without loss of generality, we are assuming that $\mathcal{A}$ opens only one facility, if at all, in each phase, because, otherwise, the competitive ratio can only be made larger.

$\mathcal{A}$: For $\mathcal{A}$, we next argue that in phase j, either it opens a new facility (which incurs a cost of f) or pays a distance cost of mD to fulfil all the m^j requests made in phase j. If a new facility is opened by $\mathcal{A}$ at v_j, then the facility-opening cost is f while the distance cost is zero. Otherwise, we know that by the construction of the sequence, in phase j at v_j there is no open facility in T_{v_j} with $\mathcal{A}$. Thus, from the second claim of Proposition 11.2.5, to fulfil each of the m^j requests made in phase j, at least a distance cost of $\dfrac{D}{m^{j-1}}$ has to be incurred. Counting the cost over the m^j requests, we get that the cost of $\mathcal{A}$ is phase j when it does not open a new facility is at least Dm. Thus, we get that the cost of $\mathcal{A}$ in phase j is at least $\min\{f, mD\}$. Counting over the $h + 1$ phases, we get the total cost of $\mathcal{A}$ is at least

$$(h + 1)\min\{f, mD\}. \tag{11.4}$$

Recall that we are free to choose m, h, and D, such that the total number of requests $\sum_{j=0}^{h} m^j \leq n$ (total number of requests). Choosing $m = h$ and $D = f/h$, comparing the cost of $\mathcal{A}$ (11.4) and OPT (11.3), we get

$$\mu_{\mathcal{A}} \geq \frac{h}{2}. \tag{11.5}$$

Since $\sum_{j=0}^{h} h^j \leq \dfrac{h^{h+1}}{h-1}$, choosing $h = \dfrac{\log n}{\log \log n}$ satisfies the constraint $\sum_{j=0}^{h} h^j \leq n$. Consequently, from (11.5), we get a lower bound on the competitive ratio of any deterministic algorithm $\mathcal{A}$ to be $\Omega\left(\dfrac{\log n}{\log \log n}\right)$.

Finally, we embed this binary tree over a one-dimensional line segment, as follows. The root is mapped to the centre of the segment. Let v be a vertex at level i mapped to $\tilde{v}$. Then, v's left child is mapped to $\tilde{v} - \dfrac{D}{m^i}$ and v's right child is mapped to $\tilde{v} + \dfrac{D}{m^i}$. It can be shown that, for any $m \geq 4$, this embedding results in a hierarchically well-separated metric space. ∎

Remark 11.2.6 *The lower bound proved in Theorem 11.2.4 applies to randomized algorithms as well, as proved in Problem 11.2.*

Remark 11.2.7 *In Theorem 11.2.4, we have derived the lower bound on the competitive ratio of any deterministic algorithm only for the uniform facility cost case. It turns out that, order-wise, this lower bound cannot be improved or strengthened with non-uniform facility cost, since algorithms with competitive ratio of $\mathcal{O}\left(\dfrac{\log n}{\log \log n}\right)$ are known for the non-uniform facility cost case. We will discuss one algorithm for a non-uniform facility cost case with a competitive ratio of $\mathcal{O}\left(\log n\right)$ in Section 11.2.5.*

Next, we discuss online algorithms to upper bound the competitive ratio for the facility location problem. We begin with a randomized algorithm that is naturally appealing in the way that it balances the facility-opening and the distance cost. A deterministic algorithm will be discussed in Section 11.2.5 for the more general setting of non-uniform facility cost.

11.2.3 Randomized Algorithm for Uniform Facility Cost

With uniform facility cost, we present a simple randomized algorithm in this section, and bound its competitive ratio for both the worst-case and the secretarial inputs.

Algorithm RFL: On arrival of the ith request at location x_i, let $d_i = d(x_i, F_{i-1})$ be the distance of x_i from the nearest open facility in set F_{i-1} just before the arrival of the ith request. Then the algorithm opens a new facility at $y_i = x_i$ with probability $\min\left\{1, \frac{d_i}{f}\right\}$, and assigns the ith request there. Otherwise, the ith request is assigned to the nearest open facility in F_{i-1}. Thus,

$$F_i = \begin{cases} F_{i-1} \cup \{x_i\} & \text{w.p. } \min\left\{1, \frac{d_i}{f}\right\}, \\ F_{i-1} & \text{w.p. } 1 - \min\left\{1, \frac{d_i}{f}\right\}. \end{cases} \tag{11.6}$$

Thus, on the ith request arrival, the expected facility-opening cost is at most d_i, and the expected distance cost is at most the expected facility-opening cost. We make this precise as follows. Let $\Delta_i = C_i - C_{i-1}$ be the expected increase in the cost (11.1) (incremental cost) of the algorithm because of the ith request arrival. Algorithm RFL ensures that

$$\mathbb{E}\{\Delta_i\} \le \frac{d_i}{f} f + \left(1 - \frac{d_i}{f}\right) d_i \le 2d_i. \tag{11.7}$$

Another important property of the algorithm RFL is summarized in the following lemma.

Lemma 11.2.8 *For any m, let m requests arrive at locations $x_i, i = 1, 2, \dots, m$. Let $X = \{x_1, \dots, x_m\}$. The expected distance cost paid by the algorithm RFL before a facility opens at a location in X is less than f.*

Proof: Let

$$X^i = \{x_i, x_{i+1}, \dots, x_m\}$$

be the $m - i + 1$ length suffix of the full sequence X. Let C^i be the expected distance cost paid by the algorithm RFL before a facility opens at any point in X^i, when the input is X^i.

The quantity we are interested in (the expected distance cost paid by the algorithm RFL before a facility opens in X) is C^1. The way we are going to bound C^1 is by writing a recursion for C^i, and iteratively bound C^m, C^{m-1}, and so on.

On arrival of the ith request at location x_i, algorithm RFL opens a new facility with probability $p_i = \min\left\{1, \frac{d_i}{f}\right\}$, where d_i is the distance from x_i to the nearest open facility. Thus, with probability p_i, it incurs a (facility) cost f, and with probability $1 - p_i$ a (distance) cost of $d_i = p_i f$ (where $p_i < 1$), independently of all the other requests $X^1 \backslash \{x_i\}$.

Thus, considering X^m, $C^m = p_m f(1 - p_m)$, since with probability $1 - p_m$ a new facility is not opened and in which case the distance cost is $p_m f$. Similarly, it follows that for $1 \le i \le k \le m$,

$$C^i = \sum_{k=i}^{m} p_k f P_i^k, \tag{11.8}$$

where $P_i^k = \prod_{\ell=i}^{k}(1 - p_\ell)$ is the probability that no facility is opened at any of the request locations $x_i, x_{i+1}, \ldots, x_k$. Let $\hat{C}^i = \frac{C^i}{f}$. From (11.8), it directly follows that

$$\hat{C}^i = (1 - p_i)(p_i + \hat{C}^{i+1}), \qquad (11.9)$$

and $\hat{C}^m = p_m(1 - p_m)$. As $0 \le p_m \le 1$, $p_m(1 - p_m) \le 1/4$ with equality at $p_m = 1/2$. Thus, we get $\hat{C}^m < 1$, which when applied inductively (i.e., $\hat{C}^{i+1} < 1$) on (11.9) gives

$$\hat{C}^i < (1 - p_i)(p_i + 1) = (1 - p_i^2).$$

Since $p_i > 0$, we get $\hat{C}^i < 1$ for all $i = 1, \ldots, m$. Thus, $C^1 = f\hat{C}^1 < f$. ∎

What Lemma 11.2.8 implies is that if the algorithm RFL opens no facilities in X (any set of requests), then the expected distance cost paid by the algorithm over the set of requests X is at most f.

We analyse the RFL algorithm in both the secretarial as well as the adversarial input setting, starting with the secretarial case as follows.

Secretarial Input

In this section, we consider the secretarial input, where the locations x_i of the ith request are chosen adversarially, but the order of arrival of requests is uniformly random. Let $X = (x_1, \ldots, x_n)$ be the locations of the n requests. Then input $\sigma = \pi(X)$, where π is a permutation that is selected uniformly randomly.

With X, consider OPT, and let it open k^* facilities located at $c_1^*, \ldots, c_{k^*}^*$. We will concentrate on any one such facility c^* and call the subset of requests among X assigned by OPT to c^* as X_{c^*}. For any $x_i \in X_{c^*}$, let the distance of x_i to c^* be d_i^*, and the sum of the distances, and the average distance of requests in X_{c^*} from c^* be $S_{c^*} = \sum_{x_i \in X_{c^*}} d_i^*$ and $A_{c^*} = \frac{S_{c^*}}{|X_{c^*}|}$, respectively.

Definition 11.2.9 *A request $x_i \in X_{c^*}$ is called **good** if it is among the closest half of the requests in X_{c^*} from c^*. A request that is not **good** is called **bad**. Thus, all good requests belong to $\mathcal{B}(c^*, 2A_{c^*})$, where $\mathcal{B}(c, r)$ is a ball centred at c with radius r.*

Lemma 11.2.10 *The total expected cost of good requests $x_i \in X_{c^*}$ with algorithm RFL is*

$$\sum_{\{x_i \in X_{c^*} : x_i \text{ is good}\}} \mathbb{E}\{\Delta_i\} \le 2f + 2S_{c^*} + 2 \sum_{\{x_i \in X_{c^*} : x_i \text{ is good}\}} d_i^*.$$

Moreover, this holds independent of the order in which the requests arrive.

Proof: Consider all the requests of X that are within a distance of $2A_{c^*}$ from c^*, i.e., $X \cap \mathcal{B}(c^*, 2A_{c^*})$, and let $X(c^*, 2A_{c^*}) = X \cap \mathcal{B}(c^*, 2A_{c^*})$.

Case I: Let algorithm RFL open no facility among the requests in $X(c^*, 2A_{c^*})$. In this case, the total expected cost accrued by all the requests of $X(c^*, 2A_{c^*})$ is at most f from Lemma 11.2.8. From Definition 11.2.9, all good requests are within a distance of $2A_{c^*}$ from c^*, i.e., $\{x_i \in X_{c^*} : x_i \text{ is good}\} \subseteq X(c^*, 2A_{c^*})$. Therefore, if algorithm RFL opens no facility among the requests in $X(c^*, 2A_{c^*})$, then algorithm RFL opens no facility at any of the good requests of X_{c^*}, and hence the total expected cost accrued by all good requests of X_{c^*} is at most f from Lemma 11.2.8.

Case II: Algorithm RFL opens a facility on the tth request (for some t before all good requests arrive) within a distance of $2A_{c*}$ from c^*. From Lemma 11.2.8, the total expected cost accrued by all the requests of $X(c^*, 2A_{c*})$ is at most f before a facility is opened by algorithm RFL, and a cost of f is paid to open the facility on the tth request's arrival. Thus, the total expected cost incurred before the arrival of the $t + 1^{st}$ request is at most $2f$.

From here on, we assume that there is an open facility within a distance of $2A_{c*}$ from c^*, and consider any good request of X_{c*} that arrives subsequently. Using the triangle inequality, it follows that the distance of any good request $x_i \in X_{c*}$ from the nearest open facility is at most $2A_{c*} + d_i^*$, as shown in Figure 11.2. From (11.7), we get that the incremental cost of any good request that arrives after the tth request is $\mathbb{E}\{\Delta_i\} \leq 2(2A_{c*} + d_i^*)$. Counting over all the good requests that arrive after the tth request, the expected cost of RFL is then

$$\leq \sum_{\{x_i \in X_{c*} : x_i \text{ is good}\}} 2(2A_{c*} + d_i^*),$$

$$\leq 2S_{c*} + \sum_{\{x_i \in X_{c*} : x_i \text{ is good}\}} 2d_i^*,$$

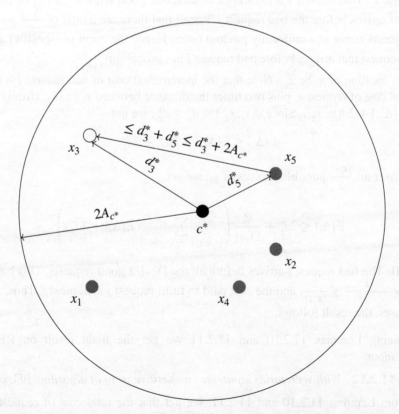

Figure 11.2 Black node is the facility opened at c^* by OPT, while empty circle node (request) x_3 is the facility opened by the RFL algorithm within a distance of $2A_{c*}$ from c^*. The request arriving after x_3, x_4, and x_5 are at most at a distance of $d_3^* + 2A_{c*}$ from x_3.

where the second inequality follows by using the definition $A_{c^*} = \frac{S_{c^*}}{|X_{c^*}|}$, and the fact that there are $|X_{c^*}|/2$ good requests.

Thus, accounting for both the cases, the total expected cost of RFL for good requests is at most

$$\sum_{\{x_i \in X_{c^*} : x_i \text{ is good}\}} \mathbb{E}\{\Delta_i\} \leq 2f + 2S_{c^*} + \sum_{\{x_i \in X_{c^*} : x_i \text{ is good}\}} 2d_i^*.$$

∎

Next, we bound the cost of bad requests, which is where we need the secretarial input condition.

Lemma 11.2.11 *The expected cost of any bad request $x_i \in X_{c^*}$ with algorithm RFL is*

$$\mathbb{E}\{\Delta_i\} \leq 2d_i^* + \frac{2}{|X_{c^*}|} \left(f + \sum_{\{x_j \in X_{c^*} : x_j \text{ is good}\}} (\mathbb{E}\{\Delta_j\} + 2d_j^*) \right).$$

Proof: Case I : Bad request i arrives after at least one good request. Let g_i be the last good request that arrives before the bad request i. Recall that there are a total of $\frac{|X_{c^*}|}{2}$ good requests and all requests arrive in a uniformly random order. Hence the event of (specific) g_i being the last good request that arrives before bad request i has probability $\frac{2}{|X_{c^*}|}$.

Let the location of g_i be x_{g_i}. Note that the incremental cost of bad request i is at most the incremental cost of request g_i plus two times the distance between x_i and x_{g_i} (from (11.7)), i.e., $\mathbb{E}\{\Delta_i\} \leq \mathbb{E}\{\Delta_{g_i}\} + 2d(x_i, x_{g_i})$. Since $d(x_i, x_{g_i}) \leq d_i^* + d_{g_i}^*$, we get

$$\mathbb{E}\{\Delta_i\} \leq \mathbb{E}\{\Delta_{g_i}\} + 2d_{g_i}^* + 2d_i^*.$$

Summing over all $\frac{|X_{c^*}|}{2}$ possible choices of g_i, we get

$$\mathbb{E}\{\Delta_i\} \leq 2d_i^* + \frac{2}{|X_{c^*}|} \left(\sum_{\{x_j \in X_{c^*} : x_j \text{ is good}\}} (\mathbb{E}\{\Delta_j\} + 2d_j^*) \right).$$

Case II: The bad request i arrives before all the $|X_{c^*}|/2$ good requests. This happens with probability $\frac{1}{|X_{c^*}|/2+1} \leq \frac{2}{|X_{c^*}|}$, and the cost paid to fulfil request i is at most f. Thus, accounting for both cases, the result follows. ∎

Combining Lemmas 11.2.10 and 11.2.11 we get the main result on RFL for the secretarial input.

Theorem 11.2.12 *With secretarial input, the competitive ratio of algorithm RFL is at most 8.*

Proof: From Lemmas 11.2.10 and 11.2.11, we get that the total cost of requests with the algorithm RFL assigned to facility c^* by the OPT is at most

$$\sum_{\{x_i \in X_{c^*} : x_i \text{ is good}\}} \mathbb{E}\{\Delta_i\} + \sum_{\{x_j \in X_{c^*} : x_j \text{is bad}\}} \mathbb{E}\{\Delta_j\} \leq 5f + 6S_{c^*} + 4 \sum_{\{x_i \in X_{c^*} : x_i \text{ is good}\}} d_i^*, \quad (11.10)$$

by using the fact that

$$\sum_{\{x_i \in X_{c^*} \,:\, x_i \text{ is good}\}} d_i^* + \sum_{\{x_j \in X_{c^*} \,:\, x_j \text{ is bad}\}} d_j^* = S_{c^*}.$$

By the definition of good requests, $\sum_{\{x_i \in X_{c^*} \,:\, x_i \text{ is good}\}} d_i^* \leq \frac{S_{c^*}}{2}$. Using this, from (11.10), we get that the total cost of requests with the algorithm RFL assigned to facility c^* by the OPT is at most

$$5f + 8S_{c^*}.$$

Recall that by definition of c^* and X_{c^*}, the cost of OPT with respect to c^* is $f + S_{c^*}$. Since the above argument is true for each facility c^* opened by OPT, we get

$$\mu_{\text{RFL}} = \frac{C_{\text{RFL}}}{C_{\text{OPT}}} \leq \frac{8(\sum_{i=1}^{k^*} f + S_{c_i^*})}{\sum_{i=1}^{k^*} f + S_{c_i^*}} \leq 8,$$

where k^* is the total number of facilities opened by OPT. ∎

11.2.4 Adversarial Input

In this section, we consider the adversarial input request sequence X, and show the following result for the algorithm RFL.

Theorem 11.2.13 *The competitive ratio of algorithm RFL with the worst-case input request sequence is at most $\mathcal{O}(\log n)$.*

The proof idea is similar to Theorem 11.2.12, where we will concentrate on any one facility c^* opened by OPT, and bound the expected cost of all requests assigned to c^* by OPT with the algorithm RFL. For the proof, whenever we use the term *cost*, it means the expected cost.

Proof: As before, consider one of the facilities c^* opened by OPT, and let the set of requests of X assigned to c^* by OPT be denoted as X_{c^*}. Recall that the sum of the distances, and the average distance of requests in X_{c^*} from c^* be $S_{c^*} = \sum_{x_i \in X_{c^*}} d_i^*$ and $A_{c^*} = \frac{S_{c^*}}{|X_{c^*}|}$, respectively.

Consider the annuli centred at c^*

$$\mathsf{A}_{c^*}(\alpha) = \mathcal{B}(c^*, 2^\alpha A_{c^*}) \backslash \mathcal{B}(c^*, 2^{\alpha-1} A_{c^*}), \quad \alpha = 1, \ldots, \log n, \tag{11.11}$$

as shown in Figure 11.3, and let the set of requests falling in $\mathsf{A}_{c^*}(\alpha)$ be denoted as $X_{c^*}^\alpha$. We leave it as an exercise in Problem 11.3, to show that $\mathsf{A}_{c^*}(\alpha)$ for $\alpha > \log n$ will contain no requests belonging to X_{c^*}, and hence restrict our attention to $\alpha \leq \log n$.

Consider an annulus $\mathsf{A}_{c^*}(\alpha)$ for any $\alpha = 1, \ldots, \log n$. From Lemma 11.2.8, the distance cost paid by all requests with locations belonging to $\mathsf{A}_{c^*}(\alpha)$ before a facility is opened by the algorithm RFL is less than f. Let algorithm RFL open a facility in $\mathsf{A}_{c^*}(\alpha)$ on the tth request arrival. Thus, the total cost until this point is at most $2f$. Let the location of the open facility in $\mathsf{A}_{c^*}(\alpha)$ be x_t^α. Clearly, x_t^α is at a distance of at most $2^\alpha A_{c^*}$ from c^*. Therefore, the $r^{th}, r > t$, request at location x_r belonging to $\mathsf{A}_{c^*}(\alpha)$ can be assigned to x_t^α, and the distance between x_r and x_t^α is at most $3d_r^*$, where $2^{\alpha-1}A_{c^*} \leq d_r^* \leq 2^\alpha A_{c^*}$ is the distance of x_r from c^*. See Figure 11.3 for reference.

Thus, the cost of assigning request x_r is at most $6d_r^*$ from (11.7). Thus, for all requests falling in $\mathsf{A}_{c^*}(\alpha)$ for $\alpha = 1, \ldots, \log n$, the total cost is at most $2f + \sum_{r:x_r \in \mathsf{A}_{c^*}(\alpha)} 6d_r^*$. Summing over all the $\log n$ annuli, we get that the total cost $\leq 2f \log n + \sum_{\alpha=1}^{\log n} \sum_{r:x_r \in \mathsf{A}_{c^*}(\alpha)} 6d_r^*$.

Only one region remains to be considered, the innermost disc $\mathcal{B}(c^*, A_{c^*})$. Similar to above, the cost paid by algorithm RFL before a facility opens in $\mathcal{B}(c^*, A_{c^*})$ is at most f (Lemma 11.2.8). Once a facility is opened in $\mathcal{B}(c^*, A_{c^*})$, the distance cost paid for assigning any future request at location $x_m \in \mathcal{B}(c^*, A_{c^*})$ by the RFL algorithm is at most $2(d_m^* + A_{c^*})$ (11.7).

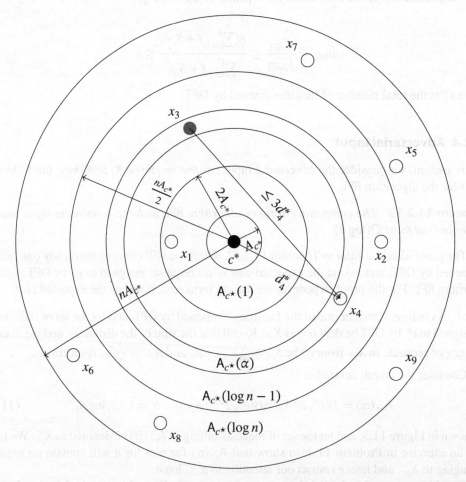

Figure 11.3 Black node is c^*, the facility opened by OPT, while the grey node (request) x_3 is the first facility opened by the RFL algorithm in $\mathsf{A}_{c^*}(\alpha)$. Let any future request belonging to $\mathsf{A}_{c^*}(\alpha)$ e.g., x_4 be at a distance of d_4^* from c^*. Then from the definition of $\mathsf{A}_{c^*}(\alpha) = \mathcal{B}(c^*, 2^\alpha A_{c^*}) \backslash \mathcal{B}(c, 2^{\alpha-1}A_{c^*})$, the distance between c^* and x_3 is at most $2d_4^*$. Thus, the distance between x_3 and x_4 is at most $3d_4^*$.

Adding the cost for requests falling in $\mathcal{B}(c^*, A_{c^*})$ and the annuli $A_{c^*}(\alpha)$ for $\alpha = 1, \ldots, \log n$, we get that the total cost for algorithm is at most $2f(1 + \log n) + 6S_{c^*} + 2S_{c^*}$. By definition, the cost paid by OPT for all requests assigned to c^* is at least $f + S_{c^*}$. Since the above argument holds, for each c^*, we get that the competitive ratio of algorithm RFL is $\mathcal{O}(\log n)$ with the worst-case input request sequence. ∎

11.2.5 Location-Dependent Facility Cost

In the previous section, we considered the case where the facility-opening cost was independent of the location at which it was opened. A more general model for the facility location problem allows the cost of opening a facility at location x to be equal to f_x. Under this setting, the modified objective function after the arrival of the ith request, compared to (11.1), is

$$C_i = \sum_{j=1}^{|F_i|} f_{y_j} + \sum_{k=1}^{i} d(x_k, F_k), \tag{11.12}$$

where F_k is the set of open facilities after the arrival of the $k^{th}, k \leq i$ request, and the location of the open facilities in set F_k is denoted by $y_1, y_2, \ldots, y_{|F_k|}$. As before, with complete input, $\sigma = (x_1, \ldots, x_n)$ having n requests, the total cost of an online algorithm $\mathcal{A}$ is then just $C_n^{\mathcal{A}}(\sigma)$.

Algorithm POTENTIALUPDATE

In this subsection, we present a deterministic online algorithm whose basic idea is as follows.

Let X be the locations of the set of requests that have arrived so far, and F be the set of facilities that are open. For each $x \in X$, $d(x, F)$ is the distance to the nearest open facility in F, while $d(x, z)$ is the distance to the point z. For each point $z \in \mathcal{M}$, define a potential

$$p(z) = \sum_{x \in X} (d(x, F) - d(x, z))^+,$$

where $(a)^+ = \max\{a, 0\}$. Let the contribution of $x \in X$ to potential $p(z)$ be $p_x(z) = (d(x, F) - d(x, z))^+$. If a new facility is opened at z, distance cost $d(x, F)$ changes to $d(x, F \cup \{z\})$, where $d(x, F \cup \{z\}) \leq d(x, F)$.

One can think of $d(x, F)$ as the credit owed by request x, which decreases on account of opening a new facility. The potential of each point z corresponds to the decrease in the requests' credit if a facility at z opens.

This algorithm proceeds as follows.

Algorithm POTENTIALUPDATE: On the arrival of a new request, consider opening a new facility at all points $z \in \mathcal{M}$ for which the decrease in the requests' credit $p(z)$ exceeds the corresponding opening cost. Among all such points, open a facility at the point that maximizes the difference. In particular, when a new request arrives, the algorithm updates the potential of all points $z \in \mathcal{M}$ and computes the point $z^\star$ maximizing $p(z) - f_z$. If $p(z^\star) > f_{z^\star}$, the algorithm opens a new facility at $z^\star$ and updates the potentials. If $p(z^\star) \leq f_{z^\star}$, no new facility opens. In either case, the newly arrived request is assigned to the nearest facility in the updated facility configuration. The pseudo code is given in Algorithm 19.

Algorithm 19 POTENTIALUPDATE

Initialize $F = \emptyset, X = \emptyset, p(z) = 0 \; \forall z \in \mathcal{M}$ %$p(z)$ is potential for point z
for on arrival of each new request at location x **do**
　　$X = X \cup \{x\}$
　　For all $z \in \mathcal{M}, p(z) = p(z) + (d(x, F) - d(x, z))^+$
　　$z^\star \leftarrow \arg\max_{z \in \mathcal{M}}(p(z) - f_z)$
　　if $p(z^\star) - f_{z^\star} > 0$ **then**
　　　　$F \leftarrow F \cup \{z^\star\}$
　　　　For all $z \in \mathcal{M}, p(z) = \sum_{x \in X}(d(x, F) - d(x, z))^+$
　　end if
　　Assign x to the nearest facility in F
end for

Theorem 11.2.14 *The competitive ratio of algorithm* POTENTIALUPDATE *is at most* $4(\log n + 1) + 2$, *with location-dependent facility cost under the adversarial model.*

We will prove Theorem 11.2.14 in Problem 11.8 by breaking it into multiple sub-problems.

11.3 k-Means Clustering

In this section, we discuss a problem closely related to the facility location problem, called the **k-means clustering**, that is a very important problem for practical applications, e.g., in unsupervised learning. Similar to the facility location problem, with k-means clustering, a set of n requests arrive online, where the ith request arrives at location $x_i \in \mathcal{M}$. We will restrict ourselves to $\mathcal{M}$ being a Euclidean space in this section.

Let the complete input be $\sigma = (x_1, \ldots, x_n)$, and $\sigma^i = (x_1, \ldots, x_i)$ be its i-length prefix. Just before the arrival of the ith request, let the first $i - 1$ requests be partitioned into k_{i-1} clusters represented by $\mathcal{C}_1, \ldots, \mathcal{C}_{k_{i-1}}$, i.e., $\cup_{i=1}^{k_{i-1}} \mathcal{C}_i = \sigma^i$ and $\mathcal{C}_i \cap \mathcal{C}_j = \emptyset$. The cost of the mth cluster $1 \leq m \leq k_{i-1}$ is defined as

$$D_m = \sum_{x_j \in \mathcal{C}_m} \|x_j - c_m\|_2^2, \tag{11.13}$$

where $c_m = \frac{1}{|\mathcal{C}_m|} \sum_{x_j \in \mathcal{C}_m} x_j$ is the (geometric) centre of cluster m. D_m should be interpreted as the squared distance cost of requests assigned to cluster $\mathcal{C}_m$ from its centre c_m.

On the arrival of each new request, an online algorithm must either add it to one of the existing clusters or open a new cluster, consisting of a single point (the newly arrived request), irrevocably. In the former case $\mathcal{C}_m = \mathcal{C}_m \cup \{x_i\}$ for some $m \in \{1, \ldots, k_{i-1}\}$, while in the latter case $\mathcal{C}_m = \mathcal{C}_m, m \in \{1, \ldots, k_{i-1}\}$ and $\mathcal{C}_{k_i} = \{x_i\}$. Consequently, the cost of clusters $D_m, m \leq k_i$ is updated appropriately.

With input σ, the cost function for algorithm $\mathcal{A}$ is

$$\mathsf{D}^{\mathcal{A}}(\sigma) = \sum_{m=1}^{k_{\mathcal{A}}} \mathsf{D}_m(\sigma), \tag{11.14}$$

where $k_{\mathcal{A}}$ is the total number of clusters created by algorithm $\mathcal{A}$.

With k-means clustering problem, k is the maximum allowable number of clusters. Thus, for any online algorithm $\mathcal{A}$, $k_{\mathcal{A}} \leq k$. Let for OPT, its cost be

$$\mathsf{D}^{\mathsf{OPT}}(\sigma) \tag{11.15}$$

with at most k clusters. The competitive ratio for $\mathcal{A}$ is defined as usual as

$$\mu_{\mathcal{A}}(\sigma) = \max_{\sigma} \frac{\mathsf{D}^{\mathcal{A}}(\sigma)}{\mathsf{D}^{\mathsf{OPT}}(\sigma)}. \tag{11.16}$$

Connection to the Facility Location Problem: The cluster centres of the k-means clustering problem correspond to the location of an open facility in the facility location problem. The cost D_m of cluster m with k-means clustering is similar to the distance cost for the facility location problem; however, there is no 'exogenous' cost for opening a new cluster or centre with the k-means problem. Without any cost for opening a new cluster or centre, ideally an algorithm should open as many clusters or centres as the number of requests to minimize the cluster cost (11.13). That is, however, precluded by an upper bound (k) on the number of maximum clusters. Thus, with k-means clustering, there is an intrinsic cost to opening a new cluster – on the arrival of a new request if a new cluster is opened, it does not increase the distance cost; however, it limits the ability of an algorithm to open more clusters in future depending on the input request sequence. Given an upper limit on the number of clusters that can be created, an online algorithm has to be judicious in opening a new cluster, similar to the decision about opening a new facility for the facility location problem.

In Problem 11.9, using a very simple input arrival sequence, we show that an online algorithm for solving the k-means clustering problem must either create an unbounded number of clusters or incur an unbounded competitive ratio (11.16) if at most k clusters are allowed to be created. Therefore, in the rest of this section, we allow an online algorithm $\mathcal{A}$ to create $k_{\mathcal{A}} \geq k$ clusters, and the quest is to find $\mathcal{A}$ that has a small competitive ratio while using as small number of clusters $k_{\mathcal{A}}$ as possible.

To describe the main ideas, we first consider a semi-online setting, where an algorithm $\mathcal{A}$ is aware of the total number of requests n, and a lower bound $\mathsf{d}^{\mathsf{OPT}}$ on the optimal cost $\mathsf{D}^{\mathsf{OPT}}$ (11.15).

The basic idea of algorithm SEMIONLINE (Algorithm 20) is similar to the RFL algorithm, where a cost f of creating a new cluster is defined, and on the arrival of a new request at location x_i, a new cluster is created with probability

$$\min \left\{ \frac{d^2(x_i, \mathsf{ClusCent}^{-x_i})}{f}, 1 \right\},$$

where ClusCent^{-x_i} is the current set of locations of the cluster centres just before the arrival of a request at x_i and $d(x, S)$ is as defined in Definition 11.2.1. In contrast to the RFL algorithm, where cost f is a constant, in algorithm SEMIONLINE, the cost f is doubled at the end of a phase, where in each phase, $3k(1 + \log n)$ new clusters are created. The doubling of cost f in each phase is chosen to restrict the total number of clusters created. The cost f is intialized to $\dfrac{\mathsf{d}^{\text{OPT}}}{k \log n}$, which is possible since both d^{OPT} and n are known to the algorithm.

Algorithm 20 SEMIONLINE

Input $k, \mathsf{d}^{\text{OPT}}, n$;   %$\mathsf{d}^{\text{OPT}}$ is a lower bound on optimal cost D^{OPT}

Initialize $\text{ClusCent} = \varnothing, \ell = 1, q_1 = 0, f_1 = \dfrac{\mathsf{d}^{\text{OPT}}}{k \log n}$

for each new request located at x **do**

    with probability $p = \min\left\{\dfrac{d^2(x, \text{ClusCent}^{-x_i})}{f\ell}, 1\right\}$

    create a new cluster centre at x, i.e., $\text{ClusCent} = \text{ClusCent} \cup \{x\}, q_\ell = q_\ell + 1$

    if $q_\ell \geq 3k(1 + \log n)$ **then**

        $\ell = \ell + 1, q_\ell = 0, f_\ell = 2f_{\ell-1}$;

    end if

    Assign x to the cluster with the nearest cluster centre in ClusCent

end for

Algorithm SEMIONLINE is a randomized algorithm, and the number of phases ℓ it runs for and the number of clusters it creates are both random variables. Let L be the phase index when algorithm SEMIONLINE terminates, and ClusCent^L be the final set of cluster centres created by algorithm SEMIONLINE. Let D^{so} be the cost (11.14) of the algorithm SEMIONLINE.

We show the following two results for algorithm SEMIONLINE, which imply that it has order-wise the same cost as OPT, while opens a multiplicative factor $(\log n) \log\left(\dfrac{\mathsf{D}^{\text{OPT}}}{\mathsf{d}^{\text{OPT}}}\right)$ more clusters than OPT.

Theorem 11.3.1

$$\mathbb{E}\{|\text{ClusCent}^L|\} = \mathcal{O}\left(k \log n \log \frac{\mathsf{D}^{\text{OPT}}}{\mathsf{d}^{\text{OPT}}}\right),$$

where D^{OPT} is the optimal cost, while d^{OPT} is a lower bound on D^{OPT}.

Theorem 11.3.2

$$\mathbb{E}\{\mathsf{D}^{\text{so}}\} = \mathcal{O}\left(\mathsf{D}^{\text{OPT}}\right).$$

To prove these two theorems, we need the following preliminaries. Recall that OPT creates exactly k-clusters. Let OPT create clusters $\mathcal{C}_1^*, \dots, \mathcal{C}_k^*$ with centres $\text{ClusCent}^{\text{OPT}} = \{c_1^*, \dots, c_k^*\}$, and let OPT's cost be

$$\mathsf{D}^{\text{OPT}} = \sum_{j=1}^{k} \mathsf{D}_j^{\text{OPT}}, \quad \mathsf{D}_j^{\text{OPT}} = \sum_{x_i \in \mathcal{C}_j^*} \left\| x_i - c_j^* \right\|_2^2,$$

where $\mathsf{D}_j^{\text{OPT}}$ is the cost of the jth cluster created by OPT.

Recall that $X = \{x_1, \ldots, x_n\}$ is the set of locations of all the requests. Similar to Section 11.2.4, consider a single cluster centre c^* opened by OPT, and let the subset of requests of X assigned to c^* by OPT be denoted as X_{c^*}. Note that in contrast to Section 11.2.4, here the object of interest is squared distance and not the distance. Thus, with abuse of notation, let $d_i^* = \|x_i - c^*\|_2^2$ for $x_i \in X_{c^*}$. Then, similar to previous sections, let the sum of the squared distances, and the average squared distance of requests in X_{c^*} from c^* be $S_{c^*} = \sum_{x_i \in X_{c^*}} d_i^*$ and $A_{c^*} = \frac{S_{c^*}}{|X_{c^*}|}$ respectively.

Consider the annuli

$$A_{c^*}(0) = \mathcal{B}(c^*, A_{c^*}) \tag{11.17}$$

and

$$A_{c^*}(\alpha) = \mathcal{B}(c^*, 2^\alpha A_{c^*}) \setminus \mathcal{B}(c^*, 2^{\alpha-1} A_{c^*}), \tag{11.18}$$

as shown in Figure 11.3, where $\alpha = 1, \ldots, \log n$, and let the set of requests of X_{c^*} belonging to (falling in) $A_{c^*}(\alpha)$ be $X_{c^*}(\alpha)$. As discussed in Section 11.2.4 and Problem 11.3, $A_{c^*}(\alpha)$ for $\alpha > \log n + 1$ is empty.

Proof: [Proof of Theorem 11.3.1] By the definition of algorithm SEMIONLINE, the cost f_ℓ is doubled in each phase, where the initial value of $f_1 = \frac{\mathsf{d}^{\mathsf{OPT}}}{k \log n}$. Consider the earliest phase ℓ' of algorithm SEMIONLINE, such that the cost

$$f_{\ell'} \geq \frac{\mathsf{D}^{\mathsf{OPT}}}{k \log n}.$$

Without loss of generality, assuming $\frac{\mathsf{D}^{\mathsf{OPT}}}{k \log n} = 2^z f_1$ for some $z \in \mathbb{N}$, we have $\ell' \leq \log\left(\frac{\mathsf{D}^{\mathsf{OPT}}}{\mathsf{d}^{\mathsf{OPT}}}\right)$. Moreover, in each phase, the number of clusters created is exactly $3k(1 + \log n)$. Thus, until phase ℓ', the total number of clusters created by algorithm SEMIONLINE is at most

$$3k(1 + \log n)\ell' = O\left(k \log n \log \frac{\mathsf{D}^{\mathsf{OPT}}}{\mathsf{d}^{\mathsf{OPT}}}\right). \tag{11.19}$$

Next, we consider phases $\ell' \leq \ell \leq L$, where recall that L is the phase index when algorithm SEMIONLINE terminates. Consider one cluster C_j^* created by OPT with centre c_j^* for some $1 \leq j \leq k$. Consider the annulus $A_{c_j^*}(\alpha)$, and let $X_{c_j^*}(\alpha) \subseteq X_{c_j^*}$ be the subset of requests among $X_{c_j^*}$ that belong to annulus $A_{c_j^*}(\alpha)$. Moreover, let $X_{c_j^*}(\alpha, \ell) \subseteq X_{c_j^*}(\alpha)$ be the subset of requests that arrive when algorithm SEMIONLINE is in phase $\ell \geq \ell'$. Suppose algorithm SEMIONLINE creates a new cluster on the arrival of a request at location $x \in X_{c_j^*}(\alpha, \ell)$ at x. Then the probability that a new cluster is created on the arrival of a future request $y \in X_{c_j^*}(\alpha, \ell)$ at y by algorithm SEMIONLINE is at most $\frac{\|x-y\|^2}{f_\ell}$.

Using the triangle inequality, we can bound

$$
\frac{\|x - y\|^2}{f_e} \leq \frac{2\|x - c_j^*\|^2 + 2\|y - c_j^*\|^2}{f_e},
$$

$$
\leq \frac{4 \cdot 2^\alpha A_{c_j^*}}{f_e}, \tag{11.20}
$$

since $A_{c_j^*}$ is the average distance of requests in cluster C_j^* with centre c_j^*, and $\|x - c_j^*\|^2 \leq 2^\alpha A_{c_j^*}$ for any $x \in X_{c_j^*}(\alpha)$.

Thus, the expected number of clusters created by algorithm SEMIONLINE for requests belonging to $X_{c_j^*}(\alpha)$ in phases after phase $\ell' - 1$ is

$$
\leq 1 + \sum_{\ell \geq \ell'} \frac{4 \cdot 2^\alpha A_{c_j^*}}{f_e} |X_{c_j^*}(\alpha, \ell)|,
$$

where the 1 corresponds to the first cluster created at any request location of $X_{c_j^*}(\alpha)$.

Thus, the expected number of clusters $\mathbb{E}\{|\mathsf{ClusCent}^{\geq \ell'}(c_j^*)|\}$ created for requests belonging to $X_{c_j^*}$ (by summing over all $\alpha = 0, \ldots, \log n$) by algorithm SEMIONLINE in phases $\ell \geq \ell'$ can be bounded as follows:

$$
\mathbb{E}\{|\mathsf{ClusCent}^{\geq \ell'}(c_j^*)|\} \leq \sum_{\alpha \geq 0} \left(1 + \sum_{\ell \geq \ell'} \frac{4 \cdot 2^\alpha A_{c_j^*} |X_{c_j^*}(\alpha, \ell)|}{f_e} \right),
$$

$$
\overset{(a)}{\leq} (1 + \log n) + \sum_{\alpha \geq 0} 4 \cdot 2^\alpha A_{c_j^*} \sum_{\ell \geq \ell'} \frac{|X_{c_j^*}(\alpha, \ell)|}{f_e},
$$

$$
\overset{(b)}{\leq} (1 + \log n) + \sum_{\alpha \geq 0} 4 \cdot 2^\alpha A_{c_j^*} \frac{|X_{c_j^*}(\alpha)|}{f_{e'}},
$$

$$
\overset{(c)}{\leq} (1 + \log n) + 4 A_{c^*} \frac{|X_{c_j^*}(0)|}{f_{e'}} + \frac{8}{f_{e'}} \sum_{\alpha \geq 1} 2^{\alpha - 1} A_{c_j^*} |X_{c_j^*}(\alpha)|,
$$

$$
\overset{(d)}{\leq} (1 + \log n) + 4 A_{c_j^*} \frac{|X_{c_j^*}|}{f_{e'}} + \frac{8}{f_{e'}} \sum_{\alpha \geq 1} \sum_{x \in X_{c_j^*}(\alpha)} \|x - c_j^*\|^2,
$$

$$
\overset{(e)}{\leq} (1 + \log n) + \frac{4 D_j^{\mathsf{OPT}}}{f_{e'}} + \frac{8 D_j^{\mathsf{OPT}}}{f_{e'}},
$$

$$
= (1 + \log n) + \frac{12 D_j^{\mathsf{OPT}}}{f_{e'}}, \tag{11.21}
$$

where (a) follows since the number of annuli A_α satisfies $\alpha \leq 1 + \log n$, (b) follows by lower bounding $f_\ell \geq f_{\ell'}$ for $\ell \geq \ell'$ since cost f doubles in each phase, and $\sum_{\ell \geq \ell'} |X_{c_j^*}(\alpha, \ell)| \leq |X_{c_j^*}(\alpha)|$. Inequality (c) follows by separating the $\alpha = 0$ term and the rest, while inequality (d) follows by upper bounding $|X_{c_j^*}(0)| \leq |X_{c_j^*}|$, and $2^{\alpha-1} A_{c_j^*} |X_{c_j^*}(\alpha)| \leq \sum_{x \in X_{c_j^*}} ||x - c_j^*||^2$ which follows by the definition of $A_{c_j^*}$. Inequality (e) is obtained by using $A_{c_j^*} |X_{c_j^*}| = \mathsf{D}_j^{\mathsf{OPT}}$ and $\sum_{\alpha \geq 1} \sum_{x \in X_{c_j^*}(\alpha)} ||x - c_j^*||^2 \leq \mathsf{D}_j^{\mathsf{OPT}}$.

Thus, the expected number of clusters $\mathbb{E}\{|\mathsf{ClusCent}^{\geq \ell'}(c_j^*)|\}$ created by algorithm SEMIONLINE after phase $\ell' - 1$ corresponding to requests belonging to cluster $\mathcal{C}_j^*$ with centre c_j^* is at most $(1 + \log n) + \dfrac{12\mathsf{D}_j^{\mathsf{OPT}}}{f_{\ell'}}$. Adding over the k clusters created by OPT, and using the fact that $\mathsf{D}^{\mathsf{OPT}} = \sum_{j=1}^{k} \mathsf{D}_j^{\mathsf{OPT}}$, from (11.21) we get

$$\sum_{j=1}^{k} \mathbb{E}\{|\mathsf{ClusCent}^{\geq \ell'}(c_j^*)|\} \leq k(1 + \log n) + \frac{12\mathsf{D}^{\mathsf{OPT}}}{f_{\ell'}}. \tag{11.22}$$

Moreover, using the fact that by the choice of ℓ', $f_{\ell'} \geq \dfrac{\mathsf{D}^{\mathsf{OPT}}}{k \log n}$, we get

$$\sum_{j=1}^{k} \mathbb{E}\{|\mathsf{ClusCent}^{\geq \ell'}|\} \leq k(1 + \log n) + 12k \log n. \tag{11.23}$$

From (11.19), the expected number of clusters created by algorithm SEMIONLINE corresponding to requests belonging to cluster $\mathcal{C}_j^*$ with centre c_j^* before phase ℓ' is at most $\mathcal{O}\left(k \log n \log \dfrac{\mathsf{D}^{\mathsf{OPT}}}{\mathsf{d}^{\mathsf{OPT}}}\right)$. Combining this with (11.23), we get that the expected number of clusters created by algorithm SEMIONLINE is

$$\mathbb{E}\{|\mathsf{ClusCent}^{L}|\} = \mathcal{O}\left(k \log n \log \frac{\mathsf{D}^{\mathsf{OPT}}}{\mathsf{d}^{\mathsf{OPT}}}\right) + \mathcal{O}\left(k \log n\right),$$

$$= \mathcal{O}\left(k \log n \log \frac{\mathsf{D}^{\mathsf{OPT}}}{\mathsf{d}^{\mathsf{OPT}}}\right). \tag{11.24}$$

∎

Next, we prove Theorem 11.3.2 with the help of Lemma 11.2.8.

Proof: [Proof of Theorem 11.3.2] Similar to the proof of Theorem 11.3.1, we will count the total cost of requests in $X_{c_j^*}(\alpha)$ defined for OPT by dividing them into two stages. The first stage is until the first cluster centre is created by algorithm SEMIONLINE for requests belonging to $X_{c^*}(\alpha)$, and the second stage for requests that arrive thereafter.

Stage I. On the arrival of a new request $x \in X_{c^*}(\alpha)$ in phase ℓ, a new cluster is created with probability at least $\min\left\{\frac{d^2(x, \text{ClusCent}^{-x})}{f_L}, 1\right\}$, where L is the phase in which algorithm SEMIONLINE terminates as $f_\ell \leq f_L$, and ClusCent^{-x} is the set of cluster centres created by algorithm SEMIONLINE just before the arrival of the request located at x. Thus, from Lemma 11.2.8, the expected cost paid by all the requests belonging to $X_{c^*}(\alpha)$ with algorithm SEMIONLINE until the first cluster is created at some location of $X_{c^*}(\alpha)$ is at most

$$f_L. \tag{11.25}$$

Stage II. Let $x \in X_{c_j^*}(\alpha)$ be the location of the first request that creates a new cluster centre in $X_{c_j^*}(\alpha)$. Then, similar to (11.20), the cost paid by any request located at $y \in X_{c_j^*}(\alpha)$ that arrives after the request with location x is at most

$$\|x - y\|_2^2 \leq 4.2^\alpha A_{c_j^*}. \tag{11.26}$$

Summing (11.25) and (11.26), over all the $1 + \log n$ annuli for $0 \leq \alpha \leq \log n$, and the k clusters created by OPT, $1 \leq j \leq k$, the expected cost paid by all the requests with algorithm SEMIONLINE is at most

$$\mathbb{E}\{D^{\text{SO}}\} \leq \mathbb{E}\{f_L\}k(1 + \log n) + \sum_{j=1}^{k} \sum_{\alpha=0}^{\log n} 4.2^\alpha A_{c_j^*} |X_{c_j^*}(\alpha)|$$

$$\leq \mathbb{E}\{f_L\}k(1 + \log n) + 12 D^{\text{OPT}}, \tag{11.27}$$

where the second inequality follows since $2^{\alpha-1} A_{c_j^*} |X_{c_j^*}(\alpha)| \leq \sum_{x \in X_{c_j^*}} \|x - c_j^*\|^2$ and the definition of D^{OPT}, similar to (11.21).

We next upper bound $\mathbb{E}\{f_L\}$ to complete the proof. Consider the earliest phase $\hat{\ell}$, such that

$$f_{\hat{\ell}} \geq \frac{36 D^{\text{OPT}}}{k(1 + \log n)}. \tag{11.28}$$

From (11.22), the expected number of clusters created by algorithm SEMIONLINE during and after phase $\hat{\ell}$ is

$$\leq k(1 + \log n) + \frac{12 D^{\text{OPT}}}{f_{\hat{\ell}}} \leq \frac{4}{3}k(1 + \log n), \tag{11.29}$$

where the second inequality follows from the definition of $\hat{\ell}$ in (11.28).

Thus, the probability of creating more than $3k(1 + \log n)$ clusters during and after phase $\hat{\ell}$ with algorithm SEMIONLINE is upper bounded by 4/9 using Markov's inequality. Hence, with probability at least 5/9, the number of clusters created by algorithm SEMIONLINE during and after phase $\hat{\ell}$ is at most $3k(1 + \log n)$. Since each phase of algorithm SEMIONLINE terminates after creating $3k(1 + \log n)$ clusters, we get that with probability at least 5/9 algorithm SEMIONLINE terminates in phase $\hat{\ell}$, i.e., $L \leq \hat{\ell}$. Let r_ℓ be the probability that the algorithm

SEMIONLINE terminates in phase ℓ, while p_ℓ be the probability that the algorithm SEMIONLINE terminates in or before phase ℓ. Then we get the following bound:

$$\mathbb{E}\{f_L\} = \sum_{\ell=1}^{\hat{\ell}-1} r_\ell f_\ell + \sum_{\ell \geq \hat{\ell}} r_\ell f_\ell,$$

$$\overset{(a)}{\leq} p_{\hat{\ell}-1} f_{\hat{\ell}-1} + (1 - p_{\hat{\ell}-1}) \sum_{\ell \geq \hat{\ell}}^{\infty} f_\ell \left(\frac{5}{9}\right) \left(\frac{4}{9}\right)^{\ell-\hat{\ell}},$$

$$\overset{(b)}{\leq} f_{\hat{\ell}} + \frac{5}{9} f_{\hat{\ell}} \sum_{i=0}^{\infty} 2^i \left(\frac{4}{9}\right)^i,$$

$$= \mathcal{O}(f_{\hat{\ell}}). \tag{11.30}$$

where (a) follows since $f_{\hat{\ell}-1} \geq f_\ell$ for all $\ell \leq \hat{\ell} - 1$, while (b) follows since $f_\ell = 2 \cdot f_{\ell-1}$, and using the simple upper bound $p_{\hat{\ell}-1} \leq 1, 1 - p_{\hat{\ell}-1} \leq 1$.

Since $\hat{\ell}$ is the smallest ℓ for which $f_\ell \geq \frac{36 \mathrm{D}^{\mathrm{OPT}}}{k(1+\log n)}$, we get $\mathbb{E}\{f_L\} = \mathcal{O}\left(\frac{\mathrm{D}^{\mathrm{OPT}}}{k(1+\log n)}\right)$. Combining this with (11.27), we get that the expected cost of algorithm SEMIONLINE is

$$\mathbb{E}\{\mathrm{D}^{\mathrm{SO}}\} \leq \mathbb{E}\{f_L\} k \log n + 12 \mathrm{D}^{\mathrm{OPT}} \leq \mathcal{O}(\mathrm{D}^{\mathrm{OPT}}),$$

completing the proof. ■

Next, we make the algorithm SEMIONLINE **fully online**, and call it ONLINE (Algorithm 21). In algorithm SEMIONLINE, two non-causal parameters n and a lower bound on $\mathrm{D}^{\mathrm{OPT}}, \mathrm{d}^{\mathrm{OPT}}$, were used to define the initial cluster creation cost f_1, and to check a condition $q_\ell \geq 3k(1 + \log(n))$ which doubles the cost of creating a new cluster.

For algorithm ONLINE, the first $k + 1$ requests are used to estimate $\mathrm{d}^{\mathrm{OPT}}$, and n is initialized as $k + 1$, that is incremented on each new request arrival starting from the $k + 2^{nd}$ arrival. In particular, let

$$\mathrm{d}^*_{k+1} = \min_{x,x' \in X_{k+1}} \|x - x'\|^2/2, \tag{11.31}$$

and $X_{k+1} = \{x_1, x_2, \dots, x_{k+1}\}$ be the set of locations of the first $k + 1$ requests. We leave it as an exercise to show that d^*_{k+1} defined in (11.31) is a lower bound on $\mathrm{D}^{\mathrm{OPT}}$, when exactly k-clusters are created by OPT (Problem 11.10). Because of this lower bound, similar to algorithm SEMIONLINE, the initial cluster creation cost f_1 is then defined as $\frac{\mathrm{d}^*_{k+1}}{k}$. Other than the definition of f_1, and n being updated sequentially, algorithm ONLINE is same as algorithm SEMIONLINE.

Let

$$\gamma = \frac{\max_{x,x' \in X} \|x - x'\|^2}{\min_{x,x' \in X} \|x - x'\|^2}$$

be the aspect ratio of the request set $X = \{x_1, \dots, x_n\}$. Since $\mathrm{d}^*_{k+1} \leq \mathrm{D}^{\mathrm{OPT}}$ and $\mathrm{D}^{\mathrm{OPT}} \leq n \max_{x,x' \in X} \|x - x'\|^2$, we have

$$\log \frac{\mathrm{D}^{\mathrm{OPT}}}{\mathrm{d}^*_{k+1}} = \log(\gamma n). \tag{11.32}$$

Algorithm 21 ONLINE

Input k

Initialize ClusCent $= \{x_1, \ldots, x_{k+1}\}$ % first $k+1$ request locations

$f_1 = \frac{d^*_{k+1}}{k}$, where $d^*_{k+1} = \min_{x,x' \in \text{ClusCent}} ||x - x'||^2/2$

Initialize $\ell = 1, q_1 = 0$,

$n = k + 1$

for each new request with location $x_i, i \geq k + 2$ **do**

    $n = n + 1$

    with probability $p = \min\left\{\dfrac{d^2(x, \text{ClusCent}^{-x_i})}{f_\ell}, 1\right\}$

    create a new cluster at x, i.e., ClusCent $=$ ClusCent $\cup \{x\}$

    $q_\ell = q_\ell + 1$

    if $q_\ell \geq 3k(1 + \log n)$ **then**

        $\ell = \ell + 1$ % phase index

        $q_\ell = 0, f_\ell = 2f_{\ell-1}$;

    end if

    Assign x_i to the cluster with the nearest cluster centre in ClusCent

end for

Thus, similar to algorithm SEMIONLINE, for algorithm ONLINE, we have the following guarantees for the number of clusters created and the incurred cost.

Theorem 11.3.3 *Let L be the phase in which algorithm ONLINE terminates, and* ClusCent^L *be the final set of cluster centres created by it. Then*

$$\mathbb{E}\{|\text{ClusCent}^L|\} = \mathcal{O}\left(k \log n \log \frac{D^{\text{OPT}}}{d^*_{k+1}}\right) = \mathcal{O}\left(k \log n \log \gamma n\right).$$

Intuitively, the larger the value of γ, the harder is the job of an algorithm for clustering. Thus, Theorem 11.3.3 has an intuitive appeal that the number of clusters created by algorithm ONLINE depends on the aspect ratio that captures how skewed the request set locations are. The proof of Theorem 11.3.3 is identical to Theorem 11.3.1, by replacing the role of d^{OPT} by d^*_{k+1}, since $d^*_{k+1} \leq D^{\text{OPT}}$, and using the relation (11.32). The fact that the final bound depends on γ is because of the upper bound $D^{\text{OPT}} \leq n \max_{x,x' \in X} ||x - x'||^2$.

The total cost D^o of algorithm ONLINE is bounded as follows.

Theorem 11.3.4

$$\mathbb{E}\{D^o\} = \mathcal{O}\left((\log n)D^{\text{OPT}}\right).$$

We next prove Theorem 11.3.4 similar to the proof of Theorem 11.3.2 as follows.

Proof: Identical to (11.27), it follows that if L is the phase in which algorithm ONLINE terminates, then the total cost paid by algorithm ONLINE till phase L is

$$\mathbb{E}\{D^o\} \leq \mathbb{E}\{f_L\}k \log n + 12D^{\text{OPT}}. \tag{11.33}$$

Next, we upper bound $\mathbb{E}\{f_L\} = \mathcal{O}(\mathrm{D^{OPT}}/k)$ to prove the theorem. Compared to algorithm SEMIONLINE where $f_1 = \dfrac{\mathrm{d^{OPT}}}{k \log n}$, with algorithm ONLINE, the initial value of $f_1 = \dfrac{\mathrm{d}^*_{k+1}}{k}$. Moreover, with algorithm ONLINE, for the condition $q_\ell \geq 3k(1 + \log n)$ that doubles the cluster creating cost, n is the number of requests seen so far and not the total number of requests as in algorithm SEMIONLINE. Thus, conceptually, computing the $\mathbb{E}\{f_L\}$ is the same as in proof of Theorem 11.3.2, and there is only a marginal analytical difference which we point out as follows.

Similar to the proof of Theorem 11.3.2, consider any one of the cluster centres c_j^* opened by OPT, and let the set of requests of X assigned to c_j^* by OPT be denoted as $X_{c_j^*}$. Consider the earliest phase $\bar{\ell}$ with algorithm ONLINE, such that

$$ f_{\bar{\ell}} \geq \frac{36\mathrm{D^{OPT}}}{k}. $$

Remark 11.3.5 *Compared to the definition of phase $\hat{\ell}$ in the semi-online setting* (11.28), *there is no* $(1 + \log n)$ *term in the denominator to define* $f_{\bar{\ell}}$, *since n is unknown. This is the primary reason for the* $\log n$ *penalty in terms of the expected cost with algorithm* ONLINE *compared to algorithm* SEMIONLINE.

For any phase $\ell \geq \bar{\ell}$, let n_ℓ be the number of requests received by the algorithm starting from phase 0 till the end of phase ℓ. From the definition of algorithm ONLINE, q_ℓ is the number of clusters created by algorithm ONLINE during phase ℓ. Among q_ℓ, let q'_ℓ be the number of clusters that were not the first to be created in their respective annuli $A_{c_j^*}(\alpha)$. At the end of phase ℓ, since the total number of requests seen are n_ℓ, for any one cluster centre c_j^*, annuli $A_{c_j^*}(\alpha)$ are empty for $\alpha \geq \log(n_\ell) + 1$ (Problem 11.3).

Thus, the total number of annuli summed across the k centres created by OPT that are non-empty is at most $k(1 + \log(n_\ell))$. Thus, we get

$$ q_\ell \leq k(1 + \log(n_\ell)) + q'_\ell, \tag{11.34} $$

since there are at most $k(1 + \log(n_\ell))$ annuli that are non-empty, and there is at most one cluster (that opens first) in each annuli. Following identical steps to derive the second term of (11.22), we get that for $\ell \geq \ell'$

$$ \mathbb{E}\{q'_\ell\} \leq \frac{12\mathrm{D^{OPT}}}{f_\ell}. $$

By the choice of $f_{\bar{\ell}} \geq \dfrac{36\mathrm{D^{OPT}}}{k}$ and $\ell \geq \bar{\ell}$, we get

$$ \mathbb{E}\{q'_\ell\} \leq \frac{k}{3}. $$

Using Markov's inequality, this implies that the probability that $q'_\ell \geq 2k \log(1 + n_\ell) \leq \dfrac{1}{6}$ for $\ell \geq \bar{\ell}$.

Algorithm ONLINE moves to phase $\ell + 1$ only when in phase ℓ, the number of clusters created $q_\ell = 3k(1 + \log n_\ell)$. Thus, from (11.34), we get that algorithm ONLINE moves to phase

$\ell + 1$ only if $q'_\ell = 2k(1 + \log n_\ell)$. Since the probability that $q'_\ell \geq 2k \log(1 + n_\ell)$ is at most $\frac{1}{6}$, we get that for any phase $\ell \geq \bar{\ell}$, the probability that the algorithm does not terminate in phase ℓ (i.e., $L \geq \ell$) is at most $1/6$.

Reusing the notation, let r_ℓ be the probability that algorithm ONLINE terminates in phase ℓ, while p_ℓ be the probability that algorithm ONLINE terminates in or before phase ℓ. Then, similar to (11.30), we get the following bound:

$$\mathbb{E}\{f_L\} \leq p_{\bar{\ell}-1} f_{\bar{\ell}-1} + (1 - p_{\bar{\ell}-1}) \sum_{\ell \geq \bar{\ell}}^{\infty} f_\ell \left(\frac{5}{6}\right)\left(\frac{1}{6}\right)^{\ell - \bar{\ell}},$$

$$\leq f_{\bar{\ell}} + \frac{5}{6} f_{\bar{\ell}} \sum_{i=0}^{\infty} 2^i \left(\frac{1}{6}\right)^i,$$

$$= \mathcal{O}(f_{\bar{\ell}}).$$

where the first inequality follows since $f_{\bar{\ell}-1} \geq f_\ell$ for all $\ell \leq \bar{\ell} - 1$, while the second inequality follows since $f_\ell = 2.f_{\ell-1}$ and using the simple upper bound $p_{\bar{\ell}-1} \leq 1, 1 - p_{\bar{\ell}-1} \leq 1$.

Since $\bar{\ell}$ is the earliest phase for which $f_{\bar{\ell}} \geq \frac{36 D^{OPT}}{k}$, we get $\mathbb{E}\{f_L\} = \mathcal{O}\left(\frac{D^{OPT}}{k}\right)$. Combining this with (11.33), we get that the expected cost of algorithm ONLINE is

$$\mathbb{E}\{D\} \leq \mathbb{E}\{f_L\} k \log n + 12 D^{OPT} \leq \mathcal{O}(\log(n) D^{OPT}),$$

completing the proof. ∎

11.4 Notes

Research on online facility location defined over a metric space was initiated in [184], where a randomized algorithm RFL was presented and analysed. Compared to the 8-competitiveness of the RFL shown in [184] for the secretarial input, in a very recent work [185], it has been shown that the best competitive ratio of RFL is in fact 4 and it is tight. Moreover, a lower bound of 2 on the competitive ratio of any randomized algorithm with the secretarial input has also been derived in [185].

Another randomized algorithm was defined in [184] when the facility-opening cost is dependent on the location, and was shown to have a constant competitive ratio for the secretarial input model. The lower bound on the competitive ratio for the facility location problem proved in Theorem 11.2.4 was derived in [186], together with a deterministic algorithm that achieves the lower bound up to a constant. Algorithm POTENTIALUPDATE discussed in Section 11.2.5, a primal–dual based deterministic algorithm, was proposed in [172]. We discuss its competitive ratio guarantee in Problem 11.8. It is worth noting that algorithm POTENTIALUPDATE has the same competitive ratio as RFL when the facility-opening cost does not depend on the location. A nice review of the results on the online facility location problem can be found in [187]. An alternate class of deterministic algorithms, which splits the area hierarchically that defines when to open a new facility depending on the current cost, was proposed in [188] and has the same performance as the primal–dual algorithm [172]. Two important variants of the online facility location problem, where facilities can be moved or deleted, have been considered in [189, 190], respectively. The best-known result for the non-metric online facility location problem can be found in [191]. Facility assignment problems with fixed facility locations has been considered in [192, 193], whose main ideas are illustrated via Problem 11.6 and Problem 11.7.

Connections of the online facility location problem and the k-means clustering problem were exposed in [194], while the analysis presented in Section 11.3 follows from [195]. An $\mathcal{O}(\log n)$ improved algorithm in terms of distance cost over the algorithm presented in Section 11.3 can be found in [196]. There are many related problems such as the k-centre (discussed in Problem 11.11) and k-median that have also been considered extensively in the literature.

PROBLEMS

11.1 [197] Recall that in Theorem 11.2.4, we chose the number of levels $h = \dfrac{\log n}{\log \log n}$ to satisfy the constraint $\sum_{j=0}^{h} h^j \leq n$, which translated into lower bound $\Omega\left(\dfrac{\log n}{\log \log n}\right)$. The choice of $h = \dfrac{\log n}{\log \log n}$, however, is not tight for $\sum_{j=0}^{h} h^j \leq n$. Let $h = g(n)$ be tight for $\sum_{j=0}^{h} h^j \leq n$. Improve the result of Theorem 11.2.4 to show that the competitive ratio of any deterministic algorithm for the facility location problem is $\Omega(g(n))$.

In converse, show that using annuli $\mathsf{A}_{c^*}(\alpha) = \mathcal{B}(c^*, m^\alpha A_{c^*}) \backslash \mathcal{B}(c^*, m^{\alpha-1} A_{c^*})$ (11.11) for the RFL algorithm's analysis in Theorem 11.2.13 with an appropriate choice of m,[2] the competitive ratio of RFL in the worst case can be shown to be $\mathcal{O}(g(n))$. Conclude that RFL is optimal and its competitive ratio is $\Theta(g(n))$ that is strictly between $\Omega\left(\dfrac{\log n}{\log \log n}\right)$ and $\mathcal{O}(\log n)$.

11.2 Using Yao's principle, show that the lower bound proved for deterministic algorithms in Theorem 11.2.4 applies to randomized algorithms as well. In particular, consider the random input to be chosen as follows. First, the root node of the binary tree as shown in Figure 11.1 is requested once in phase 0. Thereafter, if node v_i is the location of all the requests made in phase i, then any one of the two children (chosen uniformly randomly) of v_i is requested m^{i+1} times in phase $i + 1$, for $i = 0, \ldots, h$. Recall that the subtree rooted at node v is denoted by T_v.

1. With this input, show that for any deterministic algorithm $\mathcal{A}$, the expected cost incurred by $\mathcal{A}$ for requests made and facilities opened that do not belong to $T_{v_{i+1}}$ is $\min\{mD, f/2\}$ plus the expected cost for requests made and facilities opened that do not belong to T_{v_i}.

2. Using the recurrence derived in part 1, show that the total expected cost of $\mathcal{A}$ at the end of phase $h - 1$ is $h \min\{mD, f/2\}$, while the expected cost of $\mathcal{A}$ for the last phase h is $h \min\{mD, f\}$.

3. Complete the proof, by arguing that the cost of OPT for any input realization is $f + hD\dfrac{m}{m+1}$, similar to the proof of Theorem 11.2.4.

---

[2] We have used $m = 2$ in Theorem 11.2.13.

11.3 Show that for a facility c^* opened by OPT, the annulus $A_{c^*}(\alpha)$ defined in (11.11) contains no requests belonging to X_{c^*} (set of requests assigned by OPT to c^*) for $\alpha > \log n$. [Hint: Argue that otherwise, the cost of points in $A_{c^*}(\alpha)$ for $\alpha > \log n$ would exceed the cost of the entire cluster.]

11.4 With location-dependent facility-opening cost, a natural generalization of the RFL algorithm is as follows. On the arrival of the ith request at location x, open a facility at x with probability $\min\left\{\dfrac{d(x, F_{i-1})}{f_x}, 1\right\}$, where f_x is the cost of opening the facility at location x. Irrespective of whether a new facility is opened or not, assign the new request to the closest open facility. Show that the competitive ratio of the RFL algorithm is unbounded when the facility-opening cost depends on the location, and the costs f_x are arbitrary, even under the secretarial request input model.

11.5 [188] Consider the facility location problem where all request locations belong to a two-dimensional square S with side d centred at the origin. The algorithm is going to work by recursively partitioning bigger squares into smaller squares as follows. Initially S is divided into four equal-sized non-overlapping squares $S_i, i = 1, 2, 3, 4$, and a facility is opened at the centre of each S_i as soon as a request arrives whose location belongs to S_i. Subsequently, each S_i is further divided into four equal-sized squares $S_{ij}, j = 1, 2, 3, 4$, when the sum of the distance cost of all the request locations belonging to S_i exceeds $a \cdot f$, where a is a constant and f is the facility-opening cost. Similar to before, a facility is opened at the centre of S_{ij} as soon as a request arrives whose location belongs to S_{ij}. This procedure is repeated recursively to create smaller and smaller squares and facilities being opened at the centres of the newly created squares. Show that the competitive ratio of this algorithm is $\mathcal{O}(\log n)$, where n is the total number of requests.

11.6 Consider a variation of the facility location problem, where k facilities are located on a real line (fixed locations) with inter-facility distance of d. Each facility has a capacity of c, i.e., at most c customers can be served by any one facility. A facility is defined to be **eligible** if it has less than c customers assigned to it. n customer requests arrive sequentially with $n \leq kc$. Customer i's location on the real line is denoted as ℓ_i, and customer i has to be irrevocably assigned to any one of the eligible facilities on its arrival. The cost of any online algorithm is the sum of the distances between the customer's location and its assigned facility.

Consider the GREEDY algorithm that assigns a newly arrived request to the nearest eligible facility.

1. For $c = 1$, by constructing an input sequence, show that the competitive ratio of GREEDY algorithm is $\Omega(k)$.

2. Show that the GREEDY algorithm is at most $4k$-competitive for any c.

11.7 Suppose there are only two facilities that are located on the real line with location ℓ_1 and ℓ_2 with capacities c_1 and c_2, respectively. At any time, facility $i, i = 1, 2$, is defined to be

eligible if it has less than c_i customers assigned to it. Let $n = c_1 + c_2$ customer requests arrive sequentially, where request i is located at r_i on the real line. Requests have to be assigned irrevocably to any one of the eligible servers on their arrival and the objective is to minimize the sum of the distances between the customer's location and its assigned facility.

1. By constructing an input sequence, show that the competitive ratio of any deterministic online algorithm is at least 3.

2. Show that the GREEDY algorithm (that assigns a newly arrived request to the nearest eligible facility) is at most 3-competitive.

11.8 In this problem, we will prove Theorem 11.2.14 as follows. Similar to the proof of the competitive ratio upper bound of the RFL algorithm in Theorems 11.2.12 and 11.2.13, we will concentrate on facilities opened by OPT.

Let $X = (x_1, x_2, \ldots, x_n)$ be the locations of the n requests, and $F^{\text{OPT}} = \{c_1, \ldots, c_k\}$ be the set of locations of the facilities opened by OPT, where $C_i \subseteq X$ is the set of requests assigned to the open facility located at c_i, and $|C_i| = n_i$.

For each request $x \in X$, let $d_x^{\text{OPT}} = d(x, F^{\text{OPT}})$, and the total distance cost for OPT be $S^{\text{OPT}} = \sum_{x \in X} d_x^{\text{OPT}}$, while the facility-opening cost for OPT be $\text{Fac}^{\text{OPT}} = \sum_{i=1}^{k} f_{c_i}$. Distance cost restriction for a subset of requests $X' \subseteq X$, $S^{\text{OPT}}(X') = \sum_{x \in X'} d_x^{\text{OPT}}$. The corresponding quantities for algorithm POTENTIALUPDATE are denoted with a superscript $\mathcal{A}$ instead of OPT.

1. Show that with algorithm POTENTIALUPDATE, for all $z \in \mathcal{M}$, $p(z) \leq f_z$ after each new request arrives, or every time $p(z)$ is updated. Prove this via induction on the number of requests considered by the algorithm POTENTIALUPDATE. [This will show that the algorithm POTENTIALUPDATE maintains the invariant that $p(z) \leq f_z$ for all $z \in \mathcal{M}$ throughout.]

2. Let $X_t \subseteq X$ be the subset of requests that has been revealed by time t, and $F_t^{\mathcal{A}}$ be the set of locations of the opened facilities by algorithm POTENTIALUPDATE after all requests in X_t have arrived. Using part 1, show that for OPT's assignment of the set of requests in C_i to the open facility at c_i,

$$|X_t \cap C_i| d(c_i, F_t^{\mathcal{A}}) \leq f_{c_i} + 2 S^{\text{OPT}}(C_i),$$

for any $i = 1, \ldots, k$ and any t.

[Hint: Apply the invariant of part 1 for point c_i, i.e., $f_{c_i} \geq p(c_i)$ and use the definition of potential $p(c_i)$.]

3. We index $u_1, u_2, \ldots, u_{n_i}$, the n_i requests that are assigned by OPT to the opened facility c_i in order of their arrival times. Let $F_j^{\mathcal{A}}$ be the set of locations of the opened facilities by algorithm POTENTIALUPDATE after the arrival of u_j. Using part 2, show that

$$d(u_j, F_j^{\mathcal{A}}) \leq \frac{1}{j}\left(f_{c_i} + 2S^{\text{OPT}}(C_i)\right) + d_{u_j}^{\text{OPT}}.$$

Consequently, show that POTENTIALUPDATE's distance cost, $S^{\mathcal{A}} = \sum_{x \in X} d_x^{\mathcal{A}}$, is no greater than

$$\log(n+1)\text{Fac}^{\text{OPT}} + (2(\log n + 1) + 1)S^{\text{OPT}}.$$

4. Let for each request x, its loan be defined as

$$\text{loan}(x) = \min\{d(x, F_{x^-}^{\mathcal{A}}), \min_{z \in \mathcal{M}}\{f_z - p(z) + d(x, z)\}\},$$

where $F_{x^-}^{\mathcal{A}}$ denotes the set of locations of open facilities, and $p(z)$ is z's potential for POTENTIALUPDATE, just before x arrives, respectively. Show that for each new request x,

$$\text{loan}(x) = f_w - p(w) + d(x, w)$$

if POTENTIALUPDATE opens a new facility at w on the arrival of x, and $\text{loan}(x) = d(x, F_{x^-}^{\mathcal{A}})$ otherwise.

5. Recall that $X_t \subseteq X$ is the subset of requests that has been revealed by time t, and $F_t^{\mathcal{A}}$ is the set of locations of the opened facilities by algorithm POTENTIALUPDATE after all requests in X_t have arrived. Show that

$$\sum_{w \in F_t^{\mathcal{A}}} f_w \leq \sum_{x \in X_t} \text{loan}(x).$$

[Define potential $\Phi(X_t) = \sum_{x \in X_t} d(x, F_t^{\mathcal{A}})$ and relate the change in the potential $\Delta\Phi = \Phi(X_t \cup \{x\}) - \Phi(X_t)$ on the arrival of a new request located at x to loan(x) and use part 4, where $p(z)$ is the potential just before request at x arrives].

6. Using part 2, show that

$$\sum_{x \in X} \text{loan}(x) \leq (\log n + 1)\text{Fac}^{\text{OPT}} + (2\log n + 1)S^{\text{OPT}}.$$

[Hint: As before, index $u_1, u_2, \ldots, u_{n_i}$, the n_i requests that are assigned by OPT to the open facility located at c_i in order of their arrival times. Separate the first and the subsequent requests. For the first request, claim that $\text{loan}(u_1) \leq f_{c_i} + d_{u_1}^{\text{OPT}}$, while for subsequent requests $2 \leq j \leq n_i$, argue that $\text{loan}(u_j) \leq d(u_j, F_{u_j^-}^{\mathcal{A}})$ and then use part 2 to upper bound $\text{loan}(u_j)$ as

$$\text{loan}(u_j) \leq \frac{1}{j-1}[f_{c_i} + 2S^{\text{OPT}}(C_i)] + d_{u_j}^{\text{OPT}}.]$$

7. Complete the proof of Theorem 11.2.14 by combining parts 2, 5, and 6.

11.9 For the *k*-means clustering problem, show that an online algorithm must either create an unbounded number of clusters or incur an unbounded competitive ratio. [Hint: The following sequence may be helpful. Let n be the total number of requests that are unknown to begin with, and consider the sequence of request locations on $\mathbb{R}$, $1, c, c^2, \ldots, c^n$, respectively, for $c \geq 2$.]

11.10 For the *k*-means clustering problem, for a set of $k + 1$ requests, let

$$X_{k+1} = \{x_1, \ldots, x_{k+1}\} \text{ and } d^*_{k+1} = \min_{x, x' \in X_{k+1}} ||x - x'||^2 / 2.$$

Show that $d^*_{k+1} \leq D^{OPT}$, where D^{OPT} is the optimal cost of OPT when exactly *k*-clusters are created by it with request sequence X.

11.11 *k*-centre problem. Similar to the *k*-means clustering problem, let there be a maximum of *k*-clusters that can be chosen, but now the problem is to choose the location of the *k*-cluster centres so as to minimize the maximum distance of any point from its cluster centre. As before, let $X = (x_1, \ldots, x_n)$ be the location vector of all the n requests. In particular, if $c_1, \ldots, c_k$ are the cluster centres and $X_i = \{x_{i1}, \ldots, x_{im_i}\}$, $i = 1, \ldots, k$ are the locations of the (requests) points assigned to cluster i, then the radius for cluster i is R_i while diameter D_i is

$$R_i = \max_{j=1,\ldots,m_i} ||x_{ij} - c_i||, \text{ and } D_i = \max_{j,k=1,\ldots,m_i, j \neq k} ||x_{ij} - x_{ik}||, \tag{11.35}$$

and the maximum radius and diameter is

$$R = \max_{i=1,\ldots,k} R_i, \text{ and } D = \max_{i=1,\ldots,k} D_i. \tag{11.36}$$

1. [198] First, we consider the offline setting where all n points' location is known. Consider the following local algorithm to find the cluster centres: choose the k centre points sequentially, starting with an arbitrary point as the first centre. In each iteration, choose the point that is farthest from any earlier centre point to be the next centre point. Stop once k centres are selected. Show that this algorithm is 2-approximate to minimize R.

2. [194] Now we consider the online setting, where points with location x_i arrive sequentially, and an algorithm is not allowed to split any cluster, but can merge any two clusters. Consider the algorithm ALGOKCENTRE that works in phases. To begin, the algorithm waits for the first $k + 1$ points, and defines them to be the $k + 1$ cluster centres. Let $d^1_{\min}$ equal to the distance of the closest pair of points among the first $k + 1$ points.

   Next, phase 1 begins, that consists of two sub-phases: *merge* and *create*. *Merge* sub-phase: Among the $k + 1$ cluster centres, all cluster centres that are within a distance of $2d^1_{\min}$ are merged into a single cluster centre. For example, consider a pair of cluster centres c_1 and c_2 with distance at most $2d^1_{\min}$ between them. Let the set of points assigned to c_1 and c_2 be C_1 and C_2, respectively. In the merged configuration there will be only one cluster centre c_1 or c_2 (choice being immaterial) with $C_1 \cup C_2$ points assigned to that cluster centre. This process is repeated for all pairs of cluster centres with distance at most $2d^1_{min}$ between them.

Create sub-phase: As new points arrive, a new cluster is created if the newly arriving point is farther than $2d^1_{min}$ from any current cluster centre, until the number of clusters becomes $k + 1$. Once the number of clusters become $k + 1$, phase 1 ends. Phase 2 begins by setting $d^2_{min} = 2d^1_{min}$, with the above sub-phases by replacing d^1_{min} by d^2_{min}, and so on.

(a) For any i, show that at the beginning of phase i, $d^i_{min} \leq D_{OPT}$ (11.36).
(b) Show that the pairwise distance between any two cluster centres after the merging step of phase i is at least $2d^i_{min}$.
(c) Show that the radius (11.35) for any cluster at the end of phase i is at most $2d^{i+1}_{min}$.
(d) The radius (11.35) of any cluster after the merging step of phase i is at most $d^{i+1}_{min} + 2d^i_{min} \leq 2d^{i+1}_{min}$.
(e) Conclude that ALGOKCENTRE is 8-competitive for minimizing D.
(f) Conclude that ALGOKCENTRE is also 8-competitive for minimizing R.

CHAPTER 12

Load Balancing

12.1 Introduction

In this chapter, we consider the load balancing problem, which in its simplest form is to assign jobs with different sizes sequentially to multiple machines so as to minimize the maximum of the sum of the sizes of jobs assigned to any machine at any point in time.

We present some of the basic techniques developed for solving the load balancing problem under many settings of interest. We start with the simplest setting, where all machines are identical and all jobs are of equal size, and they are permanent, i.e., once they arrive, they do not leave the system. In this setting, round robin is an optimal algorithm; however, it needs to remember past decisions, requiring memory. One challenge is to devise algorithms that are memoryless but still have performance close to that of round robin. In this setting, we present the power-of-d algorithm, where a job on its arrival is assigned to the least loaded machine among d machines, where the d machines are chosen uniformly randomly from the set of all machines.

When job sizes are arbitrary, the load balancing problem is a bit more difficult. For permanent jobs with arbitrary sizes, we consider the case where machine speeds are not identical, and present a near-optimal deterministic online algorithm. Compared to the permanent jobs setting, the temporary jobs setting is more practical but challenging, where jobs arrive into the system and leave at an arbitrary time that is not necessarily known to an algorithm. In the temporary jobs case, we consider two well-studied models: (i) with machine restriction, where each job can be processed by a subset of machines while all the machines have identical speed, and (ii) without machine restriction, where any job can be processed by any machine; however, machine speeds are non-identical.

Finally, we consider the load balancing problem over a network, where each job corresponds to a source–destination pair, and fulfilling a job involves finding a path from the specified source to the destination. Assigning a job to a path means that each edge on that path carries an additional load equal to the size of the job. The goal is then to minimize the maximum sum of the loads assigned on any edge of the network. Even though this problem appears seemingly hard, a simple algorithm with elegant analysis is shown to achieve the optimal competitive ratio that is of the order of the logarithm of the number of nodes in the network.

12.2 Permanent Jobs

In this section, we consider the case where jobs are permanent, i.e., once a job arrives it stays in the system for the entire duration of interest. Before considering the worst-case analysis where job sizes can be arbitrary and can arrive in any order, we first consider the simpler setting when all job sizes are identical and all machines are identical.

12.2.1 Equal-Sized Jobs with Identical Machines

We begin the discussion on load balancing algorithms with perhaps the simplest setting, where there are m machines and m jobs, each job is of the same size, and any job can be assigned to any machine. Without loss of generality, we let the size of each job to be unity. The load on any machine is the total number of jobs assigned to it, and the objective is to minimize the maximum load across all machines. The trivial optimal algorithm round-robin (RR) is to assign one job to one machine in a round-robin manner that achieves the optimal load of unity.

To execute RR, the algorithm has to remember the index of the machine where the most recently arrived job was assigned. In practical settings, it is also important to consider memoryless algorithms that are independent of the previous assignments. One such obvious choice is the RANDOM algorithm, where each job is allocated to any one of the m machines uniformly randomly, independent of all other prior job allocations.

Even though RANDOM has low complexity, the maximum load guarantee is poor and scales as $\Theta\left(\frac{\log m}{\log \log m}\right)$ with high probability. We prove the upper bound on the maximum load next, and leave the lower bound as an exercise.

Performance Guarantee of RANDOM

Lemma 12.2.1 *With* RANDOM, *the maximum load across all machines with m machines and m jobs is* $\mathcal{O}\left(\frac{\log m}{\log \log m}\right)$ *with probability at least* $1 - 1/m$.

Proof: Let $k = \left(\frac{3 \log m}{\log \log m}\right)$. After all the m jobs are assigned, let $X_i = 1$ if machine i has at least k jobs assigned to it by RANDOM, otherwise, $X_i = 0$. Let

$$X = \sum_{i=1}^{n} X_i$$

be the number of machines that have at least k jobs assigned to it. We want to upper bound $\mathbb{P}(X \geq 1)$ by $1/m$ for $k = \left(\frac{3 \log m}{\log \log m}\right)$ to claim the result.

The probability that (a particular) machine i has at least k jobs assigned to it is

$$\mathbb{P}(X_i = 1) = \sum_{\ell=k}^{m} \binom{m}{\ell} \left(\frac{1}{m}\right)^{\ell} \left(1 - \frac{1}{m}\right)^{m-\ell} \leq \binom{m}{k} \left(\frac{1}{m}\right)^{k}. \tag{12.1}$$

Note that $\frac{m!}{m-k!} \leq m^k$. Thus, writing $\binom{m}{k} \leq \frac{m^k}{k!}$ and using Stirling's approximation $k! \geq \sqrt{2\pi k}\left(\frac{k}{e}\right)^k$, we get $\binom{m}{k} \leq \left(\frac{em}{k}\right)^k$. Using this bound in (12.1), we get

$$\mathbb{P}(X_i = 1) \leq \left(\frac{e}{k}\right)^k. \tag{12.2}$$

For $k = \left(\frac{3 \log m}{\log \log m} \right)$, the upper bound (12.2) evaluates to

$$\mathbb{P}(X_i = 1) = \left(\frac{e \log \log m}{3 \log m} \right)^{\left(\frac{3 \log m}{\log \log m} \right)},$$

$$\leq \exp \left(\frac{3 \log m}{\log \log m} (\log \log \log m - \log \log m) \right),$$

$$= \exp \left(-3 \log m + \frac{3 \log m \log \log \log m}{\log \log m} \right),$$

$$\overset{(a)}{\leq} \exp \left(-2 \log m \right),$$

$$= \frac{1}{m^2},$$

where (a) follows for large enough m.

Since there are a total of m machines, using the union bound, it follows that

$$\mathbb{P}(X \geq 1) \leq m \frac{1}{m^2}. \tag{12.3}$$

Thus, with probability at least $1 - 1/m$, $X = 0$, i.e., all machines have load at most $\left(\frac{3 \log m}{\log \log m} \right)$. ∎

To show that Lemma 12.2.1 is tight, i.e., the maximum load scales as $\Omega \left(\frac{\log m}{\log \log m} \right)$ with high probability, we have the following result, whose proof we leave as an exercise in Problem 12.1.

Lemma 12.2.2 *The maximum load with* RANDOM *is* $\Omega \left(\frac{\log m}{\log \log m} \right)$ *with probability at least* $1 - 1/m^{1/3}$.

RANDOM assigns any job to a randomly chosen machine and provides a poor performance guarantee in terms of the maximum load, since it leaves a lot of machines idle or lightly loaded. To decrease the imbalance of load across different machines, a natural extension of RANDOM is to consider $d \geq 2$ machines randomly, and choose the one with the lightest current load for assigning each new job. As d becomes closer to m, one can expect significant performance improvement on account of this algorithm getting closer to RR, but remarkably even for $d = 2$ there is an exponential decrease in the maximum load compared to when $d = 1$ (RANDOM). We discuss this new algorithm and its performance in detail in the next subsection where we have m identical unit-sized jobs that are permanent and m identical machines.

12.2.2 POWER-OF-d-CHOICES

POWER-OF-d-CHOICES ALGORITHM: Each job is assigned to the least loaded machine at the time of its assignment among $d \geq 2$ machines, where the d machines are chosen independently and uniformly at random from the set of all m machines.

The improvement in terms of the maximum load with POWER-OF-d-CHOICES in comparison to RANDOM is remarkable, as we show next.

Theorem 12.2.3 *With* POWER-OF-d-CHOICES, *the maximum load on any machine is at most* $\frac{\log \log m}{\log d} + \mathcal{O}(1)$ *with high probability.*

Recall that with RANDOM the maximum load scales $\Theta\left(\frac{\log m}{\log \log m}\right)$. Hence, even for $d = 2$, POWER-OF-d-CHOICES offers fundamental performance improvement. The basic idea behind the result is to show that if the number of machines with load at least i at any time during the execution of the POWER-OF-d-CHOICES algorithm is at most β_i, then conditioned on β_i, we can bound $\beta_{i+1} = cm\left(\frac{\beta_i}{m}\right)^d$ for some constant c, with high probability.

Essentially, conditioned on β_i, a new job is assigned to a machine with current load i, if all the d machines considered for it have a load of i. Since the d choices are made randomly, this implies that the probability of choosing a machine with current load i is $\frac{\beta_i}{m}$, and the probability that all the d machines considered for a job to have a load of i is $\left(\frac{\beta_i}{m}\right)^d$.

Thus, the number of machines with load at least i falls off exponentially with d as i increases. To make the proof rigorous, the number of machines with load at least i is shown to be stochastically dominated by a Binomial random variable corresponding to the number of heads with m independent trials with heads probability of $\left(\frac{\beta_i}{m}\right)^d$.

Proof: [Theorem 12.2.3] We consider jobs arriving sequentially at consecutive discrete time instants. Thus, time t is the same as the arrival instant of the tth job.

Definition 12.2.4 *Let the height $h(t)$ of the tth job be one more than the number of jobs already assigned to the machine at the time of the arrival of the tth job in which the tth job is placed.*

Definition 12.2.5 *Let $\mathsf{m}_i(t)$ and $\mathsf{J}_i(t)$ be the number of machines with load at least i, and the number of jobs with height at least i at time t (after the tth job's arrival), respectively.*

We want to upper bound $\mathsf{J}_i(m)$, the number of jobs with height at least i, after all the m jobs have arrived, for $i = \frac{\log \log m}{\log d} + \mathcal{O}(1)$. Towards that end, we will iteratively construct β_i's such that $\mathsf{m}_i(m) \le \beta_i$ with high probability for some chosen values of i. Let $\beta_6 = \frac{m}{2e}$ and

$$\beta_{i+1} = \frac{e}{m^{d-1}}\beta_i^d, \text{ for } i \ge 6.$$

Let

$$p_i = \left(\frac{\beta_i}{m}\right)^d. \tag{12.4}$$

Note that, by definition, $p_i m$ is a decreasing sequence in i. Let $i^\star$ be the smallest i for which

$$p_i m \le 2\log m \text{ or } \frac{\beta_i^d}{m^d} \le \frac{2\log m}{m}. \tag{12.5}$$

From the definition of β_6, it is easy to check that $\beta_{i+6} \leq m/2^{d^i}$. Consequently,

$$i^\star \leq \frac{\log\log m}{\log d} + \mathcal{O}(1).$$

To prove the theorem, we will show that after all m job arrivals, with high probability there are no jobs with height at least $i^\star + 2$, i.e., $\mathsf{J}_{i^\star+2}(m) < 1$.

Definition 12.2.6 *Let $\mathcal{E}_i$ be the event that $\mathsf{m}_i(m) \leq \beta_i$ after all the m jobs have arrived and have been assigned.*

Lemma 12.2.7 *Event $\mathcal{E}_6$ always happens.*

Proof: To see this, consider

$$\mathsf{m}_6(m) = |\{\text{machines with at least 6 jobs after all } m \text{ jobs have arrived}\}|.$$

By the pigeon-hole principle, we have $\mathsf{m}_6(m) \leq m/6$, and since $2e > 6$, we get $\mathsf{m}_6(m) \leq \beta_6$. Therefore, event $\mathcal{E}_6$ always happens. ∎

Next, we show that for $6 \leq i \leq i^\star - 1$, if event $\mathcal{E}_i$ happens with high probability, so does the event $\mathcal{E}_{i+1}$. From Lemma 12.2.7, we know that $\mathcal{E}_6$ always happens, so this is meaningful. Towards that end, consider an indicator random variable

$$Y_t = \begin{cases} 1 & \text{if and only if } h(t) \geq i+1 \text{ and } \mathsf{m}_i(t-1) \leq \beta_i, \\ 0 & \text{otherwise.} \end{cases} \tag{12.6}$$

In words, $Y_t = 1$ if the height of the tth job is at least $i+1$, and the number of machines with at least i jobs at the (just before) arrival of the tth job is at most β_i.

A job that arrives at time t has height at least $i+1$ only if the current load at each of the d random choices of machines that are made for its assignment is at least i. Given that $\mathsf{m}_i(t-1) \leq \beta_i$, i.e., the number of machines with load at least i is at most β_i at time $t-1$, the probability that each choice of the d choices of machines for the job arriving at time t has current load of at least i is $\frac{\beta_i}{m}$. Therefore, given that $\mathsf{m}_i(t-1) \leq \beta_i$, the probability that a job assigned at time t joins a machine already containing i or more jobs is at most $\left(\frac{\beta_i}{m}\right)^d$.

Let job j be allocated to machine $\mathcal{M}_j$. Then using the preceding argument, we have

$$\begin{aligned}
\mathbb{P}(Y_t = 1 | \mathcal{M}_1, \dots, \mathcal{M}_{t-1}) \\
= \mathbb{P}\left(h(t) \geq i+1 \cap \mathsf{m}_i(t-1) \leq \beta_i | \mathcal{M}_1, \dots, \mathcal{M}_{t-1}\right), \\
= \mathbb{P}\left(\mathsf{m}_i(t-1) \leq \beta_i | \mathcal{M}_1, \dots, \mathcal{M}_{t-1}\right) \\
\times \mathbb{P}\left(h(t) \geq i+1 | \mathsf{m}_i(t-1) \leq \beta_i, \mathcal{M}_1, \dots, \mathcal{M}_{t-1}\right), \\
\leq \mathbb{P}\left(h(t) \geq i+1 | \mathsf{m}_i(t-1) \leq \beta_i, \mathcal{M}_1, \dots, \mathcal{M}_{t-1}\right), \\
\leq \left(\frac{\beta_i}{m}\right)^d, \\
= p_i, \tag{12.7}
\end{aligned}$$

where the last equality follows from the definition of p_i (12.4).

To proceed further we need the following two well-known facts. Let $B(n, q)$ be the number of heads appearing in n independent coin tosses with heads probability of q.

Lemma 12.2.8 *Let $X_1, \ldots, X_n$ be arbitrary random variables, and let $Z_1, \ldots, Z_n$ be binary random variables such that $Z_i = Z_i(X_1, \ldots, X_{i-1})$.*[1] *Then if*

$$\mathbb{P}(Z_i = 1 | X_1, \ldots, X_{i-1}) \le q,$$

then

$$\mathbb{P}\left(\sum_{i=1}^n Z_i \ge k\right) \le \mathbb{P}(B(n, q) \ge k).$$

Similarly, if $\mathbb{P}(Z_i = 1 | X_1, \ldots, X_{i-1}) \ge q$, then

$$\mathbb{P}\left(\sum_{i=1}^n Z_i \le k\right) \le \mathbb{P}(B(n, q) \le k).$$

Lemma 12.2.9 *[Chernoff bounds] Let $X_1, \ldots, X_n$ be independent binary random variables, with $\mathbb{P}(X_i = 1) = q$. Then for $t \ge nq$,*

$$\mathbb{P}\left(\sum_{i=1}^n X_i \ge t\right) \le \left(\frac{nq}{t}\right)^t e^{t-nq},$$

and for $t \le nq$,

$$\mathbb{P}\left(\sum_{i=1}^n X_i \le t\right) \le \left(\frac{nq}{t}\right)^t e^{t-nq}.$$

From (12.7), and using Lemma 12.2.8, we get

$$\mathbb{P}\left(\sum_{t=1}^m Y_t \ge k\right) \le \mathbb{P}(B(m, p_i) \ge k), \tag{12.8}$$

where $p_i = \left(\frac{\beta_i}{m}\right)^d$. Moreover, notice that conditioned on event $\mathcal{E}_i$ ($m_i(m) \le \beta_i$ after all m job arrivals), $\sum_{t=1}^m Y_t = J_{i+1}(m)$, the number of jobs with height at least $i + 1$. Thus,

$$
\begin{aligned}
\mathbb{P}\left(J_{i+1}(m) \ge k | \mathcal{E}_i\right) &= \mathbb{P}\left(\sum_{t=1}^m Y_t \ge k | \mathcal{E}_i\right), \\
&\le \frac{\mathbb{P}\left(\sum_{t=1}^m Y_t \ge k\right)}{\mathbb{P}(\mathcal{E}_i)}, \\
&\le \frac{\mathbb{P}(B(m, p_i) \ge k)}{\mathbb{P}(\mathcal{E}_i)}, \tag{12.9}
\end{aligned}
$$

where the last inequality follows from (12.8).

---

[1] Z_i is a measurable function of random variables $X_1, \ldots, X_{i-1}$.

Given $\mathcal{E}_i$, the event $\mathsf{m}_{i+1}(t) \geq k$ implies the event $\mathsf{J}_{i+1}(t) \geq k$. Thus, from (12.9), we get

$$\mathbb{P}\left(\mathsf{m}_{i+1}(m) \geq k|\mathcal{E}_i\right) \leq \frac{\mathbb{P}(\mathsf{B}(m, p_i) \geq k)}{\mathbb{P}\left(\mathcal{E}_i\right)}. \tag{12.10}$$

Recall the definition of $\beta_{i+1} = \frac{e}{m^{d-1}}\beta_i^d = emp_i$, where $p_i = \left(\frac{\beta_i}{m}\right)^d$ as defined in (12.4). Choosing $k = \beta_{i+1}$, we get from (12.10)

$$\mathbb{P}\left(\mathcal{E}_{i+1}^c|\mathcal{E}_i\right) = \mathbb{P}\left(\mathsf{m}_{i+1}(m) \geq \beta_{i+1}|\mathcal{E}_i\right) \leq \frac{\mathbb{P}(\mathsf{B}(m, p_i) \geq emp_i)}{\mathbb{P}\left(\mathcal{E}_i\right)} \leq \frac{1}{e^{mp_i}\mathbb{P}\left(\mathcal{E}_i\right)}. \tag{12.11}$$

Recall that $i^\star$ is the smallest i for which $p_i m < 2\log m$. Thus, for any $i < i^\star$, $p_i m \geq 2\log m$, and we get from (12.11)

$$\mathbb{P}\left(\mathcal{E}_{i+1}^c|\mathcal{E}_i\right) \leq \frac{1}{m^2\mathbb{P}\left(\mathcal{E}_i\right)}. \tag{12.12}$$

In words, for $i < i^\star$, if the event $\mathcal{E}_i$ happens with high probability, then so does the event $\mathcal{E}_{i+1}$. Recall that $\mathbb{P}(\mathcal{E}_6) = 1$. Thus, repeatedly using the identity

$$\mathbb{P}(A^c) \leq \mathbb{P}(A^c|B)\mathbb{P}(B) + \mathbb{P}(B^c), \tag{12.13}$$

with $A = \mathcal{E}_{i+1}$ and $B = \mathcal{E}_i$ for $6 \leq i \leq i^\star - 1$ and using the relation (12.12), we can bound

$$\mathbb{P}\left(\mathcal{E}_{i+1}^c\right) \leq \frac{i-6}{m^2}. \tag{12.14}$$

Since $p_{i^\star} \leq \frac{2\log m}{m}$ from (12.5), similar to (12.10), we get

$$\mathbb{P}\left(\mathsf{m}_{i^\star+1}(m) \geq 6\log m|\mathcal{E}_{i^\star}\right) \leq \frac{\mathbb{P}\left(\mathsf{B}\left(m, \frac{2\log m}{m}\right) \geq 6\log m\right)}{\mathbb{P}\left(\mathcal{E}_{i^\star}\right)},$$

$$\leq \frac{1}{m^2\mathbb{P}\left(\mathcal{E}_{i^\star}\right)}, \tag{12.15}$$

where to obtain the second inequality, we have used Lemma 12.2.9. Using the identity (12.13) one more time with $A^c = \{\mathsf{m}_{i^\star+1}(m) \geq 6\log m\}$, and $B = \mathcal{E}_{i^\star}$ and using (12.15), we get

$$\mathbb{P}\left(\mathsf{m}_{i^\star+1}(m) \geq 6\log m\right) \leq \frac{i^\star + 1 - 6}{m^2}. \tag{12.16}$$

Thus, we have been able to bound the probability that the number of machines with at least $i^\star + 1$ jobs after all m jobs arrivals is at least $6\log m$ by $\mathcal{O}(i^\star/m^2)$, which will be sufficient since $i^\star \leq \frac{\log\log m}{\log d} + \mathcal{O}(1)$. To complete the proof of the theorem, we want to show that there are no jobs with height at least $i^\star + 2$, which we do as follows. Note that since $p_{i^\star+1} \leq \left(\frac{6\log m}{m}\right)^d$ from (12.5), thus similar to (12.9),

$$\mathbb{P}\left(J_{i^\star+2}(m) \geq 1 | m_{i^\star+1}(m) \leq 6 \log m\right) \leq \frac{\mathbb{P}\left(B\left(m, \left(\frac{6 \log m}{m}\right)^d\right) \geq 1\right)}{\mathbb{P}\left(m_{i^\star+1}(m) \leq 6 \log m\right)},$$

$$\overset{(a)}{\leq} \frac{m\left(\frac{6 \log m}{m}\right)^d}{\mathbb{P}\left(m_{i^\star+1}(m) \leq 6 \log m\right)}, \qquad (12.17)$$

where (a) follows from Markov's inequality. Using the identity (12.13), with $A^c = \{J_{i^\star+2}(m) \geq 1\}$ and $B = \{m_{i^\star+1}(m) < 6 \log m\}$, we get the unconditioned probability from (12.16) and (12.17) as

$$\mathbb{P}\left(J_{i^\star+2}(m) \geq 1\right) \leq \frac{(6 \log m)^d}{m^{d-1}} + \frac{i^\star + 1 - 6}{m^2} = \mathcal{O}\left(\frac{1}{m}\right),$$

which implies that the maximum load on any machine is at most $i^\star + 2 = \frac{\log \log m}{\log d} + \mathcal{O}(1)$ with high probability. ∎

A natural question to ask is whether the analysis (Theorem 12.2.3) for POWER-OF-d-CHOICES is tight, or can one get a smaller bound on the maximum load. It turns out that the analysis is tight, and one can show a lower bound matching the result of Theorem 12.2.3 that holds with high probability [199].

After this brief detour on the identical jobs and identical machine setting where we considered randomized assignment algorithms and obtained high probability results, we return to our worst-case analysis, the main object of interest.

12.2.3 Arbitrary Job Sizes with Identical Machines

We begin the worst-case analysis with the simplest model where n jobs arrive with arbitrary sizes that are permanent. There are a total of m machines, all of which are identical and any job can be assigned to any machine. For the rest of the chapter, the **load** on any machine is the sum of the sizes or loads of all the jobs assigned to it, and the objective is to minimize the maximum load across the m machines.

For this problem, the natural greedy algorithm that assigns an incoming job to the least loaded machine on its arrival can be shown to have a competitive ratio of at most $2 - \frac{1}{m}$. The proof is simple and we leave it as an exercise in Problem 12.3. One can also show that the competitive ratio of the greedy algorithm is at least $2 - \frac{1}{m}$ (Problem 12.4). The greedy algorithm, however, is not optimal and one can get better competitive ratios for this simple problem setting.

12.2.4 Arbitrary Job Sizes with Non-Identical Machines

In this section, we continue our discussion on permanent jobs but now the machines are not identical. Let a total of n jobs arrive sequentially, where the size of the jth job is w_j. In contrast to previous sections, there are m machines that are not identical, i.e., they are different in the sense that a job j with size w_j incurs a load of w_j/s_k on machine k. The parameter s can be interpreted as the speed of the machine, and we index the machines in increasing order of their speeds, $s_1 \leq s_2 \leq ... \leq s_m$. This setup is generally referred to as the *related machines* case. The load on any machine is the sum of the loads of the jobs assigned to it. The objective of an online algorithm is to minimize the maximum load across all machines after all n job arrivals.

When machines are identical, i.e., $s_i = s_j$ for all $i \neq j$, a greedy algorithm, which assigns a newly arrived job to the least loaded machine on its arrival, achieves a competitive ratio of $2 - 1/m$ (Problem 12.3). Unfortunately, a greedy algorithm does not perform very well in the non-identical machines case considered in this section (its competitive ratio is $\Theta(\log m)$ [200]), and we need a slightly non-trivial algorithm to achieve a constant competitive ratio, which is described next.

For OPT, let L^{OPT} be the optimal maximum load across all machines after all n jobs have arrived. We propose an algorithm called the SLOWEST-FIRST, whose basic idea is to assume the knowledge of an upper bound Λ on the optimal load L^{OPT} and, using that, define a machine to be **assignable** if after assigning a newly arrived job to the machine, its updated load is at most 2Λ. Among all the assignable machines, SLOWEST-FIRST assigns the job to the machine with the slowest speed.

Algorithm 23 SLOWEST-FIRST Algorithm

1: **Input:** speed of machines $s_1 \leq s_2 \leq ... \leq s_m$, Upper Bound Λ on L^{OPT}
2: **Initialize:** load on machine i, $\ell_i = 0$
3:
4: **for** $j = 1 : n$ (on j^{th} job arrival with size w_j) **do**
5:     Set of assignable machines for job j $M_A(j) = \{i | \ell_i + w_j/s_i \leq 2\Lambda\}$
6:     **if** $|M_A(j)| = 0$ **then**
7:         fail;
8:         break;
9:     **else**
10:         Assign job j to the slowest machine $a \in M_A(j)$,
11:         i.e., $a = \arg\min_{i \in M_A(j)} s_i$
12:         Update the load on the assigned machine $\ell_a = \ell_a + w_j/s_a$
13:     **end if**
14: **end for**

Theorem 12.2.10 *If $\Lambda \geq L^{\text{OPT}}$, then* SLOWEST-FIRST *never ends in state fail. Consequently, the load on any machine never exceeds 2Λ.*

Note that for defining SLOWEST-FIRST, we have assumed that the algorithm has the knowledge of an upper bound Λ on the optimal load L^{OPT}. If $L^{\text{OPT}} = \Lambda$, then Theorem 12.4.1 implies that the competitive ratio of the SLOWEST-FIRST algorithm is 2.

Without this 'genie-aided' assumption of $L^{\text{OPT}} \leq \Lambda$, to make the SLOWEST-FIRST algorithm realizable, we need to estimate Λ somehow from the input in a causal way. Moreover, to get a good competitive ratio guarantee, we need the estimate of Λ to be as close to L^{OPT} as possible. Towards that end, a generic technique called the doubling trick is useful that progressively updates Λ such that $L^{\text{OPT}} \leq \Lambda \leq 2L^{\text{OPT}}$ always and incurs an additional multiplicative penalty of 4 in terms of the competitive ratio. The overall competitive ratio of the SLOWEST-FIRST algorithm will be 8 after appending the doubling trick. The basic idea behind the doubling trick and the rigorous proof that it only incurs an additional multiplicative penalty of 4 in the competitive ratio is presented in Section 12.3.3. So, for the moment we let $L^{OPT} \leq \Lambda$ and proceed.

Proof: [Theorem 12.4.1] The main idea is to show that algorithm SLOWEST-FIRST never encounters the fail state when $L^{OPT} \leq \Lambda$, which implies that the load on all machines is at most 2Λ.

The proof follows a contradiction argument as follows. Let SLOWEST-FIRST encounter fail state on the jth job arrival. Let $\ell_i(j-1)$ be the load on machine i just before the jth job arrival. Consider the set of machines $E(j-1)$ with SLOWEST-FIRST just before the jth job arrival that have load at most L^{OPT}, i.e.,

$$E(j-1) = \{i|\ell_i(j-1) \leq L^{OPT}\}.$$

Among the $|E(j-1)|$ machines, consider the fastest machine, f_{j-1}, i.e., $f_{j-1} = \max\{i|i \in E(j-1)\}$ since machines are indexed in increasing order of their speeds. Note that to define $E(j-1)$, the load is compared to L^{OPT} and not 2Λ like in $M_A(j)$. It can be the case that $|E(j-1)| = 0$; in such an event we let $f_{j-1} = 0$.

Lemma 12.2.11 $f_{j-1} < m$ *(the fastest machine).*

Proof: Proof by contradiction. Suppose $f_{j-1} = m$, in which case by the definition of $E(j-1)$, the load on the mth machine

$$\ell_m(j-1) \leq L^{OPT}. \tag{12.18}$$

Moreover, since m is the fastest machine, we have $L^{OPT} \geq w_j/s_m$ since w_j has to be assigned to some machine by OPT as well, and assigning it to the fastest machine incurs the least individual load. Combining this with (12.18), we get

$$\ell_m(j-1) + w_j/s_m \leq L^{OPT} + L^{OPT} \leq 2\Lambda, \tag{12.19}$$

making the job j assignable to the mth machine, contradicting the fact that we encountered the fail state (no assignable machine) on job j's arrival. ∎

Define $O = \{i|\ell_i(j-1) > L^{OPT} \text{ with } i > f_{j-1}\}$ to be the set of overloaded machines with SLOWEST-FIRST just before the jth job arrival that are faster than machine f_{j-1}. Since $f_{j-1} < m$, $|O| > 0$. Moreover, from the definition of $E(j-1)$ and f_{j-1}, it follows that if machine $i \in O$, then machine $i + 1 \in O$ for $i + 1 \leq m$.

Among the first $j - 1$ jobs, let S_i and S_i^{OPT} be the set of jobs assigned to machine i by SLOWEST-FIRST and OPT, respectively. Consider the following load, which represents the load if all jobs of $\cup_{i \in O} S_i$ were assigned to the mth (fastest) machine:

$$\sum_{i \in O, k \in S_i} w_k/s_m = \sum_{i \in O, k \in S_i} \frac{\frac{w_k}{s_m}}{\frac{w_k}{s_i}} \frac{w_k}{s_i},$$

$$= \sum_{i \in O} \frac{s_i}{s_m} \sum_{k \in S_i} \frac{w_k}{s_i},$$

$$\overset{(a)}{>} \sum_{i \in O} \frac{s_i}{s_m} L^{\mathsf{OPT}},$$

$$\overset{(b)}{\geq} \sum_{i \in O} \frac{s_i}{s_m} \sum_{k \in S_i^{\mathsf{OPT}}} \frac{w_k}{s_i},$$

$$\overset{(c)}{=} \sum_{i \in O, k \in S_i^{\mathsf{OPT}}} w_k / s_m, \qquad (12.20)$$

where (a) follows since machine $i \in O$ and hence the load on machine $i \left(\sum_{k \in S_i} \frac{w_k}{s_i} \right)$ is more than L^{OPT} by the definition of O, while (b) follows from the optimality of OPT which has maximum load of at most L^{OPT}, while (c) is just the definition.

Multiplying both the left hand side (LHS) and the right hand side (RHS) of (12.20) by speed s_m of the fastest machine, we get

$$\sum_{i \in O, k \in S_i} w_k > \sum_{i \in O, k \in S_i^{\mathsf{OPT}}} w_k. \qquad (12.21)$$

Recall from the definition of set O that for any machine pair $i_1 \in O, i_2 \notin O$, $s_{i_1} \geq s_{i_2}$, i.e., machine i_1 is faster than i_2. Thus, (12.21) implies that there is at least one job $j' \in \cup_{i \in O} S_i$ such that $j' \notin \cup_{i \in O} S_i^{\mathsf{OPT}}$, i.e., there exists a job assigned by SLOWEST-FIRST to some machine in set O which is assigned by OPT to a machine m$'$ $\notin O$ that is slower than any machine in O.

Since OPT allocates job j' to some machine m$'$ $\notin O$, it must be that

$$w_{j'} / s_{\mathsf{m}'} \leq L^{\mathsf{OPT}} \leq \Lambda.$$

Moroever, by definition, f_{j-1} is the fastest machine among the set of machines $O^c = [m] \backslash O$, $f_{j-1} \geq \mathsf{m}'$. Therefore, we also have $w_{j'} / s_{f_{j-1}} \leq L^{\mathsf{OPT}} \leq \Lambda$. Recall that job j' is among the first $j-1$ jobs; hence it must be that the load on machine f_{j-1} just before the j'^{th} jobs's arrival is

$$\ell_{f_{j-1}}(j' - 1) \leq \ell_{f_{j-1}}(j - 1) \leq L^{\mathsf{OPT}},$$

where the second inequality follows since $f_{j-1} \in E(j-1)$. Therefore,

$$w_{j'} / s_{f_{j-1}} + \ell_{f_{j-1}}(j' - 1) \leq 2 L^{\mathsf{OPT}} \leq 2\Lambda,$$

making job j' assignable on machine f_{j-1}, where machine f_{j-1} is slower than any machine $i \in O$.

Recall that job j' has been assigned to some machine $i \in O$ by SLOWEST-FIRST since $j' \in \cup_{i \in O} S_i$. Thus, we get a contradiction, since SLOWEST-FIRST always chooses the slowest machine among all the assignable machines, but it has chosen some machine $i \in O$ to assign job j' even though job j' is assignable on machine f_{j-1}, and machine f_{j-1} is slower than any machine in $i \in O$. ∎

12.2.5 Machine Restriction

Another formulation that is of interest in the permanent jobs setting is when all machines are identical but for each job, there is a specific subset of machines where it can be processed. In this case, the natural greedy algorithm that assigns the newly arrived job to the least loaded server among the ones where it can be assigned is $\lceil \log_2 m \rceil + 1$ competitive, and any deterministic algorithm is at least $\lceil \log_2 m \rceil$ competitive [201]. We discuss the machine restriction case in detail for the temporary jobs case in the next subsection.

12.3 Temporary Jobs

In this section, we switch our attention to the more practical case of temporary jobs. In particular, we consider that once a job arrives, it remains in the system for a finite amount of time, and the departure time of a newly arrived job is not known to the algorithm, until it departs. Moreover, the speed of the assigned machine does not influence the departure time of the job. When a job departs (determined exogenously) the algorithm becomes aware of it. The setting where machine speeds can be modulated to influence the departure time of any job is referred to as *speed scaling* and is studied in Chapter 14.

12.3.1 Machine Restriction with Identical Machines

In this section, we consider the case when all machines are identical, i.e., they have the same speed, but there is a restriction that any machine can only process jobs belonging to specific subsets. In particular, let the set of m machines be denoted as $[m]$, and $M_j \subseteq [m]$ be the subset of machines that can process or serve job j.

There are a total of n jobs that arrive over time, and assigning job j to any machine belonging to M_j increases its load ℓ_j by amount w_j. Note that the load on any machine changes only when either a new job arrives or departs, referred to as an *epoch* hereafter. Let $t = 0, 1, \ldots$ be the epoch times, and the load at epoch t refers to the load of any machine right after the tth epoch. The **objective** is to assign jobs to machines so as to minimize the maximum of the loads on any machine at any epoch time.

Algorithm ROBIN-HOOD. Let $\ell_m(t)$ be the load of machine m at epoch time t.[2] The algorithm maintains an estimate $L(t)$ defined as follows. On the arrival of job j with size w_j at epoch t, set

$$L(t) = \max \left\{ L(t-1), w_j, \frac{1}{m} \left(w_j + \sum_{m \in [m]} \ell_m(t-1) \right) \right\}, \tag{12.22}$$

where the third term inside the max is the average of the load per machine in the system at epoch t (after the assignment of job j).

A machine m is defined to be *rich* at some epoch t if $\ell_m(t) \geq \sqrt{m}L(t)$, and is *poor* otherwise. If machine m is rich at epoch t, its *windfall* time is defined to be the last epoch at which it became rich, i.e., t_0 is the windfall time for machine m, if at epoch t_0^- it is was poor, and between

---

[2] By definition of epochs. ℓ_m does not change between t and $t + 1^-$.

epoch t_0 till t it remains rich throughout. Note that with this definition of $L(t)$, a rich machine can become poor and vice versa over time.

Algorithm: Assign job 1 to any arbitrary machine in M_1, and $L(1) = w_1$. Assign job j on its arrival to any poor machine of subset M_j, i.e., with $\ell_m(t-1) < \sqrt{m}L(t), m \in M_j$. If there is no poor machine available, then assign job j to a rich machine in M_j with the most recent windfall time.

If job j is assigned to machine $a \in M_j$, then the load of machine a is updated as $\ell_a(t) = \ell_a(t^-) + w_j$.

Remark 12.3.1 *From the definition of $L(t)$, $L(t) \geq \frac{1}{m}\left(w_j + \sum_{m\in[m]} \ell_m(t-1)\right)$. Thus, the total load $w_j + \sum_{m\in[m]} \ell_m(t-1)$ in the system at any epoch t on arrival of job j is at most $mL(t)$. Thus, at most $\sqrt{m}$ machines can be rich at any epoch.*

Let L^{OPT} be the optimal maximum load achieved by OPT over all epoch times t.

Lemma 12.3.2 *For any epoch t, $L(t) \leq L^{\text{OPT}}$ with the algorithm* ROBIN-HOOD.

Proof: Clearly, after assigning job 1, $L(t) \leq L^{\text{OPT}}$, since OPT also has to assign job 1 to some machine, which implies $L^{\text{OPT}} \geq w_1$ and $L(1) = w_1$ by definition. Assume that for epoch $0 \leq \tau \leq t-1$, $L(\tau) \leq L^{\text{OPT}}$. Let $L(t)$ increase at epoch t on the arrival of job j. Once again $L^{\text{OPT}} \geq w_j$.

Note that the total workload in the system just after the arrival of job j at epoch t is

$$w_j + \sum_{m\in[m]} \ell_m(t-1),$$

which at best can be equally distributed over the m machines by OPT. Hence, we have $L^{\text{OPT}} \geq \frac{1}{m}\left(w_j + \sum_{m\in[m]} \ell_m(t-1)\right)$. Thus, using the induction hypothesis, and the definition of $L(t)$, it is immediate that $L(t) \leq L^{\text{OPT}}$ at the next epoch t. ∎

Using Lemma 12.3.1, we next prove the following result.

Theorem 12.3.3 *The competitive ratio of* ROBIN-HOOD *is at most $2\sqrt{m} + 1$.*

Proof: To prove the result, we will show that at any epoch t, and for any machine $m \in M$,

$$\ell_m(t) \leq \sqrt{m}(L(t) + L^{\text{OPT}}) + L^{\text{OPT}}. \tag{12.23}$$

Combining (12.23) with Lemma 12.3.2 implies the claimed competitive ratio bound for algorithm ROBIN-HOOD.

For any poor machine at epoch t, (12.23) is true by the definition of it being poor. Consider a rich machine m at epoch t, and let S_m be the set of jobs that were assigned to it after its windfall time t_0 that have not departed till epoch t. Let $j \in S_m$ be one such job. Since machine m is rich throughout time $[t_0, t]$, all machines $M_j\backslash\{m\}$ must have become rich before time t_0, or otherwise ROBIN-HOOD would have assigned job m to one of the machines in $M_j\backslash\{m\}$. Let k be the number of machines to which any of the jobs of S_m could have been assigned, $k = |\cup_{j\in S_m} M_j|$. Since at most $\sqrt{m}$ machines are rich at any epoch (Remark 12.3.1), we get $k \leq \sqrt{m}$.

Let q be the job that made the machine m rich at epoch t_0. Trivially $w_q \leq L^{OPT}$. Moreover, by the pigeon-hole principle, $\sum_{j \in S_m} w_j \leq kL^{OPT}$. Thus, the load on machine m at time t is

$$\ell_m(t) \leq \ell_m(t_0^-) + w_q + \sum_{j \in S_m} w_j,$$

$$\overset{(a)}{\leq} \sqrt{m}L(t_0^-) + w_q + \sum_{j \in S_m} w_j,$$

$$\overset{(b)}{\leq} \sqrt{m}L(t_0^-) + L^{OPT} + kL^{OPT},$$

$$\overset{(c)}{\leq} \sqrt{m}L(t_0^-) + L^{OPT} + \sqrt{m}L^{OPT},$$

$$\overset{(d)}{\leq} \sqrt{m}L(t) + L^{OPT} + \sqrt{m}L^{OPT}, \qquad (12.24)$$

where (a) follows since machine m was poor at epoch t_0^-, (b) follows from $w_q \leq L^{OPT}$, and $\sum_{j \in S_m} w_j \leq kL^{OPT}$, while (c) follows since $k \leq \sqrt{m}$, and (d) since $L(t)$ is a non-decreasing function of time $L(t_0^-) \leq L(t)$. Combining (12.24) with Lemma 12.3.2, we get

$$\ell_m(t) \leq (2\sqrt{m} + 1)L^{OPT},$$

for any machine m at all times t, proving the claim. ∎

ROBIN-HOOD is optimal up to a multiplicative factor of $\sqrt{2}$ since one can show a lower bound on the competitive ratio for any deterministic online algorithm to be $\sqrt{m}$ [202]. Hence, the optimal competitive ratio for any deterministic online algorithm is $\Theta(\sqrt{m})$ under this setting, which is very pessimistic. The large competitive ratio is a result of the arbitrary restriction on the set of machines that any job can be assigned to. A more reasonable setting is when the machines are not identical but any job can be assigned to any machine. This relaxation fundamentally changes the optimal competitive ratios, and one can derive online algorithms with constant competitive ratios. We discuss this relaxed model in the next subsection.

12.3.2 No Machine Restriction with Non-Identical Machines

Similar to Section 12.3.1, we consider the temporary jobs setting where the departure time of jobs is unknown, and which is not impacted by any scheduling decision. In comparison to Section 12.3.1, however, we remove the machine restriction, i.e., any job can be assigned to any machine but each machine has a different speed.

Let the total number of machines be m. A total of n jobs arrive sequentially, and on the arrival of job j its size w_j is revealed, which can be assigned to any of the m machines. The speed of machine $i, i = 1, 2, \ldots, m$, is s_i, and the load exerted on machine i by assigning job j to it is $\frac{w_j}{s_i}$. The load on any machine at any time is the sum of the loads exerted by jobs assigned to it. It is worth noting that $\frac{w_j}{s_i}$ is not in any way related to the departure time of the job j.

Without loss of generality, we assume that machines are indexed in order of increasing speeds, i.e., $s_1 \leq s_2 \leq \ldots \leq s_m$.

Without knowing the departure time of any job, the problem is to assign each job to one of the machines so as to minimize the maximum of the loads on any machine across all times.

A job is defined to be **active** at time t if it has arrived by time t but has not departed by time t. For a set of machines G, define $S(G) = \sum_{g \in G} s_g$ to be the sum of the speeds of machines in set G. Let the optimal load incurred by OPT be L^{OPT}, and let this be known to any online algorithm. We will remove this restriction later using the doubling trick. The time instant just before time t is denoted as t^-. Let the load on machine g at time t^- be $\ell_g(t^-)$, which is equal to the load exerted by all active jobs at time t^- assigned to machine g.

A job j that arrives at time t is defined to be *assignable* to machine g if and only if

1. $\frac{w_j}{s_g} \leq L^{OPT}$ and

2. $\ell_g(t^-) + \frac{w_j}{s_g} \leq cL^{OPT}$ for some $c > 1$ to be chosen later.

Algorithm SLOW-FIT: Assign job j on its arrival to the **slowest** assignable machine. Break ties if necessary by assigning the job to the machine with the smallest index.

Theorem 12.3.4 *If $c \geq 5$, then the SLOW-FIT algorithm guarantees that all jobs are assignable, i.e., for each job there is at least one machine that is assignable on its arrival.*

Theorem 12.3.4 directly gives us the following upper bound on the competitive ratio of the SLOW-FIT algorithm.

Corollary 12.3.5 *The competitive ratio of the SLOW-FIT algorithm is at most 5.*

Proof: From Theorem 12.3.4, with algorithm SLOW-FIT, each job is assignable for $c \geq 5$. Consequently, by the definition of algorithm SLOW-FIT, the load on any machine is at most cL^{OPT} at any time. Thus, the maximum load across all machines at all times is upper bounded by cL^{OPT}, which implies that the competitive ratio of algorithm SLOW-FIT is at most $c \geq 5$. ∎

Remark 12.3.6 *If instead of L^{OPT}, only an upper bound $\Lambda > L^{OPT}$ is known, then replacing L^{OPT} by Λ in the algorithm definition, we will get that all jobs are assignable, and the maximum load on any machine is at most $c\Lambda$.*

Now we prove Theorem 12.3.4.

Proof: Recall that a job is defined to be active at time t if it has arrived by time t but has not departed by time t. Let the cumulative size of all active jobs (summed across all machines) with the algorithm SLOW-FIT at time t be $C_{SF}(t)$. We use contradiction to prove Theorem 12.3.4. Let at some time t_0, job q arrives that is not assignable. We will show that this will imply that at some earlier time $t' < t_0$, the cumulative size of all active jobs $C_{SF}(t')$ is more than

$$\left(\sum_{i=1}^{m} s_i \right) L^{OPT}. \tag{12.25}$$

To show that (12.25) is not possible, consider the set of all active jobs $A(t')$ at time t', and let $\mathcal{J}_j \subseteq A(t')$ be the set of jobs allocated by OPT to machine j. Then by the definition of OPT, $\sum_{i \in \mathcal{J}_j} w_i \leq s_j L^{OPT}$. Summing this across all machines j, we get that the cumulative size of all active jobs $A(t')$ at time t' satisfies the following upper bound:

$$\sum_{j=1}^{m} \sum_{i \in \mathcal{J}_j} w_i \leq \sum_{j=1}^{m} s_j L^{OPT}.$$

Since the LHS is just the total size of all active jobs and is independent of the algorithm chosen,

$$C_{SF}(t') \leq \sum_{j=1}^{m} \sum_{i \in \mathcal{J}_j} w_i.$$

Therefore, (12.25) can never be true.

To show that if some job q that arrives at time t_0 being not assignable implies (12.25), we will construct a sequence of time *epochs* t_i backwards in time $t_k < t_{k-1} < \cdots < t_1 < t_0$ and a corresponding disjoint set of machines $G_k, G_{k-1}, \ldots, G_1, G_0$ for which two properties **P1** and **P2** (listed below) will hold true.

To begin with, t_0 is the time at which job q arrives which is not assignable, and $G_0 = \{m\}$, the fastest machine. At time t_i^-, let $J(G_i)$ be the set of active jobs that are assigned by SLOW-FIT to the set of machines G_i. Using set $J(G_i)$, we will define G_{i+1} and t_{i+1} as follows.

$[G_{i+1}]$ To define G_{i+1}, consider the set of machines to which OPT assigns the jobs of $J(G_i)$, and let m_{i+1} be the slowest machine to which OPT assigns any jobs of $J(G_i)$. Then set G_{i+1} is defined as the contiguous set of machines starting from m_{i+1} till the one before the first (slowest) machine of set G_i, i.e.,

$$G_{i+1} = \{m_{i+1}, m_{i+2}, \ldots, m_i - 1\}. \tag{12.26}$$

For example, $G_1 = \{m_1, \ldots, m-1\}$ for some m_1, since $G_0 = \{m\}$. See Figure 12.1 for a pictorial illustration. It is important to note that if $m_{i+1} \geq m_i$, then set G_{i+1} is empty. If $G_{i+1} = \varnothing$, we will get a contradiction right away, as will be pointed out later. Thus, for the moment assume that G_i's are non-empty until step k, at which time G_k includes machine 1, the slowest.

Note that by definition, OPT assigns jobs of $J(G_i)$ to machines in $\cup_{0 \leq j \leq i+1} G_j$.

$[t_{i+1}]$ Consider the task q_i with the smallest size in set $J(G_i)$. Define time t_{i+1} to be the arrival time of job q_i. For a pictorial description see Figure 12.2.

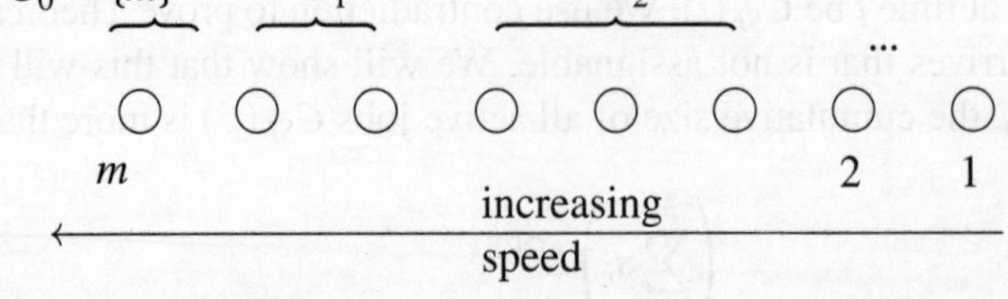

$$G_0 = \{m\} \qquad G_1 \qquad\qquad G_2$$

$$m \qquad\qquad\qquad\qquad\qquad\qquad 2 \quad 1$$

increasing
speed

Figure 12.1 Definition of G_{i+1} using contiguous blocks of machines starting from the fastest to the slowest.

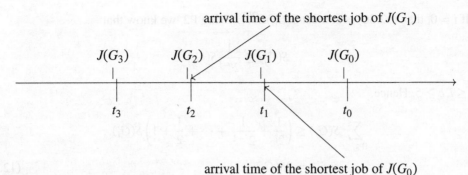

arrival time of the shortest job of $J(G_1)$

$J(G_3)$ $J(G_2)$ $J(G_1)$ $J(G_0)$

t_3 t_2 t_1 t_0

arrival time of the shortest job of $J(G_0)$

Figure 12.2 Pictorial description of definition of the time instants t_i, where $J(G_i)$ is the set of active jobs at time t_i^- with SLOW-FIT.

Next, we claim that with our definitions, the following two properties hold for each i:

P1 At time t_i^-, each machine in G_i has a load that exceeds $(c-1)L^{OPT}$.
P2 For $0 < j \le i$, $S(G_j) \ge (c-3)S(G_{j-1})$, where $S(G) = \sum_{g \in G} s_g$.

We prove them as follows. Note that for any job j, we have

$$w_j/s_m \le L^{OPT}, \tag{12.27}$$

since m is the fastest machine, and OPT assigns job j to some machine. Therefore, since job q is unassignable at time t_0 with SLOW-FIT, the load on the fastest machine at time t_0^- must be at least

$$\ell_m(t_0^-) + w_j/s_m > cL^{OPT}.$$

Using (12.27), we get

$$\ell_m(t_0^-) > (c-1)L^{OPT}. \tag{12.28}$$

Since $G_0 = \{m\}$, we have that P1 is true for t_0, while P2 is true trivially for $i = 0$.

Next, assume that P1 and P2 hold at the end of the ith iteration of defining G_i and t_i. We want to show that P1 and P2 hold for the $(i+1)^{st}$ iteration.

From P1, we know that each machine in G_i has a load greater than $(c-1)L^{OPT}$ at time t_i^-. Therefore, the cumulative size of all jobs (of set $J(G_i)$) assigned to the set of machines G_i is at least

$$(c-1)S(G_i)L^{OPT}. \tag{12.29}$$

Since all jobs of set $J(G_i)$ are active at time t_i^- (by definition), the cumulative size of jobs in $J(G_i)$ assigned to machines in set $\cup_{0 \le j \le i} G_j$ by OPT is upper bounded by

$$\sum_{0 \le j \le i} S(G_j)L^{OPT}, \tag{12.30}$$

since the maximum load on any machine with OPT is at most L^{OPT}.

If $i = 0$, then (12.30) is at most $S(G_0)L^{OPT}$. Using P2, we know that

$$S(G_j) \leq \frac{1}{2^{i-j}}S(G_i)$$

for $j \leq i, c \geq 5$. Hence,

$$\sum_{0 \leq j \leq i} S(G_j) \leq \left(\frac{1}{2^i} + \frac{1}{2^{i-1}} + \cdots + \frac{1}{2} + 1\right)S(G_i).$$

$$= 2S(G_i). \tag{12.31}$$

Hence, for $i > 0$, (12.30) is bounded by $2S(G_i)L^{OPT}$.

Recall from (12.29) that the cumulative size of active jobs in $J(G_i)$ at time t_i^- is at least $(c-1)S(G_i)L^{OPT}$. Since OPT can only assign $2S(G_i)L^{OPT}$ of it to machines in G_i, OPT has to allocate at least $(c-3)S(G_i)L^{OPT}$ amount of size of jobs in $J(G_i)$ to machines in G_{i+1}. Since the load on any machine never exceeds L^{OPT} with OPT, we have

$$(c-3)S(G_i)L^{OPT} \leq S(G_{i+1})L^{OPT}, \tag{12.32}$$

since $S(G_{i+1})L^{OPT}$ is the maximum cumulative size that machines in G_{i+1} can handle. Therefore, property P2 is proven for set G_{i+1}.

To prove property P1, recall that the job $q_i \in J(G_i)$ has the smallest size in set $J(G_i)$ whose arrival time is the next time epoch t_{i+1} (backwards). Since q_i is assigned to some machine G_i by SLOW-FIT, all machines in G_{i+1} must have been unassignable at time t_{i+1} since machines in set G_{i+1} are slower than machines in G_i, and SLOW-FIT always assigns new jobs to the slowest assignable machine.

Recall that OPT allocates some jobs of $J(G_i)$ to the slowest machine in G_{i+1}. Let job $r \in J(G_i)$ be assigned to the slowest machine m_{i+1} of G_{i+1} by OPT. Also, with OPT the load on machine m_{i+1} is at most L^{OPT}. Thus,

$$w_r/s_{\mathsf{m}_{i+1}} \leq L^{OPT}. \tag{12.33}$$

Since $q_i \in J(G_i)$ is the job with the smallest size, we have $w_{q_i} \leq w_r$. Thus, (12.34) implies that

$$\frac{w_{q_i}}{s_g} \leq L^{OPT} \tag{12.34}$$

for all $g \in G_{i+1}$ since $s_g \geq s_{\mathsf{m}_{i+1}}$ (m_{i+1} is the slowest machine among G_{i+1}). The unassignable condition of job q_i to all machines of G_{i+1} implies that

$$\ell_g(t_{i+1}^-) + \frac{w_{q_i}}{s_g} \geq cL^{OPT},$$

$$\ell_g(t_{i+1}^-) \geq (c-1)L^{OPT}, \forall g \in G_{i+1}, \tag{12.35}$$

where the second inequality follows from (12.34). This proves property P1.

Now we complete the argument to show that if a job is unassignable with SLOW-FIT, it implies (12.25). Consider iteration k, where the set G_k includes machine 1 (the slowest machine). Then from P1, we have that the cumulative size of jobs in $J(G_k)$ at time t_k^- is at least

$$\geq (c-1)S(G_k)L^{\text{OPT}},$$

$$\overset{(a)}{\geq} (c-1)\frac{\sum_{0\leq i\leq k} S(G_i)}{2}L^{\text{OPT}},$$

$$\overset{(b)}{=} \frac{c-1}{2}\left(\sum_{i=1}^{m} s_i\right)L^{\text{OPT}}, \tag{12.36}$$

where (a) follows from P2, which shows that $\sum_{0\leq i\leq k} S(G_i) \leq 2S(G_k)$, and (b) from the definition of k, i.e., $\sum_{0\leq i\leq k} S(G_i) = \sum_{i=1}^{m} s_i$. Thus, for $c \geq 5$, (12.36) is equivalent to (12.25), which we know cannot happen. Thus, we have that all jobs are assignable with SLOW-FIT for $c \geq 5$.

Finally, we argue that we get a similar contradiction if $G_i = \emptyset$, while $1 \notin \cup_{j=0}^{i-1} G_j$, i.e., the slowest machine is not part of any set $G_0, \dots, G_{i-1}$.

From P1, we know that each machine in G_{i-1} has a load greater than $(c-1)L^{\text{OPT}}$ at time t_{i-1}^-. Therefore, the cumulative size of all jobs (of set $J(G_{i-1})$) assigned to the set of machines G_{i-1} at time t_{i-1}^- is at least

$$(c-1)S(G_{i-1})L^{\text{OPT}}.$$

But since $G_i = \emptyset$, all jobs of set $J(G_{i-1})$ are assigned to machines $\cup_{0\leq j\leq i-1} G_j$. Thus, we get that the cumulative size of all jobs assigned by OPT to machines $G_0, \dots, G_{i-1}$ at time t_{i-1}^- is at least

$$(c-1)S(G_{i-1})L^{\text{OPT}}. \tag{12.37}$$

By definition of OPT, the cumulative size of all jobs assigned by OPT to machines $G_0, \dots, G_{i-1}$ at any time is

$$\sum_{0\leq j\leq i-1} S(G_j)L^{\text{OPT}} \overset{\text{P2}}{\leq} 2S(G_{i-1})L^{\text{OPT}}. \tag{12.38}$$

Since $c \geq 5$, we get a contradiction combining (12.37) and (12.38).   ∎

Next, we present the trick to remove the restriction that an online algorithm needs the knowledge of an upper bound on OPT's optimal load.

12.3.3 The Doubling Trick

Quite often in defining an online algorithm, it is useful to assume that the optimal value achieved by OPT is known, e.g. in algorithm SLOWEST-FIRST (Section 12.2.4) and algorithm SLOW-FIT (Section 12.3.2). However, to make the algorithm realizable, one needs to remove this restriction, which is typically done using a *doubling* trick, which in principle is as follows.

To start with, initialize the estimated optimal value by the corresponding size of the earliest arriving job, which is generally less or more than the actual optimal depending on whether we are solving a minimization or a maximization problem. The estimate is kept as it is as long as the algorithm remains 'feasible', and is doubled on encountering successive infeasibility. To better understand the doubling trick, we describe this idea in detail for SLOW-FIT as follows and call the algorithm modified SLOW-FIT.

Recall that SLOW-FIT needs to know the optimal load L^{OPT}. Let $\tilde{L}^{OPT}(h)$ be the estimated value of L^{OPT} in phase h (defined later) that will be used in modified SLOW-FIT. Phase 1 starts on the first job arrival, and $\tilde{L}^{OPT}(1) = w_1/s_m$, where s_m is the speed of the fastest machine. Clearly, $L^{OPT} \geq w_1/s_m$, and hence $L^{OPT} \geq \tilde{L}^{OPT}(1)$.

Execute SLOW-FIT using $\tilde{L}^{OPT}(1)$ instead of L^{OPT} until some job becomes unassignable. Let q be the first job that is unassignable. Then phase 2 begins starting from job q after updating the current estimate of L^{OPT} as $\tilde{L}^{OPT}(2) = 2\tilde{L}^{OPT}(1)$. The current load on all machines is made zero and SLOW-FIT is executed assuming that q is the first job with $L^{OPT} = \tilde{L}^{OPT}(2)$. We call this the modified SLOW-FIT algorithm.

Refer to Figure 12.3 for a simple illustration of this modified SLOW-FIT algorithm, where shaded and non-shaded rectangles represent unassignable and assignable jobs, respectively. In general, on the arrival of each unassignable job, a new phase begins after the estimate of L^{OPT} is updated as $\tilde{L}^{OPT}(h) = 2\tilde{L}^{OPT}(h-1)$, and the algorithm forgets about all prior job assignments made to any machine earlier, i.e., resets the load of each machine to be zero, and implements SLOW-FIT with the newly updated estimate $\tilde{L}^{OPT}$ of L^{OPT}. Note that whenever a job becomes unassignable to all machines at the end of phase $h-1$, we can deduce that $L^{OPT} > \tilde{L}^{OPT}(h-1)$, since otherwise the job would have been assignable (Theorem 12.3.4).

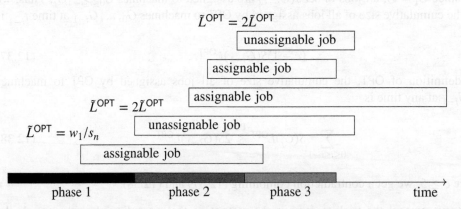

Figure 12.3 Pictorial description of modified SLOW-FIT algorithm, where the colour of the rectangle changes whenever $\tilde{L}^{OPT}$ is doubled.

Theorem 12.3.7 *The competitive ratio of modified* SLOW-FIT *is $4c$ for $c \geq 5$.*

We need the following preliminary results to prove Theorem 12.3.7.

Lemma 12.3.8 *The total number of phases is h_{Last}, where h_{Last} is the smallest integer for which $L^{OPT} \leq 2^{h_{Last}} w_1/s_m$. Moreover, the largest value of $\tilde{L}^{OPT}(h_{Last}) \leq 2L^{OPT}$.*

Proof: Let h_{Last} be the earliest phase at which $\tilde{L}^{\text{OPT}}(h_{\text{Last}})$ exceeds L^{OPT}. Then from Theorem 12.3.4 we know that all jobs that arrive after phase h_{Last} are assignable with SLOW-FIT, and hence $\tilde{L}^{\text{OPT}}(h_{\text{Last}})$ is never doubled. Since the initial value of $\tilde{L}^{\text{OPT}}(1) = w_1/s_m$, and in the beginning of each phase $\tilde{L}^{\text{OPT}}$ is doubled, the first claim follows.

For the second claim, note that a new phase h is started only if $L^{\text{OPT}} > \tilde{L}^{\text{OPT}}(h-1)$, and at which time $\tilde{L}^{\text{OPT}}$ is doubled. Let the last phase be h_{Last}, after which all jobs are assignable; then $\tilde{L}^{\text{OPT}}(h_{\text{Last}} - 1) < L^{\text{OPT}}$ and hence $\tilde{L}^{\text{OPT}}(h_{\text{Last}}) \leq 2L^{\text{OPT}}$.   ∎

Lemma 12.3.9 *For any phase h, just considering the jobs that arrive within that phase, the maximum load incurred by modified SLOW-FIT is at most $c\tilde{L}^{\text{OPT}}(h)$.*

Proof: Within any phase h, the value of $\tilde{L}^{\text{OPT}}(h)$ remains the same. Thus, from Theorem 12.3.4 all jobs arriving within that phase are assignable with the estimate $\tilde{L}^{\text{OPT}}(h)$ of the true optimal value, which implies the result from the definition of assignability.   ∎

Proof: [Theorem 12.3.7] Let the total number of phases be h_{Last}. From Lemma 12.3.9, the maximum load in any phase i is at most $c\tilde{L}^{\text{OPT}}(i) \leq 2^{i-1}c\tilde{L}^{\text{OPT}}(1)$. Jobs arriving in any phase can last for many future phases (see Figure 12.3); however, modified SLOW-FIT disregards the jobs already allocated in previous phases. Therefore, the total load at any time can be at most the sum of maximum loads across all phases, and is given by

$$\sum_{i=1}^{h_{\text{Last}}} 2^{i-1}c\tilde{L}^{\text{OPT}}(1) \leq 2^{h_{\text{Last}}}c\tilde{L}^{\text{OPT}}(1),$$

$$= c2.2^{h_{\text{Last}}-1}\tilde{L}^{\text{OPT}}(1),$$

$$= 2c\tilde{L}^{\text{OPT}}(h_{\text{Last}}),$$

$$\overset{(a)}{\leq} c2.2L^{\text{OPT}},$$

$$= 4cL^{\text{OPT}},$$

where (a) follows from the second claim of Lemma 12.3.8.   ∎

12.4 Network Load Balancing

In this section, we consider a network load balancing problem, where the network is represented by a graph $G = (V, E)$ with node set V and edge set E, with $|V| = m, |E| = n$, and each edge e has capacity $u : E \to \mathbb{R}^+$.

Jobs arrive at some $s \in V$ called the source node that is destined for some node $t \in V$ (called the destination). In particular, job i is characterized by a triplet (s_i, t_i, w_i), where s_i is the source node, t_i is the destination node, and $w_i \in \mathbb{R}^+$ is the size or resource demand that job i will put on each edge on the path between s_i and t_i that is used to serve job i. We consider the permanent jobs setting, where once the jobs arrive it stays in the system forever.

Job i is defined to be *fulfilled* once a single path P_i (no splitting is allowed) between s_i and t_i is identified for routing job i. Consequently, for each edge $e \in P_i$, an additional load of $\frac{w_i}{u(e)}$ is exerted on it. Thus, for an edge $e \in E$, its load after assigning the first j jobs is defined to be

$$\ell_e(j) = \sum_{i\,:\,e \in P_i, i \leq j} \frac{w_i}{u(e)}, \tag{12.39}$$

which represents the total load exerted on edge e by all the paths passing through it, till the jth job request.

Let path P_i be used to fulfil job i by an online algorithm $\mathcal{A}$. Let the total number of jobs that arrive sequentially be k (k need not be known to an online algorithm). Then the set of paths used by $\mathcal{A}$ to serve all the k jobs are $\mathcal{P} = \{P_1, \ldots, P_k\}$. Similar definition for OPT yields $\mathcal{P}^{\mathsf{OPT}} = \{P_1^{\mathsf{OPT}}, \ldots, P_k^{\mathsf{OPT}}\}$, where the appropriate loads on each edge with the $\mathcal{P}$ and $\mathcal{P}^{\mathsf{OPT}}$ are as given in (12.39).

Let for $\mathcal{A}$, the maximum load across all edges after $j \leq k$ job arrivals be

$$\lambda_{\mathcal{A}}(j) = \max_e \ell_e(j).$$

Similarly, $\ell_e^{\mathsf{OPT}}(j)$ and $\lambda_{\mathsf{OPT}}(j)$ are the corresponding quantities for OPT. Then the competitive ratio of $\mathcal{A}$ is defined as

$$\mu_{\mathcal{A}} = \max_{\sigma} \frac{\lambda_{\mathcal{A}}(k)}{\lambda_{\mathsf{OPT}}(k)},$$

where $\sigma = \{(s_i, t_i, w_i)\}_{i=1}^{j}, j \leq k$, represents the job input sequence. The objective is to find $\mathcal{A}$ that minimizes $\mu_{\mathcal{A}}$.

Assuming the knowledge of an upper bound Λ on the optimal load $\lambda_{\mathsf{OPT}}(k)$ i.e., $\lambda_{\mathsf{OPT}}(k) \leq \Lambda$, we normalize the resource demand and the load on each edge by Λ to get $\tilde{w} = \frac{w}{\Lambda}$ and $\tilde{\ell}_e = \frac{\ell_e}{\Lambda}$. Knowing Λ, algorithm WEIGHTED-SHORTEST-PATH assigns a weight to each edge in the network, and uses the shortest path over the network (with edge weights as cost) to serve a new job request. On each new job arrival with size w, the new weight of an edge e is updated as

$$a^{\text{old load on } e + \frac{\tilde{w}}{u_e}} - a^{\text{old load on } e}$$

for some $a > 1$. This ensures that weight increases faster for edges that are already sufficiently loaded, and following the shortest path routing with updated weights, the algorithm tries to distribute the load throughout the network in order to minimize $\lambda_{\mathcal{A}}(k)$. For some $\beta > 1$, if there exists any edge on the shortest path such that the updated load after assignment of the newest request on the computed shortest path is greater than or equal to $\beta\Lambda$, the algorithm ends in a fail state and stops.

We next show that with an appropriate choice of β, the algorithm never fails, and consequently we get a competitive ratio bound for it.

Algorithm 24 WEIGHTED-SHORTEST-PATH Algorithm

1: **Input:** Graph G, Λ (upper bound on the optimal load), $u(e)$ (capacity of edge e), β (parameter to be chosen), $a > 1$

2: Initialize $\tilde{\ell}_e = \ell_e = 0$ for all $e \in E$

3: **for** each new job request (s, t, w) **do**

4:     $\tilde{w} = w/\Lambda$

5:     $\tilde{\ell}_e = \ell_e/\Lambda$,

6:     Weight of edge e, $c_e = a^{\tilde{\ell}_e + \frac{\tilde{w}}{u(e)}} - a^{\tilde{\ell}_e}$ for all $e \in E$

7:     Let S be the shortest path from $\mathsf{s} \to \mathsf{t}$ with respect to cost c_e

8:     **if** $\exists\, e \in S : \ell_e + \frac{w}{u(e)} \geq \beta\Lambda$ **then**

9:         b=FAIL

10:     **else**

11:         b=SUCCESS.

12:         Assign job request (s, t, w) over edges of S

13:         $\forall e \in S, \ell_e = \ell_e + \frac{w}{u(e)}$, % update the load

14:     **end if**

15: **end for**

Theorem 12.4.1 *If $\lambda_{\mathsf{OPT}}(k) \leq \Lambda$, then $\exists\, \beta = \mathcal{O}(\log m)$ such that* WEIGHTED-SHORTEST-PATH *never ends in the FAIL state. Consequently, the maximum load on any edge with* WEIGHTED-SHORTEST-PATH *is at most $\beta\Lambda$.*

Remark 12.4.2 *As before, if $\lambda_{\mathsf{OPT}}(k) = \Lambda$, then the competitive ratio of algorithm* WEIGHTED-SHORTEST-PATH *is at most $\mathcal{O}(\log m)$. Even otherwise, using the doubling trick to estimate $\lambda_{\mathsf{OPT}}(k)$, the competitive ratio of algorithm* WEIGHTED-SHORTEST-PATH *is at most $\mathcal{O}(\log m)$. We briefly discuss this at the end of this subsection in Theorem 12.4.4.*

To prove Theorem 12.4.1 we once again use a potential function argument similar to many problems already encountered in the book, e.g. the MARKING algorithm for the paging problem in Chapter 5. Let $\tilde{\ell}_e(j)$ and $\tilde{\ell}_e^{\mathsf{OPT}}(j)$ be the (normalized) load on edge e with WEIGHTED-SHORTEST-PATH and OPT after j job arrivals, respectively. After the arrival of j requests, the potential function Φ is defined as

$$\Phi(j) = \sum_{e \in E} a^{\tilde{\ell}_e(j)}(\gamma - \tilde{\ell}_e^{\mathsf{OPT}}(j)) \tag{12.40}$$

for some $\gamma > 1$. The parameter $a > 1$ is the same as that used to define algorithm WEIGHTED-SHORTEST-PATH.

We will show in Lemma 12.4.3 that the potential function (12.40) with WEIGHTED-SHORTEST-PATH is non-increasing as more jobs arrive. In particular, we will show that $\Phi(j + 1) - \Phi(j) \leq 0$ for $a = 1 + \frac{1}{\gamma}$. Using Lemma 12.4.3, we complete the proof of Theorem 12.4.1.

Proof: [Proof of Theorem 12.4.1] Initially, at time 0 before the arrival of any request, $\tilde{\ell}_e(j) = \tilde{\ell}_e^{\mathsf{OPT}}(j) = 0$ and

$$\Phi(0) = \gamma|E| = \gamma n.$$

Moreover, since Φ is non-increasing (Lemma 12.4.3), after the arrival of all k jobs,

$$\Phi(k) \leq \gamma n.$$

Once the kth (last) job request arrives, by definition,

$$\Phi(k) = \sum_{e \in E} a^{\tilde{\ell}_e(k)}(\gamma - \tilde{\ell}_e^{\mathsf{OPT}}(k)). \tag{12.41}$$

Since $\tilde{\ell}_e^{\mathsf{OPT}}(k) = \dfrac{\ell_e^{\mathsf{OPT}}(k)}{\Lambda} \leq 1$,

$$\Phi(k) \geq \sum_{e \in E} a^{\tilde{\ell}_e(k)}(\gamma - 1). \tag{12.42}$$

Since $\gamma > 1$, combining (12.42) with the fact that $\Phi(k) \leq \gamma n$, we get that for each term corresponding to edge $e \in E$ of (12.42),

$$(\gamma - 1)a^{\tilde{\ell}_e(k)} \leq \gamma n. \tag{12.43}$$

Hence, the maximum load on any edge with WEIGHTED-SHORTEST-PATH,

$$\lambda(k) = \max_{e \in E} \ell_e(k) = \Lambda \max_{e \in E} \tilde{\ell}_e(k) \leq \Lambda \log_a \left(\frac{\gamma n}{\gamma - 1} \right) = \mathcal{O}\left(\Lambda \log m \right),$$

since $n \leq m^2$, where m is the number of vertices of graph G, and $a = 1 + \dfrac{1}{\gamma}$. Thus, if $\beta = \mathcal{O}(\log m)$, WEIGHTED-SHORTEST-PATH never reaches the FAIL state ∎

Next, we state and prove the critical lemma.

Lemma 12.4.3 *For any number of job arrivals j, $\Phi(j + 1) - \Phi(j) \leq 0$ for $a = 1 + \dfrac{1}{\gamma}$.*

Proof: WEIGHTED-SHORTEST-PATH uses path P_{j+1}, while OPT uses P_{j+1}^{OPT} to route the $j + 1^{st}$ job, respectively. Then the change in potential after serving job request $j + 1$ is

$$\Phi(j + 1) - \Phi(j) = \sum_{e \in E} a^{\tilde{\ell}_e(j+1)}(\gamma - \tilde{\ell}_e^{\mathsf{OPT}}(j+1)) - \sum_{e \in E} a^{\tilde{\ell}_e(j)}(\gamma - \tilde{\ell}_e^{\mathsf{OPT}}(j)).$$

Note that OPT affects only the $\tilde{\ell}_e^{\mathsf{OPT}}$ terms for $e \in \mathcal{P}^{\mathsf{OPT}}$, while algorithm WEIGHTED-SHORTEST-PATH affects only the $\tilde{\ell}_e$ terms for $e \in E$. We first account for the change $\Phi(j + 1) - \Phi(j)$ because of OPT, and then from algorithm WEIGHTED-SHORTEST-PATH.

By expanding $\tilde{\ell}_e^{\mathsf{OPT}}(j + 1) = \tilde{\ell}_e^{\mathsf{OPT}}(j) + \dfrac{\tilde{w}(j+1)}{u(e)}$ for $e \in P_{j+1}^{\mathsf{OPT}}$ and noting that $\tilde{\ell}_e^{\mathsf{OPT}}(j + 1) = \tilde{\ell}_e^{\mathsf{OPT}}(j)$ for $e \notin P_{j+1}^{\mathsf{OPT}}$ since with OPT, the load does not change for any paths other than P_{j+1}^{OPT}, we get

$$\Phi(j+1) - \Phi(j) = \sum_{e \in P_{j+1}^{\text{OPT}}} a^{\tilde{\ell}_e(j+1)} \left(\gamma - \tilde{\ell}_e^{\text{OPT}}(j) - \frac{\tilde{w}(j+1)}{u(e)} \right)$$

$$+ \sum_{e \notin P_{j+1}^{\text{OPT}}} a^{\tilde{\ell}_e(j+1)} \left(\gamma - \tilde{\ell}_e^{\text{OPT}}(j) \right) - \sum_{e \in E} a^{\tilde{\ell}_e(j)} \left(\gamma - \tilde{\ell}_e^{\text{OPT}}(j) \right),$$

$$\overset{(a)}{=} \sum_{e \in E} \left(\gamma - \tilde{\ell}_e^{\text{OPT}}(j) \right) \left(a^{\tilde{\ell}_e(j+1)} - a^{\tilde{\ell}_e(j)} \right)$$

$$- \sum_{e \in P_{j+1}^{\text{OPT}}} \frac{\tilde{w}(j+1)}{u(e)} a^{\tilde{\ell}_e(j+1)}, \tag{12.44}$$

where (a) follows by rearranging terms.

Note that WEIGHTED-SHORTEST-PATH's action impacts (12.44) only via $a^{\tilde{\ell}_e(j+1)}$ and $a^{\tilde{\ell}_e(j)}$. However, since WEIGHTED-SHORTEST-PATH is using path P_{j+1} to route the $j+1^{st}$ job, $\tilde{\ell}(j+1) \neq \tilde{\ell}(j)$ only for $e \in P_{j+1}$, while $\tilde{\ell}(j+1) = \tilde{\ell}(j)$ for $e \notin P_{j+1}$. Thus,

$$\Phi(j+1) - \Phi(j) = \sum_{e \in P_{j+1}} \left(\gamma - \tilde{\ell}_e^{\text{OPT}}(j) \right) \left(a^{\tilde{\ell}_e(j+1)} - a^{\tilde{\ell}_e(j)} \right)$$

$$- \sum_{e \in P_{j+1}^{\text{OPT}}} \frac{\tilde{w}(j+1)}{u(e)} a^{\tilde{\ell}_e(j+1)}, \tag{12.45}$$

where the contribution from both OPT and WEIGHTED-SHORTEST-PATH has been accounted for.

Dropping the $-\tilde{\ell}_e^{\text{OPT}}(j)(.)$ term from (12.45), using the fact that $a^{\tilde{\ell}_e(j+1)} \geq a^{\tilde{\ell}_e(j)}$, and expanding $\tilde{\ell}_e(j+1)$, we get from (12.45),

$$\Phi(j+1) - \Phi(j) \leq \gamma \sum_{e \in P_{j+1}} \left(a^{\tilde{\ell}_e(j) + \frac{\tilde{w}(j+1)}{u(e)}} - a^{\tilde{\ell}_e(j)} \right) - \sum_{e \in P_{j+1}^{\text{OPT}}} \frac{\tilde{w}(j+1)}{u(e)} a^{\tilde{\ell}_e(j)}. \tag{12.46}$$

Because of WEIGHTED-SHORTEST-PATH choosing the shortest path P_{j+1} for assigning job $j+1$, we have

$$\sum_{e \in P_{j+1}} \left(a^{\tilde{\ell}_e(j) + \frac{\tilde{w}(j+1)}{u(e)}} - a^{\tilde{\ell}_e(j)} \right) \leq \sum_{e \in P_{j+1}^{\text{OPT}}} \left(a^{\tilde{\ell}_e(j) + \frac{\tilde{w}(j+1)}{u(e)}} - a^{\tilde{\ell}_e(j)} \right),$$

using which in (12.46), we get

$$\Phi(j+1) - \Phi(j) \leq \gamma \sum_{e \in P_{j+1}^{\text{OPT}}} \left(a^{\tilde{\ell}_e(j) + \frac{\tilde{w}(j+1)}{u(e)}} - a^{\tilde{\ell}_e(j)} \right) - \sum_{e \in P_{j+1}^{\text{OPT}}} \frac{\tilde{w}(j+1)}{u(e)} a^{\tilde{\ell}_e(j)}. \tag{12.47}$$

Now both the summations in (12.47) are over the edges of the path selected by OPT on the arrival of job $j + 1$. Hence, rewriting (12.47),

$$\Phi(j+1) - \Phi(j) \leq a^{\tilde{\ell}_e(j)} \left(\sum_{e \in P_{j+1}^{\text{OPT}}} \left(\gamma \left(a^{\frac{\tilde{w}(j+1)}{u(e)}} - 1 \right) - \frac{\tilde{w}(j+1)}{u(e)} \right) \right). \tag{12.48}$$

Since the $j + 1^{st}$ job request is served by OPT using path P_{j+1}^{OPT}, therefore for all $e \in P_{j+1}^{\text{OPT}}$,

$$0 \leq \frac{\tilde{w}(j+1)}{u(e)} \leq \frac{\lambda_{\text{OPT}}}{\Lambda} \leq 1.$$

Let $x = \frac{\tilde{w}(j+1)}{u(e)} \leq 1$. Thus, from (12.48), to show that the $\Phi(j+1) - \Phi(j) \leq 0$, it is sufficient to show that for any $x \in (0, 1]$, $\exists\, a > 1$ such that[3]

$$\gamma(a^x - 1) - x \leq 0.$$

It is easy to check that one such choice is $a = 1 + \frac{1}{\gamma}$. Therefore, we have

$$\Phi(j+1) - \Phi(j) \leq 0$$

for $a = 1 + \frac{1}{\gamma}$, i.e., the potential function does not increase on the arrival of any new incoming request. ∎

Recall that WEIGHTED-SHORTEST-PATH requires the knowledge of an upper bound Λ on the optimal load incurred by OPT. To remove this restriction, once again we use the doubling trick to estimate Λ and call the algorithm MODIFIED WEIGHTED-SHORTEST-PATH. On the arrival of the first job with size $w(1)$, $\tilde{\Lambda}(1) = \min_{e \in E} \frac{w(1)}{u(e)}$, the load of the first job on the best edge (largest capacity). Then WEIGHTED-SHORTEST-PATH is executed with $\Lambda = \tilde{\Lambda}(1)$. Every time the algorithm reaches the FAIL state, a new phase starts and $\tilde{\Lambda}(i) = 2\tilde{\Lambda}(i - 1)$, i.e., the estimate of Λ is doubled, and at which time, WEIGHTED-SHORTEST-PATH restarts with $\Lambda = \tilde{\Lambda}(i)$, assuming no earlier jobs have been assigned.

Theorem 12.4.4 *The competitive ratio of algorithm* MODIFIED-WEIGHTED-SHORTEST-PATH *is most $\mathcal{O}(\log m)$.*

Recall that if $\Lambda = \lambda_{\text{OPT}}(k)$, then the competitive ratio of the MODIFIED-WEIGHTED-SHORTEST-PATH algorithm is $\mathcal{O}(\log m)$. The proof of Theorem 12.4.4 is identical to the proof of Theorem 12.3.7, where we get an additional multiplicative penalty of 4, and is left as an exercise.

To complement the upper bound on the competitive ratio for this network load balancing problem, in Problem 12.11, we will show that the competitive ratio of any deterministic algorithm is at least $\Omega(\log m)$. Thus, MODIFIED-WEIGHTED-SHORTEST-PATH is an optimal deterministic online algorithm up to a constant factor.

---

[3] We only need it for $x = y$.

12.5 Notes

The basic problem of minimizing the maximum load on any machine was first considered in the classical work of Graham [203]. Graham in fact studied the scheduling problem of minimizing the makespan, where each job has a processing time requirement and each machine can work at a unit speed, and each job has to be processed without preemption. Makespan is the time at which all jobs are completely processed. With identical machines, when all jobs are available at time 0, makespan is the same as the maximum load with permanent jobs. In the online setting, where jobs arrive over time, makespan (after removing the idling time of each machine) is equal to the maximum load in the permanent jobs setting.

In [203], the natural greedy algorithm that assigns an incoming job to the least loaded machine is shown to be $2 - 1/m$-competitive for minimizing the makespan. Notably this bound holds even when jobs are temporary for identical machines. For permanent jobs, more refined algorithms have been discussed in [204–206], with the best-known algorithm being 1.9201-competitive algorithm [207]. The best-known lower bound on the competitive ratio of any deterministic online algorithm is 1.88 by [208], while for the randomized case it is $e/(e - 1)$ [209, 210]. For more results on online algorithms for scheduling, we refer to survey articles [211, 212].

For the non-identical machines case, considered in Section 12.2.4–Section 12.3.2, with and without permanent jobs, the presented results follow from the seminal works [200, 213]. For the temporary jobs case with non-identical machines, a lower bound of $3 - o(1)$ on the competitive ratio of any deterministic algorithm can be found in [213]. Compared to the 8-competitiveness of the algorithm presented in Section 12.2.4, improved analysis can be found in [214, 215]. The result for network load balancing discussed in Section 12.4 can be found in [200]. The case of unrelated machines (each job has an arbitrary size on each machine) with temporary jobs (not covered in the chapter) was solved in [216], which showed a lower bound of $\Omega\left(\dfrac{m}{\log m}\right)$ for any deterministic algorithm and $\Omega\left(\dfrac{m}{(\log m)^2}\right)$ for any randomized algorithm, which is close to the competitive ratio of $\mathcal{O}(m)$ for an algorithm that assigns each job to that server that has the smallest current load. We summarize the variety of results in different models succinctly in Table 12.1.

It is easy to show that lookahead (knowing the next few arriving job sizes) does not improve the competitiveness of online algorithms for minimizing the maximum load or the makespan. For the makespan problem, however, a reordering concept is useful [217], where future arriving jobs can be assigned to machines in a different order than they arrive. In [217], it is shown that with reordering, the competitive ratio between 4/3 and 1.4659 can be obtained depending on the number of machines m for the identical machines case, when the buffer size is $\mathcal{O}(m)$. For the makespan problem, a semi-online is also considered [218, 219], where the online algorithm is aware of the sum of the sizes of all jobs from the beginning.

Allowing reassignment of jobs or job migration between machines can provide better competitive ratios and has been considered in [220]. Upon the arrival of a new job with size w_j, any online algorithm is allowed to migrate or reassign some previously assigned jobs, where the total size of the migrated jobs is bounded by βw_j. In [220], an algorithm with competitive ratio $1 + \epsilon$ and constant migration or reassignment factor $\beta(\epsilon)$ for $\epsilon > 0$ has been derived.

Table 12.1 Summary of competitive ratio results for various load balancing models

Machines	Permanent Jobs	Temporary Jobs
Identical	Greedy algorithm $2 - \frac{1}{m}$	Greedy algorithm $2 - \frac{1}{m}$
Related (non-identical machines with no machine restriction)	$\Theta(1)$	$\Theta(1)$
Restricted (identical machines with machine restriction)	$\Theta(\log_2 m)$	$\Theta(\sqrt{m})$
Unrelated (arbitrary different job sizes on different machines)	$\Theta(\log_2 m)$	$\Omega\left(\frac{m}{\log m}\right)$ (det.) $\Omega\left(\frac{m}{(\log m)^2}\right)$ (rand.)/ Greedy algorithm $\mathcal{O}(m)$

An alternate way of measuring the reassignment cost was introduced in [221] where competitiveness is measured against current load: an algorithm has a competitive ratio of α if after every job arrival, the maximum load is within an α factor of the optimal minimum load for the current set of jobs. Each incoming job j has size w_j and reassignment cost r_j. For a job, the reassignment cost has to be paid for its initial assignment and then every time it is reassigned. OPT has to pay the reassignment cost once for each job for its initial assignment. The optimal reassignment cost R is simply the sum of reassignment costs of all jobs scheduled till now. For arbitrary reassignment costs, [221] achieves a competitiveness of 3.5981 and a reassignment factor of 6.8285. Further improvements can be found in [222].

In addition to minimizing the maximum load across all machines, a more smooth objective function that captures balanced allocations is to minimize the p-norm of the load assigned to the m-machines. In particular, if L_j is the sum of the sizes of the jobs assigned to machine j, then the p-norm is

$$\left(\sum_{j=1}^{m} L_j^p\right)^{1/p}.$$

The objective studied in this chapter corresponds to the ∞-norm

$$\max_j L_j.$$

For the p-norm problem, competitive algorithms can be found in [223–225] for both the identical machines and non-identical machines case, and in [226] with reassignments.

The POWER-OF-d-CHOICES algorithm presented in Section 12.2.1 was proposed and analysed in [199], whose continuous time counterpart with stochastic arrivals has been analysed in [227–229].

Load balancing problems are also related to routing games, and there is a large body of work in this direction. For example, see [230–232] and the references therein. As is evident, there is an extremely large body of work on load balancing problems, and it is difficult to review everything. For a more comprehensive coverage, we refer the reader to reviews [211, 212, 233].

PROBLEMS

12.1 Prove Lemma 12.2.2. Try and lower bound the probability that any bin contains at least $\frac{\log m}{3 \log \log m}$ balls by $1/em^{1/3}$, and then use Chebyshev's inequality to conclude the result.

12.2 Consider that n balls are thrown in n bins uniformly randomly. Show that the expected number of *empty* bins that contain no balls is $n\left(1 - \frac{1}{n}\right)^n \sim n/e$ for large n. Show that if kn balls are thrown in n bins with $k = c \log n + d$, where c and d are constants, then with high probability all bins have at least one ball.

12.3 Show that the competitive ratio of the greedy algorithm for the load balancing problem with permanent jobs and identical machines considered in Section 12.2.3 is at most 2. Next, refine the analysis to show that the competitive ratio is at most $2 - 1/m$, where m is the number of machines.

12.4 For the greedy algorithm considered in Problem 12.3 for $m = 2$ machines, show that the competitive ratio is at least 3/2 with an input that has just three jobs of size $\{1, 1, 2\}$, matching the upper bound on the competitive ratio of 3/2 for $m = 2$. Generalize this input for an arbitrary m case, and show that the competitive ratio of the greedy algorithm is at least $2 - 1/m$ for any m.

[Hint: Considering $m(m - 1)$ jobs of size $1/m$ and a single job of size 1 should be sufficient.]

12.5 Consider a finite lookahead, i.e., at the tth job arrival, the sizes of the next ℓ (ℓ is finite) jobs that are going to arrive are also available. Show that any finite lookahead does not improve the competitive ratio of any online algorithm for minimizing the maximum load with m identical machines and permanent jobs.

[Hint: Add lots of jobs with arbitrary small sizes.]

12.6 (Unrelated machines) In this problem, we consider the arbitrary sizes case where a job j has size w_{ji} on machine i generally referred to as the unrelated machines case. Consider that the objective is to minimize the maximum of the sum of the sizes assigned to any machine where jobs are **permanent**. Show that algorithm WEIGHTED-SHORTEST-PATH (suitably defined over a simple bipartite graph between jobs and servers) proposed in Section 12.4 has a competitive ratio of at most $\mathcal{O}(\log m)$, where m is the number of machines.

[Hint: Analysis is similar to the proof of Theorem 12.4.1.]

12.7 We are given an unlimited number of identical machines, and jobs arrive one after the other, where job i has size w_i. Initially all machines are closed. Once a machine is opened, it remains open forever. At any step, an online algorithm can possibly open additional machines and then assign the job to any one of the open machines, but reassignment of a job once assigned to a machine is not allowed. The objective is to minimize the maximum load over all the open machines plus the total number of opened machines. To be precise, if an algorithm $\mathcal{A}$ opens $m_{\mathcal{A}}$ machines in total, and the final load on machine j is ℓ_j, then the cost of $\mathcal{A}$ is $c_{\mathcal{A}} = \max_{j \in \{1,\ldots,m_{\mathcal{A}}\}} \ell_j + m_{\mathcal{A}}$, and the objective is to minimize $c_{\mathcal{A}}$.

1. Let $W = \sum_{i=1}^{n} w_i$ be the sum of the sizes of all jobs. Prove that $c_{\mathrm{OPT}} \geq 2\sqrt{W}$.

2. Let the value of W be known to any online algorithm ahead of time. Propose an online algorithm with constant competitive ratio assuming that OPT never opens more than $\lceil \sqrt{W} \rceil$ machines.

   [Hint: Intuition developed for proving the bound in part 1 might be useful to propose a 'natural' online algorithm given the extra information.]

3. Remove the restriction that W is known and the assumption that OPT never opens more than $\lceil \sqrt{W} \rceil$ machines, and propose an online algorithm with constant competitive ratio.

12.8 [220] Consider that there are m identical machines, and any job can be assigned to any machine, and all jobs are permanent. Then for a set of jobs N, consider an arbitrary assignment A_N of jobs of N over the m machines, with maximum load across all machines being L_N. Show that assigning a new job j with size w_j to the least loaded machine (according to the present assignment A_N) yields an assignment with maximum load $L_{N \cup \{j\}}$ across all the m machines, where

$$L_{N \cup \{j\}} \leq \max \left\{ L_N, L_{N \cup \{j\}}^{\mathrm{OPT}} + \left(1 - \frac{1}{m}\right) w_j \right\},$$

where $L_{N \cup \{j\}}^{\mathrm{OPT}}$ is the optimal offline minimum of the maximum load across all machines possible with input $N \cup \{j\}$ set of jobs.

12.9 [220] Reassignment. In this problem, we consider the same setting as in Problem 12.8, but with reassignment. In particular, on the arrival of a new job with size w_j, a set of jobs S can be reassigned for which the sum of the sizes of jobs of S is at most βw_j, i.e., $\sum_{i \in S} w_i \leq \beta w_j$.

Algorithm: On the arrival of a new job j with size w_j, choose one of the following two options that minimizes the maximum load across all machines:

1. assign job j to the currently least loaded machine, or

2. for each machine $i = 1, \ldots, m$, let h_i (with size w_i) be the job with the maximum size assigned to machine i. Among $h_i, i = 1, \ldots, m$, find the machine $i^\star$ that has the job with the smallest size, i.e., $i^\star(j) = \arg\min_{h_i} w_i$. Choose machine $i^\star(j)$, and remove jobs from machine $i^\star(j)$ in any arbitrary order, until it is empty or the total size of the removed jobs is at most $2w_j$ ($\beta = 2$). Assign job j to machine $i^\star(j)$, and assign the removed jobs from machine $i^\star(j)$ to the machine with the least load sequentially.

With $\beta = 2$, show that this reassignment algorithm achieves a competitive ratio of at most $\frac{3}{2} - \frac{1}{2m}$ by showing the following sub-claims. The main idea is to show that if the competitive ratio of an algorithm after assigning jobs of set N is $\left(\frac{3}{2} - \frac{1}{2m}\right)$, then the same holds true after assigning jobs of set $N \cup \{j\}$ with the above algorithm.

(i) Define a job j to be **heavy** if $w_j > L_{N \cup \{j\}}^{OPT}/2$, and **light** otherwise, where L_N^{OPT} has been defined in Problem 12.8. Show that there are at most m heavy jobs in $N \cup \{j\}$.

(ii) If the newly arrived job is **light**, then show that assigning job j with option (1) of the algorithm implies that the maximum load on any machine is at most

$$\left(\frac{3}{2} - \frac{1}{2m}\right) L_{N \cup \{j\}}^{OPT}$$

using Problem 12.8.

(iii) Consider the other case, where the newly arrived job j is **heavy**. Then using part (i), argue that all jobs assigned to machine $i^\star(j)$ are **light**.

(iv) Following part (iii), show that after removing any of the light jobs from machine $i^\star(j)$ and assigning the heavy job j to machine $i^\star(j)$, the load on machine $i^\star(j)$ is at most

$$\left(\frac{3}{2} - \frac{1}{2m}\right) L_{N \cup \{j\}}^{OPT}.$$

(v) Finally, show that after reassigning all the jobs removed from machine $i^\star(j)$ to the least loaded machine sequentially, the load on any machine is at most

$$\left(\frac{3}{2} - \frac{1}{2m}\right) L_{N \cup \{j\}}^{OPT}.$$

12.10 The competitive ratio of the greedy algorithm for the load balancing problem with permanent jobs and related machines defined in Section 12.2.4 is at least $\Omega(\log m)$.

12.11 [200] In this problem, we will prove a lower bound of $\Omega(\log m)$ for any deterministic online algorithm for the network problem considered in Section 12.4, where the total number of vertices in the network is $\mathcal{O}(m)$.

Let m be some power of 2. Consider a network with a single source s, m intermediate nodes $X = \{x_1, \ldots, x_m\}$, and for level $i = 1, \ldots, \log m$, T_{ij} sinks for $j = 1, \ldots, 2^{i-1}$. Thus, the total number of nodes in the network is $\mathcal{O}(m)$. The source is connected to all nodes of X. Sink T_{11} is connected to all nodes of X, while T_{21} and T_{22} are connected to $x_1, \ldots, x_{m/2}$ and $x_{m/2+1}, \ldots, x_m$. In general, T_{ij} is connected to nodes

$$x_{(j-1)m/2^{i-1} + 1}, \ldots, x_{jm/2^{i-1}}.$$

To illustrate the idea, we consider a small network as shown in Figure 12.4, with $m = 8$, where there is a single source s from which all the job requests will originate. There are 8 intermediate nodes x_1 to x_8, and 7 sinks in three levels. At level i, there are 2^{i-1} sinks T_{ij}, for $i = 1, 2, 3$.

All job requests will originate at s.

Job arrivals: Each arriving job request has size of $w_i = 1 \; \forall \; i$, and capacity of each edge of the network is also $u(e) = 1 \; \forall \; e$. Consider any deterministic online algorithm $\mathcal{A}$.

Phase 1: $m/2$ requests arrive that originate at s with destination T_{11}.

Phase $i = 2, \dots, \log m$: $m/2^i$ requests arrive that originate at s with destination as some sink T_{ij} of level i, where j is such that the vertices of X connected to $T_{i,j}$ have an average of $(i-1)/2$ requests going through them after the end of phase $i-1$ with $\mathcal{A}$.

1. Prove the claim (used to define the algorithm) via induction, that at the end of phase $i-1$ for $i \geq 2$, there exists j_{i-1} such that the subset of vertices of X connected to $T_{i,j_{i-1}}$ has an average of $(i-1)/2$ job requests going through them.

2. Show that at the end of all $\log m$ phases, the maximum number of requests passing through some vertex $x \in X$ is $\frac{\log m}{2}$ for $\mathcal{A}$.

3. Show that for OPT, the maximum number of job requests passing through any vertex $x \in X$ is 1.

4. Conclude that the competitive ratio of any deterministic online algorithm $\mathcal{A}$ is $\Omega(\log m)$.

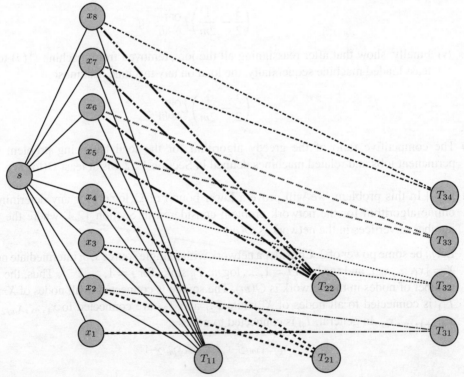

Figure 12.4 Example of a network for Problem 12.11

CHAPTER 13

Scheduling to Minimize Flow Time (Delay)

13.1 Introduction

In this chapter, we begin our discussion on the problem of scheduling jobs with multiple servers, which has widespread applications in areas of operations research, communication networks, etc. Essentially, jobs with a certain processing requirement, called size, arrive over time. There are multiple identical fixed-speed servers, and the problem is to assign jobs to fixed-speed servers so as to minimize some function of the job response time (departure minus the arrival time).

Different objectives are of interest for solving the scheduling problem that are application specific. For example, when an application depends on the time when all the jobs are finished, then *makespan* (the finishing time of the last completed job) is considered, while when the total delay is of interest, *flow* time (sum of the response times of all jobs) is the chosen objective. A special case of flow time is the *completion* time, which is defined as the sum of the departure times of all jobs, disregarding their arrival times.

As we discussed in Chapter 12, the load balancing problem with the objective of minimizing the maximum load is the same as minimizing makespan. Thus, in this chapter, we concentrate on solving the scheduling problem with the objective of minimizing the flow time. The completion time problem is simpler than the flow time problem.

For the considered scheduling problem, multiple classes of restrictions are possible, e.g., whether preemption is allowed or not, can a job be migrated between servers or not, are jobs required to be assigned to a server (which cannot be changed later) as soon as they arrive or not, whether server speeds are identical or not, and, finally, is there a job–server assignment restriction (a job can be processed by only a subset of servers). Different restrictions imply very different results on the competitive ratio for online algorithms.

In this chapter, we concentrate on the simplest setting where both preemption and job migration are allowed. Moreover, we consider that all servers are identical, having fixed speed, with no job–server assignment restriction, and a job can be assigned to a server any time after it has arrived, and not necessarily on its arrival. Some other settings are explored via problems at the end of the chapter. Scheduling problem with variable speed servers is discussed in the next chapter.

Even in this simplest setting, we will show that the power of online algorithms is limited for solving the flow time problem. In particular, we show that no online algorithm can have a competitive ratio that is independent of the system parameters, e.g., the total number of jobs n, the number of servers m, and the size of the jobs. In particular, we will show that the optimal competitive ratio for minimizing the flow time is

$$\max\left\{\Theta\left(\log(n/m)\right), \Theta\left(\log\left(w_{\max}/w_{\min}\right)\right)\right\}, \tag{13.1}$$

where w_{max} and w_{min} are the maximum and the minimum job sizes, respectively, and this lower bound is achieved by a simple algorithm called the shortest remaining processing time (SRPT), which at any time processes the m shortest (remaining size) jobs on m distinct servers.

To circumvent the negative result (13.1) on the competitive ratio for all online algorithms, we will show that if for the online SRPT algorithm, each server is allowed to operate at a slightly higher speed, $(2 - 1/m)$-times more than that for OPT, called the resource augmentation regime, then the total flow time of the SRPT algorithm is identical to that of OPT with unit speed servers.

13.2 Problem Formulation: Minimizing Flow Time with Identical Servers

Consider that there are a total of n jobs that arrive, with job j arriving at time a_j with size w_j. Size essentially reflects the amount of processing needed to complete the job. There are a total of m identical servers, where each server can process jobs at fixed speed s. Without loss of generality, we let $s = 1$. When a server processes a job for time duration t, t amount of work is completed for that job.

A job is defined to be complete at time d_j as soon as the total amount of work completed for it possibly by different servers is w_j. A job can be processed at any time on only one server, without any parallelization or splitting. The flow time of job j is defined to be $f_j = d_j - a_j$, the delay or total time it spends in the system before departure, and the total flow time is

$$F = \sum_{j=1}^{n} f_j. \tag{13.2}$$

The other two important metrics, (i) **makespan** is defined as $\max_j d_j$, the time at which all jobs are complete, and (ii) **completion time** is defined as $\sum_{j=1}^{n} d_j$, which disregards the arrival times of jobs.

There are two conditions that are relevant for job execution: **preemption** and **job migration**. Preemption means that a particular job can be suspended and restarted again at any time, while job migration allows for a job to be restarted on a different server than the one where it was preempted from, if required. Throughout this chapter, we will consider that both preemption and job migration are allowed. Disallowing preemption and migration leads to significantly different results that are reviewed at the end of the chapter.

Let $\sigma = \{w_j, a_j\}_{j=1}^{n}$ be the input sequence. Under this model, the basic question is whether the competitive ratio of an algorithm $\mathcal{A}$ that is defined as

$$\mu_{\mathcal{A}} = \max_{\sigma} \frac{F_{\mathcal{A}}(\sigma)}{F_{OPT}(\sigma)} \tag{13.3}$$

can be made independent of the system parameters, i.e., n, m, and w_j. Unfortunately, the answer turns out to be no, and we first show a lower bound that no online algorithm can achieve a competitive ratio better than

$$\max \left\{ \Omega \left(\log(n/m) \right), \Omega \left(\log \left(w_{max}/w_{min} \right) \right) \right\},$$

where $w_{max} = \max_j w_j$ and $w_{min} = \min_j w_j$. Thus, a logarithmic dependence on the number of jobs or the ratio of the maximum to minimum job sizes is unavoidable. Next, we show that the SRPT algorithm that at any time processes the m shortest (remaining size) jobs on m distinct servers can achieve the lower bound up to a constant.

We begin by reviewing the SRPT algorithm, and some of its properties, e.g., that the SRPT algorithm is an optimal algorithm to minimize the total flow time when the number of servers is one.

13.3 SRPT Algorithm

Let at time t, the remaining size of job j be $w_j(t)$. Since job j arrives at time a_j, $w_j(a_j) = w_j$. The set of incomplete jobs at time t is

$$R(t) = \{j : w_j(t) > 0, a_j \le t\}. \tag{13.4}$$

Jobs in $R(t)$ are ordered in the increasing order of their remaining sizes $w_j(t)$. At any time t, the SRPT algorithm processes the first m (shortest) jobs of the set $R(t)$ on the m servers. Note that to execute the SRPT algorithm, both preemption and job migration are required, since on the arrival of a new job, which is shorter than any of the m jobs that are currently being processed, some job will be preempted, and possibly be processed on a different server in future, depending on other job sizes.

The main intuition behind considering the SRPT algorithm can be understood by rewriting the flow time metric as follows. Let $n^{\mathcal{A}}(t) = |R_{\mathcal{A}}(t)|$ be the number of incomplete jobs with algorithm $\mathcal{A}$ at time t. Then it follows that the flow time (13.2) for any algorithm $\mathcal{A}$ is

$$F_{\mathcal{A}} = \int n^{\mathcal{A}}(t)dt. \tag{13.5}$$

For an intuitive explanation for expression (13.5), consider Figure 13.1, where there are four jobs that arrive over time and there is a single server. The projection of the shaded part of the rectangles for each job on the time (x)-axis in subfigure (a) represents the time during which that job is actually processed. The time corresponding to the unshaded part of any job's rectangle corresponds to the server processing some other job. The width of the rectangle corresponding to job j is $d_j - a_j$ (which contains both shaded and unshaded regions) and the height is taken to be 1. Clearly the flow time (13.2) is $\sum_{j=1}^{4}(d_j - a_j)$, which is also the sum of the areas of the four rectangles (shaded plus unshaded regions), counted horizontally in subfigure (a). An alternative way to count this sum is via counting vertically across time, where the height at time t is equal to the number of incomplete jobs $n^{\mathcal{A}}(t)$, and the sum is the integral over the height $= n^{\mathcal{A}}(t)$ as shown in the subfigure (b).

With flow time expression (13.5), the SRPT algorithm is essentially trying to minimize $n^{\mathcal{A}}(t)$ by processing the jobs with the shortest remaining sizes, thereby maximizing the number of departures in any time interval. It turns out that when the number of servers is 1, in fact, the online SRPT algorithm is an optimal offline algorithm OPT.

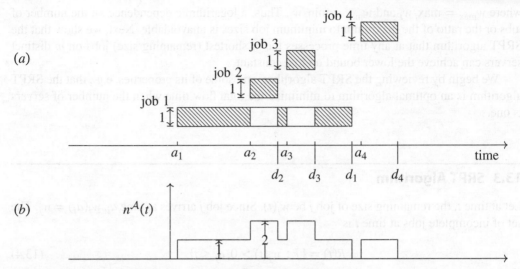

Figure 13.1 Pictorial description of the SRPT algorithm with a single server, where flow time of job j is $d_j - a_j$, and the shaded portion represents the time during which a job is processed.

Theorem 13.3.1 [234] SRPT *algorithm is* OPT *for minimizing the total flow time with a single server* $m = 1$.

It is not too hard to show this result, and we leave this an exercise in Problem 13.2.

Remark 13.3.2 *An important point to note is that when, instead of flow time, the objective is to minimize weighted flow time defined as* $F = \sum_{j=1}^{n} \alpha_j f_j$ *(where* α_j *is the weight or relative importance of job j), no online algorithm is constant competitive* [235] *even with a single server, i.e.,* $m = 1$. *In this book, we concentrate on unweighted flow time minimization problems, and refer the reader to* [235] *for more details.*

In the presence of multiple servers, one can easily construct input sequences for which the SRPT algorithm is not optimal. For example, consider two servers and three jobs that arrive together. Let the size of two jobs be one each, while the size of the third job be two. SRPT will process the two jobs of size one parallely on two servers, and schedule the job with size two on any one server once the two jobs of size one have departed. OPT on the other hand will process one of the jobs with size one and the job with size two together, and then once the job with size one departs, process the other job with size one. Thus, at time 2, with OPT there are no remaining jobs while with the SRPT one job is remaining. This can be exploited by an adversary to make the competitive ratio of SRPT larger than one by requesting lots of small jobs of size say 1/2 starting from time 2.

As we show in this chapter, however, SRPT is the 'best' online algorithm in terms of competitive ratio. We begin by showing a lower bound on the competitive ratio of the SRPT algorithm, which is then generalized to apply for all online algorithms, including randomized ones. Then to show that SRPT is an optimal online algorithm, we prove that it achieves the general lower bound up to a constant.

13.3.1 Lower Bound on the Competitive Ratio

We begin with a lower bound (13.3) on the competitive ratio of the SRPT algorithm, which will then be generalized to hold for all online algorithms.

Theorem 13.3.3 *The competitive ratio* (13.3) *of the* SRPT *algorithm is at least*

$$\max\left\{\Omega\left(\log(n/m)\right), \Omega\left(\log\left(w_{max}/w_{min}\right)\right)\right\}.$$

We will just consider two servers $m = 2$ and show this bound. As will be clear, the idea is readily generalizable to $m > 2$.

The basic idea with $m = 2$ is that at each appropriate time instant, three jobs are going to arrive, one 'big' and two 'small', where the sum of the sizes of the two small jobs is equal to the size of the big job. SRPT by definition will schedule the two small jobs parallely[1] on two servers before the big job. We will consider an alternate algorithm $\mathcal{B}$ that will schedule the big job and one small job parallely and process the second small job after finishing the other small job.

What this entails is that there exists a 'special time' where with the SRPT algorithm, there are a lot of unfinished jobs, while $\mathcal{B}$ has finished all the jobs that have arrived so far. From this special time onwards, a lot of 'tiny' jobs arrive that preempt the unfinished jobs of SRPT, making the flow time large for SRPT because of the large number of incomplete jobs at the special time. $\mathcal{B}$ pays no such penalty after the special time, since it has no unfinished jobs at the special time. The exact input sequence and arrival time instants are as follows.

For notational simplicity, let $W = \left(w_{max}/w_{min}\right)$ for the rest of this section, and, without loss of generality, let W be some power of 2.

Proof: Let $m = 2$, and consider the input where three jobs arrive at time instants $r_i = 2W\left(1 - \frac{1}{2^i}\right)$ for each $i = 0, 1, \ldots, \log W - 1$, one 'big' with size $\frac{W}{2^i}$ and two 'small' with size $\frac{W}{2^{i+1}}$. All logarithms will be base 2 unless stated otherwise. The time interval between two successive time instants r_i and r_{i+1} is $\frac{W}{2^i}$, and the final time instant $r_{\log W - 1} = 2W - 4$.

SRPT schedules at time r_i the two small jobs arriving at time r_i parallely on the two servers, which are completed by time $z_i = r_i + \frac{W}{2^{i+1}}$. Then starting at time z_i and until the time r_{i+1}, the big job that arrived at time r_i and the big job that arrived at time r_{i-1}, where both have a remaining size of $\frac{W}{2.2^{i-1}} = \frac{W}{2^i}$ at time z_i, are scheduled by SRPT. Moreover, since the time duration $[z_i, r_{i+1}]$ is less than $\frac{W}{2^i}$ (the remaining size of these two big jobs at time z_i), both of these big jobs are unfinished at time r_{i+1}. This conclusion holds true for all r_i. More importantly, at time $r_{\log W - 1} + 2 = 2(W - 1)$ also, all the big jobs that have arrived so far are unfinished with the SRPT algorithm, and there are a total of $\log W$ such big jobs. The time $2(W - 1)$ is special since as we show next, $\mathcal{B}$ (an alternate algorithm) has no unfinished jobs at time $2(W - 1)$.

Consider an alternate algorithm $\mathcal{B}$ that at time r_i schedules one big and one small job that arrives at time r_i parallely, and schedules the second small job arriving at time r_i after the first small job that arrived at time r_i is finished at time $r_i + \frac{W}{2^{i+1}}$. Thus, $\mathcal{B}$ finishes all the three jobs

---

[1] Note that a single job can be processed on any one server at any time. Thus, throughout the chapter, parallely means distinct jobs being processed by distinct servers simultaneously.

arriving at time r_i by time $r_{i+1} \forall i$. Therefore, at time $2(W-1)$, all jobs are finished by $\mathcal{B}$ that have arrived so far.

If no further jobs arrive after time $2(W-1)$, the difference between the total flow time of SRPT and that of $\mathcal{B}$ will be minimal. However, since the SRPT algorithm has $\log W$ unfinished jobs at time $2(W-1)$, if a large number of tiny (very small size) jobs arrive next, all tiny jobs will preempt the $\log W$ unfinished jobs with the SRPT algorithm. As a result, the accumulated flow time of the $\log W$ unfinished jobs can be made large without increasing the total flow time of algorithm $\mathcal{B}$ by too much as follows.

Note that the size of all the unfinished (big) jobs at time $2(W-1)$ with the SRPT algorithm is strictly more than 1. The remaining job arrival sequence is as follows: at time $2(W-1)+k$, $k = 0, \ldots, W^2 - 1$, two jobs of size one arrive. Clearly, $\log W$ unfinished jobs with the SRPT algorithm have to wait till time $2(W-1)+W^2 - 1$ to even begin their processing, leading to a flow time of at least $W^2 \log W$. Thus, the total flow time of the SRPT algorithm is $\Omega(W^2 \log W)$.

For $\mathcal{B}$, however, there are no unfinished jobs at time $2(W-1)$, and thus the total flow time for all jobs that arrived till time $2(W-1)$ is $5W^2$, while for the unit-sized jobs arriving after $2(W-1)$ the flow time is just $2W^2$, since they do not have to wait for any other job. Thus, the total flow time of algorithm $\mathcal{B}$ is $\mathcal{O}(W^2)$.

Since the total flow time of OPT is at most that of $\mathcal{B}$, the competitive ratio of the SRPT algorithm is at least $\Omega(\log W)$, where $W = (w_{\max}/w_{\min})$. By our choice of the input, the total number of jobs $n = \mathcal{O}(W^2)$, making the lower bound also $\Omega(\log n)$. We leave it as an exercise to show that in fact one can show the lower bound $\Omega(\log(n/m))$ for $m > 2$. ∎

Next, we show that the lower bound shown in Theorem 13.3.3 for the SRPT algorithm in fact holds for any randomized algorithm.

Theorem 13.3.4 *The competitive ratio* (13.3) *of any randomized algorithm is at least*

$$\max\left\{\Omega\left(\log(n/m)\right), \Omega\left(\log\left(w_{max}/w_{min}\right)\right)\right\}.$$

The basic idea to prove this result is similar to that of Theorem 13.3.3, except that now we have to construct an input sequence that can 'fool' any randomized algorithm and not just a specific one, e.g., SRPT. Essentially, we will construct the input sequence in phases, such that the expected number of unfinished jobs for any randomized algorithm at some time (called the overloaded time) is at least $\mathcal{O}(m \log W)$, where $W = w_{\max}/w_{\min}$. Then starting from the overloaded time, the input will consist of a large number of jobs with small sizes that can keep the $\mathcal{O}(m \log W)$ unfinished jobs waiting till all the small jobs are finished to get the required lower bound. For the SRPT algorithm, this was easy for a particular deterministic sequence, but in this case, with a randomized algorithm, the overloaded time is a random variable.

Proof: Compared to the proof of Theorem 13.3.3, where we used the special case of $m = 2$, in this case, we will work with general m. Recall that $W = (w_{\max}/w_{\min})$. We will need W to be large enough such that $L = \log W - 3\log(m \log W)$ (the maximum number of phases to be chosen next) is some positive integer. The first part of the input will consist of at most L phases (defined next), while the second part will depend on the decisions made by an online randomized algorithm $\mathcal{A}$ in the first L phases.

First part of the input: Consider an input with at most L phases, $i = 0, \ldots, L-1$, where the phase i starts at time $r_i = 2W\left(1 - \frac{1}{2^i}\right)$ and ends at time $r_{i+1} = 2W\left(1 - \frac{1}{2^{i+1}}\right)$, i.e., the duration

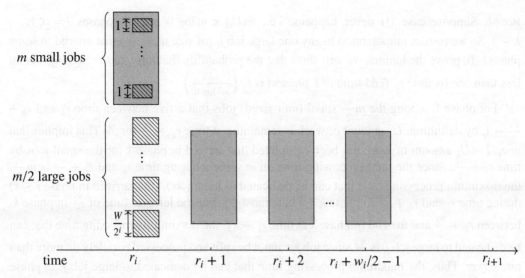

Figure 13.2 Pictorial description of the definition of phase i of the input for the lower bound for any randomized algorithm $\mathcal{A}$, where each grey rectangle consists of m small jobs of size one.

of phase i is $2W\left(\frac{1}{2^i} - \frac{1}{2^{i+1}}\right) = \frac{W}{2^i}$. During each phase, two types of jobs, large and small, arrive:
(i) $m/2$ large jobs of size $w_i = W/2^i$ arrive together at the start of the phase at time $r_i = 2W\left(1 - \frac{1}{2^i}\right)$ and
(ii) m small jobs of size $w_{ij} = 1$ arrive at each time instant $r_{ij} = r_i + j, j = 0, 1, \ldots, \frac{w_i}{2} - 1$. See Figure 13.2 for an illustration of the first part of the input.

Let

$$w_L = W/2^L. \tag{13.6}$$

Thus, in total, $m/2$ large jobs and $m\frac{w_i}{2}$ small jobs arrive in phase i. Let the set of small jobs that arrive in a phase be denoted by S_i.

For any randomized algorithm $\mathcal{A}$, let U_i be the total amount of work remaining for the set of small jobs S_i at time $r_i + \frac{w_i}{2}$ within phase i. We will try and argue next that either

(I) there exists a phase i such that $\mathbb{E}\{U_i\} \geq m \log W$ or
(II) at the end of all the L phases, any large job (that has arrived so far) has remaining size of at least 1 with high probability.

The second part of the input will be chosen depending on which case is true for $\mathcal{A}$.

Lemma 13.3.5 *For any randomized algorithm $\mathcal{A}$, either there exists a phase i such that $\mathbb{E}\{U_i\} \geq m \log W$ or the probability that any one large job has remaining size of less than 1 by time r_L (end of phase L) is upper bounded by $\mathcal{O}\left(\frac{1}{m^2 \log W}\right)$.*

Proof: Suppose case (I) never happens, i.e., $\mathbb{E}\{U_i\} < m \log W$ for all phases $i = 0, 1, \ldots, L-1$. So we restrict our attention to any one large job j_i (of size $w_i = \frac{W_i}{2^i}$) that arrived in some phase i. To prove the lemma, we will show that the probability that job j_i has remaining size of less than one by time r_L (end time of L phases) is $\mathcal{O}\left(\frac{1}{m^2 \log W}\right)$.

For phase k, among the $m\frac{w_k}{2}$ small (unit-sized) jobs that arrive between time r_k and $r_k + \frac{w_k}{2} - 1$, by definition, U_k amount of work is remaining at time $r_k + \frac{w_k}{2}$ for $\mathcal{A}$. This implies that $mw_k/2 - U_k$ amount of work has been completed that arrived in phase k for the small jobs by time $r_k + \frac{w_k}{2}$. Since the total processing time on m servers during time r_k and $r_k + \frac{w_k}{2}$ is $m\frac{w_k}{2}$, the maximum processing time that can be dedicated to large job j_i (that arrived in phase $i \leq k$) during time r_k and $r_k + \frac{w_k}{2}$ in phase $k \geq i$ is at most U_k. For the leftover time of $\frac{w_k}{2}$ in phase k, between $r_k + \frac{w_k}{2}$ and the end of phase k at time $r_k + w_k$, the maximum processing time that can be dedicated to large job j_i is $\frac{w_k}{2}$ since job j_i cannot be split and processed parallely on more than one server. Thus, the maximum processing time that can be dedicated to large job j_i in phase $k \geq i$ is $\frac{w_k}{2} + U_k$. Therefore, the large job j_i with original size w_i has remaining size of less than one at time r_L only if

$$\sum_{k=i}^{L-1} \left(\frac{w_k}{2} + U_k\right) > w_i - 1. \tag{13.7}$$

Note that

$$\sum_{k=i}^{L} \frac{w_k}{2} = \frac{w_i}{2} \sum_{i=0}^{L-i-1} \frac{1}{2^i} = \frac{w_i}{2} 2(1 - (1/2)^{L-i}) = w_i - w_L/2,$$

where w_L has been defined in (13.6). Therefore,

$$\sum_{k=i}^{L-1} \frac{w_k}{2} = \sum_{k=i}^{L} \frac{w_k}{2} - w_L/2 = w_i - w_L/2 - w_L/2 = w_i - w_L. \tag{13.8}$$

Using (13.8), event (13.7) happens with probability

$$\leq \mathbb{P}\left(w_i - w_L + \sum_{k=i}^{L-1} U_k > w_i - 1\right) = \mathbb{P}\left(\sum_{k=i}^{L-1} U_k > w_L - 1\right).$$

From our hypothesis, $\mathbb{E}\{U_i\} < m \log W$ for all phases $i = 0, 1, \ldots, L-1$. Hence, using Markov's inequality, we have

$$\mathbb{P}(U_i > m^3 (\log W)^2) \leq \frac{1}{m^2 \log W}.$$

By our choice of $L = \log W - 3 \log(m \log W)$, $L \leq \log W$, and $w_L = W/2^L = (m \log W)^3$. Thus, for $\sum_{k=i}^{L-1} U_k \geq w_L - 1 = m^3 (\log W)^3 - 1$ to be true, it must be the case that at least one among the L random variables $U_k, k = 0, \ldots, L-1$, is larger than $\frac{m^3 (\log W)^3 - 1}{L} = \mathcal{O}(m^3 (\log W)^2)$.

Thus,

$$\mathbb{P}\left(\sum_{k=i}^{L-1} U_k > w_L - 1 = m^3 (\log W)^3 - 1\right) \leq \mathbb{P}(U_k > m^3 (\log W)^2),$$

$$\leq \frac{1}{m^2 \log W}.$$

Therefore, at the end of all the L phases, any large job (that has arrived so far) has remaining size of at least one with high probability. ∎

Second part of the input: If case (I) happens in some phase $i \leq L - 1$ for $\mathcal{A}$, i.e., $\mathbb{E}\{U_i\} \geq m \log W$ in phase i, then define $t_{\text{overload}} = r_i + \frac{w_i}{2}$ within phase i as the **overloaded** time, and starting from overloaded time t_{overload}, m unit-sized jobs arrive at each time instant $t_{\text{overload}} + k$ for $k = 0, \dots, W^2 - 1$.

Recall that U_i is the total unfinished work for small jobs of S_i at time $r_i + \frac{w_i}{2}$ within phase i. Since each small job of S_i is of unit size, this also implies that the expected number of small jobs with remaining size of one is $m \log W$ at time $r_i + \frac{w_i}{2}$.

Otherwise, if case (II) happens, then at the end of all L phases at time r_L, m unit-sized jobs arrive at each time instant $r_L + k$ for $k = 0, \dots, W^2 - 1$. See Figure 13.3 for a pictorial representation of the second part of the input.

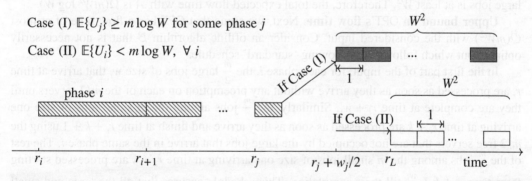

Case (I) $\mathbb{E}\{U_i\} \geq m \log W$ for some phase j

Case (II) $\mathbb{E}\{U_i\} < m \log W, \ \forall \ i$

Figure 13.3 Description of the second part of the input depending on the actions of any randomized algorithm $\mathcal{A}$ on the first part. Each white and grey rectangle represents m jobs of size one.

We will show that in either of the two cases, OPT's flow time is $\mathcal{O}(mW^2)$ while the flow time of $\mathcal{A}$ is at least $\Omega(mW^2 \log W)$.

Lower bound on Algorithm $\mathcal{A}$'s flow time: When case (I) happens, as argued earlier, the expected number of small jobs with remaining size one with $\mathcal{A}$ at the overloaded time t_{overload} is $\Omega(m \log W)$.

Starting from the overloaded time, m unit-sized jobs arrive at each time instant $r_i + \frac{w_i}{2} + k$ for $k = 0, \dots, W^2 - 1$. Since the expected number of small jobs with remaining size of one is $\Omega(m \log W)$ at the overloaded time, the expected total flow time for $\mathcal{A}$ is $\Omega(mW^2 \log W)$, since each of the m unit-sized jobs that arrive at time $r_i + \frac{w_i}{2} + k$ for $k = 0, \dots, W^2 - 1$ has to wait for at least $\Omega(\log W)$ time units.

In case (II), from Lemma 13.3.5, the remaining size of any large job is at least one at the end of the Lth phase with large enough probability, and the total number of large jobs that arrive until time r_L is $mL/2$. Thus, from Lemma 13.3.5, the expected number of large jobs that have **remaining size less than one** at time r_L is

$$\sum_{i=1}^{mL/2} i \, \mathbb{P}(i \text{ large jobs with remaining size less than one at time } r_L) \leq \frac{1}{m^2 \log W} \sum_{i=1}^{mL/2} i,$$

$$\leq \frac{\frac{mL}{2}\left(\frac{mL}{2}+1\right)/2}{m^2 \log W},$$

$$\leq \frac{\log W}{4}, \qquad (13.9)$$

where the last inequality follows since $L \leq \log W$ by the choice of L. Since the total number of large jobs that arrive by time r_L is $mL/2 = \Omega(m \log W)$, while the expected number of large jobs with remaining size less than one at time r_L is $\leq \frac{\log W}{4}$ (13.9), the expected number of large jobs with remaining size of more than one at time r_L with case (II) is $\Omega(m \log W)$.

Thus with $\mathcal{A}$, to minimize the flow time starting from time r_L, all the m unit-sized jobs that arrive at time $r_L + k$ for $k = 0, \ldots, W^2 - 1$ (second part on input in case (II)) preempt all the large jobs with remaining size at least one. Consequently, the flow time of each of the $\Omega(m \log W)$ large jobs is at least W^2. Therefore, the total expected flow time with $\mathcal{A}$ is $\Omega(mW^2 \log W)$.

Upper bound on OPT's **flow time**: Next, we argue that OPT has a flow time of at most $\mathcal{O}(mW^2)$ with the considered input. Consider an offline algorithm $\mathcal{B}$ that is not necessarily optimal, but which follows the following 'standard' schedule.

In the first part of the input, for each phase i, the $\frac{m}{2}$ large jobs of size w_i that arrive at time r_i are processed as soon as they arrive without any preemption on each of the $m/2$ servers until they are complete at time $r_i + w_i$. Similarly, the $\frac{m}{2}$ jobs among the m small jobs of size one arriving at time $r_i + k$ are processed as soon as they arrive and finish at time $r_i + k + 1$ using the $m/2$ free servers that are not occupied by the large jobs that arrive in the same phase i. The rest of the $\frac{m}{2}$ jobs among the m small jobs of size one arriving at time $r_i + k$ are processed starting from time $r_i + k + \frac{w_i}{2}$ till their completion. This schedule ensures that all the large and small jobs arriving in phase i are complete at the start of phase $i + 1$, and the total flow time of jobs arriving in phase i is $2mw_i + \frac{m}{2}\left(\frac{w_i}{2}\right)^2$.

When algorithm $\mathcal{A}$ satisfies the condition of case (I) in phase i, i.e., $\mathbb{E}\{U_i\} \geq m \log W$, in which case the second part of the input begins at time t_{overload}, then the above standard schedule is applied for OPT till phase $i - 1$ and is modified for phase i as follows. Note that since we are considering oblivious adversaries, the adversary knows the distribution used by $\mathcal{A}$. Thus, the adversary can verify whether case (I) or case (II) is true. Note that if the standard schedule is applied for phase i as well, then OPT will also satisfy $\mathbb{E}\{U_i^{\text{OPT}}\} \geq m \log W$, which needs to be avoided, since it knows the future arrivals.

The modification made by $\mathcal{B}$ for phase i is as follows. In phase i, all the m small jobs that arrive at times $r_i + k$, $k = 0, 1, \ldots, w_i/2$, are processed as soon as they arrive on the m servers till time $r_i + k + 1$. The m small jobs of size one that arrive at each time instant $r_i + w_i/2 + k$

for $k = 0, \dots, W^2 - 1$ (that are special for phase i as second part of the input), are also processed as soon as they arrive between time $r_i + w_i/2 + k$ till $r_i + w_i/2 + k + 1$ on the m servers. The total flow time of these small jobs is thus mW^2. All the m large jobs that arrive at the beginning of phase i at time r_i are processed after all the small jobs (arriving at time $r_i + w_i/2 + k$ for $k = 0, \dots, W^2 - 1$) are complete beginning at time $r_i + w_i/2 + W^2$ till their completion, since no other jobs arrive thereafter, with a total flow time of $\frac{m}{2}\left(W^2 + \frac{3}{2}w_i\right)$. Thus, by processing small jobs first in phase i compared to the standard schedule applied till phase $i - 1$, $\mathcal{B}$ (on account of knowing the input in advance) avoids incurring a large total flow time.

If case (I)'s condition is not satisfied for any phase, then the standard schedule is used for all the L phases, and all jobs arriving in each phase are completed by the end of that phase. Thus, the total flow time of all jobs arriving in the L phases is at most $\frac{m}{2}\frac{W^2}{2} + 4W$. The mW^2 jobs of size one arriving after the end of L phases (second part of input in case (II)) are processed as soon as they arrive, with a total flow time of mW^2.

Thus, in both cases, summing across all phases and the mW^2 unit-sized jobs, the flow time of $\mathcal{B}$ is at most $\mathcal{O}(mW^2)$. Since OPT is by definition as good as $\mathcal{B}$, the flow time of OPT in either case is $\mathcal{O}(mW^2)$.

Since the expected flow time of $\mathcal{A}$ is $\Omega(mW^2 \log W)$, we get the result that the competitive ratio of any randomized algorithm is at least $\Omega(\log W)$.

Note that with the input $n = \mathcal{O}(mW^2)$, the other lower bound of $\Omega(\log(n/m))$ also follows. ∎

13.3.2 Upper Bound on the Competitive Ratio of the SRPT Algorithm

In this section, we show that the SRPT algorithm is an optimal (up to a constant) online algorithm by proving the following theorem.

Theorem 13.3.6 *The competitive ratio of the* SRPT *algorithm is at most*

$$\max\left\{\mathcal{O}\left(\log(n/m)\right), \mathcal{O}\left(\log\left(w_{max}/w_{min}\right)\right)\right\}.$$

Proof: We will first prove that the competitive ratio of the SRPT algorithm is at most $\mathcal{O}\left(\log\left(w_{max}/w_{min}\right)\right)$. Recall from (13.4), the definition of the set of incomplete jobs at time t as

$$R(t) = \{j : w_j(t) > 0, a_j \le t\}, \tag{13.10}$$

where $w_j(t)$ is the remaining size of job j at time t. Since job j arrives at time a_j, $w_j(a_j) = w_j$.

For an algorithm $\mathcal{A}$, let $n^{\mathcal{A}}(t) = |R_{\mathcal{A}}(t)|$ be the number of incomplete jobs at time t, and $V^{\mathcal{A}}(t) = \sum_{j \in R_A(t)} w_j(t)$ be the volume (the total outstanding workload) at time t.

Let

$$\Delta V(t) = V^{\mathcal{A}}(t) - V^{\text{OPT}}(t) \tag{13.11}$$

and

$$\Delta n(t) = n^{\mathcal{A}}(t) - n^{\text{OPT}}(t) \tag{13.12}$$

be the difference in respective quantities between $\mathcal{A}$ and OPT. $\Delta V(t)$ can be regarded as the potential function.

At time t, let job j be classified as belonging to **class** k if its remaining size $w_j(t) \in [2^k, 2^{k+1})$ for $-\infty < k < \infty$. Job j changes its class multiple times during the time it remains in the system, and its class at its arrival time a_j is denoted as its *initial* class. We let $w_{\min} \le w_j \le w_{\max}$, $\forall j$, i.e., the shortest and the longest sizes of any job are $w_{\min}$ and $w_{\max}$, respectively. Let the ratio of $w_{\max}$ and $w_{\min}$ (as defined previously) be $W = \frac{w_{\max}}{w_{\min}}$. Let $k_{\min} = \lfloor \log(w_{\min}) \rfloor$ and $k_{\max} = \lfloor \log(w_{\max}) \rfloor$ be the initial classes of the shortest and the longest jobs.

For any quantity denoted by $Q \in \{V, \Delta V, n, \Delta n\}$, $Q_{\ge \ell, \le h}$ means the respective quantity when restricted to jobs of classes between ℓ and h, and $Q_x = Q_{\ge x, \le x}$.

Definition 13.3.7 *A server is defined to be busy at time t if it is processing some job at time t. A server that is not busy is defined to be idle.*

Busy and idle servers: Let $b^{\mathcal{A}}(t)$ be the number of busy servers (processing some job) with algorithm $\mathcal{A}$ at time t. Hence, the number of idle servers at time t with $\mathcal{A}$ is $\mathcal{I}_{\mathcal{A}}(t) = m - b^{\mathcal{A}}(t)$.

Definition 13.3.8 *The set of times t when all servers are busy with algorithm $\mathcal{A}$, i.e., $b^{\mathcal{A}}(t) = m$, is denoted as $T^b_{\mathcal{A}}$, i.e., $T^b_{\mathcal{A}} = \{t : b^{\mathcal{A}}(t) = m\}$.*

Note that the set of busy times depends on the choice of algorithm $\mathcal{A}$. For the rest of this section, we will always use $T^b_{\mathcal{A}}$ in the context of $\mathcal{A}$ being the SRPT algorithm, and thus drop the subscript $\mathcal{A}$ from $T^b_{\mathcal{A}}$ henceforth.

Recall from (13.5) that $F_{\mathcal{A}} = \int n^{\mathcal{A}}(t)dt$. Similarly, we get the following simple result, using conservation of work and the fact that the speed of each server is unity.

Lemma 13.3.9 $\int b^{\mathcal{A}}(t)dt = \sum_{j=1}^{n} w_j$,

where $w_j = w_j(a_j)$ is the original size of job j.

The following two properties are also immediate.

Lemma 13.3.10 $F_{\mathcal{A}} \ge \sum_{j=1}^{n} w_j$, *since the flow time of each job is at least $w_j = w_j(a_j)$.*

Lemma 13.3.11 *There are at most $2 + \log W$ initial classes for jobs.*

The most important ingredient for proving the $\mathcal{O}\left(\log\left(w_{\max}/w_{\min}\right)\right)$ bound on the competitive ratio of the SRPT algorithm is as follows. Using the definition of $\Delta V(t)$ and the properties of the SRPT algorithm, we will bound the number of incomplete jobs with the SRPT algorithm at any time belonging to a certain class in terms of m (the number of servers) and the number of incomplete jobs with OPT at the same time in Lemma 13.3.12 and Corollary 13.3.13.

Lemma 13.3.12 *For $k_1 \le k_2$, the number of jobs with the SRPT algorithm at time $t \in T^b$ with classes between k_1 and k_2 is*

$$n^{\mathcal{A}}_{\ge k_1, \le k_2}(t) \le m(k_2 - k_1 + 2) + 2n^{\text{OPT}}_{\le k_2}(t).$$

The proof of Lemma 13.3.12 is provided after the proof of Lemma 13.3.14. The immediate corollary of Lemma 13.3.12 is as follows, whose proof we leave as an exercise in Problem 13.3. For the rest of this section, $\mathcal{A}$ means SRPT unless otherwise mentioned.

Corollary 13.3.13 *For $t \in T^b$, $n^{\mathcal{A}}(t) \leq m(4 + \log(W)) + 2n^{\text{OPT}}(t)$.*

Using Corollary 13.3.13, we next show that the competitive ratio of the SRPT algorithm is at most $\mathcal{O}(\log W)$.

Lemma 13.3.14 *The competitive ratio of the SRPT algorithm is at most $\mathcal{O}(\log W)$. In particular,*

$$F_{\mathcal{A}} \leq (6 + \log(W))F_{\text{OPT}}.$$

Proof:

$$F_{\mathcal{A}} \overset{(a)}{=} \int n^{\mathcal{A}}(t)dt,$$

$$\overset{(b)}{=} \int_{t \notin T^b} n^{\mathcal{A}}(t)dt + \int_{t \in T^b} n^{\mathcal{A}}(t)dt,$$

$$\overset{(c)}{\leq} \int_{t \notin T^b} b^{\mathcal{A}}(t)dt + \int_{t \in T^b} (m(4 + \log(W)) + 2n^{\text{OPT}}(t))dt,$$

$$\overset{(d)}{=} \int_{t \notin T^b} b^{\mathcal{A}}(t)dt + \int_{t \in T^b} (b^{\mathcal{A}}(t)(4 + \log(W)) + 2n^{\text{OPT}}(t))dt,$$

$$\leq (4 + \log(W)) \int_t b^{\mathcal{A}}(t)dt + 2 \int_t n^{\text{OPT}}(t)dt,$$

$$\overset{(e)}{=} (4 + \log(W)) \sum_{j=1}^n w_j + 2 \int_t n^{\text{OPT}}(t)dt,$$

$$\overset{(f)}{\leq} (6 + \log(W))F_{\text{OPT}},$$

where (a) follows from (13.5), (b) follows by partitioning time into sets T^b, where all servers are busy with SRPT, and the complement of set T^b. When $t \notin T^b$, then at least one server is idle with SRPT, and hence the number of jobs $n^{\mathcal{A}}(t)$ with SRPT is the same as the number of busy servers $b^{\mathcal{A}}(t)$ at time t, which implies the first term of inequality (c). The second and third terms of inequality (c) follows from Corollary 13.3.13. Noting that for $t \in T^b$, all servers are busy and hence $b^{\mathcal{A}}(t) = m$ implies inequality (d). Inequalities (e) and (f) follow from Lemma 13.3.9 and Lemma 13.3.10, respectively. ∎

Next, we work towards proving Lemma 13.3.12.

Definition 13.3.15 *For some $t \in T^b$, consider $\hat{\imath} < t$ to be the earliest time such that $[\hat{\imath}, t) \in T^b$, i.e., for the whole time $[\hat{\imath}, t)$ all servers are busy with the SRPT algorithm. During interval $[\hat{\imath}, t)$, the latest time at which a job belonging to class greater than k is processed is defined as t_k. We let $t_k = \hat{\imath}$ if no job with class greater than k is processed in $[\hat{\imath}, t)$.*

Remark 13.3.16 *Many of the intermediate results that follow apply for generic algorithms. Thus to identify the importance of the SRPT algorithm, all results that critically depend on the SRPT algorithm will be appended with a superscript $*$.*

With these definitions, we have the following intermediate result.

Lemma 13.3.17 *For $t \in T^b$, $\Delta V_{\leq k}(t) \leq \Delta V_{\leq k}(t_k)$.*

Since $t_k \leq t$, what this result means is that the difference in the volume between SRPT and OPT for jobs with class at most k does not increase from time t_k to time t.

Proof: Since $t_k \geq \hat{t}$, $[t_k, t) \in T^b$, i.e., all servers are busy throughout the interval $[t_k, t)$ with the SRPT algorithm working on jobs with class at most k. Hence, the total amount of work done by SRPT in interval $[t_k, t)$ is $m(t - t_k)$ on jobs with class at most k.

OPT on the other hand need not have all servers busy during $[t_k, t)$, but the total work done by OPT (on any class of jobs) in $[t_k, t)$ is also upper bounded by $m(t - t_k)$. Thus, if OPT works throughout $[t_k, t)$ on jobs with class at most k, then

$$\Delta V_{\leq k}(t) \leq \Delta V_{\leq k}(t_k).$$

However, OPT could also work on jobs with class greater than k in $[t_k, t)$, potentially lowering a job's class from $k' > k$ to k. Consequently, compared to the case when OPT works throughout $[t_k, t)$ on jobs with class at most k, $V_{\leq k}^{OPT}(t)$ is only larger, and $\Delta V_{\leq k}(t)$ smaller. Hence, even in this case,

$$\Delta V_{\leq k}(t) \leq \Delta V_{\leq k}(t_k).$$

The arrival of new jobs in interval $[t_k, t)$ does not affect the above argument, since it only counts the total work done. ∎

Lemma 13.3.18 * *For $t \in T^b$, $\Delta V_{\leq k}(t_k) \leq m2^{k+1}$.*

Proof: Case I: $t_k = \hat{t}$. Thus, no job with class more than k is processed by SRPT in $[\hat{t}, t)$. The event that $t_k = \hat{t}$ also implies that at **any moment just before t_k, there is at least one idle server** which follows from the definition of $\hat{t}$ being the earliest time such that $[\hat{t}, t) \in T^b$. Thus, any moment just before t_k, the total number of jobs with SRPT is at most $m - 1$, and all these jobs belong to class at most k since $t_k = \hat{t}$.

Case II: $t_k > \hat{t}$. At any moment before t_k, $t_k - \epsilon$ for $\epsilon > 0$ small enough, let SRPT process m_1 jobs $j_1, \ldots, j_{m_1}$ with class more than k. Essentially, by the definition of t_k, these m_1 jobs change their class from $k + 1$ to k at time $t_k - \epsilon$.

Since $t_k \in T^b$, and the fact that SRPT processes the jobs belonging to the smallest class at any time, we get that there are at most $m - m_1$ jobs with class at most k at time $t_k - \epsilon$, since otherwise any of j_1 to j_{m_1} jobs of class greater than k would not have been processed. Thus, the total number of jobs at time $t_k - \epsilon$ with SRPT of class at most k is at most m.

Combining Cases I and II, we get that for any small enough $\epsilon > 0$, at time $t_k - \epsilon$, the total remaining size of all jobs of class at most k with SRPT is at most $m2^{k+1}$, since a job belonging to class k has at most remaining size 2^{k+1}, i.e.,

$$V_{\leq k}^A(t_k - \epsilon) \leq m2^{k+1}. \tag{13.13}$$

At time t_k, new jobs belonging to class at most class k can arrive; however, they do not affect $\Delta V_{\leq k}(t_k)$ since they contribute equally to both $V_{\leq k}^{\mathcal{A}}(t_k)$ and $V_{\leq k}^{\text{OPT}}(t_k)$. Thus, from (13.13), we get the required result that

$$\Delta V_{\leq k}(t_k) \leq m2^{k+1}.$$

■

Combining Lemmas 13.3.17 and 13.3.18, we get the following result.

Lemma 13.3.19 *For* $t \in T^b$, $\Delta V_{\leq k}(t) \leq m2^{k+1}$.

Using Lemma 13.3.19, we complete the proof of Lemma 13.3.12, which connects the number of incomplete jobs with the algorithm and OPT, belonging to a certain set of classes.

Proof: [Proof of Lemma 13.3.12]

$$\sum_{k=k_1}^{k_2} n_k^{\mathcal{A}}(t) \overset{(a)}{\leq} \sum_{k=k_1}^{k_2} \frac{V_k^{\mathcal{A}}(t)}{2^k},$$

$$\overset{(b)}{=} \sum_{k=k_1}^{k_2} \frac{\Delta V_k(t) + V_k^{\text{OPT}}(t)}{2^k},$$

$$= \sum_{k=k_1}^{k_2} \frac{\Delta V_{\leq k}(t) - \Delta V_{\leq k-1}(t)}{2^k} + \sum_{k=k_1}^{k_2} \frac{V_k^{\text{OPT}}(t)}{2^k},$$

$$\overset{(c)}{=} \frac{\Delta V_{\leq k_2}(t)}{2^{k_2}} + \sum_{k=k_1}^{k_2-1} \left(\frac{\Delta V_{\leq k}(t)}{2^k} - \frac{\Delta V_{\leq k}(t)}{2^{k+1}} \right) - \frac{\Delta V_{\leq k_1-1}(t)}{2^{k_1}} + \sum_{k=k_1}^{k_2} \frac{V_k^{\text{OPT}}(t)}{2^k},$$

$$\overset{(d)}{\leq} \frac{\Delta V_{\leq k_2}(t)}{2^{k_2}} + \sum_{k=k_1}^{k_2-1} \frac{\Delta V_{\leq k}(t)}{2^{k+1}} - \frac{\Delta V_{\leq k_1-1}(t)}{2^{k_1}} + 2n_{\geq k_1, \leq k_2}^{\text{OPT}}(t),$$

$$\overset{(e)}{\leq} 2m + \sum_{k=k_1}^{k_2-1} m + \frac{V_{\leq k_1-1}^{\text{OPT}}(t)}{2^{k_1}} + 2n_{\geq k_1, \leq k_2}^{\text{OPT}}(t),$$

$$\overset{(f)}{\leq} 2m + \sum_{k=k_1}^{k_2-1} m + n_{\leq k_1-1}^{\text{OPT}}(t) + 2n_{\geq k_1, \leq k_2}^{\text{OPT}}(t),$$

$$\leq m(k_2 - k_1 + 2) + 2n_{\leq k_2}^{\text{OPT}}(t),$$

where (a) follows from the definition of $V_k^{\mathcal{A}}(t)$ as the total remaining size of jobs belonging to class k at time t, and the size of each job in class k belongs to $[2^k, 2^{k+1})$, while (b) follows from the definition of $\Delta V_k = V_k^{\mathcal{A}} - V_k^{\text{OPT}}$. To get (c) we separate the telescopic sum over k_1 to k_2 into three parts: k_2, k_1 to $k_2 - 1$, and $k_1 - 1$. Inequality (d) follows from the definition of V_k^{OPT}, and the fact that the size of each job in class k belongs to $[2^k, 2^{k+1})$. Inequality (e) follows by applying Lemma 13.3.19 on the first two terms separately, and for the third term using the property that $-\Delta V_{\leq k_1 - 1}(t) \leq V^{OPT}_{\leq k_1 - 1}(t)$. Using the fact that size of each job in class k belongs to $[2^k, 2^{k+1})$ on the third term of (e), we get inequality (f).

Finally noting that

$$n^A_{\geq k_1, \leq k_2}(t) = \sum_{k=k_1}^{k_2} n^A_k(t),$$

the result stated in Lemma 13.3.12 follows.   ∎

Next, we proceed to **prove that the competitive ratio of the SRPT algorithm is at most** $\mathcal{O}\left(\log\left(\frac{n}{m}\right)\right)$. Let $\bar{k}$ be the maximum integer such that for some time $t \in T^b$ (T_b is the set of time instants where all servers are busy with SRPT),

$$n^A_{\geq \bar{k}}(t) \geq m. \tag{13.14}$$

If no such integer $\bar{k}$ exists, then let $\bar{k} = k_{min} - 1$. Condition (13.14) implies that at some time t, the number of incomplete jobs with the SRPT algorithm of class at least $\bar{k}$ is at least m and, **importantly**, for class $\bar{k} + 1$, there are at most $m - 1$ jobs for any time $t \in T^b$. We refer to (13.14) as property P1, which we will use later in the proof.

Next, we partition the time period T^b into sets T^b_k, for $k = k_{min} + 1, \dots, \bar{k}$, and $T^b_{k_{min}}, T^b_{\bar{k}+1}$, that are defined as follows.

Definition 13.3.20 *For $k = k_{min} + 1, \dots, \bar{k}$, T^b_k is defined as the set of time instants when all servers are busy, and at least one server is busy with a job of class k and no server is busy with a job of class greater than k. $T^b_{\bar{k}+1}$ is defined as the set of time instants when all servers are busy, and at least one server is busy with a job of class larger than $\bar{k}$, while $T^b_{k_{min}}$ is the set of time instants when all servers are busy with jobs of class at most k_{min}.*

Similar to before, for the SRPT algorithm $\mathcal{A}$ we can write

$$F_{\mathcal{A}} = \int_{t \notin T^b} n^A(t)dt + \int_{t \in T^b} n^A(t)dt,$$

$$= \int_{t \notin T^b} b^A(t)dt + \sum_{k=k_{min}}^{\bar{k}} \int_{t \in T^b_k} n^A(t)dt + \int_{t \in T^b_{\bar{k}+1}} n^A(t)dt. \tag{13.15}$$

By definition of T^b_k for $k = k_{min}, \dots, \bar{k} + 1$, at time $t \in T^b_k$ there are at most m jobs of class less than k, since at least one job of class k is being processed, and SRPT always processes jobs with the smallest class. Moreover, from property P1 (13.14), for $t \in T^b$, there are at most m jobs of class larger than $\bar{k}$.

Since $T^b_k \subseteq T^b$, we get that for $t \in T^b_k$ with $k = k_{min}, \dots, \bar{k}$,

$$n^A(t) = n^A_{<k}(t) + n^A_{\geq k, \leq \bar{k}}(t) + n^A_{\geq \bar{k}+1}(t) \leq 2m + n^A_{\geq k, \leq \bar{k}}(t). \tag{13.16}$$

Moreover, from the definition of $\bar{k}$, from Property P1, there are at most $m - 1$ jobs of class larger than $\bar{k}$ for any $t \in T^b$, and from the definition $t \in T^b_{\bar{k}+1}$, there is at least one job of class

$\bar{k} + 1$ being processed. These two facts together imply that the number of jobs with class at most $\bar{k} + 1$ is at most m, since SRPT always processes jobs with the smallest class. Thus, for $t \in T^b_{\bar{k}+1}$, we have

$$n^{\mathcal{A}}(t) = n^{\mathcal{A}}_{<\bar{k}+1}(t) + n^{\mathcal{A}}_{\geq \bar{k}+1}(t) \leq 2m. \tag{13.17}$$

Using (13.16) and (13.17) in (13.15), we get

$$F_{\mathcal{A}} \leq \int_{t \notin T^b} b^{\mathcal{A}}(t) dt + \sum_{k=k_{\min}}^{\bar{k}} \int_{t \in T^b_k} (2m + n^{\mathcal{A}}_{\geq k, \leq \bar{k}}(t)) dt + \int_{t \in T^b_{\bar{k}+1}} 2m \, dt$$

$$\overset{(a)}{\leq} \int_{t \notin T^b} b^{\mathcal{A}}(t) dt + \sum_{k=k_{\min}}^{\bar{k}} \int_{t \in T^b_k} (4m + m(\bar{k} - k) + 2n^{\text{OPT}}_{\leq \bar{k}}(t)) dt + \int_{t \in T^b_{\bar{k}+1}} 2m \, dt,$$

$$= \int_{t \notin T^b} b^{\mathcal{A}}(t) dt + \sum_{k=k_{\min}}^{\bar{k}} \int_{t \in T^b_k} 4m \, dt + \int_{t \in T^b_{\bar{k}+1}} 2m \, dt$$

$$+ \sum_{k=k_{\min}}^{\bar{k}} m(\bar{k} - k) \int_{t \in T^b_k} dt + 2 \sum_{k=k_{\min}}^{\bar{k}} \int_{t \in T^b_k} n^{\text{OPT}}_{\leq \bar{k}}(t) dt,$$

$$\overset{(b)}{\leq} \int_{t \notin T^b} b^{\mathcal{A}}(t) dt + \int_{t \in T^b} 4m \, dt + \sum_{k=k_{\min}}^{\bar{k}} m(\bar{k} - k) \int_{t \in T^b_k} dt + 2 \int_{t \in T^b} n^{\text{OPT}}(t) dt,$$

$$\overset{(c)}{\leq} \int_{t \notin T^b} b^{\mathcal{A}}(t) dt + \int_{t \in T^b} 4b^{\mathcal{A}}(t) \, dt + \sum_{k=k_{\min}}^{\bar{k}} m(\bar{k} - k)|T^b_k| + 2 \int_{t \in T^b} n^{\text{OPT}}(t) dt,$$

$$\overset{(d)}{\leq} \int_t 4b^{\mathcal{A}}(t) dt + \sum_{k=k_{\min}}^{\bar{k}} m(\bar{k} - k)|T^b_k| + 2 \int_t n^{\text{OPT}}(t) dt,$$

$$\overset{(e)}{\leq} \int_t 6n^{\text{OPT}}(t) dt + \sum_{k=k_{\min}}^{\bar{k}} m(\bar{k} - k)|T^b_k|,$$

$$= 6F_{\text{OPT}} + \sum_{k=k_{\min}}^{\bar{k}} m(\bar{k} - k)|T^b_k|, \tag{13.18}$$

where inequality (a) follows by applying Lemma 13.3.12 on the second term, while (b) follows by combining the second and third terms while upper bounding the third term by $\int_{t \in T^b_{\bar{k}+1}} 4m \, dt$, and upper bounding the last term involving $n^{\text{OPT}}_{\leq \bar{k}}(t)$. To get (c), we substitute $m = b^{\mathcal{A}}(t)$ since $t \in T^b$ (all servers are busy), while inequality (d) is obtained by combining the first two terms of (c) and upper bounding the last term by letting the integral to be over all times t. The final inequality (e) is obtained by using Lemmas 13.3.9 and 13.3.10 together on the first and third terms of (d).

Now, we are left with upper bounding the term $\sum_{k=k_{\min}}^{\bar{k}} m(\bar{k} - k)|T_k^b|$ in (13.18). Recall the definition of T_k^b from Definition 13.3.20, which jointly couples the events happening across multiple servers. To derive the required bound, we next define a single-server specific time instants variable $T_{k,\ell}$ as follows. For server ℓ, $T_{k,\ell}$ is the set of time instants (not necessarily in T^b, i.e., some other server might be idling) such that server ℓ is processing a job of class k with the SRPT algorithm. The following proposition connects the times T_k^b and $T_{k,\ell}$.

Proposition 13.3.21 $m|T_k^b| \le \sum_{\ell=1}^{m} |T_{k,\ell}|$.

Proof: For $t \in T_k^b$, only jobs with classes higher than k are precluded from getting processed on any server by the SRPT algorithm. Thus, $t \in T_k^b$ implies that $t \in \cup_{k' \le k} T_{k',\ell}$ for each ℓ. Since this is true for each $\ell = 1, \dots, m$, summing across the m servers, we get $m|T_k^b| \le \sum_{\ell=1}^{m} |T_{k,\ell}|$. ∎

Using Proposition 13.3.21, we get

$$\sum_{k=k_{\min}}^{\bar{k}} m(\bar{k} - k)|T_k^b| \le \sum_{k=k_{\min}}^{\bar{k}} \sum_{\ell=1}^{m} (\bar{k} - k)|T_{k,\ell}|. \tag{13.19}$$

The RHS of (13.19) essentially captures the total time spent by a job of class k across all servers scaled with $(\bar{k} - k)$. Next, rather than counting the RHS of (13.19) across multiple jobs that could belong to the same class at any time, we isolate individual jobs and count their contribution to the RHS of (13.19). In particular, we upper bound the RHS of (13.19) via considering the maximum contribution made to the RHS of (13.19) by a job j that arrives with initial class k.

Recall that there are a total of n jobs, and let n_k be the number of jobs with initial class k, for $k = k_{\min}, \dots, \bar{k} - 1$, and $n_{\bar{k}}$ be the number of jobs with initial class larger than or equal to $\bar{k}$.[2] Consider a job j that arrives with initial class $k \le \bar{k}$, and which progressively moves from class k' to $k' - 1$ for $k' = k, k-1, \dots, k_{\min}$, where the total amount of processing time for job j when it is in class k' is at most $2^{k'+1}$. Thus, the contribution of job j with initial class k to the RHS of (13.19) is at most $\sum_{k'=0}^{k-k_{\min}} (\bar{k} - k + k')2^{k-k'+1} \le 2(\bar{k} - k + 1)2^{k+1}$.

Thus, accounting for all jobs that belong to class at most $\bar{k}$, we upper bound the RHS of (13.19) as

$$\sum_{k=k_{\min}}^{\bar{k}} \sum_{\ell=1}^{m} (\bar{k} - k)|T_{k,\ell}| \le \sum_{k=k_{\min}}^{\bar{k}} 2n_k(\bar{k} - k + 1)2^{k+1},$$

$$= 4 \sum_{k=k_{\min}}^{\bar{k}} n_k(\bar{k} - k)2^k + 2 \sum_{k=k_{\min}}^{\bar{k}} n_k 2^{k+1},$$

$$\le 4 \sum_{k=k_{\min}}^{\bar{k}} n_k(\bar{k} - k)2^k + 4 \sum_{j=1}^{n} w_j, \tag{13.20}$$

---

[2] We actually only need the number of jobs with initial class equal to $\bar{k}$, but since we only need an upper bound in terms of n, we include jobs with class larger than or equal to $\bar{k}$ as well.

where the last inequality follows since each of the n_k jobs with initial class k has (original) processing time $w \geq 2^k$.

The final task is to upper bound $G = \sum_{k=k_{\min}}^{\bar{k}} n_k(\bar{k} - k)2^k$. Let $i = \bar{k} - k$ and $a_i = n_{\bar{k}-i}2^{\bar{k}-i}$. Then $G = \sum_{i=0}^{\bar{k}-k_{\min}} ia_i$. We approach this upper bound by finding what the largest value G can take under the constraint

$$\sum_{i=0}^{\bar{k}-k_{\min}} a_i \leq \sum_{j=1}^{n} w_j \tag{13.21}$$

and

$$\sum_{i=0}^{\bar{k}-k_{\min}} \frac{a_i}{2^{\bar{k}-i}} = \sum_{i=0}^{\bar{k}-k_{\min}} n_{\bar{k}-i} \leq n, \tag{13.22}$$

where constraint (13.21) follows since a job with initial class j has (original) processing time $w_j \geq 2^j$, while constraint (13.22) captures the fact that the total number of jobs is at most n.

The following proposition helps us in upper bounding G, whose proof is left as an exercise in Problem 13.4.

Proposition 13.3.22 *Given a sequence of non-negative numbers $a_1, \ldots, a_n$, such that $\sum_{i=1}^{n} a_i \leq A$ and $\sum_{i=1}^{n} 2^i a_i \leq B$, then $\sum_{i=1}^{n} ia_i \leq \log\left(\frac{4B}{A}\right)A$.*

Applying Proposition 13.3.22, with $A = \sum_{j=1}^{n} w_j$ and $B = n2^{\bar{k}}$, we get

$$G = \sum_{k=0}^{\bar{k}-k_{\min}} ia_i \leq \log\left(\frac{4n2^{\bar{k}}}{\sum_{j=1}^{n} w_j}\right) \sum_{j=1}^{n} w_j,$$

$$\leq \mathcal{O}\left(\frac{n}{m}\right) F_{\text{OPT}}, \tag{13.23}$$

where we have used the fact that $\sum_{j=1}^{n} w_j \geq m2^{\bar{k}}$, which follows from the definition of $\bar{k}$ (13.14) that implies that at some time t, the number of jobs belonging to class $\bar{k}$ are at least m, and the fact that the least size of a job belonging to class k is 2^k, and Lemma 13.3.10 that states that $F_{\text{OPT}} \geq \sum_{j=1}^{n} w_j$.

Combining (13.20) and (13.23) with (13.18), we get

$$F_A \leq \mathcal{O}\left(\frac{n}{m}\right) F_{\text{OPT}},$$

as required.   ∎

Thus, we have completed the proof of Theorem 13.3.6, which is kind of a negative result since the competitive ratio depends on the logarithm of the ratio of the relative sizes of jobs, or the logarithm of the ratio of the number of jobs and the number of servers.

In the online setting, the information available with any algorithm is seriously limited compared to the offline algorithm, and for any problem where the optimal competitive ratio depends on the parameters of the input sequence, it is worth considering whether an online algorithm can be made competitive if it is given access to more resources than OPT. For the considered scheduling problem in this chapter, the natural resource augmentation is in terms of giving the online algorithm access to servers with speed more than that of OPT. In the next section, we present a surprising result that the flow time of the SRPT algorithm when all m servers have speed $2 - 1/m$ is at most the flow time of OPT with m unit speed servers.

13.4 Speed Augmentation for SRPT

In this section, we show that if for the online SRPT algorithm, the servers are allowed to operate at a slightly higher speed of $(2 - 1/m)$-times more than that for OPT, which is called the resource augmentation regime, the flow time of the SRPT algorithm is at most the flow time of OPT with unit speed servers.

Definition 13.4.1 *An algorithm is called work conserving if it does not idle as long as there is remaining work.*

Let $\mathcal{A}(j, [t_a, t_b])$ denote the amount of work completed by an algorithm $\mathcal{A}$ for job j in time interval $[t_a, t_b]$. For a set of jobs $\mathcal{J}$, $\mathcal{A}(\mathcal{J}, [t_a, t_b]) = \sum_{j \in \mathcal{J}} \mathcal{A}(j, [t_a, t_b])$. Moreover, $\mathcal{A}(j, t)$ denotes the amount of work completed by algorithm $\mathcal{A}$ for job j by time t, i.e., $\mathcal{A}(j, t) = \mathcal{A}(j, [-\infty, t])$, while for a set of jobs $\mathcal{J}$, $\mathcal{A}(\mathcal{J}, t) = \sum_{j \in \mathcal{J}} \mathcal{A}(j, t)$.

Lemma 13.4.2 *Let $1 \leq \beta \leq (2 - 1/m)$ and $\alpha = \frac{2-1/m}{\beta} \geq 1$. Let $\mathcal{A}$ be any work-conserving algorithm that has access to m servers having speed α each, while $\mathcal{A}'$ is any algorithm that has access to m servers with unit speed. Then for any job arrival sequence σ with a complete set of jobs $\mathcal{J}$,*

$$\mathcal{A}(\mathcal{J}, \beta t) \geq \mathcal{A}'(\mathcal{J}, t).$$

Thus, the amount of work completed by any work-conserving algorithm with speed α servers by time $(2 - 1/m)t$ is at least as much as work done by OPT by time t with unit speed servers.

Proof: We will use contradiction to prove the claim. If the claim is false, then there exists a time instant t_j and job j such that the amount of work done by any work-conserving algorithm $\mathcal{A}$ with speed α servers satisfies

$$\mathcal{A}(\mathcal{J}, \beta t_j) < \mathcal{A}'(\mathcal{J}, t_j) \quad \text{and} \quad \mathcal{A}(j, \beta t_j) < \mathcal{A}'(j, t_j). \tag{13.24}$$

Among all such jobs j that satisfy (13.24), consider the job j_e that arrives the earliest at time a_e and let $t = t_{j_e}$. Then from (13.24), we know that

$$\mathcal{A}(\mathcal{J}, \beta t) < \mathcal{A}'(\mathcal{J}, t) \tag{13.25}$$

and

$$\mathcal{A}(j_e, \beta t) < \mathcal{A}'(j_e, t). \tag{13.26}$$

Moreover, since a_e is the arrival time of the earliest such job, it must be that the work done by $\mathcal{A}$ till time a_e is at least as much as the work done by $\mathcal{A}'$ until time a_e as well as time a_e/β since $\beta > 1$. Therefore, we have

$$A(\mathcal{J}, a_e) \geq A'(\mathcal{J}, a_e/\beta). \tag{13.27}$$

Thus, from (13.25) and (13.27), the total amount of work done by $\mathcal{A}$ between time a_e and time βt is strictly less than the amount of work done by $\mathcal{A}'$ between time a_e/β and t,

$$A(\mathcal{J}, [a_e, \beta t]) < A'(\mathcal{J}, [a_e/\beta, t]). \tag{13.28}$$

To complete the claim, we will show that both (13.26) and (13.28) cannot hold simultaneously for the choice of β and α as mentioned in the statement of the lemma. For $\mathcal{A}$, we will consider the time interval $[a_e, \beta t]$, while for $\mathcal{A}'$, the time interval of interest is $[a_e/\beta, t]$.

Consider the time interval $[a_e, \beta t]$, and for algorithm $\mathcal{A}$, partition this interval into two periods: overloaded, when there are more than m unfinished or active jobs in the system, and full, when at most m unfinished or active are active in the system. Let t_o and t_f be the total duration of the overloaded part and the full part in $[a_e, \beta t]$, respectively.

Since the algorithm $\mathcal{A}$ is work conserving, during the full period, job j_e was active throughout and was getting processed at speed α. Thus, $\mathcal{A}$ completes

$$t_f \alpha$$

amount of work for job j_e in the full period in $[a_e, \beta t]$. Moreover, during the overloaded period, all the m servers are busy throughout with $\mathcal{A}$ working at speed α. Therefore, the total amount of work completed by $\mathcal{A}$ in interval $[a_e, \beta t]$ is at least

$$m t_o \alpha + t_f \alpha.$$

For $\mathcal{A}'$, the amount of work that can be completed in interval $[a_e/\beta, t]$ with m servers that work at unit speed is at most $m(t - a_e/\beta)$. Moreover, the amount of work completed by $\mathcal{A}'$ for job j_e by time t is $t - a_e \leq t - a_e/\beta$, since a job is not allowed to be split and processed parallely on multiple servers.

Plugging these bounds on the work done by $\mathcal{A}$ and $\mathcal{A}'$, for job j_e, and the total amount of work done in (13.26) and (13.28), respectively, we get

$$\alpha t_f < t - \frac{a_e}{\beta} \tag{13.29}$$

and

$$\alpha \left(m t_o + t_f \right) < m \left(t - \frac{a_e}{\beta} \right). \tag{13.30}$$

Multiplying (13.29) with $(m-1)$ and adding to (13.30) yields

$$\alpha m (t_o + t_f) = \alpha \left(m t_o + t_f \right) + (m-1)\alpha t_f < \left(t - \frac{a_e}{\beta} \right) (2m-1).$$

Since $t_o + t_f = \beta t - a_e$, we get

$$\alpha m < \frac{2m - 1}{\beta},$$

making

$$\alpha\beta < 2 - 1/m,$$

contradicting the choice of $\alpha\beta = 2 - 1/m$.

Thus, (13.24) cannot be true, and the claim of the lemma follows. ∎

Definition 13.4.3 *[Augmentation Property] Let the number of jobs finished completely by an algorithm $\mathcal{A}$ with input sequence σ' by time t be k. Consider any input sequence σ'' such that $\sigma' \subseteq \sigma''$. Then $\mathcal{A}$ is defined to satisfy the augmentation property if the number of jobs finished completely by $\mathcal{A}$ with input sequence σ'' by time t is at least k.*

Lemma 13.4.4 *The* SRPT *algorithm satisfies the augmentation property.*

We leave the proof of Lemma 13.4.4 as an exercise in Problem 13.5.

Theorem 13.4.5 *The flow time of any online algorithm $\mathcal{A}$ that is work conserving and satisfies the augmentation property and has access to m servers with speed $2 - 1/m$ is at most the flow time of* OPT *with m unit speed servers.*

Proof: Let the full input job sequence be σ. Let the subset of input $\sigma_t \subseteq \sigma$ be the set of jobs that OPT with unit speed servers finishes completely by time t, when the input sequence is σ. Let $\mathcal{A}$ be any algorithm that is work conserving and satisfies the augmentation property. Therefore, from Lemma 13.4.2, if the input sequence is just σ_t, $\mathcal{A}$ finishes all $|\sigma_t|$ jobs by time $t(2 - 1/m)/\alpha$ given m servers with speed α.

Now we make use of the augmentation property of $\mathcal{A}$. Let $\sigma_t = \sigma'$ and $\sigma = \sigma''$, then the augmentation property implies that for any time t, at least $|\sigma_t|$ jobs will be completed by time $(2 - 1/m)t/\alpha$ with $\mathcal{A}$ even when the input sequence is σ.

This implies that for any k, the completion time of the kth job with $\mathcal{A}$ is no later than $(2 - 1/m)/\alpha$ times the completion time of the kth job with OPT for any job arrival sequence σ. Note that the order of departure of jobs with $\mathcal{A}$ and OPT might be different. Thus, choosing $\alpha = 2 - 1/m$, we get

$$\sum_{j \in \sigma} d_j(\text{OPT}) \geq \sum_{j \in \sigma} d_j(\mathcal{A}). \tag{13.31}$$

Recall that the flow time is $\sum_{j \in \sigma}(d_j - a_j)$ and $\sum_{j \in \sigma} a_j$ is independent of the algorithm. Thus, to claim that $F_{\text{OPT}} \geq F_{\mathcal{A}}$, it is sufficient to show that $\sum_{j \in \sigma} d_j(\text{OPT}) \geq \sum_{j \in \sigma} d_j(\mathcal{A})$, as done in (13.31). Hence, the proof is complete using (13.31). ∎

We get the result for SRPT as a corollary to Theorem 13.4.5.

Corollary 13.4.6 *The flow time of the online* SRPT *algorithm with $2 - 1/m$ speed augmentation is identical to that of* OPT *with unit speed servers.*

The proof follows since SRPT is work conserving and satisfies the augmentation property, Lemma 13.4.4.

13.5 Notes

SRPT was the first algorithm to be analysed to minimize the flow time with m identical servers in [236], where it was shown that in fact it is an optimal online algorithm. The lower bound on the competitive ratio presented in Theorem 13.3.3 was proven in [236], while the upper bound result for the competitive ratio presented in Theorem 13.3.6 follows from the simpler proof of SRPT derived in [237], compared to the original proof presented in [236].

The resource augmentation result (Corollary 13.4.6) for SRPT was proven in [238]. This result has been further improved in [239], where it has been shown that with m servers with $(1 + \epsilon)$ speed, SRPT is $4/\epsilon$-competitive with respect to OPT with m unit speed servers, for any $\epsilon > 0$.

Algorithms to minimize flow time with multiple servers that do not need job migration, unlike SRPT, with competitive ratio of

$$\max\left\{\mathcal{O}\left(\log(n)\right), \mathcal{O}\left(\log\left(w_{\max}/w_{\min}\right)\right)\right\}$$

and

$$\max\left\{\mathcal{O}\left(\log(n/m)\right), \mathcal{O}\left(\log\left(w_{\max}/w_{\min}\right)\right)\right\}$$

have been derived in [240] and [241], respectively. Algorithms that are required to dispatch or assign each arriving job to a server as soon as it arrives, and without job migration, were considered in [242], with a competitive ratio of $\max\left\{\mathcal{O}\left(\log(n)\right), \mathcal{O}\left(\log\left(w_{\max}/w_{\min}\right)\right)\right\}$.

More involved settings such as minimizing the weighted flow time has been considered in [235], while the non-clairvoyant setting, where an algorithm only knows the presence of a job but not its remaining size, has been considered in [243, 244], where it is shown that with randomization upper and lower bounds on the competitive ratio is order $\log n$. The case of related servers, where servers have different speeds, has been considered in [245, 246], where in [245] an algorithm with a competitive ratio of $\mathcal{O}\left(\log^2\left(w_{\max}/w_{\min}\right)\log(S)\right)$ was proposed, where S is the ratio of the maximum and the minimum speeds across the m servers. The competitive ratio was subsequently improved to $\mathcal{O}\left(\log^2(w_{\max}/w_{\min})\right)$ in [246]. The case of subset constraints, where each job can be assigned to only a specified subset of the servers, has been considered in [247], where it is shown that no online algorithm with a bounded competitive ratio exists, even if all job sizes are equal to one.

Other important performance metrics with scheduling are makespan (which is equivalent to minimizing the maximum load of a server and is discussed in detail in Chapter 12) and completion time (which is the sum of the times at which jobs complete, disregarding their arrival times). The completion time minimization problem is simpler than the flow time minimization problem, and has been considered in great detail in literature [248–251]. A comprehensive review of online scheduling that is relevant for this chapter, as well as Chapters 14 and 15, can be found in Chapter 3 of [252].

Most recently the scheduling problem for minimizing flow time has been considered in the presence of machine learning augmented setting for a single server in [253, 254].

PROBLEMS

13.1 In this chapter, we considered only the objective of minimizing the flow time. Another important metric is *makespan*, which is defined as the completion time of the last finished job. There are a total of m servers, each with unit speed. n jobs arrive over time, with job j having size w_j. Jobs have to be assigned to a server as soon as they arrive, and jobs cannot be preempted. Let d_j be the departure time of job j. Then the makespan is defined as $\max_j d_j$.

To minimize makespan, consider the following *greedy* algorithm (first analysed by Graham [255]) that assigns a newly arrived job to the least loaded server at that time. Show that the competitive ratio of the greedy algorithm is at most $2 - 1/m$.

[Hint: For an arbitrary job sequence $\mathcal{I} = j_1, \dots, j_n$ with n jobs, let $M(\mathcal{I})$ be the makespan for the schedule constructed by the greedy algorithm.

Let $w_{\max} = \max_j w_j$. Then try to show that

$$mM(\mathcal{I}) \le \sum_{j=1}^{n} w_j + (m-1)w_{\max}, \tag{13.32}$$

and note that both $\frac{1}{m}\sum_{j=1}^{n} w_j$ and $w_{\max}$ are a lower bound on OPT's makespan to conclude the result.]

13.2 Prove Theorem 13.3.1.

13.3 Prove Corollary 13.3.13.

[Hint] Note that all newly arriving jobs have class at least $k_{\min}$. Thus, with the SRPT algorithm, jobs belonging to class $< k_{\min}$ are never preempted. Another fact is that with the SRPT algorithm the number of jobs with class $< k_{\min}$ is at most m at any time t.

13.4 Prove Proposition 13.3.22.

13.5 Prove Lemma 13.4.4.

13.6 Suppose preemption is not allowed. Then show that no online algorithm can achieve a competitive ratio better than $\Omega(n)$ for minimizing flow time with m identical servers and a total of n jobs, with job j having size w_j arriving at time a_j.

[Remark: This is a somewhat surprising result, that without preemption the competitive ratio is worse than when preemption is allowed. The fact is that without preemption, any online algorithm is even more limited than the optimal offline algorithm, which is counter-intuitive.]

13.7 [247] In this problem, we will consider the case that each job can be assigned to only a subset of servers, and the objective is to minimize the flow time.

Consider that there are three servers, and jobs with unit size are of two types. Jobs with type I can be scheduled on servers $\{1, 2\}$, while type II jobs can be scheduled only on servers $\{2, 3\}$.

Let the input be such that at each time step $t = 0, 1, \ldots, T - 1$, two jobs of type I and two jobs of type II arrive. Let S be the system state (number of incomplete jobs) at time T for any deterministic algorithm $\mathcal{A}$.

(a) Show that with S, either (i) at least $T/2$ jobs of type I are unfinished or (ii) at least $T/2$ jobs of type II are unfinished.

(b) Depending on S in part (a), input two jobs of type I or II at $t = T, T + 1, \ldots, L$ with $L >> T$. In particular, if case (i) happens, then two jobs of type I arrive at each step $t = T, T + 1, \ldots, L$. Show that the flow time of $\mathcal{A}$ is $\Omega(T.L)$, while that of OPT is $\mathcal{O}(L)$. For case (ii) construct similar input. Conclude that the competitive ratio of $\mathcal{A}$ by considering the complete input from $t = 0, 1, \ldots, L$ is at least T.

13.8 Consider that both preemption and job migration are allowed. There are m identical servers and a total of n jobs, **and all the jobs arrive at time** $t = 0$. Job j has p_j distinct segments (called tasks), each with size $w_{jk}, k = 1, \ldots, p_j$. Job j is defined to be complete or departs at time d_j if d_j is the earliest time at which all its tasks are complete. The problem is to minimize the sum of job flow time $\sum_j (d_j - a_j) = \sum_j d_j$. Importantly, distinct tasks of the same job can be processed parallely on different servers.

Job-SRPT algorithm: For any task k of job j, let $w_{jk}(t)$ be its remaining size at time t. Then the total remaining **cumulative size** of job j at time t is defined as $w_j(t) = \sum_{k \in \text{Job}_j} w_{jk}(t)$ (sum of the sizes of all incomplete tasks).

Let $n(t)$ be the number of unfinished jobs at time t. Then index the $n(t)$ incomplete jobs at time t in increasing order of their remaining cumulative sizes. If $n(t) \geq m$, the Job-SRPT algorithm processes the m shortest jobs on the m servers, and on each server the shortest task of each job is executed.

Thus, each server is executing a task corresponding to a distinct job at each time. Otherwise, if $n(t) < m$, then the $n(t)$ distinct jobs (shortest task of that job) are executed on the $n(t)$ servers, and for the rest of $m - n(t)$ servers, the $m - n(t)$ shortest tasks (other than the ones already executing) across all incomplete $n(t)$ jobs are executed.

Show that the Job-SRPT algorithm with m servers having speed $2 - 1/m$ has the same job flow time as OPT with m unit speed servers.

[Hint: It is sufficient to show that the Job-SRPT algorithm is work conserving, and satisfies the augmentation property (Definition 13.4.3) when all jobs arrive at time 0.]

CHAPTER 14

Scheduling with Speed Scaling

14.1 Introduction

In this chapter, we supplement the problem of minimizing the flow time with multiple fixed-speed servers considered in Chapter 13 by allowing the flexibility for each server to have a tuneable speed. This setup is typically referred to as *speed scaling* in the literature. Increasing server speed decreases the flow time but comes at a cost of increased energy consumption, which is typically accounted for by defining a speed based power cost function $P(s)$ that is an increasing function of speed s.

A variety of problems can now be formulated, such as minimizing flow time subject to a constraint on the total energy cost, or minimizing a linear combination of flow time and total energy cost, etc. The most popular problem studied in literature is the linear combination of flow time and total energy cost, generally referred to as the flow time plus energy problem.

In this chapter, we consider the flow time plus energy problem and begin with the single server case. With a single server, SRPT remains an optimal scheduling algorithm, and the only non-trivial decision is the speed choice. We will show that an algorithm that chooses speed such that the power consumption at each time instant is equal to the number of incomplete jobs in the system plus one is 3-competitive, independent of the power cost function P.

Next, we consider the more challenging speed scaling problem when there are multiple identical servers, i.e., with the same power cost function P. We consider the multi-server version of the SRPT algorithm for scheduling, and the following speed choice: the total power consumption across all servers at any time instant is equal to the number of incomplete jobs in the system, and all servers process their jobs at the same speed. We show that this algorithm is constant competitive, where the constant depends only on the cost function P. Recall from Chapter 13 that the competitive ratio of the SRPT algorithm with fixed speed servers to minimize the flow time is $\Omega\left(\max\left\{\log(n/m), \log\left(w_{\max}/w_{\min}\right)\right\}\right)$, where n is the number of jobs and m is the number of servers, and $w_{\max}$ and $w_{\min}$ are the maximum and minimum job sizes. Thus, importantly, this result shows that the SRPT algorithm with and without speed scaling has a fundamentally different behaviour with multiple servers.

For most of the chapter we consider the setting where preemption is allowed. For some practical settings, preemption is costly, and fixed scheduling disciplines like first-cum-first-serve (FCFS) and last-cum-first-serve (LCFS) are mandated. We show that under FCFS and LCFS, the competitive ratio of any online algorithm for minimizing the flow time plus energy depends on the total number of jobs, and is fundamentally different from the preemptive setting.

14.2 Problem Formulation

The input description is the same as in Chapter 13. Let the input consist of n jobs, where job j arrives (is released) at time a_j and has work or size w_j. Let there be a total of $m \geq 1$ servers, all with the same power function $P(s)$, where $P(s)$ denotes the power consumed while processing a job at speed s.

The speed s is the rate at which work is processed by the server, and w amount of work is completed in time w/s by any server if it processes work at speed s throughout time w/s.

A job can be processed at any time on only one server, without any parallelization or splitting. A job is defined to be complete at time d_j as soon as the total amount of work completed for it possibly by different servers is w_j. The flow time f_j for job j is $f_j = d_j - a_j$ (completion time minus the arrival time) and the total flow time is $F = \sum_j f_j$. From here on we refer to F as just the flow time. Note that $F = \int n(t)dt$ as shown in (13.5), where $n(t)$ is the number of incomplete jobs at time t.

Let server k process its job at speed $s^k(t)$ at time t. Choosing larger speeds reduces the flow time but increases the energy cost, and we consider the sum of flow time and energy cost as the objective function, as follows:

$$C = \int n(t)dt + \int \sum_{k=1}^{m} P(s^k(t))dt, \tag{14.1}$$

where the second term is the total energy cost. A more general objective would be a weighted linear combination, i.e., $\int n(t)dt + \beta \int \sum_{k=1}^{m} P(s^k(t))dt$, where $\beta > 0$. However, note that since the factor β may be absorbed into the power function, we will work with the objective (14.1) without loss of generality.

Any online algorithm $\mathcal{A}$ has to make two causal decisions: scheduling, which specifies the job to be processed by each server, and speed selection, i.e., the speed at which to process the scheduled job. Let the cost (14.1) of $\mathcal{A}$ be $C_\mathcal{A}$. Moreover, let the cost of (14.1) for the OPT that knows the job arrival sequence σ (both a_j and w_j) in advance be C_{OPT}. Then the competitive ratio of the online algorithm $\mathcal{A}$ is defined as

$$\mu_\mathcal{A} = \max_\sigma \frac{C_\mathcal{A}(\sigma)}{C_{\text{OPT}}(\sigma)}. \tag{14.2}$$

14.2.1 Recipe for Deriving a Bound on the Competitive Ratio

For an algorithm $\mathcal{A}$ (OPT), let $n_\mathcal{A}(t)$ ($n_o(t)$) and $s^k_\mathcal{A}(t)$ ($s^k_o(t)$) denote the number of incomplete jobs and the speed of server k at time t, respectively. Let there exist a function Φ (typically called the potential function) for which the following relation is true:

$$n_\mathcal{A}(t) + \sum_{k=1}^{m} P(s^k_\mathcal{A}(t)) + \frac{d\Phi(t)}{dt} \leq c\left(n_o(t) + \sum_{k=1}^{m} P(s^k_o(t))\right) \tag{14.3}$$

for some c almost everywhere, and $\Phi(t)$ satisfies the following *boundary* conditions:

1. Before any job arrives and after all jobs are finished, potential function vanishes, i.e., $\Phi(0) = 0$ and $\Phi(\infty) = 0$ and
2. $\Phi(t)$ does not have a positive jump discontinuity at any point where it is not differentiable.

Then, integrating (14.3) with respect to t, we get

$$\int \left(n_{\mathcal{A}}(t) + \sum_{k=1}^{m} P(s_{\mathcal{A}}^k(t)) \right) dt \leq \int c \left(n_o(t) + \sum_{k=1}^{m} P(s_o^k(t)) \right) dt,$$

which is equivalent to showing

$$C_{\mathcal{A}}(\sigma) \leq c \, C_{\mathsf{OPT}}(\sigma)$$

for any input σ, implying that algorithm $\mathcal{A}$ has a competitive ratio of at most c.

This is the typical recipe that we will follow throughout this chapter, where the main challenge is to construct a potential function Φ that satisfies the boundary conditions and (14.3) for an appropriate choice of c.

Remark 14.2.1 *Relaxing the boundary conditions: Finding Φ that satisfies the first of the boundary conditions is generally easy, but making sure that it satisfies the second condition, i.e., it does not have a positive jump discontinuity at any point of non-differentiability, is sometimes hard. In case that is not possible, and if the total increase in Φ summed across all points of discontinuities of Φ is at most $d \cdot C_{\mathsf{OPT}}$, then integrating (14.3) implies*

$$C_{\mathcal{A}}(\sigma) \leq (c + d) \, C_{\mathsf{OPT}}(\sigma),$$

resulting in a competitive ratio of $c + d$. In Section 14.3.2, we will encounter one such potential function, which increases at discontinuities but is still sufficient for showing that a particular algorithm is an order-wise optimal online algorithm in terms of the competitive ratio.

14.3 Single Server

In this section, we begin with the single server case, where if the server processes a job at speed s, it consumes power $P(s)$. With a single server, we will consider several scenarios, such as where preemption is allowed, or a more rigid discipline such as FCFS or LCFS. We begin with the simplest case, when preemption is allowed.

14.3.1 With Preemption

With a single server, when preemption is allowed, processing the job with the shortest remaining processing time (SRPT) is optimal (Problem 13.2) even when the server speed is tuneable. Hence, the only non-trivial decision is at what speed to process the shortest job without knowing the future job arrivals, unlike OPT.

Let the server speed be chosen as follows. Let at time t, $A(t)$ and $O(t)$ be the set of incomplete jobs with the SRPT algorithm and OPT, respectively, with $n(t) = |A(t)|$ and $n_o(t) = |O(t)|$.

Consider an algorithm that chooses speed at time t as

$$s(t) = P^{-1}(n(t) + 1). \qquad (14.4)$$

The speed choice (14.4) with a small modification of $s(t) = P^{-1}(n(t))$ can be interpreted as follows. With $s(t) = P^{-1}(n(t))$, the power cost

$$P(s(t)) = n(t),$$

i.e., *the instantaneous power consumption is the same as the instantaneous number of incomplete jobs/flow time $n(t)$.* Thus, with this speed choice, the two terms of the objective function (14.1) are equal to each other at each time t, which is intuitively appealing when minimizing the sum of two cost functions.

Moreover, for $P(s) = s^2$, $s(t) = P^{-1}(n(t))$ is also the locally optimal speed, i.e., if no further jobs arrive in future, it is optimal to use speed of $s(t) = P^{-1}(n(t))$ (Problem 14.1). The extra $+1$ in (14.4) is included for simpler analytical tractability. In Section 14.4.1, we will show that the $+1$ is not needed and in fact removing the $+1$ results in an improved competitive ratio.

We let the power function P satisfy the following assumptions. See Remark 14.3.3 on how to remove this restriction.

Assumption 14.3.1 $P : \mathbb{R}_+ \to \mathbb{R}_+$ *is differentiable, strictly increasing, and strictly convex, such that $P(0) = 0$, $\lim_{s \to \infty} P(s) = \infty$, and $\bar{s} := \inf\{s > 0 \mid P(s) > s\} < \infty$.*

Examples of functions satisfying (14.3.1) include $P(s) = s^\alpha$, $P(s) = s \ln(1 + s)$.

Theorem 14.3.2 *The proposed speed scaling algorithm (14.4) with the SRPT algorithm is 3-competitive for minimizing the flow time plus energy with a single server.*

Remark 14.3.3 *Assumption 14.3.1 is relaxable and Theorem 14.3.2 is applicable even when $P(.)$ is non-convex or there is a limit on the maximum speed of the server. We leave it as an exercise (Problem 14.2) to prove this fact.*

Proof: To prove Theorem 14.3.2, we follow the recipe described in Section 14.2.1, where the potential function is defined as follows. At time t, let $n_o(t, q)$ and $n(t, q)$ denote the number of incomplete jobs with OPT and the SRPT algorithm, respectively, with remaining size at least q. For example, $n_o(t, 0) = n_o(t)$ and $n(t, 0) = n(t)$. For easy understanding of $n(t, q)$ refer to Figure 14.1, where there is a total of four incomplete jobs $n(t) = 4$ represented by four shades, and the height of each shade represents its remaining size. Hence, $n(t, q_1) = 4$, $n(t, q_2) = 2$, and $n(t, q_3) = 1$.

Let

$$d(t, q) = \max\{0, n(t, q) - n_o(t, q)\},$$

and define the potential function

$$\Phi(t) = c \int_0^\infty f\big(d(t, q)\big) \, dq, \qquad (14.5)$$

Job sizes q

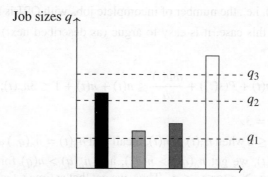

Figure 14.1 Illustration for the definition of $n(t, q)$

where $f(0) = 0$, and $\forall\ i \geq 1$, $\Delta(i) = f(i) - f(i-1) = P'(P^{-1}(i))$ (this means $P'(x)$ where $x = P^{-1}(i)$, and P' is the first derivative of P). For example, $P(s) = s^\alpha$, $\Delta(i) = \alpha\, i^{1-1/\alpha}$. The constant c in (14.5) will be chosen later.

The potential function (14.5) counts the difference between the remaining work with the algorithm and OPT evaluated via a function f. The idea is that if the work remaining with the algorithm is larger than OPT, then the rate at which Φ decreases, $d\Phi(t)/dt$, is sufficient to offset the instantaneous flow time $n(t)$ plus the energy cost $P(s(t))$ in (14.3).

Using the potential function (14.5), we will follow the recipe suggested in Section 14.2.1, and show that the speed choice (14.4) satisfies (14.3) for $c = 3$, and the boundary conditions. Consequently, we will conclude that $C_{\text{SRPT}}(\sigma) \leq 3\, C_{\text{OPT}}(\sigma)$ for any input σ as required.

Boundary Conditions: It is easy to check that Φ (14.5) satisfies the first boundary condition. To check that it satisfies the second boundary condition, we consider two types of events that can potentially increase Φ discontinuously: (i) arrival of a new job and (ii) departure of a job from either SRPT or OPT. When a new job arrives with size w, both $n(t^+, q) = n(t, q) + 1$ for $q \in [0, w]$ and $n_o(t^+, q) = n(t, q) + 1$ for $q \in [0, w]$. Thus, Φ remains unchanged.

Moreover, when a job j departs with either SRPT or OPT at time t, the remaining size of job j is arbitrarily close to zero at time $t - \epsilon$ for small enough ϵ, and hence on departure time t, $n(t, q) = n(t^+, q) - 1$ or $n_o(t^+, q) = n_o(t, q) - 1$ only at $q = 0$. Since Φ is defined as an integral over q, Φ remains unchanged on a departure by SRPT or OPT. Therefore, the second boundary condition is also satisfied.

In the rest of the proof, we try to show that (14.3) holds for $c = 3$ at all times where there is no discontinuity.

At time t, let the size of the shortest job with SRPT be q_a, and with OPT be q_o. By definition, $n_o(t) = n_o(q_o, t)$ and $n(t) = n(q_a, t)$, and SRPT and OPT are working on their respective shortest jobs with size q_a and q_o, respectively. Since we are going to consider a fixed time t, for ease of notation, we let $n(q) = n(q, t)$ and $n_o(q) = n_o(q, t)$.

Processing by SRPT at speed $s(t)$ changes $n(q)$ for $q \in [q_a - s(t)dt, q_a]$, and processing by OPT at speed $s_o(t)$ changes $n_o(q)$ for $q \in [q_o - s_o(t)dt, q_o]$, respectively.

Case I: $n_o(t) > n(t)$, i.e., the number of incomplete jobs with OPT is larger than the number of jobs with SRPT. In this case, it is easy to argue (as described next) that $\frac{d\Phi(t)}{dt} \leq 0$, which using (14.4) implies

$$n(t) + P(s(t)) + \frac{d\Phi(t)}{dt} \leq n(t) + n(t) + 1 \leq 3n_o(t); \tag{14.6}$$

thus, (14.3) holds for $c = 3$.

To show that $\frac{d\Phi(t)}{dt} \leq 0$ when $n_o(t) > n(t)$, recall that $n_o(t) = n_o(q_o)$ and $n(t) = n(q_a)$. From the fact that $n_o(t) > n(t)$, we get $n_o(q_o) > n(q_a)$, and $n_o(q) > n(q)$ for $q \in [q_o - s_o(t)dt, q_o]$ irrespective of whether $q_o \geq q_a$ or $q_o < q_a$. Thus, we get that at time $t + dt, n_o(q) \geq n(q)$ for $q \in [q_o - s_o(t)dt, q_o]$. Thus, $d(q) = \max\{0, n(q) - n_o(q)\}$ remains zero for $q \in [q_o - s_o(t)dt, q_o]$ and therefore there is no increase in Φ because of the processing (work done) by OPT. Processing by SRPT can only decrease Φ; thus, $\frac{d\Phi(t)}{dt} \leq 0$ when $n_o(t) > n(t)$.

Case II: $n_o(t) < n(t)$. We need to consider the following three cases separately depending on the size of the smallest job being processed by SRPT and OPT.

1. $q_a < q_o$. Processing by SRPT at speed $s(t)$ changes $n(q)$ for $q \in [q_a - s(t)dt, q_a]$, and hence the change in $\Phi(t)$ because of SRPT is

$$\begin{aligned} d\Phi(t) &= c\left(f(n(q_a) - 1 - n_o(q_a)) - f(n(q_a) - n_o(q_a))\right)s(t)dt, \\ &= -c\Delta(n(q_a) - n_o(q_a))s(t)dt, \\ &= -c\Delta(n(t) - n_o(t))s(t)dt, \end{aligned} \tag{14.7}$$

where the last inequality follows since $n(t) = n(q_a)$ and $n_o(q_a) = n_o(t)$ as $q_a < q_o$. Counting the contribution from OPT in $d\Phi(t)/dt$ is slightly more non-trivial. Processing by OPT at speed $s_o(t)$ changes $n_o(q)$ for $q \in [q_o - s_o(t)dt, q_o]$; hence the change in $\Phi(t)$ because of OPT is

$$\begin{aligned} d\Phi(t) &= c\left(f(n(q_o) - (n_o(q_o) - 1)) - f(n(q_o) - n_o(q_o))\right)s_o(t)dt, \\ &= c\Delta(n(q_o) - n_o(q_o) + 1)s_o(t)dt. \end{aligned} \tag{14.8}$$

Since $q_a < q_o$, we have $n(q_o) \leq n(q_a) + 1$, which implies that $n(q_o) - n_o(q_o) - 1 \leq n(q_a) - n_o(q_a) = n(t) - n_o(t)$. Since $\Delta(.)$ is an increasing function, i.e., $\Delta(x) \leq \Delta(y)$ for $x \leq y$, we get from (14.8) that

$$d\Phi(t) \leq c\Delta(n(t) - n_o(t))s_o(t)dt. \tag{14.9}$$

Combining the contribution of SRPT and OPT from (14.7) and (14.9), respectively, we get

$$d\Phi(t)/dt \leq c\Delta(n(t) - n_o(t))(-s(t) + s_o(t)). \tag{14.10}$$

2. $q_o = q_a$ In this case, we will have to consider whether the speed of SRPT $s(t)$ is more or less compared to OPT's speed $s_o(t)$. If $s(t) \geq s_o(t)$, then $d(q)$ decreases by 1 for $q \in [q - s(t)dt, q - s_o(t)dt]$, while if $s(t) < s_o(t)$, $d(q)$ increases by 1 for $q \in [q - s_o(t)dt, q - s(t)dt]$.

Counting for contributions from both SRPT and OPT together, the change in Φ in the first case is

$$d\Phi(t)/dt \le c\Delta(n(t) - n_o(t))(-s(t) - s_o(t))dt$$

while

$$d\Phi(t)/dt \le c\Delta(n(t) - n_o(t) + 1)(-s(t) + s_o(t))dt$$

in the second case.

3. $q_a > q_o$ This case is similar to the case of $q_a < q_o$. Since $q_a > q_o$, we have $n_o(q_a) \le n_o(q_o) - 1$. Plugging this in (14.7), we get that the contribution from SRPT is

$$d\Phi(t) = -c\Delta(n(t) - n_o(t) + 1)s(t)dt. \tag{14.11}$$

Moreover, since $q_a > q_o$, $n(q_o) = n(q_a) = n(t)$. Using this, from (14.8) we get

$$d\Phi(t) = c\Delta(n(t) - n_o(t) + 1)s_o(t)dt. \tag{14.12}$$

Combining (14.11) and (14.12), we get

$$d\Phi(t)/dt \le c\Delta(n(t) - n_o(t) + 1)(-s(t) + s_o(t)). \tag{14.13}$$

To recap, we have shown that as long as $n(t) > n_o(t)$,

$$d\Phi(t)/dt \le c\Delta(n(t) - n_o(t))(-s(t) + s_o(t))$$

or

$$d\Phi(t)/dt \le c\Delta(n(t) - n_o(t) + 1)(-s(t) + s_o(t)).$$

To proceed further in the proof of Theorem 14.3.2, we will require the following technical lemma.

Lemma 14.3.4 *Let $s, \tilde{s}, \beta \ge 0$. Then for any function P that is strictly increasing, strictly convex, and differentiable,*

$$\Delta(\beta)(-s + \tilde{s}) \le \left(-s + P^{-1}(\beta)\right)P'(P^{-1}(\beta)) + P(\tilde{s}) - \beta.$$

To prove Lemma 14.3.4, we need the well-known Young's inequality.

Proposition 14.3.5 (Young's Inequality) *Let g be a real-valued, continuous, and strictly increasing function on $[0, c]$ for $c > 0$. If $g(0) \ge 0$ and a, b are such that $a \in [0, c]$ and $b \in [g(0), g(c)]$, then*

$$\int_0^a g(x)dx + \int_{g(0)}^b g^{-1}(x)dx \ge ab,$$

where $g^{-1}(x)$ is the inverse function of g.

Proof: [Proof of Lemma 14.3.4] Let $g(x) = P'(x)$, $a = \tilde{s}$, and $b = P'(P^{-1}(\beta))$. Then all the conditions of Young's inequality are satisfied since P is assumed to be a strictly convex, increasing, continuous, and differentiable function. Using Young's inequality, we get

$$\tilde{s}P'(P^{-1}(\beta)) \leq \int_0^{\tilde{s}} g(x)dx + \int_{P'(0)}^{P'(P^{-1}(\beta))} g^{-1}(x)dx,$$

$$\overset{(a)}{=} P(\tilde{s}) - P(0) + xg^{-1}(x)\Big|_{g(0)}^{g(P^{-1}(\beta))} - \int_{g(0)}^{g(P^{-1}(\beta))} xd(g^{-1}(x)),$$

$$\overset{(b)}{=} P(\tilde{s}) + P^{-1}(\beta)P'(P^{-1}(\beta)) - \int_0^{P^{-1}(\beta)} g(y)dy,$$

$$= P(\tilde{s}) + P^{-1}(\beta)P'(P^{-1}(\beta)) - \beta, \tag{14.14}$$

where (a) follows by using integration by parts, and (b) follows since $P(0) = 0$ and by change of variable $y = g^{-1}(x)$. Adding $-sP'(P^{-1}(\beta))$ to both sides of (14.14), the assertion of Lemma 14.3.4 follows. ∎

Next, we complete the proof of Theorem 14.3.2 by showing that (14.3) holds for $c = 3$ using Lemma 14.3.4.

Using Lemma 14.3.4 with $\beta = n(t) - n_o(t)$ for the case $q_a < q_o$ in (14.10), we get that

$$n(t) + P(s(t)) + \frac{d\Phi(t)}{dt}$$

$$\overset{(a)}{\leq} n(t) + n(t) + 1 + \left(-s(t) + P^{-1}(\beta)\right)\Delta(\beta) + P(s_o(t)) - \beta,$$

$$\overset{(b)}{\leq} 2n(t) + 1 - c(n(t) - n_o(t) + P(s_o(t))),$$

$$\overset{(c)}{\leq} c(n_o(t) + P(s_o(t))),$$

where (a) follows since $s(t) = P^{-1}(n(t) + 1)$, (b) follows since with speed choice $s(t) = P^{-1}(n(t) + 1)$ (14.4), $(-s(t) + P^{-1}(\beta)) \leq 0$, and (c) holds for $c = 3$.

Identical analysis goes through when $q_a \geq q_o$ by applying Lemma 14.3.4 with $\beta = n(t) - n_o(t) + 1$ in (14.13), to get

$$d\Phi(t)/dt \leq c\left(-s(t) + P^{-1}(\beta)\right)\Delta(\beta) + P(s_o(t)) - \beta$$

and $n(t) + P(s(t)) + \frac{d\Phi(t)}{dt} \leq c(n_o(t) + P(s_o(t)))$ as long as $\left(-s(t) + P^{-1}(\beta)\right) < 0$.

Remark 14.3.6 *Satisfying $\left(-s(t) + P^{-1}(\beta)\right) < 0$ when $\beta = n(t) - n_o(t) + 1$ is the primary reason to choose $s(t) = P^{-1}(n(t) + 1)$ and not just $s(t) = P^{-1}(n(t))$.*

The case of $n(t) = n_o(t)$ remains, but here similar to the two cases of $n(t) < n_o(t)$ and $n(t) > n_o(t)$, we can show that either $d\Phi(t)/dt \leq 0$ if $q_a \leq q_o$ or $c\Delta(n(t) - n_o(t) + 1)(-s(t) + s_o(t))$ when $q_a > q_o$, which we leave as an exercise.

Thus, we have shown that (14.3) holds with $c = 3$ for SRPT with speed choice (14.4). Since the boundary conditions are also satisfied by the potential function (14.5), we conclude from our recipe (14.3) that the competitive ratio of the proposed speed scaling algorithm (14.4) is at most 3. ∎

Theorem 14.3.2 shows that when preemption is allowed, SRPT with a simple speed scaling choice (14.4) is 3-competitive. It turns out that if the scheduling discipline precludes executing the shortest job, it is not always possible to come up with a constant competitive online algorithm. In the next section, we consider one such example, where the scheduler is restricted to follow an FCFS discipline.

14.3.2 Without Preemption: FCFS

Consider a single server that follows an FCFS discipline for scheduling jobs. Job j with size w_j arrives at time a_j and jobs have to be processed in the order of their arrival. The only variable is the speed choice $s(t)$ at time t, and the objective is to minimize the flow time plus energy (14.1).

Consider the following speed choice that is locally optimal[1] for $P(s) = s^\alpha$ and $\alpha = 2$,

$$s(t) = P^{-1}\left(n(t)\right), \tag{14.15}$$

where $n(t)$ is the number of incomplete jobs at time t.

Lower Bound We begin by deriving a lower bound on the competitive ratio of the speed scaling algorithm (14.15) with FCFS.

Theorem 14.3.7 *With $P(s) = s^\alpha$, the competitive ratio of the speed choice* (14.15) *with FCFS is $\Omega\left(n^{\frac{\alpha-1}{\alpha}}\right)$ where n is the total number of jobs in the input.*

Proof: Consider the following input. At time 0, job 1 with size w arrives, where let w to be large. Algorithm following (14.15) will process this job at speed 1. Starting from time $w/2$, a single job with size one arrives at time $w/2 + k$ for $k = 0, 1, \ldots, w^{\frac{\alpha}{\alpha+1}} - 1$ with $P(s) = s^\alpha$. For processing job 1, algorithm (14.15) chooses speed $(k+2)^{1/\alpha}$ between time instants $w/2 + k$ and $w/2 + k + 1$, for $k = 0, 1, \ldots$, until job 1 is completed. Thus, job 1 is completed at time $\frac{w}{2} + \Omega\left(w^{\frac{\alpha}{\alpha+1}}\right)$. Therefore, the job arriving at time $\frac{w}{2} + k, k = 0, 1, \ldots, \Omega\left(w^{\frac{\alpha}{\alpha+1}}\right)$, has to wait for time at least $\Omega\left(w^{\frac{\alpha}{\alpha+1}}\right) - k$ before it can be processed. Therefore, the total flow time (counting only the wait times for jobs arriving at time $w/2 + k, k = 0, \ldots, \Omega\left(w^{\frac{\alpha}{\alpha+1}}\right)\right)$ is at least $\Omega\left(w^{\frac{2\alpha}{\alpha+1}}\right)$.

Now we consider an alternate algorithm to lower bound the flow time plus energy for OPT. Consider the speed choice for time 0 till time $w/2$ as 2, and thereafter speed 1 throughout. With this speed choice, the first job with size w that arrived at time 0 is complete at time $w/2$, the arrival time of the second job. Since the jobs arriving after time 0 are all of unit size, with this speed choice, no incoming job has to wait behind any other job. Thus, the flow time plus energy for job 1 is $w/2 + 2^\alpha w/2$, while for each of the unit sized jobs, the flow time plus energy is 2. Thus, the total flow time plus energy for all jobs with OPT is at most $2w^{\frac{\alpha}{\alpha+1}} + (2^\alpha + 1)w/2 = \mathcal{O}(w)$.

---

[1] It is optimal to use this speed assuming no further jobs are going to arrive in future. In Problem 14.1, we discuss this result for SRPT, but it is true for any fixed scheduling policy.

Therefore, the competitive ratio of the speed choice (14.15) with FCFS is $\Omega\left(w^{\frac{\alpha-1}{\alpha+1}}\right)$. Since the number of jobs $n = w^{\frac{\alpha}{\alpha+1}} + 1$, we get that the competitive ratio is at least

$$\mu_{\text{FCFS}} = \Omega\left(n^{\frac{\alpha-1}{\alpha}}\right). \tag{14.16}$$

∎

The same bound as in Theorem 14.3.10 can be shown for any other speed choice which only depends on $n(t)$, the number of incomplete jobs, by suitably changing the input, since the algorithm (14.15) is locally optimal under the causal information about the input that an online algorithm can have.

Essentially, the adversary is exploiting the fact that the algorithm is unable to process the shortest job, because of the FCFS restriction, and cannot match OPT in keeping up with it in terms of speed because of lack of future knowledge.

Upper Bound Next, we show an upper bound on the competitive ratio for the speed choice (14.15) as $\mathcal{O}(n^{(\alpha-1)/\alpha})$ for $P(s) = s^\alpha$, matching the lower bound (14.16). Towards that end, consider the following potential function. Let $A(t)$ be the set of incomplete jobs with the algorithm at time t. Recall that the job with size w_j arrives at time a_j. Let $w_j(t), t \geq a_j$ be the remaining size of the job j at time t with the algorithm ($w_j(a_j) = w_j$), and $n([a_j, t])$ be the number of incomplete jobs with the algorithm at time t that have arrived between time a_j (arrival time of job j) and t.

With $P(s) = s^\alpha$, let the potential function be

$$\Phi(t) = \frac{c}{\alpha} \sum_{j \in A(t)} \Delta(n([a_j, t]))w_j(t), \tag{14.17}$$

where $\Delta(x) = P'(P^{-1}(x))$.

Compared to (14.5), potential function (14.17) has no contribution from the respective terms of OPT, and hence the potential function (14.17) will not satisfy the second boundary condition. Thus, we take recourse in Remark 14.2.1 and bound the total increase at points of discontinuities as follows.

Lemma 14.3.8 *The total increase in $\Phi(\cdot)$ (14.17) at points of discontinuities is at most*

$$cn^{1-1/\alpha} \sum_{j=1}^{n} w_j,$$

where n is the total number of jobs.

Proof: Function $\Phi(t)$ (14.17) can have discontinuities only when either a job arrives into the system or leaves the system. First consider the arrival of a new job j at time $t = a_j$. Because of this new arrival, for every other job $k \in A(t^+)$, $n([a_k, t^+]) = n([a_k, t]) + 1$, and the potential function increases by at most

$$\frac{c}{\alpha}(\Delta(n([a_k, t]) + 1) - \Delta(n([a_k, t])))w_k.$$

By definition, at most n jobs arrive over time, and the total increase in the potential function $\Phi(.)$ for a single job k because of $n - 1$ other job arrivals is at most

$$\frac{c}{\alpha} \sum_{j=1}^{n} (\Delta(n([a_k, t]) + 1) - \Delta(n([a_k, t]))) w_k \leq \frac{c}{\alpha} \Delta(n) w_k \leq c n^{1-1/\alpha} w_k,$$

since $n([a_k, t]) \leq n$ and $\Delta(n) = P'(P^{-1}(x)) = \alpha x^{1-1/\alpha}$. Thus, summing over all jobs, we get that the total increase in $\Phi(\cdot)$ at all arrival instants is at most $\sum_{k=1}^{n} c n^{1-1/\alpha} w_k$.

Clearly, when a job departs, $w_j(t) = 0$; thus, $\Phi(\cdot)$ does not change. ∎

Let $n(t)$ be the total number of incomplete jobs with the algorithm at time t, and $s(t)$ be the speed of the algorithm at time t. Then we have the following result for the drift $d\Phi(t)/dt$ of the potential function $\Phi(t)$.

Lemma 14.3.9

$$d\Phi(t)/dt \leq \frac{c}{\alpha} \Delta(n(t))(-s(t)).$$

Proof: Because of the FCFS restriction, the algorithm will be working on its earliest arrived job j at time t. Let the earliest arrived incomplete job at time t be j that arrived at time a_j. Then $w_j(t^+) \to w_j(t) - s(t)dt$, while $n([a_j, t]) = n(t)$. Hence, the contribution in $d\Phi(t)/dt$ from the algorithm is $d\Phi(t)/dt = -\frac{c}{\alpha} \Delta(n(t)) s(t)$, as needed. ∎

Theorem 14.3.10 *With $P(s) = s^\alpha$, the proposed speed scaling algorithm (14.15) is $2\alpha(n^{1-1/\alpha} + 1)$-competitive for a single server following the FCFS discipline.*

Proof: From Lemma 14.3.9, we know that $d\Phi(t)/dt \leq 0$ always. Similar to $n(t)$, let $n_o(t)$ be the total number of incomplete jobs with OPT at time t. Let $n(t) \leq n_o(t)$, for which case upper bounding $d\Phi(t)/dt$ by 0,

$$n(t) + P(s(t)) + d\Phi(t)/dt \leq n(t) + n(t),$$
$$\leq 2n_o(t),$$

since $P(s(t)) = n(t)$ from (14.15). When $n(t) > n_o(t)$,

$$n(t) + P(s(t)) + d\Phi(t)/dt \overset{(a)}{\leq} n(t) + n(t) + \frac{c}{\alpha} \Delta(n(t))(-s(t)),$$

$$\overset{(b)}{\leq} n(t) + n(t)$$
$$+ \frac{c}{\alpha} \left((-s(t) + P^{-1}(n(t))) P'(P^{-1}(n(t))) - n(t) \right),$$

$$\overset{(c)}{\leq} n(t) + n(t) - \frac{c}{\alpha} n(t),$$

$$\overset{(d)}{\leq} 0,$$

where (a) follows from Lemma 14.3.9 and $P(s(t)) = n(t)$, (b) follows by using Lemma 14.3.4, (c) follows since $s(t) = P^{-1}(n(t))$, and (d) follows by choosing $c = 2\alpha$. Thus, in both cases $n(t) > n_o(t)$ or $n(t) \leq n_o(t)$, we have shown that (14.3) holds for $c = 2\alpha$.

Moreover, from Lemma 14.3.8, the total increase in $\Phi(\cdot)$ at points of discontinuities is at most

$$cn^{1-1/\alpha} \sum_{j=1}^{n} w_j. \tag{14.18}$$

With $P(s) = s^\alpha$, the minimum cost (flow time plus energy) incurred for any job of size w_j is $2w_j$ (the best case is when jobs arrive in such a way that no job has to wait for another and each of them is processed at the optimal speed of 1). Thus, $C_{\text{OPT}} \geq 2 \sum_{j=1}^{n} w_j$.

Using (14.18), we get that the total increase in $\Phi(\cdot)$ at points of discontinuity is at most $\frac{c}{2} n^{1-1/\alpha} C_{\text{OPT}}$. Thus, following Remark 14.2.1, defining $d = \frac{c}{2} n^{1-1/\alpha}$, where $c = 2\alpha$, we get that the competitive ratio of speed choice (14.15) is at most

$$c + d \leq \alpha(n^{1-1/\alpha} + 2)$$

with FCFS. ∎

Combining Theorems 14.3.7 and 14.3.10, we conclude that when the scheduling discipline is fixed to be FCFS, no algorithm can have competitive ratio independent of n, the number of jobs, unlike the setting where preemption is allowed (Theorem 14.3.2). This is somewhat surprising since both the algorithm and OPT have to follow FCFS; however, as it turns out, with FCFS, an online algorithm gets more restricted with respect to OPT. Similar conclusions can be drawn for the LCFS discipline as well, and we leave that as an exercise in Problem 14.3.

14.4 Multiple Servers

In this section, we generalize the results of Section 14.3, when there are multiple identical servers, each with the same power function $P(s)$ (called the homogenous setting).

In particular, let there be m servers, and any job can be processed by any of the m servers. As before, we assume that preemption is allowed, i.e., a job can be suspended and later restarted from the point at which it was suspended. Moreover, we also assume that **job migration** is allowed, i.e., if a job is preempted, it can be processed later at a different server than the one from which it was preempted. Thus, a job can be processed by different servers at different intervals, but at any given time it can be processed by only one server, i.e., no job splitting or parallel processing of a single job is allowed.

Under this setting, we will consider the multi-server SRPT algorithm for scheduling the jobs as described in Section 13.3, which at any time processes the m jobs with the shortest remaining size on the m servers.

Recall that when server speeds are fixed, the competitive ratio (also the best possible) of the SRPT algorithm with multiple identical servers is

$$\max\{\Theta(\log n/m), \Theta(w_{\max}/w_{\min})\}$$

(for the objective of minimizing the flow time), essentially a negative result. In this section, we show that when server speeds are tuneable, the competitive ratio of the multi-server SRPT algorithm (for the objective of minimizing the flow time plus energy) is a constant that only depends on the power function P, and not on $n, m,$ or w_{max}, w_{min}. This demonstrates that fixed speed and speed tuneable server setups are fundamentally different.

14.4.1 Multi-Server SRPT Algorithm

Let $A(t)$ and $O(t)$ be the set of incomplete jobs at time t with the SRPT algorithm and OPT, respectively, with $n(t) = |A(t)|$ and $n_o(t) = |O(t)|$. Recall that the SRPT algorithm maintains a single queue and processes the $\min\{m, n(t)\}$ shortest (remaining size) jobs on the $\min\{m, n(t)\}$ servers at any time t. With the SRPT algorithm, let the server speeds be chosen as follows.

The speed for server k is chosen as

$$s^k(t) = \begin{cases} P^{-1}\left(\frac{n(t)}{m}\right) & \text{if } n(t) \geq m, \\ P^{-1}(1), & \text{otherwise.} \end{cases} \quad (14.19)$$

Thus, all servers work at the same speed always. The speed scaling choice (14.19) can be interpreted as follows. Under (14.19),

$$\sum_{k=1}^{m} P(s^k(t)) = n(t),$$

i.e., the instantaneous power consumption at any time is equal to the instantaneous number of incomplete jobs.

To state the bound on the competitive ratio of the SRPT algorithm with speed choice (14.19) we need the following assumption on the power function in addition to Assumption 14.3.1.

Assumption 14.4.1 $P(xy) \leq P(x)P(y).$

Theorem 14.4.2 *Under Assumptions 14.3.1 and 14.4.1, the* SRPT *algorithm with speed scaling (14.19) is c-competitive, where*

$$c = P(2 - 1/m)\left(2 + \frac{2}{P^{-1}(1)} \max\{1, P(\bar{s})\}\right),$$

where $\bar{s}$ is defined in Assumption 14.3.1. Taking $P(s) = s^\alpha$ for $\alpha > 1$, the competitive ratio equals $4(2 - 1/m)^\alpha$. Typical relevant values of α are $2 \leq \alpha \leq 3$; thus, the derived result shows that the competitive ratio of the SRPT algorithm is modest for practical settings.

Corollary 14.4.3 *For a single server, the* SRPT *algorithm with speed scaling* $s(t) = P^{-1}(n(t))$ *(14.19) is 2-competitive.*

Proof: With a single server, the speed choice (14.19) specializes to $s(t) = P^{-1}(n(t))$. Moreover, the second term in the competitive ratio upper bound of Theorem 14.4.2, $\frac{2}{P^{-1}(1)} \max\{1, P(\bar{s})\}$, is a result of an additional potential function $\Phi_2(t)$ in (14.20) (the potential function used to prove Theorem 14.4.2) that is not needed with a single server. As a result, the second term $\frac{2}{P^{-1}(1)} \max\{1, P(\bar{s})\}$ in the competitive ratio upper bound of Theorem 14.4.2 drops out and we get a competitive ratio bound of $2P(2 - 1/m) = 2$ (with $m = 1$) for SRPT with speed scaling choice $s(t) = P^{-1}(n(t))$. ∎

Recall that in Theorem 14.3.2, we showed that with a single server, the SRPT algorithm with speed $s(t) = P^{-1}(n(t) + 1)$ is 3-competitive. Corollary 14.4.3 implies that the additional factor of $+1$ in speed is not needed, and an improved competitive ratio can be obtained for the SRPT algorithm in the single server setting with speed $s(t) = P^{-1}(n(t))$.

To prove Theorem 14.4.2, we will once again use a potential function argument, where the potential function is defined as follows. At time t, let $n_o(t, q)$ and $n(t, q)$ denote the number of incomplete jobs under OPT and the algorithm, respectively, with remaining size at least q. In particular, $n_o(t, 0) = n_o(t)$ and $n(t, 0) = n(t)$. Let

$$d(t, q) = \max\left\{0, \frac{n(t, q) - n_o(t, q)}{m}\right\}.$$

Define

$$\Phi_1(t) = c_1 \int_0^\infty f\big(d(t, q)\big)\, dq,$$

where $f(0) = 0$, and $\forall\, i \geq 1, \Delta\left(\frac{i}{m}\right) = f\left(\frac{i}{m}\right) - f\left(\frac{i-1}{m}\right) = P'\left(P^{-1}\left(\frac{i}{m}\right)\right)$ (this means $P'(x)$ where $x = P^{-1}\left(\frac{i}{m}\right)$), and

$$\Phi_2(t) = c_2 \int_0^\infty (n(t, q) - n_o(t, q))\, dq.$$

Consider the potential function

$$\Phi(t) = \Phi_1(t) + \Phi_2(t). \tag{14.20}$$

Similar to the single server case, using the drift of the potential function $d\Phi(t)/dt$, we will show that (14.3) holds for a choice of c, and Φ satisfies the boundary conditions, from which we will conclude that $C_{\mathrm{SRPT}}(\sigma) \leq c\, C_{\mathrm{OPT}}(\sigma)$ for any input σ as required.

Remark 14.4.4 *The $\Phi_1(t)$ part of the potential function is a multi-server generalization of the potential function Φ considered for the single server case in (14.5), while the $\Phi_2(t)$ part is needed to handle the case when the number of incomplete jobs with the SRPT algorithm is less than the number of servers m.*

Proposition 14.4.5 $\Phi(\cdot)$ *as defined in (14.20) satisfies both the boundary conditions.*

Proof: Proof is identical to the single server case as in Theorem 14.3.2. ∎

The main idea in proving Theorem 14.4.2 is as follows. First, we will restrict OPT to follow the SRPT algorithm for scheduling, but it can choose its speed depending on future job arrivals. Using the augmentation result of Corollary 13.4.6, we can show that the OPT that follows the

SRPT algorithm is $P(2 - 1/m)$-competitive with respect to OPT in Lemma 14.4.6. Next, we compare the performance of the SRPT algorithm with speed choice (14.19) and the OPT that follows the SRPT algorithm and chooses arbitrary speeds, via the potential function (14.20), and show that it is c (a constant)-competitive. Putting this together, we get that the SRPT algorithm with speed scaling (14.19) is $cP(2 - 1/m)$-competitive with respect to OPT itself.

Lemma 14.4.6 OPT *following the* SRPT *algorithm with an arbitrary choice of speed is* $P(2 - 1/m)$-*competitive with respect to* OPT *for minimizing* (14.1).

The proof utilizes Corollary 13.4.6, and we leave the rest of the details as part of Problem 14.4.

Note that Φ_1 in (14.20) is the same as Φ (14.5) in the single server setting, for $m = 1$. In the single server setting, both SRPT and OPT process at most one job, and in the proof of Theorem 14.3.2, it was shown that the contribution in $d\Phi_1(t)/dt$ from the processing by the SRPT algorithm and OPT can be combined in the single term to get

$$d\Phi(t)/dt \leq 3\Delta(n(t) - n_o(t))(-(s(t) + s_o(t))),$$

which on the application of Lemma 14.3.4 gives the required result. In the multi-server setting, both SRPT and OPT are processing multiple jobs simultaneously, and it is not obvious whether one can match the contribution from the SRPT algorithm and OPT to $d\Phi_1(t)/dt$ job by job. In the proof of Theorem 14.4.2, we show that the contribution of the SRPT algorithm and OPT to $d\Phi_1(t)/dt$ cannot be matched job by job, but for each job processed by SRPT which decreases the $d\Phi_1(t)/dt$, there is a 'matching' job being processed by OPT, for which we can combine their contributions to $d\Phi_1(t)/dt$, and then apply Lemma 14.3.4.

Proof: [Proof of Theorem 14.4.2] In the light of the preceding discussion, we assume throughout this proof that OPT performs SRPT scheduling, and additionally include a factor of $P(2 - 1/m)$ in the competitive ratio from Lemma 14.4.6. For simplicity, we refer to the OPT following the SRPT algorithm as simply OPT throughout this proof.

In the following, we show that (14.3) is true for a suitable choice of c for all times t at which $\Phi(t)$ is not discontinuous. To show (14.3), we bound $d\Phi(t)/dt$ via individually bounding $d\Phi_1(t)/dt$ and $d\Phi_2(t)/dt$ in Lemmas 14.4.7 and 14.4.8 below.

Let the speed of a job being processed by server k with SRPT and OPT at time t be $s^k(t)$ and $s_o^k(t)$, respectively. For the remainder of this proof, consider any such time instant t. For ease of exposition, we drop the index t from $n(t, q), n(t, q_o), n(t), n_o(t), s^k(t)$, and $s_o^k(t)$, since only a fixed (though generic) time instant t is under consideration.

In the next lemma, we bound the drift $d\Phi_1(t)/dt$ at time t depending on whether the number of incomplete jobs $n = n(t)$ with SRPT at time t is more or less than the number of servers m.

Lemma 14.4.7 *For* $n \geq m$,

$$d\Phi_1(t)/dt \leq c_1 n_o - c_1 n + c_1 \left(\frac{m-1}{2}\right) + c_1 \sum_{k \in O(t)} P(s_o^k),$$

while for $n < m$,

$$dΦ_1(t)/dt \leq c_1 n_o - c_1 \frac{n(n+1)}{2m} + c_1 \sum_{k \in O(t)} P(s_o^k).$$

Lemma 14.4.8 $dΦ_2(t)/dt \leq -c_2 \min(m,n)P^{-1}(1) + c_2 \sum_{k \in O(t)} \max\{P(\bar{s}), P(s_o^k)\}.$

Using Lemmas 14.4.7 and 14.4.8 (proved subsequently), we next show that (14.3) holds for an appropriate value of c by considering the following two cases:

[**Case 1:** $n \geq m$.] $n + \sum_{k \in A(t)} P(s^k) + dΦ(t)/dt$

$$\overset{(a)}{\leq} n + n + c_1 n_o - c_1 n + c_1 \left(\frac{m-1}{2} \right) + c_1 \sum_{k \in O(t)} P(s_o^k) - c_2 m P^{-1}(1) + c_2 \sum_{k \in O(t)} \max\{P(\bar{s}), P(s_o^k)\},$$

$$\leq (c_1 + c_2) \sum_{k \in O(t)} P(s_o^k) + (c_1 + c_2 P(\bar{s})) n_o + n(2 - c_1) + \left[c_1 \left(\frac{m-1}{2} \right) - c_2 m P^{-1}(1) \right],$$

$$\overset{(b)}{\leq} (c_1 + c_2 \max\{1, P(\bar{s})\}) \left(n_o + \sum_{k \in O(t)} P(s_o^k) \right),$$

where (a) follows from Lemmas 14.4.7 and 14.4.8, and since $P(s^k) = n/m$ when $n \geq m$ (see (14.19)), while (b) follows by setting $c_1 = 2$ and $c_2 \geq 1/P^{-1}(1)$.

[**Case 2:** $n < m$.] $n + \sum_{k \in A(t)} P(s^k) + dΦ(t)/dt$

$$\overset{(a)}{\leq} n + n + c_1 n_o - c_1 \frac{n(n+1)}{2m} + c_1 \sum_{k \in O(t)} P(s_o^k) - c_2 n P^{-1}(1) + c_2 \sum_{k \in O(t)} \max\{P(\bar{s}), P(s_o^k)\},$$

$$\leq (c_1 + c_2 \max\{1, P(\bar{s})\}) \left(n_o + \sum_{k \in O(t)} P(s_o^k) \right) + n(2 - c_2 P^{-1}(1)),$$

$$\overset{(b)}{\leq} (c_1 + c_2 \max\{1, P(\bar{s})\}) \left(n_o + \sum_{k \in O(t)} P(s_o^k) \right),$$

where once again (a) follows from Lemmas 14.4.7 and 14.4.8, and since $P(s^k) = 1$ when $n < m$ (see (14.19)), while (b) follows by setting $c_2 = 2/P^{-1}(1)$.

This proves (14.3) for

$$c = c_1 + c_2 \max\{1, P(\bar{s})\} = \left(2 + \frac{2}{P^{-1}(1)} \max\{1, P(\bar{s})\} \right).$$

$\blacksquare$

Next, we provide the remaining proofs of Lemma 14.4.7 and 14.4.8.

Proof: [Proof of Lemma 14.4.7] Recall that OPT is following SRPT. Let $q(i)$ and $q_o(i)$ denote, respectively, the size of the ith shortest job being processed by SRPT and OPT, respectively. Recalling that $n = n(t)$ is the number of incomplete jobs with SRPT, we prove the lemma for two separate cases as follows.

Case 1: $n \geq m$. Suppose that OPT is processing r jobs using r different servers at time t, where $r \leq m$. Define $\tilde{n}(q) = \max(n(q), n-r)$, and $\tilde{n}_o(q) = \max(n_o(q), n_o - r)$. The function $g(q) := \tilde{n}(q) - \tilde{n}_o(q)$ satisfies the following properties.

1. $g(0) = n - n_o$, $g(q) \to n - n_o$ as $q \to \infty$,
2. g is piecewise constant and left-continuous, with a downward jump of 1 at $q = q(i)$, $1 \leq i \leq r$, and an upward jump of 1 at $q = q_o(i)$, $1 \leq i \leq r$.[2]

Consider the change in Φ_1 because of the processing by OPT ($n_o(q) \to n_o(q) - 1$ for $q = q_o(1), \cdots, q_o(r)$):

$$
\begin{aligned}
d\Phi_1(t) &= c_1 \sum_{i=1}^{r} \left[f\left(\frac{n(q_o(i)) - n_o(q_o(i)) + 1}{m} \right) - f\left(\frac{n(q_o(i)) - n_o(q_o(i))}{m} \right) \right] s_o^i dt, \\
&\stackrel{(a)}{=} c_1 \sum_{i=1}^{r} \Delta\left(\frac{n(q_o(i)) - n_o(q_o(i)) + 1}{m} \right) s_o^i dt, \\
&\stackrel{(b)}{\leq} c_1 \sum_{i=1}^{r} \Delta\left(\frac{\tilde{n}(q_o(i)) - \tilde{n}_o(q_o(i)) + 1}{m} \right) s_o^i dt, \\
&= c_1 \sum_{i=1}^{r} \Delta\left(\frac{g(q_o(i)) + 1}{m} \right) s_o^i dt. \quad (14.21)
\end{aligned}
$$

In writing (a) we take $\Delta(i/m) = 0$ for $i \leq 0$, while (b) holds since $\tilde{n}_o(q_o(i)) = n_o(q_o(i))$ for $1 \leq i \leq r$, and $\tilde{n}(q) \geq n(q) \ \forall \ q$.

Next, consider the change in Φ_1 due to SRPT ($n(q) \to n(q) - 1$ for $q = q(1), \cdots, q(m)$) since all $n > m$ and all m servers are busy with SRPT.

$$
\begin{aligned}
d\Phi_1(t) &= c_1 \sum_{i=1}^{m} \left[f\left(\frac{n(q(i)) - 1 - n_o(q(i))}{m} \right) - f\left(\frac{n(q(i)) - n_o(q(i))}{m} \right) \right] s^i dt, \\
&= -c_1 \sum_{i=1}^{m} \Delta\left(\frac{n(q(i)) - n_o(q(i))}{m} \right) s^i dt, \\
&\stackrel{(a)}{\leq} -c_1 \sum_{i=1}^{r} \Delta\left(\frac{\tilde{n}(q(i)) - \tilde{n}_o(q(i))}{m} \right) s^i dt - c_1 \sum_{i=r+1}^{m} \Delta\left(\frac{n(q(i)) - n_o(q(i))}{m} \right) s^i dt, \\
&\stackrel{(b)}{\leq} -c_1 \sum_{i=1}^{r} \Delta\left(\frac{g(q(i))}{m} \right) s^i dt - c_1 \sum_{i=r+1}^{m} \Delta\left(\frac{n - i + 1 - n_o}{m} \right) s^i dt, \quad (14.22)
\end{aligned}
$$

where (a) follows since $n(q(i)) = \tilde{n}(q(i))$ for $1 \leq i \leq r$, and $\tilde{n}_o(q) \geq n_o(q)$ for all q, while (b) follows as $n(q(i)) \geq n - i + 1$ and $n_o(q(i)) \leq n_o$ for all i.[3]

---

[2] This assumes all jobs being served by SRPT and OPT have distinct remaining sizes. If, for example, k jobs under OPT have the same remaining size $\hat{q}$, then g would have an upward jump of k at $\hat{q}$.

[3] $n(q(i)) = n - i + 1$ if SRPT has exactly one job with the remaining size $q(i)$. If multiple jobs have the same remaining size $q(i)$ under SRPT, then we have $n(q(i)) \geq n - i + 1$.

We now combine (14.21) and (14.22) to capture the overall change in Φ_1. In doing so, we make the following crucial observation.

Claim 1: For each $i \in \{1, 2, \cdots, r\}$, one can find a unique $j \in \{1, 2, \cdots, r\}$ such that $g(q(i)) \geq g(q_o(j)) + 1$.

To see that this claim is true, note that for each job with the remaining size $q(k)$ ($1 \leq k \leq r$) being processed by SRPT contributes a downward tick of magnitude 1 in g at $q(k)$. Similarly, each job with remaining size $q_o(k)$ ($1 \leq k \leq r$) being processed by OPT contributes an upward tick of magnitude 1 in g at $q_o(k)$.[4]

It is therefore clear that each downward tick from ℓ to $\ell - 1$ in $g(.)$ can be mapped to a unique upward tick from $\ell - 1$ to ℓ. Moreover, at the downtick, say at $q(i)$, we have $g(q(i)) \geq \ell$ (because g is left-continuous), and at the corresponding upward tick, say at $q_o(j)$, we have $g(q_o(j)) \leq \ell - 1$, implying $g(q_o(j)) + 1 \leq \ell$ (again, because g is left-continuous). This proves **Claim 1**.

Based on the above observation, combining (14.21) and (14.22), we can now bound the overall change in Φ_1 as follows.

$$d\Phi_1(t)/dt \leq c_1 \sum_{i=1}^{r} \Delta\left(\frac{g(q(i))}{m}\right)(-s^i + s_o^i) - c_1 \sum_{i=r+1}^{m} \Delta\left(\frac{n-i+1-n_o}{m}\right)s^i. \qquad (14.23)$$

Applying Lemma 14.3.4 on the first summation of (14.23), we can bound

$$\Delta\left(\frac{g(q(i))}{m}\right)(-s^i + s_o^i) \leq P(s_o^i) - \frac{g(q(i))}{m},$$

since $s^k = P^{-1}\left(\frac{n}{m}\right) \geq P^{-1}\left(\frac{g(q(i))}{m}\right)$. Similarly, applying Lemma 14.3.4 on the second summation of (14.23)

$$-\Delta\left(\frac{n-i+1-n_o}{m}\right)s^i \leq -\frac{n-i+1-n_o}{m}$$

(taking s_o^k in the statement of Lemma 14.3.4 to be zero). Combining the above bounds, we get

$$d\Phi_1(t)/dt \leq c_1 \sum_{i=1}^{r}\left[P(s_o^i) - \frac{g(q(i))}{m}\right] - c_1 \sum_{i=r+1}^{m}\left(\frac{n-i+1-n_o}{m}\right).$$

Finally, noting that $g(q(i)) \geq n - i + 1 - n_o$ for $1 \leq i \leq r$, we conclude that

$$d\Phi_1(t)/dt \leq c_1 \sum_{i=1}^{r} P(s_o^i) - c_1 \sum_{i=1}^{m}\left(\frac{n-i+1-n_o}{m}\right),$$

$$= c_1 n_o - c_1 n + c_1\left(\frac{m-1}{2}\right) + c_1 \sum_{i=1}^{r} P(s_o^i).$$

---

[4] The magnitude of the discontinuity in g at q thus equals $|\{j \in R : q_o(j) = q\}| - |\{j \in [r] : q(j) = q\}|$, where $[r] = \{1, 2, \cdots, r\}$.

Case 2: $n < m$. Let r denote the number of jobs that OPT is processing at time t. Let $h(q) = n(q) - n_o(q)$. As before, the rate of change of Φ_1 can be expressed as follows:

$$\frac{d\Phi_1(t)}{dt} = c_1 \sum_{i=1}^{r} \Delta\left(\frac{h(q_o(i)) + 1}{m}\right) s_o^i - c_1 \sum_{i=1}^{n} \Delta\left(\frac{h(q(i))}{m}\right) s^i$$

$$\leq c_1 \sum_{i=1}^{n_o} \Delta\left(\frac{h(q_o(i)) + 1}{m}\right) s_o^i - c_1 \sum_{i=1}^{n} \Delta\left(\frac{h(q(i))}{m}\right) s^i$$

Claim 2: For each $i \in \{1, 2, \cdots, n_o\}$ such that $h(q_o(i)) \geq 0$, one can find a unique $j \in \{1, 2, \cdots, n\}$ such that $h(q(j)) \geq h(q_o(i)) + 1$.

The proof of **Claim 2** is similar to that of **Claim 1** for the case when $n \geq m$. Note that h is a piecewise constant and left-continuous function with $h(0) = n - n_o$, $h(q) = 0$ for large enough q. Moreover, it has upward jumps at $q_o(i)$ ($i \leq n_o$) at downward jumps at $q(i)$ ($i \leq n$). Thus, any uptick in $h(\cdot)$ from $\ell - 1$ to ℓ for $\ell \geq 1$ can be mapped to a unique downtick from ℓ to $\ell - 1$. The rest of the argument is identical to that of Claim 1.

Based on the above observation, suppose that among the set of jobs $\mathcal{S}$ being processed by SRPT, for a subset $J \subseteq \mathcal{S}$ SRPT's terms are matched with OPT terms.

$$\frac{d\Phi_1(t)}{dt} \leq c_1 \sum_{i \in J} \Delta\left(\frac{h(q(i))}{m}\right)(-s^i + s_o^i) + c_i \sum_{i \notin J} \Delta\left(\frac{h(q(i))}{m}\right)(-s^i).$$

Applying Lemma 14.3.4 similar to the case when $n > m$,

$$\frac{d\Phi_1(t)}{dt} \leq c_1 \left(\sum_{i \in J} P(s_o^i) - \frac{h(q(i))}{m}\right) - c_1 \sum_{i \notin J} \frac{h(q(i))}{m},$$

$$\leq c_1 \sum_{i \in O} P(s_o^i) - \sum_{i=1}^{n} \frac{h(q(i))}{m},$$

$$\leq c_1 \sum_{i \in O} P(s_o^i) - c_1 \sum_{i=1}^{n} \frac{n - i + 1 - n_o}{m},$$

$$\leq c_1 \sum_{i \in O} P(s_o^i) + c_1 n_o - c_1 \frac{n(n+1)}{2m}.$$

∎

Proof: [Proof of Lemma 14.4.8] The rate of change in Φ_2 is

$$d\Phi_2(t)/dt = -c_2 \sum_{k \in A(t)} s^k + c_2 \sum_{k \in O(t)} s_o^k,$$

$$\leq -c_2 \min(n, m) P^{-1}(1) + c_2 \sum_{k \in O(t)} \max(P(\bar{s}), P(s_o^k)),$$

where to bound the first term we have used $s^k \geq P^{-1}(1)$, while for the second term, we rely on the following facts (i) $s_o^k \leq P(\bar{s})$ when $s_o^k \leq \bar{s}$, and (ii) $s_o^k \leq P(s_o^k)$ when $s_o^k > \bar{s}$. ∎

14.5 Notes

The study on speed scaling began with [256] for a single server setup, where the objective was to minimize the total energy spent to finish arriving jobs by their deadline (a problem that will be discussed in detail in Chapter 15). The flow time plus energy problem became popular later [257–261]. For the single server case, the best-known competitive result of $2 + \epsilon$ was derived in [262], improving upon the $3 + \epsilon$ result of [259]. A non-rigorous lower bound of $2 - \epsilon$ on the competitive ratio is also provided in [262]. The results presented in Section 14.3 follow from [259].

The weighted flow time plus energy problem has been studied in [259, 263]. In particular, with the weighted case, a relaxation to flow time called the fractional weighted flow time is considered together with the energy cost [259] and an algorithm with a competitive ratio of $2 + \epsilon$ is derived. We present this analysis in Problem 14.5. The recipe to convert a solution for the fractional weighted flow time plus energy problem to a solution for the (integral) weighted flow time plus energy with a small increase (P dependent) in the competitive ratio can be found in [263]. Recently, [264] considered the machine learning augmented setup when the job arrival sequence is stochastic and proposed a consistent, smooth, and robust algorithm.

The multi-server case has been studied in [170, 265], where the servers are allowed to have different power functions, called the heterogeneous case. The best competitive ratio of 2α for $P(s) = s^\alpha$ is proven in [170]. Moreover, algorithms that do not require job migration are analysed in [170, 265].

The results for the multi-server SRPT algorithm with homogenous servers presented in Section 14.4 follow from [266], from which the result of [262] follows as a special case. The most general system model with speed scaling has been studied in [267], where there is a network of speed tuneable servers, and the objective is to minimize the sum of flow time plus energy for multiple source–destination pairs.

The non-clairvoyant single server problem, where jobs on arrival do not reveal their sizes, was studied in [268], whose multi-server extension has been considered in [269], where servers are allowed to be heterogenous and it is shown that with resource augmentation of $1 + \epsilon$, competitive ratio of $1/\epsilon^5$ is achievable. The flow time plus energy problem with precedence constraints has also been considered in [270, 271], while the objective of minimizing makespan with speed scaling has been studied in [272].

A tutorial on using potential functions to derive competitive algorithms for scheduling problems can be found in [273].

PROBLEMS

14.1 Let $P(s) = s^2$. Consider that there is a single server that is following SRPT for scheduling jobs. Show that if at time t, the number of incomplete jobs is $n(t)$ and no further jobs are going to arrive in the future, then the optimal speed to use that minimizes the flow time plus energy is $s(t) = P^{-1}(n(t))$.

14.2 Consider the flow time plus energy problem with a single server where preemption is allowed. Suppose that there is an upper bound of $s_{\max}$ on the maximum speed of the server. Show that the algorithm that processes jobs using SRPT while choosing speed $s(t) = \min\{P^{-1}(n+1), s_{\max}\}$ is still 3-competitive, following the same analysis as presented in the proof of Theorem 14.3.2.

(a) [274] With $n(t)$ and $n_o(t)$ as the number of incomplete jobs with the algorithm and OPT, respectively, at time t, show that $n(t) - n_o(t) + 1 \leq P(s_{\max})$. [Hint: Let at time t, $n(t) > P(s_{\max})$, and let time $t_0 \leq t$ be the last time before t when $n(t_0) \leq P(s_{\max})$. Consider interval $[t_0, t]$, where the algorithm works at the maximum speed. Use the fact that SRPT maximizes the number of departures in any interval of time with a single server, among all algorithms working at the same speed, to conclude the result.]

(b) Using part (a), show that

$$\left(-s(t) + P^{-1}(\beta)\right) \Delta(\beta) < 0$$

for both $\beta = n(t) - n_o(t) + 1$ and $\beta = n(t) - n_o(t)$.

(c) Conclude that the algorithm is still 3-competitive similar to the proof of Theorem 14.3.2.

14.3 Consider the flow time plus energy problem with a single server where LCFS discipline is enforced for scheduling jobs. Show that the speed scaling algorithm (14.15) for $P(s) = s^\alpha, \alpha > 1$, has a competitive ratio of $\Omega(n^{1-1/\alpha})$, where n is the total number of jobs in the input.

Consider the following input. Let jobs $i = 1, \dots, n-1$ have size one, while job n has a size w. Job i arrives at time $t_i, i = 1, 2, \dots, n$, where $t_1 = 1, t_i = t_{i-1} + \frac{1-\epsilon}{P^{-1}(i)}, i \geq 2, i \leq n$, where $\epsilon > 0$ is a fixed constant. The input is chosen in such a way that algorithm (14.15) cannot finish any job (following LCFS) before the arrival of the next job.

Conversely, show that using the potential function (14.24) that the speed scaling algorithm (14.15) has a competitive ratio $\mathcal{O}(n^{1-1/\alpha})$. Let $A(t)$ be the set of incomplete jobs with the algorithm at time t. For a job $j \in A(t)$, let $\text{rank}_j(t)$ be the number of jobs in $A(t)$ that have arrived before it, while $w_j(t)$ $(w_j^o(t))$ be its remaining size at time t with the algorithm (OPT). Then consider the potential function given by

$$\Phi(t) = \frac{c}{\alpha} \sum_{j \in A(t)} \Delta(\text{rank}_j)(w_j(t) - w_j^o(t)), \tag{14.24}$$

where $\Delta(x) = P'(P^{-1}(x))$, and c is a constant that can be chosen appropriately. Prove the result using the recipe prescribed in Section 14.2.1.

14.4 Prove Lemma 14.4.6.

[Hint: Use of Corollary 13.4.6 might be helpful.]

14.5 (Weighted Flow Time + Energy) [259] Let for job j, $\beta_j > 0$ be its weight that represents its relative importance with respect to other jobs. Let the arrival time of job j be a_j. Then for any time $t \geq a_j$, let $w_j(t)$ be the remaining size of job j. The fractional weight of job j at time t is defined as

$$p_j(t) = \beta_j \frac{w_j(t)}{w_j},$$

and the fractional weighted flow time of job j is $\int_{w_j(t)>0} p_j(t)dt$, the integral of fractional weight over time for which $w_j(t) > 0$.

Let a total of n jobs arrive with arbitrary sizes. Consider a single server with power function P satisfying Assumption 14.3.1. Then the weighted fractional flow time plus energy problem is to solve

$$\min \left\{ \int \sum_{j=1}^{n} p_j(t) + \int P(s(t))dt \right\}.$$

Let the density of a job be defined as the ratio of the weight and the original size, i.e., for job j its density is $\dfrac{\beta_j}{w_j(a_j)}$, and inverse density is the inverse of the density.

Consider the highest density first (HDF) algorithm $\mathcal{A}$ that, from the set of incomplete jobs, processes the job with the highest density at speed $s(t) = P^{-1}(p_{\mathcal{A}}(t))$, where $p_{\mathcal{A}}(t) = \sum_j p_j(t)$ is the total fractional weight of all jobs at time t with algorithm $\mathcal{A}$.

Consider the following potential function:

$$\Phi(t) = 2 \int_0^{\infty} h\left(d(t,m)\right) dm, \tag{14.25}$$

where $d(t,m) = (p_{\mathcal{A}}(t,m) - p_o(t,m))^+$, where $p_*(t,m)$ is the total fractional weight of incomplete jobs at time t with inverse density at least m, where $* \in \{\mathcal{A}, \mathrm{OPT}\}$, $(x)^+ = \max\{0,x\}$ and

$$\frac{d}{dp}h(p) = P'(P^{-1}(p)).$$

(a) Show that $\Phi(t)$ (14.25) satisfies the boundary conditions.

(b) Show that for any function $g(m)$, $\Phi_g(t) = 2 \int_0^{\infty} h\left(g(m)\right) dm$ satisfies

$$d\Phi_g(t)/dt = 2 \int_0^{\infty} P'\left(P^{-1}(g(m))\right) \frac{d}{dt} g(m) dm.$$

(c) Using the relation derived in part (b) with $g(m) = d(t,m)$, counting the contribution of both the algorithm $\mathcal{A}$ and OPT to the drift $d\Phi(t)/dt$, show that

$$d\Phi(t)/dt = -2P'\left(P^{-1}(p_{\mathcal{A}}(t) - p_o(t))\right)$$

for two cases: (i) when $p_A(t) > p_o(t)$ and (ii) $p_A(t) < p_o(t)$, similar to the proof of Theorem 14.3.2.

(d) For the case when $p_A(t) = p_o(t)$, count only the contribution of OPT to $d\Phi(t)/dt$ using part (b), and show that $d\Phi(t)/dt \leq P'(P^{-1}(0))s_o(t)$, where $s_o(t)$ is the speed of OPT at time t. Then use Lemma 14.3.4 to show that $d\Phi(t)/dt \leq 2P(s_o(t))$.

(e) Conclude that the above algorithm is 2-competitive, by using parts (c) and (d), and (14.3) with $c = 2$.

14.6 Equal-Sized Jobs Let there be m identical speed tuneable servers with power function $P(.)$ that is convex and differentiable. Assume that all jobs have equal sizes. In particular, let the size of all jobs be one, without loss of generality. The objective is to minimize the flow time plus energy and preemption is allowed.

1. Show that the round-robin algorithm that assigns a job to a server irrevocably on its arrival following the round-robin rule (without considering outstanding job sizes or number of jobs in any server) is an optimal scheduling algorithm.

2. With the round-robin algorithm, let the speed choice for server k at time t be $s^k(t) = P^{-1}(n_k(t))$, where $n_k(t)$ is the number of incomplete jobs that have been assigned to server k. Show that this algorithm is 2-competitive.

14.7 Let there be m identical speed tuneable servers with power function $P(.)$, and let the job sizes be arbitrary. The objective is to minimize the flow time plus energy, and preemption is allowed.

1. Consider the class of algorithms that routes an incoming job to a server with the least sum of remaining job sizes. Note that this algorithm assigns the job to a server on its arrival and does not migrate jobs between servers ever. Show that all algorithms in this class have a competitive ratio that is $\Omega(m^{1-1/\alpha})$.

2. Consider the class of algorithms that route an incoming job to a server with the least number of queued jobs (join the shortest queue (JSQ)). Note that this algorithm assigns the job to a server on its arrival and does not migrate jobs between servers ever. Show that all algorithms in this class have a competitive ratio that is $\Omega(m^{1-1/\alpha})$.

CHAPTER 15

Scheduling to Minimize Energy with Job Deadlines

15.1 Introduction

In Chapter 13, we considered the problem of minimizing flow time for both single and multiple servers, when server speeds were fixed, and the only decision variable was which job to schedule or process at each time. With speed tuneable servers, a natural extension of this problem, called speed scaling, was studied in Chapter 14, where the problem of minimizing flow time plus energy was studied, with two decision variables: which job to schedule or process and its processing speed.

In this chapter, we consider an alternate formulation of the speed scaling problem, where jobs have deadlines, and server speeds are tuneable with corresponding power functions. The problem is to find which job to schedule or process at each time, and its processing speed, so as to minimize the total energy used, such that each job is complete by its deadline. For this formulation, both the common deadline case (all deadlines are identical) and the individual deadline case are of interest.

With a single server, for the commonly used power function $P(s) = s^{\alpha}, \alpha > 1$ with speed s, we present an online algorithm for both the common and the individual deadlines case, for which the competitive ratio is upper bounded by α^{α}, and the upper bound is also tight for the considered algorithm. For $P(s) = s^{\alpha}, \alpha > 1$, we also consider the more modern paradigm of machine learning augmented algorithm for going beyond the worst case, where prediction about job arrival times and their sizes is available, but with uncertain accuracy.

Another power function of interest, motivated by information theory, is given by $P(s) = 2^s - 1$, which results in fundamentally different results than $P(s) = s^{\alpha}$. For $P(s) = 2^s - 1$, with a single server, we present an online algorithm whose competitive ratio is at most 3 only for the common deadline case. For the common deadline case, we also show how to extend results from the single server case to the multiple server case without changing the competitive ratio.

15.2 Arbitrary Deadlines with a Single Server

The problem description is similar to that of Chapter 14, where there is a total of n jobs that arrive in the system, with job j arriving at time a_j (called release time) with size w_j. The distinguishing feature with respect to Chapter 14 is that job j has a **deadline** d_j by which it has to be completed by any algorithm.

There is a single server with power function $P(s)$, where $P(s)$ denotes the power consumed while processing at speed s. The speed s is the rate at which work is processed by the server, and w amount of work is completed in time w/s by the server if processing at speed s throughout time w/s. A job j is defined to be complete at time c_j if w_j amount of work has been completed for it. Thus, the deadline constraint forces that $c_j \leq d_j$, and the objective function is the total energy used,

$$E = \int P(s(t))dt. \tag{15.1}$$

Therefore, the optimization problem is

$$\begin{aligned} \min \quad & E \\ \text{s.t.} \quad & c_j \leq d_j, \ \forall j. \end{aligned} \tag{15.2}$$

15.2.1 Optimal Offline Algorithm – YDS

We first present an optimal offline algorithm for solving (15.2). For any $t_1 \leq t_2$, let $S(t_1, t_2)$ denote the subset of jobs that have release time at least t_1 and deadline at most t_2. Let $w(t_1, t_2)$ be the sum of the sizes of all jobs (called work) belonging to $S(t_1, t_2)$. Thus, $w(t_1, t_2)$ counts the total amount of work that arrives at or after t_1, and has a deadline at or before t_2. Since each job has to be completed by its deadline, clearly, any algorithm has to finish at least $w(t_1, t_2)$ amount of work in the interval $[t_1, t_2]$ for any t_1, t_2.

Define the **intensity** of interval $[t_1, t_2]$ to be $I_{t_1 t_2} = \frac{w(t_1, t_2)}{(t_2 - t_1)}$.

Algorithm YDS: Repeat the following steps until all jobs are scheduled:

1. Let $\left[t_1^c, t_2^c \right]$ be the interval with the maximum intensity, called **critical**, among all relevant[1] intervals.

2. Choose constant speed $s(t) = \frac{w(t_1^c, t_2^c)}{(t_2^c - t_1^c)}$ for $t \in \left[t_1^c, t_2^c \right]$, and complete all jobs that comprise the work $w\left(t_1^c, t_2^c \right)$ within the critical interval $\left[t_1^c, t_2^c \right]$, with always scheduling the job with the earliest deadline that has already been released.

3. Remove the critical interval $\left[t_1^c, t_2^c \right]$ and the jobs that comprise the critical interval $\left(\text{belonging to } S\left(t_1^c, t_2^c \right) \right)$ from the problem instance. In particular, for all jobs j other than those that belong to $S\left(t_1^c, t_2^c \right)$ such that $d_j \in \left(t_1^c, t_2^c \right)$ reset the deadline as $d_j = t_1^c$, while for jobs j, with $a_j < t_1^c$ and $d_j > t_2^c$, reset the deadline as $d_j = d_j - \left(t_2^c - t_1^c \right)$. The arrival times for jobs j with $a_j > t_1^c$ are reassigned as $a_j = \max\left\{ t_1, a_j - \left(t_2^c - t_1^c \right) \right\}$. Go to Step 1.

A pictorial description of the definition of the critical interval, and the execution of the algorithm YDS for a simple problem instance is given in Figure 15.1.

---

[1] The only intervals that need to be considered have the left limit as possible release times and the right limit as possible deadlines.

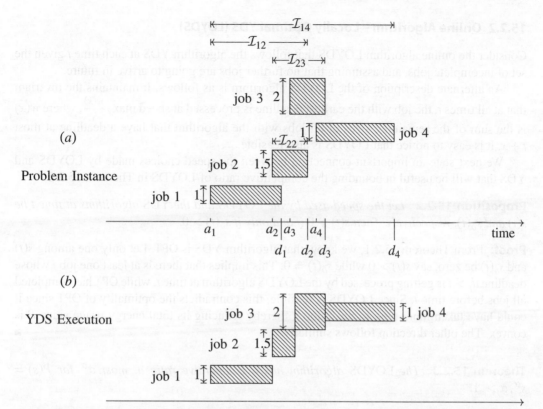

Figure 15.1 Pictorial description of the YDS algorithm, where the height of the rectangle represents the size of the job, and $\mathcal{I}_{xy}$ represents the interval with arrival time at least a_x and deadline at most d_y. Let $a_1 = 0$, $d_1 = 5.5$, $a_2 = 5, d_2 = 6$, $a_3 = 5.5, d_3 = 6.5$, and $a_4 = 6.25$, $d_4 = 8.5$, as shown in subfigure (a). Clearly, interval $\mathcal{I}_{23}$ has the highest intensity of $3.5/1.5 = 2.33$ among all the intervals. Hence, jobs 2 and 3 are scheduled in interval $\mathcal{I}_{23}$ with speed 2.33 throughout, where job 2 is processed first followed by job 3 as shown in subfigure (b). Consequently, job 1's deadline is then moved to $d_1 = a_2 = 5$ and arrival time of job 4 is moved to $a_4 = d_3 = 6.5$, as shown in subfigure (b).

We summarize all the properties of algorithm YDS as follows.

Theorem 15.2.1

- *Algorithm* YDS *is optimal for solving* (15.2) *for any convex power cost function P(.).*

- *Each job is processed at a fixed speed by algorithm* YDS.

- *Algorithm* YDS *minimizes the maximum of the energy used by any algorithm across all times to solve* (15.2).

We will outline how to prove the first property in Problem 15.2. The second property is immediate, while we leave the proof of the third property as an exercise. Next, using the offline algorithm YDS, we propose an online algorithm that, at each time t, executes YDS, assuming no further jobs are going to arrive in the future.

15.2.2 Online Algorithm – Locally Optimal YDS (LOYDS)

Consider the online algorithm LOYDS that follows the algorithm YDS at each time t given the set of incomplete jobs, and assuming that no further jobs are going to arrive in future.

An alternate description of the LOYDS algorithm is as follows. It maintains the invariant that at all times t, the job with the earliest deadline is processed at speed $\max_x \frac{w(x)}{x}$, where $w(x)$ is the sum of the remaining sizes of all jobs with the algorithm that have a deadline at most $t + x$. It is easy to notice that LOYDS is also feasible.

We next state an important connection between the speed choices made by LOYDS and YDS that will be useful in bounding the competitive ratio of LOYDS in Theorem 15.2.3.

Proposition 15.2.2 *Let the speed used by the* LOYDS *and the* YDS *algorithms at time t be* $s(t)$ *and* $s_o(t)$, *respectively. Then* $s(t) > 0$ *if and only if* $s_o(t) > 0$.

Proof: From Theorem 15.2.1, we know that algorithm YDS is OPT. Let only one among $s(t)$ and $s_o(t)$ be zero, say $s(t) > 0$ while $s_o(t) = 0$. This implies that there is at least one job j whose deadline $d_j > t$ is getting processed by the LOYDS algorithm at time t, while OPT has completed all jobs before time t. Since LOYDS is feasible, this contradicts the optimality of OPT since it could have taken more time to finish job j, thereby reducing its total energy usage since P is convex. The other direction follows similarly. ∎

Theorem 15.2.3 *The* LOYDS *algorithm has a competitive ratio at most* α^α *for* $P(s) = s^\alpha, \alpha > 1$.

To show that Theorem 15.2.3 is tight, we also have the following converse result whose proof we leave as an exercise in Problem 15.3.

Theorem 15.2.4 *The competitive ratio of the* LOYDS *algorithm is at least* α^α *for* $P(s) = s^\alpha$, $\alpha > 1$, *even when all jobs have a common deadline.*

Note that unlike most of the other lower bounds derived in other chapters, Theorem 15.2.4 is not an algorithm independent lower bound, but is only valid for the LOYDS algorithm. Moreover, the lower bound derived in Theorem 15.2.4 holds for the common deadline case. Since the upper bound on the competitive ratio of the LOYDS algorithm (Theorem 15.2.3) with individual deadlines matches this lower bound, no improvement can be obtained in the competitive ratio of the LOYDS algorithm with common deadlines.

Next, we present the proof of Theorem 15.2.3. We will use the potential function recipe as described in Section 14.2.1, and propose a potential function Φ that satisfies the boundary conditions (14.2.1), and show that

$$P(s(t)) + \frac{d\Phi(t)}{dt} \leq \alpha^\alpha P(s_o(t)), \tag{15.3}$$

where $s(t)$ and $s_o(t)$ is the speed of algorithm $\mathcal{A}$ (LOYDS) and OPT, respectively, at time t, to conclude that algorithm $\mathcal{A}$ has a competitive ratio of at most α^α for $P(s) = s^\alpha$.

Defining the potential function: To define the potential function, we need the following preliminaries depending on the algorithm LOYDS. Let at time t, $w(t, t')$ be the sum of the remaining sizes of jobs at time t with the LOYDS algorithm having a deadline in $(t, t']$. For each time t, we will inductively define a sequence of instances $t_0, t_1, \ldots$ as follows. Initialize $t_0 = t$. Given t_{i-1}, define t_i as follows:

$$t_i = \arg \max_{t' \geq t_{i-1}} \frac{w(t_{i-1}, t')}{t' - t_{i-1}}. \tag{15.4}$$

Thus, the first instance t_1 so found corresponds to essentially the critical interval with the highest intensity used by the YDS algorithm that begins at time t_0. t_i is defined similarly depending on t_{i-1}.[2]

With this definition of t_i, which depends on the current time t, let

$$s(t_i) = \frac{w(t_{i-1}, t_i)}{t_i - t_{i-1}}.$$

The **speed** chosen by the LOYDS algorithm at time t' for $t_i < t' \leq t_{i+1}$ is simply

$$s(t') = s(t_i)$$

as long as no new job arrivals happen. On a new job arrival, the instances t_i's and the speed to be followed in the future are recomputed using (15.4).

Definition 15.2.5 *The successive intervals $(t_i, t_{i+1}]$ (15.4) are defined as local critical intervals (LCI). For an LCI i, i.e., $(t_i, t_{i+1}]$, its intensity is defined as $s(t_i) = \frac{w(t_i, t_{i+1})}{t_{i+1} - t_i}$.*

The following lemma is easy to prove from the definition (15.4), and will be useful for analysing the change in the potential function.

Lemma 15.2.6 *Speeds or intensities $s(t_i)$ defined at time t for instances $t_0, t_1, \ldots$ form a non-increasing sequence in $i \geq 1$.*

Let $w_o(t, t')$ be the sum of the remaining sizes of jobs at time t with OPT having a deadline in $(t, t']$. Then we define the potential function using (15.4), which depends on the LOYDS algorithm, as follows.

$$\Phi(t) = \alpha \sum_{i \geq 0} s(t_i)^{\alpha-1} \left(w(t_i, t_{i+1}) - \alpha w_o(t_i, t_{i+1}) \right). \tag{15.5}$$

It is important to note that for each t, the definition of t_i (15.4) can change. Therefore, $\Phi(t)$ can possibly change arbitrarily on the arrival of a new job. We will show in Lemma 15.2.7 that the change in $\Phi(t)$ on any new job arrival is negative to satisfy the second boundary condition (14.2.1).

---

[2] $(t_i, t_{i+1}]$ computed at time t is equivalent to $(t_0, t_1]$ when computed at time t_i if no new jobs arrive after time t.

Lemma 15.2.7 *Potential function* (15.5) *satisfies both the boundary conditions* (14.2.1).

Proof: It is easy to see that the first of the boundary conditions is satisfied, i.e., $\Phi(t) = 0$ (15.5) before any job arrives and after all jobs are complete. The second condition needs to be checked for possibly two events: (a) arrival of a new job and (b) departure or completion of a job or completion of a critical interval.

Case (b) is easy to verify, as follows. Note that both $w(t_i, t_{i+1})$ and $w_o(t_i, t_{i+1})$ decrease continuously by their very definitions. Thus, when a job j is completed by either the LOYDS algorithm or OPT, there is no discontinuity. The only real source of discontinuity can be the multiplier term $s(t_i)^{\alpha-1}$ that can abruptly change on the completion of a critical interval. However, on the completion of a critical interval, $t_{i+1} - t_i$ approaches 0 and, more importantly, both $w(t_i, t_{i+1})$ and $w_o(t_i, t_{i+1})$ also approach 0, since t_{i+1} is a deadline for a job in both $w(t_i, t_{i+1})$ and $w_o(t_i, t_{i+1})$, and both algorithms have to finish all the jobs with deadline t_{i+1} by time t_{i+1}. Thus, there is no discontinuity in $\Phi(t)$ on the completion of a critical interval.

Next, we consider the case of the arrival of a new job. Let a new job j_x arrive at time t with size x and **deadline** t_d. The arrival of job j_x can change the potential function (15.5) via changing the definition of t_i's (15.4), thereby changing the LCIs (Definition 15.2.5). Let the deadline of job j_x, t_d be such that for LCIs $(t_1, t_2], (t_2, t_3] \ldots$ defined for the current time t, $t_i < t_d \leq t_{i+1}$ for some i.

Recall the definition of an LCI from Definition 15.2.5. The arrival of a job can either change both the LCIs and their intensities or keep the LCIs the same but change their intensities. We distinguish between these two cases for proving the lemma.

Case I: LCIs remain the same but their intensities change. Since $t_i < t_d \leq t_{i+1}$, in this case only the intensity $s(t_i)$ (Definition 15.2.5) of LCI i changes (15.5) to $\frac{w(t_i, t_{i+1})+x}{t_{i+1}-t_i}$. Moreover, the term $\left(w(t_i, t_{i+1}) - \alpha w_o(t_i, t_{i+1})\right)$ of (15.5) decreases by $(\alpha - 1)x$. Thus, the total change in the potential function is

$$\Delta\Phi = \alpha \left(\frac{w(t_i, t_{i+1}) + x}{t_{i+1} - t_i}\right)^{\alpha-1} \cdot \left((w(t_i, t_{i+1}) + x) - \alpha(w_o(t_i, t_{i+1}) + x)\right)$$

$$- \alpha \left(\frac{w(t_i, t_{i+1})}{t_{i+1} - t_i}\right)^{\alpha-1} \cdot \left(w(t_i, t_{i+1}) - \alpha w_o(t_i, t_{i+1})\right). \tag{15.6}$$

Let $a = w(t_i, t_{i+1})$ and $b = w_o(t_i, t_{i+1})$; we have from (15.6)

$$\Delta\Phi = \frac{\alpha\left((a+x)^{\alpha-1}(a - \alpha b - (\alpha-1)x) - a^{\alpha-1}(a - \alpha b)\right)}{(t_{i+1} - t_i)^{\alpha-1}} \leq 0, \tag{15.7}$$

where the second inequality follows from Lemma 15.2.8. Thus, we have shown that if the LCIs do not change on the arrival of a new job, the change in the potential function is non-positive.

Lemma 15.2.8 *Let* $a, b, x \geq 0$ *and* $\alpha \geq 1$. *Then*

$$\left((a+x)^{\alpha-1}(a - \alpha b - (\alpha-1)x) - a^{\alpha-1}(a - \alpha b)\right) \leq 0.$$

The proof of lemma 15.2.8 follows from basic calculus and we omit its proof.

Case II: Both the LCIs and their intensities change. Recall that a new job j_x arrives at time t with size x and **deadline** t_d, with $t_i < t_d \leq t_{i+1}$. Instead of thinking of this new job as a single entity of size x, we are going to consider decomposing j_x into jobs of smaller size x' such that the sum of the sizes of the decomposed jobs is equal to x. Clearly, the problem (15.1) remains unaffected whether one job of size x with deadline d arrives at time t or two jobs of sizes x_1, x_2, where $x_1 + x_2 = x$, with identical deadlines d, arrive at time t. Using this decomposition of job j_x into smaller sized jobs of size x', consider that we increase the job size of the new job from 0 gradually. Doing so, at some (possibly different for the four cases) critical value of x' either of the following four events will happen regarding the LCIs and their intensities.

1. No merging or splitting of any LCI. As x' increases, the intensity of LCI i increases but it remains a critical interval. Since the intensity of LCI $i-1$ is at least as much as that of LCI i, either the intensity of LCI i is (a) strictly less than the intensity of LCI $i-1$ or (b) becomes equal to the intensity of LCI $i-1$. Option (a) is identical to Case I considered above, while for option (b) we get that the critical x^c is such that the 'new' intensity of LCI i is equal to the intensity of LCI $i-1$, i.e., $s(t_{i-1}) = \frac{w(t_i, t_{i+1}) + x^c}{t_{i+1} - t_i}$.

2. As we increase x', let at $x' = x^c$, the LCI i splits into two LCIs, i' with $(t_i, t']$ and i'' with $(t', t_{i+1}]$ for some $t_i \leq t' < t_{i+1}$. Since x^c is the smallest such x', and for any value of x' just below x^c there is no change in the LCI configuration, i.e., there is a single LCI i, and at x^c it splits, by the definition of intensities, the intensities of LCIs i' and i'' are equal, in particular, equal to $\frac{w(t_i, t_{i+1}) + x'}{t_{i+1} - t_i}$.

   To see this concretely, consider an example, where at time t, let there be two incomplete jobs with remaining sizes w_1 and w_2, with deadlines d_1 and d_2, respectively, where $d_2 > d_1$. Moreover, let there be only a single LCI, LCI 0 that spans the time interval $(t, d_2]$. In particular, by the definition of LCIs, this means

$$\frac{w_1}{d_1 - t} < \frac{w_1 + w_2}{d_2 - t} \quad \text{and} \quad \frac{w_2}{d_2 - d_1} > \frac{w_1}{d_1 - t}.$$

Next, consider that a new job (job 3 with size w_3) arrives at time t with deadline $d_3, d_1 < d_3 < d_2$. Let job 3 split the LCI 0 into two LCIs, $0'$ spanning interval $(t, d_3]$ and $0''$ spanning interval $(d_3, d_2]$ as we increase w_3 from 0 at x^c for the first time. For any size $x' < x^c$ for job 3, there is a single LCI, which means

$$\frac{w_1 + x'}{d_3 - t} < \frac{w_1 + w_2 + x'}{d_2 - t}, \quad \text{and} \quad \frac{w_1}{d_1 - t} < \frac{w_1 + w_2 + x'}{d_2 - t},$$

while at x^c,

$$\frac{w_1 + x^c}{d_3 - t} \geq \frac{w_1 + w_2 + x^c}{d_2 - t}$$

and

$$\frac{w_1 + x^c}{d_3 - t} \geq \frac{w_2}{d_2 - d_3},$$

where the last inequality follows from Lemma 15.2.6.

The intensity of LCI $0'$ is $\frac{w_1 + x^c}{d_3 - t}$, while that of LCI $0''$ is $\frac{w_2}{d_2 - d_3}$. Thus, using all the inequalities above and the fact that $d_3 < d_2$, for the split to happen at x^c, x^c satisfies

$$\frac{w_1 + x^c}{d_3 - t} = \frac{w_2}{d_2 - d_3} = \frac{w_1 + w_2 + x^c}{d_2 - t},$$

i.e., the intensities of the two split LCIs are equal.

3. As we increase x', let at $x' = x^c$, a sequence of contiguous LCIs $0, \ldots, i$ merge into a single LCI, which can be thought of as pairwise merging of LCIs $i - 1$ and i to get a new LCI $i - 1'$, and so on. In particular, just before the merging, we have two LCIs $i - 1$ and i spanning time intervals $(t_{i-1}, t_i]$ and $(t_i, t_{i+1}]$, respectively. Since LCI $i - 1$ and i are two distinct LCIs just before $x' = x^c$, we have $\frac{w(t_{i-1}, t_i)}{t_i - t_{i-1}} > \frac{w(t_{i-1}, t_{i+1})}{t_{i+1} - t_{i-1}}$, where $w(.,.)$ includes the size $x' < x^c$ of the new job.

When $x' = x^c$, at which point the merging happens, we have a new LCI $(i - 1)'$ spanning interval $(t_{i-1}, t_{i+1}]$, with intensity

$$\frac{w(t_{i-1}, t_{i+1})}{t_{i+1} - t_i} = \frac{w(t_{i-1}, t_i)}{t_i - t_{i-1}} = \frac{w(t_i, t_{i+1})}{t_{i+1} - t_i}, \tag{15.8}$$

i.e., the intensity of the new LCI $(i - 1)'$ is equal to the intensity of LCI i and $i - 1$, i.e., the intensity of LCI $(i - 1)'$ is equal to the intensity of LCI i and $i - 1$. To see this concretely, one can use the same example (used in the previous part) in the reverse direction.

4. Finally, it can happen that LCI i splits into two parts, i' and i'', and i' merges with LCI $i - 1$. This is a combination of events 2 and 3 above, and similar conclusion can be drawn about the new intervals having equal intensities.

For the first event, since LCIs do not change, it is sufficient to replace x by x' in (15.7) to conclude that $\Delta\Phi \leq 0$. For the second and third events, since the intensities of merged or split intervals are all equal, and these intervals are contiguous, these intervals can still be considered together as far as the potential function (15.5) is concerned. Thus, once again we can use (15.7) by replacing x by x' to conclude that $\Delta\Phi \leq 0$. Repeating this argument over the all the x^c sized smaller decomposed jobs of job j_x with total size x, we conclude that $\Delta\Phi \leq 0$, and the second boundary condition is satisfied by $\Phi(t)$. Since the fourth event is a combination of the second and the third event, the same conclusion holds for it as well.

If the size of the new job x is less than any of x^c's described above, then the LCIs do not change and Case I is sufficient for analysis. ∎

Next, to complete the proof of Theorem 15.2.3, we prove that (15.3) holds for the LOYDS algorithm.

Lemma 15.2.9 *For the potential function (15.5),* $P(s(t)) + \frac{d\Phi(t)}{dt} \leq \alpha^\alpha P(s_o(t))$.

Proof: Consider any time t when neither a new job arrives or an existing job is completed by the LOYDS or OPT. For such time t, we want to show $P(s(t)) + \frac{d\Phi(t)}{dt} \leq \alpha^\alpha P(s_o(t))$, which is equivalent to

$$s(t_0)^\alpha + \frac{d}{dt}\left(\alpha \sum_{i \geq 0} s(t_i)^{\alpha-1}\left(w(t_i, t_{i+1}) - \alpha w_o(t_i, t_{i+1})\right)\right) \leq \alpha^\alpha s_o(t_0)^\alpha, \qquad (15.9)$$

since by definition, $t_0 = t$. Rewriting (15.9),

$$s(t_0)^\alpha - \alpha^\alpha s_o(t_0)^\alpha + \frac{d}{dt}\left(\alpha \sum_{i \geq 0} s(t_i)^{\alpha-1}\left(w(t_i, t_{i+1}) - \alpha w_o(t_i, t_{i+1})\right)\right) \leq 0. \qquad (15.10)$$

Next, we consider the contribution of the LOYDS algorithm and OPT to $\frac{d\Phi(t)}{dt}$. By definition, the LOYDS algorithm reduces $w(t_0, t_1)$ at a rate of $s(t_0)$, i.e., $\frac{d}{dt}w(t_0, t_1) = s(t_0)$ and $\frac{d}{dt}w(t_i, t_{i+1}) = 0$ for $i \geq 1$. For OPT, let $k \geq 0$ be the smallest index such that $w_o(t_k, t_{k+1}) > 0$ at time t, where t_k's are defined using the LOYDS algorithm in (15.4). That is, for LCIs $(t_i, t_{i+1}]$ defined via (15.4), the kth LCI is the earliest LCI that has a non-zero amount of work left with OPT. Given the YDS (that is OPT) algorithm's description, we know that YDS always processes a single job with the earliest deadline at any point in time. Since t_i's form a non-decreasing function, we get from the definition of k being the smallest index such that $w_o(t_k, t_{k+1}) > 0$, that YDS is reducing $w_o(t_k, t_{k+1})$ at the rate $s_o(t) = s_o(t_0)$, and $w_o(t_i, t_{i+1})$ remains unchanged for $i \neq k$, i.e., $\frac{d}{dt}w_o(t_k, t_{k+1}) = s_o(t_0)$ and $\frac{d}{dt}w_o(t_i, t_{i+1}) = 0$ for $i \neq k$.

Using this, from (15.10), we get

$$s(t_0)^\alpha - \alpha^\alpha s_o(t_0)^\alpha - \alpha s(t_0)^{\alpha-1}s(t_0) + \alpha^2 s(t_k)^{\alpha-1}s_o(t_0) \leq 0. \qquad (15.11)$$

From Lemma 15.2.6, we know that $s(t_k) \leq s(t_0)$, using which, (15.11) would be true if

$$s(t_0)^\alpha - \alpha^\alpha s_o(t)^\alpha - \alpha s(t_0)^{\alpha-1}s(t_0) + \alpha^2 s(t_0)^{\alpha-1}s_o(t_0) \leq 0. \qquad (15.12)$$

Rearranging (15.12), we get

$$(1 - \alpha)s(t_0)^\alpha + \alpha^2 s(t_0)^{\alpha-1}s_o(t_0) - \alpha^\alpha s_o(t_0)^\alpha \leq 0. \qquad (15.13)$$

Now we take recourse to some simple calculus-based formulation to show that (15.13) is true. Let $z = \frac{s(t_0)}{s_o(t_0)}$, where recall that because of Proposition 15.2.2, $z \neq 0, \infty$. Then (15.13) is equivalent to

$$p(z) = (1 - \alpha)z^\alpha + \alpha^2 z^{\alpha-1} - \alpha^\alpha \leq 0. \qquad (15.14)$$

Differentiating $p(z)$ with respect to z, we get

$$p'(z) = \alpha(1 - \alpha)z^{\alpha-1} + \alpha^2(\alpha - 1)z^{\alpha-2}.$$

Now $p'(z) = 0$ for $z = \alpha$ which is unique. Importantly, note that since we are only interested in $\alpha > 1$, $p'(z) \geq 0$ for $z \leq \alpha$ and $p'(z) \leq 0$ for $z \geq \alpha$. Moreover, note that $p(0) = -\alpha^\alpha$ and $p(+\infty) = -\infty$. This together implies that $p(z)$ is maximized at $z = \alpha$ and clearly $p(\alpha) = 0$.

Hence, we get that $p(z) \leq 0$ for $z \geq 0$, which is what we wanted to prove, i.e., (15.9) is true, and, consequently, the proof is complete. ∎

Note that for the proof we have not explicitly used the exact speed chosen by the LOYDS algorithm or the YDS algorithm; instead, we have only relied on the structural properties of the two algorithms.

A simpler algorithm than LOYDS for Problem 15.2 is called the average rate (AVR), which is defined as follows. Recall from Problem 15.2 that job j arrives at time a_j with deadline d_j and has size w_j. Let the intensity of job j be defined as $\dfrac{w_j}{d_j - a_j}$. Let a step function for job j be

$$
u_j(t) = \begin{cases} \dfrac{w_j}{d_j - a_j} & \text{for } t \in [a_j, d_j], \\ 0 & \text{otherwise.} \end{cases} \tag{15.15}
$$

Then algorithm AVR chooses speed $s(t) = \sum_j u_j(t)$ at time t, and one job is processed at a time, where the job with the earliest deadline is processed first. Alternatively, AVR can be described as multiple jobs being processed parallely, where each job j is processed at constant speed $u_j(t)$ throughout time $t \in [a_j, d_j]$. With $P(s) = s^\alpha$, the competitive ratio of AVR for Problem 15.2 is $2^{\alpha-1}\alpha^\alpha$ [256].

15.2.3 Beyond the Worst-Case Input: Incorporating Predictions

In this section, we will consider the presence of a machine learning (ML) algorithm or an oracle that can predict the input $\{a_j, w_j\}$, but the quality of the prediction is unknown. In this setup, the goal is to design an online algorithm whose competitive ratio is close to unity when the prediction is accurate, while remaining bounded (similar to the setup that we have considered throughout the book) when there is no bound on the prediction error. This is not a trivial task, and in this section, we consider a simpler problem than (15.2), called the uniform deadline problem, and present an algorithm that can achieve both these objectives simultaneously.

Definition 15.2.10 *Uniform Deadline Problem: Let time be discrete, and at time $\tau = 0, 1, \ldots, T - D$, a single job with size w_τ arrives that has a deadline $D + \tau$, and the total time horizon is T. Thus, all jobs have the same relative deadline D, and the only uncertainty is about the job sizes w_τ arriving in future. We define an instance of the problem as a triple $(\mathbf{w}, D, T)$, where $\mathbf{w} = (w_0, \ldots, w_{T-D})$.*

As before, at time $t \in [0, T]$, $P(s(t))$ denotes the power consumed while processing at speed $s(t)$, where $s(t) = \sum_{i \in A(t)} s_i(t)$, $A(t)$ is the set of jobs being processed simultaneously, and $s_i(t)$ is the speed at which job $i \in A(t)$ is processed, respectively, at time t.

A job that arrives at time τ is defined to be complete at time c_τ if w_τ amount of work has been completed for it. Thus, the deadline constraint forces that $c_\tau \leq \tau + D$, and the problem is to solve

$$
\min \quad E = \int P(s(t))dt \tag{15.16}
$$
$$
s.t. \quad c_\tau \leq \tau + D, \ \forall \tau \in [0, 1, \ldots, T - D].
$$

Prediction and Error Model

Let $(\mathbf{w}^{\text{real}}, D, T)$ be the real problem instance, where $\mathbf{w}^{\text{real}} = \left(w_0^{\text{real}}, \dots, w_{T-D}^{\text{real}}\right)$, while $(\mathbf{w}^{\text{pred}}, D, T)$ is the predicted instance by the ML algorithm at time 0, where $\mathbf{w}^{\text{pred}} = \left(w_0^{\text{pred}}, \dots, w_{T-D}^{\text{pred}}\right)$.

The error between $\mathbf{w}^{\text{real}}$ and $\mathbf{w}^{\text{pred}}$ is defined as

$$\eta = \sum_{i=0}^{T-D} |w_i^{\text{pred}} - w_i^{\text{real}}|^\alpha, \tag{15.17}$$

where α is such that $P(s) = s^\alpha$. Ideally, one would like to replace α in (15.17) by any arbitrary number; however, it turns out that for any number below α, there is no useful way of using the prediction [275]. Notice that the guarantee with any number higher than α in (15.17) will be weaker.

Define the work difference between the real and the predicted size of job i as $w_i^+ = \max\left\{w_i^{\text{real}} - w_i^{\text{pred}}, 0\right\}$ and $w_i^- = \max\left\{w_i^{\text{pred}} - w_i^{\text{real}}, 0\right\}$. Let $\mathbf{w}^+ = \left(w_0^+, \dots, w_{T-D}^+\right)$ and $\mathbf{w}^- = \left(w_0^-, \dots, w_{T-D}^-\right)$, and the full instance be $(\mathbf{w}^+, D, T)$, and $(\mathbf{w}^-, D, T)$.

Using these definitions, the following proposition connects the energy used by OPT on these work difference instances and error η.

Proposition 15.2.11 *Let $E_{\text{OPT}}(\mathbf{w}, D, T)$ be the optimal energy consumed by OPT for the Problem (15.16) with instance $(\mathbf{w}, D, T)$. Then*

$$E_{\text{OPT}}(\mathbf{w}^+, D, T) + E_{\text{OPT}}(\mathbf{w}^-, D, T) \le \eta. \tag{15.18}$$

Proof: Note that for any i, only one among w_i^+ or w_i^- is greater than 0. Thus, the two instances $(\mathbf{w}^+, D, T), (\mathbf{w}^-, D, T)$ can be combined to form a single instance where the corresponding non-zero quantity among w_i^+ and w_i^- is considered, denoted by $w_i^\pm$. For this combined instance, consider an algorithm $\mathcal{A}$ that completely processes the job of size $w_i^\pm$ arriving at time τ by time $\tau + 1$ at speed $w_i^\pm$. Thus, the total energy usage of $\mathcal{A}$

$$E_{\mathcal{A}}(\mathbf{w}^+, D, T) + E_{\mathcal{A}}(\mathbf{w}^-, D, T) = \sum_{i=0}^{T-D} |w_i^\pm|^\alpha = \sum_{i=0}^{T-D} |w_i^{\text{pred}} - w_i^{\text{real}}|^\alpha,$$

which by definition (15.17) is equal to η. Since OPT is at least as good as any algorithm, we get the result. ∎

For this ML augmented model, let $\epsilon > 0$ be the tradeoff parameter an algorithm uses to weigh between leaning on the predicted input and preparing for the worst-case input to ensure robustness. The smaller the value of ϵ, more is the trust shown by the algorithm in the prediction, and as ϵ increases the algorithm leans towards the uncertain future input.

Definition 15.2.12 (Consistent Algorithm) *With perfect prediction, i.e., $\eta = 0$, an algorithm $\mathcal{A}$ is called consistent if its cost $C_{\mathcal{A}} \le c(\alpha, \epsilon) C_{\text{OPT}}$, where $c(\alpha, \epsilon)$ tends to 1 as ϵ approaches 0.*

Essentially, consistency means that if ϵ is chosen small enough, the algorithm's cost is very close to that of OPT, when the prediction error is zero. Thus, it is a natural requirement for a reasonable algorithm.

Definition 15.2.13 (Smooth Algorithm) *To ensure that the algorithm's performance deteriorates smoothly as the prediction error η increases, an algorithm $\mathcal{A}$ is called smooth if its cost $C_{\mathcal{A}} \leq c(\alpha, \epsilon)C_{\mathrm{OPT}} + f(\alpha, \epsilon, \eta)$, where $f(\alpha, \epsilon, 0) = 0$ for any α, ϵ.*

With error $\eta = 0$, smoothness is same as consistency.

Definition 15.2.14 (Robust Algorithm) *To ensure that an algorithm's competitive ratio should always be bounded even for arbitrarily bad (adversarial) predictions, algorithm $\mathcal{A}$ is called robust if its cost $C_{\mathcal{A}} \leq r(\alpha, \epsilon)C_{\mathrm{OPT}}$ for some function $r(\alpha, \epsilon)$.*

Ideally, we would have liked $r(\alpha, \epsilon)$ to be independent of ϵ, but that is generally not the case, and $r(\alpha, \epsilon)$ increases as ϵ becomes smaller (when prediction is valued more by the algorithm).

Using these definitions, the competitive ratio of algorithm $\mathcal{A}$, which is consistent, smooth, and robust, is at most

$$\mu_{\mathcal{A}} \leq \min\left\{c(\alpha, \epsilon) + \frac{f(\alpha, \epsilon, \eta)}{E_{\mathrm{OPT}}}, r(\alpha, \epsilon)\right\}.$$

A Consistent and Smooth Algorithm

For the uniform deadline problem, we will propose an algorithm (LAS-TRUST) using OPT (YDS) on the predicted input, which is adjusted using the AVR algorithm when the real input deviates from the predicted input.

Since Problem (15.16) is simpler than Problem (15.2), where all jobs arrive at integral times, and all have the same relative deadline, we first show that the AVR algorithm has an improved competitive ratio of 2^{α} compared to the general case of $2^{\alpha-1}\alpha^{\alpha}$.

Theorem 15.2.15 *For the uniform deadline problem (Problem (15.16)), the competitive ratio of the AVR algorithm is at most 2^{α}.*

Proof: The proof is simple, and we defer that to Problem 15.4. ∎

Algorithm LAS-TRUST: For instance $(\mathbf{w}^{\mathrm{pred}}, D, T)$, which is known ahead of time, use offline YDS algorithm for scheduling and choosing the speed $s^{\mathrm{YDS}}(t)$. From the definition of the YDS algorithm, we know that at any time t, only one job is scheduled, and the speed for job i that is scheduled at time t is

$$s_i^{\mathrm{YDS}}(t) = s^{\mathrm{YDS}}(t) = \frac{w_i^{\mathrm{pred}}}{e_i - b_i}$$

throughout the interval $t \in [b_i, e_i]$, where b_i and e_i are the start and the end time for processing of job i by YDS.

Making the algorithm **online**. On the arrival of job i at time τ_i, job i is scheduled in interval $[b_i, e_i]$ at speed $s'(t) = \min\left\{\frac{w_i^{\mathrm{real}}}{e_i-b_i}, s^{\mathrm{YDS}}(t)\right\}$ for $t \in [b_i, e_i]$. The min is needed in case $w_i^{\mathrm{pred}} > w_i^{\mathrm{true}}$.

Since w_i^{real} can be larger than w_i^{pred}, choosing speed $s'(t)$ for interval $[b_i, e_i]$ may not finish job i by its deadline. To take care of this, the leftover work instance $(\mathbf{w}^+, D, T)$ is scheduled using the AVR algorithm in addition. Let the speed output by algorithm AVR on $(\mathbf{w}^+, D, T)$ for any time $t \in [\tau_i, \tau_i + D]$ be $s''(t)$.

Thus, the total speed of the algorithm at time t is

$$s(t) = s'(t) + s''(t).$$

In terms of speed s_i dedicated to job i, we can write $s_i(t) = s_i'(t) + s_i''(t)$, where

$$s_i'(t) = \begin{cases} \min\left\{\dfrac{w_i^{\text{real}}}{e_i - b_i}, s_i^{\text{YDS}}(t)\right\} & \text{for} \quad t \in [b_i, e_i], \\ 0 & \text{otherwise}, \end{cases} \tag{15.19}$$

and

$$s_i''(t) = \begin{cases} \dfrac{\max\{w_i^{\text{real}} - w_i^{\text{pred}}, 0\}}{D} & \text{for} \quad t \in [\tau_i, \tau_i + D], \\ 0 & \text{otherwise}. \end{cases} \tag{15.20}$$

Remark 15.2.16 *Algorithm* LAS-TRUST *is consistent since if* $(\mathbf{w}^{pred}, D, T)$ *is identical to* $(\mathbf{w}^{real}, D, T)$, *then the algorithm collapses to* YDS, *which is* OPT.

To characterize the smoothness of algorithm LAS-TRUST, we have the following result.

Theorem 15.2.17 *Let* $\mathcal{A}$ *be the algorithm* LAS-TRUST. *For any* $0 < \delta \le 1$,

$$E_{\mathcal{A}}(\mathbf{w}^{real}, D, T) \le (1 + \delta)^\alpha E_{\text{OPT}}(\mathbf{w}^{real}, D, T) + \left(\frac{24}{\delta}\right)^\alpha \eta.$$

Proof: From the definition of algorithm LAS-TRUST, we know that $s'(t) \le s^{\text{YDS}}(t)$ at all times t, where $s^{\text{YDS}}(t)$ is the optimal speed for instance $(\mathbf{w}^{\text{pred}}, D, T)$.

Moreover, $s''(t)$ is the speed profile of algorithm AVR on input $\mathbf{w}^+ = (w_0^+, \ldots, w_{T-D}^+)$. Since algorithm AVR is 2^α-competitive (Theorem 15.2.15), we get that the energy used in executing speed profile $s_i''(t)$ is

$$\int P(s''(t))dt \le 2^\alpha E_{\text{OPT}}(\mathbf{w}^+, D, T).$$

Thus, the total energy used by algorithm LAS-TRUST is

$$E_{\mathcal{A}}(\mathbf{w}^{\text{real}}, D, T) = \int P(s'(t) + s''(t))dt,$$

$$\overset{(a)}{\le} (1 + \delta/3)^\alpha \int P(s'(t))dt + (6/\delta)^\alpha \int P(s''(t))dt, \tag{15.21}$$

$$\le (1 + \delta/3)^\alpha E_{\text{OPT}}(\mathbf{w}^{\text{pred}}, D, T) + (6/\delta)^\alpha 2^\alpha E_{\text{OPT}}(\mathbf{w}^+, D, T), \tag{15.22}$$

where (a) follows from Proposition 15.2.18, with $\gamma = \delta/3$.

Proposition 15.2.18 *For $P(s) = s^\alpha$, and any $s_1, s_2, \geq 0, 0 < \gamma \leq 1$,*

$$P(s_1 + s_2) \leq (1 + \gamma)^\alpha P(s_1) + (2/\gamma)^\alpha P(s_2).$$

Scheduling instance $(\mathbf{w}^{\text{real}}, D, T)$ using YDS, and then scheduling instance $(\mathbf{w}^-, D, T)$ in addition using AVR, is a feasible schedule for $(\mathbf{w}^{\text{pred}}, D, T)$. Thus, similar to (15.22), we get

$$E_{\text{OPT}}(\mathbf{w}^{\text{pred}}, D, T) \leq E_{\mathcal{A}}(\mathbf{w}^{\text{pred}}, D, T) \leq (1 + \delta/3)^\alpha E_{\text{OPT}}(\mathbf{w}^{\text{real}}, D, T)$$
$$+ (6/\delta)^\alpha 2^\alpha E_{\text{OPT}}(\mathbf{w}^-, D, T). \tag{15.23}$$

Combining (15.22) and (15.23), we get

$$E_{\mathcal{A}}(\mathbf{w}^{\text{real}}, D, T) \overset{(a)}{\leq} (1 + \delta/3)^{2\alpha} E_{\text{OPT}}(\mathbf{w}^{\text{real}}, D, T)$$
$$+ (24/\delta)^\alpha (E_{\text{OPT}}(\mathbf{w}^+, D, T) + E_{\text{OPT}}(\mathbf{w}^-, D, T)),$$
$$\overset{(b)}{\leq} (1 + \delta/3)^{2\alpha} E_{\text{OPT}}(\mathbf{w}^{\text{real}}, D, T) + (24/\delta)^\alpha \eta,$$
$$\overset{(c)}{\leq} (1 + \delta)^\alpha E_{\text{OPT}}(\mathbf{w}^{\text{real}}, D, T) + (24/\delta)^\alpha \eta,$$

where (a) follows since $0 \leq \delta \leq 1$, (b) follows from Proposition 15.2.11, while (c) follows since $(1 + x/3)^2 \leq (1 + x)$ for $0 \leq x \leq 1$. ∎

A Consistent, Smooth, and Robust Algorithm

Next, we work towards making algorithm LAS-TRUST robust, where the idea is to modify the speed proposed by algorithm LAS-TRUST in such a way that it is comparable with the speed choice made by algorithm AVR (Lemma 15.2.21). Since algorithm AVR is 2^α-competitive, the resulting robustness guarantee will follow.

Given an instance of the uniform deadline problem $(\mathbf{w}, D, T)$, consider a modified problem instance $(\mathbf{w}, (1 - \delta)D, T)$ where all deadlines have been reduced by a fraction $(1 - \delta)$. If $s(t)$ is a feasible speed profile for $(\mathbf{w}, D, T)$, then speed profile $s'(t) = \frac{s(t)}{1-\delta}$ is feasible for $(\mathbf{w}, (1 - \delta)D, T)$, but with $s'(t)$, the time for which non-zero speed is used is also reduced by a fraction $1 - \delta$. Thus, we get

$$E_{\text{OPT}}(\mathbf{w}, (1 - \delta)D, T) \leq \frac{1}{(1-\delta)^{\alpha-1}} E_{\text{OPT}}(\mathbf{w}, D, T). \tag{15.24}$$

For a feasible speed profile $s(t)$ for $(\mathbf{w}^{\text{real}}, (1 - \delta)D, T)$, where job i is processed at speed $s_i(t)$ at time t, consider a modified speed profile given by

$$s_i^\delta(t) = \frac{1}{\delta D} \int_{t-\delta D}^{t} s_i(x) dx, \tag{15.25}$$

where s_i^δ is the speed dedicated to the ith job in speed profile $s^\delta(t)$ at time t. The following properties are immediate, and their proofs are left as exercises in Problems 15.5, 15.6, and 15.7.

Lemma 15.2.19 *Speed profile $s^\delta(t)$ is feasible for $(\mathbf{w}^{real}, D, T)$.*

Lemma 15.2.20 *The energy consumed by speed profile $s^\delta(t)$ is not higher than that of $s(t)$, i.e.,*

$$\int (s^\delta(t))^\alpha dt \le \int (s(t))^\alpha dt.$$

Recall that with the AVR algorithm, for instance $(\mathbf{w}^{\text{real}}, D, T)$ multiple jobs are processed parallely, where job i is processed at speed $u_i(t) = \frac{w_i^{\text{real}}}{D}$ at time $t \in [\tau_i, \tau_i + D]$ and total speed at time t is $u(t) = \sum_i u_i(t)$.

Lemma 15.2.21 *Speed profile $s_i^\delta(t)$ satisfies $s_i^\delta(t) \le \frac{1}{\delta} u_i(t)$.*

Lemma 15.2.21 directly implies the following bound on the energy with speed profile $s^\delta(t)$.

$$\int (s^\delta(t))^\alpha dt \le \left(\frac{1}{\delta}\right)^\alpha \int (u(t))^\alpha dt \le \left(\frac{2}{\delta}\right)^\alpha E_{\text{OPT}}(\mathbf{w}^{\text{real}}, D, T), \qquad (15.26)$$

where the second inequality follows since AVR is 2^α-competitive (Theorem 15.2.15). Combining Lemma 15.2.20 and (15.26), we get

$$\int (s^\delta(t))^\alpha dt \le \min\left\{\int (s(t))^\alpha dt, \left(\frac{2}{\delta}\right)^\alpha E_{\text{OPT}}(\mathbf{w}^{\text{real}}, D, T)\right\}. \qquad (15.27)$$

Algorithm 25 ML-Aug Algorithm

1: **Input:** $T, D, \mathbf{w}^{\text{pred}}, \mathbf{w}^{\text{real}}, \alpha$
2: Choice of trust or tradeoff parameter $\epsilon > 0$
3: Choose $\delta > 0$, such that $\left(\frac{1+\delta}{1-\delta}\right)^\alpha = 1 + \epsilon$
4: Precompute schedule using YDS algorithm on the instance $(\mathbf{w}^{\text{pred}}, (1-\delta)D, T)$ to get constant speed s_i^{YDS} for job i that is processed between $[b_i, e_i]$.
5: On the arrival of job i at time τ_i

$$s_i'(t) = \begin{cases} \min\left\{\frac{w_i^{\text{real}}}{e_i - b_i}, s_i^{\text{YDS}}\right\} & \text{for } t \in [b_i, e_i], \\ 0 & \text{otherwise}, \end{cases} \qquad (15.28)$$

and

$$s_i''(t) = \begin{cases} \frac{\max\{w_i^{\text{real}} - w_i^{\text{pred}}, 0\}}{(1-\delta)D} & \text{for } t \in [\tau_i, \tau_i + (1-\delta)D], \\ 0 & \text{otherwise}. \end{cases} \qquad (15.29)$$

6: Set the final speed for job i $s_i(t) = \frac{1}{\delta D} \int_{t-\delta D}^{t} (s_i'(x) + s_i''(x))dx$
7: Process job i at time t for which $s_i(t) > 0$ at speed $s_i(t)$

We next propose an algorithm called ML-Aug that will be consistent, smooth, and robust, whose pseudo-code is given in Algorithm 25. ML-Aug is essentially the same as the LAS-Trust algorithm with speed choice $s(t)$ replaced by $s^\delta(t)$, where the particular choice of δ is influenced by the trust parameter ϵ.

Algorithm ML-Aug produces a feasible schedule for $(\mathbf{w}^{real}, D, T)$ by combining the fact that the speed choice $s_i'(t) + s_i''(t)$ is feasible for $(\mathbf{w}^{real}, (1-\delta)D, T)$ following (15.19) and (15.20), and Lemma 15.2.19.

Theorem 15.2.22 *With $\epsilon > 0$, the competitive ratio of algorithm ML-Aug is at most*

$$\mu_{ML-Aug} \le \min\left\{(1+\epsilon) + \mathcal{O}\left(\frac{\alpha}{\epsilon}\right)^\alpha \frac{\eta}{E_{OPT}(\mathbf{w}^{real}, D, T)}, \mathcal{O}\left(\frac{\alpha}{\epsilon}\right)^\alpha\right\}.$$

The choice of trust or tradeoff parameter ϵ critically controls the competitive ratio of the ML-Aug algorithm. If ϵ is chosen close to 0 and η is small, then we get a competitive ratio close to 1. However, if η is large, then the competitive ratio transitions to the robust regime where the competitive ratio is $\mathcal{O}\left(\frac{\alpha}{\epsilon}\right)^\alpha$. Thus, compared to the algorithm (AVR for example) that disregards prediction, the competitive ratio is $\mathcal{O}\left(\frac{\alpha}{\epsilon}\right)^\alpha$ compared to 2^α for AVR.

Proof: The energy used by algorithm ML-Aug is

$$E_{ML-Aug}(\mathbf{w}^{real}, D, T) = \int (s^\delta(t))^\alpha dt,$$

$$\stackrel{(a)}{\le} \min\left\{\int (s'(t) + s''(t))^\alpha dt, \left(\frac{2}{\delta}\right)^\alpha E_{OPT}(\mathbf{w}^{real}, D, T)\right\},$$

$$\stackrel{(b)}{\le} \min\left\{(1+\delta)^\alpha E_{OPT}(\mathbf{w}^{real}, (1-\delta)D, T)) + (24/\delta)^\alpha \eta, \right.$$
$$\left. \left(\frac{2}{\delta}\right)^\alpha E_{OPT}(\mathbf{w}^{real}, D, T)\right\},$$

$$\stackrel{(c)}{\le} \min\left\{\left(\frac{1+\delta}{1-\delta}\right)^\alpha E_{OPT}(\mathbf{w}^{real}, D, T) + (24/\delta)^\alpha \eta, \right.$$
$$\left. \left(\frac{2}{\delta}\right)^\alpha E_{OPT}(\mathbf{w}^{real}, D, T)\right\},$$

where (a) follows from (15.27), (b) follows from Theorem 15.2.17 since the speed $s'(t) + s''(t)$ chosen in ML-Aug is equal to the speed of LAS-Trust with instance $(\mathbf{w}^{real}, (1-\delta)D, T)$, and (c) follows from (15.24). With $\left(\frac{1+\delta}{1-\delta}\right)^\alpha = 1 + \epsilon$, which implies $\delta = \mathcal{O}\left(\frac{\epsilon}{\alpha}\right)$, we get

$$E_{ML-Aug}(\mathbf{w}^{real}, D, T) \le \min\left\{(1+\epsilon)E_{OPT}(\mathbf{w}^{real}, D, T) + \mathcal{O}\left(\frac{\alpha}{\epsilon}\right)^\alpha \eta, \mathcal{O}\left(\frac{\alpha}{\epsilon}\right)^\alpha E_{OPT}(\mathbf{w}^{real}, D, T)\right\}.$$

∎

This completes the proof of Theorem 15.2.22 that shows that in the uniform deadlines case it is possible to devise a consistent, smooth, and robust online algorithm in the presence of predictions about input but with uncertain accuracy. In general, this is a challenging problem, for example, when deadlines are arbitrary.

In this section, we focussed entirely on the power function $P(s) = s^\alpha$. Different applications give rise to distinct power functions. In the next section, we encounter one such power function that is motivated by communication systems, for which we will derive an entirely different set of results.

15.3 Common Deadline with a Single Server and Shannon Rate Based Power Function

In this section, we consider the special case of Problem (15.1), where all jobs have the same common deadline. As before, a total of n jobs arrive, with job j arriving at time a_j, and all jobs have a common deadline d. Moreover, we consider a different power cost function than the one considered in Section 15.2 ($P(s) = s^\alpha$), which is relevant for communication settings.

From Shannon theory [276], the number of bits B transmitted using constant power P for time duration t is given by

$$B = t \log(1 + P) \text{ bits.}$$

Thus, considering B/t as speed, we get that $P(s) = 2^s - 1$, and the energy needed to send B bits in time duration t is $g(t) = t(2^{B/t} - 1)$. As we will see next, this power function exhibits very different properties compared to $P(s) = s^\alpha$ as studied in Section 15.2.

Instead of counting the total energy as an integral over time $E = \int P(s(t))dt$ as in (15.1), in this section, we will count E as the sum of the energy needed to process or transmit each of the n jobs.

With a common deadline, without loss of generality, let the first job arrive at $t = 0$, and the inter-arrival time between the ith and the $(i+1)^{st}$ job be given by $x_i = a_{i+1} - a_i$. Thus, a job arrival sequence is represented as

$$\sigma = (x_1, x_2, x_3, \ldots, x_{n-1}, x_n),$$

where, $x_i \geq 0$ and $\sum_{i=1}^{n-1} x_i < d$ and $\sum_{i=1}^{n} x_i = d$. We have introduced the extra time x_n that accounts for the time difference between the last (n^{th}) job arrival at time $\sum_{i=1}^{n-1} x_i$ and the common deadline d. Let S be the set of sequences representing job inter-arrival times with the total number of jobs equal to n, i.e.,

$$S = \left\{ (x_1, x_2, x_3, \ldots, x_n) \mid x_i \geq 0, \sum_{i=1}^{n} x_i = d \right\}.$$

Assumption 15.3.1 *We let the size of each job be* **equal**. *This will ensure that jobs are processed in order of their arrival, and without preemption. Let the size of any job be B bits. Generalizing the analysis presented next with unequal job sizes is challenging.*

Definition 15.3.2 *Since jobs are processed in the order of their arrival and without preemption, with an algorithm* $\mathcal{A}$, *for job i, let its processing begin at time* b_i *and finish at time* c_i. *Note that* $b_i \geq \sum_{j=1}^{i-1} x_j$ *since a job can be processed only after it arrives. Then* $f_i = c_i - b_i$ *is defined as the* **transmission time** *during which job i is processed. The respective quantities with* OPT *are denoted with a superscript o.*

Definition 15.3.3 *With job transmission times* f_i, *the total energy* (15.1) *used by an online algorithm* $\mathcal{A}$ *to transmit n jobs is given by*

$$E_{\mathcal{A}} = \sum_{i=0}^{n-1} g(f_i),$$

where $g(t) = t(2^{B/t} - 1)$ *is the energy needed to transmit a job of size B bits in time duration t. Similarly, for* OPT, $E_{\text{OPT}} = \sum_{i=0}^{n-1} g(f_i^{\text{OPT}})$.

Thus, the competitive ratio of any online algorithm $\mathcal{A}$ is

$$\mu_{\mathcal{A}} = \max_{\sigma} \frac{E_{\mathcal{A}}(\sigma)}{E_{\text{OPT}}(\sigma)}.$$

15.3.1 Optimal Offline Algorithm

Note that $P(s) = 2^s - 1$ is a convex function of s similar to $P(s) = s^{\alpha}$. Moreover, the common deadline case is a special case of the individual deadline case considered in Section 15.2. Thus, the YDS algorithm that is OPT with individual deadlines for convex power functions P continues to be OPT for the considered problem in this section. However, with a single common deadline, YDS simplifies to the following algorithm denoted as YDS-COMMON.

- For each k, compute the average of k-partial sums of inter-arrival times $\text{avg}_k = \frac{1}{k} \sum_{i=1}^{k} x_i$.

- Define $m_1 = \max_k \text{avg}_k$ to be the maximum of the average of k-partial sums. Let $k_1 = \arg\max_k \text{avg}_k$.

- Set transmission time equal to m_1 for each of the first (indexed in order of their arrival times) k_1 jobs.

- Repeat the same procedure while only considering jobs with indices greater than k_1.

The pseudo code of the YDS-COMMON algorithm is provided in Algorithm 26.

Algorithm 26 YDS-COMMON

---

initialize $k_0 = 0$

for $j := 0$ to $n - 1$ **do**

$$m_{j+1} = \max_{k \in \{1,2,3,\dots,n-k_j\}} \left\{ \frac{1}{k} \sum_{i=1}^{k} x_{k_j+i} \right\}$$

$$k_{j+1} = \max_{k \in \{1,2,3,\dots,n-k_j\}} \left\{ k : \frac{1}{k} \sum_{i=1}^{k} x_{k_j+i} = m_{j+1} \right\}$$

end for

for $i := 0$ to $n - 1$ **do**

Set transmission time $f_i = m_j$ such that $k_{j-1} < i \le k_j$

end for return $(f_0, f_1, \dots, f_{n-1})$

Since all jobs are of the same size, the basic idea of YDS-COMMON is to equate the transmission times of each job as far as possible, subject to feasibility conditions on the arrival times. See Figure 15.2 for a pictorial description of YDS-COMMON for four jobs.

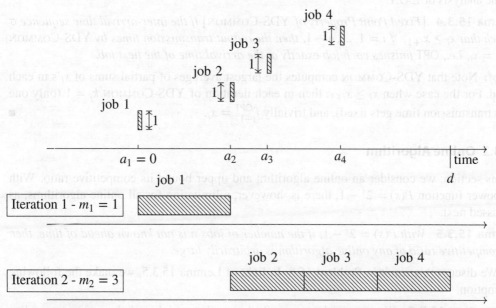

Figure 15.2 Pictorial description of YDS-COMMON for four jobs each with size one (represented by their heights). In the first iteration, only the first job is considered, since $x_1 = a_2 - a_1$ is the largest. Once job 1 is scheduled or processed, then in iteration 2, m_2 is maximized when all the three remaining jobs are considered together, and, thus, all the three remaining jobs get equal transmission time over the remaining time $d - a_2$.

We collect some of the properties of YDS-COMMON as follows. Since the inter-arrival time sequence σ is known ahead of time, YDS-COMMON makes sure that it never idles by processing at a rate (slower or faster) depending on the next job arrival times (long or short). Therefore, the job transmission times output by YDS-COMMON, f_i's, are such that $\sum_{i=0}^{n-1} f_i = d$.

Also, since the transmission of the ith job cannot start before its arrival, we also have

$$\sum_{i=1}^{\ell} f_i \geq \sum_{i=1}^{\ell} x_i, \tag{15.30}$$

for any $0 \leq \ell \leq n - 1$. Moreover, another useful property (which is easy to prove) of YDS-COMMON is

$$f_i \geq f_{i+1} \; \forall i = 0, 1, \dots n - 1, \tag{15.31}$$

i.e., the transmission times do not increase with the index of the jobs, which is intuitive, since otherwise we could stretch the transmission time and decrease the energy usage. We will make use of (15.31) repeatedly while analysing the competitive ratio of the online algorithm (called LAZY) proposed in Section 15.3.2.

Next, we present an important (fixed-point) property of YDS-COMMON that will be useful for the analysis of LAZY.

Lemma 15.3.4 [*Fixed Point Property of* YDS-COMMON] *If the inter-arrival time sequence σ is such that $x_i \geq x_{i+1}$, $\forall i = 1, \dots, n - 1$, then the output transmission times by YDS-COMMON $f_{i-1}^{OPT} = x_i$, i.e.,* OPT *finishes each job exactly at the arrival time of the next job.*

Proof: Note that YDS-COMMON computes the largest averages of partial sums of x_i's in each round. For the case when $x_i \geq x_{i+1}$, then in each iteration of YDS-COMMON $k_j = 1$ (only one job's transmission time gets fixed), and trivially $f_{i-1}^{OPT} = x_i$. ∎

15.3.2 Online Algorithm

In this section, we consider an online algorithm and upper bound its competitive ratio. With the power function $P(s) = 2^s - 1$, there is, however, a limitation for all online algorithms, as discussed next.

Lemma 15.3.5 *With $P(s) = 2^s - 1$, if the number of jobs n is not known ahead of time, then the competitive ratio of any online algorithm is arbitrarily large.*

We discuss this result in Problem 15.8. In light of Lemma 15.3.5, we make the following assumption.

Assumption 15.3.6 *We assume that at $t = 0$, the number of jobs n is known to any online algorithm together with the common deadline d, but the arrival instants are known to the algorithm only causally.*

Algorithm LAZY: The transmission time of the first job that is available at time 0 is chosen to be $\frac{d}{n}$. If the second job arrives before the finish time of the first job, the second job is added to the queue and waits for job 1 to finish. Once the first job is complete at time $\frac{d}{n}$, the transmission time for the second job is chosen to be $\frac{d}{n}$, the same as that of the first job. Similarly, for the ith job: if it arrives before time $t = (i-1)\frac{d}{n}$, it is added to the queue and transmitted, starting from the time at which the $(i-1)^{th}$ job's transmission got completed with transmission time $\frac{d}{n}$. If suppose the jth job arrives after the finish time of the $(j-1)^{th}$ job. Then for the time between the arrival of the jth job and the finish time of the $(j-1)^{th}$ job, the algorithm idles, and does not consume any power. In such a case, at the time of the arrival of the jth job at time $\sum_{i=1}^{j} x_i$, we update:

$$d \leftarrow d - \sum_{i=1}^{j} x_i,$$

$$n \leftarrow n - j.$$

The algorithm now repeats the same procedure with the new d and n, and outputs job transmission times $f_i, i = j, \dots, n-1$.

With algorithm LAZY, the transmission time for the ith job is given by

$$f_i = \min\left(f_{i-1}, \frac{d - \sum_{j=1}^{i} x_j}{n - i}\right),$$

with $f_1 = d/n$.

The basic motivation behind algorithm LAZY is that if $n(t)$ is the number of jobs yet to arrive at time t, it assumes that those $n(t)$ jobs are going to arrive at equal intervals in the left-over time of $T - t$, and chooses a transmission time of $\frac{T-t}{n(t)+1}$ for the current job.

Let the ratio of the remaining time and the number of jobs yet to arrive at the ℓth job arrival be $y_\ell = \dfrac{d - \sum_{j=1}^{\ell} x_j}{n-\ell}$ $\forall 0 \le \ell \le n-1$. Then the transmission time f_i with the algorithm LAZY can be expressed as

$$f_i = \min_{\ell \le i} \left(y_\ell\right). \tag{15.32}$$

Algorithm 27 LAZY

Initialize $f_0 = \dfrac{T}{n}$
for $i := 0$ to $n-2$ **do**
$$f_{i+1} = \min\left(f_i, \frac{d - \sum_{n=1}^{i} x_n}{n-i}\right)$$
end for
Return $(f_0, f_1, \dots, f_{n-1})$

We now show that the worst-case inter-arrival sequence (x_i's) for algorithm LAZY in terms of its competitive ratio is such that $x_i \geq x_{i+1}$. This condition essentially implies that algorithm LAZY has to idle after finishing transmission of every single job. To prove this, we show that, given any inter-arrival sequence σ, we can construct another feasible inter-arrival sequence σ' for which $x_i \geq x_{i+1}$, where, importantly for OPT, the energy usage remains the same $E_{OPT}(\sigma) = E_{OPT}(\sigma')$, while the energy spent by LAZY increases in the latter case, i.e., $E_L(\sigma) \leq E_L(\sigma')$.

Remark 15.3.7 *Note that the inter-arrival sequence σ is an n-length sequence, but the last element of σ is auxiliary, since job 0 starts at time 0, and only the first $n - 1$ elements represent the inter-arrival times of $n - 1$ other jobs. With input σ, the output of OPT is a set of transmission times for the n jobs $\left\{ f_0^{OPT}, \ldots, f_{n-1}^{OPT} \right\}$ which is of cardinality n. Thus, we can consider $\sigma' = \text{OPT}(\sigma) = \left\{ f_0^{OPT}, \ldots, f_{n-1}^{OPT} \right\}$ as a valid inter-arrival sequence, with $x'_{i+1} = f_i$ for $i = 0, \ldots, n - 1$ and $x'_n = d - \sum_{i=1}^{n-1} x'_i$.*

Moreover, note that, from (15.31), the elements of σ' are such that $f_0^{OPT} \geq f_1^{OPT} \geq \ldots \geq f_{n-1}^{OPT}$.

Lemma 15.3.8 *Let σ' be the inter-arrival sequence that is output (job transmission times) by YDS-COMMON with inter-arrival sequence $\sigma \in S$ as the input, i.e., $\sigma' \leftarrow \text{OPT}(\sigma)$. Then, we have*

$$E_L(\sigma') \geq E_L(\sigma), \tag{15.33}$$

$$E_{OPT}(\sigma') = E_{OPT}(\sigma), \tag{15.34}$$

where $E_L(\sigma)$ stands for the total energy used by algorithm LAZY with input σ.

Thus, Lemma 15.3.8 shows that the ratio of the energy used by LAZY and OPT is larger with σ' than σ.

Proof: [Proof of Lemma 15.3.8] We prove this by showing that the job transmission times for OPT remain the same with σ or σ', whereas they decrease for LAZY with σ' in comparison with σ.

For any $\sigma \in S$, let $\sigma' = \text{OPT}(\sigma) = \left(f_0^{OPT}, f_1^{OPT}, \ldots, f_{n-1}^{OPT} \right)$, where $f_i^{OPT} \geq f_{i+1}^{OPT}$, $\forall$ i and $\sum_{i=0}^{n-1} f_i^{OPT} = d$ (from Remark 15.3.7). Thus, σ' is a valid job arrival sequence, and therefore $\sigma' \in S$.

From (15.32), we know that for job inter-arrival time sequence $\sigma = (x_0, \ldots, x_n)$ and $\sigma' = \text{OPT}(\sigma) = \left(f_0^{OPT}, \ldots, f_n^{OPT} \right)$, respectively, the transmission times with algorithm LAZY are

$$y_\ell = \frac{d - \sum_{j=1}^{\ell} x_j}{n - \ell},$$

$$f_i = \min_{\ell \leq i}(y_\ell), \tag{15.35}$$

and

$$y'_\ell = \frac{d - \sum_{j=1}^{\ell} f_j^{OPT}}{n - \ell},$$
$$f'_i = \min_{\ell \leq i}(y'_\ell). \tag{15.36}$$

Thus, $(f_i)_{i=1}^n$ and $(f'_i)_{i=1}^n$ are the job transmission times output by algorithm LAZY with input σ and σ', respectively.

We first prove that the energy consumed by algorithm LAZY with σ' as the input is greater than when input is σ, by showing that the transmission times for each job with input σ' is at most as much as with input σ. Using (15.30), we have

$$\frac{d - \sum_{j=1}^{\ell} x_j}{n - \ell} \geq \frac{d - \sum_{j=1}^{\ell} f_j^{OPT}}{n - \ell}, \ \forall \ell.$$

Hence, from (15.35) and (15.36), $y_\ell \geq y'_\ell$, $\forall \ell$. Therefore,

$$\min_{\ell \leq i}(y_\ell) \geq \min_{\ell \leq i}(y'_\ell) \ \forall i,$$
$$\implies f_i \geq f'_i \ \forall i.$$

Since the energy function $g(t)$ is inversely proportional to the transmission time, for algorithm LAZY,

$$g(f'_i) \geq g(f_i) \ \forall i,$$
$$\sum_{i=0}^{n-1} g(f'_i) \geq \sum_{i=0}^{n-1} g(f_i),$$
$$E_L(\sigma') \geq E_L(\sigma),$$

where g is the energy function (Definition 15.3.3). Thus, we have proved (15.33).

From (15.31), we know that $\sigma' = \{f_0^{OPT}, \dots, f_{n-1}^{OPT}\}$ is such that $f_i^{OPT} \geq f_{i+1}^{OPT}$. Therefore, from Lemma 15.3.4, we have that with OPT (YDS-COMMON), the transmission times remain the same for both input job sequences σ and σ'. Hence, OPT uses identical energy for σ or σ', i.e., $E_{OPT}(\sigma') = E_{OPT}(\sigma)$ proving (15.34). ∎

Next, using Lemma 15.3.8, where we have connected the energy cost of algorithm LAZY and that of OPT, with σ and OPT(σ) as the input, respectively, we show that the worst-case inter-arrival sequence that maximizes the competitive ratio of LAZY is such that x_i's are non-increasing.

Theorem 15.3.9 *Let $\mathcal{X} = \{\sigma \in S : \mu_L(\sigma) \geq \mu_L(\sigma'), \forall \sigma' \in S\}$ be the set of inter-arrival time sequences that have the worst competitive ratio for algorithm* LAZY. *Let $S_D \subseteq S$ be such that*

$$S_D = \left\{(x_1, x_2, \dots, x_n) \mid x_i \geq x_{i+1}, \sum_{i=1}^n x_i = d\right\},$$

$\forall i \in \{1, \ldots, n\}$. *Then*

$$\mathcal{X} \cap S_D \neq \phi.$$

Theorem 15.3.9 implies that at least one of the worst inter-arrival sequences belongs to the set S_D.

Proof: Let $\sigma \in \mathcal{X}$. Then consider

$$\sigma^{new} \leftarrow \text{OPT}(\sigma),$$

i.e., σ^{new} is the output of OPT given the input $\sigma \in \mathcal{X}$. Note that $\sigma^{new} \in S_D$ from (15.31). Using Lemma 15.3.8, we have that for algorithm LAZY, $E_L(\sigma^{new}) \geq E_L(\sigma)$, while for OPT, $E_{\text{OPT}}(\sigma^{new}) = E_{\text{OPT}}(\sigma)$.

Hence,

$$\frac{E_L(\sigma^{new})}{E_{\text{OPT}}(\sigma^{new})} \geq \frac{E_L(\sigma)}{E_{\text{OPT}}(\sigma)},$$

and in particular

$$\frac{E_L(\sigma^{new})}{E_{\text{OPT}}(\sigma^{new})} \geq \frac{E_L(\sigma')}{E_{\text{OPT}}(\sigma')},$$

for any $\sigma' \in S$ by the definition of $\mathcal{X}$. Therefore, σ^{new} also belongs to $\mathcal{X}$, and

$$\mathcal{X} \cap S_D \neq \phi.$$

$\blacksquare$

In the light of Theorem 15.3.9, we restrict our attention to the input inter-arrival sequences of the form

$$S_D = \left\{ (x_1, x_2, \ldots, x_n) \mid x_i \geq x_{i+1}, \sum_{i=1}^{n} x_i = d \right\},$$

and prove the following theorem.

Theorem 15.3.10 *The competitive ratio of algorithm* LAZY *is at most e.*

Proof: Note that for $\sigma \in S_D$, the transmission times chosen by algorithm LAZY simplify to

$$f_i = \frac{d - \sum_{k=1}^{i} x_k}{n - i} = \frac{\sum_{k=i+1}^{n} x_k}{n - i},$$

while for OPT $f_i^{\text{OPT}} = x_{i+1}$. Recall that $g(t) = t\left(2^{B/t} - 1\right)$. Thus, the competitive ratio of algorithm LAZY is

$$\mu_L \overset{(a)}{\le} \max_{\sigma \in S_D} \frac{\sum_{i=1}^{n} g(f_i)}{\sum_{i=1}^{n} g(f_i^{OPT})},$$

$$= \max_{\sigma \in S_D} \frac{\sum_{i=1}^{n} g\left(\frac{\sum_{k=i+1}^{n} x_k}{n-i}\right)}{\sum_{i=1}^{n} g(x_{i+1})},$$

$$= \max_{\sigma \in S_D} \frac{g(x_n) + g\left(\frac{x_n + x_{n-1}}{2}\right) + \cdots g\left(\frac{x_n + \cdots + x_1}{n}\right)}{g(x_n) + \cdots + g(x_1)},$$

$$\overset{(b)}{\le} \max_{\sigma \in S_D} \frac{e(g(x_n) + \cdots + g(x_1))}{g(x_n) + \cdots + g(x_1)},$$

$$\le e,$$

where (a) follows from Theorem 15.3.9, while (b) follows since

$$g(x_n) + g\left(\frac{x_n + x_{n-1}}{2}\right) + \cdots g\left(\frac{x_n + \cdots + x_1}{n}\right) \le e \sum_{i=1}^{n} g(x_n)$$

from Lemma 15.3.11. Thus, the competitive ratio of algorithm LAZY is at most e. ∎

Lemma 15.3.11 *Let* $g(x) = x(e^{B/x} - 1)$ *for some constant B. Then for any positive real numbers* $z_1, \ldots, z_n$, *we have*

$$\sum_{j=1}^{n} g\left(\frac{1}{j} \sum_{i=1}^{j} z_i\right) \le e \sum_{j=1}^{n} g(z_j).$$

Proof: Using the expansion for $\exp(x)$, we get

$$g(x) = x\left(\sum_{k=0}^{\infty} \frac{(B/x)^k}{k!} - 1\right) = \sum_{k=1}^{\infty} \frac{C_k}{x^{k-1}},$$

where $C_k = B^k/k!$ for all $k \ge 1$. Let $\psi_k(x) = 1/x^k$ for $k = 0, 1, 2, \ldots$. Then $g(x) = \sum_{k=1}^{\infty} C_k \psi_k(x)$. Thus, to claim the result, it is sufficient to prove that

$$\sum_{j=1}^{n} \psi_k\left(\frac{1}{j} \sum_{i=1}^{j} z_i\right) \le e \sum_{j=1}^{n} \psi_k(z_j). \tag{15.37}$$

It is easy to see that (15.37) is real for $k = 0$ since $\psi_k = 0$. For $k > 0$, the following result is known that follows from an inequality due to [277] – see editorial note in [278], with an explicit proof in [279]:

$$\sum_{j=1}^{n} \psi_k\left(\frac{1}{j} \sum_{i=1}^{j} z_i\right) \le \left(1 + \frac{1}{k}\right)^k \sum_{j=1}^{n} \psi_k(z_j),$$

which implies (15.37) since $\left(1 + \frac{1}{k}\right)^k \le e$. ∎

15.4 Common Deadline with Multiple Servers

In this section, we consider the case where there are multiple identical servers (with the same power function P) to which any incoming job (all jobs are of the same size) can be assigned, and the objective is to minimize the total energy needed to complete all jobs by their common deadline d. Thus, in addition to deciding the transmission time for each job, the algorithm also has to find which job should be processed by which server. We consider the offline case first, and because of the structure of the offline optimal job–server assignment, it will turn out that we can apply algorithm LAZY in each of the servers individually.

The notation is the same as considered in Section 15.3. We describe the theorem only for the case of two servers, but it extends to multiple servers in a straightforward manner. Let the jobs be ordered in terms of their arrival times, and numbered $1, 2, \ldots, n$.

Theorem 15.4.1 *With common deadline d for all jobs, when the common power function P for all servers is convex, there exists an optimal offline schedule where odd-numbered (indexed in order of arrival times) jobs are scheduled on server 1 whereas even-numbered jobs are scheduled on server 2.*

Remark 15.4.2 *The great advantage of Theorem 15.4.1 is that an online algorithm that assigns arriving jobs in a round-robin format to the two servers (odd-numbered jobs to server 1, and even-numbered jobs to server 2), and implements algorithm LAZY in both the servers simultaneously, has a competitive ratio that is same as that of an online algorithm with a single server. For example, at most e from Theorem 15.3.10 for $P(s) = 2^s - 1$. Thus, no extra work is needed for finding an online algorithm in the multiple server case compared to the single server case.*

Proof: [Proof of Theorem 15.4.1] We will use contradiction to prove the result. Let k be the largest job index such that both the kth and the $k + 1^{st}$ jobs have been assigned to the same server; let that be server 1. It is easy to see that since job sizes are the same, and there is a common deadline, any optimal offline algorithm schedules job in the order of their arrival. Let s_k be the time at which the processing of job k starts. Thus, at the time of the start of processing of job k, s_k, some other job, say $k - \ell$ for $\ell \in \{1, \ldots, k - 1\}$, is being processed on server 2. More importantly, job $k - \ell$ is not complete before the start of job $k + 1$, since otherwise, job $k + 1$ would be processed on server 2. Thus, in particular for job $k - \ell$, the transmission time $f_{k-\ell} \geq s_{k+1} - s_k$. See Figure 15.3.

Let $\mathcal{S}_i(t, d)$ be the job processing schedule of server $i = 1, 2$ from time t till the deadline d. We are going to swap $\mathcal{S}_1(s_{k+1}, d)$ with $\mathcal{S}_2(s_{k+2}, d)$, and change or adjust only the transmission time of job $k - \ell$ and job k as shown in Figure 15.3. Let the transmission time of the jth job after swapping be f'_j. In the swapped schedule, the transmission times of only jobs $k - \ell$ and k are changed to

$$f'_{k-\ell} = s_{k+1} - s_{k-\ell}, \text{ and } f'_k = s_{k+2} - s_k,$$

where, importantly,

$$f'_{k-\ell} < f_{k-\ell}, \quad f'_k > f_k, \text{ and } f'_k + f'_{k-\ell} = f_k + f_{k-\ell},$$

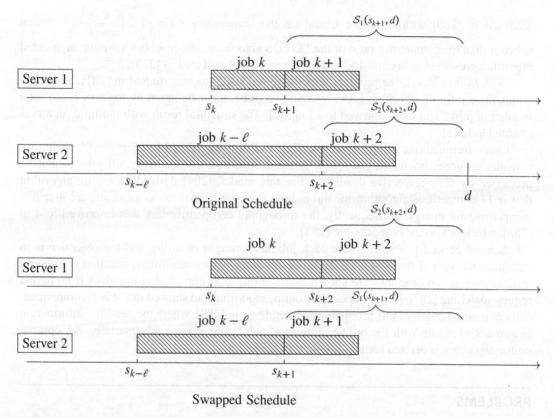

Figure 15.3 Pictorial description of the argument for proving Theorem 15.4.1.

while all other transmission times remain the same as before. Thus, the sum of the transmission times of jobs $k - \ell$ and k remain the same, while $\min\{f'_k, f'_{k-\ell}\} > \min\{f_k, f_{k-\ell}\}$. Thus, the energy used with the swapped schedule is $g(f'_k) + g(f'_{k-\ell}) < g(f_k) + g(f_{k-\ell})$ since the energy function $g(t) = t(2^{B/t} - 1)$ is a convex function.

Thus, we reach a contradiction to the choice of k being the largest index such that both the kth and the $k + 1^{st}$ jobs have been assigned to the same server. ∎

15.5 Notes

The study on speed scaling with deadline constraints discussed in Section 15.2.1 began with [256] for a single server, where the optimal offline algorithm YDS was proposed, and an online algorithm whose competitive ratio was shown to be at most $\alpha^\alpha 2^{\alpha-1}$ for power function $P(s) = s^\alpha$. The LOYDS algorithm was also discussed in [256], for which only a lower bound of α^α was derived on its competitive ratio. The upper bound on the competitive ratio of the LOYDS algorithm (presented in Section 15.2.2) that matches the lower bound was derived in [280]. An alternate algorithm has also been analysed in [280] with an upper bound on the competitive ratio of $2\left(\dfrac{\alpha}{\alpha-1}\right)^{\alpha} e^{\alpha}$, which is better than the competitive ratio of the LOYDS algorithm. The machine learning augmented algorithm presented in Section 15.2.3 was proposed and analysed in [275].

With $P(s) = 2^s - 1$, the problem with common deadlines was studied in [281], where the competitive ratio of algorithm LAZY was shown to be upper bounded by $\log n$ (n is the total number of jobs), and was improved to e in [282]. The structural result with multiple servers is credited to [283].

Other formulations of the speed scaling problem to minimize energy with deadlines consider an upper bound on the speed of the server, and, consequently, all jobs cannot be processed by their respective deadlines. For this model, [284] derived an online algorithm that is 14-competitive algorithm for throughput (number of processed jobs) and $\alpha^{\alpha} + \alpha^2 4^{\alpha}$-competitive for energy. Subsequently, the throughput competitiveness was improved to 4 in [258], which is also the best possible [285].

A more general problem, where each job has a weight or utility and the objective is to maximize the sum of the weight of the processed jobs by their deadlines, was first considered in [286], where job deadlines are known to the online algorithm. Using the ideas from online request matching [287], [286] proposed an online algorithm and showed that it is 2-competitive. A more robust version of this problem was considered in [288], where the deadline information is also not available with the online algorithm and can be chosen adversarially. An optimal online algorithm is derived for this problem in [288].

PROBLEMS

15.1 [289] A brute force implementation of the YDS algorithm, by considering only the arrival and deadline instants for intervals, has complexity $\mathcal{O}(n^3)$, where n is the number of jobs. Show that the YDS algorithm can be implemented with complexity $\mathcal{O}(n^2 \log n)$.

15.2 [280] In this problem we will work towards showing that algorithm YDS is an optimal **offline** algorithm for solving (15.2) for any convex P. We will, however, specialize it for $P(s) = s^{\alpha}$. For a general convex function P, the same procedure applies with a little more work. For $P(s) = s^{\alpha}$, we will write (15.2) as a convex program as follows and consider its KKT conditions.

Let the job arrival time a_j and deadline time d_j sequence be interlaced to form the following sequence $t_0, t_1, t_2, \ldots, t_m$, where $t_i = a_j$ or $t_i = d_j$ for some j and $t_i \leq t_{i+1}$. Thus, $t_0, t_1, t_2, \ldots, t_m$ is an increasing sequence where each instant is either an arrival time or a deadline for some job. Because of the convexity of P, it is easy to argue that the speed chosen by OPT will remain constant throughout $(t_i, t_{i+1}]$. Let $J(i)$ be the set of jobs that can be processed during interval $[t_i, t_{i+1}]$, and $J^{-1}(j)$ be the intervals during which a job j can be processed. Then we can write (15.1) as the following convex optimization problem for $P(s) = s^\alpha$, where w_{ij} represents the work done on task j during time $[t_i, t_{i+1}]$:

$$\min_{w_{ij}} \quad E = \int P(s(t))dt \tag{15.38}$$

$$\text{s.t.} \quad w_j \leq \sum_{i \in J^{-1}(j)} w_{ij}, \, j = 1, \dots, n, \tag{15.39}$$

$$\sum_{i=1}^{m} \left(\frac{\sum_{j \in J(i)} w_{ij}}{t_{i+1} - t_i} \right)^\alpha (t_{i+1} - t_i) \leq E, \tag{15.40}$$

$$w_{ij} \geq 0, \, i = 1, \dots, m, \, j \in J(i), \tag{15.41}$$

where (15.39) captures the constraint that job j has to be complete by its deadline, (15.41) controls the total energy used to satisfy (15.39) where the LHS is the total energy used, and (15.41) ensures that the solution produced by the convex program is non-trivial. Associating a dual variable with each of the three constraints, and enforcing the complementary slackness conditions, show that YDS is an optimal offline algorithm.

15.3 The competitive ratio of the LOYDS algorithm is at least α^α for $P(s) = s^\alpha, \alpha > 1$, even when all jobs have a common deadline. The following input sequence might be helpful.

Let a total of n jobs arrive, with job $i = 0, \dots, n - 1$ arriving at time i with size $\left(\frac{1}{n-i} \right)^{\frac{1}{\alpha}}$. All jobs have the same common deadline of n.

15.4 [275] Prove Theorem 15.2.15 by showing that if the speed of the AVR algorithm is $u(t)$ and that of OPT is $s_o(t)$ at time t, then

$$u(t) = \sum_{j : \tau_j \leq t \leq \tau_j + D} \frac{w_j}{D} \leq 2s_o(t).$$

In particular, prove the following parts by justifying the following inequalities: (15.42), (15.43), and (15.44).

You can use the following information about YDS: YDS processes only one job at a time, and each job throughout its processing time is processed at some constant speed. In particular, with YDS, let $p_j^\star$ be the time for which job j is processed at constant speed $s_j^\star(t) = \frac{w_j}{p_j^\star}$. At time t, with YDS, let job j_t be processed with speed $s_{j_t}^\star(t) = \frac{w_{j_t}}{p_{j_t}^\star}$.

1. Let j be some job with $a_j \leq t \leq a_j + D$. Then

$$\frac{w_j}{p_j^\star} \leq \frac{w_{j_t}}{p_{j_t}^\star} = s_o(t). \tag{15.42}$$

Essentially, show that speed is a non-decreasing function for 'overlapping' jobs.

[Hint: Use the convexity of P, by separating into two cases: jobs that have been completed by time t, and jobs that have arrived by time t but are yet to start getting processed.]

2.

$$\sum_{j:a_j \leq t \leq a_j + D} p_j^\star \leq 2D. \tag{15.43}$$

3.

$$\sum_{j:a_j \leq t \leq a_j + D} w_j \leq s_o(t) \left(\sum_{j:a_j \leq t \leq a_j + D} p_j^\star \right) \leq 2D s_o(t). \tag{15.44}$$

4. Conclude that

$$u(t) = \sum_{j:a_j \leq t \leq a_j + D} \frac{w_j}{D} \leq 2s_o(t). \tag{15.45}$$

15.5 [275] Justify the following inequalities to prove Lemma 15.2.19:

$$\int_{\tau_i}^{\tau_i + D} s_i^\delta(t) dt = \int_{\tau_i}^{\tau_i + D} \frac{1}{\delta D} \left(\int_{t-\delta D}^{t} s_i(t') dt' \right) dt,$$

$$= \int_{\tau_i}^{\tau_i + (1-\delta)D} s_i(t') \left(\int_{t'}^{t'+\delta D} \frac{1}{\delta D} dt \right) dt' = w_i.$$

15.6 [275] Justify the following inequalities to prove Lemma 15.2.20:

$$\int_0^T (s^\delta(t))^\alpha dt = \int_0^T \left(\frac{1}{\delta D} \int_{t-\delta D}^{t} s(t') dt' \right)^\alpha dt,$$

$$\leq \int_0^T \frac{1}{\delta D} \left(\int_{t-\delta D}^{t} (s(t'))^\alpha dt' \right) dt,$$

$$= \int_0^T (s(t))^\alpha \left(\int_{t'}^{t'+\delta D} \frac{1}{\delta D} dt' \right) dt' = \int_0^T (s(t))^\alpha dt.$$

15.7 [275] Justify the following inequalities to prove Lemma 15.2.21:

$$s_i^\delta(t) = \frac{1}{\delta D} \int_{t-\delta D}^{t} s_i(t') dt \leq \frac{1}{\delta D} \int_{\tau_i}^{\tau_i + D} s_i(t') dt' = \frac{w_i}{\delta D} = \frac{u_i(t)}{\delta}.$$

15.8 With $P(s) = 2^s - 1$, if the number of jobs n is not known ahead of time, then the competitive ratio of any online algorithm with the common deadline case is arbitrarily large even when all jobs have the same size of B bits.

[Hint: Consider either $n = 1$ or 2 packets, and common deadline $d = 1$. Consider the number of bits remaining to be transmitted at time $1/2$ and argue that irrespective of the choice made by an online algorithm, the competitive ratio grows exponentially in B.]

15.9 Consider the common deadline problem, where each job has the same size w and a common deadline d, but processing job j requires power given by function P_j. Let there be only two jobs $n = 2$ that arrive at arbitrary times before d, and both $P_j, j = 1, 2$ are convex, but not necessarily equal. Find the optimal offline algorithm for this $n = 2$ case – call it OPT_2 – as a function of P_1, P_2. Iteratively using OPT_2, derive an optimal offline algorithm for the n jobs case, with possibly distinct P_j's for $j = 1, \ldots, n$. The optimal offline algorithm is called MOVERIGHT [290].

CHAPTER 16

Travelling Salesman

16.1 Introduction

In this chapter, we visit a classical combinatorial problem, the travelling salesman problem (TSP). In the offline case, TSP is formulated over an undirected graph, where each edge has a weight, and the objective is to minimize the total edge weight of the tour that starts and ends at the same vertex and visits each vertex of the graph at least once. TSP in the offline case is a very rich problem and has been an object of intense study. In the online setting, TSP can be posed in multiple ways, and we study two of the most prominent versions in this chapter.

The first version we consider involves sites to be visited that belong to a metric space. Consider a walker that can walk at most unit speed. Starting at a fixed site, sites (locations) to be visited in the future belonging to a metric space are revealed sequentially, while the walker is travelling. The goal of the walker is to visit all sites and return to the starting site in the minimum time possible while ensuring that a site is visited only after it has been revealed. This version captures some of the online counterparts of the usual offline TSP applications. For this version, we first show that the competitive ratio of any online algorithm is at least 2, and then present a simple algorithm that achieves the lower bound.

The second version we consider is an exploration problem over an unknown graph. Assume that a walker is at a particular (starting) vertex of an unknown undirected edge weighted graph G. The walker's objective is to visit all the vertices of G and return to the starting vertex over the shortest path. The online restriction is that at any time, only the neighbours of all the visited vertices so far and the associated edge weights are revealed. Thus, each time a walker reaches a new vertex, it has to decide which vertex to visit next, given the partial graph information. This unknown graph exploration version is seemingly more difficult than the site exploration version, and we present the best-known online algorithm with the competitive ratio of at most 16.

16.2 Metric Based Problem Formulation

Consider a metric space $\mathcal{M}$ endowed with a distance measure d, as defined in Definition 6.2.1. Initially, the position of the walker is at the origin o. A set of n requests arrive sequentially, where the ith request arrives at location $\ell_i \in \mathcal{M}$ at time t_i. Thus, a request i is captured by a tuple (ℓ_i, t_i).

The walker can move with at most unit speed and the objective is to visit the locations of all the n requests and return to the origin (called **tour**) in minimum time possible. Since the request

i arrives at time t_i, it can be visited only at time $t \geq t_i$. We call this minimization problem the online travelling salesman problem (OTSP).

Let for an online algorithm $\mathcal{A}$, the total time taken by it to complete the tour be $T_{\mathcal{A}}$. Then the competitive ratio of $\mathcal{A}$ for solving the OTSP is

$$\mu_{\mathcal{A}} = \max_{\sigma} \frac{T_{\mathcal{A}}(\sigma)}{T_{\text{OPT}}(\sigma)}, \tag{16.1}$$

where σ is the arrival sequence of the n requests.

We assume that the metric space $\mathcal{M}$ has the property that the shortest path from x to y, $x, y \in \mathcal{M}$, is continuous, formed by points in $\mathcal{M}$ and has length $d(x, y)$.

Definition 16.2.1 *For any path $P \in \mathcal{M}$, let $|P|$ denote its length. In particular, if path $P = (x_1, x_2, \ldots, x_n)$ in order, then $|P| = \sum_{i=1}^{n-1} d(x_i, x_{i+1})$. Moreover, $|P| \geq d(x_1, x_n)$ from the triangle inequality.*

16.2.1 Lower Bounds

We begin with a simple lower bound that shows that no deterministic online algorithm can have a competitive ratio better than 3/2 for the OTSP.

Lemma 16.2.2 *The competitive ratio of any deterministic online algorithm is at least 3/2 for the OTSP.*

Proof: Consider $\mathcal{M}$ as the real line. Recall that at time 0, the walker is at the origin o. Let there be only one request $n = 1$ at time $t_1 = 1$ with location possibly being either $+1$ or -1. Knowing the request sequence in advance, OPT moves its location to $+1$ (-1) in time 0 to 1 walking at unit speed, and then comes back to the origin at time 2, walking at unit speed from time 1 to 2. Thus, OPT's cost is 2 irrespective of whether the location of the request is $+1$ or -1.

Without knowing where the request is going to arrive, let the location of an online algorithm $\mathcal{A}$ at time 1 be $\ell_{\mathcal{A}}(1)$. If $\ell_{\mathcal{A}}(1) \leq 0$, the request arrives at $+1$, otherwise if $\ell_{\mathcal{A}}(1) > 0$, then the request arrives at -1. In the best case for $\mathcal{A}$, $\ell_{\mathcal{A}}(1) = 0$. Thus, one unit of time has already expired, and $\mathcal{A}$'s location is still the origin. Then to complete the tour it has to travel two units of distance. Since the speed is at most 1, the earliest time at which $\mathcal{A}$ can complete the tour is 3. Thus, the competitive ratio of $\mathcal{A}$, $\mu_{\mathcal{A}} \geq 3/2$. ∎

This lower bound can be generalized for randomized algorithms against oblivious adversaries and we leave that as an exercise in Problem 16.1.

A more non-trivial lower bound even when $\mathcal{M}$ is chosen to be the real line is derived as follows.

Lemma 16.2.3 *With $\mathcal{M}$ as the real line, the competitive ratio of any deterministic online algorithm is at least $\frac{9+\sqrt{17}}{8}$ for the OTSP.*

Proof: Consider $\mathcal{M}$ as the real line. The main idea of the proof is to show that for an algorithm $\mathcal{A}$ if $\mu_{\mathcal{A}} \leq c$ for some constant c, then we construct input that contradicts the choice of c.

The largest value of c for which the contradiction works will give us the best lower bound. In particular, let $c^\star = \frac{9+\sqrt{17}}{8}$, and let for an algorithm $\mathcal{A}$, $\mu_\mathcal{A} \leq c$, where $c < c^\star$.

The request sequence is then constructed as follows. Until time $t = 1$ no requests are made. Then for $\mathcal{A}$ to have $\mu_\mathcal{A} \leq c$, it must be that the location of $\mathcal{A}$ at time 1, $\ell_\mathcal{A}(1) \in [-(2c-3), 2c-3]$, where $2c - 3 < 1$ since $c < c^\star$. To prove this claim, assume to the contrary, and let $\ell_\mathcal{A}(1) > 2c - 3$. Then a request can be made at time 1 at location -1, and the cost of $\mathcal{A}$ will comprise of three terms, the time elapsed till the request, i.e., 1, the time needed for moving from $2c - 3$ to -1, and then from -1 to o, and the total cost for $\mathcal{A}$ is $1 + 2c - 3 + 2 = 2c$. The cost of OPT, however, is only 2. Thus, $\mu_\mathcal{A} \geq c$ contradicts the hypothesis that $\mu_\mathcal{A} \leq c$ if $\ell_\mathcal{A}(1) > 2c - 3$. Switching the signs, we can show similarly that $\ell_\mathcal{A}(1) \geq -(2c - 3)$.

Next, let $\ell_\mathcal{A}(1) \in [-(2c-3), 2c-3]$. At time 1, **two requests are made simultaneously with locations at $+1$ and -1**. Thus, at time $t = 3$, $\mathcal{A}$ cannot have visited both requests made at time 1. Without loss of generality, assume that $\mathcal{A}$ has not visited the requested location -1.

In this case, we show that if $-(7 - 4c) < \ell_\mathcal{A}(3) < 7 - 4c$, then $\mathcal{A}$ cannot have $\mu_\mathcal{A} \leq c$, where again $7 - 4c < 1$ since $c < c^\star$. To prove the claim, let $0 < \ell_\mathcal{A}(3) = 7 - 4c - \delta$. Let one more request arrive at time 3 for location $+1$. Then, starting from $t = 3$, when $\mathcal{A}$ is at $7 - 4c - \delta$, it has to visit location 1 starting from $\ell_\mathcal{A}(3)$, and then visit -1 starting from location $+1$, and then visit o from location -1. Thus, the total cost of $\mathcal{A} = 3 + 1 + (7 - 4c + \delta) + 2 + 1 = 4c + \delta$. The cost of OPT, however, is just 4; OPT could have been at -1 at time 1, reached $+1$ at time 3 (served both requests for $+1$), and returned to o at time 4. Therefore, if $\ell_\mathcal{A}(3) = 7 - 4c - \delta$, then $\mu_\mathcal{A} > c$.

Thus, either $-1 \leq \ell_\mathcal{A}(3) \leq -(7 - 4c)$ or $7 - 4c \leq \ell_\mathcal{A}(3) \leq 1$.

Case 1: $\mathcal{A}$ has not visited $+1$ (that arrived at time 1) by time $t = 3$ and $-1 \leq \ell_\mathcal{A}(3) \leq -(7 - 4c)$ or $7 - 4c \leq \ell_\mathcal{A}(3) \leq 1$.

Case 2: $\mathcal{A}$ has visited $+1$ (that arrived at time 1) by time $t = 3$ and $7 - 4c \leq \ell_\mathcal{A}(3) \leq 1$. Note that we are ruling out the possibility of $\ell_\mathcal{A}(3) < -(7 - 4c)$, since $\mathcal{A}$ has started moving towards $+1$ at time $t = 1$ from a location that is to the left of $(2c - 3)$ and the current time is 3, since $1 + (1 - (2c - 3)) + (1 + (2c - 3)) = 3$. Given the fact that $\mathcal{A}$ has visited $+1$, it cannot be the case that $\ell_\mathcal{A}(3) < -(2c - 3)$, and hence $\ell_\mathcal{A}(3) < -(7 - 4c)$ is not possible.

In both cases, essentially $\mathcal{A}$ is within a distance of $1 - (7 - 4c)$ of either $+1$ or -1 at time $t = 3$ and has not visited -1 and $+1$, respectively. So we consider the case when $\mathcal{A}$ is within a distance of $1 - (7 - 4c)$ of $+1$ at time $t = 3$ and has not visited -1. The other case follows similarly.

Recall that in the case considered, $T_{\text{OPT}} = 4$, where OPT has visited -1 and is currently located at $+1$ at time 3. Thus, for $\mathcal{A}$ to be c-competitive, it has to cross the origin (from right to left) no later than time $4c - 2$, since otherwise, the total cost of $\mathcal{A}$ will be at least $4c + \delta$ (crossing the origin at time $4c - 2 + \delta$, and going to -1 and coming back to the origin) for some $\delta > 0$, making $\mu_\mathcal{A} > c$. Let the time at which $\mathcal{A}$ crosses the origin be $3 + q$. Thus, $3 + q < 4c - 2$ and we get

$$q < 4c - 5. \tag{16.2}$$

At time $3 + q$, **a new request arrives at location** $1 + q$.

Since OPT is at location $+1$ at time 3, it can visit this new request that arrives at time $3 + q$ by moving to location $(1 + q)$ at time $3 + q$ and return to o at time $4 + 2q$. Thus, $T_{\text{OPT}} = 4 + 2q$.

Algorithm $\mathcal{A}$ on the other hand has to incur a cost $T_A = 3 + q + 2(1 + q) + 2 = 7 + 3q$. Thus, the competitive ratio of $\mathcal{A}$ is

$$\mu_A \geq \frac{7 + 3q}{4 + 2q}.$$

Using (16.2), we get

$$c \geq \frac{7 + 3(4c - 5)}{4 + 2(4c - 5)}, \tag{16.3}$$

since by hypothesis, $\mu_A \leq c$ and $\frac{7+3q}{4+2q}$ is a monotonically decreasing function of q. The smallest value of c that satisfies (16.3) is $c^\star = \frac{9 + \sqrt{17}}{8}$, completing the proof. ∎

Next, we present a stronger lower bound of $2 - \epsilon$ for any $\epsilon > 0$ for a special metric space that is defined as the boundary of the unit square.

Lemma 16.2.4 *There exists a metric space $\mathcal{M}$ for which the competitive ratio of any deterministic online algorithm is at least $2 - \epsilon$ for the OTSP, for any $\epsilon > 0$.*

Proof: Consider the boundary $\mathcal{B}$ of a **unit** square as the metric space $\mathcal{M}$, with corner points a, b, c, d, as shown in Figure 16.1. Thus, the locations of all the requests will belong to $\mathcal{B}$, and the walker is only allowed to walk on the boundary $\mathcal{B}$.

Consider the following sets of locations for requests that arrive over time. Let (x, y) be the x and y coordinates of a location. Let $S_{a \to b} = \{(i/n, 0), i = 0, \dots, n\}$, $S_{b \to c} = \{(1, i/n), i = 0, \dots, n\}$, $S_{c \to d} = \{(i/n, 1), i = 0, \dots, n\}$ and $S_{d \to a} = \{(0, i/n), i = 0, \dots, n\}$. We will let n to be large later.

At time 0, $4(n + 1)$ requests arrive, one each for locations in $S_{a \to b} \cup S_{b \to c} \cup S_{c \to d} \cup S_{d \to a}$.

Consider any online algorithm $\mathcal{A}$. Given the request sequence that arrived at time 0, it is easy to see that if $\mathcal{A}$ starts walking along $a \to b$ $(a \to d)$ then it will continue on the path $a \to b \to c \to d \to a$ $(a \to d \to c \to b \to a)$ in sequence to visit all the $4(n + 1)$ request locations, or $\mathcal{A}$ will have a competitive ratio of > 2 (see Problem 16.2). That is, if $\mathcal{A}$ walks by switching between adjacent edges, e.g. (a, b) and (a, d), it will incur more than twice the cost of OPT.

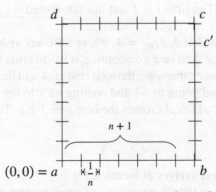

Figure 16.1 Illustration of the metric space as the boundary of the unit square and the location of the input sequence

Thus, we restrict our attention to $\mathcal{A}$ that walks either $a \to b \to c \to d \to a$ or $a \to d \to c \to b \to a$ in sequence, and without loss of generality we assume that $\mathcal{A}$ walks from $a \to b \to c \to d \to a$.

Consider time $2 - 1/n$, when $\mathcal{A}$ is at location $c' = (1, n - 1/n)$, since the walker walks nonstop at speed 1 along $a \to b \to c \to d \to a$. At this time $2 - 1/n$, an additional set of $2(n + 1)$ requests arrive, one each for locations of $S_{a \to b} \cup S_{b \to c}$ that have already been visited by $\mathcal{A}$. Thus, the decision for $\mathcal{A}$ to make at time $2 - 1/n$ is whether to continue on its current path and reach vertex a via $c' \to c \to d \to a$, and then walk from $a \to b \to c'$ and back to a, or first walk backwards along $c' \to b \to a$ and then visit requests belonging to edges (a, d) and (d, c) and reach a again.

Either of the choices that $\mathcal{A}$ has incurs an equal cost, and we count the cost of the first option as follows. From location c' reaching a back following path $c' \to b \to a$ incurs a cost of $2 - 1/n$, and then walking from $a \to d \to c \to d \to a$ incurs an additional cost of 4. Including the cost till time $2 - 1/n$, the total cost of $\mathcal{A}$ is $2 - 1/n + 2 - 1/n + 4 = 8 - 2/n$.

OPT, on the other hand, knowing the request sequence arriving in advance at time $2 - \frac{1}{n}$, follows the path $a \to d \to c \to b \to a$ and incurs a total cost of 4.

Thus, the competitive ratio of $\mathcal{A}$ is

$$\mu_{\mathcal{A}} \geq \frac{8 - 2/n}{4} = 2 - \epsilon,$$

where $\epsilon > 0$ can be made arbitrarily small by choosing a large enough n. ∎

In the next section, we consider a specific greedy algorithm and bound its competitive ratio.

16.2.2 Upper Bounds

Algorithm: Plan at Home (PAH)

1. Whenever the walker is at the origin, it starts to follow an optimal route that visits all the arrived (revealed) requests so far that are yet to be visited, and comes back to the origin o.

2. If at time t a new request is revealed with location x, then the algorithm takes one of the following two actions depending on its current position c, i.e., $\ell_{\mathcal{A}}(t) = c$:

   (a) If $d(x, o) > d(c, o)$, then the server goes back to the origin (following the shortest path from c to o, and next follows the rule specified in Case 1.

   (b) If $d(x, o) \leq d(c, o)$, then the server ignores the new request, and continues on its current tour until it arrives at the origin, and next follows the rule specified in Case 1.

Algorithm PAH is essentially a greedy algorithm, that tries to follow the optimal solution to the TSP given the current set of unvisited locations, and takes a detour at a new request arrival only if it is better to restart the tour than to continue on the current one, given the updated set of unvisited locations.

Remark 16.2.5 *Algorithm PAH is not a polynomial time algorithm, since it involves finding an optimal solution to the TSP for a given set of requests. In Problem 16.4, we discuss a polynomial time algorithm and upper bound its competitive ratio.*

Theorem 16.2.6 *Algorithm PAH is 2-competitive for the OTSP.*

Proof: The main idea of the proof is to concentrate on the time and the location of the last, the nth, request, and using which, we find an upper bound on the cost of the PAH algorithm as a function of a lower bound on the cost of OPT.

Using our notation t_n is the time at which the last request arrives at location x_n. Let $\mathcal{T}^{OPT}$ be OPT's tour or path with the least cost that starts at the origin, visits all requested locations, and returns to the origin. Then we have $T_{OPT} \geq \max\{t_n, |\mathcal{T}^{OPT}|\}$, since the nth request cannot be visited before its arrival time t_n, and trivially by definition $T_{OPT} \geq |\mathcal{T}^{OPT}|$, since the walker speed is at most unity.

In the following, we analyse the PAH algorithm's cost with respect to that of OPT depending on the location of the PAH algorithm at time t_n.

1. PAH is at the origin at time t_n. Let the set of request locations that PAH algorithm has not visited till time t_n be U_n. In this case, by the definition of the PAH algorithm, it starts an optimal tour $\mathcal{T}_n^{PAH}$ beginning from the origin at time t_n and visits all locations in $U_n \cup \{x_n\}$ and returns to the origin. Clearly, since $U_n \cup \{x_n\} \subseteq \{x_1, \ldots, x_n\}$, the cost of the partial optimal tour made by the PAH algorithm $|\mathcal{T}_n^{PAH}| \leq |\mathcal{T}^{OPT}|$. Therefore,

$$T_{PAH} = t_n + |\mathcal{T}_n^{PAH}| \leq t_n + |\mathcal{T}^{OPT}| \leq 2T_{OPT}.$$

2. PAH is not at the origin at time t_n. Let the current location of algorithm PAH at time t_n be c_n. Then depending on c_n, we consider further two sub-cases.

   (a) $d(o, x_n) > d(o, c_n)$. In this case, the current location of PAH is closer to the origin than the nth request's location. Hence, algorithm PAH will go back to the origin and attempt to start an optimal tour of the currently unvisited locations. PAH will reach the origin at time $t_n + d(o, c_n) \leq t_n + d(o, x_n)$. Once PAH reaches the origin, and since x_n is the last requested location, PAH undertakes the last optimal tour $\mathcal{T}_n^{PAH}$ starting from the origin thereafter. As in case 1 above, $|\mathcal{T}_n^{PAH}| \leq |\mathcal{T}^{OPT}|$, and the cost of the PAH algorithm is

$$t_n + d(o, c_n) + |\mathcal{T}_n^{PAH}| \leq t_n + d(o, x_n) + |\mathcal{T}^{OPT}| \leq t_n + d(o, x_n) + T_{OPT}. \quad (16.4)$$

   For OPT, we claim that

$$T_{OPT} \geq t_n + d(o, x_n), \quad (16.5)$$

   since the nth request cannot be visited before its arrival time t_n, and after visiting x_n, OPT has to return to the origin. Comparing (16.4) and (16.5), we get the required result that $T_{PAH} \leq 2T_{OPT}$.

   (b) $d(o, x_n) \leq d(o, c_n)$. In this case, algorithm PAH ignores the last arrived request at x_n and continues on its optimal tour that it started when it visited the origin the last time, and the optimal tour finishes at the origin. Let at time t_n, the tour or path be $\mathcal{T}_n^{PAH}$ that algorithm PAH has embarked upon when it visited the origin the last time. Let I_n be the set of request locations that PAH has ignored since beginning the tour $\mathcal{T}_n^{PAH}$, where most recently it has ignored x_n, i.e., $x_n \in I_n$.

   Among the request locations that belong to I_n, let x_f be the location that OPT visits the earliest, and let the arrival time of the request located at x_f be $t_f \leq t_n$. Let $P_{I_n}^{\star}$ be the shortest path that starts at x_f, visits all locations in I_n and terminates at o. Then following the argument above,

$$T_{\text{OPT}} \geq t_f + |P^\star_{I_n}|. \tag{16.6}$$

Next, we upper bound the cost of the PAH algorithm. Consider time t_f, where algorithm PAH ignored the request that arrived at location x_f and continued on its path $\mathcal{T}_n^{PAH}$. Since PAH ignores x_f that arrives at time t_f, from the definition of the PAH algorithm we have

$$d(o, x_f) \leq d(o, c_f),$$

where c_f is the location of the PAH algorithm at time t_f. This implies that PAH has travelled at least a distance of $d(o, x_f)$ in path $\mathcal{T}_n^{PAH}$. Therefore, at time t_f, the distance that PAH has to cover following $\mathcal{T}_n^{PAH}$ to reach the origin for the first time is at most $|\mathcal{T}_n^{PAH}| - d(o, x_f)$, since $|\mathcal{T}_n^{PAH}|$ is the total length of the path $\mathcal{T}_n^{PAH}$ that starts and ends at the origin. Thus, we get that PAH arrives at the origin at the end of $\mathcal{T}_n^{PAH}$ at time no later than $t_f + |\mathcal{T}_n^{PAH}| - d(o, x_f)$.

Once PAH reaches the origin, it embarks on its last tour or path $\mathcal{T}_{n+1}^{PAH}$ to cover all the uncovered request locations belonging to I_n using an optimal tour or path. By the definition of $P^\star_{I_n}$, we have

$$|\mathcal{T}_{n+1}^{PAH}| \leq d(o, x_f) + |P^\star_{I_n}|.$$

Thus, the overall cost of the PAH algorithm is

$$
\begin{aligned}
T_{\text{PAH}} &\leq t_f + |\mathcal{T}_n^{PAH}| - d(o, x_f) + |\mathcal{T}_{n+1}^{PAH}|, \\
&\leq t_f + |\mathcal{T}_n^{PAH}| - d(o, x_f) + d(o, x_f) + |P^\star_{I_n}|, \\
&= t_f + |\mathcal{T}_n^{PAH}| + |P^\star_{I_n}|. \tag{16.7}
\end{aligned}
$$

Clearly, $|\mathcal{T}_n^{PAH}| \leq T_{\text{OPT}}$. Combining this with (16.6) and (16.7), we get the required result that

$$T_{\text{PAH}} \leq 2T_{\text{OPT}}.$$

■

Thus, in the light of Lemma 16.2.4, we conclude that algorithm PAH is an optimal online algorithm over arbitrary metric spaces. In the next section, we discuss an alternate formulation of the online TSP problem where it is cast as an exploration problem over unknown graphs.

16.3 Graph Based Problem Formulation

In this section, we consider a graph based formulation for the OTSP, and call it G-OTSP. Let $G = (V, E)$ be an undirected connected graph. Each edge $e = (u, v) \in E$ has a non-negative real weight w_e, also called the length or the cost of edge e. The walker starts at a particular node

$s \in V$, and the goal of the walker is to visit all nodes of V and return to s while covering the smallest total length.

The online-ness of the problem is enforced via the constraint that the walker at time t is only aware of the edges e (and their lengths) for which it has visited at least one end-point of e by time t. Whenever a walker visits a node v it becomes aware of all edges (and their lengths) that are incident on v, and all the neighbours of v. Traversing an edge, the walker incurs a cost equal to the edge length, and the problem is to find a tour or path that visits all vertices of V and returns to the start vertex s with minimum total length.

For an online algorithm $\mathcal{A}$, let its total length be $L_{\mathcal{A}}$ to solve G-OTSP. Then the competitive ratio of $\mathcal{A}$ for the G-OTSP is

$$\mu_{\mathcal{A}} = \max_{\sigma} \frac{L_{\mathcal{A}}(\sigma)}{L_{\text{OPT}}(\sigma)}. \tag{16.8}$$

16.3.1 Identical Edge Lengths

When the lengths of all edges are equal, we consider the depth-first-search (DFS) algorithm and show that it achieves a competitive ratio of at most 2. The DFS algorithm chooses any one unexplored neighbour (if it exists) of the current node and visits it. If there is no unexplored neighbour, then the algorithm backtracks to the previous node (using the edge it used to get to the current node) and performs the same procedure. It is easy to construct graphs for which DFS is not OPT.

Algorithm 28 Algorithm DFS

Intialize $x = o$ the starting vertex and $\mathbf{s} = \varnothing$
Search (x (vertex), $\mathbf{s}$ (sequence of vertices))
The walker is currently at vertex x
if there is an unvisited vertex node z that is a neighbour of x **then**
    visit z, and execute Search (z, $\mathbf{s} = \mathbf{s} \cup \{x\}$) % x is appended to $\mathbf{s}$ in order
else
    if $\mathbf{s} \neq \varnothing$ **then**,
        let $\mathbf{s}' = \mathbf{s} \backslash \{y\}$ where y is the last vertex of $\mathbf{s}$,
        i.e., $\mathbf{s}'$ is the sequence of vertices obtained by removing y from $\mathbf{s}$.
        go back to y, execute Search (y, $\mathbf{s}'$)
    else
        Halt
    end if
end if

Theorem 16.3.1 DFS *is 2-competitive for the G-OTSP when all edge lengths are equal.*

Proof: Without loss of generality, assume that each edge length is one. With graph $G = (V, E)$, let the set of edges that the algorithm DFS visits be S. Clearly, S is a spanning tree[1] of G,

---

[1] A spanning tree T of an undirected graph $G = (V, E)$ is a subgraph that is a tree which includes all of the vertices of G, and T has $|V| - 1$ edges.

and algorithm DFS traverses each edge exactly twice. Thus, the cost of algorithm DFS is $= 2(|V| - 1)$. Moreover, for OPT, $L_{OPT} \geq |V|$, since each vertex has to be visited (thus at least $|V| - 1$ edges have to be traversed), and the algorithm has to return to the starting vertex paying an additional cost equal to the edge length. Thus,

$$\mu_{DFS} \leq 2.$$

■

A complementary lower bound to Theorem 16.3.2 is presented next.

Theorem 16.3.2 [291] *The competitive ratio of any algorithm for the G-OTSP when all edge lengths are equal is at least $2 - \epsilon$ for any $\epsilon > 0$.*

16.3.2 Planar Graphs with Arbitrary Edge Costs

In this section, we generalize the restriction of equal edge weights made in Section 16.3.1 for the case when the underlying graph is planar. With unequal edge weights, we will consider algorithm SHORTCUT, whose definition needs the following preliminaries.

Definition 16.3.3 *Throughout the execution of the algorithm, a vertex of V will be classified in one of three mutually exclusive ways:*

- **visited** *A vertex that has been visited by the walker is called a **visited** vertex.*

- **boundary** *An unvisited vertex that is a neighbour of a visited vertex is called a **boundary** vertex.*

- **unknown** *A vertex that is neither a visited nor a boundary vertex is an **unknown** vertex.*

Definition 16.3.4 *Throughout the execution of the algorithm, an edge of E will be classified in one of three mutually exclusive ways:*

- **explored** *An edge is an **explored** edge if both its endpoints are visited.*

- **boundary** *An edge is a **boundary** edge if exactly one of its endpoints is visited.*

- **unknown** *An edge that is neither explored nor a boundary edge is an **unknown** edge.*

Definition 16.3.5 *For two vertices u, v that have an edge between them, $|(u, v)|$ denotes the length of the edge between u and v.*

Definition 16.3.6 *At any time t, let $d(u, v)$ be the length of the shortest path known between vertices u and v using only the explored and the boundary edges at time t.*

The next definition is crucial for defining and analysing SHORTCUT.

Definition 16.3.7 *A boundary edge (u, v) blocks a boundary edge (y, z) if*

$$|(u, v)| < |(y, z)| \quad and \quad d(y, u) + |(u, v)| < (1 + \delta)|(y, z)|$$

*for some $\delta > 0$. A boundary edge (y, z) is called a **shortcut** if no other boundary edge blocks (y, z).*

> ## Example 16.3.8
>
> *For an example of a shortcut edge or a blocked edge, see Figures 16.2 and 16.3.*

Now we are ready to define the algorithm SHORTCUT. The pseudocode for SHORTCUT is given in Algorithm 29, where the set Block(v, w) is the set of edges that block the edge (v, w), and Incident(y) is the set of edges incident to y.

The basic idea of SHORTCUT is that the walker is going to conduct a DFS but with conditional jumps. DFS is conducted as long as the edge is not a blocked edge. Let the walker be at vertex v and considering traversing a boundary edge (v, w). If (v, w) is a shortcut, then (v, w) is traversed at this time by the walker. Otherwise, if (v, w) is not a shortcut, then the traversal of (v, w) is deferred.

Continuing like this, if the walker traverses a boundary edge (x, y) at time t, that makes y visited and (x, y) explored. Because of the traversal of (x, y), some other boundary edge, say (a, b), might become a shortcut. Then, for edge (a, b), a **jump** edge is added from y to b. Jump edge essentially stands for the shortest path between y and b that the algorithm is aware of at that time. If the algorithm directs the jump edge y to b to be traversed at any time, then the walker will traverse the shortest path between y and b that it is aware of at that time.

Two examples of the execution of the SHORTCUT algorithm are provided in Figures 16.2 and 16.3.

Remark 16.3.9 *An edge which has become unblocked, after having previously been blocked, may become blocked again. This may be the case if a new shorter path from an unblocked edge to another boundary edge is discovered because of visiting new vertices. If this is the case, then the jump edge created on the first unblocking time is deleted. If the jump edge is not deleted on an edge becoming blocked again, Example 1 [292] shows that the competitive ratio of SHORTCUT can be arbitrarily large.*

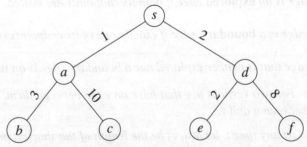

Figure 16.2 s is the starting node. Beginning at s, edge (s, a) is a shortcut, and edge (s, d) is blocked by edge (s, a) for any $\delta > 0$. Thus, SHORTCUT traverses edge (s, a) first. On reaching a, edge (a, b) is a shortcut, while edge (a, c) is blocked by edge (a, b). Thus, edge (a, b) is traversed. Once (a, b) is traversed, (a, c) is unblocked and a jump edge between b and c is added and traversed. Continuing on, the path followed by the SHORTCUT algorithm is $s \to a \to b \to a \to c \to a \to s \to d \to e \to d \to f \to d \to s$.

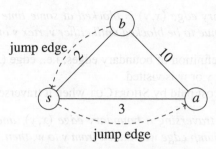

Figure 16.3 s is the starting node, and both a and b are boundary nodes. To begin with, edge (s, b) is a shortcut, while (s, a) is blocked by (s, b). Thus, the SHORTCUT algorithm traverses (s, b). Reaching b, (s, a) is now unblocked since edge (s, b) has been explored and no longer a boundary edge, and (s, a) becomes a shortcut. Hence, a jump edge $(b \rightarrow s \rightarrow a)$ is added (since that is the shortest path) and not (b, a), and is traversed next. Finally, the algorithm returns to s from a.

Algorithm 29 SHORTCUT

Input δ

Procedure ShortCut $(x, y \in V, G = (V, E))$

% Traveling from x, the searcher visits y for the first time

for each boundary edge (v, w) **do**

    if visiting y caused the set Block(v, w) to become empty **then**

        add a jump edge (y, w) at the end of Incident(y) and Incident(w)

    end if

end for

for each boundary edge $(y, z) \in$ Incident(y) **do**

    if z is a boundary vertex and (y, z) is a SHORTCUT **then**

        Traverse the edge (y, z)

        ShortCut (y, z, G)

    else if z is a boundary vertex and (y, z) is a jump edge

        Traverse the shortest known path between y and z

        ShortCut (y, z, G)

    end if

end for

Return to x along the shortest known path

Lemma 16.3.10 *The walker using* SHORTCUT *visits all the nodes of V.*

The proof is simple by following the definition and can be proven using contradiction, and we leave it as an exercise in Problem 16.5.

Next, we identify an important property of SHORTCUT.

Fact 16.3.11 *If a boundary edge (x, y) is blocked at some time by another boundary edge (v, w), then (x, y) will continue to be blocked until either vertex y or w is visited.*

This is true from the definition of boundary edges, i.e., edge (x, y) and edge (v, w) remain boundary edges until either y or w is visited.

Next, we quantify the cost paid by SHORTCUT when it traverses a jump edge.

Lemma 16.3.12 *If after traversing a boundary edge (x, y), another boundary edge (v, w) becomes a shortcut, and a jump edge was added from y to w, then*

$$d(y, w) \leq (2 + \delta)|(v, w)|.$$

Proof: Since edge (v, w) became a shortcut after the traversal of edge (x, y), no other edge blocks edge (v, w) after the visit of y. From Fact 16.3.11, this implies that before y was visited, there was an edge incident on y, say (y, z), that blocked edge (v, w). Therefore, from Definition 16.3.7, we have

$$d(y, v) < (1 + \delta)|(v, w)|,$$

discounting $|(y, z)|$ which is ≥ 0. Therefore, using the triangle inequality,

$$d(y, w) \leq |(v, w)| + d(y, v) < (2 + \delta)|(v, w)|.$$

∎

Next, we present the main result of this section, which needs the following definition.

Definition 16.3.13 *An edge is defined to be **charged** in two ways. When the edge (x, y) is a shortcut and is traversed, then it is called charged. In this case, the charge is just the length of the shortcut edge (x, y). Consider the case when after traversing a boundary edge (x, y), another boundary edge (v, w) became a shortcut, and a jump edge was added from y to w. Moreover, if the jump edge y to w is traversed, then the edge (v, w) is defined to be charged, and the charge is the length of the shortest path from y to w. The sum of the lengths of the charged edges is essentially the total length of SHORTCUT.*

Theorem 16.3.14 SHORTCUT *is 16-competitive for the G-OTSP.*

Proof: For the cost of SHORTCUT, we will count the length of the charged edges. Let the set of charged edges, Definition 16.3.13, be C. For a set S of edges, we denote $L(S) = \sum_{(x,y) \in S} |(x, y)|$.

Consider any edge $(x, y) \in C$. If (x, y) was a shortcut, then its charge was just the length $|(x, y)|$, while if it was a jump edge, then its charge was $d(w, y)$ for some vertex w. Thus, in both cases, from Lemma 16.3.12, we know that the charge for any edge (x, y) that is part of C is at most $(2 + \delta)|(x, y)|$. Thus, the total length or charge of the path chosen by SHORTCUT is at most

$$\sum_{(x,y) \in C} 2(2 + \delta)|(x, y)| \leq 2(2 + \delta)L(C), \tag{16.9}$$

where the additional factor of 2 accounts for the fact that DFS that returns to the starting vertex s traverses each edge in C twice, once in each direction.

Consider any minimum spanning tree (MST) denoted as MST of G, and among all such MST's choose the one that maximizes the number of edges shared between MST and C, or minimizes the number of edges in C\MST, and call it $MST^\star$. In particular,

$$MST^\star = \arg\min_{MST(G)} \text{Edges(C\textbackslash MST)}. \tag{16.10}$$

Consider the claim (proved in Lemma 16.3.15)

$$L(C) \le (1 + 2/\delta)L(MST^\star). \tag{16.11}$$

Clearly, for OPT, $L_{OPT} \ge |MST(G)|$ for any $MST(G)$, since all vertices of G have to be explored. Then choosing $\delta = 2$, from (16.9) and (16.11), we get that SHORTCUT is 16-competitive. ∎

From here on, we concentrate on proving the following main result.

Lemma 16.3.15 $L(C) \le (1 + 2/\delta)L(MST^\star)$.

Proof: Consider a fixed planar embedding[2] of $MST^\star \cup C$. An edge in $C\backslash MST^\star$ is called a **chord**. Chords are essentially edges used by the SHORTCUT algorithm that are not part of $MST^\star$. For an illustration, see Figure 16.4. Let W be a closed walk obtained by walking around the planar embedding of $MST^\star$ as shown in Figure 16.5, where note that each edge of $MST^\star$ is included twice in W, and

$$L(W) = 2L(MST^\star). \tag{16.12}$$

To visualize, W can be thought of as a perimeter of a polygon by inflating W outwards, and chords are the extra connections made between vertices of V, as shown in Figure 16.6. When we refer to W as a simple curve, we essentially cut W at one of its vertices and make W an open curve. For example, if we cut W at d in Figure 16.6, then $W = da'ea''ca'''f''bf'''sfad$.

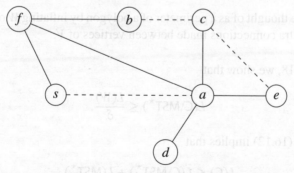

Figure 16.4 Solid edges represent the $MST^\star$ while dashed edges (called chords) represent $C\backslash MST^\star$.

---

[2] A graph $G = (V, E)$ is said to be planar if it can be drawn on the plane such that no two edges of G intersect at a point other than a vertex. Such a drawing of a planar graph is called a planar embedding of the graph.

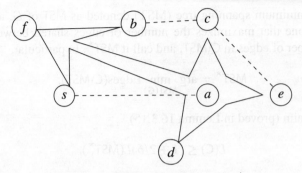

Figure 16.5 Solid edges represent the closed walk W over MST*.

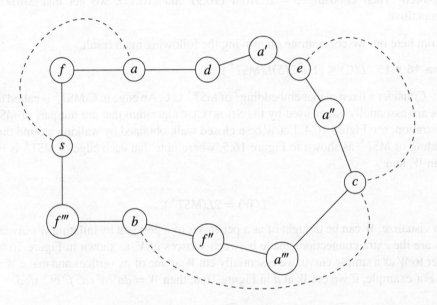

Figure 16.6 W can be thought of as a perimeter of a polygon by inflating W outwards, and chords (dashed lines) are extra connections made between vertices of V.

In Lemma 16.3.18, we show that

$$L(C \backslash MST^\star) \leq \frac{L(W)}{\delta}, \tag{16.13}$$

which together with (16.12) implies that

$$
\begin{aligned}
L(C) &\leq L(C \backslash MST^\star) + L(MST^\star), \\
&\leq L(MST^\star)/\delta + L(MST^\star), \\
&\leq (2 + 2/\delta)L(MST^\star).
\end{aligned}
$$

∎

Now only the proof of Lemma 16.3.18 remains. Before proving Lemma 16.3.18, we need to prove an intermediate Lemma 16.3.17, which we do as follows. Let a chord (x, y) be called **inside** of another chord (v, w) if in traversing W, the vertices are encountered in any of the following orders, $vxyw, vyxw, wyxv,$ or $wxyv$.

Consider any chord (x, y), and denote by $W(x, y)$ the portion of W between x and y. For example, as shown in Figure 16.6, for chord (b, c), $W(b, c) = (b, f'', a''', c)$ and $|W(b, c)| = |(b, f'')| + |(f'', a''')| + |(a''', c)|$.

Definition 16.3.16 *We define a chord (x, y) to be* **good** *if*

$$L(W(x, y)) \geq (1 + \delta)|(x, y)|.$$

Essentially, a good chord means that compared to the path from x to y in MST* *(that has length $L(W(x, y)))$, chord (x, y) has a smaller length.*

We next prove that all chords are good.

Lemma 16.3.17 *All chords are good.*

Proof: We use contradiction to prove this claim, i.e., chord (x, y) is not good, $L(W(x, y)) < (1 + \delta)|(x, y)|$. We define an edge (v, w) to be **heavy** if $(v, w) \in W(x, y)$ and $|(v, w)| \geq |(x, y)|$. We will show that there is **at least one heavy edge in** $W(x, y)$. Consider the time t when (x, y) was charged, or equivalently the time that y was first visited. We claim that at time t, there must be another boundary edge in $W(x, y)$, since $W(x, y)$ is a path from a visited vertex x to a boundary vertex y. For example, it could be either (x, z) for some z or some (v, w) as shown in Figure 16.7.

Let (v, w) be the first such boundary edge encountered when travelling from x to y on $W(x, y)$. It is easy to see that $d(x, v) + |(v, w)| \leq L(W(x, y))$, and since $L(W(x, y)) < (1 + \delta)|(x, y)|$ from the contradiction hypothesis, we have

$$d(x, v) + |(v, w)| < (1 + \delta)|(x, y)|. \tag{16.14}$$

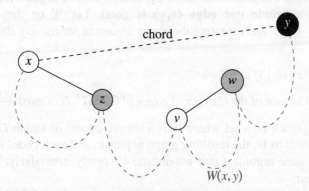

Figure 16.7 Grey shaded vertices are possible boundary vertices. Since (x, y) is charged and traversed, x was a visited vertex and y was a boundary vertex just before it was visited. If z is unvisited, then (x, z) is a boundary edge. Otherwise, starting from (x, z), find the first unvisited vertex w on $W(x, y)$. It could be that $w = y$. Then the edge incident on w, (v, w), is a boundary edge.

Recall that edge (x, y) is a charged edge, i.e., it must have been a shortcut at the time when it was charged. Combining (16.14) with the definition of an edge being a shortcut, Definition 16.3.13, we get

$$|(x, y)| \leq |(v, w)|, \tag{16.15}$$

since otherwise edge (x, y) would have been blocked by edge (v, w), and hence not charged. Thus, there is at least one (v, w) heavy edge in $W(x, y)$.

Next, we want to show that there is at **least one heavy edge of** $W(x, y)$ **that has not been charged**. We again follow a contradiction argument and assume that all heavy edges of $W(x, y)$ have been charged. Among the heavy edges of $W(x, y)$, let (v, w) be the edge that is charged last, where, without loss of generality, let v be visited before w, and consider time t' when edge (v, w) was charged.

Remove edge (v, w) and add edge (x, y) to $W(x, y)$ and call it $W' = W(x, y) \cup (x, y) \backslash (v, w)$. Consider a path p_{vw} from v to w in W', and let (a, b) be the first boundary edge encountered on p_{vw}. Simple argument shows that

$$d(v, a) + |(a, b)| \leq L(W(x, y)) + |(x, y)| - |(v, w)|.$$

Using (16.15), and the hypothesis that we began with that $L(W(x, y)) < (1 + \delta)|(x, y)|$, we can conclude that

$$d(v, a) + |(a, b)| < (1 + \delta)|(v, w)|.$$

Now, since (v, w) is a charged heavy edge by hypothesis, it must be the case that $|(a, b)| \geq |(v, w)|$, since otherwise (a, b) would have blocked by (v, w) (Definition 16.3.7).

This implies that (a, b) is a heavy edge (since $|(a, b)| \geq |(v, w)| \geq |(x, y)|$), and (a, b) by definition is a boundary edge and hence not charged by SHORTCUT. Therefore, $(a, b) \in \text{MST}^{\star}$.

Thus, we get that either $\text{MST}^{\star} \cup (x, y) \backslash (v, w)$ which is an MST that has a lower cost than MST $\text{MST}^{\star}$ when $|(v, w)| > |(x, y)|$, contradicting the fact that $\text{MST}^{\star}$ is an MST, or $\#\text{Edges}(C \backslash \text{MST}^{\star} \cup (x, y) \backslash (v, w)) < \#\text{Edges}(C \backslash \text{MST}^{\star})$ when $|(v, w)| = |(x, y)|$, contradicting the fact that $\text{MST}^{\star}$ satisfies (16.10).

Therefore, we reach a contradiction to the hypothesis that we began with, i.e., $L(W(x, y)) < (1 + \delta)|(x, y)|$, and conclude that **edge** (x, y) **is good**. Let W be the curve formed by replacing $W(x, y)$ by (x, y), and repeating the above argument recursively shows that all chords are good. ∎

Finally, we prove (16.13) as follows.

Lemma 16.3.18 *The sum of the charges of edges of* $C \backslash \text{MST}^{\star}$ *is at most* $\frac{L(W)}{\delta}$.

Proof: Let $\mathcal{W}_k = \{(W, k)\}$ be a set where W is a simple curve[3] of length $L(W)$, and adding a set $c_1, \ldots, c_k$ of k chords to W, the resulting graph is planar, and each chord is good (Definition 16.3.16), using the same argument that we did most recently, recursively. Then consider the optimization problem

$$T(L(W), k) = \sup_{\mathcal{W}_k} \sum_{i=1}^{k} |c_i|,$$

---

[3] Recall that W is the closed walk obtained by walking around the planar embedding of $\text{MST}^{\star}$ as shown in Figure 16.5.

where $|c_i|$ is the length of chord $i \in \mathcal{W}_k$. To re-emphasize, the supremum is over $\mathcal{W}_k$, i.e., all possible simple curves W and all possible ways of adding k chords to W the resulting graph is planar, and each chord is good.

It is an easy exercise (Problem 16.6) to show that $T(L(W), k)$ follows the following recursive relation

$$T(L(W), 0) = 0 \quad \text{and}$$

$$T(L(W), k) \leq T(L(W) - (1 + \delta)|(x, y)| + |(x, y)|, k - 1) + |x, y|, \tag{16.16}$$

where (x, y) is a good chord. Moreover, the solution of this recurrence satisfies

$$T(L(W), k) \leq \frac{L(W)}{\delta}. \tag{16.17}$$

Note that the bound in (16.17) is independent on k which appears counter-intuitive. The bound is inherently capturing the fact that there is an in-built limitation to how many good chords can be added to any simple curve W.

Notice that SHORTCUT is essentially adding chords belonging to set $\mathcal{W}_k$, since each chord it creates is good, and the graph MST $\cup$ C is planar. Thus, the sum of the charges of edges of $C \backslash MST^\star = T(L(W), k')$ for an appropriate k', which is at most $\max_k T(L(W), k) \leq \frac{L(W)}{\delta}$, proving (16.13), from which Lemma 16.3.15 follows.   ∎

16.4 Notes

The metric based problem formulation was considered in [293], where the PAH algorithm, together with the lower bounds presented in the chapter, were derived. Subsequently, [294], showed the existence of a polynomial–time algorithm for general metric spaces which is 2.65-competitive, while for Euclidean metric spaces it is $2 + \epsilon$-competitive for any $\epsilon > 0$. An optimal algorithm for the real line was derived in [295] with a competitive ratio of 1.64. For the non-negative real line, [296] gives an optimal online algorithm with a competitive ratio of 3/2.

For the G-OTSP, the SHORTCUT algorithm that is 16-competitive was proposed in [297] for planar graphs. In [292], a simpler analysis was provided for the SHORTCUT algorithm, where it was shown that its competitive ratio is at most 16 even for any class of graphs with bounded genus. The fact that the SHORTCUT algorithm is not constant competitive for arbitrary graphs was also shown in [292]. The 2-competitive DFS based algorithm presented in Section 16.3.1 for the equal edge weights was analysed in [291]. A lower bound of $2 - \epsilon$ is also shown for the equal edge weights in [291] by constructing F-shaped graphs, where the topmost corner point is the starting vertex.

Non-trivial lower bounds of 5/2 and 10/3 on the competitive ratio for any online algorithm for the G-OTSP have been derived in [298] and [299], respectively. Nearest neighbour (NN) algorithm is also considered for this model, which repeatedly visits the unexplored vertex that is closest to the current vertex. The competitive ratio for the greedy algorithm is $\mathcal{O}(\log n)$ as shown by [300] that is discussed in Problem 16.8. This analysis for NN is tight even on planar unit-weight graphs [301].

PROBLEMS

16.1 Extend Lemma 16.2.2 to randomized algorithms.

16.2 Recall the input sequence arriving at time 0 in the proof of Lemma 16.2.4. Show that if any online algorithm $\mathcal{A}$ starts walking along $a \to b$ ($a \to d$), then it will continue on path $a \to b \to c \to d \to a$ ($a \to d \to c \to b \to a$) in sequence to visit all the $4(n+1)$ request locations, or $\mathcal{A}$ will have a competitive ratio of > 2.

16.3 Show that if the metric space is the whole of the unit square and not just its boundary, the competitive ratio of any deterministic online algorithm is at least $\frac{4+2\sqrt{2}}{4} - \epsilon$ for the OTSP, for any $\epsilon > 0$.

16.4 [293] (Polynomial-time algorithm for OTSP) Let APPROX be a polynomial–time offline algorithm that can approximate the length of the optimal TSP tour over any set of locations belonging to S with an approximation ratio a. Let $T_{\text{APPROX}}(S)$ be the optimal tour over the set of locations in S starting and terminating at the origin.

Algorithm $\mathcal{A}$ for the OTSP: At any time t, when a new request is presented, let the server be travelling from point x to point y (some two requested locations), and S_t be the set of requests that have not yet been served by an online algorithm $\mathcal{A}$ (including the newly arrived request), plus the origin o. $\mathcal{A}$ abandons the current tour and follows the shortest route to the origin o via x or y, and then embarks on a-approximate tour over S_t using algorithm APPROX.

Show that the competitive ratio of $\mathcal{A}$ is at most $3/2 + \mathsf{a}$.

[Hint: Similar to the proof of Theorem 16.2.6, consider the arrival time t_n of the last request and let $\ell(t_n)$ be the location of $\mathcal{A}$ at time t_n when it is travelling between x and y. Consider $D = d(o,x) + d(o,y) + d(x,y)$ and show that $T_{\text{OPT}} \geq D$, and $d(o, \ell(t_n)) \leq D/2$. Next, show that $T_{\mathcal{A}} \leq t_n + d(o, \ell(t_n)) + T_{\text{APPROX}}(S_{t_n})$ to conclude the result.]

16.5 Prove Lemma 16.3.10.

16.6 Prove (16.16) and (16.17).

16.7 In this problem, we consider a new online problem called the **Steiner Tree** that is defined as follows. Let the input be a graph $G(V, E)$ with weight $w(e)$ for each edge $e \in E$ that is completely known to begin with. There is a special subset of vertices $S \subseteq V$, called the terminal vertex set. At time $i = 1, \ldots |S|$, one terminal vertex $s_i \in S$ is revealed. Let the set of terminal vertices revealed just before s_i be S^{-i}, and an existing tree connecting all vertices of S^{-i} be T^{-i}. On the arrival of s_i at time i, a new tree $T^{-(i+1)}$ has to be output that connects all vertices of $S^{-i} \cup \{s_i\}$ and is only an augmentation of T^{-i}, i.e., edges selected in T^{-i} have to be part of $T^{-(i+1)}$. The objective is to minimize the weight of the tree output at the end of all $|S|$ terminal vertex arrivals.

[302] Show that GREEDY (Algorithm 30) is $\mathcal{O}(\log n)$-competitive[4] as follows. Let $c(i)$ denote the cost of the path P_i found in the ith iteration by Algorithm 30 on terminal s_i's arrival. Order the indices of terminals such that $c(i_1) \geq c(i_2) \geq \ldots \geq c(i_{|S|})$.

Show that for each j, the cost

$$c(i_j) \leq \frac{2C_{\text{OPT}}}{j}, \tag{16.18}$$

where C_{OPT} is the cost of OPT. To show (16.18), use a contradiction argument as follows. Let (16.18) be false for some j. Then consider the set of vertices $S_j = \{s_{i_1}, \ldots, s_{i_j}\}$, where for each vertex $i_k, k = 1, \ldots, j, c(i_k) \geq \frac{2C_{\text{OPT}}}{j}$.

1. Argue that the distance between any two vertices of the set $S_j \cup \{s_1\}$ is at least $\frac{2C_{\text{OPT}}}{j}$ if (16.18) is false for some j.

2. Argue using part 1 that the cost of a minimum spanning tree (MST) for the set of vertices $S_j \cup \{s_1\}$ is at least $2C_{\text{OPT}}$ if (16.18) is false for some j.

3. Using part 2, complete the contradiction argument to show (16.18) using the following fact (which you do not have to necessarily prove). The cost of the MST of a subset of the full terminal set S cannot be more than $2C_{\text{OPT}}$.

4. Using (16.18), complete the proof that the competitive ratio of Algorithm 30 is $\mathcal{O}(H_{|S|})$, where H_n is the harmonic number with index n.

Algorithm 30 Algorithm GREEDY

Input $G = (V, E), S \subseteq V$
Let $S = \{s_1, s_2, \ldots, s_{|S|}\}$ be the terminal vertices indexed in order of their arrival time
$T \leftarrow \{s_1\}$
for $\{i = 2$ to $|S|\}$ **do**
    Let P_i be the shortest path in G from s_i to T
    Add P_i to T
end for
Output T as the Steiner Tree

16.8 [300, 301] Consider the nearest neighbour (NN) algorithm (Algorithm 31) for the G-OTSP where the total number of vertices $|V| = n$.

---

[4] A lower bound of $\Omega(\log n)$ is also known from [302]. Thus, the greedy algorithm is order-wise optimal.

Algorithm 31 Algorithm NN

Input $G = (V, E), w(e) \; \forall \; e \in E$

Starting vertex s

while (there are unvisited vertices) **do**

From the current vertex u, visit the nearest unvisited neighbour (shortest length) v of u

end while

Return to s.

Show that the NN algorithm has a competitive ratio of $\mathcal{O}(\log(n))$.[5] First, show that the weight of the optimal cost of the travelling salesman problem for any subset $S \subseteq V$ must be at least that of the best Steiner tree for S and cannot exceed it by a factor of two. Next, to prove this result, connect the execution of the NN algorithm with Algorithm 30 for the Steiner Tree problem, and use the result of Problem 16.7.

CHAPTER 17

Convex Optimization (Server Provisioning in Cloud Computing)

17.1 Introduction

In this chapter, we consider an important practical problem in modern data centres: how many servers to provision, given the uncertain demand, in the presence of a switching cost incurred in increasing or decreasing the number of active servers over time.

At a data centre, let the demand at time t be $D(t)$ that is revealed causally over time. Dedicating $S(t)$ number of servers at time t to support this demand, two types of costs are incurred; the quality of service cost depending on $D(t), S(t)$ and the energy cost required to run the $S(t)$ servers. The two costs are combined to produce a single cost function $f_t(S_t, D_t)$. In addition, because of obvious practical limitations, there is a penalty in changing the number of servers across time slots, captured by cost function $c(S(t-1), S(t))$, where c is a specific function that increases with $|S(t-1) - S(t)|$. Overall, the optimization problem is to choose $S(t)$ with uncertain demand $D(t)$ so as to minimize $f_t(S_t, D_t) + c(S(t-1), S(t))$ summed across time. This problem is popularly known as **server provisioning** for power-proportional data centers.

To model this popular and important problem, in this chapter, we consider a general framework of online convex optimization (OCO) with switching cost, where at each discrete time t, a convex function $f_t : \mathbb{R}^d \to \mathbb{R}^+$ is revealed, and an algorithm has to choose an action x_t knowing all $f_\tau, \tau \le t$. The cost of choosing action x_t at time t is the sum of the sub-optimality/hitting cost $f_t(x_t)$, and the switching cost $c(x_{t-1}, x_t)$. The goal is to choose $x_t, 1 \le t \le T$ such that the overall cost summed over T slots is minimized. Note that for the server provisioning problem, $d = 1$.

17.2 Problem Formulation

At each discrete time $1 \le t \le T$, a non-negative convex function f_t arrives such that $f_t : \mathbb{R}^d \to \mathbb{R}^+$. Let $x_t^\star = \arg\min_x f_t(x)$. Let x_0 be fixed for time 0. On the arrival of the function f_t at time t, the decision is to move from the current action x_{t-1} to a new action x_t, where the total cost is the sum of two types of costs: (i) hitting cost $f_t(x_t)$ and (ii) switching cost $c(x_{t-1}, x_t)$. In particular, moving the action to x_t from x_{t-1} there is an effort cost $c(x_{t-1}, x_t)$ that is increasing in $|x_{t-1} - x_t|$, while $f_t(x_t)$ is the sub-optimality or hitting cost that counts how far away x_t is compared to the optimal action $x_t^\star$ that minimizes $f_t(x)$.

An online algorithm $\mathcal{A}$ has to choose actions x_t in response to functions $f_\tau, \tau \leq t$ revealed or arriving sequentially, and the overall cost of $\mathcal{A}$ is

$$C_{\mathcal{A}} = \sum_{t=1}^{T} f_t(x_t) + c(x_{t-1}, x_t), \tag{17.1}$$

where T is the total time horizon.

We will call Problem 17.1 as the OCO-S problem. Even without the switching cost, the OCO problem is quite meaningful and has widespread applications, where the actions x_t have to be chosen before the function f_t is revealed using information about $f_\tau, \tau \leq t - 1$ only, and the overall cost is just $C_{\mathcal{A}} = \sum_{t=1}^{T} f_t(x_t)$. We discuss the OCO problem in Problem 17.8.

Remark 17.2.1 *The OCO-S problem is a special case of the MTS studied in Chapter 6, but where the state space is continuous. For MTS, the general lower bound (Theorem 6.3.1) on the competitive ratio of any deterministic online algorithm is unbounded for a continuous state space. In this chapter, we will show that by exploiting the strong convexity of f_t's, a deterministic online algorithm with a constant competitive ratio is possible.*

Remark 17.2.2 *The OCO-S problem has elements similar to the facility location problem considered in Chapter 11, where on each request's arrival, the algorithm has to either assign it to an existing open facility, incurring an assignment cost (that is similar to the switching cost with the OCO-S problem), or open a new facility paying a fixed facility opening cost (that corresponds to the hitting cost of the OCO-S). One major distinction compared to the facility action problem is that with the OCO-S problem, the hitting cost is a variable depending on the function f_t and the chosen action x_t, while the facility opening cost with the facility action problem is a fixed constant or is location dependent.*

We will assume for the rest of the chapter that $\|.\|$ represents the 2-norm. Moreover, each f_t is assumed to be m-strongly convex with respect to the 2-norm, i.e.,

$$(\nabla f_t(x) - \nabla f_t(y))^T (x - y) \geq m\|x - y\|^2, \tag{17.2}$$

as well as

$$f(y) \geq f(x) + \nabla f(x)^T (y - x) + \frac{m}{2}\|y - x\|^2,$$

and the switching or effort cost is **quadratic**

$$c(x, y) = \frac{1}{2}\|x - y\|^2.$$

Remark 17.2.3 *The reason for assuming that f_t's are strongly convex is that if functions f_t's are just convex, then no deterministic algorithm has a bounded competitve ratio for solving (17.1). We discuss this issue in more detail in Problem 17.1.*

Remark 17.2.4 *Without loss of generality, for competitive ratio analysis we consider the case that $f_t(x_t^\star) = 0$ for all t.*

Any online algorithm for solving the OCO-S problem has to balance the hitting cost and the switching cost on the arrival of each function f_t. Towards that end, we next discuss an algorithm called the online balanced descent (OBD) that uses the concept of a level-set of function f_t defined as follows. The level-set of function f_t with level ℓ is

$$L_t(\ell) = \{x \in \mathbb{R}^d : f_t(x) \leq \ell\}. \tag{17.3}$$

Definition 17.2.5 *Let* $\mathcal{P}_{L_t(\ell)}$ *be the projection map onto the level-set* $L_t(\ell)$, *i.e.,*

$$\mathcal{P}_{L_t(\ell)}(x) = \arg\min_{y \in L_t(\ell)} \|x - y\|^2.$$

Since f_t *is strictly convex, the level-set* $L_t(\ell)$ (17.3) *is a closed convex set, and hence the projection is unique and belongs to the boundary of the level-set* $L_t(\ell)$.

We next describe the algorithm OBD. At time t, let the previously chosen action by OBD be x_{t-1}, and the newly arrived function be f_t. On the arrival of each new function f_t at time t, initialize $\ell = f_t(x_t^\star)$, the optimal value with respect to f_t. Thus, $L_t(\ell) = \{x_t^\star\}$ is a singleton to begin with since each f_t is strongly convex. At each step $x(\ell) = \mathcal{P}_{L_t(\ell)}(x_{t-1})$.

The algorithm stops right away if $x(\ell) = x_{t-1}$. Otherwise, ℓ is increased iteratively to enlarge the set $L_t(\ell)$, and this process of incrementing ℓ continues until $\frac{1}{2}\|x(\ell) - x_{t-1}\|^2 = \beta\ell$. A pictorial description of the algorithm can be seen in Figure 17.1.

Thus, OBD tries to balance the switching cost and the hitting cost up to a scaled parameter β, i.e., the switching cost is at most β times the hitting cost (since $f_t(x_t^\star) = 0$, the hitting cost $f_t(x(\ell)) = \ell$). Note that since, without loss of generality, we are considering $f_t(x_t^\star) = 0$, the initial value of ℓ will be 0.

The pseudo-code of OBD is provided in Algorithm 32, where note that since the function $g(\ell) = \|x(\ell) - x_{t-1}\|$ is continuous in ℓ, the algorithm can be implemented efficiently.

Algorithm 32 Online Balanced Descent OBD

Initialize x_0 and $\beta > 0$.
for On arrival of a new function f_t **do**
    $x_t^\star = \arg\min_x f_t(x)$
    Initialize $\ell = f_t(x_t^\star)$
    $x(\ell) = \mathcal{P}_{L_t(\ell)}(x_{t-1})$
    Stop if
    $x(\ell) = x_{t-1}$,
    Otherwise, increase ℓ incrementally until $\frac{1}{2}\|x(\ell) - x_{t-1}\|^2 = \beta\ell$

    If $\ell_f = \ell$ when the algorithm terminates, assign $x_t = x(\ell_f)$
end for

The basic intuition behind OBD is to minimize the switching cost such that the newly found action x_t belongs to an appropriately chosen level-set (choice of ℓ) of f_t (the newly arrived function) that gives an upper bound on the hitting cost. E.g., $x_t = \arg\min_{x \in L_t(\ell)} \frac{1}{2}\|x - x_{t-1}\|_2^2$. By the definition of the level set, this means that with OBD the switching cost is minimized given that the hitting cost is bounded by ℓ (since $f_t(x_t^\star) = 0$).

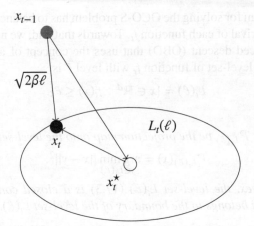

Figure 17.1 Illustration of projection of x_{t-1} onto $L_t(\ell)$ with $\frac{1}{2}||x(\ell) - x_{t-1}||^2 = \beta\ell$.

Definition 17.2.6 *Let $H_t = f_t(x_t)$ and $M_t = \frac{1}{2}||x_t - x_{t-1}||^2$ be the hitting cost and the switching cost paid by* OBD *at time t, respectively. For* OPT, *let H_t^{OPT} and M_t^{OPT} be the corresponding costs at time t.*

Fact 17.2.7 *When $f_t(x_t^\star) = 0$ for all t, then by the definition of* OBD, *$M_t = \beta H_t$. This follows since initially at each time t, $\ell = 0$ and if $x(\ell) = x_{t-1}$, then trivially, $M_t = \beta H_t$. Otherwise, if ℓ_f is the level at which* OBD *terminates for time t, then by definition of* OBD, *$M_t = \frac{1}{2}||x(\ell_f) - x_{t-1}||^2 = \beta\ell_f = \beta H_t$.*

The main result of this chapter for OBD is as follows.

Theorem 17.2.8 *For $\beta = 2 + \frac{10}{m}$, where m is the strong convexity parameter of all functions f_t, the competitive ratio of* OBD *is at most $3 + O\left(\frac{1}{m}\right)$. Importantly, the competitive ratio bound is independent of the dimension (d) of actions.*

Proof: To prove Theorem 17.2.8, we will make use of a potential function argument, and use the following potential function. For $x, y \in \mathbb{R}^d$,

$$\Phi(x, y) = \eta||x - y||^2, \tag{17.4}$$

where η is a constant to be chosen later. In the analysis, the first (x) and the second argument (y) of $\Phi(x, y)$ will be the actions x_t and x_t^{OPT} chosen by the algorithm and OPT, respectively, for solving the OCO-S problem. Note that $\Phi(x, y) \geq 0$, $\forall x, y$, and importantly $\Phi(x_0, x_0^{OPT}) = 0$ since the initial starting point is the same for both the algorithm and OPT.

For the potential function Φ (17.4), the following useful properties are derived next.

Lemma 17.2.9 *For $a, b, c \in \mathbb{R}^d$, if the angle θ between vectors $a - c$ and $b - c$ lies in $[\pi/2, 3\pi/2]$, then*

$$\Phi(a, c) - \Phi(a, b) \leq -\Phi(b, c).$$

Proof: Consider the triangle with vertices a, b, and c. Using Cosines Law,

$$||a - b||^2 = ||a - c||^2 + ||b - c||^2 - 2||a - c||\,||b - c||\cos\theta,$$

which implies

$$||a - c||^2 - ||a - b||^2 = -||b - c||^2 + 2||a - c||\,||b - c||\cos\theta.$$

Since $\theta \in [\pi/2, 3\pi/2]$, $2||a - c||\,||b - c||\cos\theta \leq 0$, and the result follows. ∎

Lemma 17.2.10 *For $a, b, c \in \mathbb{R}^d$,*

$$\Phi(a, c) - \Phi(a, b) \leq 2\Phi(b, c) + \Phi(a, b).$$

Proof: Using Cosines Law,

$$||a - c||^2 - ||a - b||^2 = ||b - c||^2 - 2||a - b||\,||b - c||\cos\theta, \tag{17.5}$$

where θ is the angle between $a - b$ and $b - c$. Clearly,

$$-2||a - b||\,||b - c||\cos\theta \leq 2||a - b||\,||b - c||,$$

$$\leq 2\frac{||a - b||^2 + ||b - c||^2}{2}, \tag{17.6}$$

where the second inequality follows from the arithmetic mean (AM)–geometric mean (GM) inequality $\sqrt{uv} \leq \frac{u+v}{2}$. Using (17.6), from (17.5)

$$||a - c||^2 - ||a - b||^2 \leq ||b - c||^2 + ||a - b||^2 + ||b - c||^2,$$
$$\implies \Phi(a, c) - \Phi(a, b) \leq 2\Phi(b, c) + \Phi(a, b).$$

∎

Lemma 17.2.11 *Let x_t and x_t^{OPT} be the actions chosen by OBD and OPT, respectively, at time t. Then for each time $t = 1, \ldots, T$,*

$$\Phi(x_t, x_t^{\mathsf{OPT}}) \leq \frac{4\eta}{m}H_t + \frac{4\eta}{m}H_t^{\mathsf{OPT}},$$

where H_t and H_t^{OPT} are the hitting costs of OBD and OPT, respectively (Definition 17.2.6).

Proof: From the definition of the potential function Φ (17.4)

$$\Phi(x_t, x_t^{\mathsf{OPT}}) = \eta||x_t - x_t^{\mathsf{OPT}}||^2,$$

$$\overset{(a)}{\leq} \eta(||x_t - x_t^\star|| + ||x_t^{\mathsf{OPT}} - x_t^\star||)^2,$$

$$= \eta(||x_t - x_t^\star||^2 + ||x_t^{\mathsf{OPT}} - x_t^\star||^2 + 2||x_t - x_t^\star||\,||x_t^{\mathsf{OPT}} - x_t^\star||),$$

$$\overset{(b)}{\leq} 2\eta(||x_t - x_t^\star||^2 + ||x_t^{\mathsf{OPT}} - x_t^\star||^2),$$

$$\overset{(c)}{\leq} \frac{4\eta}{m}H_t + \frac{4\eta}{m}H_t^{\mathsf{OPT}},$$

where (a) follows from the triangle inequality and $x_t^\star = \arg\min_x f_t(x)$, while (b) follows since $\|x_t - x_t^\star\|\|x_t^{OPT} - x_t^\star\| \le \frac{\|x_t - x_t^\star\|^2 + \|x_t^{OPT} - x_t^\star\|^2}{2}$ from the AM–GM inequality, while for getting (c) we use the m-strongly convex property of functions f_t which implies $f_t(x) \ge \frac{m}{2}\|x - x_t^\star\|^2 \ \forall \ x$ since $f_t(x_t^\star) = 0$, and the definition of H_t and H_t^{OPT}. $\blacksquare$

To complete the proof of Theorem 17.2.8, we will bound $H_t + M_t + \Delta\Phi$, which we break up into two cases.

Case I: $H_t \le H_t^{OPT}$. Note that

$$\Delta\Phi_t = \Phi(x_t, x_t^{OPT}) - \Phi(x_{t-1}, x_{t-1}^{OPT}),$$

$$\le \Phi(x_t, x_t^{OPT}),$$

$$\le \frac{4\eta}{m}H_t + \frac{4\eta}{m}H_t^{OPT},$$

where the last inequality follows from Lemma 17.2.11. Thus, we have

$$H_t + M_t + \Delta\Phi_t \le H_t + M_t + \frac{4\eta}{m}H_t + \frac{4\eta}{m}H_t^{OPT},$$

$$\le \left(1 + \beta + \frac{8\eta}{m}\right)H_t^{OPT}, \tag{17.7}$$

where we have used Fact 17.2.7, $M_t = \beta H_t$, and the condition that $H_t \le H_t^{OPT}$.

Case II: $H_t > H_t^{OPT}$. In this case, we will use specific properties of OBD. On the arrival of the function f_t at time t, let ℓ_f be the level that OBD stops at, and (final chosen action at time t) x_t is the projection of action x_{t-1} on the level-set $L_t(\ell_f)$. Note that since $H_t > H_t^{OPT}$, $H_t > 0$. $H_t > H_t^{OPT}$ also implies that x_t^{OPT} must lie in the interior of $L_t(\ell_f)$, while x_t always by definition lies on the boundary of $L_t(\ell_f)$. Thus, we get that the angle θ between vector $x_{t-1} - x_t$ and $x_t^{OPT} - x_t$ is obtuse, as shown in Figure 17.2. Hence, Lemma 17.2.9 becomes applicable and will be used as follows.

$$\Delta\Phi_t = \Phi(x_t, x_t^{OPT}) - \Phi(x_{t-1}, x_{t-1}^{OPT}),$$

$$\overset{(a)}{=} (\Phi(x_t, x_t^{OPT}) - \Phi(x_{t-1}, x_t^{OPT})) + (\Phi(x_{t-1}, x_t^{OPT}) - \Phi(x_{t-1}, x_{t-1}^{OPT})),$$

$$\overset{(b)}{\le} -\Phi(x_t, x_{t-1}) + 2\Phi(x_t^{OPT}, x_{t-1}^{OPT}) + \Phi(x_{t-1}, x_{t-1}^{OPT}), \tag{17.8}$$

where in (a) we have added and subtracted $\Phi(x_{t-1}, x_t^{OPT})$, while in (b) to bound $(\Phi(x_t, x_t^{OPT}) - \Phi(x_{t-1}, x_t^{OPT}))$ we have used Lemma 17.2.9 (with $a = x_t^{OPT}, b = x_{t-1}, c = x_t$) since the angle θ between vector $x_{t-1} - x_t$ and $x_t^{OPT} - x_t$ (as shown in Figure 17.2) is obtuse as discussed above, and for bounding $\Phi(x_{t-1}, x_t^{OPT}) - \Phi(x_{t-1}, x_{t-1}^{OPT})$ we have used Lemma 17.2.10. The bound from Lemma 17.2.9 to get inequality (b)

$$(\Phi(x_t, x_t^{OPT}) - \Phi(x_{t-1}, x_t^{OPT})) \le -\Phi(x_t, x_{t-1})$$

is really the key step of this proof, which can be seen graphically in Figure 17.2.

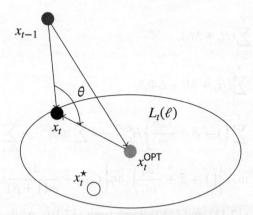

Figure 17.2 Illustration of projection of x_{t-1} onto $L_t(\ell)$, where x_t^{OPT} is in the interior of $L_t(\ell)$.

Using the definition of M_t (Definition 17.2.6) and the potential function Φ for OBD, $\Phi(x_t, x_{t-1}) = 2\eta M_t$, and for OPT, $\Phi(x_t^{\text{OPT}}, x_{t-1}^{\text{OPT}}) = 2\eta M_t^{\text{OPT}}$. Hence, we get from (17.8)

$$\Delta\Phi_t = -2\eta M_t + 4\eta M_t^{\text{OPT}} + \Phi(x_{t-1}, x_{t-1}^{\text{OPT}}).$$

Therefore,

$$H_t + M_t + \Delta\Phi_t \leq H_t + M_t - 2\eta M_t + 4\eta M_t^{\text{OPT}} + \Phi(x_{t-1}, x_{t-1}^{\text{OPT}}),$$

$$\leq \left(1 + \frac{1}{\beta} - 2\eta\right)M_t + 4\eta M_t^{\text{OPT}} + \frac{4\eta}{m}H_{t-1} + \frac{4\eta}{m}H_{t-1}^{\text{OPT}}, \qquad (17.9)$$

where the last inequality follows since $M_t = \beta H_t$ (Fact 17.2.7), and using Lemma 17.2.11 on $\Phi(x_{t-1}, x_{t-1}^{\text{OPT}})$.

Combining (17.7) and (17.9) that covers both the cases, when $H_t \leq H_t^{\text{OPT}}$ and $H_t > H_t^{\text{OPT}}$, and choosing $\eta \geq \dfrac{1 + \frac{1}{\beta}}{2}$, we get that for any t,

$$H_t + M_t + \Delta\Phi_t \leq \left(1 + \beta + \frac{8\eta}{m}\right)H_t^{\text{OPT}} + 4\eta M_t^{\text{OPT}} + \frac{4\eta}{m}H_{t-1} + \frac{4\eta}{m}H_{t-1}^{\text{OPT}}. \qquad (17.10)$$

Note that

$$\sum_{t=1}^{T} \Delta\Phi_t = \Phi_T(x_t, x_t^{\text{OPT}}) - \Phi(x_0, x_0^{\text{OPT}}) \geq 0, \qquad (17.11)$$

since $\Phi(x_0, x_0^{\text{OPT}}) = 0$ as the initial starting point is the same for both the algorithm and OPT, and $\Phi_T(x_t, x_t^{\text{OPT}}) \geq 0$ for any x_t, x_t^{OPT}.

Using (17.11), and summing (17.10) over all $t = 1$ to $t = T$, we get an upper bound on the cost (17.1) of OBD, as follows.

$$C_{\text{OBD}} = \sum_{t=1}^{T} (H_t + M_t),$$

$$\overset{(a)}{\leq} \sum_{t=1}^{T} (H_t + M_t + \Delta\Phi_t),$$

$$\overset{(b)}{\leq} \sum_{t=1}^{T} \left(1 + \beta + \frac{12\eta}{m}\right) H_t^{\text{OPT}} + 4\sum_{t=1}^{T} \eta M_t^{\text{OPT}} + \sum_{t=1}^{T} \frac{4\eta}{m} H_{t-1},$$

$$\overset{(c)}{\leq} \max\left\{\left(1 + \beta + \frac{12\eta}{m}\right), 4\eta\right\} C_{\text{OPT}} + \frac{4\eta}{m(1+\beta)} C_{\text{OBD}}, \qquad (17.12)$$

where (a) follows from (17.11) and (b) follows from (17.10), while to get inequality (c) we have used $H_t = \frac{1}{1+\beta}(H_t + M_t)$ that follows since $M_t = \beta H_t$ (Fact 17.2.7).

Thus, the competitive ratio of OBD is upper bounded by

$$\mu_{\text{OBD}} \leq \frac{\max\left\{\left(1 + \beta + \frac{12\eta}{m}\right), 4\eta\right\}}{1 - \frac{4\eta}{m(1+\beta)}},$$

with $\frac{4\eta}{m(1+\beta)} < 1$ where recall that $\eta \geq \frac{1+\frac{1}{\beta}}{2}$.

Choosing $\eta = \frac{1+\frac{1}{\beta}}{2}$, we get $\frac{4\eta}{m(1+\beta)} = \frac{2}{m\beta}$. Choosing $\beta = 2 + 10/m$, $1 - \frac{4\eta}{m(1+\beta)} = \frac{8+2m}{10+2m}$ and $\eta = \frac{1+\frac{1}{\beta}}{2} = \frac{3m+10}{2(2m+10)}$.

Therefore,

$$\frac{\max\left\{\left(1 + \beta + \frac{12\eta}{m}\right), 4\eta\right\}}{1 - \frac{4\eta}{m(1+\beta)}} \leq \frac{\max\left\{1 + \frac{m}{2m+10} + \frac{12}{m}\frac{3m+10}{2(2m+10)}, 4\frac{3m+10}{2(2m+10)}\right\}}{\frac{8+2m}{10+2m}},$$

$$\leq 3 + \mathcal{O}(1/m).$$

Thus, we get $\mu_{\text{OBD}} \leq 3 + O(1/m)$ as required. ∎

17.3 Notes

The server provisioning problem for power-proportional data centres was first studied in [303–306], which is a one-dimensional version of the OCO-S problem studied in this chapter, i.e., each $f_t : \mathbb{R} \to \mathbb{R}$ and the switching cost is linear. For the one-dimensional OCO-S problem with linear switching cost, a 3-competitive algorithm was proposed in [303], while in [305], a $1 + \mathcal{O}(1/w)$-competitive algorithm is provided, where w is the lookahead window, i.e., at time t, the functions that are going to arrive at $t, t+1, \dots, t+w$ are available in advance. Improvements with lookahead can be found in [307]. With linear switching cost, a 2-competitive algorithm was derived in [308] for the one-dimensional problem, together with a lower bound of 1.86 on any online algorithm. An improved lower bound of 2 has been derived in [309]. The OCO-S problem can also be seen as a continuous version of the metrical task system problem [77, 310], whose popular special case is the k-server problem considered in Chapter 5. For the one-dimensional case with linear switching cost, when the number of servers chosen is required to be integral, an optimal deterministic online algorithm with competitive ratio 3 and an optimal randomized algorithm with competitive ratio 2 have been derived in [309] together with the lower bounds.

A multi-dimensional OCO-S problem when functions f_t are polyhedral and the switching cost is quadratic was considered in [311], and a constant competitive algorithm was derived. When functions f_t are m-strongly convex and the switching cost is quadratic, a $3 + \mathcal{O}(1/m)$ competitive algorithm (presented in this chapter) was derived in [312] for the multi-dimensional OCO-S problem. Importantly, the competitive ratios of the algorithms in [311, 312] are independent of the dimension of the OCO-S problem. An improved algorithm with competitive ratio $\mathcal{O}\left(\frac{1}{\sqrt{\mu}}\right)$ as $\mu \to 0$ has been derived in [362] that meets the lower bound of $\Omega\left(\frac{1}{\sqrt{\mu}}\right)$ [362] on the competitive ratio of all online algorithms.

Moving beyond convex functions f_t's, recently in [313] the multi-dimensional OCO-S problem with non-convex functions and lookahead was considered, where a $1 + \mathcal{O}(1/w)$-competitive algorithm with w-lookahead is derived, as long as the function f satisfies the following two conditions: (i) *order of growth* condition that ensures the hitting cost functions grow at least as quickly as the switching costs as one moves away from the minimizer and (ii) the switching costs satisfy an approximate version of the triangle inequality. Going beyond the worst case, the OCO-S problem has been considered in [264] when predictions with unknown accuracy are available, and consistent and robust algorithms have been proposed. A related problem to the OCO-S problem is called the convex body chasing problem, where at each time a convex body arrives, and the algorithm has to move a point inside the newly arrived convex body with the objective of minimizing the sum of all the movements. This problem was introduced in [314] and later studied in [315–318]. We discuss the convex body chasing problem in Problem 17.7.

PROBLEMS

17.1 Show that if the functions f_t's are just convex, then the competitive ratio of any deterministic online algorithm to solve (17.1) is unbounded.

[Hint: Consider $f_t(x) = 0$, $\forall x$ for $t = 1, \ldots, T'$ and $f_{T'+1}(x) = (x-1)^2$ and choose T' large.]

17.2 Consider the convex optimization problem where at each time $t = 1, \ldots, T$, a non-negative convex function $f_t : \mathbb{R} \to \mathbb{R}^+$ which has a unique minimizer is revealed. Once the function f_t is revealed, an action $x_t \in \mathbb{R}$ is chosen (possibly using all the information revealed so far) to **minimize**

$$\sum_{t=1}^{T} f_t(x_t) + \sum_{t=1}^{T} |x_t - x_{t-1}|.$$

Show that Algorithm 33 is 3-competitive for this problem by considering the potential function

$$\Phi(x_t, x_t^{\text{OPT}}) = 3|x_t - x_t^{\text{OPT}}|,$$

where x_t is the action chosen by an algorithm, while x_t^{OPT} is the OPT's action, at time t.

Algorithm 33

On arrival of the new function f_t, compute $x_t^\star = \arg\min_x f_t(x)$. [minimizer is unique]
Move from the previous location x_{t-1} towards $x_t^\star$ until
either (a) reach point x such that $|x - x_{t-1}| = f_t(x)/2$ or (b) reach $x_t^\star$
Whichever location is reached first, choose that as x_t.

Let $H_t = f_t(x_t)$ and $H_t^{\text{OPT}} = f_t(x_t^{\text{OPT}})$, while $M_t = |x_t - x_{t-1}|$ and $M_t^{\text{OPT}} = |x_t^{\text{OPT}} - x_{t-1}^{\text{OPT}}|$, and $\Delta\Phi_t = \Phi(x_t, x_t^{\text{OPT}}) - \Phi(x_{t-1}, x_{t-1}^{\text{OPT}})$.

1. Show that $\Phi(x_{t-1}, x_t^{\text{OPT}}) - \Phi(x_{t-1}, x_{t-1}^{\text{OPT}}) \leq 3|x_t^{\text{OPT}} - x_{t-1}^{\text{OPT}}|$, and $\Phi(x_t, x_t^{\text{OPT}}) - \Phi(x_{t-1}, x_t^{\text{OPT}}) \leq 3|x_t - x_{t-1}|$.

2. Using part 1 and the algorithm definition, when $H_t \leq H_t^{\text{OPT}}$, show that

$$H_t + M_t + \Delta\Phi_t \leq 3H_t^{\text{OPT}} + 3M_t^{\text{OPT}}.$$

3. When $H_t > H_t^{\text{OPT}}$, improve part 1 to show that

$$\Phi(x_t, x_t^{\text{OPT}}) - \Phi(x_{t-1}, x_t^{\text{OPT}}) \leq -3M_t.$$

4. Establish an exact (equality) relationship between M_t and H_t when $H_t > H_t^{\text{OPT}}$.

5. Using parts 1, 3 and 4, show that $H_t + M_t + \Delta\Phi_t \leq 3H_t^{\text{OPT}} + 3M_t^{\text{OPT}}$ when $H_t > H_t^{\text{OPT}}$.

6. Conclude that the algorithm is 3-competitive.

17.3 While considering problem (17.1) we did not insist that any algorithm return to the starting point x_0 at time T. In the spirit of server provisioning for data centres, once all the demands are met the number of servers should ideally be 0 and to do so, a switching cost has to be paid at time T. Thus, in this problem for (17.1) we enforce the constraint that at time T (chosen by the adversary), any algorithm has to return to the starting point x_0, which without loss of generality, let $x_0 = 0$.

Consider the OBD algorithm (Algorithm 32) until time step $T - 1$ as is, and return to $\mathbf{0}$ at time T from the current location x_{T-1} paying a cost of $||x_{T-1}||^2$. Show that this algorithm has a competitive ratio of at most a constant times more than the competitive ratio of OBD without enforcing this constraint derived in Theorem 17.2.8.

Essentially, the analysis of OBD remains the same until time $T - 1$. To prove the claim, for time T show the following.

1.
$$M_T = ||x_{T-1} - 0||^2,$$

$$\leq ||x_{T-1} - x_{T-1}^{OPT}||^2 + M_T^{OPT} + 2\sqrt{||x_{T-1} - x_{T-1}^{OPT}||^2 M_T^{OPT}},$$

$$\leq 2||x_{T-1} - x_{T-1}^{OPT}||^2 + 2M_T^{OPT}. \tag{17.13}$$

2. For the potential function Φ defined in (17.4), using (17.13) show that

$$\Delta\Phi_T = \Phi(0,0) - \Phi(x_{T-1}, x_{T-1}^{OPT}) = -\frac{\eta}{2} M_T + \eta M_T^{OPT}.$$

Conclude the result using the above two statements similar to Theorem 17.2.8.

17.4 Show that if a randomized algorithm is c-competitive for the OCO-S problem, then there is a c-competitive deterministic algorithm.

[Hint: For the deterministic algorithm, use $x_t = \mathbb{E}_{\mathcal{R}}\{x\}$, where $\mathcal{R}$ is the probability distribution of the randomized algorithm, and then use Jensen's inequality to conclude the result.]

17.5 Show that the ski-rental problem considered in Chapter 2 is a special case of the OCO-S problem.

17.6 Show that in the offline case, the OCO-S problem can be cast as a convex program.

17.7 In this problem, we will consider a $0 - \infty$ version of the OCO-S problem, which is known as the *convex body chasing* problem. Let $\chi \subset \mathbb{R}^d$ be a convex, compact, and bounded set. At each time t, a function f_t and a convex set $\chi_t \subset \chi$ are revealed, such that

$$f_t(x) = \begin{cases} 0 & \text{if } x \in \chi_t, \\ \infty & \text{otherwise.} \end{cases} \tag{17.14}$$

Choosing x_t at time t, let the cost of $\mathcal{A}$ be

$$C_{\mathcal{A}} = \sum_{t=1}^{T} f_t(x_t) + \sum_{t=1}^{T} ||x_t - x_{t-1}||. \tag{17.15}$$

Note that we are choosing the switching cost as just the distance here, and not the distance squared as before. With cost function (17.15), any $\mathcal{A}$ is forced to choose the action $x_t \in \chi_t$, and the cost (17.15) of $\mathcal{A}$ is simply

$$C_{\mathcal{A}} = \sum_{t=1}^{T} ||x_t - x_{t-1}||.$$

1. For $d = 1$, where χ_t's are just intervals, show that the following algorithm is optimal:

$$x_{t+1} = \text{Proj}\left(x_t, \chi_{t+1}\right),$$

where $\text{Proj}\left(x, \chi\right)$ is the projection of x on a convex set χ.

2. For $d = 2$, show using just one-dimensional line segments as the convex sets χ_t that the lower bound on the competitive ratio of any online algorithm is at least $\sqrt{2}$.

3. Generalize part 2 for any $d \geq 2$ to show that the lower bound on the competitive ratio of any online algorithm is at least $\Omega(\sqrt{d})$.

4. [317] For $d = 2$, consider a special case of the problem, called the *nested* convex body chasing problem, where $\chi_t \subseteq \chi_{t-1}$ for all t. Let $\chi_1 = \mathcal{B}(0, r)$ be a ball with radius r. Show that the following algorithm

$$x_{t+1} = \begin{cases} x_t & \text{if } x_t \in \chi_{t+1}, \\ \text{Centroid of } \chi_{t+1}, & \text{otherwise,} \end{cases} \quad (17.16)$$

has a constant competitive ratio. The following result may be helpful.

Lemma 17.3.1 (Grünbaum[319]) *With $d = 2$, for any bounded convex set χ, let L be any line that passes through the centroid of χ, and H_1 and H_2 be the two partitions of χ induced by L. Then*

$$\max\{A(H_1), A(H_2)\} \leq \left(1 - \frac{1}{e}\right) A(\chi),$$

where $A(.)$ represents the area.

17.8 In this problem, we will consider the OCO problem where there is no switching cost for changing the actions, but now f_t is revealed after action a_t is chosen. In particular, let at time t an action a_t be chosen using the knowledge of $f_\tau, \tau \leq t - 1$, after which a convex function f_t is revealed, and the cost of the action a_t is $f_t(a_t)$. Let the feasible set for each time t be χ that is a closed, convex, and bounded. Let the optimizer for f_t over χ be $x_t^\star$, i.e., $x_t^\star = \arg\min_{x \in \chi} f_t(x)$, and let each f_t be Lipschitz with constant L, i.e., $|f_t(x) - f_t(y)| \leq L|x - y|$.

The performance metric for an online algorithm for this problem is defined as the *dynamic regret* (the accumulated penalty)

$$\sum_{t=1}^{T} |f_t(x_t^\star) - f_t(a_t)|. \quad (17.17)$$

Dynamic means that OPT is allowed to choose optimal decisions at each time t. There is also a static version of regret where OPT is constrained to choose a single action for all time $1 \leq t \leq T$ knowing all $f_t, 1 \leq t \leq T$ in advance. We will look at the static regret problem in Problem 17.10.

Show that the following online algorithm that chooses

$$a_t = x^\star_{t-1}$$

(the optimal decision for the previous time slot) has dynamic regret (17.17) at most LV, where $V = \sum_{t=2}^{T} |x^\star_t - x^\star_{t-1}|$.

Conversely, choosing $f_t(x) = b_t x$, where $b_t = \pm 1$ with equal probability, show that the expected dynamic regret (17.17) of any online algorithm is at least $\Omega(V)$.

17.9 In this problem, we will show that the $\mathcal{O}(V)$ dynamic regret (17.17) can be obtained for Problem 17.8, even if full function f_t is not revealed at time t and only the gradient of f_t at the point a_t (previous action) is available after a_t has been chosen, as long as each f_t is strongly convex and smooth. Recall that a m-strongly convex function satisfies

$$f(y) \geq f(x) + \nabla f(x)^T (y - x) + \frac{m}{2}||x - y||^2,$$

while a β-smooth function satisfies

$$||\nabla f(y) - \nabla f(x)|| \leq \beta ||y - x||, \ \forall \, x, y \in \chi.$$

Let χ (feasible set) be convex, bounded, and closed over which all actions are restricted to lie. Consider the following algorithm. Let the current action be a_t, then a_{t+1} be chosen as

$$a_{t+1} = \text{Proj}\left(a_t - \frac{1}{\gamma} \nabla f_t(a_t), \chi\right),$$

where $\text{Proj}(x, \chi)$ is the projection of x on a convex set χ.

1. For this algorithm, show that for each time slot t,

$$||a_{t+1} - x^\star_t|| \leq c ||a_t - x^\star_t|| \tag{17.18}$$

for some $c < 1$. Thus, at each step, there is contraction towards the optimizer of the 'previous' step. In preparation towards proving this result, first show that

$$\left(\nabla f_t(x) - \nabla f_t(y)\right)^T (x - y) \geq \frac{m\beta}{m + \beta}||x - y||^2 + \frac{1}{m + \beta}||\nabla f_t(x) - \nabla f_t(y)||^2. \tag{17.19}$$

[Hint: Use of function $g_t(x) = f_t(x) - \frac{m}{2}||x||^2$ will be useful. Show that g is $\beta - m$ smooth. By definition, $m \leq \beta$. For $\beta = m$, show the claim directly where $||\nabla f(y) - \nabla f(x)|| \leq m||y - x||$. For $m < \beta$, show that

$$\left(\nabla g_t(x) - \nabla g_t(y)\right)^T (x - y) \geq \frac{1}{\beta - m}||\nabla g_t(x) - \nabla g_t(y)||^2,$$

from which the claim follows using some algebraic manipulations.]

Next, to prove (17.18), justify the following steps, where $\Delta_t = \|a_t - x_t^\star\|$,

$$\Delta_{t+1}^2 \leq \left(1 - \frac{2}{\gamma}\frac{m\beta}{m+\beta} + \beta^2\left(\frac{1}{\gamma^2} - \frac{2}{\gamma}\frac{1}{m+\beta}\right)\right)\Delta_t^2. \tag{17.20}$$

Choosing $\gamma = \frac{\beta+m}{2}$ in (17.20), we get the required contraction.

2. Use part 1, triangle inequality, and algebraic manipulations to show that

$$\sum_{t=1}^{T} \|x_t^\star - a_t\| \leq \|x_1^\star - a_1\| - c\|x_T^\star - a_T\|$$

$$+ c\sum_{t=1}^{T} \|x_t^\star - a_t\| + \sum_{t=2}^{T} \|x_t^\star - x_{t-1}^\star\|, \tag{17.21}$$

Thus, regrouping terms, we get

$$\sum_{t=1}^{T} \|x_t^\star - a_t\| \leq \frac{\|x_1^\star - a_1\| - c\|x_T^\star - a_T\|}{1-c} + \frac{1}{1-c}\sum_{t=2}^{T} \|x_t^\star - x_{t-1}^\star\|. \tag{17.22}$$

3. Using the Lipschitz condition on f_t, conclude that the dynamic regret (17.17) is $\mathcal{O}(V)$.

17.10 [320] In this problem, we consider the static regret problem compared to the dynamic regret problem which we studied in Problem 17.8. With static regret, the objective function is

$$\sum_{t=1}^{T} |f_t(x_t^\star) - f_t(a_t)|,$$

where OPT is choosing a single action $x^\star$ for all time slots $1 \leq t \leq T$ knowing all $f_t's$ for $1 \leq t \leq T$ that minimizes

$$x^\star = \arg\min_{x \in \chi} \sum_{t=1}^{T} f_t(x),$$

where χ (feasible set) is convex, bounded, and closed over which all actions are restricted to lie. Consider the following online gradient descent algorithm for choosing action a_t as follows.

Let each f_t be m-strongly convex, and choose $\eta_t = \frac{1}{mt}$. Show that ONLINE-GRADIENTDESCENT has static regret

$$\leq \frac{G^2}{2m}(1 + \log(T)),$$

where $\max_{t=1,\dots,T} \|\nabla f_t\| \leq G$.[1]

---

[1] If functions f_t are only convex and not strongly convex, then the optimal static regret is $\Theta(\sqrt{T})$, and is achieved by FOLLOWTHEPERTURBEDLEADER algorithm [320].

Algorithm 34 Algorithm ONLINEGRADIENTDESCENT

Input: feasible set χ, initial point a_0, learning rates η_t
for $t = 1$ to T **do**
    Let $y_t = a_{t-1} - \eta_{t-1}\nabla f_t(a_{t-1})$
    $a_t = \text{Proj}(y_t, \chi)$
end for

Proof is simple by using the following contraction property of projection

$$\|a_t - x^\star\| = \|\text{Proj}(a_{t-1} - \eta_{t-1}\nabla f_t(a_{t-1}), \chi) - x^\star\|,$$
$$\leq \|a_{t-1} - \eta_{t-1}\nabla f_t(a_{t-1}) - x^\star\|,$$

and the strong-convexity property

$$2(f_t(a_t) - f_t(x^\star)) \leq 2\nabla f_t^T(a_t)(a_t - x^\star) - m\|x^\star - a_t\|^2.$$

CHAPTER 18

Multi-Commodity Flow Routing

18.1 Introduction

In this chapter, we consider a canonical network flow problem, popularly known as *multi-commodity routing*, where the network is represented as a directed graph. Each flow request identifies a source–destination pair and a flow demand, i.e., the amount of flow going from the source to the destination (possibly over multiple paths of the graph) should be at least as much as the demand. Each edge of the graph is equipped with a latency function, and the cost of an edge is equal to the latency function evaluated at the total flow passing through it. Requests arrive sequentially or in an online manner, and have to be routed irrevocably using only the causal information, and the goal is to minimize the sum of the cost of all edges after all request arrivals.

Unlike many other problems considered in this book, the offline optimal solution is easy to find by solving a convex program. On the online front, however, an optimal online algorithm is not known. We consider both the splittable and the unsplittable cases (where only one path can be used to route the demand for each source–destination pair). For both cases, we consider affine latency functions and present the best-known guarantees on the competitive ratio that are achieved by a locally optimal algorithm that solves a convex program on each request arrival given the past routing decisions.

It is worthwhile noting that the unsplittable problem considered in this chapter is similar to the network load balancing problem studied in Section 12.4, where the objective was to minimize the maximum load exerted on any one edge of the network. Compared to that objective, in this chapter, we consider minimizing the sum of the 'loads' exerted on all edges of the network via summing the latency functions of each edge evaluated at their flow allocation. This new cost function has a fundamentally different competitive ratio guarantee compared to the network load balancing problem. In particular, we showed in Chapter 12 that the best competitive ratio for the network load balancing problem scales as $\Theta(\log(n))$, where n is the number of vertices in the network graph. In contrast, we will show that for affine latency functions, a simple algorithm is constant competitive.

18.2 Problem Formulation

Consider a directed graph (network) $G = (V, E)$ with vertex set V and edge set E. Each edge $e \in E$ has an associated cost function $C^e(.)$ that will be defined in (18.4). A set of requests σ, with $|\sigma| = K$, arrive sequentially, where request k originates at source s_k and is destined for sink t_k, where $s_k, t_k \in V$. The demand for request k is denoted by d_k, which represents the amount of flow that needs to be routed from s_k to t_k.

We will consider both the splittable and the unsplittable flow cases, where in the splittable case, demand d_k can be split over multiple paths of G, while in the unsplittable case, demand d_k has to be routed over a single path of G. On the arrival of request k, the routing decision has to be made irrevocably, which can only depend on the first k requests. Requests are assumed to be permanent, i.e., once they arrive they remain active for the time period of interest.

Let the amount of flow belonging to request k passing through edge $e \in E$ be f_e^k. Then the feasible flow constraints for each vertex $v \in V$ are given by

$$\sum_{e \in \delta^+(v)} f_e^k - \sum_{e \in \delta^-(v)} f_e^k = 0, \text{ for } v \neq s_k, t_k, \forall\, k = 1, \dots, K \tag{18.1}$$

$$\sum_{e \in \delta^+(v)} f_e^k - \sum_{e \in \delta^-(v)} f_e^k = d_k \text{ for } v = s_k, \; k = 1, \dots, K, \tag{18.2}$$

$$\sum_{e \in \delta^+(v)} f_e^k - \sum_{e \in \delta^-(v)} f_e^k = -d_k \text{ for } v = t_k, \; k = 1, \dots, K, \tag{18.3}$$

where $\delta^+(v)(\delta^-(v))$ are the outgoing (incoming) edges of node $v \in V$. Constraint (18.1) captures the fact that for a vertex that is neither a source nor a destination, the net flow through it should be zero. For a vertex that is either a source or a destination, the net out-flow or net in-flow should be equal to the demand and is captured by (18.2) and (18.3).

Let $\mathcal{F}_e^{k-1} = (f_e^1, \dots, f_e^{k-1})$ be the vector that represents the amount of flow passing through edge e for the first $k - 1$ requests. The cost of assigning flow f_e^k on edge e given $\mathcal{F}_e^{k-1}$ is given by

$$C^e(f_e^k; \mathcal{F}_e^{k-1}) = \int_0^{f_e^k} \ell_e\left(\sum_{i=1}^{k-1} f_e^i + z\right) dz, \tag{18.4}$$

where ℓ_e is a non-decreasing function, representing the per-edge latency cost. The cost (18.4) captures the incremental increase in cost as the flow is added infinitesimally slowly (from $z = 0$ to $z = f_e^k$) for any request k, given the prior request flow assignments.

Popular examples of edge-latency functions include constant functions $\ell_e(x) = c$, affine $\ell_e(x) = a_e x + b_e$, and polynomial functions $\ell_e(x) = \sum_{i=0}^{n} a_i x^i$.

The cost of any online algorithm for the kth request (with assignment f_e^k) is given by summing (18.4) across all edges,

$$C_k = \sum_{e \in E} C^e(f_e^k; \mathcal{F}_e^{k-1}). \tag{18.5}$$

Remark 18.2.1 *C_k is a convex function of f_e^k, since ℓ_e is a non-decreasing function.*

Thus, the overall cost of any online algorithm with total K request arrivals is

$$C = \sum_{k=1}^{K} C_k, \tag{18.6}$$

and the competitive ratio of an online algorithm $\mathcal{A}$ is

$$\mu_{\mathcal{A}} = \max_{\sigma} \frac{C^{\mathcal{A}}(\sigma)}{C^{\mathrm{OPT}}(\sigma)}.$$

The objective we consider in the chapter is to minimize $\mu_{\mathcal{A}}$ for two cases: when the flow for each request can be split among multiple paths, and also when each request's flow has to be routed over a single path, the unsplittable case.

Example 18.2.2

To illustrate the limitation of any online algorithm $\mathcal{A}$, consider the network shown in Figure 18.1. Consider that node 1 is the source node for all requests, while the destination can be either node 2, 3, or 4. In particular, consider that the first request is for node pair $(1, 4)$ with unit demand. If $\mathcal{A}$ chooses a single path $1 \rightarrow 3 \rightarrow 4$ $(1 \rightarrow 2 \rightarrow 4)$ to fulfil the unit demand, then the second request is for node pair $(1, 3)$ $((1, 2))$, with unit demand. Thus, $\mathcal{A}$ will route two units of flow through at least one edge. OPT, on the other hand, knowing the request sequence in advance, will route the two requests over disjoint paths, routing unit flow through all edges. The same conclusion can be drawn if $\mathcal{A}$ splits the demand over multiple paths.

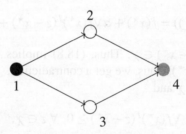

Figure 18.1 Black node is the source node for all requests, while the destinations are either a white node or a grey node.

18.3 Splittable Flow

In this section, we consider the case when the demand d_k of request k can be split over multiple paths of G. For this case, we begin with the following negative result.

Lemma 18.3.1 *For the splittable flow problem for polynomial latency functions $\ell_e(x) = ax^b, a > 0, b > 1$, the competitive ratio of any deterministic algorithm increases exponentially with b.*

We will discuss the proof of Lemma 18.3.1 in Problem 18.1. In the light of Lemma 18.3.1, in this chapter, we restrict our attention to ℓ_e being affine functions of the form $\ell_e(x) = a_e x + b_e$. For this case, we propose algorithm GREEDY and upper bound its competitive ratio as follows.

On arrival of the kth request, given the past routing decisions, $\mathcal{F}_e^{k-1}$, algorithm GREEDY solves the following optimization problem:

$$\min_{f_e^k \geq 0, e \in E} \quad C_k = \sum_{e \in E} C^e(f_e^k; \mathcal{F}_e^{k-1}), \tag{18.7}$$

satisfying $(18.1), (18.2), (18.3)$.

Recall from Remark 18.2.1 that C_k is a convex function of f_e^k, and hence (18.7) is a convex program. Next, we state a useful property of an optimal solution of a convex program.

Lemma 18.3.2 *Let f be a continuously differentiable convex function, and let $\chi \subset \mathbb{R}^n$ be a closed convex set. Then for the problem*

$$\min_{x \in \chi} f(x),$$

$x^\star$ *is optimal if and only if $x^\star \in \chi$ and $\nabla f(x^\star)^T(z - x^\star) \geq 0$ for all $z \in \chi$.*

Proof: Proof by contradiction. Let $x^\star$ be the optimal solution to $\min_{x \in \chi} f(x)$, while $\nabla f(x^\star)^T$ $(z - x^\star) < 0$ for some $z \in \chi$. Using the Taylor expansion for f, we get that for small enough $\alpha > 0$,

$$f(x^\star + \alpha(z - x^\star)) = f(x^\star) + \alpha \nabla f(x^\star)^T(z - x^\star) + o(\alpha) < f(x^\star). \tag{18.8}$$

Since χ is convex, $x^\star + \alpha(z - x^\star) \in \chi$. Thus, (18.8) implies that $f(x^\star + \alpha(z - x^\star))$ has a smaller function value than $f(x^\star)$. Thus, we get a contradiction.

For the converse, let $x^\star \in \chi$ and

$$\nabla f(x^\star)^T(z - x^\star) \geq 0, \ \forall z \in \chi. \tag{18.9}$$

From the convexity of f, we get

$$f(x^\star) + \nabla f(x^\star)^T(z - x^\star) \leq f(z), \ \forall z \in \chi,$$

implying that

$$\nabla f(x^\star)^T(z - x^\star) \leq f(z) - f(x^\star), \ \forall z \in \chi. \tag{18.10}$$

Equations (18.9) and (18.10) together imply that

$$f(z) - f(x^\star) \geq 0, \ \forall z \in \chi, \tag{18.11}$$

proving the optimality of $x^\star$. ∎

Notice that from (18.4),

$$\frac{dC_k}{df_e^k} = \ell_e\left(\sum_{i=1}^{k} f_e^i\right), \tag{18.12}$$

Thus, applying Lemma 18.3.2 to Problem 18.7, given the current solution $\mathcal{F}_e^{k-1}$, the optimal solution f_e^k of (18.7) for the kth-request satisfies

$$\sum_{e\in E} \ell_e\left(\sum_{i=1}^{k} f_e^i\right) f_e^k \leq \sum_{e\in E} \ell_e\left(\sum_{i=1}^{k} f_e^i\right) x_e^k, \tag{18.13}$$

where x_e^k is any other feasible flow for the kth request.

Another property that follows from the KKT conditions[1] for the convex program is

$$\sum_{e\in P} \ell_e\left(\sum_{i=1}^{k} f_e^i\right) \leq \sum_{e\in Q} \ell_e\left(\sum_{i=1}^{k} f_e^i\right), \tag{18.14}$$

where P and Q are any two paths in G from s_k to t_k, where P carries non-zero flow for request k in the optimal solution of (18.7). The proof of this property can be found in [321]. Condition (18.14) has an intuitive appeal that a path carrying non-zero flow with the optimal solution should have a lower cost than any other path from s_k to t_k, respectively.

Compared to the GREEDY algorithm, OPT will jointly find $f_e^k \geq 0, k = 1, \ldots, K$, for all the K requests by solving

$$\min_{\substack{f_e^k \geq 0, k=1,\ldots,K, \\ e\in E}} \quad C = \sum_{k=1}^{K} \sum_{e\in E} C^e(f_e^k; \mathcal{F}_e^{k-1}),$$

$$\text{satisfying} \quad (18.1), (18.2), (18.3), \tag{18.15}$$

only once.

Next, we analyse the competitive ratio of the GREEDY algorithm.

Theorem 18.3.3 *For affine latency functions, the competitive ratio of* GREEDY *is at most* $\frac{4K^2}{(1+K)^2}$, *where K is the total number of requests.*

The proof is remarkably simple and uses some elementary analysis, which is presented as follows.

Proof: With affine latency function $\ell_e(x) = a_e x + b_e$, the cost for satisfying flow request k using assignment f_e^k given $\mathcal{F}_e^{k-1}$ from (18.4) is

$$C_k(f_e^k; \mathcal{F}_e^{k-1}) = \sum_{e\in E} a_e\left(\sum_{i=1}^{k-1} f_e^i + \frac{1}{2}f_e^k\right) f_e^k + \sum_{e\in E} b_e f_e^k.$$

The optimality condition (18.13) implies that

$$\sum_{e\in E} a_e\left(\sum_{i=1}^{k} f_e^i + b_e\right)\left(f_e^k - x_e^k\right) \leq 0, \tag{18.16}$$

---

[1] Refer to Section A.2.

for an optimal solution f_e^k of (18.7) and any other feasible solution x_e^k.

Let $1 \leq \alpha \leq \beta \leq 2$, and consider for each edge e

$$\left(\alpha \sum_{i=1}^{K} f_e^i - \beta \sum_{i=1}^{K} x_e^i \right)^2 \geq 0,$$

$$\implies \alpha^2 \sum_{i=1}^{K} \sum_{j=1}^{K} f_e^i f_e^j - 2\alpha\beta \sum_{i=1}^{K} \sum_{j=1}^{K} f_e^i x_e^j + \beta^2 \sum_{i=1}^{K} \sum_{j=1}^{K} x_e^i x_e^j \geq 0. \tag{18.17}$$

This is a general recipe for evaluating the performance of an algorithm $\mathcal{A}$, where the main idea is to weigh the cost of algorithm $\mathcal{A}$ and any other feasible solution with different weights (α and β), and then invoke properties of algorithm $\mathcal{A}$.

Using the following elementary relation

$$\sum_{k=1}^{K} \sum_{j=1}^{K} f_e^k f_e^j = 2 \sum_{k=1}^{K} \left(\sum_{j=1}^{k-1} f_e^j + \frac{1}{2} f_e^k \right) f_e^k, \tag{18.18}$$

on the first and third terms of (18.17), we get

$$2\alpha^2 \sum_{k=1}^{K} \left(\sum_{j=1}^{k-1} f_e^j + \frac{1}{2} f_e^k \right) f_e^k - 2\alpha\beta \sum_{i=1}^{K} \sum_{j=1}^{K} f_e^i x_e^j + 2\beta^2 \sum_{k=1}^{K} \left(\sum_{j=1}^{k-1} x_e^j + \frac{1}{2} x_e^k \right) x_e^k \geq 0. \tag{18.19}$$

Multiplying (18.19) with a_e, and adding over all edges $e \in E$, we get

$$\sum_{e \in E} a_e \left(2\alpha^2 \sum_{k=1}^{K} \left(\sum_{j=1}^{k-1} f_e^j + \frac{1}{2} f_e^k \right) f_e^k - 2\alpha\beta \sum_{i=1}^{K} \sum_{j=1}^{K} f_e^i x_e^j + \sum_{k=1}^{K} \left(2\beta^2 \sum_{j=1}^{k-1} x_e^j + \frac{1}{2} x_e^k \right) x_e^k \right) \geq 0. \tag{18.20}$$

Consider two elementary relations

$$2\alpha^2 - \frac{2\alpha\beta}{K} \geq 2\alpha^2 - \alpha\beta \geq 0, \tag{18.21}$$

for $1 \leq \alpha \leq \beta \leq 2$ and $K \geq 2$, and

$$2\beta^2 - 2\alpha\beta \geq 2\beta^2 - 2\beta^2 \geq 0. \tag{18.22}$$

Multiplying $b_e f_e^k$ with $2\alpha^2 - \frac{2\alpha\beta}{K}$, and multiplying $b_e x_e^k$ with $2\beta^2 - 2\alpha\beta$ and adding them together, and summing over all edges e and all requests $k = 1, \ldots, K$, we get

$$\sum_{e \in E} \sum_{k=1}^{K} \left(\left(2\alpha^2 - \frac{2\alpha\beta}{K} \right) b_e f_e^k + (2\beta^2 - 2\alpha\beta) b_e x_e^k \right) \geq 0,$$

$$\implies \sum_{e \in E} \sum_{k=1}^{K} (2\alpha^2 b_e f_e^k - 2\alpha\beta b_e x_e^k + 2\beta^2 b_e x_e^k) - \frac{2\alpha\beta}{K} \sum_{e \in E} \sum_{k=1}^{K} b_e f_e^k \geq 0. \tag{18.23}$$

Let $\mathbf{x}$ be any flow vector (that captures x_e^k for all $e \in E$ and all $k = 1, \ldots, K$). For GREEDY, $\mathbf{x} = \mathbf{f}$. Then from (18.6) we can write the total cost

$$C(\mathbf{f}) = \sum_{k=1}^{K} \left(\sum_{e \in E} a_e \left(\sum_{j=1}^{k-1} f_e^j + \frac{1}{2} f_e^k \right) f_e^k + b_e f_e^k \right).$$

Using this definition, adding (18.20) and (18.23), we get

$$2\alpha^2 C(\mathbf{f}) - 2\alpha\beta \sum_{e \in E} \sum_{k=1}^{K} \left(a_e \sum_{j=1}^{K} f_e^j + b_e \right) x_e^k + 2\beta^2 C(\mathbf{x}) - \frac{2\alpha\beta}{K} \sum_{e \in E} \sum_{k=1}^{K} b_e f_e^k \geq 0. \quad (18.24)$$

Applying the optimality condition (18.16) for the flow $\mathbf{f}$ (GREEDY) on second term $2\alpha\beta \sum_{e \in E} \sum_{k=1}^{K} \left(a_e \sum_{j=1}^{k} f_e^j + b_e \right) x_e^k$ of (18.24), we get

$$2\alpha\beta \sum_{e \in E} \sum_{k=1}^{K} \left(a_e \sum_{j=1}^{k} f_e^j + b_e \right) x_e^k \geq 2\alpha\beta \sum_{e \in E} \sum_{k=1}^{K} \left(a_e \sum_{j=1}^{k} f_e^j + b_e \right) f_e^k,$$

$$= 2\alpha\beta \sum_{e \in E} \sum_{k=1}^{K} \left(a_e \left(\sum_{j=1}^{k-1} f_e^j + \frac{1}{2} f_e^k + \frac{1}{2} f_e^k \right) + b_e \right) f_e^k,$$

$$= 2\alpha\beta C(\mathbf{f}) + 2\alpha\beta \sum_{e \in E} a_e \sum_{k=1}^{K} \frac{1}{2} f_e^k f_e^k.$$

Using this in (18.24) and considering the innermost sum over index j (18.24) from 1 to k instead of 1 to K, we get

$$(2\alpha^2 - 2\alpha\beta)C(\mathbf{f}) - \alpha\beta \sum_{e \in E} a_e \sum_{k=1}^{K} f_e^k f_e^k + 2\beta^2 C(\mathbf{x}) - \frac{2\alpha\beta}{K} \sum_{e \in E} \sum_{k=1}^{K} b_e f_e^k \geq 0. \quad (18.25)$$

Using Cauchy–Schwarz inequality $\sum_{k=1}^{K} \left(f_e^k \right)^2 \geq \frac{1}{K} \left(\sum_{k=1}^{K} f_e^k \right)^2$ on the second term in (18.25), we get

$$(2\alpha^2 - 2\alpha\beta)C(\mathbf{f}) - \frac{\alpha\beta}{K} \sum_{e \in E} a_e \left(\sum_{k=1}^{K} f_e^k \right)^2 + 2\beta^2 C(\mathbf{x}) - \frac{2\alpha\beta}{K} \sum_{e \in E} \sum_{k=1}^{K} b_e f_e^k \geq 0,$$

$$\implies (2\alpha^2 - 2\alpha\beta)C(\mathbf{f}) + 2\beta^2 C(\mathbf{x}) - \frac{2\alpha\beta}{K} C(\mathbf{f}) \geq 0, \quad (18.26)$$

where the second equality follows from the fact that the sum of the second and fourth terms is equal to $C(\mathbf{f})$.

It is easy to see that (18.26) is equivalent to

$$C(\mathbf{f}) \le \frac{\beta^2}{-\alpha^2 + \alpha\beta + \frac{\alpha\beta}{K}} C(\mathbf{x}).$$

Recall that the only conditions on α, β are $1 \le \alpha \le \beta \le 2$. Thus, choosing $\alpha = 1 + 1/K$ and $\beta = 2$, we get

$$C(\mathbf{f}) \le \frac{4K^2}{(1+K)^2} C(\mathbf{x}). \tag{18.27}$$

Since (18.27) is true for any feasible solution $\mathbf{x}$, letting $\mathbf{x}$ to be the OPT solution, we get the result. $\blacksquare$

Thus, for affine edge latency functions ℓ_e, GREEDY is constant (≤ 4 for large K) competitive. In Problem 18.2, we discuss a lower bound on the competitive ratio of GREEDY with affine edge latency functions. Next, we consider the unsplittable flow case, where only one path can be used to route demand for any source–destination pair.

18.4 Unsplittable Flow

In this section, we consider problem (18.7) with an additional constraint that demand for any request cannot be split over multiple paths, and has to be satisfied using a single path.

Similar to Lemma 18.3.1, we get the following negative result for the unsplittable case as well.

Lemma 18.4.1 *With unsplittable flow when $\ell_e(x) = ax^b, a > 0, b > 1$, the competitive ratio of any deterministic online algorithm increases exponentially in b.*

We will discuss the proof of Lemma 18.4.1 in Problem 18.5. Once again we restrict our attention to ℓ_e being affine functions of the form $\ell_e(x) = a_e x + b_e$.

Similar to the optimality conditions (18.13) for the splittable case, the following is the necessary and sufficient condition for optimality of flow $\mathbf{f}$ in the unsplittable case. Given unsplittable flows $f_1, \dots, f_{k-1}$, a feasible unsplit flow f_e^k for request k is optimal if and only if

$$\sum_{e \in E} \int_0^{f_e^k} \ell_e \left(\sum_{i=1}^{k-1} f_e^i + z \right) dz \le \sum_{e \in E} \int_0^{x_e^k} \ell_e \left(\sum_{i=1}^{k-1} f_e^i + z \right) dz, \tag{18.28}$$

where x_e^k is any other feasible flow for the kth request. In the case of affine functions this specializes to

$$\sum_{e \in E} a_e \left(\sum_{i=1}^{k-1} f_e^i + \frac{1}{2} f_e^k \right) f_e^k + \sum_{e \in E} b_e f_e^k \le \sum_{e \in E} a_e \left(\sum_{i=1}^{k-1} f_e^i + \frac{1}{2} f_e^k \right) x_e^k + \sum_{e \in E} b_e x_e^k. \tag{18.29}$$

GREEDY: On the arrival of the kth request, solve (18.7) given the prior flows f_e^i, $i = 1, \ldots, k - 1$, with the additional constraint that the flow has to be unsplittable. Thus, the output of GREEDY f_e^k satisfies (18.29) for each $k = 1, \ldots, K$.

Remark 18.4.2 *Under the unsplittable constraint, problem* (18.7) *is equivalent to solving the shortest path problem on a directed graph, and hence can be solved in polynomial time.*

Theorem 18.4.3 *For affine latency functions, the competitive ratio of* GREEDY *in the unsplittable case is at most* $3 + 2\sqrt{2}$.

Proof: Recall from (18.6) that the total cost of an algorithm with optimal flow (vector) $\mathbf{f} = \{f_e^k\}$ is

$$C(\mathbf{f}) = \sum_{k=1}^{K} \left(\sum_{e \in E} a_e \left(\sum_{j=1}^{k-1} f_e^j + \frac{1}{2} f_e^k \right) f_e^k + b_e f_e^k \right),$$

$$= \sum_{e \in E} a_e \frac{1}{2} \left(\sum_{k=1}^{K} f_e^k \right)^2 + \sum_{e \in E} b_e f_e^k, \tag{18.30}$$

where the second equality follows from (18.18).

From the optimality condition for GREEDY (18.29), we have

$$C(\mathbf{f}) \leq \sum_{k=1}^{K} \left(\sum_{e \in E} a_e \left(\sum_{j=1}^{k-1} f_e^j + \frac{1}{2} x_e^k \right) x_e^k + b_e x_e^k \right). \tag{18.31}$$

Using $\sum_{k=1}^{K} x_e^k x_e^k \leq \left(\sum_{k=1}^{K} x_e^k \right)^2$, and increasing the limit of the inner sum from $j = 1$ to $k - 1$ to $j = 1$ to $K - 1$ in (18.31), we get

$$C(\mathbf{f}) \leq \sum_{k=1}^{K} \left(\sum_{e \in E} a_e \left(\sum_{j=1}^{K-1} f_e^j x_e^k + \frac{1}{2} \left(\sum_{k=1}^{K} x_e^k \right)^2 \right) + b_e x_e^k \right).$$

Next using the elementary relation (18.18), and the definition of $C(\mathbf{x})$ (18.30), we get

$$C(\mathbf{f}) \leq C(\mathbf{x}) + \sum_{e \in E} a_e \sum_{k=1}^{K} \sum_{j=1}^{K} f_e^j x_e^k.$$

Let $\lambda > 1$, and adding and subtracting $\lambda C(\mathbf{x})$ to the RHS, and using (18.30) to write out $-\lambda C(\mathbf{x})$, we get

$$C(\mathbf{f}) \leq (1 + \lambda)C(\mathbf{x}) + \sum_{e \in E} a_e \left(\sum_{k=1}^{K} \sum_{j=1}^{K} f_e^j x_e^k - \frac{\lambda}{2} \left(\sum_{k=1}^{K} x_e^k \right)^2 \right) - \lambda b_e \sum_{k=1}^{K} x_e^k.$$

Dropping the last term, we get

$$C(\mathbf{f}) \leq (1 + \lambda)C(\mathbf{x}) + \sum_{e \in E} a_e \left(\sum_{k=1}^{K} \sum_{j=1}^{K} f_e^j x_e^k - \frac{\lambda}{2} \left(\sum_{k=1}^{K} x_e^k \right)^2 \right). \tag{18.32}$$

Consider

$$\left(\frac{1}{\sqrt{2\lambda}} \sum_{k=1}^{K} f_e^k - \frac{\sqrt{\lambda}}{\sqrt{2}} \sum_{k=1}^{K} x_e^k \right)^2 \geq 0,$$

$$\implies \frac{1}{2\lambda} \left(\sum_{k=1}^{K} f_e^k \right)^2 - \sum_{k=1}^{K} \sum_{j=1}^{K} f_e^j x_e^k + \frac{\lambda}{2} \left(\sum_{k=1}^{K} x_e^k \right)^2 \geq 0. \tag{18.33}$$

Multiplying (18.33) with a_e and summing over $e \in E$, and adding to (18.32), we get

$$C(\mathbf{f}) \leq (1 + \lambda)C(\mathbf{x}) + \frac{1}{2\lambda} \sum_{e \in E} a_e \left(\sum_{k=1}^{K} f_e^k \right)^2,$$

$$\overset{(a)}{\leq} (1 + \lambda)C(\mathbf{x}) + \frac{1}{2\lambda} \sum_{e \in E} a_e \left(\sum_{k=1}^{K} f_e^k \right)^2 + \frac{1}{\lambda} \sum_{e \in E} b_e \sum_{k=1}^{K} f_e^k,$$

$$\overset{(b)}{=} (1 + \lambda)C(\mathbf{x}) + \frac{1}{\lambda}C(\mathbf{f}),$$

where (a) follows since $\sum_{e \in E} b_e \sum_{k=1}^{K} f_e^k \geq 0$ and (b) follows from the definition of $C(\mathbf{f})$ (18.30).

Thus,

$$C(\mathbf{f}) \leq \frac{1 + \lambda}{\lambda - 1} \lambda C(\mathbf{x}).$$

Optimizing over λ, we get $\lambda^\star = 1 + \sqrt{2}$, and the competitive ratio of GREEDY is at most $3 + 2\sqrt{2}$. ∎

18.5 Notes

The results presented in this chapter follow from [322]. A lower bound matching the upper bound of $3 + 2\sqrt{2}$ presented in the chapter for the unsplittable flow case can be found in [323]. Extensions of the results presented in this chapter to polynomial latency function with degree $d > 1$ can be found in [324]. A lower bound of $\Omega \left(\left(\frac{d}{\ln 2} \right)^{d+1} \right)$ has been derived in [324], while an upper bound as a function of the solutions of the equation $(d + 1)(x + 1)^d = x^{d+1}$ were provided in [325]. Improvements to these were made in [326, 327]. For most recent and best-known results with $d > 1$, we refer to [328].

Some more advances in the direction of minimizing network load can be found in [326, 329, 330]. A related online load balancing problem has been considered in [325], where the objective is to minimize the L_p norm of the sum of the loads on all the servers. In [331], a routing algorithm for admission control is considered, where the objective is to admit as many requests as possible to maximize the profit subject to satisfying the capacity constraint of each edge. The algorithm analysed in [331] has the same flavour as the algorithm considered in Section 12.4 to minimize the maximum load on any edge.

Game theoretic treatment of routing problems involves minimizing the price of anarchy of routing games [332–335], but there is no online aspect to that. The price of anarchy for the unsplittable game has been considered in [333], with affine latency functions studied in [334, 335]. Greedy algorithms similar to the one considered in the chapter have also been considered to maximize social welfare in routing games [336–338].

PROBLEMS

18.1 In the splittable flow case with general latency functions ℓ_e, show that the competitive ratio of any deterministic online algorithm is unbounded.[2] Consider $\ell_e(x) = m \cdot x^{m-1}$ for $m > 2$, and a four-node network shown in Figure 18.1.

18.2 In the splittable flow case with affine latency function $\ell_e(x) = a_e x + b_e$ show that the competitive ratio of GREEDY is at least $\frac{2K-1}{K}$. Consider the network shown in Figure 18.2 with latency functions $\ell_{(s_i, s)}(x) = 0$, $\ell_{(t, t_i)}(x) = 0$, $\ell_{(s_i, t_i)}(x) = i$ for $i = 1, \ldots, n$ and $\ell_{(s,t)}(x) = x$. The input is such that for $i = 1, \ldots, n$, a demand of unit size is requested from s_i to t_i sequentially.

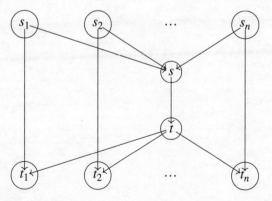

Figure 18.2 Network for Problem 18.2.

---

[2] All the problems in this chapter are credited to [322].

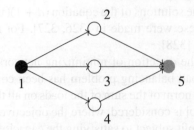

Figure 18.3 Black node is the source for all requests, while the destinations are either a white node or a grey node.

18.3 In the splittable flow case with linear latency functions $\ell_e(x) = a_e x$, show that the competitive ratio of GREEDY is at least $\frac{4}{3}$. Consider the network shown in Figure 18.3, where for all outgoing edges e from node 1 $\ell_e(x) = 4x$, while for all other edges $\ell_e(x) = 0$.

18.4 In the unsplittable flow case with general latency functions ℓ_e, show that the competitive ratio of any deterministic online algorithm is unbounded. Consider $\ell_e(x) = m \cdot x^{m-1}$ for $m > 2$, and the same network example as considered in Problem 18.1 is sufficient.

18.5 In the unsplittable flow case with linear latency function $\ell_e(x) = a_e x$, show that the competitive ratio of any deterministic algorithm is at least 2. The network shown in Figure 18.1 can be useful with $\ell_e(x) = 2x$.

CHAPTER 19

Resource Constrained Scheduling (Energy Harvesting Communication)

19.1 Introduction

In this chapter, we consider a more complicated scheduling problem than Chapter 15, where the resource needed for the processing of packets, energy, itself arrives over time, and the algorithm has only causal knowledge about it. This paradigm is relevant for communication systems powered by renewable energy sources, where the amount of energy arriving at each time slot is unpredictable. This scenario also models scheduling problems on factory floors where the availability time of, say, raw materials or multiple machines needed to complete a complicated job is uncertain and is revealed causally to the algorithm.

Conventionally, in online scheduling, unlimited energy is available, and the objective is to minimize a combination of energy used and relevant performance metrics, e.g., makespan, completion time, flow time, and the only uncertainty is about the packet or job arrival times and their sizes. For the online scheduling problem considered in the chapter, both the amount of energy and its arrival slots in the future are unknown to the algorithm and are possibly controlled by the adversary. With energy arriving over time and in arbitrary amounts, the generic scheduling problem is to minimize any performance metric, subject to the energy neutrality constraint, i.e., the amount of energy used by any time is at most the amount of energy that has arrived so far.

With arbitrary energy arrivals, we consider a canonical problem of transmitting a single packet (with a fixed number of bits) to minimize its completion time. Without loss of generality, we assume that the total amount of energy that arrives over time is sufficient to transmit the packet completely by the optimal offline algorithm OPT. The challenge is to propose an algorithm that can compete with OPT. We show that a LAZY algorithm has a competitive ratio of 2, which is also the best possible.

The considered problem in this chapter is fairly versatile. For example, it can model a scheduling paradigm where there are multiple servers but their availability is unknown, and the amount of work done in each slot is a concave function of the number of servers used in that slot. Then a scheduling problem (with any usual performance metric such as flow time, makespan, completion time) emerges where the decision is: how many servers to use among the available ones at each time.

19.2 Problem Formulation

Consider a source that has a single packet of size B bits which it intends to transmit to its destination. We consider slotted time, and each slot width is assumed to be equal to 1. The source receives energy over time, where the slots in which energy arrives are denoted as τ_k, and the energy that the source receives in slot τ_k is denoted as E_k. We denote the total accumulated energy received till slot t as

$$\text{acc}(t) = \sum_{k=1}^{F(t)} E_k,$$

where $F(t) = \max\{\tau_k | \tau_k \le t\}$. The sequence $\{\tau_k, E_k\}$ is arbitrary (can be chosen by an adversary), and known to the source only causally.

The channel between the source and the destination is assumed to be an additive white Gaussian noise channel, for which the number of bits $B(t,p)$ sent in a time duration t using energy E at constant power $p = E/t$ is given by the Shannon formula [276]

$$B(t,p) = t \log_2 \left(1 + p\right) \text{ bits.} \tag{19.1}$$

Let e_i be the energy used by the source at time slot i to transmit power p_i (recall that slot duration is 1, so $e_i = p_i$) that corresponds to transmitting

$$B_i = \log_2(1 + p_i) \text{ bits}$$

in time slot i using (19.1). The problem that the source wants to solve is: how much power p_i to transmit in time slot i, given the causal information about the sequence $\{\tau_k, E_k\}$, that minimizes the time by which all B bits are received by the destination, called the completion time problem.

Let $B(k) = \sum_{i=1}^{k} B_i$ be the total number of bits sent by any algorithm till slot k. Then, formally, the problem is

$$\min_{p_i} \quad T$$

$$\text{s.t.} \quad \sum_{i=1}^{k} e_i \le \text{acc}(k),$$

$$B(T) \ge \text{B}, \tag{19.2}$$

$$\forall k \le T.$$

The constraint $\sum_{i=1}^{k} e_i \le \text{acc}(k)$ is called the **energy neutrality constraint**, i.e., the amount of energy consumed by any time slot cannot be more than the total energy that has arrived till that slot.

The competitive ratio for any online algorithm $\mathcal{A}$ is then

$$\mu_{\mathcal{A}} = \max_{\sigma = \{\tau_k, E_k\}} \frac{T_{\mathcal{A}}(\sigma)}{T_{\text{OPT}}(\sigma)}.$$

Remark 19.2.1 *For any time slot t, a natural greedy algorithm that consumes all the available energy in a single slot has an unbounded competitive ratio. The main reason for this is that the number of bits transmitted in a slot (19.1) is a concave function of the energy consumed. To show this result concretely, consider an energy arrival sequence, where energy E arrives only in the first time slot, such that*

$$\lim_{t \to \infty} t \log_2 \left(1 + \frac{E}{t} \right) > B, \text{ and } \log_2 (1 + E) < B.$$

Let t_{OPT} be the smallest t such that $t \log_2 \left(1 + \frac{E}{t} \right) = B$. Then, OPT will transmit B bits in time t_{OPT} (consuming E at a slow rate taking advantage of the log function), while the greedy algorithm cannot finish the transmission of B bits ever, since it consumes all the energy E in the first slot which is insufficient to transmit the B bits.

19.3 Online Algorithm

In the light of Remark 19.2.1, we consider a non-trivial algorithm called LAZY that at each new energy arrival slot τ_k computes whether is it possible to send all the B bits using all the energy that has arrived till time τ_k at all or not, i.e., if

$$\lim_{t \to \infty} t \log_2 \left(1 + \frac{\sum_{i=1}^{\tau_k} E_i}{t} \right) \geq B \qquad (19.3)$$

or not.

If it is not possible, then the algorithm waits till the next energy arrival slot, and makes no transmission until then. Otherwise, the source starts to transmit with constant power

$$p_j = \frac{\sum_{i=1}^{\tau_k} E_i}{t^\star} \qquad (19.4)$$

in each time slot $j \geq \tau_k$, where $t^\star$ satisfies

$$t^\star \log_2 \left(1 + \frac{\sum_{i=1}^{\tau_k} E_i}{t^\star} \right) = B. \qquad (19.5)$$

Thus, the algorithm is trying to transmit the B bits in the shortest time possible assuming that no further energy is going to arrive in future.

Subsequently, on any new energy arrival, $t^\star$ is recomputed given the total remaining energy (leftover + newly arrived) and the remaining number of bits, and the constant transmit power (19.4) for each subsequent slot is updated.

For LAZY, we show that if T_{OPT} is OPT's completion time, then the time at which LAZY starts transmission is at most T_{OPT}, and once LAZY starts, it finishes its transmission in a time duration that is at most T_{OPT}. Thus, the total completion time for LAZY is at most $2T_{OPT}$, which gives us the following result.

Theorem 19.3.1 *The competitive ratio of* LAZY *is at most* 2.

In Theorem 19.4.1 we show that the competitive ratio of any online algorithm for solving the completion time problem (Problem 19.2) with energy arriving over time is at least $2 - \epsilon$ for any $\epsilon > 0$, showing that LAZY is an optimal online algorithm.

Proof: [Proof of Theorem 19.3.1] First, we show that LAZY starts its transmission by time T_{OPT}, i.e., (19.3) is satisfied for some $\tau_k \leq T_{\text{OPT}}$. We prove this by contradiction. Recall that with LAZY, transmission can begin only at the time when a new energy arrival happens. Let that time be $T_s = \tau_k$ for some k. From the contradiction hypothesis $T_s > T_{\text{OPT}}$.

$T_s = \tau_k$ together with the definition of LAZY implies that

$$t \log\left(1 + \frac{\text{acc}(\tau_{k-1})}{t}\right) < B \quad \forall t \text{ and,} \tag{19.6}$$

$$t \log\left(1 + \frac{\text{acc}(\tau_k)}{t}\right) \geq B \quad \text{for some } t,$$

since transmission began only at time τ_k and not at τ_{k-1}, where the total accumulated energy at time τ_k is $\text{acc}(\tau_k)$.

Let for OPT, whose completion time is T_{OPT}, the energy or power[1] transmitted in slot j be $p_j^\star$. Then, by definition of Problem 19.2,

$$B = \sum_{j=1}^{T_{\text{OPT}}} \log(1 + p_j^\star). \tag{19.7}$$

Let $g(x) = \log(1 + x)$. Then, by Jenson's inequality,

$$\sum_{j=1}^{T_{\text{OPT}}} \log(1 + p_j^\star) \leq T_{\text{OPT}}\, g\left(\frac{\sum_{j=1}^{T_{\text{OPT}}} p_j^\star}{T_{\text{OPT}}}\right),$$

$$\overset{(a)}{\leq} T_{\text{OPT}}\, g\left(\frac{\text{acc}(T_{\text{OPT}})}{T_{\text{OPT}}}\right),$$

$$\overset{(b)}{<} T_{\text{OPT}}\, g\left(\frac{\text{acc}(\tau_{k-1})}{T_{\text{OPT}}}\right). \tag{19.8}$$

(a) follows since even for OPT $\sum_{j=1}^{T_{\text{OPT}}} p_j^\star \leq \text{acc}(T_{\text{OPT}})$, the total energy arrived till then, and (b) follows from our hypothesis that the completion time of OPT $T_{\text{OPT}} < \tau_k = T_s$, which implies that the total energy that OPT can use is at most the energy that arrives till time τ_{k-1}, which is $\text{acc}(\tau_{k-1})$. Combining (19.6) and (19.8), we get

$$\sum_{j=1}^{T_{\text{OPT}}} \log(1 + p_j^\star) < B,$$

---

[1] Energy consumed or power transmitted in a slot are equal to each other since slot width is one.

contradicting (19.7). Thus, if $T_s > T_{OPT}$, then the transmission of B bits is not feasible with OPT by time T_{OPT}, implying the contradiction.

To complete the proof, next we show that once LAZY starts transmission, it finishes sending B bits in time duration of at most T_{OPT}.

Let τ_{last} be the last energy arrival slot before T_{OPT}, the time at which OPT finishes its transmission. Note that the maximum number of bits that can be transmitted using energy $acc(\tau_{last})$ in time duration T_{OPT} is at most $T_{OPT}g\left(\dfrac{acc(\tau_{last})}{T_{OPT}}\right)$. Since OPT can use only the energy that has arrived till time τ_{last}, necessarily the following has to be satisfied:

$$B \le T_{OPT}g\left(\frac{acc(\tau_{last})}{T_{OPT}}\right). \tag{19.9}$$

By definition, LAZY begins transmission at some energy arrival slot, and from the previous argument, we know that such energy arrival slot is before or at time T_{OPT}. Consequently, it is easy to argue that the worst-case input for LAZY that maximizes its competitive ratio is when LAZY begins its transmission only at time τ_{last}. We consider this scenario henceforth to upper bound the competitive ratio of LAZY.

Consider an alternate online algorithm $\mathcal{A}$ that begins to transmit at time τ_{last}, with constant power $\dfrac{acc(\tau_{last})}{T'}$ for time duration T' where

$$T'g\left(\frac{acc(\tau_{last})}{T'}\right) = B, \tag{19.10}$$

and discards any energy that arrives after time τ_{last}. Note that there exists a T' that satisfies (19.10), since we know that LAZY begins transmission at time τ_{last}, which in particular means that $t^\star$ satisfying (19.5) exists for $\sum_{i=1}^{\tau_{last}} E_i = acc(\tau_{last})$.

Let T_{on} be the transmission time (actual time for which the B bits are transmitted) for LAZY. Note that LAZY is identical to $\mathcal{A}$ if no energy arrives after τ_{last}, while if energy arrives after τ_{last}, LAZY transmits bits at a faster rate than $\mathcal{A}$, and hence will complete transmission before $\mathcal{A}$. Thus, we have

$$T_{on} \le T'. \tag{19.11}$$

Comparing (19.9) and (19.10), we get

$$T' \le T_{OPT}. \tag{19.12}$$

Thus,

$$T_{on} \le T_{OPT},$$

and recall that we have already proven that $T_s \le T_{OPT}$. Hence, the competitive ratio of LAZY can be upper bounded by

$$\mu_{LAZY} = \max_{\sigma=(\tau_k, E_k)}\left(\frac{T_{LAZY}}{T_{off}}\right) = \frac{T_s + T_{on}}{T_{OPT}},$$

$$\le \frac{2T_{OPT}}{T_{OPT}} = 2.$$

∎

19.4 Lower Bound

Theorem 19.4.1 *The competitive ratio of any algorithm to solve Problem 19.2 is at least $2 - \epsilon$ for any $\epsilon > 0$.*

Proof: To prove this result, we will consider two input sequences $\sigma_1 = \{\tau_0, E_0\}$ and $\sigma_2 = \{(\tau_0, E_0), (\tau_1, E_1)\}$, where with σ_1 there is just one energy arrival, while with σ_2 there is an additional energy arrival of amount E_1 at time τ_1. Let $\tau_0 = 0$ and $\tau_1 = 1$. With these two input sequences, we will try to show

$$\min_{\mathcal{A}} \max_{\sigma_i, i=1,2} \frac{T_{\mathcal{A}}(\sigma_i)}{T_{\mathsf{OPT}}(\sigma_i)} \geq 2 - \epsilon, \tag{19.13}$$

for any $\epsilon > 0$, over all online algorithms $\mathcal{A}$, which implies the required lower bound.

Recall that $g(x) = \log(1 + x)$. Since we are looking for a lower bound, we can choose any value for E_0, E_1, and B (even depending on each other). For σ_1, σ_2, let the value of E_0, E_1, and B be chosen as follows. Let E_0 be such that $\mathsf{B} = Tg\left(\frac{E_0}{T}\right)$ for some large T, and let E_1 be such that $\mathsf{B} = \tau_1 g\left(\frac{E_0 + E_1}{\tau_1}\right)$. This choice is made to ensure that using only energy E_0, it takes a long time to finish transmitting B bits, while using both $E_0 + E_1$ it takes only a unit amount of time, and $E_1 > E_0$. This information will be critically utilized by OPT but not by $\mathcal{A}$, since the latter gets to see energy arrival information only causally.

With σ_1, OPT will finish at time T_1, where

$$T_1 g\left(\frac{E_0}{T_1}\right) = \mathsf{B}.$$

Note that by the choice of input $T_1 = T$.

With σ_2, OPT will finish at time T_2, where T_2 is defined as follows. Since $E_1 > E_0$, OPT will completely consume energy E_0 by time $\tau_1 = 1$ to transmit $\mathsf{B}_1 = \tau_1 g\left(\frac{E_0}{\tau_1}\right)$ bits in the first slot, and then use the newly arriving energy E_1 in time $T_2 - \tau_1$ to transmit the leftover bits $\mathsf{B} - \mathsf{B}_1$, where $T_2 - \tau_1$ is such that

$$(T_2 - \tau_1)g\left(\frac{E_1}{(T_2 - \tau_1)}\right) = \mathsf{B} - \mathsf{B}_1,$$

as shown in Figure 19.1.

Any online algorithm $\mathcal{A}$ until time τ_1 cannot distinguish between σ_1 and σ_2, and thus consumes an α fraction of energy E_0 that is available at time $\tau_0 = 0$ by time τ_1. Thus, we can index all online algorithms by a single parameter α, where the lower bound on the competitive ratio is

$$\min_{\alpha \in [0,1]} \max_{\sigma_i, i=1,2} \frac{T_{\mathcal{A}}(\sigma_i)}{T_{\mathsf{OPT}}(\sigma_i)}. \tag{19.14}$$

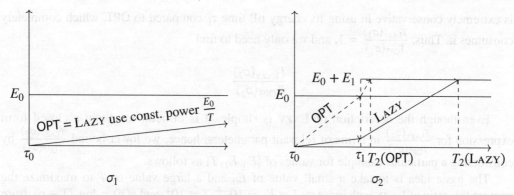

Figure 19.1 Illustration of the power/energy profile used by OPT and LAZY for σ_1 and σ_2.

The maximum number of bits that can be transmitted by $\mathcal{A}$ with particular choice of α with input σ_1 is given by

$$B_\alpha = \tau_1 g\left(\frac{\alpha E_0}{\tau_1}\right) + \lim_{t\to\infty}(t-\tau_1)g\left(\frac{(1-\alpha)E_0}{t-\tau_1}\right). \tag{19.15}$$

Recall from the choice made for B, T, E_0, E_1, $B = Tg\left(\frac{E_0}{T}\right)$ for some large T. Then, from the concavity of function g, we get from (19.15)

$$B_\alpha \leq B$$

with equality only at $\alpha = 1 - \frac{\tau_1}{T}$.

Therefore, we can conclude that $\mathcal{A}$ will not be able to complete the transmission of B bits if the input sequence is σ_1, and if it makes a choice of $\alpha \neq 1 - \frac{\tau_1}{T}$. Alternatively, if $\alpha \neq 1 - \frac{\tau_1}{T}$, then the competitive ratio of $\mathcal{A}$ is ∞, since the adversary can decide between σ_1 and σ_2 depending on the choice of α by $\mathcal{A}$. Remarkably, $\alpha = 1 - \frac{\tau_1}{T}$ is the choice made by LAZY described in the previous section.

Note that since the input is either σ_1 or σ_2 at time τ_1, $\mathcal{A}$ has complete information. Therefore, starting at time τ_1 $\mathcal{A}$ can make the optimal decision, and the only non-trivial decision for $\mathcal{A}$ is: how much energy to consume (α) until time τ_1 without the exact knowledge of σ_1 or σ_2. From the previous discussion, we know that the only non-trivial choice is $\alpha = 1 - \frac{\tau_1}{T}$. Since that equals the choice made by LAZY, we can restrict our attention to LAZY to derive the lower bound (19.14). Hence,

$$\min_{\mathcal{A}} \max_{\sigma_i, i=1,2} \frac{T_{\mathcal{A}}(\sigma_i)}{T_{\text{OPT}}(\sigma_i)} \geq \max_{\sigma_i, i=1,2} \frac{T_{\text{LAZY}}(\sigma_i)}{T_{\text{OPT}}(\sigma_i)}. \tag{19.16}$$

The behaviour of LAZY with input σ_1 and σ_2 is illustrated in Figure 19.1 in comparison to OPT, where we see that LAZY is identical to OPT with input σ_1, while when the input is σ_2, it is extremely conservative in using its energy till time τ_1 compared to OPT, which completely consumes it. Thus, $\frac{T_{\text{LAZY}}(\sigma_1)}{T_{\text{OPT}}(\sigma_1)} = 1$, and we only need to find

$$\frac{T_{\text{LAZY}}(\sigma_2)}{T_{\text{OPT}}(\sigma_2)}.$$

Even though the description of LAZY is simple, it is difficult to obtain a closed form expression for $\frac{T_{\text{LAZY}}(\sigma_2)}{T_{\text{OPT}}(\sigma_2)}$ in terms of relevant parameters; hence, we lower bound $\frac{T_{\text{LAZY}}(\sigma_2)}{T_{\text{OPT}}(\sigma_2)}$ by considering a particular example for values of $\{E_0, E_1, T\}$ as follows.

The basic idea is to take a small value of E_0 and a large value of T to maximize the competitive ratio of LAZY with input σ_2. Let $E_0 = 10^{-4}$, $T = 10^4$, and $g(p) = \log_2(1 + p)$, from which we can extract the values of B and E_1, with $B = Tg\left(\frac{E_0}{T}\right)$ and $B = \tau_1 g\left(\frac{E_0 + E_1}{\tau_1}\right)$, where $\tau_1 = 1$ from the construction. With this choice $\frac{T_{\text{LAZY}}(\sigma_2)}{T_{\text{OPT}}(\sigma_2)} = 2 - 2.49 \times 10^{-4}$. By increasing T and decreasing E_0 towards 0, we can keep pushing $\frac{T_{\text{LAZY}}(\sigma_2)}{T_{\text{OPT}}(\sigma_2)}$ arbitrarily close to 2. This completes the proof. ∎

19.5 Notes

The problem presented in this chapter was first considered in [339], where an upper bound of 2 was derived on the competitive ratio of LAZY. The matching lower bound of $2 - \epsilon$ for $\epsilon > 0$ presented in this chapter follows from [340], while the OPT for the problem considered in the chapter can be found in [341]. Generalized versions of this problem were considered in [340, 342], where both the source and the destination consume energy for communication and energy availability is unknown at both terminals. [340, 342]. The most general formulation of this problem is over a network modelled by a directed graph, where each vertex or node in the network has energy availability uncertainty, and the objective is to minimize the completion time of a packet between a single source and a destination. Even for this generalized setting, remarkably a 2-competitive algorithm has been derived in [343] via solving a non-polymatroidal maximum flow problem over a graph. We present the main ingredient (an algorithm to solve the non-polymatroidal max-flow problem) of this algorithm in Problem 19.3, which can be used repeatedly to get a 2-competitive algorithm Problem 19.2 defined over a network. For a special case of a many-to-one communication network, the OPT has been derived in [344].

PROBLEMS

19.1 (Optimal Offline Algorithm) In this problem, we consider the offline setting (where both E_k, τ_k are known for all slots $k \geq 1$) for Problem 19.2, and derive some necessary conditions that an OPT has to satisfy. For the OPT, let N be the number of times when the transmit power changes until the transmission of B bits is complete. In particular, let constant power p_i be used between time slot t_i and $t_{i+1} - 1$, where $t_1 = 1$, and $i = 1, \dots, N$.

Prove the following using contradiction.

1. With OPT, the transmission power remains constant between energy arrivals, i.e., t_i's coincide with some energy arrival slot τ_k.

2. With OPT, the transmission powers increase monotonically, i.e., $p_1 \leq p_2 \leq \cdots \leq p_N$.

3. With OPT, whenever the transmission power changes in slot t, the energy consumed up to time slot t equals the energy harvested up to that time slot, i.e., $\sum_{i=1}^{t} e_i = \mathrm{acc}(t)$.

19.2 Motivated by the necessary conditions derived in Problem 19.1, consider the following offline algorithm for solving Problem 19.2. Given the future knowledge of arriving energy, i.e., $\mathrm{acc}(t)$ for each t, find the earliest energy arrival slot $\tau_{k^\star}$ at which the accumulated energy $\mathrm{acc}(k^\star)$ is sufficient to transmit B bits by time $\tau_{k^\star+1}^-$.[2] In particular, let

$$T_1^\star \log\left(1 + \frac{\mathrm{acc}(k^\star)}{T_1^\star}\right) = \mathrm{B}, \tag{19.17}$$

where $\tau_{k^\star} \leq T_1^\star \leq \tau_{k^\star+1}^-$.

Then assume that all the energy $\mathrm{acc}(k^\star)$ is available at time 0, and choose transmit power $p_1^{\mathrm{temp}} = \mathrm{acc}(k^\star)/T_1^\star$.

If no such $\tau_{k^\star}$ exists that satisfies (19.17), then we will set $p_1^{\mathrm{temp}} = \mathrm{acc}(\mathrm{last})/t_{\mathrm{last}}$, where $\mathrm{acc}(\mathrm{last})$ is the sum of total energy that arrives ever, and t_{last} is the earliest time for which

$$t_{\mathrm{last}} \log\left(1 + \frac{\mathrm{acc}(\mathrm{last})}{t_{\mathrm{last}}}\right) = \mathrm{B}. \tag{19.18}$$

Consider the earliest time slot t at which using power allocation p_1^{temp} from time 0 to t violates the energy neutrality constraint, i.e., $\sum_{i=1}^{t} p_1^{\mathrm{temp}} > \mathrm{acc}(t)$. If no such slot exists, use transmit power p_1^{temp} from time slot 1 till $T_1^\star$ or t_{last}.

Let the earliest energy arrival slot after time t be $t_{\mathrm{first}} = \min\{\tau_k | \tau_k \geq t\}$. Then choose transmit power as $p_1 = \mathrm{acc}(t_{\mathrm{first}})/t_{\mathrm{first}}$ from time slot 1 till time slot t_{first}, i.e., consume all the energy by time t_{first} that arrives by time t_{first} at uniform power rate. Repeat the above process starting from time slot $t_{\mathrm{first}} + 1$ with the remaining number of bits at slot $t_{\mathrm{first}} + 1$ and future energy arrivals.

Prove that this algorithm is OPT.

19.3 [Non-polymatroidal maximum flow problem] For the network shown in Figure 19.2, consider the following problem: maximize the rate of communication or throughput from the source s to the destination d. In Figure 19.2, an arrow between two nodes represents an

---

[2] Just before the next energy arrival slot.

edge between them over which communication is possible. Node k can assign power $P_{k\ell}$ on the ℓth outgoing edge subject to the sum-power constraint of P_k, i.e., with O_k as the set of outgoing edges from node k with total power constraint $\sum_{\ell \in O_k} P_{k\ell} \leq \mathsf{P}_k$. Moreover, the rate $r_{k\ell}$ achieved on edge $k\ell$ when assigned power $P_{k\ell}$ is

$$r_{k\ell} = \log(1 + P_{k\ell}).$$

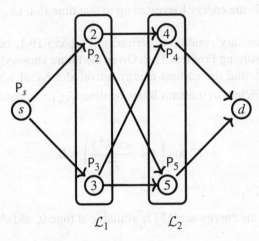

Figure 19.2 A two-layer network.

Formally, the problem can be stated as

$$\max \quad R \tag{19.19}$$

$$\text{s.t. } r_{k\ell} = \log(1 + P_{k\ell}), \sum_{\ell \in O_k} P_{k\ell} \leq P_k \tag{19.20}$$

$$r_{24} + r_{25} \leq r_{s2}, r_{34} + r_{35} \leq r_{s3}, r_{4d} \leq r_{24} + r_{34}, r_{5d} \leq r_{25} + r_{35} \tag{19.21}$$

$$r_{s2} + r_{s3} = r_{4d} + r_{5d} = R, \tag{19.22}$$

where in (19.20) r_{kl} is the rate achieved on each of the outgoing links $\ell \in O_k$ of node k, while (19.21) captures the flow conservation constraints at each node other than the source and the destination, while in (19.22) R is the out-going and in-coming rate at the source and the destination, respectively, that represents the throughput.

[Note: In the *polymatroidal* max-flow problem for a directed graph [345, 346], the set of rates possible on outgoing links of any node are defined as the intersection of hyperplanes. However, the rate constraints (19.20), (19.21), and (19.22) are not polymatroidal, which can be seen as follows. The out-degree of node s is 2 with total power P_s. Hence, the rate constraints on the two outgoing links will result in a region $(r_1, r_2) = (\log(1 + \alpha P_s), \log(1 + (1 - \alpha)P_s))$ whose boundary is traced by $0 \leq \alpha \leq 1$ as shown in Figure 19.3, which is clearly non-polymatroidal. In the following, we will propose an algorithm that can solve this *non-polymatroidal* max-flow problem for the network shown in Figure 19.2.]

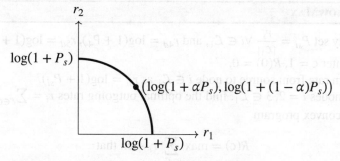

Figure 19.3 Rate region for out-degree 2 with total power P_s.

Consider the following algorithm FLOWMAX to solve the problem (19.19), whose main idea is as follows. First, note that the power allocation from nodes 4 and 5 in $\mathcal{L}_2$ towards the destination is trivial since they have only one outgoing edge. In particular, the rate from nodes 4 and 5 to d is fixed to be $r_{4d} = \log(1 + \mathsf{P}_4)$ and $r_{5d} = \log(1 + \mathsf{P}_5)$, respectively.

Initially assign equal power $\mathsf{P}_s/2$ from the source to both its outgoing edges to nodes 2 and 3 of $\mathcal{L}_1$ in **Step II**. With equal power allocation, let $r_{si}, i \in \mathcal{L}_1$, be the incoming rate into node $i = 2, 3 \in \mathcal{L}_1$ from the source. Subject to incoming constraints r_{si} for nodes $i \in \mathcal{L}_1$ and outgoing rate constraints of r_{4d}, r_{5d} to the destination, in **Step III**, find the optimal sum-rate between nodes of layer $\mathcal{L}_1$ and $\mathcal{L}_2$, where the optimal outgoing rate from nodes $i \in \mathcal{L}_1$ is denoted by r_i.

The set of nodes $i \in \mathcal{L}_1$ for which the out-rate r_i computed in **Step III** is lower than the incoming rate r_{si} they are currently receiving from the source is called U. In the next iteration, power from the source is reduced towards nodes of U and increased towards U^c to update r_{si}, i.e., r_{si} is increased for nodes $i \in U^c$ and decreased for $i \in U$. One important point is that even after updating, FLOWMAX keeps $r_{si} > r_i$ to avoid technical difficulties that can possibly arise otherwise.

If in any iteration $|U| = |\mathcal{L}_1|$ or $|U| = 0$, the algorithm terminates. Otherwise, the algorithm terminates at convergence.

1. Show that the sum-rate $R(c)$ computed from layer 1 to 2 in **Step III** is non-decreasing in iteration index c.

2. Show that if in iteration c, $U(c) = |\mathcal{L}_1|$, then $R(c)$ is optimal.

3. Show that $\forall c \geq 2, |U(c)| > 0$.

4. Show that if $|U(1)| = 0$, then the rate obtained in the first iteration $R(1)$ is optimal for solving (19.19).

5. Show that if the sum-rate (19.19) satisfies $R(c + 1) = R(c)$ for any iteration c, then the rate vector $\mathbf{r}(c) = [r_2(c)\ r_3(c)]$ is a global maxima, and $R(c)$ is the optimal sum-rate.

6. Combining parts 1 to 5, conclude that algorithm FLOWMAX converges to the optimal solution of (19.19).

Algorithm FLOWMAX

Step I: Initially set $P_{si} = \frac{P_s}{|\mathcal{L}_1|} \; \forall i \in \mathcal{L}_1$, and $r_{4d} = \log(1 + P_4), r_{5d} = \log(1 + P_5)$.
Initialize, counter $c = 1, R(0) = 0$.
Step II: Assign rate from source to node $i \in \mathcal{L}_1$ as $r_{si} = \log(1 + P_{si})$.
Step III: For nodes $i = 2, 3 \in \mathcal{L}_1$, find the optimal outgoing rates $r_i = \sum_{\ell \in O_i} r_{i\ell}$ by solving the following convex program

$$R(c) = \max \sum_{i \in \mathcal{L}_1} r_i \text{ such that}$$

$r_i \leq r_{si}$ and $\sum_{i=2}^{3} r_{ij} \leq r_{jd}, j \in 4, 5$.
Step IV: Define $U(c) = \{i \in \mathcal{L}_1 : r_i < r_{si}\}$
If $\Big(|U(c)| = 0 \text{ or } |U(c)| = |\mathcal{L}_1| \text{ or } |R(c) - R(c-1)| \leq \epsilon \Big)$ **break;**
Else
Compute the effective unused source power

$$\Delta = \left(\sum_{i \in U(c)} (P_{si} - e^{r_i} + 1) \right).$$

Redistribute the unused power as

- for each $j \in U(c)^c$, $P_{sj} = P_{sj} + \frac{\Delta}{|\mathcal{L}_1|}$.

- for each $i \in U(c)$, $P_{si} = e^{r_i} - 1 + \frac{\Delta}{|\mathcal{L}_1|}$.

$c = c + 1$, Go back to Step II
EndIf

CHAPTER 20

Submodular Partitioning for Welfare Maximization

20.1 Introduction

In this chapter, we consider a combinatorial resource allocation problem, called the *submodular partition* or *welfare* problem, where the objective is to divide or partition a given set of resources among multiple agents (with a possibly different valuation for each subset of resources), such that the sum of the agents' valuation (for resources assigned to them) is maximized.

When the agents' valuations of the subsets of resources is arbitrary, this problem is not only NP-hard, but also APX hard, i.e., it is hard to find even a good approximate solution. Thus, a natural, submodularity assumption is made on the agent valuations, that essentially captures the diminishing returns property, i.e., the incremental increase in any agents' valuation decreases as more and more resources are assigned to it. Important examples of this problem include combinatorial auctions, e.g., spectrum allocation among various cellular telephone service providers, advertisement-display slot assignments on web platforms, public utility allocations, etc.

Under the submodularity assumption, the partitioning problem becomes approximable. Early research in this direction considered an offline setting, but surprisingly the same ideas are applicable in the online setting as well, but with a slightly weaker guarantee.

In this chapter, for the online submodular partitioning problem, we present a simple greedy algorithm, and derive its competitive ratio, as a function of the **curvature** of the submodular valuation functions and a new metric called the **discriminant**. Curvature measures the 'distance' as to how far the valuation function is from being linear, while the discriminant counts the amount of improvement made by the greedy algorithm in each iteration. We also discuss some important applications of the submodular partition problem.

20.2 Submodular Partition Problem

We begin with a formal definition of a submodular function.

Definition 20.2.1 (*Monotone and Submodular Function*) *Let* $[N] = \{1, 2, \ldots, N\}$ *be a ground set. A set function* $Z : 2^N \to \mathbb{R}$ *is defined to be* **monotone** *if for* $S \subset T \subseteq [N]$,

$$Z(S) \leq Z(T),$$

and **submodular** *if for all $T \subseteq [N], S \subset T$ and $x \notin T$,*

$$Z(T \cup \{x\}) - Z(T) \leq Z(S \cup \{x\}) - Z(S).$$

Without loss of generality, we assume $Z(\emptyset) = 0$ ($\Rightarrow Z(S) \geq 0, \forall S \subseteq [N]$).

Submodularity captures the *diminishing returns* property exhibited by or expected to hold for natural utility metrics, i.e., the rate of increase of utility function decreases with an increase in the size of the allocated set.

Alternate and equivalent definitions of submodularity are as follows.

Definition 20.2.2 *A function f is submodular if*

1. *for every $S, T \subseteq [N]$ we have $f(S) + f(T) \geq f(S \cup T) + f(S \cap T)$ or*
2. *for every $X \subseteq [N]$ and $x_1, x_2 \in [N] \backslash X$ such that $x_1 \neq x_2$ we have $f(X \cup \{x_1\}) + f(X \cup \{x_2\}) \geq f(X \cup \{x_1, x_2\}) + f(X)$.*

Important examples of submodular functions include set union, entropy, mutual information [347], number of edges crossing a graph cut [348], etc. Showing these quantities are submodular can be easy or hard depending on the choice of the three definitions one chooses. For example, showing that the number of edges crossing a graph cut is submodular is very easy if one uses Definition 20.2.2 (1), and difficult otherwise.

More involved examples of submodular functions that are important in practice are spectrum allocation in wireless communication [349], where the function is the rate obtained by any agent over the allocated frequency bins, and influence maximization in networks [350]. For a detailed review of applications of submodular functions, see [351].

One important property of a submodular function is its curvature, which is defined as follows. Let the increment in valuation of a set S upon addition of element q to S be defined as

$$\rho_q(S) = f(S \cup \{q\}) - f(S).$$

Definition 20.2.3 *The **curvature** c of a monotone and submodular valuation function f is defined as*

$$c(f) = 1 - \min_{S, j \in S^*} \frac{\rho_j(S)}{\rho_j(\emptyset)}, \quad \text{where } S^* = \{j : j \in N \setminus S, \rho_j(\emptyset) > 0\}. \tag{20.1}$$

It is easy to see that by definition

$$0 \leq c(f) \leq 1.$$

An equivalent definition of curvature that follows from the submodularity of f is

$$c(f) = 1 - \min_{i \in [N]} \frac{f([N]) - f([N] \backslash \{i\})}{f(\{i\}) - f(\emptyset)},$$

where $[N] = \{1, 2, \dots, N\}$ is the ground set.

One simple consequence of Definition 20.2.3 is that

$$f(\{i\}) - f(\emptyset) \geq f(S \cup \{i\}) - f(S) \geq (1 - c(f))f(\{i\}) - f(\emptyset),$$

where the first inequality follows from the submodularity of f. Note that the smaller the curvature, the closer is the function f to being linear, e.g., when $c(f) = 0$, f is in fact linear.

In this chapter, we consider a **rich combinatorial** problem, where the objective is to partition a set of resources among distinct agents that have monotone increasing and submodular valuation for each subset of resources, such that the sum of the valuation of each agent is maximized. The formal definition of the problem is as follows.

Problem 20.2.4 *Let the set of allocable resources be $\mathcal{R}$ with $|\mathcal{R}| = n$, and the set of agents be denoted by $\mathcal{U}$ with $|\mathcal{U}| = m$. For $S \subseteq \mathcal{R}$, each agent u has a monotone and submodular valuation function $Z_u(S) : 2^{\mathcal{R}} \to \mathbb{R}$, where, without loss of generality, $Z_u(\emptyset) = 0, \forall u \in \mathcal{U}$.*

*The **submodular partition problem** is to find a partition of the set of resources $\mathcal{R}$ among the set of agents $\mathcal{U}$ such that the sum of the valuations of individual agents is maximized. Formally:*

$$max \sum_{u \in \mathcal{U}} Z_u(S_u), \text{subject to: } S_u \subseteq \mathcal{R} \quad \forall u, \ S_{u_i} \cap S_{u_j} = \emptyset, \text{for } u_i \neq u_j.$$

For each agent u, c_u is the curvature for agent u's that is defined by (20.2.3) using valuation function Z_u, and $c_{\max} = \max\limits_{u \in \mathcal{U}} c_u$.

Before we proceed further, we first introduce a combinatorial object called a **matroid** and a general optimization problem over it, which generalizes the submodular partition problem.

Definition 20.2.5 *(Matroid) A matroid over a finite ground set $[N]$ is a pair $([N], \mathcal{M})$, where $\mathcal{M} \subseteq 2^N$ (power set of $[N]$) that satisfies the following properties:*

1. *$\emptyset \in \mathcal{M}$.*
2. *If $T \in \mathcal{M}$ and $S \subset T \Rightarrow S \in \mathcal{M}$ [independence property].*
3. *If $S, T \in \mathcal{M} : |T| > |S| \Rightarrow \exists \ x \in T \setminus S : S \cup \{x\} \in \mathcal{M}$ [augmentation property]. $\mathcal{M}$ is called the family of independent sets.*

Definition 20.2.6 *(Rank of a matroid) For any subset $S \in 2^N$, the rank function of a matroid $([N], \mathcal{M})$ is defined as $r(S) = \max\{|M| : M \subseteq S, \text{ for } M \in \mathcal{M}\}$, and rank of the matroid is $\max_S r(S)$, the cardinality of the largest independent set. For a matroid to have rank K, there must exist no independent sets of cardinality $K + 1$.*

For many applications, two special cases of matroids are of interest, namely the uniform and the partition matroid that are defined as follows.

Definition 20.2.7 *(Uniform Matroid) For some $K > 0$, the uniform matroid over a ground set $[N]$ is defined as $([N], \mathcal{M}^u)$, where $\mathcal{M}^u = \{S : S \subseteq [N], |S| \leq K\}$.*

The uniform matroid corresponds to all subsets of a set of size at most K.

Definition 20.2.8 *(Partition Matroid) A ground set $[N]$, and its partition $\{P_i : i = 1, 2, ..., p\}$, i.e., $\cup_i P_i = [N]$, and $P_i \cap P_j = \emptyset, i \neq j$ are given. Given integers $k_i : 1 \leq k_i \leq |P_i|$, the partition* *matroid over* $[N]$ *is defined as* $([N], \mathcal{M}^p)$, *where* $\mathcal{M}^p = \{S : S \subseteq [N] \text{ and } |S \cap P_i| \leq k_i \text{ for } i = 1, 2, \dots, p\}$.

A generalized version of Problem 20.2.4 that is defined over a matroid is as follows.

Problem 20.2.9   *Given a matroid* $([N], \mathcal{M})$ *of rank* K, *and a monotone and submodular function* $Z : 2^{[N]} \to \mathbb{R}$, *the problem is to find* $\max \{Z(S) : S \in \mathcal{M}\}$.

Remark 20.2.10   *The problem of interest in this chapter, Problem 20.2.4 is a special case of Problem 20.2.9, where the matroid is the partition matroid* $(\mathcal{R}, \mathcal{M}^p)$,

$$\mathcal{M}^p = \{S : S \subseteq \mathcal{V}, \ |S \cap \mathcal{V}_r| \leq 1 \quad \forall r \in \mathcal{R}\}, \tag{20.2}$$

where $\mathcal{V} = \mathcal{U} \times \mathcal{R} = \{(u, r) : u \in \mathcal{U}, r \in \mathcal{R}\}$ *(agent-resource pairs), and* $\mathcal{V}_r = \{(u, r) : u \in \mathcal{U}\}$ *and*

$$Z(S) = \sum_{u \in \mathcal{U}} Z_u(S_u) \tag{20.3}$$

is submodular, since the sum of submodular functions is submodular (Problem 20.1). Note that S_u *is the restriction of* S *to agent* u.

Note that (20.2) corresponds to the constraint that each resource can be assigned to at most one agent. For this special case (the only problem considered in the rest of the chapter), we denote the increment in valuation by allocating resource r *to agent* u *given the existing set* S *as*

$$\rho_{(u,r)}(S) := Z(S \cup \{(u, r)\}) - Z(S) = Z_u(S_u \cup \{r\}) - Z_u(S_u). \tag{20.4}$$

Next, we describe the online setting for the partition problem, which is of primary interest.

20.2.1 Online Submodular Partition Problem

Problem 20.2.11   *This problem is identical to Problem 20.2.4, except that now, at each time index* $t = 1, 2, \dots, |\mathcal{R}|$, *one resource* $j_t \in \mathcal{R}, |\mathcal{R}| = n$ *arrives, which must immediately be allocated to exactly one of the agents and the decision is irrevocable.*

For the rest of the chapter, we will concentrate on solving Problem 20.2.11 and work with the cumulative valuation function Z (20.3), and the incremental valuation $\rho_r^u(S)$ over Z (20.4).

Let the arrival sequence of resources be σ, a permutation over the $|\mathcal{R}| = n$ resources. For input σ, let for an online algorithm $\mathcal{A}$, the set partition of $\mathcal{R}$ be $S_{\mathcal{A}}(\sigma)$. Then the competitive ratio for an online algorithm $\mathcal{A}$ is

$$\mu_{\mathcal{A}} = \min_{\sigma} \frac{Z(S_{\mathcal{A}}(\sigma))}{Z(S_{\text{OPT}}(\sigma))}.$$

We propose a simple greedy algorithm called GREEDY-ON for the online submodular partition problem, that on each resource's arrival assigns it to that agent that has the largest incremental utility, given the current allocation. The tie-breaking rule of GREEDY-ON (allocate resource j_t to agent u with least c_u) is also chosen to maximize the incremental utility, since the smaller the curvature, more is the incremental utility of that agent.

Algorithm 34 Greedy Algorithm for the Online Monotone Submodular Partition problem

---

1: **procedure** GREEDY-ON
2:     **Initialize:** $G^0 = \varnothing, t = 1$
3:     **while** $t \leq |\mathcal{R}| = n$, on arrival of resource j_t at time t **do**
4:         Allocate j_t to agent u_t if
5:         $u_t = \underset{u}{\text{argmax}} \left\{ \rho_{j_t}^u(G^{t-1}) \right\}$
6:         **Tie:** Allocate resource j_t to agent u with least c_u
7:         $G^t \leftarrow G^{t-1} \cup \{(u_t, j_t)\}$
8:         $t \leftarrow t + 1$
9:     **end while**
10:     **Return** $G = G^n$
11: **end procedure**

To derive a lower bound on the competitive ratio of the GREEDY-ON algorithm, we define a quantity called the *discriminant* as follows.

Definition 20.2.12 *For iteration t of* GREEDY-ON, *where resource j_t arrives and the current allocated set is G^{t-1}, the **discriminant** at iteration t, d_t is defined as*

$$d_t = \frac{\rho_{(u^\star, j_t)}(G^{t-1})}{\underset{u' \neq u^\star}{max}\, \rho_{(u', j_t)}(G^{t-1})}, \quad where\ u^\star = \underset{u}{argmax}\, \rho_{(u, j_t)}(G^{t-1}).$$

At iteration t, discriminant d_t is the ratio of the increment due to the best local agent chosen by the GREEDY-ON algorithm for allocating the resource j_t and the increment possible if the resource j_t is allocated to the agent who values it the second most. Since the numerator is always greater than the denominator, $\forall t$, $d_t \geq 1$.

Next, we present the guarantee on the competitive ratio of the GREEDY-ON algorithm as a function of the curvature and the discriminant.

Theorem 20.2.13 *For any arrival sequence σ over the $|\mathcal{R}| = n$ resources, the competitive ratio of the* GREEDY-ON *algorithm for Problem 20.2.11 is bounded by*

$$\mu_{\text{GREEDY-ON}} \geq min \left(1, \frac{1}{\left(\underset{t}{max} \left\{ \frac{1}{d_t} + c_{u_t} \right\} \right)} \right),$$

where d_t is the discriminant and c_{u_t} is the curvature of the agent chosen, in iteration t, respectively, for $t \in \{1, 2, \ldots, |\mathcal{R}|\}$.

In classical work, algorithm GREEDY-ON is known to have a competitive ratio of at least $1/2$ ([352]), which was improved to $1/(1 + c_{max})$ using the curvature information in [353] since $0 \leq c_{u_t} \leq 1$. Theorem 20.2.13 subsumes (since $d_t \geq 1$) both these results and lower bounds the competitive ratio of algorithm GREEDY-ON as a function of both the curvature and the discriminant.

In the rest of the chapter, we will prove Theorem 20.2.13, for which we restate the following notation:

1. Agent chosen by the GREEDY-ON algorithm at time t for allocating resource j_t: u_t.
2. With u_t as the agent chosen in iteration t, let the GREEDY-ON allocation (set partition of $\mathcal{R} = (j_1, \ldots, j_n)$) be

$$G^t = \{(u_1, j_1), (u_2, j_2), \ldots, (u_t, j_t)\},$$

and after all n resource arrivals

$$G^n = \{(u_1, j_1), (u_2, j_2), \ldots, (u_n, j_n)\},$$

and OPT's allocation be

$$S_{\text{OPT}} = \{(\hat{u}_1, j_1), (\hat{u}_2, j_2), \ldots, (\hat{u}_n, j_n)\},$$

where OPT allocates resource j_i to user $\hat{u}_i$.

3. Partition matroid $\mathcal{M}^p$ as defined in (20.2). Then, $\sum_{u \in \mathcal{U}} Z_u(S_u) \equiv Z(S)$ for $S \in \mathcal{M}^p$.
4. The set of all agent–resource pairs involving the resource j_t that arrives at time t: $U^t = \{(u, j_t) : \forall u \in \mathcal{U}\}$.
5. $\Psi^t = S_{\text{OPT}} \cap U^t$ and $\xi^t = G^n \cap U^t$.

Remark 20.2.14 *Note that $|\Psi^t \cap \xi^t| \leq 1$, since at every time t only a single resource is allocated ($|\Psi^t| = |\xi^t| = 1$).*

Lemma 20.2.15 *For $t_1 \neq t_2$, $\Psi^{t_1} \cap \Psi^{t_2} = \xi^{t_1} \cap \xi^{t_2} = \Psi^{t_1} \cap \xi^{t_2} = \emptyset$.*

Proof: It follows from the definition that $\Psi^t \subseteq U^t$ and $\xi^t \subseteq U^t$. Since $U^{t_1} \cap U^{t_2} = \emptyset$, the result follows. ∎

Lemma 20.2.16 *$G^n \setminus S_{\text{OPT}}$ and $S_{\text{OPT}} \setminus G^n$ can be decomposed as*

$$G^n \setminus S_{\text{OPT}} = \bigcup_{t=1}^{n} \xi^t \setminus \Psi^t, \quad \text{and} \quad S_{\text{OPT}} \setminus G^n = \bigcup_{t=1}^{n} \Psi^t \setminus \xi^t.$$

Proof: From the definition of Ψ^t and ξ^t, it follows that $G^n = \bigcup_{t=1}^{n} \xi^t$, and $S_{\text{OPT}} = \bigcup_{t=1}^{n} \Psi^t$. The proof concludes using Lemma 20.2.15. ∎

Lemma 20.2.17 *For any two resource–agent allocations $A, B \in \mathcal{M}^p$ (20.2),[1] the following is true:*

$$Z(A \cup B) \leq Z(A) + \sum_{i : b_i \in B \setminus A} \rho_{b_i}(A).$$

---

[1] A or B is a specific resource–user allocation.

Proof: Order B as $(b_1, b_2, \ldots, b_{|B|})$ arbitrarily and denote the partial ordered sets $B^t = (b_1, b_2, \ldots, b_t)$ [with $B^0 = \varnothing$]; then we have:

$$Z(A \cup B) = Z(A) + \sum_{i: b_i \in B \setminus A} \rho_{b_i}(A \cup B^{i-1}),$$

$$\overset{(i)}{\leq} Z(A) + \sum_{i: b_i \in B \setminus A} \rho_{b_i}(A),$$

where (i) follows by submodularity of Z. ∎

Now we are ready to prove Theorem 20.2.13.

Proof of Theorem 20.2.13

Proof: From Lemma 20.2.17, we have

$$Z(S_{OPT} \cup G^n) \leq Z(G^n) + \sum_{q \in S_{OPT} \setminus G^n} \rho_q(G^n),$$

$$\overset{(i)}{=} Z(G^n) + \sum_{t=1}^{n} \sum_{q \in \Psi^t \setminus \xi^t} \rho_q(G^n),$$

$$\overset{(ii)}{\leq} Z(G^n) + \sum_{t=1}^{n} \sum_{q \in \Psi^t \setminus \xi^t} \rho_q(G^{t-1}), \tag{20.5}$$

where (i) follows from Lemma 20.2.16 and Remark 20.2.15, and (ii) follows from the submodularity of Z, since $G^{t-1} \subseteq G^n$.

We can also expand $Z(S_{OPT} \cup G^n)$ in an alternate way as follows.

$$Z(S_{OPT} \cup G^n) = Z(S_{OPT}) + \sum_{t=1}^{n} \rho_{(u_t, j_t)}(S_{OPT} \cup G^{t-1}),$$

$$= Z(S_{OPT}) + \sum_{t=1}^{n} \sum_{q \in \xi^t \setminus \Psi^t} \rho_q(S_{OPT} \cup G^{t-1}), \tag{20.6}$$

where the second equality follows by again applying Lemma 20.2.16 and Remark 20.2.15. Combining (20.5) and (20.6),

$$Z(S_{OPT}) \leq Z(G^n) + \sum_{t=1}^{n} \sum_{q \in \Psi^t \setminus \xi^t} \rho_q(G^{t-1}) - \sum_{t=1}^{n} \sum_{q \in \xi^t \setminus \Psi^t} \rho_q(S_{OPT} \cap G^{t-1}). \tag{20.7}$$

From the definition of curvature (Definition 20.2.3), for any $q = (u_t, j_t)$,

$$\rho_q(S_{OPT} \cap G^{t-1}) \geq (1 - c_{u_t}) \rho_q(G^{t-1}). \tag{20.8}$$

Expanding $Z(G^n)$ in (20.7) as $Z(G^n) = \sum_{t=1}^{n} \sum_{q \in \xi^t} \rho_q(G^{t-1})$, using (20.8) on the third term of (20.7), we have

$$Z(S_{\text{OPT}}) \le \sum_{t=1}^{n} \sum_{q \in \xi^t} \rho_q(G^{t-1}) + \sum_{t=1}^{n} \sum_{q \in \Psi^t \setminus \xi^t} \rho_q(G^{t-1}) - \sum_{t=1}^{n} \sum_{\substack{q \in \xi^t \setminus \Psi^t \\ q=(u_t,j_t)}} (1 - c_{u_t})\rho_q(G^{t-1}). \quad (20.9)$$

Cancelling identical terms in the first and the last summations in (20.9), we get

$$Z(S_{\text{OPT}}) \le \sum_{t=1}^{n} \sum_{q \in \xi^t \cap \Psi^t} \rho_q(G^{t-1}) + \sum_{t=1}^{n} \sum_{q \in \Psi^t \setminus \xi^t} \rho_q(G^{t-1}) + \sum_{t=1}^{n} \sum_{\substack{q \in \xi^t \setminus \Psi^t \\ q=(u_t,j_t)}} c_{u_t}.\rho_q(G^{t-1}). \quad (20.10)$$

Next, we consider time t, where resource j_t is assigned by OPT to $\hat{u}_t$ such that $\hat{u}_t \ne u_t$, i.e., the algorithm GREEDY-ON and OPT assign resource j_t to different agents, and use the definition of discriminant to bound the second term in the RHS of (20.10). For $q = (\hat{u}_t, j_t) \in \Psi^t \setminus \xi^t$ (i.e., part of OPT's allocation but not in GREEDY-ON's allocation):

1. Then $(\hat{u}_t, j_t) \notin \xi^t$ by definition. But ξ_t contains (u_t, j_t) (since it is equal to $G^n \cap U^t$), and hence we conclude that $\hat{u}_t \ne u_t$.
2. We also note that $G^{t-1} \cup (\gamma_{n-1}, j_t) \in \mathcal{M}^p$, $\forall \gamma_{n-1} \in \mathcal{U}$ (since j_t has not been allocated in G^{t-1}), and hence $G^{t-1} \cup (\hat{u}_t, j_t) \in \mathcal{M}^p$. Essentially agent $\hat{u}_t$ is eligible to be assigned resource j_t by algorithm GREEDY-ON.

Therefore from the definition of the discriminant (Definition 20.2.12), we can write for $q \in \Psi^t \setminus \xi^t$,

$$\rho_q(G^{t-1}) \le \frac{\rho_{(u_t,j_t)}(G^{t-1})}{d_t}. \quad (20.11)$$

Using (20.11) on the second term of the RHS of (20.10), we have

$$Z(S_{\text{OPT}}) \le \sum_{t=1}^{n} \left(\sum_{q \in \xi^t \cap \Psi^t} \rho_q + \sum_{q \in \Psi^t \setminus \xi^t} \frac{\rho_q}{d_t} + \sum_{\substack{q \in \xi^t \setminus \Psi^t \\ q=(u_t,j_t)}} c_{u_t}.\rho_q \right). \quad (20.12)$$

Note that $\Psi^t = \{(\hat{u}_t, j_t)\}$ and $\xi^t = \{(u_t, j_t)\}$. Thus, if $\xi^t \setminus \Psi^t \ne \emptyset$, then it is clear that $\Psi^t \setminus \xi^t \ne \emptyset$. Thus, we combine together the last two summations in (20.12) to get

$$Z(S_{\text{OPT}}) \le \sum_{t=1}^{n} \sum_{q \in \xi^t \cap \Psi^t} \rho_q + \sum_{t=1}^{n} \sum_{\substack{q \in \xi^t \setminus \Psi^t \\ q=(u_t,j_t)}} \left(c_{u_t} + \frac{1}{d_t} \right) \rho_q.$$

Bringing $c_{u_t} + \frac{1}{d_t}$ out of the summation by defining $\Lambda = \max_t \left(c_{u_t} + \frac{1}{d_t} \right)$, we get

$$Z(S_{OPT}) \leq \sum_{t=1}^{n} \sum_{q \in \xi^t \cap \Psi^t} \rho_q + \Lambda \sum_{t=1}^{n} \sum_{\substack{q \in \xi^t \setminus \Psi^t \\ q = (u_t, j_t)}} \rho_q. \tag{20.13}$$

We can further reduce the RHS of (20.13) to

$$Z(S_{OPT}) \leq \max(1, \Lambda) \sum_{t=1}^{n} \sum_{q \in \xi^t \cap \Psi^t} \rho_q + \max(1, \Lambda) \sum_{t=1}^{n} \sum_{\substack{q \in \xi^t \setminus \Psi^t \\ q = (u_t, j_t)}} \rho_q,$$

$$= \max(1, \Lambda) \sum_{t=1}^{n} \sum_{q \in \xi^t} \rho_q,$$

$$= \max(1, \Lambda) Z(G^n).$$

This gives the required bound:

$$\frac{Z(G^n)}{Z(S_{OPT})} \geq \min \left(1, \frac{1}{\Lambda} \right) = \min \left(1, \frac{1}{\max_t \left(c_{u_t} + \frac{1}{d_t} \right)} \right).$$

∎

20.3 Applications

We discuss two applications of the online submodular partition problem as follows.

20.3.1 Unweighted Bipartite Matching and AdWords Problem

Recall the unweighted bipartite matching problem studied in Chapter 9. The unweighted bipartite matching problem can be considered as a submodular partitioning problem by defining the valuation of a left vertex as $v(\ell) = \min\{1, |R_\ell|\}$, when subset R_ℓ of the right vertices is assigned to the left vertex ℓ. Clearly, $v(\ell) = \min\{1, |R_\ell|\}$ is sub-modular, and hence the unweighted bipartite matching problem is an instance of Problem 20.2.11.

Similarly, for the AdWords problem discussed in Chapter 10, on user i's arrival if it is allocated the set of ads A_i, then the valuation is $r(i) = \min\{B_i, \sum_{j \in A_i} v_{ij}\}$, where B_i is the total budget of user i, while v_{ij} is the bid of user i for ad j. Once again, it is easy to verify that $r(i)$ is a submodular set function; hence the AdWords problem is an instance of Problem 20.2.11.

20.3.2 Assigning Mobile Users to Basestations

An important problem to solve in a cellular wireless network is the assignment of each mobile user to a single basestation, among the set of all basestations, which can depend on the distance, wireless channel conditions, etc. Moreover, this problem is well modelled as an online problem, where mobile users arrive sequentially into the system, and on their arrival, they have to be assigned to a basestation irrevocably.

Let there be a total of m basestations and n mobile users that will arrive sequentially. On the arrival of user i, it has to be irrevocably assigned to one of the basestations. The channel gain between user i and basestation j is represented as $h_{ij} \geq 0$, which is revealed only on the arrival of user i. Let the set of users assigned to basestation j be A_j. Each basestation has a total power constraint of P_j, and it assigns power P_{ij} to its connected user $i \in A_j$. Then the sum-rate obtained by basestation j is

$$R(A_j) = \max_{P_{ij}, \sum_{i \in A_j} P_{ij} \leq P_j} \sum_{i \in A_j} \log(1 + P_{ij} h_{ij}). \tag{20.14}$$

The problem is to partition the set of users among m basestations such that

$$\max_{A_j, A_j \cap A_k = \emptyset} \sum_{j=1}^{m} R(A_j). \tag{20.15}$$

In Problem 20.6, we show that $R(A_j)$ (20.14) is a monotone increasing submodular function, and hence problem (20.15) can be solved using the GREEDY-ON algorithm with a competitive ratio of $\min\left(1, \dfrac{1}{\max\limits_{t}\left(c_{u_t} + \dfrac{1}{d_t}\right)}\right)$. Computing both the d_t and c_{u_t} for this problem are interesting exercises.

20.4 Notes

The earliest theoretical results on the performance of the greedy algorithm for the submodular partitioning problem date back to the seminal work of [354, 355, 352] that studied the offline version of the problem and derived a 1/2-approximation [352]. Surprisingly, the same guarantee holds for the online case as well for the greedy algorithm. The first instance-dependent guarantee was derived in [353], which improved the competitive ratio guarantee for the greedy algorithm to be $\dfrac{1}{1+c}$, where $c \geq 1$ is the curvature that captures the distance of the function from being linear. The recent improvement of this result is the $(1 - \gamma_h/e - \epsilon)$-competitive algorithm [356], for any $\epsilon > 0$ where γ_h is the h-curvature. A randomized algorithm, called the continuous greedy algorithm, was proposed in [358] to improve the instance-dependent guarantee to $(1 - e^{-c})/c$. The results presented in this chapter can be found in [359]. Most of the theoretical work on the greedy algorithm assumes the value oracle model, where a polynomial algorithm is assumed to exist that can compute the optimal increment in each iteration. To obviate this possibly restrictive assumption, approximate greedy algorithms were considered by [357], where the increment is only available up to a certain approximation guarantee.

PROBLEMS

20.1 Show that the sum of two submodular functions is submodular.

20.2 Show that the maximum of two submodular functions is not necessarily submodular.

20.3 For a random vector X, its entropy $H(X) = -\sum_{X \in \mathcal{X}} p_X \log p_X$, where $\mathcal{X}$ is the support of X, while for two random vectors X, Y, the conditional entropy

$$H(X|Y) = - \sum_{X \in \mathcal{X}, Y \in \mathcal{Y}} p_{X,Y} \log p_{X|Y}.$$

The mutual information between X and Y is defined as

$$I(X;Y) = H(X) - H(X|Y) = H(Y) - H(Y|X) = - \sum_{X \in \mathcal{X}, Y \in \mathcal{Y}} p_{X,Y} \log \frac{p_{X,Y}}{p_X p_Y}.$$

Show that entropy is monotone and submodular, while mutual information is non-monotone but submodular.

[Hint: Take a vector X and append an extra element x to get a new vector $X \cup \{x\}$ and use Definition 20.2.1.]

20.4 Consider a positive semidefinite matrix $X \in \mathbb{R}^{n \times n}$, and let $X[S, S]$ be the submatrix of X with row and column indices belonging to subset $S \subseteq [n]$. Consider the set function $f(S) = \log(\det(X[S, S]))$. Show that the curvature of f,

$$c(f) \leq 1 - \frac{1}{\lambda_{\min}(X)},$$

where $\lambda_{\min}(X)$ is the minimum eigenvalue of X.[2]

20.5 [350] [Influence maximization with independent cascade model] Consider a directed graph $G = (V, E)$ where each directed edge $(u, v) \in E$ has an associated probability $0 \leq p_{uv} \leq 1$. The information spread model over G is as follows. When node v first becomes active in time step t, it is given a single chance to activate each of its currently inactive neighbour w, and it succeeds with a probability p_{vw} independently of the history. (If w has multiple newly activated neighbours, their attempts are sequenced in an arbitrary order.) If v succeeds in activating w, then w will become active in step $t + 1$, but whether or not v succeeds, v cannot make any further attempts to activate w in subsequent rounds. A node once activated remains active throughout. The process continues until no new activations are possible.

---

[2] Functions of the form $f(S) = \log(\det(X[S, S]))$ capture the entropy or mutual information in inference problems. Solving

$$\max_{S : |S| = k} f(S)$$

is highly important in feature or subset selection and given this bound on the curvature, one can get improved guarantees on the performance of a greedy algorithm.

Let A be the initially activated subset of nodes of V, while S_A be the random set of activated nodes at the end of the process starting from A. Then the problem to solve is

$$\max_{|A|=k} \mathbb{E}\{|S_A|\},$$

i.e., find the subset A of size k to be initially activated that maximizes the expected number of activated nodes.

Show that $\mathbb{E}\{|S_A|\}$ is a submodular set function by proving the following. Instead of flipping coins with probability p_{vw} only after v becomes active, flip coins for all edges $e = (v, w) \in E$ with probability p_{vw} once at the beginning and store their outcomes in $O(E) \in \{0, 1\}^E$. An edge e for which $O(e) = 1$ is defined as *live*, while $O(e) = 0$ is defined as *blocked*.

1. Fix the outcomes of the coin flips $O(E)$, and then activate the initial set A. Show that a node $x \in V \setminus A$ ends up becoming active at some time in the original process if and only if there is a path from some node in A to x consisting entirely of live edges. (Call such a path a live-edge path.)

2. For a fixed choice of coin flips $O(E)$, let $|S_A(O(E))|$ be the deterministic set of activated nodes at the end of the process starting with A. Show that for a fixed $O(E)$, $|S_A(O(E))|$ is submodular.

3. For a fixed $O(E)$, let the set of nodes that can be reached from any node v using only a live-edge path be $R(v, O(E))$. Using part 1, claim that $|S_A(O(E))| = \cup_{v \in A} R(v, O(E))$.

4. Using part 2 and the fact that

$$\mathbb{E}\{|S_A|\} = \sum_{\text{outcome} \in O(E)} \mathbb{P}(\text{outcome})|S_A(O(E))|,$$

conclude that $\mathbb{E}\{|S_A|\}$ is submodular.

20.6 Consider the Shannon capacity function of a set S of channels

$$C(S) = \max_{p_i \geq 0, \sum_{i \in S} p_i \leq 1} \sum_{i \in S} \log(1 + h_i p_i),$$

where there are $|S|$ channels, and the gain of channel $i \in S$ is $h_i > 0$, and p_i is the power allocated to channel $i \in S$ with the sum-power constraint of $\sum_{i \in S} p_i \leq 1$. The optimal solution $p_i^\star$ is called water-filling, and is given by

$$p_i^\star = \left(\gamma - \frac{1}{h_i}\right)^+,$$

where γ is called the water-level that satisfies $\sum_{i \in S} p_i = 1$, and $(x)^+ = \max\{x, 0\}$. Show that $C(S)$ is a monotone increasing submodular function.

[Hint: Using Definition 20.2.2 (1) might be helpful.[3]]

---

[3] Proof in [349] follows a different approach using Karamata's inequality.

Appendix

A.1 Types of Adversaries and Their Relationships

Definition A.1.1 *For randomized online algorithms, the* **oblivious adversary** *has to generate the entire input sequence in advance (using only the information about distribution used by the randomized algorithm) before any requests are served by the online algorithm. Thus, the adversary has no access to the random choices made by the algorithm. Moreover,* OPT*'s cost is equal to the cost of the optimal offline algorithm knowing the entire input sequence in advance.*

Let the oblivious adversary be denoted as Q_o. Then Q_o knows the distribution D used by the randomized algorithm $\mathcal{R}$, but does not know the actual random choices made by $\mathcal{R}$. Another way to describe this interaction is that Q_o chooses input $\sigma_1, \sigma_2, \ldots$, which is processed by $\mathcal{R}$ sequentially with decisions $d_1, d_2, \ldots$ and Q_o has to make request σ_i without any knowledge of $d_1, d_2, \ldots, d_{i-1}$.

Definition A.1.2 *For a minimization problem, a randomized algorithm $\mathcal{R}$ is μ-competitive against an oblivious adversary Q_o if*

$$\mathbb{E}\{C_{\mathcal{R}}(\sigma)\} \leq \mu C_{Q_o}(\sigma), \tag{A.1}$$

where σ is the input generated by Q_o.

Definition A.1.3 *Adaptive adversary Q_a: Adversary is allowed to observe the online algorithm's decisions (random choices) and generate the next request based on that. Thus, Q_a's request σ_i can depend on $d_1, d_2, \ldots, d_{i-1}$*

Definition A.1.4 *Adaptive offline adversary Q_{af}: Adversary is allowed to observe the online algorithm's decisions (random choices) and generate the next request based on that. Moreover,* OPT *is allowed access to this sequence offline and hence is charged the optimum offline cost for that sequence. Thus, once $\mathcal{R}$ has made its sequential decisions $d_1, d_2, \ldots, d_n$ that can be used to generate $\sigma_1, \sigma_2, \ldots, \sigma_n$,* OPT*'s cost is the cost incurred by the optimal offline algorithm knowing the full sequence $\sigma_1, \sigma_2, \ldots, \sigma_n$ ahead of time.*

A slightly weaker definition is as follows.

Definition A.1.5 *Adaptive online adversary Q_{ao}: Adversary is allowed to observe the online algorithm's decisions (random choices) and generate the next request based on that.* OPT, *however, also must serve each request online, i.e., before knowing the random choices made by the online algorithm on the present request, which in turn possibly influences the next request made by the adversary. Thus,* OPT *also has to make sequential decisions after each σ_i.*

For a randomized algorithm $\mathcal{R}$, its decisions $d_1, d_2, \ldots, d_n$ are random, and with an adaptive adversary, request σ_i can depend on $d_1, d_2, \ldots, d_{i-1}$. Consequently, $Q_a = \{\sigma_1, \ldots, \sigma_n\}$ is potentially a random sequence. Thus, it is useful to denote the cost of $\mathcal{R}$ as $\mathbb{E}\{C_{\mathcal{R}}(Q_a)\}$. Similarly, for OPT we write its cost as $\mathbb{E}\{C_{Q_a}(\mathcal{R})\}$, where we are including $\mathcal{R}$ to represent that the input is influenced by the decisions made by the algorithm $\mathcal{R}$, and that OPT also uses the same resources and identical initial conditions as $\mathcal{R}$. Using this, for a minimization problem, we can define the competitive ratio of $\mathcal{R}$ as follows.

Definition A.1.6 *A randomized algorithm $\mathcal{R}$ is μ-competitive against an adaptive (offline or online) adversary if*

$$\mathbb{E}\{C_{\mathcal{R}}(Q_a)\} \le \mu \mathbb{E}\{C_{Q_a}(\mathcal{R})\}. \tag{A.2}$$

Remark A.1.7 *It is worthwhile noting that with respect to a deterministic online algorithm $\mathcal{A}$, oblivious, adaptive online and adaptive offline adversaries are the same since they all know $\mathcal{A}$'s decisions for any input ahead of time. Thus, when we say a deterministic online algorithm has competitive ratio μ, we do not need to specify against which adversary.*

We next state the main result that shows that an adaptive offline adversary is too powerful, and randomization is not principally useful.

Theorem A.1.8 [98] *If there is a randomized online algorithm that is μ-competitive against an adaptive offline adversary, then there also exists a μ-competitive deterministic online algorithm.*

Proof: Recall that a randomized algorithm $\mathcal{R}$ is simply a probability distribution D over the set of deterministic algorithms $A \in \mathsf{A}$. Thus, from (A.2), for any adaptive offline adversary, we get

$$\mathbb{E}_A\{C_A(Q_a)\} - \mu \mathbb{E}_A\{C_{Q_a}(A)\} \le 0.$$

Let the first input request made by the adversary be σ_1. Then, we have

$$\max_{Q_a}\{\mathbb{E}_A\{C_A(Q_a)\} - \mu \mathbb{E}_A\{C_{Q_a}(A)\}\} \le 0,$$

where the maximum is over all adversaries where the first input is σ_1. Given σ_1, $\mathcal{R}$ produces a decision, let that be d_1. Thus, conditioning over d_1, since the adversary is allowed access to d_1 before requesting σ_2, we get

$$\mathbb{E}_{d_1}\{\max_{Q_a}\{\mathbb{E}_A\{C_A(Q_a)|d_1\} - \mu \mathbb{E}_A\{C_{Q_a}(A)|d_1\}\}\} \le 0.$$

Since this expectation is non-positive, there exists a deterministic decision d_1^* for which the random variable inside the expectation is non-positive. Therefore,

$$\max_{Q_a}\{\mathbb{E}_A\{C_A(Q_a)|d_1^*\} - \mu \mathbb{E}_A\{C_{Q_a}(A)|d_1^*\}\} \le 0.$$

This d_1^* will be the first decision made by a deterministic algorithm on input request σ_1. We continue this procedure as follows. Let Q_a requests σ_2 next, and restricting to all such adversaries, and conditioning on the decision d_2 made by $\mathcal{R}$, we have

$$\mathbb{E}_{d_2}\{\max_{Q_a}\{\mathbb{E}_A\{C_A(Q_a)|d_1^*, d_2\} - \mu \mathbb{E}_A\{C_{Q_a}(A)|d_1^*, d_2\}\}\} \le 0,$$

where the maximum is over adversaries that first request σ_1, and on decision d_1^* by $\mathcal{R}$ requests σ_2. As before, there thus exists d_2^* for which

$$\max_{Q_a}\{\mathbb{E}_A\{C_A(Q_a)|d_1^*, d_2^*\} - \mu\mathbb{E}_A\{C_{Q_a}(A)|d_1^*, d_2^*\}\} \leq 0.$$

The second decision made by the deterministic algorithm is then d_2^*.

Continuing this way, we obtain a deterministic sequence $d_1^*, d_2^*, \dots, d_i^*$ for which

$$\max_{Q_a}\{\mathbb{E}_A\{C_A(Q_a)|d_1^*, d_2^*, \dots, d_i^*\} - \mu\mathbb{E}_A\{C_{Q_a}(A)|d_1^*, d_2^*, \dots, d_i^*\}\} \leq 0, \qquad \text{(A.3)}$$

until the final request σ_{i+1} is a special STOP request.

Thus, for the input sequence $\sigma = (\sigma_1, \sigma_2, \dots, \sigma_{i+1})$, the first term of (A.3) is the cost of the constructed deterministic algorithm on σ, while the second term is the OPT cost $C_{\text{OPT}}(\sigma)$ since with deterministic decisions $d_1^*, d_2^*, \dots, d_i^*$, σ can be characterized offline and consequently OPT's cost is the cost $C_{\text{OPT}}(\sigma)$ of an offline optimal algorithm on input σ. Thus, we get the required result, that the deterministic algorithm is also μ-competitive. ∎

Note that this proof is existential, and does not provide any recipe on how to convert a randomized algorithm into a deterministic one. The proof presented here follows from [360].

Theorem A.1.9 [98] *If $\mathcal{R}_1$ is a μ-competitive randomized algorithm against an adaptive online adversary, and $\mathcal{R}_2$ is a λ-competitive algorithm against an oblivious adversary, then $\mathcal{R}_1$ is $(\mu\lambda)$-competitive against the adaptive offline adversary.*

Proof: Let Q_a be an adaptive offline adversary, and $\mathcal{R}_1$ and $\mathcal{R}_2$ be two randomized algorithms with distributions D_1 and D_2 over $A \in \mathsf{A}$ (all deterministic algorithms). Suppose Q_a is interacting with $\mathcal{R}_1$, i.e., it is an adaptive offline adversary with respect to decisions made by $\mathcal{R}_1$. We denote this explicitly by denoting Q_a as Q_{a1}. Then with respect to $\mathcal{R}_2$, Q_{a1} is an oblivious adversary. Hence, from (A.1), since $\mathcal{R}_2$ is a λ-competitive algorithm against an oblivious adversary, we have

$$\mathbb{E}_{D_2}\{C_A(Q_{a1})\} \leq \lambda C_{Q_{a1}}(\mathcal{R}_1),$$

where we are denoting the cost of the optimal offline solution as $C_{Q_{a1}}(\mathcal{R}_1)$, since Q_{a1} is an adaptive adversary with respect to decisions made by $\mathcal{R}_1$, and input requested by Q_{a1} depends on the decisions made by $\mathcal{R}_1$.

Taking expectation over D_1, we get

$$\mathbb{E}_{D_1}\{\mathbb{E}_{D_2}\{C_A(Q_{a1})\}\} \leq \lambda\mathbb{E}_{D_1}\{C_{Q_{a1}}(\mathcal{R}_1)\}. \qquad \text{(A.4)}$$

Next, we consider an **online adaptive** adversary Q' using Q and $\mathcal{R}_2$. In particular, the input requests with Q' are the same as that with Q_{a1} (i.e., adaptive adversary with respect to $\mathcal{R}_1$), while the decisions its corresponding OPT makes are the same as that of $\mathcal{R}_2$. Thus, the cost of OPT with Q' that corresponds to $\mathcal{R}_1$ is $C_{\mathcal{R}_2}(Q_{a1})$, while the cost of $\mathcal{R}_1$ is $C_{\mathcal{R}_1}(Q_{a1})$. Since by definition, $\mathcal{R}_1$ is μ-competitive against any online adaptive adversary, we get

$$\mathbb{E}_{D_1}\{C_{\mathcal{R}_1}(Q_{a1})\} \leq \mu\mathbb{E}_{D_1}\{C_{\mathcal{R}_2}(Q_{a1})\}$$

and

$$\mathbb{E}_{D_2}\{\mathbb{E}_{D_1}\{C_{\mathcal{R}_1}(Q_{a1})\}\} \leq \mu\mathbb{E}_{D_2}\{\mathbb{E}_{D_1}\{C_{\mathcal{R}_2}(Q_{a1})\}\}.$$

Importantly, the LHS of the above relation does not depend on D_2, and swapping the order of expectations on the RHS, we get

$$\mathbb{E}_{D_1}\{C_{\mathcal{R}_1}(Q_{a1})\} \leq \mu\mathbb{E}_{D_1}\{\mathbb{E}_{D_2}\{C_{\mathcal{R}_2}(Q_{a1})\}\}. \tag{A.5}$$

Combining (A.4) and (A.5), we get

$$\mathbb{E}_{D_1}\{C_{\mathcal{R}_1}(Q_{a1})\} \leq \mu\lambda\mathbb{E}_{D_1}\{C_{Q_{a1}}(\mathcal{R}_1)\},$$

implying that $\mathcal{R}_1$ is $\mu\lambda$-competitive against an adaptive offline adversary. ■

An immediate consequence of the above two theorems is:

Corollary A.1.10 *With the same assumptions as in Theorem A.1.9, there exists a $\mu\lambda$-competitive deterministic algorithm.*

A.2 KKT Conditions for Convex Optimization Problems

Consider the following optimization problem:

$$\begin{aligned}
\min_{x} \quad & f_0(\mathbf{x}) \\
\text{s.t.} \quad & f_i(\mathbf{x}) \leq 0, i = 1, \dots, n \\
& h_j(\mathbf{x}) = 0, j = 1, \dots, m \\
& \mathbf{x} \in \mathbb{R}^d,
\end{aligned} \tag{A.6}$$

where f_0, f_i are all convex functions, while h_j are affine functions of the form $\mathbf{a}_i^T \mathbf{x} = \mathbf{b}_j$. Let the domain $\mathcal{D} = \cap_{i=0}^n \text{DOM}(f_i) \cap \cap_{j=1}^m \text{DOM}(h_j) \neq \varnothing$, and let the optimal value of (A.6) be $p^\star$. Problem (A.6) is called the primal problem, and any feasible solution to it is called a primal solution. For notational simplicity, in the rest of this section, we constrain ourselves to $x \in \mathbb{R}$, i.e., $d = 1$.

The corresponding Lagrangian dual to (A.6) is given by

$$L(x, \lambda, \mu) = f_0(x) + \sum_{i=1}^n \lambda_i f_i(x) + \sum_{j=1}^m \mu_j h_j(x), \tag{A.7}$$

where λ_i and μ_j are the Lagrange multipliers associated with constraint $f_i(x) \leq 0$ and $h_j(x) = 0$, respectively.

The Lagrange dual function is defined as

$$g(\lambda, \mu) = \inf_{x \in \mathcal{D}} L(x, \lambda, \mu). \tag{A.8}$$

It is worthwhile noting that the dual function $g(\lambda, \mu)$ is always concave even if (A.6) is not convex. A simple but powerful relationship holds between the dual function and $p^\star$, given by

$$p^\star \geq g(\lambda, \mu) \tag{A.9}$$

for any $\lambda > 0$ and μ, which follows directly from the definitions. Since the lower bound (A.9) holds for all $\lambda > 0$ and μ, an immediate question is how large can this lower bound be. This question is formulated as the following problem, called the Lagrange dual problem.

$$\max_{\lambda, \mu} \quad g(\lambda, \mu)$$
$$\text{s.t.} \quad \lambda_i \geq 0, i = 1, \dots, n \tag{A.10}$$

Problem (A.10) is called the dual problem, and any feasible solution to it is called the dual solution. Let the optimal value of (A.10) be $d^\star$. From (A.9), we know that

$$p^\star \geq d^\star, \tag{A.11}$$

which is known as the weak duality property. When

$$p^\star = d^\star, \tag{A.12}$$

it is known as the strong duality property, in which case the duality gap $p^\star - d^\star = 0$. The main quest in optimization is to find the necessary and sufficient conditions when there is no duality gap. For convex optimization, one such characterization is what is known as the Karush–Kuhn–Tucker (KKT) conditions which we state below. Let all f_i's be differentiable. Let there exist x', λ', μ' such that the following properties hold:

$$f_i(x') \leq 0 \; \forall \, i = 0, \dots, n, \tag{A.13}$$
$$h_j(x') = 0 \; \forall \, j = 1, \dots, m, \tag{A.14}$$
$$\lambda_i' \geq 0 \; \forall \, i = 1, \dots, n, \tag{A.15}$$
$$\lambda_i' f_i(x') \geq 0 \; \forall \, i = 1, \dots, n, \tag{A.16}$$
$$\nabla f_0(x') + \sum_{i=1}^{n} \lambda_i' \nabla f_i(x') + \sum_{j=1}^{m} \mu_j' \nabla h_j(x') = 0, \tag{A.17}$$

then x' and (λ', μ') are primal and dual optimal solutions with zero duality gap.

Equation (A.17) means that the gradient of $L(x, \lambda', \mu')$ vanishes at $x = x'$. Since $L(x, \lambda', \mu')$ is concave, this implies that x' optimizes $L(x, \lambda', \mu')$ over x. Moreover, condition (A.16) is known as *complementary slackness*, which implies that the ith optimal Lagrange multiplier is zero unless the ith constraint is tight at the optimum. Under these conditions, we have

$$g(\lambda', \mu') = L(x', \lambda', \mu'), \tag{A.18}$$

$$= f_0(x') + \sum_{i=1}^{n} \lambda_i' f_i(x') + \sum_{j=1}^{m} \mu_j' h_j(x'), \tag{A.19}$$

$$= f_0(x'), \tag{A.20}$$

proving strong duality and zero duality gap, where the second equality is by definition, while the third equality follows since $\lambda_i' f_i(x') = 0$ and $h_j(x') = 0 \; \forall j = 1, \dots, m$.

In addition, if Slater's condition is satisfied, i.e., there exists a strictly feasible point x, $f_i(x) < 0$ for all $i = 1, \dots, n$, then the KKT conditions are also necessary for optimality. For more details on convex optimization, please see [361].

Bibliography

[1] V. V. Vazirani, *Approximation algorithms*. Springer, 2001, vol. 1.

[2] A. R. Karlin, M. S. Manasse, L. Rudolph, and D. D. Sleator, "Competitive snoopy caching," *Algorithmica*, vol. 3, no. 1–4, pp. 79–119, 1988.

[3] A. R. Karlin, M. S. Manasse, L. A. McGeoch, and S. Owicki, "Competitive randomized algorithms for nonuniform problems," *Algorithmica*, vol. 11, no. 6, pp. 542–571, 1994.

[4] H. Fujiwara and K. Iwama, "Average-case competitive analyses for ski-rental problems," *Algorithmica*, vol. 42, no. 1, pp. 95–107, 2005.

[5] A. Khanafer, M. Kodialam, and K. P. N. Puttaswamy, "The constrained ski-rental problem and its application to online cloud cost optimization," in *2013 Proceedings IEEE INFOCOM*, 2013, pp. 1492–1500.

[6] Z. Lotker, B. Patt-Shamir, and D. Rawitz, "Ski rental with two general options," *Information Processing Letters*, vol. 108, no. 6, pp. 365–368, 2008.

[7] ——, "Rent, lease, or buy: Randomized algorithms for multislope ski rental," *SIAM Journal on Discrete Mathematics*, vol. 26, no. 2, pp. 718–736, 2012.

[8] A. Levi and B. Patt-Shamir, "Non-additive two-option ski rental," *Theoretical Computer Science*, vol. 584, pp. 42–52, 2015.

[9] M. Hu, W. Xu, H. Li, and X. Chen, "Competitive analysis for discrete multiple online rental problems," *Journal of Management Science and Engineering*, vol. 3, no. 3, pp. 125–140, 2018.

[10] B. Patt-Shamir and E. Yadai, "Non-linear ski rental," in *Proceedings of the 32nd ACM Symposium on Parallelism in Algorithms and Architectures*, 2020, pp. 431–440.

[11] D. R. Dooly, S. A. Goldman, and S. D. Scott, "TCP dynamic acknowledgment delay (extended abstract) theory and practice," in *Proceedings of the Thirtieth Annual ACM symposium on Theory of Computing*, 1998, pp. 389–398.

[12] R. Fleischer, "On the bahncard problem," *Theoretical Computer Science*, vol. 268, no. 1, pp. 161–174, 2001.

[13] S. S. Seiden, "A guessing game and randomized online algorithms," in *Proceedings of the Thirty-second Annual ACM Symposium on Theory of Computing*, 2000, pp. 592–601.

[14] A. R. Karlin, C. Kenyon, and D. Randall, "Dynamic tcp acknowledgement and other stories about e/(e-1)," in *Proceedings of the Thirty-third Annual ACM Symposium on Theory of Computing*, 2001, pp. 502–509.

[15] N. Buchbinder, K. Jain, and J. S. Naor, "Online primal–dual algorithms for maximizing ad-auctions revenue," in *European Symposium on Algorithms*. Springer, 2007, pp. 253–264.

[16] É. Bamas, A. Maggiori, and O. Svensson, "The primal–dual method for learning augmented algorithms," *Advances in Neural Information Processing Systems*, vol. 33, pp. 20 083–20 094, 2020.

[17] R. Kumar, M. Purohit, and Z. Svitkina, "Improving online algorithms via ml predictions," in *Proceedings of the 32nd International Conference on Neural Information Processing Systems*, 2018, pp. 9684–9693.

[18] D. D. Sleator and R. E. Tarjan, "Amortized efficiency of list update and paging rules," *Communications of the ACM*, vol. 28, no. 2, pp. 202–208, 1985.

[19] S. Irani, "Two results on the list update problem," *Information Processing Letters*, vol. 38, no. 6, pp. 301–306, 1991.

[20] R. Karp and P. Raghavan, "Personal communication reported by Irani [1991]," 1990.

[21] S. Albers, "Improved randomized on-line algorithms for the list update problem," *SIAM Journal on Computing*, vol. 27, no. 3, pp. 682–693, 1998.

[22] N. Reingold, J. Westbrook, and D. D. Sleator, "Randomized competitive algorithms for the list update problem," *Algorithmica*, vol. 11, no. 1, pp. 15–32, 1994.

[23] S. Albers, B. Von Stengel, and R. Werchner, "A combined BIT and TIMESTAMP algorithm for the list update problem," *Information Processing Letters*, vol. 56, no. 3, pp. 135–139, 1995.

[24] B. Teia, "A lower bound for randomized list update algorithms," *Information Processing Letters*, vol. 47, no. 1, pp. 5–9, 1993.

[25] C. Ambühl, B. Gärtner, and B. Von Stengel, "A new lower bound for the list update problem in the partial cost model," *Theoretical Computer Science*, vol. 268, no. 1, pp. 3–16, 2001.

[26] R. Bachrach, R. El-Yaniv, and M. Reinstadtler, "On the competitive theory and practice of online list accessing algorithms," *Algorithmica*, vol. 32, no. 2, pp. 201–245, 2002.

[27] E. Timnat and S. Naor, "The list update problem," Ph.D. dissertation, Computer Science Department, Technion, 2016.

[28] S. Albers and M. Mitzenmacher, "Average case analyses of list update algorithms, with applications to data compression," *Algorithmica*, vol. 21, no. 3, pp. 312–329, 1998.

[29] S. Albers, "A competitive analysis of the list update problem with lookahead," *Theoretical Computer Science*, vol. 197, no. 1-2, pp. 95–109, 1998.

[30] N. Reingold and J. Westbrook, "Off-line algorithms for the list update problem," *Information Processing Letters*, vol. 60, no. 2, pp. 75–80, 1996.

[31] C. Ambühl, "Offline list update is NP-hard," in *European Symposium on Algorithms*. Springer, 2000, pp. 42–51.

[32] S. Kamali and A. López-Ortiz, "A survey of algorithms and models for list update," in *Space-Efficient Data Structures, Streams, and Algorithms*. Springer, 2013, pp. 251–266.

[33] J. L. Bentley and C. C. McGeoch, "Amortized analyses of self-organizing sequential search heuristics," *Communications of the ACM*, vol. 28, no. 4, pp. 404–411, 1985.

[34] S. S. Seiden, "On the online bin packing problem," *Journal of the ACM (JACM)*, vol. 49, no. 5, pp. 640–671, 2002.

[35] J. Balogh, J. Békési, G. Dósa, J. Sgall, and R. v. Stee, "The optimal absolute ratio for online bin packing," in *Proceedings of the Twenty-sixth Annual ACM-SIAM Symposium on Discrete Algorithms*. SIAM, 2014, pp. 1425–1438.

[36] B. Chandra, "Does randomization help in on-line bin packing?" *Information Processing Letters*, vol. 43, no. 1, pp. 15–19, 1992.

[37] Jeffrey D. Ullman, "The performance of a memory allocation algorithm, Princeton University, Department of Electrical Engineering," *Computer Science Laboratory*, vol. 47, 1971.

[38] M. R. Garey, R. L. Graham, and J. D. Ullman, "Worst-case analysis of memory allocation algorithms," in *Proceedings of the Fourth Annual ACM Symposium on Theory of Computing*, 1972, pp. 143–150.

[39] D. S. Johnson, A. Demers, J. D. Ullman, M. R. Garey, and R. L. Graham, "Worst-case performance bounds for simple one-dimensional packing algorithms," *SIAM Journal on Computing*, vol. 3, no. 4, pp. 299–325, 1974.

[40] G. Dósa and J. Sgall, "First Fit bin packing: A tight analysis," in *30th International Symposium on Theoretical Aspects of Computer Science (STACS 2013)*, ser. Leibniz International Proceedings in Informatics (LIPIcs), N. Portier and T. Wilke, eds., vol. 20. Dagstuhl, Germany: Schloss Dagstuhl–Leibniz-Zentrum fuer Informatik, 2013, pp. 538–549. [Online]. Available: http://drops.dagstuhl.de/opus/volltexte/2013/3963.

[41] M. R. Garey, R. L. Graham, D. S. Johnson, and A. C.-C. Yao, "Resource constrained scheduling as generalized bin packing," *Journal of Combinatorial Theory, Series A*, vol. 21, no. 3, pp. 257–298, 1976.

[42] G. Dósa and J. Sgall, "Optimal analysis of best fit bin packing," in *International Colloquium on Automata, Languages, and Programming*. Springer, 2014, pp. 429–441.

[43] C. C. Lee and D.-T. Lee, "A simple on-line bin-packing algorithm," *Journal of the ACM (JACM)*, vol. 32, no. 3, pp. 562–572, 1985.

[44] J. Balogh, J. Békési, and G. Galambos, "New lower bounds for certain classes of bin packing algorithms," *Theoretical Computer Science*, vol. 440, pp. 1–13, 2012.

[45] A. van Vliet, "An improved lower bound for on-line bin packing algorithms," *Information Processing Letters*, vol. 43, no. 5, pp. 277–284, 1992.

[46] G. Galambos and J. Frenk, "A simple proof of liang's lower bound for on-line bin packing and the extension to the parametric case," *Discrete Applied Mathematics*, vol. 41, no. 2, pp. 173–178, 1993.

[47] E. C. man Jr, M. Garey, and D. Johnson, "Approximation algorithms for bin packing: A survey," *Approximation Algorithms for NP-hard Problems*, pp. 46–93, 1996.

[48] G. Galambos and G. J. Woeginger, "On-line bin packing: A restricted survey," *Zeitschrift für Operations Research*, vol. 42, no. 1, pp. 25–45, 1995.

[49] H. I. Christensen, A. Khan, S. Pokutta, and P. Tetali, "Approximation and online algorithms for multidimensional bin packing: A survey," *Comput. Sci. Rev.*, vol. 24, pp. 63–79, 2017. [Online]. Available: https://doi.org/10.1016/j.cosrev.2016.12.001.

[50] E. F. Grove, "Online bin packing with lookahead," in *Proceedings of the Sixth Annual ACM-SIAM Symposium on Discrete Algorithms*, 1995, pp. 430–436.

[51] J. Boyar, S. Kamali, K. S. Larsen, and A. López-Ortiz, "Online bin packing with advice," *Algorithmica*, vol. 74, no. 1, pp. 507–527, 2016.

[52] P. W. Shor, "How to pack better than best fit: Tight bounds for average-case online bin packing," in *[1991] Proceedings 32nd Annual Symposium of Foundations of Computer Science*. IEEE Computer Society, 1991, pp. 752–759.

[53] ——, "The average-case analysis of some on-line algorithms for bin packing," *Combinatorica*, vol. 6, no. 2, pp. 179–200, 1986.

[54] S. Albers and M. Mitzenmacher, "Average-case analyses of first fit and random fit bin packing," *Random Structures & Algorithms*, vol. 16, no. 3, pp. 240–259, 2000.

[55] J. Csirik, D. S. Johnson, C. Kenyon, J. B. Orlin, P. W. Shor, and R. R. Weber, "On the sum-of-squares algorithm for bin packing," *Journal of the ACM (JACM)*, vol. 53, no. 1, pp. 1–65, 2006.

[56] V. Gupta and A. Radovanovic, "Online stochastic bin packing," *arXiv preprint arXiv:1211.2687*, 2012.

[57] S. Banerjee and D. Freund, "Uniform loss algorithms for online stochastic decision-making with applications to bin packing," in *Abstracts of the 2020 SIGMETRICS/Performance Joint International Conference on Measurement and Modeling of Computer Systems*, 2020, pp. 1–2.

[58] C. Kenyon *et al.*, "Best-fit bin-packing with random order," in *SODA*, vol. 96, 1996, pp. 359–364.

[59] Z. Ivković and E. L. Lloyd, "A fundamental restriction on fully dynamic maintenance of bin packing," *Information Processing Letters*, vol. 59, no. 4, pp. 229–232, 1996.

[60] J. Balogh, J. Békési, G. Galambos, and G. Reinelt, "Lower bound for the online bin packing problem with restricted repacking," *SIAM Journal on Computing*, vol. 38, no. 1, pp. 398–410, 2008.

[61] ——, "On-line bin packing with restricted repacking," *Journal of Combinatorial Optimization*, vol. 27, no. 1, pp. 115–131, 2014.

[62] E. Cinlar, "Markov renewal theory," *Advances in Applied Probability*, vol. 1, no. 2, pp. 123–187, 1969.

[63] L. A. McGeoch and D. D. Sleator, "A strongly competitive randomized paging algorithm," *Algorithmica*, vol. 6, no. 1–6, pp. 816–825, 1991.

[64] A. R. Karlin, S. J. Phillips, and P. Raghavan, "Markov paging," *SIAM Journal on Computing*, vol. 30, no. 3, pp. 906–922, 2000.

[65] R. Vaze and S. Moharir, "Paging with multiple caches," in *2016 14th International Symposium on Modeling and Optimization in Mobile, Ad Hoc, and Wireless Networks (WiOpt)*. IEEE, 2016, pp. 1–8.

[66] L. A. Belady, "A study of replacement algorithms for a virtual-storage computer," *IBM Systems Journal*, vol. 5, no. 2, pp. 78–101, 1966.

[67] D. D. Sleator and R. E. Tarjan, "Amortized efficiency of list update and paging rules," *Communications of the ACM*, vol. 28, no. 2, pp. 202–208, 1985.

[68] A. Fiat, R. M. Karp, M. Luby, L. A. McGeoch, D. D. Sleator, and N. E. Young, "Competitive paging algorithms," *Journal of Algorithms*, vol. 12, no. 4, pp. 685–699, 1991.

[69] P. Raghavan and M. Snir, "Memory versus randomization in on-line algorithms," in *International Colloquium on Automata, Languages, and Programming*. Springer, 1989, pp. 687–703.

[70] D. Achlioptas, M. Chrobak, and J. Noga, "Competitive analysis of randomized paging algorithms," *Theoretical Computer Science*, vol. 234, no. 1–2, pp. 203–218, 2000.

[71] M. Chrobak and L. L. Larmore, "An optimal on-line algorithm for k servers on trees," *SIAM Journal on Computing*, vol. 20, no. 1, pp. 144–148, 1991.

[72] N. Bansal, N. Buchbinder, and J. Naor, "A primal–dual randomized algorithm for weighted paging," *Journal of the ACM (JACM)*, vol. 59, no. 4, pp. 1–24, 2012.

[73] E. Koutsoupias and C. H. Papadimitriou, "Beyond competitive analysis," *SIAM Journal on Computing*, vol. 30, no. 1, pp. 300–317, 2000.

[74] T. Lykouris and S. Vassilvtiskii, "Competitive caching with machine learned advice," in *International Conference on Machine Learning*. PMLR, 2018, pp. 3296–3305.

[75] D. Rohatgi, "Near-optimal bounds for online caching with machine learned advice," in *Proceedings of the Fourteenth Annual ACM-SIAM Symposium on Discrete Algorithms*. SIAM, 2020, pp. 1834–1845.

[76] P. Raghavan and M. Snir, "Memory versus randomization in on-line algorithms," in *International Colloquium on Automata, Languages, and Programming*. Springer, 1989, pp. 687–703.

[77] A. Borodin, N. Linial, and M. E. Saks, "An optimal on-line algorithm for metrical task system," *Journal of the ACM (JACM)*, vol. 39, no. 4, pp. 745–763, 1992.

[78] E. F. Grove, "The harmonic online k-server algorithm is competitive," in *Proceedings of the Twenty-third Annual ACM Symposium on Theory of Computing*, 1991, pp. 260–266.

[79] E. Koutsoupias and C. H. Papadimitriou, "On the k-server conjecture," *Journal of the ACM (JACM)*, vol. 42, no. 5, pp. 971–983, 1995.

[80] A. Fiat, R. M. Karp, M. Luby, L. A. McGeoch, D. D. Sleator, and N. E. Young, "Competitive paging algorithms," *Journal of Algorithms*, vol. 12, no. 4, pp. 685–699, 1991.

[81] Y. Bartal, N. Linial, M. Mendel, and A. Naor, "On metric ramsey-type phenomena," in *Proceedings of the Thirty-fifth Annual ACM Symposium on Theory of Computing*, 2003, pp. 463–472.

[82] Y. Bartal, B. Bollobás, and M. Mendel, "Ramsey-type theorems for metric spaces with applications to online problems," *Journal of Computer and System Sciences*, vol. 72, no. 5, pp. 890–921, 2006.

[83] S. Bubeck, M. B. Cohen, J. R. Lee, and Y. T. Lee, "Metrical task systems on trees via mirror descent and unfair gluing," *SIAM Journal on Computing*, vol. 50, no. 3, pp. 909–923, 2021.

[84] A. Antoniadis, C. Coester, M. Elias, A. Polak, and B. Simon, "Online metric algorithms with untrusted predictions," in *International Conference on Machine Learning*. PMLR, 2020, pp. 345–355.

[85] S. Seiden, "Unfair problems and randomized algorithms for metrical task systems," *Information and Computation*, vol. 148, no. 2, pp. 219–240, 1999.

[86] M. S. Manasse, L. A. McGeoch, and D. D. Sleator, "Competitive algorithms for server problems," *Journal of Algorithms*, vol. 11, no. 2, pp. 208–230, 1990.

[87] A. Fiat, Y. Rabani, and Y. Ravid, "Competitive k-server algorithms," *Journal of Computer and System Sciences*, vol. 48, no. 3, pp. 410–428, 1994.

[88] M. Chrobak and L. L. Larmore, "Generosity helps or an 11-competitive algorithm for three servers," *Journal of Algorithms*, vol. 16, no. 2, pp. 234–263, 1994.

[89] ——, "On fast algorithms for two servers," *Journal of Algorithms*, vol. 12, no. 4, pp. 607–614, 1991.

[90] ——, "An optimal on-line algorithm for k servers on trees," *SIAM Journal on Computing*, vol. 20, no. 1, pp. 144–148, 1991.

[91] A. Fiat, Y. Rabani, Y. Ravid, and B. Schieber, "A deterministic $O(k^3)$-competitive k-server algorithm for the circle," *Algorithmica*, vol. 11, no. 6, pp. 572–578, 1994.

[92] M. Chrobak and L. L. Larmore, "The server problem and on-line games." *On-line Algorithms*, vol. 7, pp. 11–64, 1991.

[93] B. Csaba, "Note on the work function algorithm," *Acta Cybernetica*, vol. 14, no. 3, pp. 503–506, 2000.

[94] E. Koutsoupias, "The k-server problem," *Computer Science Review*, vol. 3, no. 2, pp. 105–118, 2009.

[95] ——, "Weak adversaries for the k-server problem," in *40th Annual Symposium on Foundations of Computer Science (Cat. No. 99CB37039)*. IEEE, 1999, pp. 444–449.

[96] S. Irani and R. Rubinfeld, "A competitive 2-server algorithm," *Information Processing Letters*, vol. 39, no. 2, pp. 85–91, 1991.

[97] J. M. Kleinberg, "A lower bound for two-server balancing algorithms," *Information Processing Letters*, vol. 52, no. 1, pp. 39–43, 1994.

[98] S. Ben-David, A. Borodin, R. Karp, G. Tardos, and A. Wigderson, "On the power of randomization in on-line algorithms," *Algorithmica*, vol. 11, no. 1, pp. 2–14, 1994.

[99] N. Bansal, N. Buchbinder, A. Madry, and J. Naor, "A polylogarithmic-competitive algorithm for the k-server problem," in *2011 IEEE 52nd Annual Symposium on Foundations of Computer Science*. IEEE, 2011, pp. 267–276.

[100] M. Chrobak, H. Karloof, T. Payne, and S. Vishwnathan, "New ressults on server problems," *SIAM Journal on Discrete Mathematics*, vol. 4, no. 2, pp. 172–181, 1991.

[101] A. Fiat, Y. Rabani, and Y. Ravid, "Competitive k-server algorithms," *Journal of Computer and System Sciences*, vol. 48, no. 3, pp. 410–428, 1994.

[102] Y. Azar, A. Z. Broder, and M. S. Manasse, "On-line choice of on-line algorithms," in *SODA*, 1993, pp. 432–440.

[103] A. Borodin and R. El-Yaniv, *Online Computation and Competitive Analysis*. Cambridge University Press, 2005.

[104] P. Rajhavan and M. Snir, "Memory versus randomization in on-line algorithms," *IBM Journal of Research and Development*, vol. 38, no. 6, pp. 683–707, 1994.

[105] M. Smith and J. Deely, "A secretary problem with finite memory," *Journal of the American Statistical Association*, vol. 70, no. 350, pp. 357–361, 1975.

[106] E. L. Presman and I. M. Sonin, "The best choice problem for a random number of objects," *Theory of Probability & Its Applications*, vol. 17, no. 4, pp. 657–668, 1973.

[107] M. Gardner, "Mathematical games," *Scientific American*, vol. 202, no. 5, pp. 174–188, 1960.

[108] J. P. Gilbert and F. Mosteller, "Recognizing the maximum of a sequence," in *Selected Papers of Frederick Mosteller*. Springer, 2006, pp. 355–398.

[109] T. S. Ferguson *et al.*, "Who solved the secretary problem?" *Statistical science*, vol. 4, no. 3, pp. 282–289, 1989.

[110] D. V. Lindley, "Dynamic programming and decision theory," *Journal of the Royal Statistical Society: Series C (Applied Statistics)*, vol. 10, no. 1, pp. 39–51, 1961.

[111] A. Cayley, "Mathematical questions with their solutions," *The Educational Times*, vol. 23, pp. 18–19, 1875.

[112] L. Moser, "On a problem of cayley," *Scripta Math*, vol. 22, pp. 289–292, 1956.

[113] I. Guttman, "On a problem of l. moser," *Canadian Mathematical Bulletin*, vol. 3, no. 1, pp. 35–39, 1960.

[114] E. B. Dynkin, "Optimal choice of the stopping moment of a markov process," in *Doklady Akademii Nauk*, vol. 150, no. 2. Russian Academy of Sciences, 1963, pp. 238–240.

[115] P. Freeman, "The secretary problem and its extensions: A review," *International Statistical Review/Revue Internationale de Statistique*, pp. 189–206, 1983.

[116] R. Kleinberg, "A multiple-choice secretary algorithm with applications to online auctions," in *Proceedings of the Sixteenth Annual ACM-SIAM Symposium on Discrete Algorithms*. Citeseer, 2005, pp. 630–631.

[117] M. Babaioff, N. Immorlica, D. Kempe, and R. Kleinberg, "A knapsack secretary problem with applications," in *Approximation, Randomization, and Combinatorial Optimization: Algorithms and Techniques*. Springer, 2007, pp. 16–28.

[118] M. Bateni, M. Hajiaghayi, and M. Zadimoghaddam, "Submodular secretary problem and extensions," in *Approximation, Randomization, and Combinatorial Optimization: Algorithms and Techniques*. Springer, 2010, pp. 39–52.

[119] M. Babaioff, N. Immorlica, and R. Kleinberg, "Matroids, secretary problems, and online mechanisms," in *Proceedings of the Eighteenth Annual ACM-SIAM Symposium on Discrete Algorithms*. Society for Industrial and Applied Mathematics, 2007, pp. 434–443.

[120] S. O. Gharan and J. Vondrák, "On variants of the matroid secretary problem," *Algorithmica*, vol. 67, no. 4, pp. 472–497, 2013.

[121] R. Vaze, "Online knapsack problem under expected capacity constraint," in *IEEE INFOCOM 2018-IEEE Conference on Computer Communications*. IEEE, 2018, pp. 2159–2167.

[122] S. Barman, S. Umboh, S. Chawla, and D. Malec, "Secretary problems with convex costs," in *International Colloquium on Automata, Languages, and Programming*. Springer, 2012, pp. 75–87.

[123] A. Gupta, R. Mehta, and M. Molinaro, "Maximizing profit with convex costs in the random-order model," *arXiv preprint arXiv:1804.08172*, 2018.

[124] H. Esfandiari, M. Hajiaghayi, V. Liaghat, and M. Monemizadeh, "Prophet secretary," *SIAM Journal on Discrete Mathematics*, vol. 31, no. 3, pp. 1685–1701, 2017.

[125] Y. Azar, A. Chiplunkar, and H. Kaplan, "Prophet secretary: Surpassing the 1-1/e barrier," in *Proceedings of the 2018 ACM Conference on Economics and Computation*, 2018, pp. 303–318.

[126] H. Esfandiari, M. Hajiaghayi, B. Lucier, and M. Mitzenmacher, "Prophets, secretaries, and maximizing the probability of choosing the best," in *International Conference on Artificial Intelligence and Statistics*, 2020, pp. 3717–3727.

[127] T. Kesselheim, R. Kleinberg, and R. Niazadeh, "Secretary problems with non-uniform arrival order," in *Proceedings of the Forty-seventh Annual ACM Symposium on Theory of Computing*, 2015, pp. 879–888.

[128] D. Bradac, A. Gupta, S. Singla, and G. Zuzic, "Robust algorithms for the secretary problem," *arXiv preprint arXiv:1911.07352*, 2019.

[129] A. Antoniadis, T. Gouleakis, P. Kleer, and P. Kolev, "Secretary and online matching problems with machine learned advice," *arXiv preprint arXiv:2006.01026*, 2020.

[130] A. Gupta and S. Singla, "Random-order models," *CoRR*, vol. abs/2002.12159, 2020, [Online]. Available: https://arxiv.org/abs/2002.12159, https://dblp.org/rec/journals/corr/abs-2002-12159.bib, dblp computer science bibliography, https://dblp.org

[131] R. El-Yaniv, A. Fiat, R. M. Karp, and G. Turpin, "Optimal search and one-way trading online algorithms," *Algorithmica*, vol. 30, no. 1, pp. 101–139, 2001.

[132] T. Kesselheim, K. Radke, A. Tonnis, and B. Vocking, "Primal beats dual on online packing LPs in the random-order model," *SIAM Journal on Computing*, vol. 47, no. 5, pp. 1939–1964, 2018.

[133] S. Albers, A. Khan, and L. Ladewig, "Improved online algorithms for knapsack and gap in the random order model," *Algorithmica*, pp. 1–36, 2021.

[134] R. Vaze, "Online knapsack problem and budgeted truthful bipartite matching," in *IEEE INFOCOM 2017-IEEE Conference on Computer Communications*. IEEE, 2017, pp. 1–9.

[135] A. Marchetti-Spaccamela and C. Vercellis, "Stochastic on-line knapsack problems," *Mathematical Programming*, vol. 68, no. 1, pp. 73–104, 1995.

[136] G. S. Lueker, "Average-case analysis of off-line and on-line knapsack problems," *Journal of Algorithms*, vol. 29, no. 2, pp. 277–305, 1998.

[137] Y. Zhou, D. Chakrabarty, and R. Lukose, "Budget constrained bidding in keyword auctions and online knapsack problems," in *International Workshop on Internet and Network Economics*. Springer, 2008, pp. 566–576.

[138] N. R. Devanur, K. Jain, B. Sivan, and C. A. Wilkens, "Near optimal online algorithms and fast approximation algorithms for resource allocation problems," *Journal of the ACM (JACM)*, vol. 66, no. 1, pp. 1–41, 2019.

[139] L. Yang, A. Zeynali, M. H. Hajiesmaili, R. K. Sitaraman, and D. Towsley, "Competitive algorithms for online multidimensional knapsack problems," in *Proceedings of the ACM on Measurement and Analysis of Computing Systems*, vol. 5, no. 3, pp. 1–30, 2021.

[140] K. Iwama and S. Taketomi, "Removable online knapsack problems," in *International Colloquium on Automata, Languages, and Programming*. Springer, 2002, pp. 293–305.

[141] X. Han, Y. Kawase, and K. Makino, "Randomized algorithms for online knapsack problems," *Theoretical Computer Science*, vol. 562, pp. 395–405, 2015.

[142] K. Iwama and G. Zhang, "Online knapsack with resource augmentation," *Information Processing Letters*, vol. 110, no. 22, pp. 1016–1020, 2010.

[143] H.-J. Böckenhauer, D. Komm, R. Královič, and P. Rossmanith, "The online knapsack problem: Advice and randomization," *Theoretical Computer Science*, vol. 527, pp. 61–72, 2014.

[144] M. Cygan, Ł. Jeż, and J. Sgall, "Online knapsack revisited," *Theory of Computing Systems*, vol. 58, no. 1, pp. 153–190, 2016.

[145] M. Bienkowski, M. Pacut, and K. Piecuch, "An optimal algorithm for online multiple knapsack," *arXiv preprint arXiv:2002.04543*, 2020.

[146] H. W. Kuhn, "The hungarian method for the assignment problem," *Naval Research Logistics Quarterly*, vol. 2, no. 1–2, pp. 83–97, 1955.

[147] J. Munkres, "Algorithms for the assignment and transportation problems," *Journal of the Society for Industrial and Applied Mathematics*, vol. 5, no. 1, pp. 32–38, 1957.

[148] T. G. Kurtz, "Solutions of ordinary differential equations as limits of pure jump markov processes," *Journal of Applied Probability*, vol. 7, no. 1, pp. 49–58, 1970.

[149] R. M. Karp, U. V. Vazirani, and V. V. Vazirani, "An optimal algorithm for on-line bipartite matching," in *Proceedings of the Twenty-second Annual ACM Symposium on Theory of Computing*, 1990, pp. 352–358.

[150] G. Goel and A. Mehta, "Online budgeted matching in random input models with applications to adwords," in *SODA*, vol. 8, 2008, pp. 982–991.

[151] B. Birnbaum and C. Mathieu, "On-line bipartite matching made simple," *Acm Sigact News*, vol. 39, no. 1, pp. 80–87, 2008.

[152] N. R. Devanur, K. Jain, and R. D. Kleinberg, "Randomized primal-dual analysis of ranking for online bipartite matching," in *Proceedings of the Twenty-fourth Annual ACM-SIAM Symposium on Discrete Algorithms*. SIAM, 2013, pp. 101–107.

[153] C. Karande, A. Mehta, and P. Tripathi, "Online bipartite matching with unknown distributions," in *Proceedings of the Forty-third Annual ACM Symposium on Theory of Computing*, 2011, pp. 587–596.

[154] M. Mahdian and Q. Yan, "Online bipartite matching with random arrivals: an approach based on strongly factor-revealing lps," in *Proceedings of the Forty-third Annual ACM Symposium on Theory of Computing*, 2011, pp. 597–606.

[155] A. Mehta *et al.*, "Foundations and trends® in theoretical computer science," *Foundations and Trends® in Theoretical Computer Science*, vol. 8, no. 4, pp. 265–368, 2013.

[156] N. Korula and M. Pál, "Algorithms for secretary problems on graphs and hypergraphs," in *International Colloquium on Automata, Languages, and Programming*. Springer, 2009, pp. 508–520.

[157] T. Kesselheim, K. Radke, A. Tönnis, and B. Vöcking, "An optimal online algorithm for weighted bipartite matching and extensions to combinatorial auctions," in *European Symposium on Algorithms*. Springer, 2013, pp. 589–600.

[158] G. Aggarwal, G. Goel, C. Karande, and A. Mehta, "Online vertex-weighted bipartite matching and single-bid budgeted allocations," in *Proceedings of the Twenty-second Annual ACM-SIAM Symposium on Discrete Algorithms*. SIAM, 2011, pp. 1253–1264.

[159] Z. Huang, N. Kang, Z. G. Tang, X. Wu, Y. Zhang, and X. Zhu, "Fully online matching," *Journal of the ACM (JACM)*, vol. 67, no. 3, pp. 1–25, 2020.

[160] B. Gamlath, M. Kapralov, A. Maggiori, O. Svensson, and D. Wajc, "Online matching with general arrivals," in *2019 IEEE 60th Annual Symposium on Foundations of Computer Science (FOCS)*. IEEE, 2019, pp. 26–37.

[161] M. Fahrbach, Z. Huang, R. Tao, and M. Zadimoghaddam, "Edge-weighted online bipartite matching," in *2020 IEEE 61st Annual Symposium on Foundations of Computer Science (FOCS)*, 2020, pp. 412–423.

[162] K. Chaudhuri, C. Daskalakis, R. D. Kleinberg, and H. Lin, "Online bipartite perfect matching with augmentations," in *IEEE INFOCOM 2009*. IEEE, 2009, pp. 1044–1052.

[163] R. A. Baezayates, J. C. Culberson, and G. J. Rawlins, "Searching in the plane," *Information and Computation*, vol. 106, no. 2, pp. 234–252, 1993.

[164] N. Buchbinder and J. Naor, "Online primal-dual algorithms for covering and packing," *Mathematics of Operations Research*, vol. 34, no. 2, pp. 270–286, 2009.

[165] ——, *The Design of Competitive Online Algorithms via a Primal–Dual Approach*. Now Publishers Inc, 2009.

[166] T. Kesselheim, A. Tönnis, K. Radke, and B. Vöcking, "Primal beats dual on online packing lps in the random-order model," in *Proceedings of the Forty-sixth Annual ACM Symposium on Theory of Computing*, 2014, pp. 303–312.

[167] A. Mehta, A. Saberi, U. Vazirani, and V. Vazirani, "Adwords and generalized online matching," *Journal of the ACM (JACM)*, vol. 54, no. 5, pp. 22–es, 2007.

[168] S. Agrawal and N. R. Devanur, "Fast algorithms for online stochastic convex programming," in *Proceedings of the Twenty-sixth Annual ACM-SIAM Symposium on Discrete Algorithms*. SIAM, 2014, pp. 1405–1424.

[169] X. Wei, H. Yu, and M. J. Neely, "Online primal-dual mirror descent under stochastic constraints," in *Abstracts of the 2020 SIGMETRICS/Performance Joint International Conference on Measurement and Modeling of Computer Systems*, 2020, pp. 3–4.

[170] N. R. Devanur and Z. Huang, "Primal dual gives almost optimal energy-efficient online algorithms," *ACM Transactions on Algorithms (TALG)*, vol. 14, no. 1, pp. 1–30, 2017.

[171] Z. Huang and Q. Zhang, "Online primal dual meets online matching with stochastic rewards: configuration LP to the rescue," in *Proceedings of the 52nd Annual ACM SIGACT Symposium on Theory of Computing*, 2020, pp. 1153–1164.

[172] D. Fotakis, "A primal-dual algorithm for online non-uniform facility location," *Journal of Discrete Algorithms*, vol. 5, no. 1, pp. 141–148, 2007.

[173] S. Shalev-Shwartz and Y. Singer, "A primal–dual perspective of online learning algorithms," *Machine Learning*, vol. 69, no. 2–3, pp. 115–142, 2007.

[174] N. Garg, A. Gupta, A. Kumar, and S. Singla, "Non-clairvoyant precedence constrained scheduling," in *46th International Colloquium on Automata, Languages, and Programming (ICALP 2019)*. Schloss Dagstuhl-Leibniz-Zentrum fuer Informatik, 2019.

[175] N. Alon, B. Awerbuch, Y. Azar, N. Buchbinder, and J. Naor, "The online set cover problem," *SIAM Journal on Computing*, vol. 39, no. 2, pp. 361–370, 2009.

[176] A. Pananjady, V. K. Bagaria, and R. Vaze, "The online disjoint set cover problem and its applications," in *2015 IEEE Conference on Computer Communications (INFOCOM)*. IEEE, 2015, pp. 1221–1229.

[177] Y. Emek, A. Goldbraikh, and E. Kantor, "Online disjoint set cover without prior knowledge," in *27th Annual European Symposium on Algorithms (ESA 2019)*. Schloss Dagstuhl-Leibniz-Zentrum fuer Informatik, 2019.

[178] N. R. Devanur and T. P. Hayes, "The adwords problem: Online keyword matching with budgeted bidders under random permutations," in *Proceedings of the 10th ACM conference on Electronic Commerce*, 2009, pp. 71–78.

[179] U. Bhaskar, A. Jalal, and R. Vaze, "The Adwords Problem with Strict Capacity Constraints," in *36th IARCS Annual Conference on Foundations of Software Technology and Theoretical Computer Science (FSTTCS 2016)*, ser. Leibniz International Proceedings in Informatics (LIPIcs), A. Lal, S. Akshay, S. Saurabh, and S. Sen, eds., vol. 65. Dagstuhl, Germany: Schloss Dagstuhl–Leibniz-Zentrum fuer Informatik, 2016, pp. 30:1–30:14. [Online]. Available: http://drops.dagstuhl.de/opus/volltexte/2016/6865

[180] N. R. Devanur and K. Jain, "Online matching with concave returns," in *Proceedings of the Forty-fourth Annual ACM Symposium on Theory of Computing*, 2012, pp. 137–144.

[181] Z. Huang and A. Kim, "Welfare maximization with production costs: A primal dual approach," in *Proceedings of the Twenty-Sixth Annual ACM-SIAM Symposium on Discrete Algorithms*. SIAM, 2014, pp. 59–72.

[182] Z. Huang, "Sigact news online algorithms column 25: Online primal dual: Beyond linear programs," *ACM SIGACT News*, vol. 45, no. 4, pp. 105–119, 2014.

[183] T. Kesselheim. [Online]. Available: https://ls2-www.cs.tu-dortmund.de/grav/de/grav_files/people/kesselheim/AuU/skript05.pdf.

[184] A. Meyerson, "Online facility location," in *Proceedings 42nd IEEE Symposium on Foundations of Computer Science*. IEEE, 2001, pp. 426–431.

[185] H. Kaplan, D. Naori, and D. Raz, "Almost tight bounds for online facility location in the random-order model," 2022. [Online]. Available: https://arxiv.org/abs/2207.08783

[186] D. Fotakis, "On the competitive ratio for online facility location," *Algorithmica*, vol. 50, no. 1, pp. 1–57, 2008.

[187] ——, "Online and incremental algorithms for facility location," *ACM SIGACT News*, vol. 42, no. 1, pp. 97–131, 2011.

[188] A. Anagnostopoulos, R. Bent, E. Upfal, and P. Van Hentenryck, "A simple and deterministic competitive algorithm for online facility location," *Information and Computation*, vol. 194, no. 2, pp. 175–202, 2004.

[189] G. Divéki and C. Imreh, "Online facility location with facility movements," *Central European Journal of Operations Research*, vol. 19, no. 2, pp. 191–200, 2011.

[190] M. Cygan, A. Czumaj, M. Mucha, and P. Sankowski, "Online facility location with deletions," *arXiv preprint arXiv:1807.03839*, 2018.

[191] M. Bienkowski, B. Feldkord, and P. Schmidt, "A nearly optimal deterministic online algorithm for non-metric facility location," *arXiv preprint arXiv:2007.07025*, 2020.

[192] A. R. Ahmed, M. S. Rahman, and S. Kobourov, "Online facility assignment," *Theoretical Computer Science*, vol. 806, pp. 455–467, 2020.

[193] T. Itoh, S. Miyazaki, and M. Satake, "Competitive analysis for two variants of online metric matching problem," *Discrete Mathematics, Algorithms and Applications*, vol. 13, no. 06, p. 2150156, 2021.

[194] M. Charikar, C. Chekuri, T. Feder, and R. Motwani, "Incremental clustering and dynamic information retrieval," *SIAM Journal on Computing*, vol. 33, no. 6, pp. 1417–1440, 2004.

[195] E. Liberty, R. Sriharsha, and M. Sviridenko, "An algorithm for online *k*-means clustering," in *2016 Proceedings of the Eighteenth Workshop on Algorithm Engineering and Experiments (ALENEX)*. SIAM, 2016, pp. 81–89.

[196] A. Bhaskara and A. K. Rwanpathirana, "Robust algorithms for online *k*-means clustering," in *Algorithmic Learning Theory*. PMLR, 2020, pp. 148–173.

[197] A. Chakraborty, "Personal communication."

[198] T. F. Gonzalez, "Clustering to minimize the maximum intercluster distance," *Theoretical Computer Science*, vol. 38, pp. 293–306, 1985.

[199] Y. Azar, A. Z. Broder, A. R. Karlin, and E. Upfal, "Balanced allocations," in *Proceedings of the Twenty-sixth Annual ACM Symposium on Theory of Computing*, 1994, pp. 593–602.

[200] J. Aspnes, Y. Azar, A. Fiat, S. Plotkin, and O. Waarts, "On-line routing of virtual circuits with applications to load balancing and machine scheduling," *Journal of the ACM (JACM)*, vol. 44, no. 3, pp. 486–504, 1997.

[201] Y. Azar, J. Naor, and R. Rom, "The competitiveness of on-line assignments," *Journal of Algorithms*, vol. 18, no. 2, pp. 221–237, 1995.

[202] Y. Azar, A. Z. Broder, and A. R. Karlin, "On-line load balancing," *Theoretical Computer Science*, vol. 130, no. 1, pp. 73–84, 1994.

[203] R. L. Graham, "Bounds for certain multiprocessing anomalies," *Bell System Technical Journal*, vol. 45, no. 9, pp. 1563–1581, 1966.

[204] Y. Bartal, A. Fiat, H. Karloff, and R. Vohra, "New algorithms for an ancient scheduling problem," in *Proceedings of the Twenty-fourth Annual ACM Symposium on Theory of Computing*, 1992, pp. 51–58.

[205] D. R. Karger, S. J. Phillips, and E. Torng, "A better algorithm for an ancient scheduling problem," *Journal of Algorithms*, vol. 20, no. 2, pp. 400–430, 1996.

[206] S. Albers, "Better bounds for online scheduling," *SIAM Journal on Computing*, vol. 29, no. 2, pp. 459–473, 1999.

[207] R. Fleischer and M. Wahl, "On-line scheduling revisited," *Journal of Scheduling*, vol. 3, no. 6, pp. 343–353, 2000.

[208] J. F. Rudin III and R. Chandrasekaran, "Improved bounds for the online scheduling problem," *SIAM Journal on Computing*, vol. 32, no. 3, pp. 717–735, 2003.

[209] B. Chen, A. van Vliet, and G. J. Woeginger, "A lower bound for randomized on-line scheduling algorithms," *Information Processing Letters*, vol. 51, no. 5, pp. 219–222, 1994.

[210] J. Sgall, "A lower bound for randomized on-line multiprocessor scheduling," *Information Processing Letters*, vol. 63, no. 1, pp. 51–55, 1997.

[211] K. Pruhs, J. Sgall, and E. Torng, "Online scheduling." 2004. [Online]. Available: https://citeseerx.ist.psu.edu/viewdoc/download?doi=10.1.1.10.992&rep=rep1&type=pdf.

[212] J. Sgall, "On-line scheduling," in *Online algorithms: The State of the Art*, 1998, vol. 1442, pp. 196–231.

[213] Y. Azar, B. Kalyanasundaram, S. Plotkin, K. R. Pruhs, and O. Waarts, "On-line load balancing of temporary tasks," *Journal of Algorithms*, vol. 22, no. 1, pp. 93–110, 1997.

[214] P. Berman, M. Charikar, and M. Karpinski, "On-line load balancing for related machines," *Journal of Algorithms*, vol. 35, no. 1, pp. 108–121, 2000.

[215] I. Caragiannis, "Better bounds for online load balancing on unrelated machines," in *Proceedings of the Nineteenth Annual ACM-SIAM Symposium on Discrete Algorithms*, 2008, pp. 972–981.

[216] A. Armon, Y. Azar, L. Epstein, and O. Regev, "Temporary tasks assignment resolved," *Algorithmica*, vol. 36, no. 3, pp. 295–314, 2003.

[217] M. Englert, D. Özmen, and M. Westermann, "The power of reordering for online minimum makespan scheduling," in *2008 49th Annual IEEE Symposium on Foundations of Computer Science*. IEEE, 2008, pp. 603–612.

[218] H. Kellerer, V. Kotov, M. G. Speranza, and Z. Tuza, "Semi on-line algorithms for the partition problem," *Operations Research Letters*, vol. 21, no. 5, pp. 235–242, 1997.

[219] S. Albers and M. Hellwig, "Semi-online scheduling revisited," *Theoretical Computer Science*, vol. 443, pp. 1–9, 2012.

[220] P. Sanders, N. Sivadasan, and M. Skutella, "Online scheduling with bounded migration," *Mathematics of Operations Research*, vol. 34, no. 2, pp. 481–498, 2009.

[221] J. Westbrook, "Load balancing for response time," *Journal of Algorithms*, vol. 35, no. 1, pp. 1–16, 2000.

[222] M. Andrews, M. X. Goemans, and L. Zhang, "Improved bounds for on-line load balancing," *Algorithmica*, vol. 23, no. 4, pp. 278–301, 1999.

[223] B. Awerbuch, Y. Azar, E. F. Grove, M.-Y. Kao, P. Krishnan, and J. S. Vitter, "Load balancing in the ℓ_p norm," in *Proceedings of IEEE 36th Annual Foundations of Computer Science*. IEEE, 1995, pp. 383–391.

[224] A. Avidor, Y. Azar, and J. Sgall, "Ancient and new algorithms for load balancing in the ℓ_p norm," *Algorithmica*, vol. 29, no. 3, pp. 422–441, 2001.

[225] S. Im, N. Kell, D. Panigrahi, and M. Shadloo, "Online load balancing on related machines," in *Proceedings of the 50th Annual ACM SIGACT Symposium on Theory of Computing*, 2018, pp. 30–43.

[226] A. Bernstein, T. Kopelowitz, S. Pettie, E. Porat, and C. Stein, "Simultaneously load balancing for every p-norm, with reassignments," in *8th Innovations in Theoretical Computer Science Conference (ITCS 2017)*. Schloss Dagstuhl-Leibniz-Zentrum fuer Informatik, 2017.

[227] N. D. Vvedenskaya, R. L. Dobrushin, and F. I. Karpelevich, "Queueing system with selection of the shortest of two queues: An asymptotic approach," *Problemy Peredachi Informatsii*, vol. 32, no. 1, pp. 20–34, 1996.

[228] M. Mitzenmacher, "The power of two choices in randomized load balancing," *IEEE Transactions on Parallel and Distributed Systems*, vol. 12, no. 10, pp. 1094–1104, 2001.

[229] L. Ying, R. Srikant, and X. Kang, "The power of slightly more than one sample in randomized load balancing," *Mathematics of Operations Research*, vol. 42, no. 3, pp. 692–722, 2017.

[230] I. Caragiannis, M. Flammini, C. Kaklamanis, P. Kanellopoulos, and L. Moscardelli, "Tight bounds for selfish and greedy load balancing," in *International Colloquium on Automata, Languages, and Programming*. Springer, 2006, pp. 311–322.

[231] B. Vöcking, "Selfish load balancing," *Algorithmic Game Theory*, vol. 20, pp. 517–542, 2007.

[232] T. Roughgarden, "Routing games," *Algorithmic Game Theory*, vol. 18, pp. 459–484, 2007.

[233] Y. Azar, "On-line load balancing," in *Online Algorithms: The State of the Art*. Springer, 1998, pp. 178–195.

[234] L. Schrage, "Letter to the editor: A proof of the optimality of the shortest remaining processing time discipline," *Operations Research*, vol. 16, no. 3, pp. 687–690, 1968.

[235] N. Bansal and H.-L. Chan, "Weighted flow time does not admit o (1)-competitive algorithms," in *Proceedings of the Twentieth Annual ACM-SIAM Symposium on Discrete Algorithms*. SIAM, 2009, pp. 1238–1244.

[236] S. Leonardi and D. Raz, "Approximating total flow time on parallel machines," *Journal of Computer and System Sciences*, vol. 73, no. 6, pp. 875–891, 2007.

[237] S. Leonardi, "A simpler proof of preemptive total flow time approximation on parallel machines," in *Efficient Approximation and Online Algorithms*. Springer, 2006, pp. 203–212.

[238] C. A. Phillips, C. Stein, E. Torng, and J. Wein, "Optimal time-critical scheduling via resource augmentation," in *Proceedings of the Twenty-ninth Annual ACM Symposium on Theory of Computing*, 1997, pp. 140–149.

[239] K. Fox and B. Moseley, "Online scheduling on identical machines using SRPT," in *Proceedings of the Twenty-second Annual ACM-SIAM Symposium on Discrete Algorithms*. SIAM, 2011, pp. 120–128.

[240] B. Awerbuch, Y. Azar, S. Leonardi, and O. Regev, "Minimizing the flow time without migration," *SIAM Journal on Computing*, vol. 31, no. 5, pp. 1370–1382, 2002.

[241] C. Chekuri, S. Khanna, and A. Zhu, "Algorithms for minimizing weighted flow time," in *Proceedings of the Thirty-third Annual ACM Symposium on Theory of Computing*, 2001, pp. 84–93.

[242] N. Avrahami and Y. Azar, "Minimizing total flow time and total completion time with immediate dispatching," *Algorithmica*, vol. 47, no. 3, pp. 253–268, 2007.

[243] L. Becchetti and S. Leonardi, "Non-clairvoyant scheduling to minimize the average flow time on single and parallel machines," in *Proceedings of the Thirty-third Annual ACM Symposium on Theory of Computing*, 2001, pp. 94–103.

[244] R. Motwani, S. Phillips, and E. Torng, "Nonclairvoyant scheduling," *Theoretical Computer Science*, vol. 130, no. 1, pp. 17–47, 1994.

[245] N. Garg and A. Kumar, "Minimizing average flow time on related machines," in *Proceedings of the Thirty-eighth Annual ACM Symposium on Theory of Computing*, 2006, pp. 730–738.

[246] ——, "Better algorithms for minimizing average flow-time on related machines," in *International Colloquium on Automata, Languages, and Programming*. Springer, 2006, pp. 181–190.

[247] ——, "Minimizing average flow-time: Upper and lower bounds," in *48th Annual IEEE Symposium on Foundations of Computer Science (FOCS'07)*. IEEE, 2007, pp. 603–613.

[248] L. A. Hall, A. S. Schulz, D. B. Shmoys, and J. Wein, "Scheduling to minimize average completion time: Off-line and on-line approximation algorithms," *Mathematics of Operations Research*, vol. 22, no. 3, pp. 513–544, 1997.

[249] N. Garg, A. Kumar, and V. Pandit, "Order scheduling models: hardness and algorithms," in *International Conference on Foundations of Software Technology and Theoretical Computer Science*. Springer, 2007, pp. 96–107.

[250] E. Günther, O. Maurer, N. Megow, and A. Wiese, "A new approach to online scheduling: Approximating the optimal competitive ratio," in *Proceedings of the Twenty-fourth Annual ACM-SIAM Symposium on Discrete Algorithms*. SIAM, 2013, pp. 118–128.

[251] S. Khuller, J. Li, P. Sturmfels, K. Sun, and P. Venkat, "Select and permute: An improved online framework for scheduling to minimize weighted completion time," *Theoretical Computer Science*, vol. 795, pp. 420–431, 2019.

[252] Y. Robert and F. Vivien, *Introduction to Scheduling*. CRC Press, 2009.

[253] Y. Azar, S. Leonardi, and N. Touitou, "Flow time scheduling with uncertain processing time," in *Proceedings of the 53rd Annual ACM SIGACT Symposium on Theory of Computing*, 2021, pp. 1070–1080.

[254] Y. Azar, S. Leonardi, and N. Touitou, "Distortion-oblivious algorithms for minimizing flow time," *Proceedings of the 2022 Annual ACM-SIAM Symposium on Discrete Algorithms (SODA)*, SIAM, 2022, pp. 252–274.

[255] R. L. Graham, "Bounds for certain multiprocessing anomalies," *Bell System Technical Journal*, vol. 45, no. 9, pp. 1563–1581, 1966.

[256] F. Yao, A. Demers, and S. Shenker, "A scheduling model for reduced cpu energy," in *Proceedings of IEEE 36th Annual Foundations of Computer Science*. IEEE, 1995, pp. 374–382.

[257] S. Irani and K. R. Pruhs, "Algorithmic problems in power management," *ACM Sigact News*, vol. 36, no. 2, pp. 63–76, 2005.

[258] N. Bansal, H.-L. Chan, T.-W. Lam, and L.-K. Lee, "Scheduling for speed bounded processors," in *International Colloquium on Automata, Languages, and Programming*. Springer, 2008, pp. 409–420.

[259] N. Bansal, H.-L. Chan, and K. Pruhs, "Speed scaling with an arbitrary power function," in *Proceedings of the Twentieth Annual ACM-SIAM Symposium on Discrete Algorithms*. SIAM, 2009, pp. 693–701.

[260] A. Wierman, L. L. H. Andrew, and A. Tang, "Power-aware speed scaling in processor sharing systems," in *Proc. IEEE INFOCOM*, Rio de Janeiro, Brazil, 20–25 April 2009, pp. 2007–2015. [Online]. Available: http://users.monash.edu/~lachlana/pubs/SpeedScalingPS.pdf.

[261] ——, "Power-aware speed scaling in processor sharing systems: Optimality and robustness," *Performance Evaluation*, vol. 69, pp. 601–622, 2012. [Online]. Available: http://users.monash.edu/~lachlana/pubs/PSscaling.pdf.

[262] L. L. Andrew, M. Lin, and A. Wierman, "Optimality, fairness, and robustness in speed scaling designs," in *Proceedings of the ACM SIGMETRICS International Conference on Measurement and Modeling of Computer Systems*, 2010, pp. 37–48.

[263] N. Bansal, K. Pruhs, and C. Stein, "Speed scaling for weighted flow time," *SIAM Journal on Computing*, vol. 39, no. 4, pp. 1294–1308, 2010.

[264] D. Rutten and D. Mukherjee, "A new approach to capacity scaling augmented with unreliable machine learning predictions," *arXiv preprint arXiv:2101.12160*, 2021.

[265] A. Gupta, R. Krishnaswamy, and K. Pruhs, "Scalably scheduling power-heterogeneous processors," in *International Colloquium on Automata, Languages, and Programming*. Springer, 2010, pp. 312–323.

[266] R. Vaze and J. Nair, "Multiple server SRPT with speed scaling is competitive," *IEEE/ACM Transactions on Networking*, vol. 28, no. 4, pp. 1739–1751, 2020.

[267] R. Vaze and J. Nair, "Network speed scaling," *Performance Evaluation*, vol. 144, p. 102145, 2020.

[268] S.-H. Chan, T.-W. Lam, and L.-K. Lee, "Non-clairvoyant speed scaling for weighted flow time," in *European Symposium on Algorithms*. Springer, 2010, pp. 23–35.

[269] A. Gupta, S. Im, R. Krishnaswamy, B. Moseley, and K. Pruhs, "Scheduling heterogeneous processors isn't as easy as you think," in *Proceedings of the Twenty-third Annual ACM-SIAM Symposium on Discrete Algorithms*. SIAM, 2012, pp. 1242–1253.

[270] K. Pruhs, R. van Stee, and P. Uthaisombut, "Speed scaling of tasks with precedence constraints," *Theory of Computing Systems*, vol. 43, no. 1, pp. 67–80, 2008.

[271] R. Vaze and J. Nair, "Speed scaling on parallel servers with mapreduce type precedence constraints," *IEEE/ACM Transactions on Networking*, pp. 1–16, 2022.

[272] D. P. Bunde, "Power-aware scheduling for makespan and flow," *Journal of Scheduling*, vol. 12, no. 5, pp. 489–500, 2009.

[273] S. Im, B. Moseley, and K. Pruhs, "A tutorial on amortized local competitiveness in online scheduling," *ACM SIGACT News*, vol. 42, no. 2, pp. 83–97, 2011.

[274] T.-W. Lam, L.-K. Lee, I. K. To, and P. W. Wong, "Speed scaling functions for flow time scheduling based on active job count," in *European Symposium on Algorithms*. Springer, 2008, pp. 647–659.

[275] E. Bamas, A. Maggiori, L. Rohwedder, and O. Svensson, "Learning augmented energy minimization via speed scaling," *arXiv preprint arXiv:2010.11629*, 2020.

[276] T. M. Cover, *Elements of Information Theory*. John Wiley & Sons, 1999.

[277] K. Knopp, "Über reihen mit positiven gliedern," *Journal of the London Mathematical Society*, vol. 1, no. 3, pp. 205–211, 1928.

[278] J. Zinn and G. Bennett, "A sum inequality: 11145," *The American Mathematical Monthly*, vol. 113, no. 8, pp. 766–766, 2006.

[279] J. D'Aurizio, *About a Possible Hardy-type Inequality for Negative Exponents*, November 2012. [Online]. Available: https://math.stackexchange.com/questions/242123/about-a-possible-hardy-type-inequality-for-negative-exponents.

[280] N. Bansal, T. Kimbrel, and K. Pruhs, "Speed scaling to manage energy and temperature," *Journal of the ACM (JACM)*, vol. 54, no. 1, pp. 1–39, 2007.

[281] A. Deshmukh and R. Vaze, "Online energy-efficient packet scheduling for a common deadline with and without energy harvesting," *IEEE Journal on Selected Areas in Communications*, vol. 34, no. 12, pp. 3661–3674, 2016.

[282] H. Rahman, A. Vinayachandran, S. R. B. Pillai, K. Appaiah, R. Vaze, and N. Kashyap, "Deadline constrained packet scheduling in the presence of an energy harvesting jammer," *IEEE Transactions on Green Communications and Networking*, IEEE, vol. 5, no. 1, pp. 278–290, 2020.

[283] S. R. Pillai, Personal communication.

[284] H.-L. Chan, J. W.-T. Chan, T.-W. Lam, L.-K. Lee, K.-S. Mak, and P. W. Wong, "Optimizing throughput and energy in online deadline scheduling," *ACM Transactions on Algorithms (TALG)*, vol. 6, no. 1, p. 10, 2009.

[285] S. Baruah, G. Koren, B. Mishra, A. Raghunathan, L. Rosier, and D. Shasha, "On-line scheduling in the presence of overload," in *Foundations of Computer Science, 1991. Proceedings., 32nd Annual Symposium on*. IEEE, 1991, pp. 100–110.

[286] A. Coté, A. Meyerson, A. Roytman, M. Shindler, and B. Tagiku, "Energy-efficient online scheduling with deadlines," unpublished manuscript, 2010.

[287] M. Riedel, "Online request server matching," *Theoretical computer science*, vol. 268, no. 1, pp. 145–160, 2001.

[288] G. Reddy and R. Vaze, "Robust online speed scaling with deadline uncertainty," in *Approximation, Randomization, and Combinatorial Optimization. Algorithms and Techniques (APPROX/RANDOM 2018)*. Schloss Dagstuhl-Leibniz-Zentrum fuer Informatik, 2018.

[289] M. Li, A. C. Yao, and F. F. Yao, "Discrete and continuous min-energy schedules for variable voltage processors," in *Proceedings of the National Academy of Sciences*, vol. 103, no. 11, pp. 3983–3987, 2006.

[290] A. El Gamal, C. Nair, B. Prabhakar, E. Uysal-Biyikoglu, and S. Zahedi, "Energy-efficient scheduling of packet transmissions over wireless networks," in *Proceedings. Twenty-First Annual Joint Conference of the IEEE Computer and Communications Societies*, vol. 3. IEEE, 2002, pp. 1773–1782.

[291] S. Miyazaki, N. Morimoto, and Y. Okabe, "The online graph exploration problem on restricted graphs," *IEICE Transactions on Information and Systems*, vol. 92, no. 9, pp. 1620–1627, 2009.

[292] N. Megow, K. Mehlhorn, and P. Schweitzer, "Online graph exploration: New results on old and new algorithms," *Theoretical Computer Science*, vol. 463, pp. 62–72, 2012.

[293] G. Ausiello, E. Feuerstein, S. Leonardi, L. Stougie, and M. Talamo, "Algorithms for the on-line travelling salesman," *Algorithmica*, vol. 29, no. 4, pp. 560–581, 2001.

[294] N. Ascheuer, S. O. Krumke, and J. Rambau, "Online dial-a-ride problems: Minimizing the completion time," in *Annual Symposium on Theoretical Aspects of Computer Science*. Springer, 2000, pp. 639–650.

[295] M. Lipmann, "On-line routing," Ph.D. Thesis, Technische Universiteit Eindhoven, 2003.

[296] M. Blom, S. O. Krumke, W. E. de Paepe, and L. Stougie, "The online TSP against fair adversaries," *INFORMS Journal on Computing*, vol. 13, no. 2, pp. 138–148, 2001.

[297] B. Kalyanasundaram and K. R. Pruhs, "Constructing competitive tours from local information," *Theoretical Computer Science*, vol. 130, no. 1, pp. 125–138, 1994.

[298] S. Dobrev, R. Královič, and E. Markou, "Online graph exploration with advice," in *International Colloquium on Structural Information and Communication Complexity*. Springer, 2012, pp. 267–278.

[299] A. Birx, Y. Disser, A. V. Hopp, and C. Karousatou, "An improved lower bound for competitive graph exploration," *Theoretical Computer Science*, vol. 868, pp. 65–86, 2021.

[300] D. J. Rosenkrantz, R. E. Stearns, and P. M. Lewis, II, "An analysis of several heuristics for the traveling salesman problem," *SIAM Journal on Computing*, vol. 6, no. 3, pp. 563–581, 1977.

[301] C. A. Hurkens and G. J. Woeginger, "On the nearest neighbor rule for the traveling salesman problem," *Operations Research Letters*, vol. 32, no. 1, pp. 1–4, 2004.

[302] M. Imase and B. M. Waxman, "Dynamic steiner tree problem," *SIAM Journal on Discrete Mathematics*, vol. 4, no. 3, pp. 369–384, 1991.

[303] M. Lin, A. Wierman, L. L. Andrew, and E. Thereska, "Dynamic right-sizing for power-proportional data centers," *IEEE/ACM Transactions on Networking*, vol. 21, no. 5, pp. 1378–1391, 2012.

[304] M. Lin, A. Wierman, A. Roytman, A. Meyerson, and L. L. Andrew, "Online optimization with switching cost," *ACM SIGMETRICS Performance Evaluation Review*, vol. 40, no. 3, pp. 98–100, 2012.

[305] M. Lin, Z. Liu, A. Wierman, and L. L. Andrew, "Online algorithms for geographical load balancing," in *2012 International Green Computing Conference (IGCC)*. IEEE, 2012, pp. 1–10.

[306] L. Andrew, S. Barman, K. Ligett, M. Lin, A. Meyerson, A. Roytman, and A. Wierman, "A tale of two metrics: Simultaneous bounds on competitiveness and regret," in *Conference on Learning Theory*, 2013, pp. 741–763.

[307] Y. Li, G. Qu, and N. Li, "Online optimization with predictions and switching costs: Fast algorithms and the fundamental limit," *IEEE Transactions on Automatic Control*, 2020.

[308] N. Bansal, A. Gupta, R. Krishnaswamy, K. Pruhs, K. Schewior, and C. Stein, "A 2-competitive algorithm for online convex optimization with switching costs," in *Approximation, Randomization, and Combinatorial Optimization. Algorithms and Techniques (APPROX/RANDOM 2015)*. Schloss Dagstuhl-Leibniz-Zentrum fuer Informatik, 2015.

[309] S. Albers and J. Quedenfeld, "Optimal algorithms for right-sizing data centers - extended version," *CoRR*, vol. abs/1807.05112, 2018. [Online]. Available: http://arxiv.org/abs/1807.05112.

[310] A. Blum and C. Burch, "On-line learning and the metrical task system problem," *Machine Learning*, vol. 39, no. 1, pp. 35–58, 2000.

[311] N. Chen, G. Goel, and A. Wierman, "Smoothed online convex optimization in high dimensions via online balanced descent," in *Conference On Learning Theory*. PMLR, 2018, pp. 1574–1594.

[312] G. Goel and A. Wierman, "An online algorithm for smoothed regression and LQR control," *Proceedings of Machine Learning Research*, vol. 89, pp. 2504–2513, 2019.

[313] Y. Lin, G. Goel, and A. Wierman, "Online optimization with predictions and non-convex losses," *Proceedings of the ACM on Measurement and Analysis of Computing Systems*, vol. 4, no. 1, pp. 1–32, 2020.

[314] J. Friedman and N. Linial, "On convex body chasing," *Discrete & Computational Geometry*, vol. 9, no. 3, pp. 293–321, 1993.

[315] A. Antoniadis, N. Barcelo, M. Nugent, K. Pruhs, K. Schewior, and M. Scquizzato, "Chasing convex bodies and functions," in *LATIN 2016: Theoretical Informatics*. Springer, 2016, pp. 68–81.

[316] N. Bansal, M. Böhm, M. Eliáš, G. Koumoutsos, and S. W. Umboh, "Nested convex bodies are chaseable," *Algorithmica*, pp. 1–14, 2019.

[317] C. Argue, S. Bubeck, M. B. Cohen, A. Gupta, and Y. T. Lee, "A nearly-linear bound for chasing nested convex bodies," in *Proceedings of the Thirtieth Annual ACM-SIAM Symposium on Discrete Algorithms*. SIAM, 2019, pp. 117–122.

[318] C. Argue, A. Gupta, G. Guruganesh, and Z. Tang, "Chasing convex bodies with linear competitive ratio," in *Proceedings of the Fourteenth Annual ACM-SIAM Symposium on Discrete Algorithms*. SIAM, 2020, pp. 1519–1524.

[319] B. Grünbaum, V. Klee, M. A. Perles, and G. C. Shephard, *Convex polytopes*. Springer, 1967, vol. 16.

[320] E. Hazan, A. Agarwal, and S. Kale, "Logarithmic regret algorithms for online convex optimization," *Machine Learning*, vol. 69, no. 2-3, pp. 169–192, 2007.

[321] S. C. Dafermos and F. T. Sparrow, "The traffic assignment problem for a general network," *Journal of Research of the National Bureau of Standards B*, vol. 73, no. 2, pp. 91–118, 1969.

[322] T. Harks, S. Heinz, and M. E. Pfetsch, "Competitive online multicommodity routing," *Theory of Computing Systems*, vol. 45, no. 3, pp. 533–554, 2009.

[323] I. Caragiannis, M. Flammini, C. Kaklamanis, P. Kanellopoulos, and L. Moscardelli, "Tight bounds for selfish and greedy load balancing," in *International Colloquium on Automata, Languages, and Programming*. Springer, 2006, pp. 311–322.

[324] I. Caragiannis, "Better bounds for online load balancing on unrelated machines," in *Proceedings of the Nineteenth Annual ACM-SIAM Symposium on Discrete Algorithms*. Citeseer, 2008, pp. 972–981.

[325] B. Awerbuch, Y. Azar, E. F. Grove, M.-Y. Kao, P. Krishnan, and J. S. Vitter, "Load balancing in the l/sub p/norm," in *Proceedings of IEEE 36th Annual Foundations of Computer Science*. IEEE, 1995, pp. 383–391.

[326] T. Harks, S. Heinz, M. E. Pfetsch, and T. Vredeveld, "Online multicommodity routing with time windows," 2007. [Online]. Available: ZIBReport07-22, ZuseInstituteBerlin(2007).

[327] V. Bilò and C. Vinci, "On the impact of singleton strategies in congestion games," in *25th Annual European Symposium on Algorithms (ESA 2017)*. Schloss Dagstuhl-Leibniz-Zentrum fuer Informatik, 2017.

[328] M. Klimm, D. Schmand, and A. Tönnis, "The online best reply algorithm for resource allocation problems," in *International Symposium on Algorithmic Game Theory*. Springer, 2019, pp. 200–215.

[329] N. Olver, "The price of anarchy and a priority-based model of routing," Ph.D. dissertation, McGill University Libraries, 2006.

[330] B. Farzad, N. Olver, and A. Vetta, "A priority-based model of routing," *Chicago Journal of Theoretical Computer Science*, vol. 1, 2008.

[331] B. Awerbuch, Y. Azar, and S. Plotkin, "Throughput-competitive on-line routing," in *Proceedings of 1993 IEEE 34th Annual Foundations of Computer Science*. IEEE, 1993, pp. 32–40.

[332] E. Altman, T. Basar, T. Jimenez, and N. Shimkin, "Competitive routing in networks with polynomial costs," *IEEE Transactions on automatic control*, vol. 47, no. 1, pp. 92–96, 2002.

[333] T. Roughgarden and É. Tardos, "How bad is selfish routing?" *Journal of the ACM (JACM)*, vol. 49, no. 2, pp. 236–259, 2002.

[334] B. Awerbuch, Y. Azar, and A. Epstein, "The price of routing unsplittable flow," *SIAM Journal on Computing*, vol. 42, no. 1, pp. 160–177, 2013.

[335] G. Christodoulou and E. Koutsoupias, "The price of anarchy of finite congestion games," in *Proceedings of the Thirty-seventh Annual ACM Symposium on Theory of Computing*, 2005, pp. 67–73.

[336] V. S. Mirrokni and A. Vetta, "Convergence issues in competitive games," in *Approximation, Randomization, and Combinatorial optimization: Algorithms and Techniques*. Springer, 2004, pp. 183–194.

[337] A. Bjelde, M. Klimm, and D. Schmand, "Brief announcement: Approximation algorithms for unsplittable resource allocation problems with diseconomies of scale," in *Proceedings of the 29th ACM Symposium on Parallelism in Algorithms and Architectures*, 2017, pp. 227–229.

[338] J. B. Orlin, A. P. Punnen, and A. S. Schulz, "Approximate local search in combinatorial optimization," *SIAM Journal on Computing*, vol. 33, no. 5, pp. 1201–1214, 2004.

[339] R. Vaze, "Competitive ratio analysis of online algorithms to minimize packet transmission time in energy harvesting communication system," in *2013 Proceedings IEEE INFOCOM*. IEEE, 2013, pp. 115–1123.

[340] S. Satpathi, R. Nagda, and R. Vaze, "Optimal offline and competitive online strategies for transmitter-receiver energy harvesting," *IEEE Transactions on Information Theory*, vol. 62, no. 8, pp. 4674–4695, 2016.

[341] J. Yang and S. Ulukus, "Optimal packet scheduling in an energy harvesting communication system," *IEEE Transactions on Communications*, vol. 60, no. 1, pp. 220–230, 2011.

[342] A. Marathe, S. R. B. Pillai, and R. Vaze, "Opportunistic scheduling in two-way wireless communication with energy harvesting," in *2017 15th International Symposium on Modeling and Optimization in Mobile, Ad Hoc, and Wireless Networks (WiOpt)*. IEEE, 2017, pp. 1–8.

[343] R. Vaze and S. R. B. Pillai, "Online energy harvesting problem over an arbitrary directed acyclic graph network," *IEEE Transactions on Green Communications and Networking*, vol. 3, no. 4, pp. 1106–1116, 2019.

[344] J. Yang and S. Ulukus, "Optimal packet scheduling in a multiple access channel with energy harvesting transmitters," *Journal of Communications and Networks*, vol. 14, no. 2, pp. 140–150, 2012.

[345] E. L. Lawler and C. U. Martel, "Computing maximal 'polymatroidal' network flows," *Mathematics of Operations Research*, vol. 7, no. 3, pp. 334–347, 1982.

[346] C. Chekuri, S. Kannan, A. Raja, and P. Viswanath, "Multicommodity flows and cuts in polymatroidal networks," *SIAM Journal on Computing*, vol. 44, no. 4, pp. 912–943, 2015.

[347] T. M. Cover, *Elements of Information Theory*. John Wiley & Sons, 1999.

[348] M. X. Goemans, "Lecture notes." [Online]. Available: http://math.mit.edu/~goemans/18453S17/flowcuts.pdf.

[349] K. Thekumparampil, A. Thangaraj, and R. Vaze, "Combinatorial resource allocation using submodularity of waterfilling," *IEEE Transactions on Wireless Communications*, vol. 15, no. 1, pp. 206–216, 2016.

[350] D. Kempe, J. Kleinberg, and É. Tardos, "Maximizing the spread of influence through a social network," in *Proceedings of the Ninth ACM SIGKDD International Conference on Knowledge Discovery and Data Mining*, 2003, pp. 137–146.

[351] E. Tohidi, R. Amiri, M. Coutino, D. Gesbert, G. Leus, and A. Karbasi, "Submodularity in action: From machine learning to signal processing applications," *IEEE Signal Processing Magazine*, vol. 37, no. 5, pp. 120–133, 2020.

[352] M. L. Fisher, G. L. Nemhauser, and L. A. Wolsey, *An Analysis of Approximations for Maximizing Submodular Set Functions—II*. Berlin, Heidelberg: Springer Berlin Heidelberg, 1978, pp. 73–87. [Online]. Available: https://doi.org/10.1007/BFb0121195.

[353] M. Conforti and G. Cornuéjols, "Submodular set functions, matroids and the greedy algorithm: Tight worst-case bounds and some generalizations of the rado-edmonds theorem," *Discrete Applied Mathematics*, vol. 7, no. 3, pp. 251–274, 1984. [Online]. Available: http://www.sciencedirect.com/science/article/pii/0166218X84900039.

[354] J. Edmonds, "Matroids and the greedy algorithm," *Mathematical programming*, vol. 1, no. 1, pp. 127–136, 1971.

[355] G. L. Nemhauser and L. A. Wolsey, "Best algorithms for approximating the maximum of a submodular set function," *Mathematics of Operations Research*, vol. 3, no. 3, pp. 177–188, 1978.

[356] T. Soma and Y. Yoshida, "A new approximation guarantee for monotone submodular function maximization via discrete convexity," *CoRR*, vol. abs/1709.02910, 2017. [Online]. Available: http://arxiv.org/abs/1709.02910.

[357] P. R. Goundan and A. S. Schulz, "Revisiting the greedy approach to submodular set function maximization," *Optimization Online*, pp. 1–25, 2007.

[358] G. Calinescu, C. Chekuri, M. Pál, and J. Vondrák, "Maximizing a monotone submodular function subject to a matroid constraint," *SIAM J. Comput.*, vol. 40, no. 6, pp. 1740–1766, December 2011. [Online]. Available: http://dx.doi.org/10.1137/080733991.

[359] N. Rajaraman and R. Vaze, "Submodular maximization under A matroid constraint: Asking more from an old friend, the greedy algorithm," *CoRR*, vol. abs/1810.12861, 2018. [Online]. Available: http://arxiv.org/abs/1810.12861.

[360] M. X. Goemans et al., *Advanced Algorithms*. Citeseer, 1994.

[361] S. Boyd, S. P. Boyd, and L. Vandenberghe, *Convex Optimization*. Cambridge University Press, 2004.

[362] G. Goel, Y. Lin, H. Sun, and A. Wireman, "Beyond Online Balanced Descent: An Optimal Algorithm for Smoothed Online Optimization," *Advances in Neural Information Processing Systems*, vol. 32, 2019. Curran Associates, Inc., https://proceedings.neurips.cc/paper/2019/file/9f36407ead0629fc166f14dde7970f68-Paper.pdf